THE ITALIAN REGIONAL COOKBOOK

Valentina Harris

Lorenz Books

CONTENTS

FOREWORD

Although I have been living in England for most of my adult life, the place that is home to me is still Italy, in particular the corner of Tuscany that is called Garfagnana. Years ago, I was fortunate enough to be commissioned by the BBC to present a television series about the regional food of Italy, which resulted in my spending many months travelling around the country to discover the secrets of each region's cuisine. The material that was filmed was then woven into a six-part television series, but it was all the research that was undertaken to make the programme that gave me the opportunity to travel the length and breadth of the country, exploring the kitchens, meeting the cooks and producers, and learning so much about what makes up the huge richness and diversity of Italian food.

My enduring fascination with the different regional food habits and traditional cuisine of each and every of the 20 regions of Italy has always been at the heart of my great love for Italian cuisine. I am so pleased to be able to now bring you this beautiful new book illustrating just how diverse and inspiring these recipes are, and how intriguing are the stories and facts that have helped to create them.

From the extraordinary mountain cheeses of the highest Alps to the fiery chillies, olive oil and garlic-based specialities of the far south; or the thinnest pizza emerging from a Neapolitan wood-fired oven to a plate of the yellowest-possible thin ribbons of pasta, slick with butter and cream and encrusted with a shaving of white Alba truffles – Italian food is constantly changing depending upon where you are, adapting itself to the climate and geography of the land, but also revealing so much about its history and how this has influenced the specific use of ingredients. Once one begins to look, one can learn so much about Italy's history and culture simply through the food that appears on one's plate, and this journey of discovery continues to be mesmerising for me; it is the anecdotes and history behind the recipes that really brings them to life and makes them memorable.

I hope that in the pages of this book you will not only find many delicious recipes that you will instantly want to prepare and eat, but that you will also gain something of an insight into what lies behind their existence.

Italians of all ages recognise that their regional cuisine and the stories surrounding them are as much a part of their cultural heritage, their patrimony, as the Coliseum or the Rialto Bridge. Many of the rustic dishes were born out of a basic need to feed hungry mouths with whatever was available locally and seasonally, but even these are often extraordinarily imaginative and skilfully created. The more sophisticated dishes were originally the fruits of the grand banquets prepared by a huge team of cooks working for the nobility, which made the most of great quantities and a huge variety of ingredients that were well out of reach of the pocket of the 'contadini'. Put together and seasoned with history, they are all what makes Italian food so exciting and so dearly loved the world over. Only the Italians could have thought to put flour and water together to create something so hugely popular as a plate of simple spaghetti!

I wish you happy cooking and happy reading as you explore the delicious and diverse recipes of this fabulous country. Buon Appetito!

Valentina Harris

A LAND OF CONTRASTS

From the northern mountaintops of the Italian Alps to the southern tip of Sicily, the amazing variety of the Italian landscape is reflected in its food and drink. The country measures around 1,200 kilometres (750 miles) from north to south; its familiar shape resembles a boot with a high heel kicking the football of Sicily. With all the different ingredients available between one end of the country and the other, Italian cooks have plenty of scope for their undeniable flair in the kitchen.

A VARIED LANDSCAPE

The regions that make up the north of Italy could not be more different from those of the centre and south. In the north, large urban hubs and widespread industry contrast sharply with the landscape of the high mountain peaks of the Dolomites and the Alps, which are peppered with tiny, remote villages, and the flat plains where farming flourishes.

Central Italy sits between the two extremes of northern and southern Italy, taking traditions and culinary habits from both, but keeping its own wonderful cuisine. Abundant green pastures and vineyards flourish in the warmer, moist climate, giving scope for all kinds of delicious ingredients destined for the Italian table.

Further south, the harsher climate requires a different kind of farming based on hardy crops and animals. Citrus fruits, olives, grapevines and sheep dot the rocky landscape, and life can be hard for the shepherd out on the hillside in the baking heat, or the workers picking olives and grapes. However, the intensity of the flavours of the local crops and the warm winter weather can compensate for the lack of refreshing rain.

OPPOSITE *The long coastline of mainland Italy and the rugged shores of the islands abound with pretty towns, such as Bosa in Sardinia.*

RIGHT *The familiar 'boot' shape of Italy is surrounded by seas, which provide plentiful supplies of fish and shellfish to the coastal towns, while inland the foods vary as much as the country's topography, and have shaped the local cuisines.*

THRIFTY INGENUITY

Generally speaking, the north of Italy is wealthier than the south, something that is reflected both in the lifestyle of the inhabitants and in many of the ingredients used in the regional cuisines. However, in the more remote mountainous or rural areas, traditional dishes have a tendency to remind us of times when life in these parts was not quite as bountiful, and there was a very real need to make the best out of the few local ingredients available. The local cuisine is a testament to the intrinsic skill that almost all Italians seem to be born with – making even the most simple of ingredients taste delicious and offer nourishment.

STAPLE INGREDIENTS

From a gastronomic point of view, the Italian regions share a love for many of the same core ingredients, but they are used in individual recipes and in styles that subtly define the culinary culture of each place. Reflected in these dishes are the historical influences of each area's colourful past, its geography and climate, and the fantastic local produce.

Apart from the light and floral olive oil of Liguria, the north features butter and pork fat as its cooking fats of choice, and fresh pasta, risotto and polenta instead of durum-wheat pasta; homely herbs such as sage and juniper instead of basil; the subtler, softer flavours of cream and cheese instead of garlic, tomatoes and olive oil; and gentle spices such as cinnamon and nutmeg instead of the fire of the chilli pepper.

The central and southern regions begin to reflect the hot climate found there in their use of stronger flavours and more tender crops such as citrus fruits, olives, chilli peppers and a veritable cornucopia of vegetables. Olive oil is without a doubt the favourite cooking fat, with some of the very best, most fragrant olive oil made in the deep southern region of Puglia. While pork is found everywhere in Italy, southern Italians generally tend to eat less meat than their northern cousins, and it is often eked out with large quantities of pasta, bread and vegetables.

VALE

Regional specialities

Each of the regions of Italy has a particular ingredient, a style or even a cooking utensil that is symbolic of that cuisine, and cannot be confused with the food of any other place.

Piedmont truffles In Piedmont, the majestic white truffle is dug up at certain times of the year by specially trained dogs. This delicious fungus has an inimitable perfume and a very distinctive and special flavour, making it far more expensive than the more common black variety.

Aosta Valley conviviality This tiny region in the far north of Italy has an unusual drinking vessel called a grolla. This many-spouted wooden cup is used for the consumption of alcoholic coffee laced with grappa and lemon and orange zest, and is passed around at the end of a meal for everyone to enjoy.

Ligurian pesto Deep emerald-green pesto is Liguria's most significant culinary speciality. This fragrant sauce of basil, garlic, Parmesan cheese and pine nuts, pounded to a smooth texture and used to dress pasta, is perfumed by a variety of very special basil that is unique to the city of Genoa. This grows well in the warm sea breezes that flow around south-facing Liguria.

Lombardy bresaola This cured and air-dried fillet of beef typifies the intensely meaty yet elegant dishes of Lombardy. The region is relatively wealthy, hence the common use of meat in its cuisine, but the climate can be quite difficult, with humid summers and cold winters; however this means that excellent risotto rice can be grown here.

Famous fresh pasta from Emilia-Romagna
Although one could choose from many culinary delights of Emilia-Romagna, the most obvious symbol must be the fresh pasta – la sfoglia – that was first created here and is enjoyed in all its shapes and sizes, cooked in many different ways.

Risotto from the Veneto The creaminess of soft risotto, perhaps cooked with seafood from the lagoon and enlivened with a touch of those spices famously traded by the Venetian merchants, typifies the low-lying plains of the Veneto.

Austrian links With its high mountain peaks and a cuisine that still bears the strong influence of its historical links with Austria, Trentino-Alto Adige is proud of its speck, the local version of cured ham, lightly smoked over a wood fire, and flattened under weights to give delicately flavoured, paper-thin slices. In Friuli-Venezia Giulia, the Austro-Hungarian Empire is evident in the ingredients that are seldom used elsewhere, such as poppy seeds, beets, paprika and horseradish.

Suckling pig of Sardinia Sardinia has a typical dish that is, strangely, nothing to do with the sea that surrounds this lovely, remote island, but rather a lot to do with the islanders' fear of the sea, and of who or what might come out of it (storms, Saracens, unfriendly pirates). This dish is porceddu, a roast suckling pig, which nowadays is cooked on a spit over an open fire, but long ago would have been cooked in a pit beneath the ground, with only a thin wisp of smoke escaping, to avoid attracting the attention of invaders.

BELOW *Flavoursome bresaola is a highly prized speciality from Lombardy.*

BELOW RIGHT *Seafood such as scallops is a feature of the menus in Venice and the Veneto, as well as in other coastal parts of Italy.*

FAR LEFT *La chitarra is a piece of equipment used only in Abruzzo for making thick, square spaghetti.*

LEFT *Pungent flavours such as chilli and onion are a key feature of the gutsy, flavoursome dishes on the menus in the south of Italy.*

Tuscan beans The inhabitants of Tuscany are known as 'Toscani mangiafagioli' (Tuscan bean-eaters), a term that refers to both their delicious cuisine, which features the eponymous legumes, and their moneymaking skills.

Hidden treasures of Umbria and Le Marche
The culinary symbol of land-locked, densely wooded Umbria is the delicious and intensely flavoured black truffle, which is used with such generosity to perfume the local dishes. Next door, in Le Marche, there is a love of food that is stuffed with tempting ingredients, such as olive ascolane or ricotta-stuffed ravioli.

City life in Lazio The cuisine of Lazio, the region that surrounds Rome, is in essence that of the Eternal City, which dominates the area now just as it did in the past. The city's kitchens reflect all of Lazio's local culinary traditions, including those of the Roman Jewish population. Easily available local ingredients, particularly offal, are prepared in a delicious way, without fuss.

Pasta treats from Abruzzo and Molise Moving further south to Abruzzo, this is the only area that has a gadget for making the region's unique type of pasta. Spaghetti alla chitarra are made using a hollow wooden box with strings drawn tightly across it, over which the pasta dough is rolled. The strings cut the pasta into thick, square spaghetti. Next door, the region of Molise has always been renowned for producing some of the very best dried pasta in the country.

The deep south Campania's culinary symbols are of course the tomato, first cooked here after its arrival from the New World, and its perfect time-honoured companions, dried pasta and pizza. For Basilicata, which sits like the instep of the boot between the 'toe' (Calabria) and the 'heel' (Puglia) of Italy, the most important culinary symbol must surely be the chilli pepper, used to spice up all the local dishes and also to make 'holy oil', a bowl of olive oil in which chillies are steeped until almost black. This fiery concoction is then sprinkled liberally over food as a condiment.

The region of Puglia, with its beautiful coastline, is a land of shepherds and fishermen, but perhaps the most interesting feature of its cuisine is its link with its neighbours over the sea, Greece and Albania, which is evident in the use of ingredients such as almonds, olives and honey. In Calabria, the main culinary symbol is pork meat and pork fat, used to make all kinds of local cured meat specialities including the fiery 'nduja, a soft, spreadable sausage.

Spices of Sicily This island has the most exotic and varied of all the cuisines of the south of Italy. With culinary influences from Arabia, North Africa, Greece and Spain, Sicilian food is different from that of anywhere else in Italy. The very hot and dry climate and warm winters mean that tender crops such as aubergines/eggplants, tomatoes, olives, citrus fruits and grapes thrive, and these feature heavily in the local dishes. The main culinary symbol is probably the ornately decorated, intensely sweet cake called cassata alla Siciliana.

THE ITALIAN KITCHEN

PASTA

BELOW *La sfoglia, the Italian name for the rich fresh pasta made with eggs and 00 soft wheat flour, comes from Emilia-Romagna in northern Italy.*

Scholars have credited the Chinese with making pasta, using rice or millet flour and water, as far back as 1700BCE. However, Italians believe that real pasta dates back to their own ancestors, the ancient Etruscans, who inhabited central Italy (now comprising Tuscany, Lazio and Umbria) from the Iron Age in the 11th century BCE to Roman times. The Etruscans made lasagna-type noodles from water and spelt flour, which they baked or fried; later, the Romans made lagane (wide strips a bit like large pappardelle) from a similar dough.

THE ARAB INFLUENCE

The idea of boiling pasta is generally considered to have come from Arabian traders, who carried dried pasta with them to make simple meals on their long journeys along the famous Silk Road to China. They are thought to have introduced the concept and the foodstuff to Sicily during the Arab invasions of the 9th century AD, after which time dried pasta began to be produced in great quantities in Sicily. The word 'macarone' is said to derive from the Sicilian term for making dough using strong arms; early pasta-making was a very labour-intensive process until more efficient industrial methods were introduced.

PASTA BECOMES ITALIAN

What Italian cooks can certainly be credited for is creating pasta dishes with sauces, which was the next step in the evolution of this great Italian staple. It is also believed that the first recipes for pasta dough made using eggs and flour, originally to shape into ravioli and other filled pasta, came into being during the Middle Ages in northern Italy. This fresh pasta is as much a part of the cuisine of the northern regions as dairy produce and meat, which are often combined together and used to dress the pasta.

THE FRESH PASTA OF EMILIA-ROMAGNA

The northern region of Emilia-Romagna is considered to be the birthplace of fresh pasta, known throughout Italy as la sfoglia. It is a speciality of the ancient and beautiful city of Bologna and its environs, and to a lesser extent of the neighbouring city of Parma and its province. La sfoglia is made using 00 soft wheat flour blended with eggs to make a golden-yellow, elastic dough that is then lovingly rolled out to near-transparency, using either a long, strong rolling pin or a classic hand-cranked pasta machine, or nowadays sometimes an electric pasta machine for speed.

OPPOSITE: TOP, FROM LEFT TO RIGHT *maccheroncini, maltagliati, trenette* **MIDDLE, FROM LEFT TO RIGHT** *lasagne, spaghetti, conchigliette* **BOTTOM, FROM LEFT TO RIGHT** *orecchiette, garganelli, anelli.*

PASTA DI NAPOLI

There is something fabulously opulent about the stuffed shapes such as tortellini and ravioli, multi-layered lasagne, filled cannelloni and cascades of ribbons of tagliatelle that speaks volumes about the prosperity of Emilia-Romagna and its neighbours, and of an unbounded generosity of spirit when it comes to settling down to enjoy this most simple, yet perfectly delicious food.

OTHER NORTHERN SPECIALITIES

These days, dried durum-wheat pasta is of course eaten all over Italy, but some of the northern regions use mainly fresh pasta, and others, such as Aosta Valley, Friuli-Venezia Giulia, Trentino-Alto Adige and Lombardy, have no real tradition of cooking pasta at all, preferring polenta or rice as their staple starch.

Piedmont has its own fresh pasta, called tagliolini or taglierini, known in the local dialect as tajarin, which is very fine strips of very rich, eggy pasta, often made using only egg yolks instead of whole eggs. This region also has one of the most elaborate filled pastas, agnolotti alla Piemontese, containing many ingredients, including rice.

In Liguria, fresh pasta is made using 00 flour and water, and sometimes chopped fresh herbs such as borage, to make fine ribbons of pasta called trenette, or small twisted shapes called trofie, both of which are traditionally dressed with pesto.

The Veneto has two types of traditional pasta: bigoli, which are thick, whole-wheat spaghetti, and a tiny rice grain-shaped pasta used to enrich and thicken their own version of pasta e fagioli.

CENTRAL AND SOUTHERN PASTA

The fresh egg pasta so loved in most northern regions is mostly replaced in the central and southern areas of Italy by good-quality dried durum-wheat pasta. This is usually factory-made (for shapes such as fine spaghetti), or if made at home, it tends to be in more rustic, simple flour-and-water versions such as orecchiette. This division between northern and southern types of pasta becomes clearer further towards the toe of Italy: in Sicily, for instance, fresh egg pasta is virtually unheard of. However, some of the central regions do use fresh pasta in a number of their traditional dishes, for example vincisgrassi, the lasagna of Le Marche.

Durum wheat has always been grown in large quantities in southern Italy – it is so well suited to the dry soil and hot weather found most of the year round in Sicily, Campania and other southern regions. Naples, the capital city of Campania, also has an ideal climate for drying pasta once it is made. Here, mild sea breezes alternate with hot winds from Mount Vesuvius.

In the early pasta factories of Campania, the pasta was shaped into hollow tubes (a task accomplished by a large screw press powered by two men or one horse) and dried outdoors. Soft winds and plenty of sunshine ensured that the pasta would not dry too slowly and become mouldy, or dry too fast and crack. A thriving pasta industry thus developed in the region thanks to the proximity of plentiful durum-wheat supplies and this beneficial climate.

Milled durum wheat, also known as semola, is granular like sugar, not powdery like other softer flours. It must be kneaded for a long time to create an even-textured dough that will not split or become sticky once it is cooked. The Murgia, the plateau that lies just over the border from Campania in Puglia, was in the past one of the areas of the south best suited for growing top-quality durum wheat. These days, with worldwide demand far outstripping the local production, durum wheat for pasta is often imported into Italy from North America and Canada.

According to Italian law, dried pasta must be made with 100 per cent durum semolina flour and water, a practice that almost all pasta-makers worldwide have since adhered to. Despite this simple recipe, seemingly available for anyone to imitate, there are two factors in Italian dried pasta that make it better than most other products: the shaping of the dough, and the all-important drying methods.

Dried pasta, especially the more complex shapes, is designed for grabbing and holding on to sauces. Dried tubular pasta often has ridges on its surface to keep the pasta sauce adhering around it. These ridges are created during the extrusion process, when the pasta is forced out of a copper mould and cut to the desired length before it is dried. These special moulds, while expensive to buy and prone to wearing out, are favoured for making premium dried pasta.

Once the pasta is cut to the shape required, it must be dried using a process of specific temperature and time. Traditionally, for the best results, pasta is allowed to dry slowly (for up to 50 hours) at a low, constant temperature. It can only be packaged after it is fully dried. The result is a product that has a much better texture, quicker cooking time, and greatly superior sauce-holding qualities than inferior types.

FLAVOURED PASTA

Both fresh and dried pasta can carry other flavours, and favourite inclusions are purées made from spinach, tomato, roasted vegetables, mushrooms, or soft herbs such as basil, as well as the squid ink that produces distinctive jet-black pasta.

OPPOSITE *Pasta comes in many different types, shapes, sizes and colours, and the cooking methods vary accordingly. Fresh pasta, for instance, is much more tender than the dried type, and requires far less cooking. It is also more delicate and requires careful handling, especially if it is stuffed.*

LA SFOGLIA

Without question, it is the golden-yellow, silky smooth fresh pasta of Emilia-Romagna that says it all when it comes to the fresh pasta traditions of Italy and this is a good basic pasta dough recipe to use.

MAKES ABOUT 450G/1LB (ABOUT 4 SERVINGS)

400g/14oz/3½ cups 00 soft wheat flour (see Cook's tip)
4 large eggs

1 Measure out the flour and tip it on to the work surface. Make a hollow in the pile of flour with your fist.

2 Beat the egg lightly in a bowl, just enough to blend the yolk and white together, and pour into the hollow.

3 Blend the egg and flour together with your fingertips until a lumpy mass has been formed, then pull everything together with your hands.

4 Knead the mixture into a smooth ball of dough. Do not press the dough down hard on to the work surface, or stretch it as you knead. The technique simply involves a rolling and light squeezing action with both hands. When the dough feels cool and waxy and springs back immediately when lightly pressed with a finger, it is ready. Do not be tempted to over-knead or the dough will lose all its elasticity.

5 Wrap the dough in clear film/plastic wrap or a clean cloth, and leave to rest for at least 20 minutes before starting to roll it out for cutting (see opposite).

Cook's tip Use 00 soft wheat flour mixed (about half and half) with semola flour (durum-wheat flour) for a stiffer, slightly grittier, drier dough. If semola is hard to come by, use the finest possible semolina instead.

ORECCHIETTE

To make orecchiette the traditional way, precise quantities are seldom used; the old guideline is to use roughly one handful of flour per person, but obviously this depends on the size of your hands.

MAKES 400G/14OZ (ABOUT 4 SERVINGS)

about 400g/14oz/3½ cups hard durum-wheat flour
tepid water

1 Set aside a handful of flour for dusting, then mound the rest of the flour on to the work surface. Make a hollow in the middle of the mound. Add tepid water to the hollow. Using your hands, gradually mix the water with the surrounding flour to make a dough, adding more flour from the reserved quantity, if needed. The dough is ready for kneading when a thumb, inserted into it, comes away cleanly. Knead for 10 minutes, then form into a ball.

2 Squash the ball of dough on one side until it forms a point, applying your body's weight while rolling it. Continue rolling the point until it forms a long tubular shape. Roll this until a long string of dough, the thickness of your little finger, stretches out from the side of the ball, an arm's length long.

3 Using a non-serrated knife, cut the length of dough into sections the size of a finger joint from tip to knuckle.

4 With the blade at an angle of 30 degrees, press down on the dough while pulling it backwards. This thins the dough and rolls it around the knife to form an oval. Invert it to look like an ear. Shape the remaining dough.

5 Place the orecchiette on a clean, floured cloth and leave to dry slightly before cooking. Alternatively, fully dry them out, then store in sealed jars for up to 1 year.

ROLLING OUT BY HAND

Roll out the rested la sfoglia dough (see page 18) as thinly as possible with a strong, long rolling pin. Keep rolling it, moving it around to be sure it isn't sticking to the work surface, until it is really elastic, smooth and shiny. It should cool down considerably as you work it, and you will feel a drop in its temperature as you roll it.

When it is ready, the sheet of dough should feel like a brand-new, slightly damp chamois leather, but it must not be brittle or it will just crack when you cut it. You can keep it pliable by covering it with a slightly moist clean cloth when you are not working with it, though the real secret to stopping it from drying out is to work as fast as possible.

CUTTING PASTA

You can cut your pasta into the desired shape as soon as it is dry enough to roll up without it sticking to itself, either by hand using a sharp knife or with a special wheel, or using the cutter on a pasta machine. Once cut, you can use the pasta immediately, or let it dry out further by leaving it exposed to the air for about 30 minutes. Some people like to drape long strands of pasta over a rolling pin or similar, so it is suspended and the air flows more readily around it.

If you are making a stuffed pasta shape such as ravioli you must use soft, moist pasta, otherwise it will not be possible to close each parcel securely and thus keep the filling inside while it is being cooked. Once the ravioli are filled and properly sealed, leave the shapes to dry, spaced out evenly on a floured surface.

WHAT TO ADD?

The marriage of sauce and pasta is the final part of the whole process. There are some shapes that automatically need to be cooked with specific sauces, such as bucatini (hollow, thick spaghetti), which are traditionally paired with amatriciana sauce, a delicious strong tomato sauce spiked with bell peppers and pancetta. As an overall rule, short shapes are best with chunky sauces, and flat ribbon shapes or spaghetti-like shapes are best with smooth sauces – but there are so many exceptions! Another rule of thumb is that strong, garlicky, spicy sauces are not considered the best accompaniments for the delicate richness of fresh egg pasta, since they overpower it, but are perfect with dried durum-wheat pasta, whereas creamy, cheesy sauces will suit either type. On the whole, though, so long as the sauce wraps itself around the pasta, to embrace and engulf it, rather than staying behind as a separate element in the pan or serving bowl, then the partnership has worked.

ROLLING OUT USING A PASTA MACHINE

1 If using a pasta machine, break off a piece of rested la sfoglia dough (see page 18) the size of a small fist, then flatten it out with your hands.

2 Push the dough through the widest setting on your pasta machine. Fold this in half and repeat.

3 Do this three times or until the air pocket, which should form at the fold, audibly pops. This means the right surface tension has been achieved and there is no need to fold it again. In Italian they say 'la pasta canta!' ('the pasta sings!') when they hear this little sound.

4 Move the pasta machine down to the next (narrower) setting and continue to wind it through the rollers to the last or penultimate setting on the machine, depending on how fine you want it to be, rolling the dough twice on each setting.

5 Lay the finished sheet of pasta carefully on to a floured surface. If you are going to make filled pasta, use it immediately while it still contains moisture. If you are going to make ribbons of pasta, such as tagliatelle, leave the uncut sheet of pasta to dry out to a parchment texture before you cut it.

6 Now take another lump of dough the size of a small fist, flatten it, and begin again exactly as described in step 1. Do this with all the pasta you have made.

7 Keep an eye on the sheets of pasta you have rolled out. Put them on a floured surface to dry, but remember they will not be easy to cut if they are too dry. To keep them moist, cover with moist, clean cloths.

WHITE SAUCE

MAKES ABOUT 600ML/1 PINT/2½ CUPS

75g/3oz/6 tbsp unsalted butter
60ml/4 tbsp plain/all-purpose flour
600ml/1 pint/2½ cups milk
pinch of sea salt
pinch of freshly grated nutmeg

1 Melt the butter in a pan, then stir in the flour over a low heat using a wooden spoon until a paste (roux) is formed.

2 Pour in all the milk, stirring or whisking constantly to prevent lumps forming.

3 Add the salt and nutmeg to taste, then simmer gently for about 15 minutes, stirring constantly.

4 When the sauce is thick enough to coat the back of the spoon, remove from the heat.

5 Cover the surface with a little cold water to prevent a skin forming. Set aside until required.

BASIC TOMATO SAUCE

MAKES ABOUT 600ML/1 PINT/2½ CUPS

900g/2lb fresh tomatoes, skinned (see Cook's tip) and quartered, or 2 x 400g/14oz cans tomatoes, drained and quartered
1 small onion, quartered
1 carrot, quartered
1 celery stick, quartered
1 large fresh parsley sprig
10 fresh basil leaves
sea salt
45ml/3 tbsp extra virgin olive oil (optional)

1 Put the tomatoes, onion, carrot, celery, parsley and basil into a large pan. Cover with a lid and bring to the boil, then simmer for 30 minutes.

2 Remove the lid and continue to simmer for 20 minutes more, or until most of the liquid has evaporated.

3 Remove the pan from the heat and push the mixture through a food mill or sieve or strainer. Season to taste with salt, and reheat, adding the oil, if using, just before serving, or use the sauce as required in a recipe.

Cook's tip To skin the tomatoes, plunge them into boiling water for 30 seconds, then refresh in cold water. Peel away the skins.

L'ARRABBIATA

MAKES ABOUT 600ML/1 PINT/2½ CUPS

60ml/4 tbsp extra virgin olive oil
4 garlic cloves, finely chopped
1–4 dried red chillies (see Cook's tips)
2 x 400g/14oz cans chopped tomatoes, drained
sea salt
5ml/1 tsp chopped fresh parsley, to serve

1 Heat the olive oil in a large, heavy pan and add the garlic and chillies. Fry for 3–4 minutes until both the garlic and chillies are well browned.

2 Remove the chillies and garlic with a slotted spoon and discard them.

3 Add the tomatoes to the pan and season to taste with salt. Simmer over a low heat for about 20 minutes, until the sauce is thick and flavoursome.

4 Sprinkle with chopped parsley and serve with cooked pasta or as a dipping sauce.

Cook's tips

- The number of chillies that you use depends upon their strength as well as how hot you want the sauce to be. To achieve maximum heat, include the seeds.
- In Italy, cheese is not normally served when l'arrabbiata is part of a dish, but if you do want to add some, it should be aged, peppery pecorino if possible.

RAGÙ

SERVES 4 (ENOUGH FOR 400G/14OZ DRIED PASTA)

25g/1oz dried porcini mushrooms (optional)
90ml/6 tbsp olive oil or vegetable oil
1 onion, finely chopped
2 celery sticks, finely chopped
1 carrot, finely chopped
1 garlic clove, finely chopped
50g/2oz fat prosciutto crudo or streaky/fatty bacon, finely diced
450g/1lb/2 cups lean minced/ground beef
200ml/7fl oz/scant 1 cup red wine
15ml/1 tsp tomato paste diluted with 90ml/6 tbsp water
400g/14oz passata/bottled strained tomatoes
sea salt and ground black pepper

1 If using the porcini, soak them in warm water to cover for 15 minutes, then drain. Discard the stems and slice the caps.

2 Heat the oil in a pan and fry the onion, celery, carrot and garlic for 10 minutes until the onion is soft and translucent. Add the prosciutto or bacon, stir and cook over low heat for 4 minutes.

3 Add the prepared porcini (if using) and the beef. Brown the beef over a medium heat, without letting it go crisp, then pour in the wine and raise the heat to the maximum.

4 Pour in the diluted tomato paste and the passata. Stir, season to taste, lower the heat and cover. Simmer very slowly for about 2 hours, stirring frequently and adding water if necessary.

RICE, GRAINS AND PULSES

In the south of Italy, the baking summer heat and dry, mild winters are ideal for growing the strong durum wheat that is used to make dried pasta and bread, whereas in the north of the country the gentler, mistier summers and colder, snowy winters provide perfect conditions for growing rice and all kinds of pulses, such as lentils and beans. That said, rice fields can still be found further south too, such as in Sicily, where ancient Arab irrigation channels are used to ensure a plentiful supply of water in this hot, dry island.

NORTHERN RISOTTO

The chalky kind of rice that is essential for making risotto has been grown all over the north of Italy at least since the 15th century. In this cooler, wetter region of Italy, the flat, foggy rice fields of the inland north-west are fed by the snowmelt of the surrounding Alps and the Dolomites, with an intricate canal system to keep the water fresh. Further east, paddy fields lie in the vast marshy areas of the Po delta.

In the northern parts of the country, even though the rice is mainly of the risotto variety, there are some differences between the kinds of rice grown in the east and those produced in the west. The variations in climate and geography mean that some varieties will generally do better on one side of the country or the other, and these different kinds of rice do behave differently in the cooking process with resulting subtle changes in the finished dish.

To the east, in the Veneto and Friuli-Venezia Giulia, the preferred varieties tend to be vialone nano, or vialone gigante, while western cooks in Lombardy and Piedmont like to use carnaroli or arborio rice. Vialone, with its smaller, harder grain, will give a much soupier, wetter texture compared to the stiffer, tighter, drier results of cooking with carnaroli or arborio. With care, though, both give a deliciously creamy result.

THE ORIGINS OF RISOTTO

The historical route of risotto as we know it today would appear to originate from a basic gruel called malamiga, possibly from Romania, to which rice flour was added as a thickener. This was considered a very tasty, warming dish. At some point after its arrival in Italy, the original recipe was re-created using rice grains instead of the rice flour, and so the first risotto recipes began to emerge. During the 19th century, cooking techniques became more sophisticated, and rice found its way into the kitchens of the upper classes. At this stage, the idea of toasting the rice grains in butter at the start of the recipe was introduced in order to keep the firm texture of the finished dish and maximise flavour.

SICILIAN RICE HARVESTS

During the Arab domination of Sicily from AD827 to AD1060, agriculture on the island was greatly developed. The Arabs improved the utilization of the island's water resources, creating a proper system of irrigation that was very beneficial to the local agriculture. This allowed for the cultivation of citrus fruits, new vegetables and, most importantly, the introduction of rice. The system gave enough water for the crop to flourish, and the rice was then exported to Europe, where this staple food was hitherto unknown.

For centuries, Sicilian farmers had a monopoly on rice farming in southern Europe – it took more than 300 years for the crop to spread even as far as the Italian peninsula, though once it did reach the mainland the north took over as the primary producer. Subsequently, its nutritional and culinary value was understood – rice is more nutritious than many other grains – and it was grown widely.

SOUTHERN RICE DISHES

Although risotto, the nation's great rice dish, is immensely popular all over the north of Italy, there are many different rice dishes to be found in the south, particularly in Sicily. This may owe something to the influence of ingredients and traditions brought over from the island's neighbour, North Africa. The most popular street food in Sicily is arancini di riso, which are tasty, small golden balls of rice mixed with meat or vegetables. These resemble oranges after deep-frying, hence the name 'arancini'.

Some of the less well-known recipes using rice in Sicilian cooking include a rice and tomato soup; a very rustic combination of boiled rice with dried, boiled chestnuts and beans; and deliciously elegant and often colourful rice timbales. In Neapolitan cuisine, rice also appears on the menu in the form of timbales, or in classic dishes such as sartu di riso, a rice-covered mound of meat and vegetables. In Tuscany, rice is used for making cakes and pastries, such as the little oval cakes sold in every pasticceria throughout the city of Florence, which are known as budini di riso (rice puddings).

OPPOSITE *Golden fields of rice such as this one in Lombardy are a common sight in much of Italy. Types vary according to region, and this is reflected in the local dishes that put the humble grain centre stage.*

ABOVE *Arborio rice, the favoured grain (together with carnaroli) in Lombardy and Piedmont, is perhaps the most common type of risotto rice found in supermarkets outside Italy.*

TOP TIPS FOR MAKING RISOTTO

• Think about the pan you are going to make the risotto in – a deep sauté pan is perfect, but it must have a lid.

• Do not let the onion, garlic or other vegetables brown during the initial 'soffritto' (softening) process, or the rice during the toasting process – keep the heat really low.

• Remember to wait patiently before adding the first ladleful of stock or the wine to the risotto. Those rice grains need to really heat through so their inner shell is sealed off. This is what will help most when it comes to avoiding overcooking the risotto and making a savoury rice pudding instead!

• Each one of the rice grains will absorb five times its own volume during the cooking process, so make sure that whatever the rice is absorbing is delicious and appropriate to the dish – good fish stock for a fishy risotto, rich chicken stock or full-flavoured vegetable stock for wild mushrooms, and so on.

• Never add more liquid to the risotto until your spoon opens up a clear channel behind itself as you draw it through the grains.

• The risotto is cooked when the texture is velvety but the grains will still hold your teeth together for a count of 2 seconds when you test it. It should not be chalky or brittle, nor too soft and pappy.

• Remember to rest the risotto for 4 minutes once cooked. This process, called 'mantecare', is very important when it comes to making the risotto really creamy and silky – the texture known as il velluto (velvet).

POLENTA

The other important carbohydrate of the northern regions, apart from rice, is polenta. This is made from a special variety of ground maize, called 'granoturco' in Italian. It can be white or yellow, and comes in several different grades: fine-ground, medium or coarse. It is usually served in a slab with the dressing laid or poured over it, but it can also be cooked much softer and served in a bowl with the stew, dressing, sauce or cheese on the top. As it is very bland in flavour, it acts as a good, filling base for flavoursome dishes such as game stews, strong cheeses, casseroled fish, and so on. This dish forms no part of the southern cuisine – it is a real northern speciality.

Because it takes such a long time to cook, the tradition would have been to make one large batch of polenta for use during the whole week. It would be eaten first freshly made, then allowed to set until solid and rubbery, at which stage it can then be sliced, and either fried or grilled or broiled. The quick-cook variety, which is widely available, is frowned upon by purists, who claim that only the real thing, which requires up to an hour of constant stirring, will really have the right flavour.

Polenta flour is also popular for making deliciously crumbly cakes and cookies, and is often added to bread dough for a lovely yellow hint of colour and a slightly gritty texture. It also helps to keep the bread fresher for longer.

PULSES AND GRAINS

Beans and lentils are an important part of the menu all over Italy, included in soups and stews for extra nourishment or in some cases as a replacement for meat. Grains, such as rye, oats and buckwheat, are also added to bread, soups or cakes to lend substance and fibre.

Dried pulses and grains are first reconstituted by soaking them in water and then boiling in water or stock. This is the thrifty Italian cook's traditional way of unlocking all the goodness of these carefully stored ingredients, and adding flavourful bulk to a meat or vegetable stew during the cold winter months.

Chickpeas, lentils and beans of all varieties are particularly popular throughout Tuscany and Umbria. Other Italians know Tuscans as 'bean eaters', and it is true that the region excels in the simple preparation of humble pulses, which often need no more than a little salt, a sprig of rosemary and plenty of green olive oil to lift them from their basic rusticity into a memorable dish.

BASIC POLENTA

SERVES 6

1.75 litres/3 pints/7½ cups cold water
sea salt
250g/8oz/1⅓ cups ground polenta/cornmeal

1 Pour the water into a wide, heavy, preferably copper pan and place it over a high heat. Bring the water to the boil.

2 Trickle the polenta into the boiling water in a fine rain with one hand, and whisk constantly with the other.

3 When all the polenta has been whisked into the water, reduce the heat to a medium to low flame and then begin to stir with a strong, long-handled wooden spoon until the polenta comes away from the sides of the pan. This will take 40–50 minutes and requires patience, energy and a strong elbow.

4 Turn out the polenta on to a wooden board and smooth it into a mounded shape with spatulas.

5 Leave it to stand for about 5 minutes, then cut it into slabs and serve hot with its accompanying stew, fricassee or casserole, or with a slice of very strong-flavoured cheese such as Gorgonzola.

6 Alternatively, leave it to go completely cold, then slice it like bread and grill, broil, fry or bake it as required.

ABOVE *In addition to being cooked and used whole, chickpeas can also be ground to make a flour, which is used in the Lugurian speciality farinata (a thin pancake).*

OPPOSITE *The fields of lentils burst into a dazzling rainbow riot of colour around the hilltop town of Castelluccio, which is famous for its superlative lentils – deemed by many to be the best in Italy.*

In Umbria, lentils really come into their own, especially in the little town of Castelluccio. These are generally considered to be the best lentils in the whole country. Small, rounded and dark brown, these deliciously nutty pulses are used in soups, with pasta, as a side dish or just dressed with olive oil and eaten on their own. It used to be the tradition in Castelluccio to go on a pilgrimage every late June to Norcia, to the church of St Scholastica, in order to plead with the saint for rain to fall on the year's lentil crop. The lentil fields are famous for their blooming wild flowers from late May to late July – with yellows, reds and blues.

In Rome, lentils are considered so important that they take pride of place on New Year's Eve, where they form a delicious bed underneath cotechino or zampone, the traditional pig's trotter sausages that are served on this occasion. It is said that every lentil eaten on the last day of the year represents a golden sovereign that will come your way in the New Year.

Chickpeas are one of the oldest pulses known to us. There is evidence of their presence in the Middle East 7,500 years ago; there have even been carbonised chickpeas with rice found at the archaeological site of the Roman legion fort at Neuss. We know that the soldiers of the Roman legions ate them in various forms, but most importantly with an early form of pasta in a dish called laganum et ciceris. The list of ingredients, and probably the dish itself, is very similar to the popular pasta and chickpea dish still eaten in Rome today, known as pasta e ceci.

FARRO – A SOUTHERN SPECIALITY

The grain known as farro (Triticum dicoccum) is extremely popular in some parts of central Italy, and also in Puglia. There is much confusion and ongoing disagreement about what farro actually is. Spelt, emmer or einkorn, different varieties of grain from elsewhere in Europe, are all called farro in Italy. Sometimes, but not always, these are further distinguished as farro grande (large), farro medio (medium) and farro piccolo (small).

Regional differences as to what is, and always has been, grown locally and eaten as farro, may also help to explain the confusion. According to the experts, although it may look like spelt, it is not the same grain. For a start, farro always needs to be soaked before use, whereas spelt can be cooked without soaking.

One thing people do agree on is that farro is nutritious, being high in fibre and a good source of protein. In the central and southern regions the grain, once soaked, rinsed and thoroughly cooked, is used to make soups and salads, and can also be ground into flour and used to make bread. It can even be used like rice, to make a farro version of northern risotto.

COOKING PULSES AND GRAINS

- To reconstitute dried pulses and grains, soak them in cold water for several hours, preferably overnight, draining them and changing the water several times if possible. Once soaked, they should be rinsed in fresh water, then put into a large pan with fresh, cold water to cover them and brought to a fast boil. Boil vigorously for 5 minutes, then drain the pulses in a sieve or strainer, rinse under running cold water and return to the pan. Cover with fresh cold water and boil again until soft and tender.

- Do not add any salt to the pan of water until the very end of the cooking process, or the salt will toughen the skins of the pulses, making them indigestible.

DAIRY PRODUCTS

While the north of Italy is ideal cattle-farming land, with its wide plains to the east and plentiful grazing land formed from the rich silt of the Po river delta, the south is not the right terrain for raising cows. Moreover, the southern climate is too fierce and the grass too sparse for dairy herds. Instead, hardy sheep and goats roam the rocky hillsides here, just as their northern counterparts do in the cooler environment of the Italian Alps and Dolomites, and their milk is used to make some wonderful cheeses.

REGIONAL VARIATIONS

Thanks to the generally mild, relatively damp climate of northern Italy, and the flatter terrain, dairy farming is a much easier prospect than in the dry south, and so all kinds of wonderful dairy products are a traditional part of northern cuisine. Milk, butter and cream are widely used in both sweet and savoury dishes everywhere here, and of course cheese is a prized ingredient that can stand on its own or be combined with other foods in a huge range of recipes.

BELOW *Wonderfully rich cow's milk forms the basis of various dairy products in the cooler northern parts of Italy, including the wide range of famous cheeses produced there.*

The cheeses of the central and southern areas are predominantly made from ewe's milk. They tend to be pale in colour and quite soft. The most famous are pecorino, mozzarella, and ewe's milk ricotta, all of which are now exported around the world. In the south of Italy, butter and cream are rarely used; olive oil is the cooking fat of choice and is also used for making salad dressings and marinades, and as a dip for bread.

MILK AND CREAM

While milk is not really drunk fresh and is only rarely added to coffee or tea in Italy – apart from for the breakfast cappuccino – it is often turned into cream or butter in the northern and central regions. One of the country's most prized and well-known desserts, the delicate panna cotta – a light and smooth baked custard – originates from Piedmont and is made with the cream produced on this region's dairy farms.

BUTTER

In the north, butter is extensively employed as a cooking fat, although pork fat is also used for more rustic dishes that benefit from its full flavour. Italian butter is generally made without salting and is quite light and sweet in flavour, and very pale in colour. It is ideal for cooking lighter dishes of fish and vegetables and, of course, for lavishly spreading on fresh bread.

CHEESE

While the south of Italy revels in its production and use of mozzarella, the cheeses of the north are much more plentiful and very varied in character and flavour. Many of them are made from cow's milk, which is widely available in the cooler regions.

Mascarpone This delicate soft cheese is essential for making tiramisù, probably Italy's most famous dessert, first created in the Veneto. Mascarpone is actually a by-product of hard Parmigiano Reggiano and Grana Padano, made from the cream that is skimmed off the first milking.

Ricotta This comes from the same process of hard cheesemaking as mascarpone. This light, pale, soft cheese was originally made in Rome as a by-product of Pecorino Romano, the hard, salty and slightly peppery ewe's milk cheese that is made in the region and is used as a table cheese or grated over pasta, or added as an ingredient in many local dishes. The early Pecorino Romano-makers discovered that when whey is re-heated, the whey protein particles fuse together to create a curd. This curd, after draining, turns into ricotta. It can of course also be made from cow's milk, since whey naturally occurs in cheesemaking, whatever kind of animal the milk comes from. Ricotta literally translates as 're-cooked', an apt description of the process.

This soft cheese is used all over Italy in many inventive ways. It is ideal for absorbing all kinds of flavours and lending bulk to sweet and savoury recipes. Even the whey, the thin liquid left over at the end of the cheesemaking process, has its uses – it is fed to the neighbouring pigs.

Ricotta is used to make cakes and pastries, as a base for dressing pasta, and as an ingredient in many savoury dishes too, where it adds richness and takes on the other flavours. In Sicily, it is the key ingredient of the famous cassata alla Siciliana, or is used as the filling for cannoli, little deep-fried stuffed pastry shells. In Campania, it is blended with boiled wheat to make the ancient cake known as la pastiera.

ABOVE *Hardy sheep thrive in mountainous regions of the north of Italy, as well as in the arid south, and produce the milk that is used to make many notable cheeses, such as mozzarella and Pecorino Romano.*

ABOVE *Strong-tasting Parmigiano Reggiano is perhaps one of Italy's most famous foodstuffs, and is used in all manner of sauces as well as on top of some pasta dishes.*

ABOVE RIGHT *Stretchy, mild-flavoured mozzarella is a key ingredient in Italy's other famous export: pizza, although it is also enjoyed raw in salads.*

UNUSUAL VARIETIES OF RICOTTA

As well as its basic light, almost spreadable form, ricotta is also made in other versions, which ensure a longer shelf life. The pressed, salted, dried and aged variety of the cheese is known as ricotta salata. This very white, firm cheese is traditionally decorated with a delicate basket-weave pattern and is used for grating or shaving.

Ricotta infornata, sometimes known as ricotta al forno, is produced by placing soft ricotta in the oven until it develops a brown, lightly charred crust, or sometimes even until it becomes sandy brown all the way through. This is popular mainly in Sicily and Sardinia. Another delicious variation, ricotta affumicata, is very similar to ricotta infornata and is produced by placing soft ricotta in a smoker until it develops a grey crust and acquires a charred-wood scent.

Ricotta scanta is the process of letting the ricotta go sour in a controlled manner for about a week, then stirring it every 2 to 3 days, salting occasionally and allowing the liquid to flow away. After as much as 100 days of patient watching and stirring, the ricotta has the consistency of cream cheese, with a distinct, pungent, piquant aroma.

Mozzarella This light, mild and yet tasty cheese, made from either cow's milk or buffalo milk, is originally from the region of Campania. One theory tells us that water buffalo were brought to Italy by the Goths during the early medieval period; another legend tells us a rather more romantic story. Apparently when Antony and Cleopatra fell in love, they spent many idyllic hours cruising the Nile on barges pulled by water buffalo, eating sumptuous meals and feasting on cheese made from the milk of the water buffalo. The Egyptians, seeing the passion between the two, came to regard the cheese as a key to their mad affair. Antony became so fond of this cheese that he sent some water buffalo back to Rome as a gift for Caesar, with his instructions on how to make the milk into mozzarella. Overnight, the cheese became a staple of the Roman diet and then spread further into southern Italy. Ever since that time, water buffalo have become a familiar sight in the countryside between Rome and Naples.

In the early days, because it was not made from pasteurised milk and there was no way to keep it really cool and stop it spoiling, the cheese had a very short shelf life, and therefore it seldom left the regions where it was produced. However, as better cheese technology, refrigeration and transportation systems developed, mozzarella spread to other regions of Italy.

Mild and white in colour, this delicate cheese is made by the special 'pasta filata' or stretched-curd method, whereby the soft, stretchy curd is dipped into hot whey and then kneaded to the desired consistency. As it cools down again it is shaped in cold water. Historians say that it first came about as a result of some curds accidentally falling into a bucket of hot water – the resulting mixture was found to be quite delicious and of a tempting consistency. While cow's milk mozzarella, known as fiordilatte, is not considered as special as the buffalo version, the really important thing about mozzarella is that it should be as fresh as possible.

Parmesan Parmigiano Reggiano and Grana Padano are perhaps the best known of all the famous cheeses of Italy. Made using similar methods, they are mainly different because of where they come from in the north. They vary slightly in flavour and texture as a result of the fodder that the farmers provide for their cows. The focus is on well-bred, well-fed animals that give the right kind of milk for cheese production. It is made by blending an evening batch of milk, which is left to stand overnight and then skimmed, with a morning milking that is added whole and thoroughly mixed with the evening's skimmed milk.

Perhaps the more well-known of these two hard cheeses, Parmigiano Reggiano comes from the province of Parma, in Emilia-Romagna, and is linked with Parma ham – prosciutto di Parma – which comes from the same area. The pigs bred for the production of Parma ham according to law must be fed the whey from the cheese production in order to be certified as pigs suitable for Parma ham. So, they achieve a delightful and fruitful symbiosis – one cannot exist without the other.

Grana Padano comes from the Pianura Padana area of Lombardy, just north of the Parmigiano Reggiano area, and tends to be slightly more

STORING PARMESAN

To keep this cheese at its best, wrap it in foil, baking parchment or cloth rather than clear film or plastic wrap (which will cause it to sweat and become slightly oily). Store it in the bottom part of the refrigerator.

BELOW *Distinctive caciocavallo from southern Italy is made with the same pasta filata or stretched-curd method as is used for making mozzarella.*

Pecorino
del
pastore

buttery and dense than its cousin. It has the same kinds of uses in northern Italian recipes, being a hard grating cheese with a sharp, full flavour. Both these cheeses are used extensively in cooking all over Italy, and are also respected as cheeses suitable for the table on their own.

Another rare version of a similar grating cheese is Grana Trentino, which is produced in much more limited quantities than Parmesan and Grano Padano, in Trentino-Alto Adige in the foothills and mountains of the far north of Italy.

Local specialities Lombardy is of course the home of Gorgonzola, a famous blue cheese made in both piccante (strong and sharp) and dolce (milder) versions. Friuli-Venezia Giulia in the far north-east of the country has a host of small cheesemakers producing goat's and ewe's milk cheeses, some smoked, of which it is deservedly very proud.

Piedmont, which only 150 years or so ago was part of France, naturally has an absolutely vast range of delicious cheeses, including the very strong-tasting Castelmagno, the origins of which date back to the 13th century; creamy robiola; tasty Taleggio (which is also made in Lombardy) and a long list of cheeses of the Toma style. Emilia-Romagna and Lombardy share in the production of soft, slightly fermented stretched-curd cheeses such as stracchino.

Trentino-Alto Adige produces a whole range of mountain cheeses, many of which are made in very limited quantity and only sold locally, and have decidedly German names, such as Hoch Pustertaler and Graukäse.

The rocky coastal strip of Liguria has no especially famous cheeses that are known outside the area, but its artisan cheesemakers do produce some very special types of cheese for local consumption, including the delicate (and almost unpronounceable) prescinseua.

Other cheeses that come from the northern regions include a delicious semi-hard cheese called Asiago, from the low-lying Veneto region, and a buttery Fontina from the Aosta Valley in the far north-west.

The southern regions of Sardinia, Tuscany, Lazio and Sicily all produce famous versions of pecorino cheese from ewe's milk. Pecorino Romano is made in the largest blocks. Cheeses of this type are all more or less similar, with a characteristic flavour: salty, with a fruity tang that becomes steadily more robust as the cheese ages. Pecorino is made between November and late June, when the sheep can feed on fresh spring grass in these hot, dry parts of Italy and subsequently produce the best milk.

EGGS

Though not strictly a dairy product, eggs are often linked with milk, butter and cheese in recipes, and are generally used more frequently in northern regional cuisine than in that of the south. Apart from their inclusion in fresh pasta-making, they are also used in the northern tradition of patisserie, doubtless influenced by the culinary traditions of the neighbouring countries of Austria and Switzerland. They are also found in countless traditional recipes including the famously delicious frittata, a flat omelette that is often made with cheese, cured meat, fresh herbs or vegetables, or even filled with leftover pasta. Frittata can be thick or thin, small or large, and can be eaten hot or cold. It is loved all over Italy, used for taking to picnics, as a sandwich filling or just as a way of recycling leftovers into a tasty snack.

OPPOSITE *Pecorino, a salty cheese made with ewe's milk in southern Italy, is available in various forms and aged for different lengths of time.*

BELOW *Fresh eggs lend richness and colour to pasta and are indispensible in many dishes, not least the versatile frittata.*

CURED MEATS

Salumi is the collective term in Italian for all cured meats, whether they are made from pork (as indeed most of them are) or from other meats, such as beef or venison. A speciality store selling these products is called a salumeria, and an expert merchant of these wonderfully tasty products is known as a salumiere. Italian cooks take great pride in choosing and using the perfect cured meat for each occasion and particular dish, with the advice of the salumiere always on hand if required.

VARIETIES OF HAM

The Italian word for ham is 'prosciutto'. Ham can be cured, prosciutto crudo, or cooked, prosciutto cotto. These days, Italian and European Union legislation grants a PDO (Protected Designation of Origin) certification – called DOP (Denominazione di Origine Protetta) in Italy – to many of the country's cured hams, which specify where and how these are produced so that cheap copies, possibly using inferior ingredients, cannot be sold as the authentic article. There are several such PDO hams from Italy, each one with its own production process.

Parma ham, prosciutto di Parma, is made by almost 200 producers who are concentrated in the province of Parma, in Emilia-Romagna. A consortium of producers has been formed to endorse all the qualifying products within this distinctive brand and to regulate its production. Very large, fresh hams are used, weighing 12–13kg (26½–28½lb) each.

The actual curing process for Parma ham uses proportionately small amounts of salt, the only other ingredient being the air that is used to dry out the meat. The perfect microclimate for making this kind of cured ham occurs naturally in the Langhirano valley. After salting, the meat is sealed on the open side – that is, the side not protected by the leg's fat and skin – with pig fat mixed with a large amount of ground black pepper. This slows down the drying process, stopping cracking and prevents the ham from attracting insects. The meat is then cured in the fresh air over a period of 12 to 15 months, without the addition of any nitrates or flavourings, to produce an intensely flavoured ham.

Prosciutto di San Daniele, from San Daniele in Friuli-Venezia Giulia, is similar to Parma ham, especially in terms of the small quantity of salt used, and is one of the most prized hams in Italy.

Tuscany and Le Marche both produce their own versions of cured ham, prosciutto crudo. The Tuscan one is simply known as prosciutto Toscano and tends to be coarser and saltier than some of the more refined varieties such as Parma ham.

Le Marche produces a very fine and elegant cured ham called prosciutto di Carpegna, from the area around the town of Montefeltro in the province of Pesaro Urbino. Some people claim this is the finest cured ham made in Italy.

Elsewhere in Italy there are many cured hams called 'nostrani' or 'nazionali', which, like prosciutto Toscano, tend to be more strongly flavoured and are produced using more salt, which makes them less delicate than Parma ham – slightly more robust and rustic in flavour.

Prosciutto di Praga, although originally from Prague in the Czech Republic, is now one of the best-known Italian cooked hams, and is produced in the north-eastern province of Trieste, which, like Prague, was part of the Austro-Hungarian Empire until 1918.

SALAME

Salame has long been appreciated as a cured meat in Italy. Evidence shows that the Etruscans made it well before Roman times, and passed on their skills to the Romans. Even the ancient Egyptians living more than 3,000 years ago are known to have enjoyed this cured sausage. Traces of cured meats that appear to be very much like salame have been found in the tomb of Rameses III, dating back to 1166BCE.

There are many kinds of salame, but the main ones are salame Milano, salame Ungherese, salame Napoli (with chilli), salame Felino (a long and very thin salame) and salame cacciatore, which is short and squat, ideal for picnics and originally made for hunters to take with them as an easily transportable snack. The English use of the word is often in the plural, salami.

A SPECIAL TREAT FROM PARMA

Culatello di Zibello is one of the most popular, and also the most complicated of all the salumi. Making and serving culatello requires very special attention throughout the process, making it very expensive and sought after. It originates from Zibello in the province of Parma, and is a little masterpiece devised by the producers of

OPPOSITE *Parma ham is one of Italy's most prized products, and is protected by a PDO categorization. Cured with just a little salt and by a lengthy hanging time, the delicate flesh has an intense flavour.*

ABOVE *Meat from wild boar (cinghiale) is used to make small, dry-cured salumi called cacciatorini, which are more intensely flavoured and gamey than salumi made with standard cured pork.*

prosciutto di Parma. While both products, culatello and Parma ham, are made from the leg of the animal, only a particular portion of the leg is made into culatello. The meat is salt-cured for 3 days, massaged and then allowed to rest before being encased. After being aged for up to a year, the outer skin of culatello must be carefully cut and scraped away, and the meat is then moistened by being wrapped in a wine-soaked cloth. After a couple of days the skin and fat are removed and the culatello is sliced thinly to serve. This is truly a regional delicacy and the care taken in its preparation is unequalled elsewhere in Italy. The process and sale of the prestigious Culatello di Zibello is now protected by a PDO certification.

COPPA, CAPOCOLLO AND SOPPRESSA

The three regional products known as coppa, capocollo and soppressa are examples of encased salumi, similar to salame. However the process in making these differs in that the meat is not ground and mixed with fat. All three are made in a manner rather like the production of prosciutto crudo. They share similar ingredients and a common method, using mostly neck portions of the pig and adding wine, salt and a spice mix. The blend is allowed to rest for 10 days before being encased and then aged.

Coppa hails from Piacenza, while capocollo originates from Calabria; both are protected by PDO certification. Soppressa is the variety made in the Veneto region, and uses shoulder and leg portions as well as red wine. It is also aged for longer than the others, up to a year. All varieties have a texture that is reminiscent of a prosciutto with a deep red colour and pale veins of fat. The flavour ranges from delicate and mellow to robust and spicy.

SPECK, MORTADELLA AND PANCETTA

Speck is an ancient product of German origin, originally called 'bachen' (similar to the English word 'bacon'). Historical evidence shows that it has been made in Trentino-Alto Adige in the far north of Italy since at least 1239. This is a ham with a distinctive juniper flavour, which is salted, smoked and then cured.

Mortadella di Bologna is another cured meat from Emilia-Romagna that has proven origins dating back to the Ancient Romans, who were fond of 'farcimen myrtatum', a mixture of ground pork meat blended with myrtle that is considered the ancestor of modern-day mortadella.

Also produced in Emilia-Romagna, though used extensively all over Italy, is the tasty meat known as pancetta. This is streaky/fatty bacon made from the belly of the pork. Another variety, used in the same sort of way in Italian cuisine, is called guanciale, and is made from the pig's cheek. Pancetta is usually sold plain, after salting, and can be rolled or flat. It can also be flavoured with herbs and black pepper, or made fiery hot with chilli. Pancetta is very important to the cuisine of the Italy and is widely used chopped small in pasta sauces, as part of a soffritto (the base mixture of meat and vegetables for soups and sauces), or to flavour stews and other meat dishes.

LARDO FROM TUSCANY

Tuscany has a very special cured pork product that uses two great local products: the white marble from the Apuan Alps, and locally reared pork. Marble caves have existed in the mountains of Tuscany since the Roman Age, and another use was found for this smooth, chilly stone.

STORING CURED MEATS

Most cured meats last a long time, if they aren't sliced. Once cut, they must be consumed quickly to prevent flavour and moisture loss, so it is best to buy only what you can eat in a short time. In the case of bresaola, it must be eaten as soon as possible after being sliced. The same is true of culatello and speck, since both dry out very quickly.

The Barbarians who ruled in the area after the Romans raised pigs and used them to make cured products, including lardo (lard, or solidified pork fat). The best lardo in the world is undoubtedly produced in Colonnata, a small village in the hinterland behind Carrara, in the Apuan Alps. The constant mountain wind found in Colonnata creates the ideal microclimate for ageing the fresh fat, which is placed in marble tubs or basins, which are perfectly porous, and is then left to cure with wine, salt and a combination of herbs for about 6 months.

HOW TO SERVE CURED MEATS ITALIAN-STYLE
Most cured meats are served as antipasti on their own or with other ingredients such as bread, olives, fruit, pickles or salad, and should be sliced very thinly so that their flavour and aroma can be fully appreciated. The more bacon-like varieties, pancetta, guanciale and speck, can be sliced thinly or diced since they are often used in cooking.

BRESAOLA FROM LOMBARDY

This is the one major exception to the all-pork range of cured Italian meats and is made in the Valtellina area of Lombardy. Whole beef fillets are mixed with salt, pepper, bay leaves and cloves. The meat is then covered and allowed to mature for about 3 months. Bresaola is dark red and should have almost no fat. To serve, it is sliced very thin as an antipasto, dressed with olive oil and a squeeze of lemon.

SOFT PORK SAUSAGE FROM LE MARCHE

Ciauscolo is produced in and around Macerata, and in areas reaching all the way across the central parts of Italy. Traditionally, the lean pork meat used to make this almost spreadable cured pork sausage from Le Marche was chopped by hand with a meat cleaver. Today, the meat is passed through a meat grinder three times using increasingly small screens. The meat comes from the tastiest cuts of pork, and extra fat is ground with it. The mixture is flavoured with garlic, pepper and salt, pounded together in a mortar. Sometimes, some wine is added as well for extra flavour. The meat is put into a natural casing and then smoked over juniper wood for 2 days. After that it is aged in a cellar for 2 or 3 months, and finally it is ready to eat.

SALUMI FROM CALABRIA

Calabria is certainly the most important producer of cured pork in the southern regions. Capocollo, soppressata, salsiccia Calabrese and 'nduja are all typical salumi that are made here. Capocollo dates back to the time of the colonists from Magna Graecia (the southern parts of Italy that were part of the ancient Greek Empire), who first introduced stuffed pork sausages to Calabria. Pork and pork products are made everywhere in this region and are considered part of the local culture. The traditional pig breeds raised in the area are large, robust animals, such as the Calabrese or the Large White. Capocollo is made from the top part of the loin from specific pigs that weigh no less than 135kg (300lb) and are at least 8 months old.

Salsiccia Calabrese is the local version of salame, made with minced/ground pork flavoured with chilli, fennel seed, salt and pepper. The Calabrian soppressata is made with coarsely ground pork, which is then pressed. This gives it an uneven, rustic appearance when sliced. This is a speciality of southern Italy, and like salsiccia, it usually includes some fiery chilli. The cured soppressata is often stored in jars of olive oil for extra keeping qualities. It is made in Basilicata, Puglia and Calabria, where the one produced in Decollatura is especially renowned and holds a PDO certification.

'Nduja is typically Calabrian and is traditionally made from pork trimmings not used for salame or other products. Its name probably comes from the French word 'andouillette', which is a type of sausage made with the pig's innards, tripe, lung and liver, boiled with vegetables and spices. The French may have brought this type of sausage to southern Italy when they were defending the land against the invading Spanish. In Calabria, 'nduja are made with liver, lung and the fatty parts of the pig and are grilled or broiled, cooked in sauce or eaten raw, flavoured with chilli. Because it is so soft, 'nduja can be spread on toast as an antipasto.

BELOW LEFT *Mortadella is a delicate cured meat flavoured with black pepper and myrtle berries, and studded with green pistachios and small cubes of pork fat.*

BELOW *Pancetta is widely used in cooking, usually diced into small cubes and employed to add intensity of flavour to dishes.*

MEAT, POULTRY AND GAME

Meat is much more widely served in the north of Italy compared to the south. The flat plains of the agricultural north are ideal for raising cattle, with plenty of space for them to roam. This means that succulent beef and veal cuts can be produced, to be made into all kinds of hot and cold dishes. On the other hand, the south has access to delicious lamb, mutton and goat, and everywhere in Italy pork is very popular, whether it is served freshly cooked or made into tasty ham, sausages or other delicacies.

PORK, BEEF AND VEAL

Pigs can be raised almost anywhere in Italy, but the north-east has its own particular recipes using fresh pork, such as the Venetian dish of pork cooked in milk. However, much of the pork from the region goes to make the range of cured hams and other delicacies, as described previously.

La porchetta, a whole pig flavoured with herbs, garlic and pepper, is one of the most delicious forms of street food in the central and southern regions, and particularly in Sardinia; many of the local markets sell pork cooked in this way, freshly sliced and tucked inside bread to eat at leisure.

Veal usually appears either as thin escalopes, such as the famous scaloppina al Marsala or vitello tonnato from Piedmont, or in a larger joint such as the stuffed roast veal dish from Liguria called punta ripiena. Beef is often braised in red wine, giving it a particularly rich flavour and succulent texture – one example is the famous Piedmontese speciality of brasato al Barolo.

In Tuscany, beef and veal from the prized Chianina breed of cattle often feature on the menu, in particular as the vast bistecca alla Fiorentina, the enormous T-bone steak often weighing up to 1kg (more than 2lb).

LA PIGNATA

A typical dish of Basilicata is la pignata, which consists of chunks of lamb or mutton stewed in a terracotta pot with vegetables, potatoes, cubed soppressata (the local sausage) and wine. The pot is sealed with a layer of wet clay or raw bread dough, and buried in the hot embers of the fire until the lamb is cooked through, which keeps all the juices inside the pot to make a delicious sauce. As a final flourish, the stew is served sprinkled with grated pecorino cheese.

LAMB AND MUTTON

In the north, very few recipes exist for lamb, whereas in the south, lamb and mutton are much more popular, mainly because sheep are better suited to the terrain than larger, less sure-footed animals like beef cattle. There is an ancient tradition for cooking lamb whole, turned on a spit or stewed in the oven. In Puglia and Basilicata, one of the most popular local specialities consists of the guts of a small lamb, threaded and woven on to sticks and then roasted over the fire.

BELOW *Juicy, flavoursome T-bone steaks, especially those from the Chianina cattle of Tuscany, are highly prized in Italy.*

BELOW MIDDLE *Pork that hasn't been turned into ham or sausages is cooked whole in milk, in Venice.*

BELOW RIGHT *Recipes featuring lamb are mostly found in the south of Italy.*

LEFT *Shaggy highland cattle fed on lush pastures in the high meadows of the Dolomite mountain range in Trentino-Alto Adige produce beef that is used to make hearty stews, robust steaks and carne salata – marinated beef that can be cooked in butter and served with polenta and beans, or sliced and eaten raw.*

POULTRY AND GAME

The Veneto is the main region for poultry dishes, such as Venetian stuffed chicken. Alongside its many chicken classics, the region also excels in its recipes for duck, goose and other waterfowl. These are to be found in abundance in the marshy Po delta. Another favourite of the Veneto is guinea fowl in red wine, a combination of two local ingredients that come together in splendid harmony in one dish.

In Le Marche, chicken is very popular both as a main dish and in soup, and in countrified Umbria, game birds such as quail and woodpigeon are widely used and much appreciated. Often, market stalls will have dozens of golden chickens turning on the spit, and busy householders can take one or two home for a quick meal for their family.

Game also plays a big part in Italian cuisine. Many Italians enjoy traditional hunting, not just for sport but also for the table. There is certainly no shortage of game, from hare and venison to pheasant, snipe, partridge, guinea fowl and many more. These are often served as rich stews and casseroles, made with robust red or sometimes white wine, such as the classic lepre al arneis (hare in wine) from Piedmont. Rabbit is popular all over the country, but particularly in the northern regions, where it is stewed slowly until tender and served with polenta. Wild boar sausages are also very popular in Umbria, Tuscany and Le Marche,

HOW TO BONE A CHICKEN

Many recipes call for chicken pieces. Rather than buying these ready-cut, you can easily cut your own from a whole chicken. The method below initially gives four large portions of chicken, which is ideal for most recipes, although these can be cut into smaller pieces as required.

- Using a sharp boning knife, cut through the skin between the leg and the carcass.
- Twist the leg away from the body to pop the leg bone from the backbone, and then cut the leg free.
- Repeat the process on the other side.
- To remove the breast and wing, run the knife down the breastbone to the wishbone. Separate the meat from the carcass by running the knife down the breast, following the contours of the breastbone to cut the fillet away.
- Cut through the joint that attaches the wing to the carcass, keeping it attached to the breast.
- Repeat the process on the other side.
- You can portion the chicken into smaller pieces by separating the thighs, drumsticks, breasts and wings with the boning knife or using a sharp, strong pair of scissors.

OPPOSITE *Chicken is less popular in Italy than other types of meat, and is mostly eaten in the Veneto and Le Marche. Their eggs, however, are much more widely used.*

ROMAN OFFAL COOKERY

The tradition of focusing on offal in Roman cuisine is linked to the central slaughterhouse in an area of Rome called Il Testaccio. This quarter of the city has ancient origins indeed, defined most clearly and obviously by the hill called Monte dei Cocci, which stands over the site of the old slaughterhouse. This mound is actually formed from broken Roman amphorae, large clay jars, which were dumped here after the arrival of goods such as the oil, grain and wine that would arrive at the nearby river port from Africa, Spain and even further afield.

During the 1800s, peasants from the nearby countryside, the fertile area known as La Campagna Romana, would bring their animals to market to sell to the highest bidder. The animals would then be slaughtered and butchered, and the finest cuts of meat would be taken up to the grand houses of the rich. Any remaining meat would be left for the locals to pick over, and often all that remained would be the offal, among other discarded cuts such as the heads and tails. In this way the wily locals would turn the kidneys, heart, spleen and other internal organs into tasty dishes to feed their families, and dishes such as coda alla vaccinara, oxtail stewed with celery and wine, became one of Rome's most famous dishes.

One problem, however, was the lack of refrigeration and the fact that Rome gets extremely hot during the summer months. To disguise the smell of meat that might not be entirely fresh, the Roman cooks of the 1800s developed a great love for intensely flavoured and highly perfumed ingredients such as garlic, rosemary, sage, mint, oregano and cloves, and used them cleverly in their cuisine. This is still very much the case when it comes to cooking these dishes today: the same ingredients still feature in many of the offal recipes that have been handed down for centuries.

usually served with polenta, or grilled/broiled over the embers of a fire. In Tuscany, sausages are often threaded on to strong, long rosemary branches and cooked upright, so that the fat drains out of the meat and the flavour of the rosemary permeates it while it is cooking.

RAW MEAT DELICACIES

There are two very special and delicious recipes for serving raw beef or veal that come from two different regions of northern Italy: carne cruda (literally translated as raw meat) and carpaccio. The first of these is the Piedmontese version of steak tartare, from the north-west. The rule for making this dish successfully is to use extremely fresh beef, hand-chopped at the very last minute. The meat should be cut into tiny pieces using a very sharp, heavy cook's knife, simply chopping away until it is fine enough. The texture will only be right if the meat is chopped by hand with great patience, so don't even think about using a food processor for this process as all the flavour will be destroyed, along with the fine texture.

The other famous Italian raw meat dish is the delicately flavoured carpaccio from Venice. This has a charming story behind it, going back to the original Cipriani bar and café in Venice. Mr Cipriani, the owner of the café, made the dish for a certain Contessa, a favourite customer of his, who was suffering from anaemia. He sliced some pale-pink milk-fed veal as thinly as he dared, laid it out on a plate and sprinkled it with extra virgin olive oil, lemon juice and black pepper, then added some shavings of fresh Parmesan cheese. In great trepidation, he put the plate down in front of La Contessa, who fell upon it enthusiastically. 'How delicious!' she cried. 'But tell me, Mr Cipriani, what is this marvellous dish called?' Quickly, he tried to think of a name for his new invention, and remembered that there was an exhibition of works by the painter Carpaccio going on nearby. The pink tones of his dish reminded him of the colours that feature in many of the pictures. 'Carpaccio!' he said, 'My dish shall be called Carpaccio!'

BELOW *Carpaccio is a simple dish made from the finest veal or beef, which is sliced very thinly and finished with top-quality olive oil, lemon juice and black pepper, and often dressed with rocket/arugula, capers or other pickes, and shavings of fresh Parmesan.*

FISH AND SHELLFISH

The quantity and type of fish that is available varies tremendously from one end of Italy to the other. The central areas of the north and landlocked central Umbria are very far from the sea, and therefore cooks in those parts traditionally rely more on freshwater fish or preserved fish brought in from other areas, and indeed other countries. In total contrast, the coastlines of some northern regions and most of the south are rich sources of sea fish and shellfish, which are eaten fresh the day they are caught.

FROM SEA TO TABLE

Going out 'a mangiar' pesce', to eat fish, is something that many Italians love to do whenever they can. They view it as a special occasion, an opportunity to enjoy a real feast, although it is not really about complicated sauces or cooking methods – what matters most is that the fish should be as fresh as possible, and cooked very simply, so that the flavour and texture of the main ingredient is what carries each dish and makes the whole thing a triumph.

TASTY FRIED MORSELS

Fritto misto or fritto di mare is a dish that is common to almost every region of Italy. It involves as wide a mixture of fish as possible, all floured lightly and then dropped into sizzling-hot oil for just a few moments before being served, crisp and piping hot, with just a wedge of lemon to squeeze over it. The common denominators are always rings of tender squid or cuttlefish, prawns/shrimps, and whitebait. After that, each cook adds his or her own touch, such as a chunk of red mullet fillet, a few strips of edible seaweed, or whatever else might be available and considered suitable to blend with the other ingredients.

SALTWATER FISH

Prized, special and expensive fish and shellfish, such as sea bass, lobster, lemon sole or scallops, are not considered suitable for fritto misto. For these, other cooking methods are reserved, such as simple grilling/broiling over a scented fire, or poaching or baking in the oven. This keeps all the taste and texture of these more rarefied fish so that each mouthful can be savoured.

The Ligurians are mad about anchovies and the other small blue fish that have always been so plentiful in the waters between Liguria and Corsica, which are considered to be some of the best in the whole of Italy. They are filleted and made into delicious layered baked dishes, or used to form part of a local version of fritto misto.

From 1 December to 30 April every year, bianchetti (whitebait) are fished all along the Ligurian coast and are then crisply fried in a dusting of flour, and served with just a squeeze of lemon juice. The coastline here is very rocky, so rock fish are plentiful, and are made into delicious soups such as the typical buridda. Also found in this part of the Tyrrhenian Sea are red mullet and gurnard, locally known as gallinella – the 'chicken of the sea' – for its firm, meaty texture.

BELOW *Freshwater fish such as gilthead bream are delicious baked whole and served simply with garlic and potatoes.*

BELOW MIDDLE *Red mullet is quite bony, so it is often cooked whole, baked in a parcel, with just a few flavourings.*

BELOW RIGHT *Freshly caught sardines are stuffed and baked in Sicily to make a tasty dish called sarde e beccafico.*

FRESHWATER FISH

Many different freshwater fish are caught and cooked in the lakes and waterways of Italy's inland regions, where saltwater fish are harder to come by. Varieties include freshwater bream, which is a good eating fish, if terribly bony. It is suitable for frying, roasting or poaching. Carp is a large lake fish and is good baked and served whole.

Perch is a fish that is widely available in many northern regions, often sold as firm pink fillets that can be cooked in numerous different ways. The fillets are especially delicious dusted with flour, fried in butter and served atop creamy risotto. As a whole fish it is very bony, so it is best to buy it prepared by the fishmonger if possible.

Trout is plentiful in the fresh, clear waters of the streams and lakes of Trentino-Alto Adige, one of the more mountainous regions of the north. Trout from these pure waters has a delicious, delicate flavour and is rightfully considered to be a local speciality.

Eel is extremely popular in the Veneto, where it is plentiful in the low marshy terrain, living in small streams, ponds and rivers. It finds its way into all kinds of dishes, including an amazing rice dish called risi e bisati, made with meaty chunks of eel, rice, garlic and tomatoes.

PRESERVED FISH

Baccalà and stoccafisso are two types of cured, dried cod. The former is preserved only in salt; the latter is first preserved in salt and then air-dried. These, along with salted anchovies and other forms of preserved, salted fish, were the only way in which inhabitants of the regions far away from the coastline could ever introduce fish into their diet, and there is a strong tradition of cooking with this kind of fish in regions such as Piedmont and inland Veneto. Baccalà and stoccafisso need to be soaked for several days in fresh water to reconstitute them, at which point they can be treated more or less like fresh fish. In Liguria, according to ancient tradition, the salt cod is always put into fresh water to soak on a Thursday, which means it will be ready to cook on a Monday, when (owing to the rule of no fishing on a Sunday) there would be no fresh fish to eat. Anchovies may require just a brief soak before being used in dishes.

SEAFOOD

All of the various members of the cephalopod family are held dear by Italian fish cooks and connoisseurs. One of the most popular Tuscan ways of cooking the biggest of these, the octopus, is simply to boil it until softened, and then to serve it warm with cubed boiled potatoes, lots of olive oil, lemon juice and handfuls of finely chopped fresh flat leaf parsley; but countless

ABOVE *All manner of different fish and shellfish can go into making fritto misto – the main priority is that the produce is as fresh as possible.*

SUSTAINING FISH SOUP

Every region of Italy on either coast has its own local version of a fish soup or stew, which makes the most of what is to hand. The common name for them all is zuppa di pesce, but in Le Marche it is called brodetto, and in Tuscany it becomes cacciucco. The story of the latter version goes that a local fisherman's wife, having lost her husband at sea in a big storm, went round to all her neighbours and pleaded with them to help her to feed her children. With the few ingredients she managed to collect, she created this delicious speciality of the city of Livorno, which must contain five varieties or more of fresh fish, one each to represent the five 'C's in the recipe's name.

ABOVE *Scallops – both of the king and queen variety – are highly prized in Italy and are normally served simply so their flavour can be fully appreciated.*

OPPOSITE *Colourful traditional fishing nets are hung up to dry and so that they can be inspected for holes and repaired if necessary.*

recipes exist for the preparation of octopus, which is often considered a bit rubbery and chewy unless cooked with the utmost care. To avoid this bouncy texture, the best tip is to add a handful of used wine corks to the pot while it is cooking – in a mysterious fashion this helps to tenderise the flesh. Moscardini, which are tiny, newborn octopus, are also extremely popular along the Tuscan coast, and are usually served deep-fried or stewed.

Squid and cuttlefish are part of the same family and are available at fish stores and market stalls all over coastal Italy in a bewildering variety of shapes and sizes. Whether they are stuffed and baked or braised, fried, grilled, broiled or boiled, Italians really love these fish for their sweetness and texture and their ability to take on other flavours, from spicy to sour. Relatively cheap and easy to prepare, squid and cuttlefish are popular with all ages because they have no bones or scales to worry about and are very nutritious.

HOW TO PREPARE VONGOLE (CLAMS)

The best way to clean and prepare vongole so that there is no mud or sand left lurking inside their shells, which would spoil the dish, is to use fresh seawater. If you don't live near the sea, it is available to buy online, at least in some countries, or you can prepare a good substitute using still mineral water (unless you are lucky enough to live in a place where the water has no added chlorine or other chemicals). Add 36g/1½oz fine sea salt to every 1 litre/1¾ pints/ 4 cups of water. Check that the water is at room temperature, and stir the salt into the water until it completely dissolves. Cover the vongole in the salty water – they should be about 2.5cm/1in below the surface. Leave them to soak in the water for about 4 hours, in a cool place, but preferably not in the fridge. Remove them from the water after this time, rinse quickly with still mineral water and then proceed to cook them immediately in your chosen recipe.

King scallops, or capesante as they are called in Italy, are a rare and special form of seafood that is mostly found in the north of Italy, particularly around the Gulf of Venice. Southern Italians eat the much smaller, very sweet and delicious queen scallops that are found in the warm seas around their coastline.

When it comes to molluscs, carpet clams or vongole are considered to be one of the best treasures the sea has to offer. The people of Naples have a particular passion for these little shellfish, not only evident in the celebrated pairing of spaghetti alle vongole, both with and without tomatoes, but also in the delicious dish of sartu alle vongole, in which fresh vongole are steamed open with white wine, parsley and garlic.

Cozze, muscoli, or mussels, are eaten in a wide variety of dishes, often with pasta, but in Naples and Puglia they are also enjoyed raw, with just a simple squeeze of lemon juice.

Some of the more unusual shellfish are popular in regions such as the Veneto. These include moleche, the small soft-shelled crabs that are on sale at the Rialto market in Venice when they are available during the moulting periods, when their carapaces fall away and they are ready to eat. This happens in April and May, and again in October and November. The Venetians also love to eat the huge spider crab, locally known as granseola. This spiny crab is popular both in the Veneto and around the coast of Trieste in Friuli-Venezia Giulia.

VEGETABLES

The food of the north of Italy is very different from the world-famous Mediterranean diet of the south, where vegetables such as tomatoes, bell peppers and aubergines are key ingredients. In the north other, perhaps blander, vegetables come into their own, such as radicchio, white asparagus and cabbage. Of course the reason for this is that they grow well in the mild climate of northern Italy, while tomatoes and bell peppers really need to be bathed in the hot sunshine of the southern summer.

STAPLE VEGETABLES OF THE NORTH

With the notable exception of bagna caùda, the famous warm garlic dip of Piedmont, onions are generally used more extensively than garlic in the north, and are often served as a vegetable in their own right – stuffed and baked, for example. In the Veneto, the famous dish of fegato alla Veneziana, liver cooked in the Venetian style, should always be served on a deep bed of soft, sweet, gently caramelised red onions.

Potatoes are also used a great deal in northern Italian cuisine. Piedmont is purportedly one of the two regions that first gave us potato gnocchi, the other being Lazio, the area around Rome in central Italy. Turnips are also popular in the north, although they are seldom seen elsewhere in Italy. Other, more common vegetables, such as leeks, courgettes/zucchini, carrots and celery are also used all over the north.

BASIC VEGETABLES OF THE SOUTH

There is a much more widespread use of garlic in the south compared to the far north. Here, it is the ideal partner for chilli peppers and olive oil, and marries well with the many traditional, uncomplicated fish, vegetable and pasta dishes. One of the most popular ways to serve plain vegetables such as sprouting broccoli or chicory is to cook them first in salted water, then toss them in a frying pan with olive oil, chilli, garlic and sometimes anchovies, until heated through.

The tomato really comes into its own in the southern regions. Although it is of course also immensely popular in central Italian cuisine, it is in Naples that it is known quite simply as 'oro rosso' (red gold). Its cultivation in the region of Campania has brought prosperity to this region in a way that no other vegetable ever has. Perhaps it is the added richness in the soil, thanks to the presence of volcanic soil deposited by Vesuvius, or the sea breezes around the coast, or the hot summer sun; for whatever reason, it is true that tomatoes flourish here in a quite remarkable way. Many of them are processed for canning or turned into concentrated tomato paste, but while the season lasts, they are also enjoyed fresh in salads and cooking. There is even a variety that lasts well into the winter, hanging in bunches from the ceilings of restaurant and home kitchens all over the region. Although strictly speaking it is a fruit, the pomo d'oro, or golden apple, as the tomato is also called, has been adored in and around Naples since its introduction from the New World in the 17th century, and it seems to capture the very essence of the cooking of Campania.

THE MEDITERRANEAN DIET

Researchers have discovered that people in the countries bordering the Mediterranean Sea, especially in southern Italy, exhibit strikingly low rates of heart disease compared with Americans or Northern Europeans. Meals consist of grains, fruits, pulses and above all lavish quantities of vegetables, with just a little meat, cheese and fish. The main fat is olive oil, which is used for dressings and for cooking, instead of butter. The garlic that appears in many dishes as a major flavour enhancer may help to prevent blood clots, lower cholesterol and protect against cancer.

SOFFRITTO

The supporting foundations of many Italian dishes come from the balanced use of celery, carrot and onion – whether chopped fine, cut into chunks or left whole – which release the base-note flavour to soups, stews, sauces and stocks that is essential to so many Italian dishes from every region.

OPPOSITE: TOP, FROM LEFT TO RIGHT *garlic, green cabbage, red onions;* **MIDDLE, FROM LEFT TO RIGHT** *green asparagus, tomatoes, pumpkin;* **BOTTOM, FROM LEFT TO RIGHT** *bell peppers, potatoes, beetroots.*

Regional vegetables

The huge variety in the climate and terrain in Italy brings with it a corresponding diversity in the vegetables that are favoured in each region. Specialities abound, for which Italian cooks have created so many mouthwatering dishes.

Calabrian onions Calabria, the long peninsula lapped by the Mediterranean Sea in the far south (the toe of the boot), is famous all over Italy for its amazing red onions, cipolle di tropea, which are considered to be the sweetest and most delicious onions grown anywhere. This region also produces the most dense, sweet and succulent red and yellow bell peppers under its baking-hot sun.

Sicilian aubergines/eggplants The aubergine is the most important vegetable on the island of Sicily, where countless recipes have been created for its preparation. La melanzana, as it is called in Italy, was introduced to Sicily during the Arab domination of the island, along with cotton, jasmine, citrus fruits and other crops that have since become synonymous with the island. However, it is the aubergine that appears to have really captured the palate and the imagination of the Sicilians – so much so that it has even been known to turn up fried and covered in melted chocolate as an accompaniment to a main-course meat dish.

A rarity from Puglia Some of the more unusual vegetables grown in Italy are virtually unheard of in any of the other regions, or indeed elsewhere in Europe. In Puglia, for example, lampascioni, the bulb of a wild hyacinth that grows on the Karst Plateau of the Murghe, are considered a real delicacy. Whether roasted in the embers of a fire, boiled, fried, stewed, added to one of the local lamb casseroles, preserved in olive oil or pickled, these unusual and ugly-looking little bitter vegetables are only eaten in this area.

Roman artichokes and cardoons In Rome and the Lazio region there is a passion for globe artichokes that is almost unparalleled, even though other regions do of course also use this delicious, metallic-tasting vegetable. Jerusalem artichokes, known in Italy by their French name of topinambour, are only really known and eaten in Piedmont, but the globe artichoke and its first cousin the cardoon, 'cardo', is prepared with great love and reverence in and around Rome. The cardoon is also very popular in Umbria and in Abruzzo. This long-stemmed, slightly furry vegetable is not unlike a large, overgrown head of celery in appearance, but tastes more like artichoke heart.

Both cardoons and artichokes are high in iron and are considered very good for the liver, thanks to the minerals they contain. In the spring, when the artichokes and cardoons first come into season, they are sold by the side of the road in great leafy bundles by the local farmers all over the countryside, especially in the rich and fertile area known as La Campagna Romana, which has been supplying Rome and the whole region with myriad superb vegetables since Roman times.

The white asparagus of the north One of the most intriguing and typical vegetables found in Italy is the delicious white asparagus. This is a much-prized ingredient with a long history, which is equally revered in Belgium, the Netherlands and Germany though not traditionally so well known elsewhere in Europe. Back in Italy, the Consortium of the White Asparagus of Bassano, which exists to protect and promote this precious vegetable, is situated in the province of Vicenza in the town of Bassano del Grappa, in the Veneto. It was established in 1980, although local legend suggests that the discovery of this particular variety of asparagus goes back to the 16th century. The story goes that a local farmer, having seem his entire crop of green asparagus destroyed by a violent hailstorm unleashed by Mother Nature, uncovered and dug up the white asparagus shoots that were still underground, undamaged. To his great surprise he discovered that they were very tasty and fully ripe, and so he began the local tradition of intentionally producing white asparagus.

The inhabitants of Venice and its surrounding area are particularly fond of white asparagus, and serve it either simply on its own, or as part of a creamy risotto or a chunky frittata. Umbria also produces thin-stemmed wild green asparagus, which is also sold in neat bundles by the side of the road by local foragers during the very brief season.

Purple radicchio Radicchio is another real northern favourite that is not half so well known outside Italy, although it is beginning to grow in popularity as traditional Italian cookery is becoming better understood and appreciated. There are eight different versions of this wonderful purple-coloured member of the chicory family, the best of which is Trevisano, also known as fiore d'inverno, or winter flower. This is the most precious and expensive kind of radicchio. Others include the rounded Chioggia variety, and the floppy-leafed Verona. All of them are at their best in the cold winter months. Despite its bitterness, it is easily digestible and is packed full of vitamins and minerals. The ancient Romans ate radicchio raw as a bitter salad leaf, but since the 19th century, countless recipes for cooking radicchio have been created, including risotto, encased in pastry, grilled over a barbecue or braised with butter and white wine, to mention but a few treatments.

Cabbage from the mountains In the northern regions of Friuli-Venezia Giulia and Trentino-Alto Adige, close to the Austrian and Slovenian borders, cabbage is often transformed into the local version of sauerkraut, known locally as crauti, which is usually served with sausages or dumplings or as the basis for Trieste's famous speciality soup, la jota. In previous centuries, this was a good way of preserving the goodness of cabbage for use in lean times, something that still holds true today. Moreover, this priobiotic-rich food is good for gut health, as well as containing fibre and numerous vitamins, meaning that it is as beneficial for health as it is for the palate – perhaps something that people realised hundreds of years ago.

MUSHROOMS AND TRUFFLES

Mushrooms and truffles can be found growing wild in the woods, particularly in the northern and central regions, and they certainly impart a special flavour to many dishes. Where truffles do grow, they are used in quantity to make a real impact rather than being shaved finely, as might happen with imported truffles elsewhere in Europe. In Trentino-Alto Adige there are even some policemen who are trained mycologists, whom mushroom pickers can ask to check their bounty, to make sure it is completely safe to eat.

BELOW *Special knives for cutting mushrooms avoid damaging the fungus left behind in the earth. This one features a brush that is ideal for gently cleaning off any soil.*

MUSHROOM GATHERING IN ITALY

The damp climate and the dense woodland of northern Italy's upland areas give the perfect conditions for wild mushrooms to flourish, and there is no shortage of pickers to take advantage of this fact. Local stores sell special knives for cutting the mushrooms so as not to damage the fungi. There is also a sacrosanct rule of collecting the picked fungi in a woven wicker basket, so that the spores can fall back through the weave and into the surrounding soil as you walk, ready to form next year's crop.

The wooded slopes around Borgotaro, a small town in the mountains of Liguria, is considered one of the best places in the whole of Italy to find the much-prized Boletus edulis, also known as porcini, or ceps, and when the season starts the woods and hills of this area are the target for mushroom foragers from far and wide.

The woodlands on the borders of Tuscany and Emilia-Romagna are also marvellous areas for finding wild fungi, in particular the precious porcini. In early to late September, if the season has been a good one, with wet, rainy nights followed by warm sunny days, the local restaurants in the hills below the Apennine ridge will serve these large mushrooms whole, like a slab of meat, grilled or broiled to perfection and just dressed with a hint of garlic and herbs and a slick of the very best extra virgin olive oil. If visiting tourists are inspired to go and find these lovely treats for themselves, they should please remember that mushroom foraging in Italy requires a permit from the local authorities.

AMANITA CAESAREA

One of the most extraordinary and very special mushrooms is found in Piedmont as well as in other northern regions. Known as the ovulo, Caesar's mushroom, or Amanita caesarea, to give it its proper botanical name, this is an amazing mushroom that starts off looking like a whole white egg, and gradually opens to reveal a yolk-coloured yellow cap. It is at its very best served sliced thinly as a salad, with Parmesan and white truffle shavings.

DRIED MUSHROOMS

Porcini mushrooms can be bought dried. These need to be soaked in warm water to reconstitute them before they are added to a dish. The soaking water can be used in the recipe too, but it needs filtering carefully through a fine sieve or strainer, since residues of sand, grit and forest vegetation are often left behind in the liquid.

ABOVE *The fertile earth of a forest floor is the ideal territory for fungi such as these parasol mushrooms growing in Alto Adige in northern Italy.*

TRUFFLES

A vital part of the Piedmontese food scene is the precious white truffle of Alba. Rare and terribly expensive, these truffles have a unique flavour, which is celebrated throughout Italy and far beyond. Their scent is delicate, but pungent and powerful at the same time. Unlike the more common black truffles, white truffles are served only raw, finely grated in beautifully veined shavings that fall like rain over a bed of risotto, or with tajarin, the Piedmontese version of tagliatelle. Mixed with grated Parmesan cheese for a wonderful blend of strong flavours, they make delicious canapés. Black truffles are also sometimes found in Piedmont, but the quality and value of their white cousin far outshines these darker ones.

The black truffle of Norcia, in Umbria, means that this tiny little landlocked region has its own very special local ingredient. Less expensive, and considered less refined in flavour, compared with the white truffles, these black truffles are treated with casual abandon by the local cooks, who chop them up like parsley, liberally sprinkling them into all manner of pasta, meat and game dishes. Due to their cost elsewhere, a less generous hand may be expedient.

Truffle hunters go out in the gloomy light of the early dawn from October to February, using a highly trained and hence very valuable pale coloured dog (pale dogs are perfect for truffle hunting because they can be seen in the half-darkness). The dog's sensitive nose seeks out the spot where the precious fungus is growing beneath the earth, and starts to dig. The truffle hunter then has to quickly restrain the dog, whose aim is to expose and eat the delicious-smelling truffle, and continue to dig gently until the truffle can be eased out of the soil. Brushed clean, the truffle is then ready to use.

FRUITS AND NUTS

As with the vegetable harvest, very different kinds of fruits flourish in the various parts of Italy, from the apples, pears and berries of the north to the more exotic melons, figs and lemons of southern regions. Nuts also thrive in the north, and there is a well-established tradition of using these in both sweet and savoury dishes, often alongside dried fruits. One fruit found nearly everywhere in Italy is grapes, which are of course made into wine.

BELOW *Surely one of the country's most iconic fruits, the humble olive plays such an important role in the daily lives of many Italians, primarily as olive oil, but also in its cured form at the table.*

FRUITS OF THE NORTHERN REGIONS

The climate of northern Italy is rather similar to that of France – it has a far more temperate, gentler weather pattern than the south of Italy. Succulent apples and pears and juicy peaches are grown in the orchards of the sunny foothills of the most northern regions: Piedmont, Aosta Valley and Lombardy. These fruits are ideal for making desserts, and are usually treated quite simply by being baked whole or simmered in red wine for a wonderful pink-coloured sweet treat.

In the cooler uplands of northern Italy, woodland berries flourish on hillsides and in forests, and are gathered by the local inhabitants in the late summer and early autumn. Myrtles, whortleberries, tiny, fragrant, wild strawberries and raspberries ripen in the clear air and sunshine, and are made into cakes, tarts, ice creams and jams, preserving the essence of summer for cooler winter days.

Olives, which grow on the rocky Ligurian hills and in small areas on the shores of Lake Garda and Lake Como, are a member of the drupe family, a fruit with a fleshy part surrounding a hard central stone, such as cherries, plums, mangoes and peaches. Olives can be crushed to produce olive oil, of course, but are also eaten cured as part of an antipasto, or as a snack on their own. Their distinctive flavour also adds a highlight to all kinds of recipes, particularly simple fish dishes.

PERFECT FRUITS OF THE SOUTH

The southern and central regions are fortunate to be able to produce the delicious, aromatic peaches and nectarines that grow in such tremendous profusion all over Basilicata, Puglia, Calabria and Sicily. China is where the peach was first discovered by the Persians, who then passed it on to the Romans, and thus the fruit found its way around the world. By the 17th century, Spanish explorers had taken the fruit back with them from Europe to the New World, where it grew well in the warm southern parts of the USA and South America. During Queen Victoria's reign it was considered a very special treat with which to end a meal; as the British climate was not ideal for peaches, they were imported at some expense.

Italy is one of the three largest producers of peaches worldwide, after the USA, along with Greece and China. When peaches are perfectly ripe and juicy, they really need no embellishment. In Tuscany, a popular way to create a simple dessert at the table is simply to slice a beautifully ripe peach into a glass of red wine.

Melons grow abundantly all over Sicily, and are the ideal cooler on a hot day. Different varieties are in season at different times, even in winter, when the hard-skinned winter melons come into

their own. The perfect partner for melon, and also for peaches, is some thinly sliced prosciutto – still one of the most popular antipasti all over these southern parts.

Of equal importance of course are the citrus fruits, such as oranges and lemons, which take over as favourite fruits in the winter months once the summer varieties have finished. The famous Amalfi lemons that grow in great profusion on the slopes of the coastline south of Naples are particularly prized for their intense perfume and delicious flavour.

Figs are another fruit that is abundant in the southern parts, especially in Calabria, and their sweet, soft flesh is best enjoyed simply, on its own or perhaps partnered with some prosciutto, mozzarella and basil to make a wonderful salad.

SWEET AND SAVOURY NUTS

Piedmont produces some of the most highly prized hazelnuts in the world, the rounded, richly flavoured tonda gentile, which is produced in the provinces of Cuneo, Asti and Alessandria. This precious nut holds an Protected Geographical Indication (PGI) certification, which guarantees its authenticity and proves that it comes from these particular areas. Ground hazelnuts are blended with chocolate to make the famous gianduja chocolates, as well as the smooth chocolate spread called Nutella, which is so popular in Italy that it is even used to make a sweet pizza. Hazelnuts also feature in intensely flavoured nocciola ice cream, and are turned into praline for all kinds of pastries and confectionery, including hard and brittle or soft and chewy torrone (nougat).

In neighbouring Liguria, walnuts are used extensively to make a winter pesto – pesto d'inverno – by adding bread softened in milk, garlic and olive oil to walnuts pounded to a paste in a pestle and mortar. This is used in Liguria to dress pasta in the months when the local basil is not in season. Walnuts are often used in this way as a substitute for pine nuts, and their strong, slightly bitter flavour blends well with other savoury ingredients, particularly cheese, in little canapés to be eaten with a glass of wine. In both Liguria and Piedmont, walnuts are also used to make sweets and candies.

Almonds are a vital ingredient in many savoury and sweet dishes that form part of the menu in the central and southern regions. These recipes include the hard cantucci biscuits of Tuscany, specially made to be dipped into sweet vin santo, and the savoury almond pesto of Trapani. Other nuts, such as hazelnuts, pine kernels and pistachios, which are famously grown in and around the village of Bronte on the slopes of Mount Etna, are also widely used in a whole variety of sweet and savoury recipes.

AN UNUSUAL DELICACY

One of the most unusual fruits that is very popular in all central regions is the loquat, or nespola, which comes into season along with cherries. This slightly sour, orange fruit was much loved by the Romans and is harvested in the late autumn, then allowed to ripen slowly over the winter.

ABOVE LEFT *A wonderful array of fruits is available during the summer and early autumn months in Italy – from cherries, nectarines, peaches and apricots to pears, apples, figs and melons.*

ABOVE *Nuts and dried fruits such as apricots appear in both savoury and sweet dishes in many parts of Italy.*

HERBS AND SEASONINGS

Italians use lots of herbs and spices in their cooking. It is taken for granted that these will almost always be fresh – and in fact when tender herbs such as basil are unavailable during the chilly winter months, Italian cooks simply make a different dish. The only herb that really improves in flavour with drying is oregano, which finds its way into many savoury recipes, and which really recalls the aroma of sun-baked Italian hills.

FRUITS OF THE NORTHERN REGIONS

The kind of flavourings favoured by the cooks of northern Italy include sage, which is often chopped and melted with butter to make a simple dressing for pasta. This same sage-infused butter imparts a special flavour to quickly fried liver or veal escalopes.

Tuscany is the region that makes the greatest use of rosemary to flavour and perfume its regional cuisine. It is sometimes used in sweet dishes, such as the chewy chestnut-flour cake caked castagnaccio, but mainly to flavour the much-loved roasted meats of this region. These tiny spikes permeate the meat as it is cooking to give it a special taste. This is also the only region that has a traditional use of tarragon in its repertoire of dishes, here, as in the rest of Italy, known as dragoncello. In Le Marche, freshly picked wild herbs are still very commonly used in cooking, especially wild fennel, which is also hugely popular in Sardinian and Sicilian cuisine.

Oregano is a native plant to southern Italy, where its perfume hangs in the air. Not only does its aroma heighten and flavour many pasta, cheese, meat and fish dishes all around Italy, but it is also an immensely practical herb for cooks living in the city, as it is always used dry, unlike most other herbs, which are best picked and used fresh. Oregano is often confused with marjoram, to which it is related, although true oregano has a stronger flavour. This useful herb, whose botanical name is Origanum vulgare, and meaning 'joy of the mountains' in the original Greek, can be bought in local stores and markets in bunches ready to store in a cool, dry cupboard.

REGIONAL SPECIALITIES

Some herbs have such fragrant qualities that they almost embody the whole cuisine of a particular region. Ligurian basil is one such typical herb, and it grows incredibly well on the somewhat windswept, sunny coastline, thriving in the strong sea breezes. Much of the cuisine of Liguria is based around this fragrant herb, including of course the famous recipe for pesto, a simple, delicious sauce for pasta made with basil, pine nuts, garlic, Parmesan cheese and plenty of peppery olive oil. Ligurian cooks often add to the flavour by pouring pesto on top of pasta that has been made with mixed chopped herbs or, most traditionally, with borage.

Another rarity not found elsewhere in Italy is myrtle leaves in Sardinia. These are traditionally used to flavour a delicious poached chicken dish,

BELOW *Pungent, tender basil is used freely throughout Italy in all manner of dishes, but especially in the famous pesto from Liguria.*

BELOW MIDDLE *Robust, woody rosemary appears most often in northern dishes, either finely chopped or in little sprigs that are used to stud meat.*

BELOW RIGHT *Herbs and spices, such as bay leaves, juniper and black pepper, add depth of flavour to rib-sticking stews.*

in which the bird is wrapped in myrtle to flavour the meat as it cools. It is also an integral flavour in the island's signature dish of roast suckling piglet, and makes an intriguing liqueur.

SPICES

These flavourings really come into their own in the Veneto, thanks to the historical tradition of Venice as the European centre for spice traders from faraway lands. Ground ginger, cinnamon, mace, nutmeg and juniper are all favourites in savoury as well as sweet dishes. Saffron, which in Italy is usually sold in little sachets in a powdered form, is essential for making the classic golden risotto alla Milanese. Zafferano dell'Aquila from the Navelli Valley in Abruzzo is especially prized for its pungent flavour and intense aroma.

CHILLI PEPPERS

The hot red chilli pepper, known as diavolicchio or diavolino (little devil), is extremely popular in the regions of the far south, such as Calabria, Campania, Basilicata and Abruzzo. Historically, during the plague it was thought to be a cure for the disease – it certainly has a fierce effect. Today, it is used to enliven all kinds of dishes – from pasta sauces to meat and fish – and the southerners have developed a great resistance to its heat, which travellers from cooler climates may find overwhelming. Like oregano, it is almost never used in its fresh form, but dried first, then chopped or crumbled or used whole according to the individual recipe. As ever with recipes that include chilli, it is best to add a little to start with, test the dish for heat, and then add more as required to suit your palate. You can always add more, but you can't take it away once it is there!

SICILIAN SALT

There are records that date back to 1154 of the production and export of salt from the famous salt flats near Trapani, although the trade is known to have existed for much longer than that, dating to the time of the Phoenicians, well before the Roman Empire. The salt flats lie within a nature reserve and it is a remarkable place to visit, with lots of rare flora and fauna that are unique to this environment. There is also a salt museum. Salt from this special place is considered to be of the highest quality.

BELOW *Expensive but intensely flavoured, saffron is usually sold in powdered form in Italy and is most famously used in risotto.*

BELOW MIDDLE *The warm, fragrant notes of cinnamon and nutmeg enhance and lend depth to savoury dishes as well as flavouring sweet ones.*

BELOW RIGHT *Fiery dried red chillies are used with a generous hand in the cooking of the south in many dishes, including l'arrabbiata sauce.*

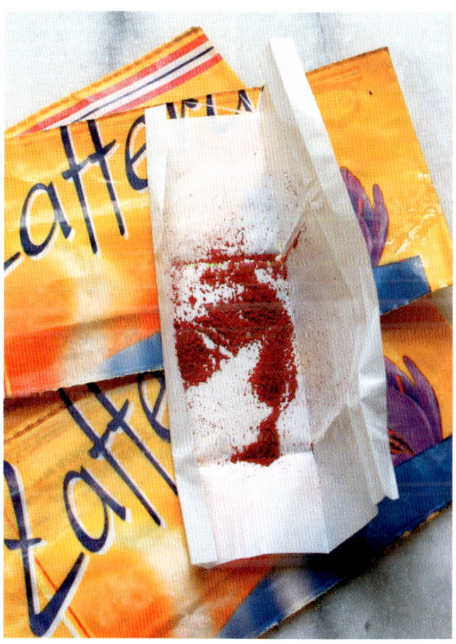

OILS AND VINEGARS

Olive oil is the cooking fat of choice in central and southern Italian cuisine, whereas further north, butter or pork fat is more commonly used. The local aromatic olive oil permeates southern Italian cooking, and is one of the healthiest and most delicious flavourings to be found in these regions. Vinegar is an everyday staple of the northern and central regions, made from the local red or white wine and used as a flavouring or to preserve ingredients.

OPPOSITE *Good-quality olive oil and balsamic vinegar – along with key ingredients such as fresh garlic and tomatoes – are a mainstay of Italian food, with different types being used according to how they are served: the best is reserved for drizzling, while cheaper types are used in cooking.*

VARIETIES OF OLIVE OIL

Most regions of Italy produce olive oil, apart from those in the far north. The most prolific is possibly Puglia in the south, where the olive groves stretch all the way down to the long coastline, with mile after mile of enormous, chunky trees that are quite different from the much smaller, twisted trees of more northerly regions such as Liguria, or even Tuscany. Legend has it that Cleopatra was immensely fond of the olive oil from Bitonto, near Bari, and that Mark Antony would always make sure he brought her some when he visited Egypt.

Sicily is also a major producer of olive oil, the trees thriving on the very arid landscape and fertile volcanic soil that makes up so much of the island. As in all the hot regions of the south, the harvest happens earlier than in the north of Italy, so the first pressed olive oil, the fiore, is usually available for the household to enjoy by October. Varieties grown on the island today include carolea, nocellara and biancolilla. The first domesticated olive cultivar brought to the island by the ancient Greeks was the kalamata, its memory preserved today as a single ancient tree in the eastern part of Sicily.

Tuscan olive oil is deep green with a grassy aroma of newly mown lawns and a very peppery taste that tends to catch at the back of the throat. It has always been considered one of the best olive oils produced anywhere in the world. There are usually as many as five types of olive pressed together to create its unique qualities, the most important variety being frantoio.

Liguria is the largest producer of olive oil in the northern regions. A fine-quality oil is made every year from the olive trees that cling so tenaciously to the hillsides in steep groves, often very close to the edges of the region's magnificent cliffs. The less intense heat and the different varieties of olive grown here mean that the oil of Liguria is quite different to that of southern and central regions. Lighter and more flowery in character, it has none of the full-bodied qualities of the oils from the deep south, nor the unmistakeably peppery characteristics of Tuscan olive oil; nor is it as complex in flavour and aroma as the olive oils from Umbria or Le Marche in central Italy.

OIL FOR DEEP-FRYING

The illustrious tradition of deep-frying all kinds of ingredients in Italy does not rely on delicate, precious olive oil. Instead, blander sunflower oil or vegetable oil is used, or in some cases strutto or lard/white cooking fat. These paler, subtler oils and fats work best when frying a batch of different seafood for fritto misto, for example, where olive oil might overpower the fishy flavours.

BALSAMIC VINEGAR

Although all kinds of vinegar, made from red or white wine, are used in many recipes from Italy – as well as for pickling and preserving all manner of vegetables for the winter – it is really balsamic vinegar that takes centre stage. This dark, sweet vinegar comes originally from Emilia-Romagna, and in particular from Modena, where the best-quality balsamic goes by the name 'aceto balsamico tradizionale di Modena'. It is the word 'tradizionale' that denotes it as being the really expensive, home-made variety. It is still made in the lofts and attics of people's homes, where the temperatures are hottest in summer and coldest in winter, and tends to be the total responsibility of the men of the household.

Traditionally, when a daughter married, some of her father's balsamic vinegar store would form part of her dowry, and passed on to her husband, and so on. A new barrel would be added to the collection with the birth of each new baby into the family.

While industrially produced balsamic vinegar is widely available, in a variety of qualities, ages and corresponding price brackets, there is no comparison between this and the tradizionale, left to mature in the attic for future generations to use.

PRESERVING IN OIL

Italians have a tradition of preserving vegetables, mushrooms, fish, cured meats and even certain kinds of cheese 'sott'olio' (under oil), to lock in both freshness and flavour, ready to be eaten during the winter. They are often served as part of an antipasto.

STORECUPBOARD INGREDIENTS

There is a long list of ingredients that will be found in any Italian kitchen cupboard or pantry, all of them vital components of the essential dishes of Italian cuisine. A thrifty cook's larder might contain rows of jars containing home-made preserved summer fruits, pickled vegetables, goat's cheese and salumi as well as packets of rice, spices, dried herbs, dried pasta, canned tomatoes, passata and other dry goods. Some of the most common items to be found are described below.

DRIED GOODS

While risotto rice is an absolute staple of the northern Italian kitchen, long grain rice is a common ingredient everywhere in Italy, because it is so useful for adding to soups, or for serving plain as an accompaniment.

Unusual pasta shapes can be found in southern Italian kitchens, where dried durum-wheat pasta is a daily necessity. In Sicily, one of the favourite shapes is anelli (rings), which look like little golden wedding rings. In Puglia, Basilicata and Calabria, rustic varieties are popular, such as orecchiette (little ears) or strascinati (meaning 'dragged', referring to the way the pasta is made). For the cooking of Lazio and Campania, spaghetti, maccheroni and bucatini are important to have to hand, as well as penne – the only really acceptable partner for the popular and fiery l'arrabbiata, one of Lazio's most famous and popular sauces.

Dried beans, peas and lentils, as well as grains such as barley and farro, are key ingredients in many regions, lending substance and nutrition to a wide range of dishes. In addition to being extremely cheap, they also keep very well and although some kinds require soaking and pre-cooking, they are nevertheless extremely convenient and useful to keep in stock.

Various types of flour – including plain/all-purpose, self-raising/self-rising, pasta and bread flours and cornflour/cornstarch – are a mainstay of every pantry, and form the basis of many of the nation's favourite foods, from pasta and pizza to sauces, cakes and cookies. These may be leavened with yeast, or using a raising agent such as baking powder or bicarbonate of soda/baking soda, giving rise to all manner of delectable home-baked treats.

Polenta flour, in the fine, medium or coarse ground versions, and coloured yellow or white, is also fundamental to northern cuisine; southern kitchens are more likely to stock couscous and plenty of good-quality Italian breadcrumbs, or more thriftily, stale bread carefully stored to turn into breadcrumbs later.

SEASONINGS AND SAUCES

Dried oregano, strings of garlic, dried red chilli peppers, anchovies, capers and different varieties of olives are essential items in any Italian pantry. Dried spices would include cinnamon, cloves and nutmeg; like dried pasta, these have a shelf life, and will lose potency if kept too long or not stored in airtight containers, so be sure to use them up and replace those that are past their best.

BELOW *Rice, whether of the long grain or risotto variety, is a staple in many Italian pantries.*

BELOW MIDDLE *Making breadcrumbs is a thrifty way to use up stale bread, and can be frozen very successfully for use at a future date.*

BELOW RIGHT *Italians normally keep in stock several different types of flour, ranging from fine 00 pasta flour to strong white bread flour and plain/all-purpose or self-raising/self-rising flour for making cakes and cookies.*

FAR LEFT *Mostarda di Cremona is simultaneously sweet, peppery and fruity, and cuts through the richness of meat dishes as well as enhancing the flavour of strong cheeses.*

LEFT *The flavour and character of honey varies tremendously depending on where it is from. The first Italian honey to gain PDO certification was that from Lunigiana in northern Tuscany, and this product is available in chestnut and acacia varieties, reflecting the flora found in the area.*

The mixture known as mostarda di Cremona (or mostarda di frutta) is the nearest thing Italy has to chutney, and consists of glacé/candied fruits preserved in thick, sweet mustard syrup. The combination of intense sweetness and fiery pepperiness makes it an ideal partner for many northern meat specialities, including bollito misto, and for certain types of very strong cheese.

Pesto, that delicious, emerald-green sauce from Liguria made by pounding basil with garlic, pine nuts, cheese and oil, can be made and eaten fresh, or it can be prepared in large batches and kept in jars with a thick layer of oil over the top of the sauce to exclude contact with the air and thus keep it from fermenting.

Salsa peverada is a Venetian sauce made from anchovies and chicken livers. It may seem quite peculiar to blend the flavours of this sauce with the already very intense taste of game, but it works surprisingly well. Although the sauce is created specifically for roasted game, it is also fabulous with roasted chicken and duck.

PRESERVED FOOD

Pickling or preserving vegetables, fruit, fish, cheese or even cured meat is a long-standing tradition in Italy. Anything that is pickled, such as capers or vegetables, is known as 'sott'aceto' (in vinegar). Food preserved in olive oil, such as goat's cheese, wild mushrooms, tiny salami, vegetables such as peppers and many others are referred to as 'sott'olio' (in oil). Some northern areas use pork fat instead of oil, covering the food and then sealing the jars to keep it moist and fresh.

The tomato harvest is so plentiful and so vital to southern cuisine that all kinds of useful ways have been devised of preserving tomatoes for the winter and spring: good supplies of pelati (canned tomatoes) and concentrato di pomodoro (concentrated tomato purée) are essential items.

SWEET FLAVOURINGS

When it comes to the necessary ingredients for making sweet things, the cook needs to keep in stock candied fruit, honey, cooking chocolate, cocoa powder, orange blossom water and icing/confectioners' sugar, which is called zucchero vanigliato, because it is flavoured with vanilla. Wild fruits such as berries can be preserved in grappa or other alcoholic liquids. Finally, there will be a selection of sticky liqueurs to give cakes, cookies and desserts their distinctive flavour.

Piedmont, particularly the city of Turin, is the base for chocolate making in the northern regions. This chocolate is eaten just as it is, but it can also be used in all sorts of delicious desserts, such as chocolate pudding blended with coffee and amaretti, or in a dark rich cake, or combined with chestnut purée and meringues in a confection known as Il Montebianco, or the white mountain.

JASMINE FLOWERS AND ORANGE BLOSSOM

Sweet-smelling jasmine flowers are used to flavour and scent ice cream and jellies in many Sicilian dessert recipes. An extract of orange blossom is also used, and adds a strong, fragrant taste to cakes and pastries.

SALSA PEVERADA

SERVES 4

3 anchovy fillets, boned and finely chopped
115g/4oz chicken livers, trimmed and finely chopped
2 rashers/strips unsmoked lean back bacon, very finely chopped
grated rind of I lemon
1 garlic clove, peeled
90ml/6 tbsp olive oil
15ml/1 tbsp white wine vinegar
sea salt and ground black pepper

1 Put the anchovy fillets into a small pan and add the chicken livers, bacon, lemon rind, garlic and olive oil.

2 Cook over a low heat, stirring frequently, for 15 minutes, or until soft and cooked through. The texture of the sauce should be as smooth as possible.

3 Remove and discard the clove of garlic. Sprinkle the sauce with the white wine vinegar, season it with salt and pepper, then stir it well. Serve the sauce hot.

PESTO

MAKES ABOUT 300ML/½PINT/1¾ CUPS

about 75g/3oz fresh basil leaves, washed but not bruised, dried carefully
large pinch of sea salt
3 garlic cloves, peeled and cut in half
100g/3¾oz pine kernels
25g/1oz/⅓ cup grated Parmesan or pecorino (or a mixture of the two)
200ml/7fl oz/scant 1 cup extra virgin olive oil
sea salt and ground black pepper

1 Put the basil, salt and garlic into a mortar and crush with a pestle until reduced to a smooth green paste. Alternatively, use a food processor.

2 Add the pine kernels and grated cheese and pound or process again until the pine kernels are all crushed.

3 Add the oil, a little at a time, stirring with a spoon, until you have reached a smooth, creamy texture. You may not need to use all of the oil. Season to taste, and use as required.

Cook's tip The ingredients in this recipe do not need to be exact – taste the pesto as you prepare it so you can adjust or alter the quantities according to personal taste.

BASIC PIZZA DOUGH

MAKES 6 SINGLE-PORTION PIZZAS OR FOCACCIAS

25g/1oz fresh/compressed yeast
200ml/7fl oz/scant 1 cup warm water
pinch sugar
2.5ml/½ tsp sea salt
400g/14oz/3½ cups strong white bread flour
10–15ml/2–3 tsp olive oil

1 Mix the yeast and water together with the sugar, and add about 30ml/2 tbsp of the flour. Put the yeast mixture in a lightly floured bowl and place it somewhere warm to rise for about 10–20 minutes.

2 Place the rest of the flour in a mound on a clean work surface, make a hollow in the centre and add the salt. Stir the yeast mixture thoroughly, and then pour it into the hollow and knead it into the rest of the flour, adding more water if required to make a soft dough.

3 Add the oil and knead together for 10–20 minutes. The dough should stretch to a length of about 25cm/10in without snapping.

4 Transfer this mixture to a large floured bowl and return it to a warm place to rise again for about 1 hour or until the dough has doubled in size.

5 Use as required in the recipe. Alternatively, roll it out into rounds, spread with passata/bottled strained tomatoes, then sprinkle with toppings, such as garlic, oregano, basil and cheese. Bake for 5–10 minutes at 220°C/425°F/Gas 7.

BASIC BREAD DOUGH

MAKES ABOUT 450G/1LB OF DOUGH

35g/1¼oz fresh/compressed yeast
300ml/½ pint/1¼ cups warm water
pinch of sugar
450g/1lb/4 cups strong white bread flour, plus extra for dusting
5ml/1 tsp sea salt
15ml/1 tbsp olive oil, plus extra for greasing

1 Mix the yeast and water together in a small bowl. Add the sugar and 30ml/2 tbsp of the flour. Leave in a warm place for about 30 minutes, or until it becomes frothy.

2 Put the remaining flour on to the work surface. Make a well in the middle and pour in the yeast mixture. Work the yeast mixture into the flour, then add the salt and the oil and knead for 10 minutes, or until the dough becomes soft and elastic.

3 Transfer the dough to a large floured bowl, cover with lightly oiled clear film or plastic wrap and leave to rise in a warm place for 2 hours, or until doubled in size.

Cook's tip This dough can be used in a variety of recipes, but you can also simply cook the bread as it is. Preheat the oven to 220°C/425°F/Gas 7. Oil a large baking sheet and sprinkle with polenta. Knock back or punch down the dough, then divide it into six pieces. Shape it into rolls, rounds, or long, narrow shapes or braids, then lay them on the oiled baking sheet. Brush the surface gently with a little olive oil mixed with water. Bake for 15 minutes, or until light golden and the underneath sounds hollow when tapped. Allow to cool on a wire rack.

Regional breads and cakes

Bread is a really important part of the whole eating ritual in Italy, particularly in central and southern regions, where the local durum wheat makes such fantastic light loaves. Nothing is wasted; even stale bread can be made into breadcrumbs and is a vital ingredient in many southern dishes. The softer kind of flour grown in northern Italy makes delicious cakes and pastries – something that cooks of these regions have turned to their full advantage and that has given rise, along with influences from nearby countries, to a thriving café scene where delectable cakes and cookies are plentiful.

Tuscan toast In Tuscany, sliced crusty bread is turned into crostini and bruschetta by toasting it, rubbing it with garlic, drizzling with olive oil and then adding a topping of meat, vegetables, cheese or fish and serving as an antipasto or a snack. It is also the custom to line soup bowls with slices of bread to make the dish more substantial, as well as to use up slightly stale bread.

Roman roses In Rome, bread is often made into rolls called rosette (little roses). They are hollow on the inside, but have a dense crust with a soft, squidgy lining, divided into petals to resemble rosebuds.

Thrifty breadcrumbs In the poorer regions of the south, bread is valued as a staple food, and stale bread is always recycled as breadcrumbs in all sorts of ways: as a coating for fried food, as a crisp topping on baked dishes, as part of a stuffing or to bulk out other ingredients such as minced/ground meat when making meatballs. Some southern areas produce bread that has reached worldwide fame, such as the thin and crisp carta da musica (literally, sheet music) bread of Sardinia and pane di altamura from Puglia.

Northern breads In the northern areas closest to the Austrian border such as Trentino-Alto Adige and Friuli-Venezia Giulia, denser brown breads in the Austrian style tend to be more common, featuring dark grains such as rye. The region of Emilia-Romagna has the delicious flatbread called piadina, which is perfect when eaten warm, folded over a few slices of the local charcuterie.

Northern café culture Polenta flour is used in baking in many of the northern regions, including Lombardy, Emilia-Romagna and the Veneto, to make crumbly, golden-yellow cakes and biscuits. The polenta flour adds an interesting texture to the mix. Cooks in the northern areas of Italy also traditionally use more sugar and spices in their recipes than southern cooks – these ingredients were brought by traders to Venice and thence to all the northern regions. Another reason why so many delicacies are found in the northern industrial centres and major cities is the long tradition of café society in cities such as Trieste, Milan and Turin, a fact that reflects the greater wealth traditionally associated with these cities.

The Austrian influence In Friuli-Venezia Giulia, whose border runs alongside Austria, many traditional sweet recipes use spices and dried or candied fruits to great effect in pastries and cakes. These are doubtless influenced by the centuries-old link with the Austro-Hungarian Empire and its fantastic sweet creations. The Lombardy town of Saronno is where the famous crunchy almond biscuits called amaretti come from, as well as the liqueur of almost the same name.

Traditional Tuscan treats Tuscany, in central Italy, is famous for the hard dunking biscuits called cantuccini, which are made to serve with vin santo, and also for a flat cake from Siena called panforte, which is rich in almonds and candied fruits. The traditional topping of pepper has been replaced these days by a coating of pure white icing/confectioners' sugar.

Umbrian chocolate Tuscany's neighbour, Umbria, is famous for its chocolate industry, especially in the regional capital Perugia, which produces the famous Baci chocolate made with ground hazelnuts. The most famous cake of the region is probably torciglione, made from ground almonds, sugar and flour and formed in the shape of a snake, or the local rustic version of a twisted strudel known as rocciata.

Sicilian sweets Sicily can really hold its own when it comes to cakes and desserts. Canola, cassata, pasta di mandorle, frutta di martorana, buccellato, torta pinolata, biscotti al pistacchio, pignolata … all these are part of the rich variety of Sicilian sweet cakes and cookies. All Sicilians adore ice cream or gelato, and some people even eat it for breakfast, tucked inside a large brioche bun.

Venetian patisserie Venice has a whole range of pastries linked to the festivities of carnevale, the yearly opportunity for Venetians and visitors to let down their hair, eating, drinking and dancing. These include the classic carnival treat fritole, fried dough balls containing candied fruit, raisins and pine nuts, the origins of which date back to the Renaissance and that in 1700 became the national cake of the Venetian state. Verona, also in the Veneto, is where the tall, star-shaped Christmas cake called pandoro was first created. The name 'pan d'oro' means 'bread of gold', which reflects the fact that the white flour used to make it was once extremely costly and families had to save up all year to be able to make this special treat.

Milanese festive bakes Milan, in Lombardy, is the birthplace of that other well-known traditional Christmas enriched, sweet bread, the deliciously soft and delicately sweet panettone, and its dove-shaped Easter counterpart, la colomba.

Christmas pastries in Molise At Christmas time in Molise there are cauciuni, little parcels of deep-fried pastry which contain a filling of chestnut purée, chocolate, honey, almonds, candied fruits and rum.

DRINKS

Italy is renowned for its fantastic varieties of wine, produced from both red and white grapes. The full-bodied wines of southern Italy also form the base for vermouth-type drinks made by companies such as Carpano, Campari and Martini e Rossi. But there are other alcoholic drinks made here too, mostly based on wine or the by-products of the wine-making process, such as grappa, a clear spirit made from leftover grape skins, stems and seeds. Some of these spirits and herbal digestifs are quite bitter in flavour, with a definite palate-cleansing effect, while others are sweet and best served at the end of a meal.

BELOW *Italy produces a wonderful range of top-quality wines, which, like all wines, vary according to the terroir of the area in which they are made. Barolo is the most famous type from Piedmont.*

REGIONAL WINE SPECIALITIES

Friuli-Venezia Giulia, in the far north-east of Italy, has a reputation both in Italy and abroad for light and refreshing white wines, often made using German grape varieties such as Riesling and Müller-Thurgau. One particular speciality is Picolit, an extraordinary sweet wine developed in the 1700s as a substitute for the sweet Hungarian wine Tokay.

The Veneto has emerged in recent times as Italy's largest producer of wine. Leading the flow is Verona's trio of world-famous wines, Soave, Valpolicella and Bardolino, closely followed by Prosecco, the light, sparkling wine from the Conegliano area.

The main grape variety grown in Piedmont is Nebbiolo; the name derives from the word 'nebbia' (fog). At the peak of the fruits' ripening in September, heavy morning fog is a much hoped-for event, as the natural humidity improves the quality of this region's renowned red wines, including Barolo.

Tuscany is of course world famous for the red wines of the Chianti area, but the whole region produces wines that are respected and well known outside its borders.

Frascati is Rome's signature wine. The ancient Romans referred to it as 'the golden wine', both for its colour and for its value. It has been said that Frascati is the most often-mentioned wine in Italian literature – not surprising, considering that it is so popular both in Rome and countrywide.

DESSERT WINES

The south of Italy has also always been well known for its 'vini da meditazione', which literally translates as wines for meditation, wines that require a moment of calm reflection in order for them to be properly appreciated. These are sweet dessert wines, made from native varieties of grapes such as Malvasia and Moscato, which are turned into wines such as Passito. They are ideal for drinking with dessert or for lingering around the table with friends at the end of a meal.

AMARO

This dark brown, syrupy drink is sometimes consumed as a 'digestif' at the end of a meal. It is made with a variety of unknown ingredients together with local herbs and tastes slightly medicinal. The name means 'bitter', which indeed describes it well.

FAR LEFT *Sticky, sweet and intensely lemony, limoncello can be enjoyed neat or included in cakes and desserts.*

LEFT *Refreshing drinks like beer and cocktails made with spirits such as Campari are very popular in Italy, especially during the heat of the summer when they can be enjoyed outside with friends.*

SPIRITS

The strong, clear distilled spirit known as grappa is made by distilling the grape residue (mainly the skins, but also the stems and seeds) left over from winemaking after pressing, and is between 37.5% and 60% alcohol by volume. The flavour of grappa, like wine, depends on the type and quality of the grape used as well as the fine details of the distillation process. In the Veneto, after finishing a cup of espresso with sugar, a few drops of grappa are poured into the nearly empty cup, swirled, and drunk down in one mouthful.

Piedmont has a tradition for making vermouth dating back to the 17th century. The classic Martini cocktail takes its name from the most well-known producer of vermouth, Martini & Rossi. The Campari group, based in Milan, not only makes the well-known bitter red drink so popular in many cocktails, but also a lighter flavoured aperitif called Aperol and the artichoke-based Cynar.

Amaretto di Saronno is a rich liqueur that has a lineage dating back to the Renaissance. In 1525, the artist Bernardino Luini was commissioned to paint a fresco of the Madonna of the Miracles in Saronno. He chose as his model a beautiful local innkeeper, and in gratitude she prepared a special gift of apricot kernels steeped in brandy and presented the resulting concoction to the artist. This bittersweet amber-coloured liqueur is still popular today.

HERBAL AND FRUIT LIQUEURS

The Val Gardena, in Trentino-Alto Adige, is renowned for being the best area in Italy for the production of herbal liqueurs, although the rest of Italy also traditionally makes them – juniper, gentian, rhubarb and wild Alpine flowers are all mixed with alcohol and distilled to make a range of very special drinks to round off a meal.

Centerbe, a very local liqueur from Abruzzo, is a strong herb-based drink that was once peddled as a cure for the plague, and is even now drunk as an aid to digestion. Its name means 'one hundred herbs'. Fernet-Branca is another bitter, aromatic spirit made from a number of herbs and spices that can include myrrh, rhubarb, chamomile, cardamom, aloe and saffron. It is usually drunk at the end of a meal.

Limoncello is a sticky, sweet drink made from the perfumed lemons of Campania, harvested from the delightful Amalfi and Positano coastline, and is extremely popular to round off a meal and for flavouring cakes and desserts.

BEER

It is hardly surprising that beer is extremely popular in the north-east of Italy, given its close geographical and historical links with Austria. Beer is drunk with food and is as also used an ingredient in many dishes throughout the north-east, especially in the cuisine of Friuli-Venezia Giulia.

NORTH-WEST ITALY

AN ALPINE LANDSCAPE

In the north-west of Italy lie the five regions of Lombardy, Piedmont, Liguria, Emilia-Romagna and the tiny Aosta Valley. The contrasts between these close neighbours are astonishing: the modern metropolitan centres of Milan, Turin and Bologna, the thriving independent port of Genoa, the ancient cities of Mantua and Cremona and the remote mountain villages of the Aosta Valley all lie within close proximity of each other, nestling between the Apennines and the Alps. It is the landscape created by this rugged backdrop that binds these regions together. The mountainous exterior surrounds the fertile basin of the river Po, where many ingredients are grown, and these form the basis of the area's culinary heritage.

THE MIGHTY RIVER PO

From its source in the mountains near the French border to its estuary on the Adriatic coast, the Po is the lifeline of the north-west, gathering in all the water that flows from the Apennines and the Alps. The river is prone to flooding and is polluted, so fresh water for agriculture and drinking comes from thousands of wells dotted throughout this low-lying landscape. These natural springs and the fertile silt deposited by the river over centuries have led to the Po basin becoming the centre of Italian industry, with an almost continuous urban development stretching 550km/342 miles from Turin to Trieste. Fields of crops fill the basin, as do large-scale food factories, which make this area one of Italy's most important food producers.

THRIVING LOMBARDY

Lombardy lies in the centre of northern Italy, bordering Switzerland. One-sixth of Italy's population lives here, many in the regional capital, Milan. The summers are humid, and the winters can be cold, foggy and rainy. The great lakes – Garda, Maggiore, Lugano and Como – which, apart from Garda, lie in the high mountains on the border with Switzerland, are favourite tourist destinations. The microclimate around the lakes allows the cultivation of typically Mediterranean produce such as olives and citrus fruit, even in these high regions. South of the Alps lie gentle hills, dotted with small, fertile plateaux where sheep and cows can graze. Lower down, modern agriculture takes over. This area is Italy's major farming centre, with countless fields of wheat, rice and other grains, interspersed with protected parks of astonishing natural beauty.

BELOW *The north-west of Italy is framed by mountains to the north, west and south, with a fertile river basin running through the centre. Liguria and Emilia-Romagna enjoy beautiful coastlines on opposite sides of Italy.*

MOUNTAINS AND PLAINS OF PIEDMONT

The name of this region is a contraction of the Italian phrase 'ai piedi del monte', meaning 'at the foot of the mountain'. The area is surrounded on three sides by the Alps. From the highest peaks the land slopes down to hilly areas, with an occasional sudden drop where the mountains meet the plains. Farming is a major industry in the low-lying areas beneath the mountain slopes, with vast fields of rice and maize as well as some of the best vineyards in Italy, which produce top-class wines. The regional capital, Turin, is one of the biggest and busiest cities in Italy.

LOCAL LANGUAGES

The people in the north-western regions bordering France and Switzerland speak many dialects, some far removed from the 'classical' Italian of Rome and Florence. Examples include: Western and Eastern Lombard, Piedmontese, Emilian and Franco-Provençal. These languages are proudly maintained and are in daily use, particularly in the mountainous areas of the Aosta Valley near the border.

ABOVE *Lake Como, in Lombardy, is a tourist hot spot, boasting a benign climate much of the year, and dazzling views of the majestic Alps.*

SPECTACULAR LIGURIA

Liguria is renowned for its stunning beaches and towns and delicious food. It winds around the coast in a narrow band, and has a temperate year-round climate due to the warm waters of the Ligurian Sea, as well as the natural barrier that is created by the mountains, protecting Liguria from the cold northerly winds. Rainfall can be abundant, giving the region a green landscape. The vast majority of the population lives and works in the thin strip of habitable land around the coast, and this is where Liguria's specialist farmers produce their top-quality olive oil and flowers, which are exported all around Europe.

HARD-WORKING EMILIA-ROMAGNA

The lower plains of the rivers Po and Adige form the region of Emilia-Romagna (actually two distinct regions of Italy combined into one). The landscape has been farmed from Etruscan and Roman times; since the Middle Ages the local people have been almost entirely focused on agriculture as a business, with organised trading opportunities provided by monastic orders, feudal lords and free communes. The co-operative farming system is still in working order today.

The produce of Emilia-Romagna is extremely varied and ranges from fruits and vegetables of countless kinds to grains and livestock, not to mention grapes, which are used to produce many splendid wines in the region.

THE REMOTE AOSTA VALLEY

Italy's tiniest region, Aosta Valley, is tucked away into the highest corner of the Alps, north of Piedmont. It borders both France and Switzerland, neighbours who have always strongly influenced the cooking of the largely French-speaking population. It is now an autonomous region, meaning that it controls its own finances and planning. Farmers mainly concentrate on raising dairy cattle in the high Alpine pastures, producing milk for the various wonderful cheeses made here, as well as growing grapes to make some top-quality wines.

In recent years much has been made of the tourism opportunities in this picturesque area, with winter sports, such as skiing, and summer walking holidays proving very popular. The breathtaking landscape, fabulously clear air and excellent food culture make it a tremendously sought-after destination.

A HISTORY OF POWER

The rich heritage of the northern part of Italy can be seen everywhere in these five regions. Empires rose and fell, trading links were forged and battles were fought over this land. The valleys are so fertile and the hills and mountains so spectacular that it is no surprise to find that many tribes have settled here. Meanwhile, traders from the north passed through these regions on their way farther south, bringing exciting new foodstuffs and recipes with them, and Ligurian ports, such as Genoa, were gateways into Italy for exotic spices, fruits and vegetables. Roman ruins dot the landscape of northern Italy, medieval towns nestle in the hills and beautiful Renaissance architecture embellishes the cities.

LOMBARDY – FINANCIAL POWERHOUSE

The city of Milan, centre of the Lombardy region, was founded by Celtic tribes who then extended their rule all the way to the Adriatic Sea. From 194BCE, Roman culture overwhelmed the Celtic civilization, and in the years that followed, Lombardy became one of the richest areas of Italy, with the construction of good roads and the swift development of agriculture and trade. Taking full advantage of the flourishing economy, Lombardy continued to trade and make deals until it became the financial centre of Europe. The word 'Lombard' in Renaissance England came to mean any merchant or banker from northern Italy.

From the Renaissance to the Napoleonic era, this thriving region was fought over with gusto by its neighbours, France and Austria, but finally, in 1859, Lombardy was officially reunited with the rest of Italy and confirmed its status as the powerhouse of Italian finance. Its busy regional capital, Milan, is the centre of its economy, as well as its food culture, being home to some of the most characteristic Lombard dishes: for example the saffron-flavoured risotto, which takes a little time to cook but is well worth the effort. The general rule in this hectic city is that making money must never take precedence over a good dinner!

BELOW *Ussel Castle in the Aosta Valley is a fine example of the splendid medieval architecture that remains in the region.*

PIEDMONT – ANCIENT REPUBLIC

Like Lombardy, Piedmont was vulnerable to attack from France and Austria. It was inhabited in early historic times by Celtic-Ligurian tribes and later conquered by the Romans.

In the Middle Ages and through the Renaissance, some Piedmontese areas remained independent, such as Asti (now famed for its sparkling wine), Alessandria, Saluzzo and Montferrat. At the Congress of Vienna in 1814–15, the Kingdom of Piedmont-Sardinia also took charge of the Republic of Genoa (now in Liguria) as a barrier against French invasion.

Piedmont was the initial springboard for Italy's unification in 1859–61, and Turin briefly became the capital of Italy. Today, Piedmont manages to preserve ancient traditions amid the fast pace of modern life, including its food cultures. It is famous for its 'Slow Food' movement, which symbolises this trend.

LIGURIA – SEAFARING REGION

The isolated coastline of Liguria has been open to marauding Saracens, Normans or pirates arriving by sea since the 5th century BCE, when the Ligurian people first arrived to give the region its name. By the Middle Ages, the port of Genoa dominated all of Liguria and had become a powerful maritime republic, in many ways stronger than its rivals in Pisa and Venice. Eventually, Genoa faltered and lost most of its power, and Liguria was annexed by Napoleon and given to the House of Savoy. This loss of independence inspired patriots such as Mazzini and Garibaldi to start the Italian Risorgimento, which in turn led to the establishment of the modern nation of Italy.

In the first years of the 20th century the region's economic growth was remarkable, and specialised industries such as olive and herb farming flourished all along the coast. During the Second World War, Liguria experienced two years of privation under occupation by German troops. However, when Allied troops reached Genoa towards the end of the war they were surprised to find Italian partisans welcoming them. In a successful insurrection, they had freed the city, and Genoa was awarded a gold medal for military valour.

AOSTA VALLEY – PROUDLY INDEPENDENT

In common with the other northern regions, the Aosta Valley was overrun by tribes from north and south, including early Celts and Ligurians. The Romans arrived around 25BCE and improved links with other regions by building roads and passes through the mountains. However, the Aosta Valley always tried to preserve its independence and

LEFT *Milan's elegant and imposing Gothic cathedral showcases the power wielded by this regional capital, which to this day remains the financial hub of the whole country.*

traditional culinary customs, which means it is different from the southern parts of Italy. Its cuisine focuses on local ingredients, such as the many cow's milk cheeses made by cattle farmers in the high mountains. The Aosta Valley joined the Kingdom of Italy in 1861, but has retained its independent status as an autonomous region.

EMILIA-ROMAGNA – CENTRE OF TRADE

The name Emilia-Romagna has its history in the Roman legacy of this area. The region was named after the Aemilian Way, a Roman highway built at the height of the Roman empire. During the Middle Ages, trading activities, politics, culture and religion flourished in the monasteries and in the University of Bologna, which is the oldest university in Europe.

In the 16th century, most of the small dukedoms became part of the Papal States, but the territories of Parma, Piacenza and Modena remained independent until Emilia-Romagna became part of the Italian kingdom in 1859, one of the first regions to commit to the new regime. Emilia-Romagna covers most of the Po valley, reaching from west to east, which has to led to great wealth in terms of agriculture and industry, as well as a fine gastronomic tradition.

A CLASSIC CUISINE

The complicated history of northern Italy, as well as its proximity to cooler European countries, means that the food is different from the cuisine of the south. Instead of eating pasta at every meal, the inhabitants tend to vary it with substantial amounts of rice and polenta. The foggy, damp plains of the Po valley are ideal places to grow rice, maize and buckwheat, rather than the durum wheat that makes the best dried pasta. (With that said, Emilia-Romagna is the famous home of delectable fresh egg pasta, which is made in all sorts of shapes.) A multitude of other world-famous products hail from this region, including balsamic vinegar from Modena, and Parma ham and Parmesan cheese from Parma.

THE COOKING OF LOMBARDY AND MILAN

Lombardy has acted as a pathway for many different tribes to pass through the Alps, some of whom stayed long enough to leave their mark on the local cuisine. Common elements link all of Lombardy's gastronomy. Generous use of butter is the main hallmark of Milanese and Lombard cooking, as is the general preference for rice or polenta over pasta. Meat, especially veal, is considered the king of the dinner table.

Rice is generally transformed into risotto with tender spring asparagus or freshwater shrimps, turned golden by the addition of saffron, and scented with herbs such as rosemary or sage. Cream is frequently on hand to make rich and sumptuous sauces to dress hearty pasta dishes such as ravioli filled with sausage meat, potatoes, Swiss chard and herbs.

A popular dish for hot summer days is vitello tonnato, a cold dish of poached veal in a sauce of tuna, mayonnaise and capers. When the weather is cooler, Lombard cooks excel at making costolette alla Milanese (breaded and butter-fried veal chops, rather like Austrian Wiener schnitzel); bollito misto, where various cuts of beef, pork, poultry, offal and veal are cooked together in a rich broth; or cassoeula, a stew of pig trotters and ears, sausage and cabbage, typically accompanied by

BELOW *These flooded rice fields in Piedmont provide excellent rice for making rich risottos.*

steaming-hot polenta. In this region polenta is made of both maize and buckwheat flour, for example in the popular dish polenta taragna, served with lots of melting cheese.

Desserts include countless crumbly, buttery or crisp cookies, of which the world-famous Amaretti di Saronno, crisp almond macaroons, is perhaps the most addictive.

CULINARY DELIGHTS OF PIEDMONT

Gastronomy is an everyday passion in Piedmont. The inhabitants are fiercely proud of having at their fingertips many of the world's finest ingredients, such as red wines that rival the greatest that France can offer, and a fantastic range of cheeses and other dairy products, not to mention the luxury of white truffles and award-winning chocolate.

Piedmont's cuisine, like that of its neighbour Lombardy, is rich, with thick white sauces predominating over red tomato-based ones. They are proud of their exquisite pastry-making tradition and careful attention to detail, which are known and respected throughout Italy. Although pasta in Piedmont is delicious, silky, soft and usually handmade, rice and polenta tend to be more prevalent. Garlic appears mainly in the salty bagna caùda, a savoury 'warm bath' in which vegetables are dipped, which is one of the region's flagship dishes. The idea is that everybody at the table dips chopped vegetables such as carrots, fennel, bell peppers and Piedmont cardoons into a mouthwatering bowl of warm olive oil, garlic, cream, butter and anchovies.

Another vital part of the Piedmontese food scene is precious white truffles. Rare and expensive, they have a unique flavour, which is celebrated throughout Italy. Their scent is delicate, but pungent and powerful at the same time. Unlike the more common black truffles, white truffles are served only raw, finely grated in beautifully veined shavings that fall like rain over a bed of risotto, or with tajarin, the Piedmontese version of tagliatelle, made with an outrageously rich, eggy dough.

Piedmont grows the world's most sought-after hazelnuts, Tonda Gentile delle Langhe. Experts pay a premium for these because of their subtle flavour. Once blended with silky chocolate, hazelnuts become Nutella, the addictive spread born in Piedmont only 40 years ago. The city of Turin can rightfully claim to have perfected the art of chocolate in Italy. Many cafés and artisan chocolate stores throughout Piedmont offer their own versions of chocolate specialities such as gianduiotti. These stores reflect the recipes and techniques passed down through local families since the 1600s.

It is no accident that the movement known as Slow Food, aimed at promoting traditional cuisine, was born, and still has its internationally powerful base, in Piedmont.

ABOVE LEFT *White truffles are sought out with dogs in the countryside around the town of Alba, in the hills of Piedmont.*

ABOVE *The Langhe area of Piedmont is awash with vineyard-covered rolling hills, where fabulous wines are produced.*

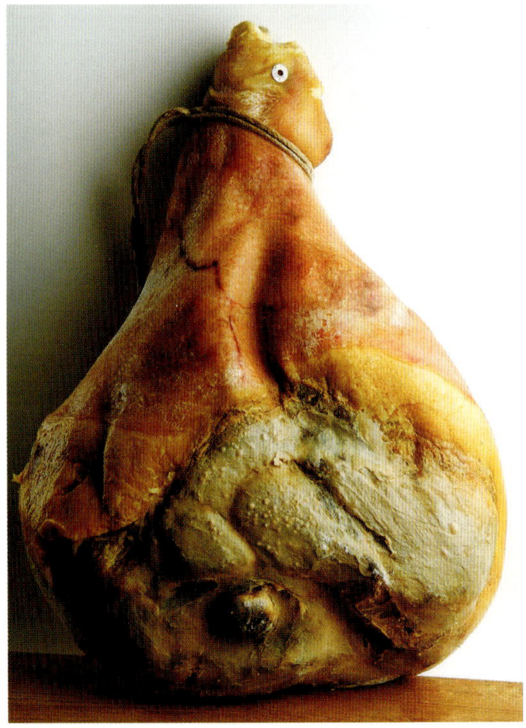

ABOVE *Parmesan cheese, or Parmigiano Reggiano, is aged in huge storage facilities in Emilia-Romagna, where it is monitored by inspectors.*

ABOVE RIGHT *Parma ham, or prosciutto di Parma, is yet another wonderful product from Emilia-Romagna.*

FRESH TASTES OF LIGURIA

It would be natural to presume that the local cuisine of coastal Liguria would be characterised by fish dishes, plus all the spices, tomatoes and other ingredients first brought to Genoa by traders in the 15th and 16th centuries, yet these are missing from the traditional repertoire. This is because it was not the Ligurian bankers or spice merchants who shaped the local menu, but the sailors of its maritime fleet. The food on board ship was restricted to ingredients that would keep indefinitely, along with fish caught on the journey. When the sailors returned to Genoa, they didn't want to eat more fish. Instead, they craved fruit and vegetables, and herbs such as fresh basil. It is the historic and commercial tradition of Genoa as a major port, along with the pleasant and temperate climate, that has created the region's unique gastronomy, harmonising the products of the sea, the vegetable garden and the woods.

The cuisine's most notable feature is the use of aromatic herbs, including bay leaves, marjoram and, most importantly, basil. Basil and Liguria are inextricably linked due to the famous sauce pesto, which originated in Genoa. The Genoese have a special passion for basil, and most people grow a pot of this fragrant herb on a sunny windowsill. Some say that the best basil grows only around Genoa, where cool winds from the mountains meet salty sea breezes, giving the basil its distinctive aroma. Undeniably, the basil in Genoa makes its pesto totally unique.

Among other specialities are farinata (a thin pancake made from chickpea flour) and the famous focaccia alla Genovese (a flat bread loaf). Both of these are served by the hundreds of local bakeries, and are consumed as snacks at any time of day, a sort of Italian fast food made with a few natural ingredients: flour, olive oil, salt and water.

Last but by no means least come the products of the green wooded hills tucked away behind the coastline: chestnuts, mushrooms and truffles, as well as small berries, such as strawberries, whortleberries and raspberries, which are used in a medley of tasty desserts and cakes.

RICH FOOD OF EMILIA-ROMAGNA

The city of Bologna is famous throughout the world for its superb cuisine. Perhaps less well known is the fact that it lies at the heart of Emilia-Romagna, a region celebrated throughout Italy for the range and quality of its ingredients and dishes. From the Adriatic coast to the inland plains and river valleys, the whole area is blessed with excellent products and a wonderful culinary heritage. Now one of the richest areas of Europe, Emilia-Romagna has developed a strong economy based on the building of cars and motorcycles. Agriculture, however, is still important. Crops, including cereals, potatoes, maize, tomatoes and onions grow well here, along with many varieties of fruit and grapes used in the production of wine. Cattle and pig breeding are also highly developed, and farm co-operatives are successful here.

Emilia-Romagna is the region that gives us exquisite fresh egg pasta in a multitude of shapes, such as tagliatelle, tortellini, garganelli and lasagne. It is also the birthplace of balsamic vinegar, Parma ham, Parmesan cheese, mortadella and a wealth of other cured meats. With this abundance of rich food from the surrounding towns and countryside, it is no wonder that Bologna has aquired the nickname Bologna la Grassa, meaning 'Bologna the fat one'.

THE CUISINE OF THE AOSTA VALLEY

People from the Aosta Valley enjoy a robust cuisine based on cheese, meat, rye bread, potatoes, polenta, gnocchi, risotto and soups. Cows grazing on the lofty Alpine meadows provide fine butter and many excellent cheeses, such as Toma, Robiola and, above all, fontina, which features in many a local recipe. Perhaps the classic cheese dish from this region is fondua, which is similar to Piedmont's fonduta or a Swiss fondue, made with milk, egg yolks and fontina cheese. Another local cheese is Fromadzo, a firm cow's milk cheese (sometimes with the addition of ewe's milk) that has been made in the valley since the 15th century. Cheese is also added to polenta, risotto and thick soups, whose ingredients range beyond the usual vegetables, meat, rice and potatoes to include mushrooms, chestnuts and almonds.

Aostans make good use of the freshwater trout that abounds in the mountain streams, and have developed plenty of recipes for this fish. Local game, such as partridge, grouse, hare and venison, is also put to use in a medley of regional specialities. The local pork products are justly famous, including a prosciutto called Jambon de Bosses, spicy blood sausages called boudins, and the local salame, which is preserved in pork fat. A strange local curiosity is tetouns, which is made of a cow's udder, salt-cured with herbs, then cooked, pressed and sliced fine like ham.

The Alpine climate in the Aosta Valley lends a fresh flavour to berries and fruit, especially apples and pears, which are poached in local red wine to make a really tasty dessert. This region is also noted for fragrant mountain honey, almond cookies (tegole) and butter crisps known as torcetti.

Meals often conclude with the passing of the grolla, a roughly carved wooden pot containing caffé alla valdostana (coffee with red wine, grappa and lemon peel), sipped from numerous spouts in a truly friendly fashion.

BELOW *Cold freshwater streams flow through the mountains of the Aosta region, bearing the delicately flavoured trout that are so appreciated by the locals.*

FESTIVALS AND CELEBRATIONS

As in other regions of Italy, there is an abundance of small local festivals in the north-west of the country, focusing on local produce when it is coming into season and at its peak of freshness. During these festivals, the cooks demonstrate huge inventiveness in using the products in a medley of fabulous recipes. Religious festivals also give an opportunity for cooks to show off their expertise, with a particular focus on feasts and special local foods at Christmas, such as Milanese panettone, soft almond macaroons and chocolate treats from Piedmont. At Easter, too, there are plenty of local delicacies to be found, such as the lovely soft Easter cake, colomba Pasquale (Easter dove), which is made in the city of Pavia.

FOOD FESTIVALS OF MILAN AND LOMBARDY

The celebration known as Sagra dell'Asparago (Asparagus Feast), which dates back to 1940, is one of the region's main gastronomic events. For 4 days, the town of Cantello offers asparagus tasting, and local restaurants create a range of special asparagus-based dishes.

In June and September, the Pizzoccheri Festival takes place in Teglio. Pizzoccheri is a pasta shape similar to tagliatelle and is made of buckwheat. It is usually cooked with vegetables and served in broth, topped with butter and cheese.

DELIGHTS OF PIEDMONT

One of the most famous festivals in Piedmont is the Truffle Festival of Alba, celebrated in October and November. This event has been running for more than 75 years and draws chefs from around the world. During the festival, the wholesale truffle market opens to the public so people can inspect, and even buy, the delicious white truffles.

The Raschera and Brus Cheese Festival is held at Frabosa Soprana in August. Raschera cheese has an ivory colour and a delicate flavour, which becomes quite pungent when it is left to mature. Brus is a fermented cheese made from both cow's and sheep's milk, with a very strong flavour, and is particularly sought after by gourmets.

The Pumpkin Festival in Piozzo in October each year features more than 120 types of pumpkin, in many shapes and sizes, which are displayed on stalls and wagons throughout the town. Visitors to Piozzo can sample both traditional and modern pumpkin-based dishes in every restaurant.

BELOW *Precious white truffles are collected and weighed in rural Piedmont, where every autumn there is a truffle festival in in the town of Alba.*

CULINARY FEASTS OF LIGURIA

The Biscette Festival at Solva di Alassio in March celebrates this typical cake from the Loanese area, made with hazelnuts, flour and sugar, bound together with orange flower water and then fried in olive oil. It is shaped to resemble a snake.

In June, nursery owners display and sell their plants and herbs – especially Ligurian basil – in the streets of Andora. The town of Savignone holds an annual pesto festival using this fragrant local basil. Later in the summer, there is a celebration of red garlic in Vessalico. This rare vegetable is limited in production to only 3,000 braids of garlic, each with 24 heads, per year.

The Trenette Festival (trenette are flat, thin ribbons of pasta) is held in August in Loano, where a wonderful assortment of local dishes is served, displaying Ligurian food at its most authentic.

SARTIRANA LOMELLINA FROG FESTIVAL

The most unusual food festival in Lombardy has to be the Frog Festival at Sartirana Lomellina in September, where delicacies such as rice with frog liver are served.

THE ORIGINS OF PANETTONE

The story of the origin of panettone – the traditional sweet bread served at Christmas time, which originates in Milan – is buried in mystery, but several legends give us various different possibilities. The most widely believed tells us that at the end of the Christmas feast in the Sforza (my Italian ancestors!) household the moment had arrived for the cook to present the dessert. Unfortunately, the oven had overheated and the expected dessert was burned and inedible. The utterly devastated cook was just about to enter the dining hall to apologise to the diners, when his assistant, Toni, presented his own creation – a sweet bread that he had made out of the various leftovers around the kitchen. The first panettone was thus carried into the dining room where it was received with great delight. The cook was an honest man and he confessed that this was not his own work but that of his assistant. It was, in short, 'il pan de Toni', which has since been renamed panettone.

Another common legend tells of a young falconer named Ughetto Atellani, who was perennially in love with a young baker called Algisa, whose bakery was in a street near to the Chiesa delle Grazie. Business was not good: Christmas was coming, but customers were not. In a bid to help, Ughetto spent every last penny he had on butter, sugar, eggs and sultanas/golden raisins, mixed it all up with the best flour he could buy and created a hugely successful sweet bread for Algisa to sell. The conclusion to the tale changes according to which version you read. In the happy one, Algisa was overcome with love for the generous Ughetto and they married and lived happily ever after. In the other one, the not-so-happy ending is that Algisa's bakery took off and she became a very successful businesswoman – but spurned poor Ughetto!

A third story dates back to the 13th century, when there was a tiny convent on the outskirts of Milan. In this damp and foggy place there lived a few nuns, their meagre existence entirely dependent upon charity. One year, the citizens of Milan had not been very generous towards them and by Christmas Eve there was little left in the pantry except for flour with which to make bread. When the Mother Superior blessed the little loaf, it miraculously turned into a fragrant, sweet panettone.

All these stories and legends remind us that this is definitely bread, and not a cake. It is enriched with butter, sugar, eggs, sultanas, candied fruit and vanilla, and its light, fluffy texture is down to the use of natural yeast. The first mention of a sweet, enriched bread very similar to panettone as we now know it dates back to the end of the 15th century, during the rule of one of the most famous Sforza men, the mighty Ludovico il Moro.

FORGOTTEN FRUITS IN EMILIA-ROMAGNA

An unusual plant known as rampion is celebrated at Borghi on the first Sunday after Easter. Rampion is found growing wild in the fields. Its leaves are edible; they have a pleasant, slightly sweet taste and are often used in salads or boiled and served with vinegar.

The Tortellino Festival (Sagra del Tortellino Tipico) is held annually in Reno Centese, in the province of Ferrara, at the end of June. Here, the keen gourmet can eat tortellini stuffed with everything from truffles to wild herbs, dressed with ragù, melted butter or cream, and also watch the experts make them. This little pasta parcel is supposed to resemble the belly button of Venus, the most beautiful goddess.

Garlic is the king of the Garlic Festival at Voghiera in July, where it is celebrated with garlic-based foods and dishes, garlic tastings, and many traditional activities and games.

At the aptly named Forgotten Fruits Festival at Casola Valsenio in October, it is possible to taste the flavours of exotic and neglected fruits from the area, such as cornelian cherries, vulpine pears, Neapolitan medlars, and many others.

FESTIVALS OF THE AOSTA VALLEY

At the end of June, the town of Avise dedicates itself entirely to a festival known as La Fiocca, entirely devoted to whipped cream – ideal for those with a sweet tooth. After this, in the second week of July, at Saint-Rhémy-en-Bosses, there is an annual festival in celebration of the local ham, the Jambon de Bosses. The French names of the ham and the town give an indication of how close this region is to the French/Swiss border.

BELOW *Piedmont and in particular affluent Milan is home to some truly wonderful chocolate stores, from which a dazzling array of sweet confections can be bought.*

PIEDMONT & THE AOSTA VALLEY

'Piemonte' owes its name to its geographical position, sitting as it does at the foot of the mountains – 'ai piedi dei monti' – and it has been known by this name since the Middle Ages. With Torino as its regional capital, the region is made up of the provinces of Cuneo, Verbano-Cusio-Ossola, Alessandria, Biella, Novara, Vercelli and Torino. It is bordered by France, Switzerland, Liguria, Lombardia and Emilia-Romagna.

Famous for its industry, its ski tourism, and its food and wine, Piedmont is also the region where the plans for the Unification of Italy were born. The first Prime Minister of Italy was Camillo Benso, Count of Cavour, who went on to declare Victor Emmanuel II Italy's first King since the 6th century, a title he held until his death in 1946. Cavour, along with Mazzini and Garibaldi, is considered to be one of the 'fathers' of the new Italy.

In culinary terms, the area is important not only because it is where the Slow Food Movement began, but also for some world-renowned produce. This includes razza bovina Piemontese, beef that is known for its high standard of breeding as well as its unusually low cholesterol content; the famous, eye-wateringly expensive and much-revered Alba white truffle, tartufo bianco d'Alba; great risottos made with the prized carnaroli rice which grows so well on the flatlands that the region is Europe's prominent supplier; and for wines such as Barolo, Freisa, Barbaresco, Nebbiolo and Dolcetto. And then there are the cheeses, many of which hold a DOC or DOP status, such as Raschera, Castelmagno, Bra, Robiola di Roccaverano and Toma Piemontese; the abundance of hazelnuts – the region is the birthplace of Nutella, although it is also used to make a variety of many local cakes, biscuits and desserts; and the chocolate, especially gianduja, which contains about 30 per cent ground hazelnut paste.

More everyday foods include 'tajarin', or taglierini, which is long, thin ribbon pasta that is similar, but much narrower, than the tagliatelle of Emilia-Romagna; and a pasta dish called agnolotti dal plin, traditionally a very small version of stuffed pasta. Bagna caùda, a warm sauce of olive oil, anchovies and garlic is an absolute staple. Meaning 'hot bath' in Piedmontese dialect, this is served with platters of raw and cooked vegetables that are dipped into the sauce.

North-west of Piedmont is Val d'Aosta, a region bordered by France to the west, Switzerland to the north and Piedmont to the south-east. It is the smallest, least-populated part of Italy, and is the only Italian region with no provinces. The name means 'Valley of Augustus', after the Roman name for the city of Aosta – Augusta Prætoria Salassorum – founded after the Romans conquered the region from the Salassi tribe around 25BCE. The area has always been vital for its mountain passes, and the Romans built many of the bridges and roads that still wind through the mountains. The great modern tunnels of Gran San Bernardo and Mont Blanc that run between Italy and France highlight the region's importance as an intersection between Italy and the rest of Europe, and the many medieval castles and fortresses are testament to the various populations who have made this valley their home. It is also the site of the glorious Gran Paradiso National Park, as well as world-class ski resorts such as Courmayeur and Cervinia, and many of Europe's highest mountains, including Mont Blanc, the Matterhorn, Monte Rosa and Gran Paradiso.

The people have always been renowned for their skills in both hunting and alpine farming, which helps to explain their traditional food products, and the meat-heavy nature of the menu where the influence of classic French cooking methods is clear. For practical reasons, given the climate and geography of Val d'Aosta, there is a long tradition of curing meat and game. The most well-known regional game salume is mocetta, which nowadays is usually made using venison or sometimes beef, although once it was made with the rigorously protected ibex. Pork is also a feature, with two cured products standing out: the delicious Jambon de Bosses and the incredibly sweet Lard d'Arnad.

As in other mountain regions of northern Italy, polenta is very popular, often served smothered with plenty of melted cheese. There is also a wide use of rye and chestnut flour, used to prepare bread and dumplings that add extra bulk to rib-sticking soups. Many of the amazing local cheeses include Fontina, Fromadzo, reblec, séras and many others.The mountains of Val d'Aosta are also perfect for growing apples and pears – and many of the local cakes and desserts centre around these fruits – but are not ideal for grapes or viticulture.

SERVES 4

- ½ tomato
- 4 large red or yellow bell peppers
- 250ml/8fl oz/1 cup milk
- 10 garlic cloves, peeled and left whole
- 150ml/¼ pint/⅔ cup olive oil
- 10 anchovies preserved in salt, cleaned and boned
- 50g/2oz/¼ cup unsalted butter
- 45ml/3 tbsp double/heavy cream
- ground black pepper

COOK'S TIP

The sauce should be served as a dip, with raw and cooked vegetables, cut into pieces for easy dipping.

BAGNA CAÙDA CON PEPERONI
BAGNA CAÙDA WITH ROASTED PEPPERS

The delicious Piedmontese speciality, bagna caùda, is traditionally served as a hot sauce in a glazed terracotta container warmed over a night-light, into which vegetables are dipped. In this more elegant version, the potently flavoured sauce (which literally translates as 'hot bath') is used to smother roasted sweet peppers. The classic dip is served to celebrate the end of the grape harvest, and the final dregs are added to beaten eggs, which would subsequently be scrambled and scooped up with hunks of bread.

1 Plunge the tomato into boiling water for 30 seconds, then refresh in cold water. Peel away the skin, then chop the flesh.

2 Put the peppers under a hot grill or broiler, turning occasionally, until blackened and burnt all over. Put them on a board and cover with an upturned bowl. Leave to cool.

3 Peel and remove the seeds from the peppers and cut the flesh into neat strips. Arrange the pepper strips on a platter and keep them to one side while you make the bagna caùda.

4 In a small pan, cook the milk with the garlic over a low heat until the garlic is completely softened, then mash the garlic into the milk.

5 Put the oil in a pan and add the anchovies. Heat slowly over a low heat, stirring, until the anchovies have dissolved into the oil, then stir in the butter and add pepper to taste.

6 Whisk the milk and garlic into the anchovy mixture, then add the chopped tomato and cream. Stir and heat through briefly until hot. Serve the sauce, poured over the sliced roasted peppers.

LA FARINATA
BAKED CHICKPEA FLOUR PANCAKES

When you first make farinata you will be more than a little alarmed at quite how liquid the batter seems to be. Fear not, it will pull together quite magically into a smooth pancake as it bakes. This is the cheapest of foods – just finely ground chickpeas, water, oil, salt and pepper – and yet it manages to be utterly moreish. Farinata is wonderful with stracchino cheese, or with salame, or just by itself – but it's always best served warm from the oven.

SERVES 6

225g/8oz/2 cups chickpea flour
60ml/4 tbsp olive oil
1.5 litres/2½ pints/6¼ cups water
sea salt and ground black pepper

1 Put the chickpea flour into a large mixing bowl and add the water. Mix using a whisk. Season with salt and ground black pepper, then add half the olive oil.

2 Cover the bowl and leave the farinata mixture to stand for at least 1 hour or preferably overnight.

3 Preheat the oven to 200°C/400°F/Gas 6.

4 Use the remaining olive oil to lightly grease a shallow baking tray or pan and pour in the farinata mixture to a depth of no more than 2.5cm/1in.

5 Bake for 30 minutes, or until crisp on the outside but still soft in the middle.

6 Slice into wide strips and roll up, then serve while warm.

SERVES 4

200g/7oz fresh soft goat's cheese
115g/4oz/1¼ cups freshly grated Parmesan cheese
75g/3oz/¾ cup walnuts, finely chopped
65g/2½oz/1 cup dried breadcrumbs
90ml/6 tbsp extra virgin olive oil
5ml/1 tsp mustard, such as savora or Dijon
200g/7oz mixed salad leaves
sea salt and ground black pepper

POLPETTINE DI FORMAGGIO CON LE NOCI
CHEESE AND WALNUT PATTIES

This is a traditional recipe from the province of Cuneo in Piedmont and is usually served as an antipasto. These little patties contain two different types of strongly flavoured cheese and the richness is perfectly offset by fresh salad leaves in a mustardy dressing.

1 Mix together the goat's cheese, freshly grated Parmesan cheese and walnuts to form a thick paste.

2 Shape the cheesy paste into cherry-sized balls using dampened hands and flatten them slightly to make little patties. Coat the patties in the breadcrumbs.

3 Heat half the oil over a medium-high heat in a frying pan and fry the patties for about 5 minutes, turning them over once or twice, until golden and crisp all over.

4 In a screw-top jar or dressing bottle, mix together the remaining oil with the mustard and a little salt and pepper. Shake well to combine. Alternatively use a fork or whisk and a small bowl.

5 Use the dressing to dress the salad leaves lightly, then arrange the leaves on four serving plates.

6 Place the sizzling hot cheese and walnut patties on top of the dressed salad leaves and serve immediately.

SERVES 4

450g/1lb Fontina cheese, cubed
15ml/1 tbsp plain/all-purpose flour or polenta flour
200ml/7fl oz/scant 1 cup cold milk
4 egg yolks
115g/4oz/½ cup butter
toasted bread, to serve

FONDUTA ALLA PIEMONTESE
PIEDMONTESE FONDUTA

The Italian version of a Swiss cheese fondue, fonduta, is served as a dip or over pasta, polenta or risotto. It is incredibly rich, so only a small amount is needed to make you feel really full! It also tastes good with toasted or fried bread, grissini, breadsticks or some vegetable crudités.

1 In a deep bowl, mix the cheese and the flour or polenta together thoroughly. Cover with the milk and leave the cheese to soften for 30 minutes. Drain the cheese.

2 Put the egg yolks and butter into the top half of a double boiler, or in a heatproof bowl over simmering water.

3 Add the cheese, and stir constantly until the cheese has melted. The eggs must be allowed to set softly.

4 As soon as the fonduta is velvety smooth and piping hot, serve it in warmed soup plates or shallow bowls with slices of toasted bread for dipping.

TARTINE AL PARMIGIANO REGGIANO
PARMESAN AND TRUFFLE CANAPÉS

Piedmont is truly the land of truffles, and there are myriad recipes using them, such as these rich and filling little canapés. Truffles are a luxurious ingredient and can be very expensive, but this is a perfect recipe for an indulgent dinner party since they can be made in advance and taste divine.

SERVES 6

9 slices white or brown bread
115g/4oz/1¼ cups freshly grated Parmesan cheese
115g/4oz/½ cup unsalted butter, softened
30g/1¼oz finely chopped truffle
a few slices of truffle, to garnish

1 Cut 18 circles out of the slices of bread using a 7.5cm/3in round pastry or cookie cutter and toast them all lightly.

2 Mix the freshly grated Parmesan cheese with the softened butter and stir in the finely chopped truffle.

3 Spread or pipe this mixture on to the rounds of toast.

4 Just before you are ready to serve the canapés, garnish each one with a slice or two of truffle.

CARCIOFI ALLA CAVOUR
CAVOUR ARTICHOKES

This classic Piedmontese recipe for artichokes has lots of flavour, created from a rich sauce of anchovies and eggs. Serve it as an appetizer or as a side dish to accompany a simple meat dish or a roast chicken.

SERVES 4

8 small, tender artichokes, trimmed
40g/1½oz/3 tbsp unsalted butter, melted
60ml/4 tbsp freshly grated Parmesan cheese, plus extra to serve

FOR THE SAUCE

50g/2oz/¼ cup unsalted butter
2 salted anchovies, boned and finely chopped
2 hard-boiled eggs, finely chopped
45ml/3 tbsp finely chopped fresh flat leaf parsley
sea salt

1 Preheat the oven to 180°C/350°F/Gas 4. Trim the artichokes by cutting off the spiny tops and removing some of the tough other leaves, then cut away the tough exterior of the stalks. Boil for 10–15 minutes in lightly salted water, until tender. Drain thoroughly.

2 Put the artichokes into an ovenproof dish. Cover with the melted butter and Parmesan, then transfer to the oven to keep warm.

3 To make the sauce, melt the butter in a small pan over a medium heat until just sizzling, then add the chopped anchovies, hard-boiled eggs and parsley and stir together thoroughly. Cook for 3–4 minutes to heat through.

4 Pour the buttery sauce over the artichokes and serve immediately, sprinkled with extra grated Parmesan.

SERVES 6

1 rabbit, jointed, approx 1.8kg/4lb
15ml/1 tbsp vinegar
2 carrots
2 celery sticks
1 onion
1 sprig rosemary
2 garlic cloves, thinly sliced
8 bay leaves
8 juniper berries
12 black peppercorns
sea salt
about 600ml/1 pint/2½ cups extra virgin olive oil

VARIATION

If you can't get hold of or prefer not to use rabbit, then you could use a jointed chicken instead.

ANTIPASTO DI CONIGLIO
RABBIT ANTIPASTO

A lovely recipe from Piedmont, this antipasto needs to be prepared about 3 days in advance. It ends up like a rustic version of a terrine and is absolutely delicious served with hunks of crusty bread to mop up the juices. Rabbit meat is cheap and tasty, and very low in fat. The flavour and tenderness are greatly improved by soaking overnight, or at least for a few hours, in water and vinegar. Wild rabbit is best soaked in milk due to the intensity of its aroma and taste.

1 Put the jointed rabbit into a large bowl and cover with water. Add the vinegar and leave overnight.

2 The next day, put the carrots, celery, onion and rosemary into a large pan, and cover with water and bring to the boil.

3 Add the jointed rabbit and return to the boil. Reduce the heat and simmer gently for 90 minutes, or until the rabbit is cooked through and completely tender. Turn off the heat and leave the rabbit to cool down completely in the stock.

4 When the rabbit is cold, remove all the meat from the bones.

5 Put a quarter of the meat in a layer in the base of a terrine and cover with a quarter of the garlic, bay leaves, juniper berries and black peppercorns, and a sprinkling of salt.

6 Repeat the layering process with the remaining ingredients, creating four layers. Cover with olive oil, and chill for 2–3 days.

7 Serve on a platter, removing the garlic, peppercorns and bay leaves as you eat.

CANNELLONI AI FUNGHI E FORMAGGIO
CHEESE AND MUSHROOM CANNELLONI

This is a very rich version of this classic baked pasta dish, made lighter with the addition of a tomato sauce and some fresh basil. Vary the taste of this perfect supper recipe by using different kinds of mushrooms and cheese.

1 Preheat the oven to 160°C/325°F/Gas 3. Brush the butter over the base and sides of a large shallow ovenproof dish.

2 Blanch the pasta sheets in salted boiling water and drop them into cold water to prevent them sticking to each other.

3 Heat the oil in a pan and add the garlic. Fry until the garlic is just pungent, then discard.

4 Add the chopped onions and the mushrooms to the garlicky oil. Cook for about 10 minutes or until both have softened.

5 Transfer the onions and mushrooms to a mixing bowl, season with salt and pepper, and gently stir in the cream cheese.

6 Take a sheet of pasta and drain and blot it carefully. Place it flat on a board and add a tablespoonful of the mushroom filling. Roll up the pasta and place it in the buttered dish. Repeat with the remaining pasta sheets and filling.

7 To make the sauce, melt the butter in a separate pan and add the tomatoes. Simmer over a low heat for about 10 minutes.

8 Season with salt and ground black pepper and add the cream, half the Parmesan cheese and the basil, then remove from the heat.

9 Pour the sauce over the filled cannelloni. Sprinkle with the remaining Parmesan cheese and bake for 15–20 minutes, until golden and bubbling.

10 Leave to stand for 5 minutes before serving with extra Parmesan and basil on top.

SERVES 4

25g/1oz/2 tbsp butter, melted
250g/9oz fresh pasta sheets
45ml/3 tbsp olive oil
1 garlic clove, lightly crushed
3 small onions, chopped
500g/1¼lb/8 cups mushrooms, roughly chopped
115g/4oz/½ cup cream cheese

FOR THE SAUCE

25g/1oz/2 tbsp unsalted butter
250g/9oz drained canned tomatoes, seeded and coarsely chopped
200ml/7fl oz/scant 1 cup single/light cream
150g/5oz/1½ cups freshly grated Parmesan cheese, plus extra to serve
8 fresh basil leaves, torn, plus extra to serve
sea salt and ground black pepper

COOK'S TIP

You can use any cultivated or wild mushrooms you have to hand for this recipe, so long as they are flavoursome.

GNOCCHI AL GORGONZOLA
GNOCCHI WITH GORGONZOLA

This is the ultimate cold-weather dish – comforting, rich, sublimely tasty and very hearty! Gorgonzola comes in two varieties: 'dolce', which is gentle and creamy or 'piccante' which is slightly drier and salty. Either can be used here.

SERVES 6

1kg/2¼lb floury potatoes, scrubbed
3 eggs, beaten
about 300g/11oz/2⅔ cups plain/all-purpose flour
185g/6½oz Gorgonzola cheese
400ml/14fl oz/1⅔ cups milk
about 105ml/7 tbsp sunflower oil
about 30 sage leaves
butter, for greasing
salt
freshly grated Parmesan cheese, to serve (optional)

COOK'S TIPS

• The amount of flour you'll need will depend on the texture of the potatoes.
• The gnocchi must not be made in a food processor or the texture will be too heavy.

1 Boil the potatoes until soft, then drain and peel quickly. Press through a potato ricer, mouli or a wide-meshed sieve or strainer twice. Blend in the eggs.

2 Working carefully and quickly, gradually add just enough flour for the mixture to hold its shape, handling it as little as possible. Form a soft dough with your hands, then roll it all into long thumb-thick cylinders.

3 Cut the cylinders into 2.5cm/1in sections (you should make about 72) and form into small concave gnocchi shapes by pressing them against the back of a fork or a flat cheese grater. Spread them out on a large board and set aside until required.

4 Put the Gorgonzola cheese and the milk into a bowl and set it over a pan of simmering water. Stir together gently so that the milk does not curdle (which will make the sauce granular), until the cheese melts into the milk.

5 Bring a large pan of salted water to the boil, carefully drop in the gnocchi and allow them to cook until they float on the surface. This should take about 1 minute if the gnocchi are really light.

6 While the gnocchi are cooking, heat the sunflower oil in a pan until sizzling and fry the sage leaves for 20 seconds or until crisp. Drain the leaves on kitchen paper and set aside until required.

7 Scoop out the gnocchi with a slotted spoon and arrange them in a warm, well-buttered ovenproof dish. You need about 12 gnocchi per person.

8 Dress the drained gnocchi with the melted Gorgonzola cheese as soon as they come out of the pan, and toss together very gently.

9 Garnish with a few fried sage leaves to serve. Offer freshly grated Parmesan cheese separately at the table, if you like.

RISOTTO AL BAROLO
BAROLO RISOTTO

This is a very old recipe for making a traditional Piedmontese dish. Although it is more complicated than some of the more modern versions of similar risotto dishes, the end result is utterly delicious and hugely filling and satisfying, containing not just the rice and the wine, but also beans, meat and vegetables. Barolo is a rather expensive but wonderful wine, and imparts intense flavour in this dish, so is worth the outlay for a special occasion. The borlotti beans will need to be soaked overnight whether they are dried or fresh.

1 Drain and rinse the beans, then cover with water and bring to the boil. Boil hard for 5 minutes. Drain again, then cover with water and simmer gently until tender. (Do not add salt, as it will make the skins toughen.) Strain the beans and set aside until required.

2 Put the stewing veal into a large pan with the whole onion, the celery and the carrot. Cover with 1.2 litres/2 pints/5 cups cold water, add a little salt and boil slowly for 2 hours, skimming occasionally.

3 Remove the meat and the vegetables from the pan. Trim the meat, then chop the meat and vegetables finely. Set them aside and strain the stock into a clean pan. Adjust the seasoning to taste, bring to the boil and allow to simmer.

4 Heat half the butter in a large, heavy pan. Fry the chopped onion gently for about 5 minutes, until soft and golden. Add all the rice and toast it quickly in the hot butter and onion. When it is well coated, shiny and hot, add about 175ml/6fl oz/$^{3}/_{4}$ cup Barolo.

5 Stir the rice and allow the alcohol to evaporate, then add a ladleful of hot stock. Stir and allow the rice to absorb the liquid, then add another 175ml/6fl oz/$^{3}/_{4}$ cup Barolo. Continue in this way, adding wine and stock alternately and stirring in between each addition, until the rice is half cooked. This should take about 10 minutes.

6 Add salt and pepper to taste, then add the beans with more wine and stock. Cook for 4 minutes more, then add the chopped meat and vegetables. Continue as before until the risotto is creamy and velvety, but the rice grains are still firm to the bite: it should take about 20 minutes to cook. Remove from the heat.

7 Add the remaining butter and the Parmesan cheese. Stir together thoroughly, then cover with a lid and leave to stand for 5 minutes before serving, sprinkled with extra Parmesan cheese.

SERVES 6

- 200g/7oz fresh or dried borlotti beans, soaked overnight
- 300g/11oz stewing veal
- 1 onion, whole and 1 onion, finely chopped
- 1 celery stick
- 1 carrot
- 115g/4oz/$^{1}/_{2}$ cup unsalted butter
- 500g/1$^{1}/_{4}$lb/scant 3 cups risotto rice
- 750ml/1$^{1}/_{4}$ pints/3 cups Barolo wine
- 90g/3$^{1}/_{2}$oz/generous 1 cup freshly grated Parmesan cheese, plus extra to serve
- sea salt and ground black pepper

COOK'S TIP

You can use a 400g/14oz can of borlotti beans, drained, rather than fresh or dried ones, if you prefer.

RISOTTO ALLA PIEMONTESE
PIEDMONTESE RISOTTO

This recipe is all about the luxurious truffle: the more the better! The other vital ingredient is, of course, the stock. This is particularly important because this is a very old risotto recipe and the rice is effectively gently boiled and then dressed, rather than being toasted before the stock is gradually added until the rice is cooked and creamy. Unlike most risottos, the Piedmontese risotto is very wet in consistency and served almost like a soup.

SERVES 6

- 2 litres/3½ pints/9 cups good-quality beef or veal stock
- 500g/1¼lb carnaroli rice
- 65g/2½oz/¾ cup freshly grated Parmesan cheese
- 65g/2½oz/5 tbsp unsalted butter
- 65g/2½oz finely sliced black or white truffle
- pinch of grated nutmeg
- sea salt
- shavings of Parmesan cheese and black or white truffle, to serve

1 Bring the stock to a gentle boil in a large pan. Add the rice and stir. Simmer, stirring occasionally for about 20 minutes, until the rice is creamy but has bite in the middle. It should be quite wet. Remove from the heat.

2 Add the Parmesan, butter, truffle and nutmeg. Taste and adjust the seasoning. Cover and rest for 4 minutes, then stir and serve in deep soup plates or bowls, with Parmesan and truffle shavings on top.

SERVES 4

1 whole chicken, about 1.6kg/ 3½lb, jointed
2 large ripe tomatoes
115g/4oz streaky/fatty bacon, lard or white cooking fat, chopped
1 large onion, finely chopped
1 small bunch celery leaves, chopped
1 small sprig each of fresh rosemary, sage and parsley, leaves chopped
50g/2oz juniper berries, lightly crushed
250ml/8fl oz/1 cup dry red wine
250ml/8fl oz/1 cup chicken stock
salt and ground black pepper
chopped fresh parsley, to garnish
mashed potatoes or soft polenta, to serve

POLLO AL GINEPRO
CHICKEN WITH JUNIPER

This is a chicken casserole from the Aosta Valley that contains lots of really flavoursome ingredients, including red wine and scented herbs, as well as lightly crushed juniper berries, which have a warming quality. Serve with a mound of soft polenta or mashed potatoes to soak up the wonderful juices.

1 Pat dry the chicken on kitchen paper.

2 Plunge the tomatoes into boiling water for 30 seconds, then refresh in cold water. Peel away the skins, remove the seeds and chop the flesh. Discard the skin and seeds, and set the chopped flesh aside.

3 Heat the bacon or fat in a large frying pan, add the onion, celery leaves, herbs and juniper berries and cook over a medium heat for 5 minutes or until the onion is soft.

4 Add the chicken joints and brown them thoroughly on all sides. Pour the wine over the chicken and cook for 3–4 minutes to allow the alcohol to burn off. Add the tomatoes and the stock, then stir well.

5 Season with salt and pepper, then cover and simmer for 90 minutes, basting occasionally with the hot stock, until the chicken is cooked through and tender. Serve on mashed potatoes or polenta, sprinkled with chopped parsley.

POLLO ALLA MARENGO
CHICKEN MARENGO

This dish was apparently served to Napoleon and his officers at the end of the Battle of Marengo, using only what remained on the cook's cart. This explains, one can only presume, the slightly weird combination of ingredients. They taste good, nevertheless. This dish is often served with prawns on top of each egg. If you want to add them, cook the unpeeled shellfish in white wine with a good pinch of salt for about 5 minutes until cooked through.

SERVES 4

1.2kg/2½lb chicken, jointed
60ml/4 tbsp plain/all-purpose flour
175ml/6fl oz/¾ cup, plus 60ml/ 4 tbsp, olive oil, plus extra if needed
400g/14oz canned tomatoes, seeded and chopped
5 basil leaves, tied together with white cotton
175ml/6fl oz/¾ cup dry white wine
1 garlic clove, crushed
200g/7oz/3 cups mushrooms, thickly sliced
4 slices white bread, such as ciabatta
4 eggs
30ml/2 tbsp finely chopped parsley, plus extra to garnish
juice of 1 lemon, strained
sea salt and ground black pepper

1 Wash the chicken joints and pat them dry with kitchen paper. Put the flour on a plate or in a plastic bag and use to dust the chicken all over. Season with salt and pepper.

2 Heat the 175ml/6fl oz/¾ cup oil in a wide frying pan, add the floured chicken and fry for 15 minutes, turning occasionally, until browned all over.

3 Add the tomatoes, basil and wine, then add the crushed garlic and a little salt. Stir and cover, then cook for a further 15 minutes.

4 Add the mushrooms, cover again and cook for 10 minutes more.

5 Heat the 60ml/4 tbsp oil in a separate frying pan, add the bread and fry until crisp and golden. Remove and set aside. Fry the eggs in the same frying pan; you may need a little more oil.

6 Sprinkle the parsley over the chicken, pour over the lemon juice and stir.

7 Using a slotted spoon, remove the chicken from the pan and arrange on a platter. Discard the basil. Surround with the sauce and mushrooms, then arrange the fried bread around the edge. Put an egg on each slice of bread. Serve immediately, sprinkled with extra chopped parsley.

SERVES 4

1 guinea fowl, about 1kg/2¼lb
10g/¼oz/2 tbsp dried porcini mushrooms
50g/2oz pork fat, chopped
50g/2oz/¼ cup unsalted butter
200g/7oz shallots or baby/pearl onions, chopped
20g/¾oz/3 tbsp plain/all-purpose flour
1 litre/1¾ pints/4 cups Barolo wine
60ml/4 tbsp grappa
pinch of grated nutmeg
1 luganega sausage, peeled and chopped
sea salt and ground black pepper
mashed potatoes, to serve
chopped fresh parsley, to garnish

FARAONA AL BAROLO
GUINEA FOWL WITH BAROLO

For people who are not sure about game, guinea fowl is the perfect bird because it has only a slight gamey flavour. If you cannot find any, the same dish works well with a small, free-range chicken. For a larger chicken, just increase the ingredients and cooking time accordingly.

1 Wipe the guinea fowl and joint it. Set aside. Put the porcini mushrooms in 200ml/7fl oz/scant 1 cup warm water to soak.

2 Put the pork fat and half the butter in a large frying pan and cook the onions for 10 minutes, until soft.

3 Add the guinea fowl and cook briefly on all sides, then sprinkle with flour and turn the pieces until the flour is absorbed into the fat. Pour over the wine and grappa, and stir. Add the nutmeg and seasoning.

4 Boil for 2 minutes, then reduce the heat and simmer for 1 hour, or until tender. Remove the joints from the pan, set aside and keep warm.

5 Increase the heat under the sauce and reduce it by one-third. Add the drained porcini and the sausage. Cook together for 15 minutes, or until the sauce has thickened and the sausage is cooked.

6 Serve the guinea fowl on mashed potatoes, with the sauce, garnished with parsley.

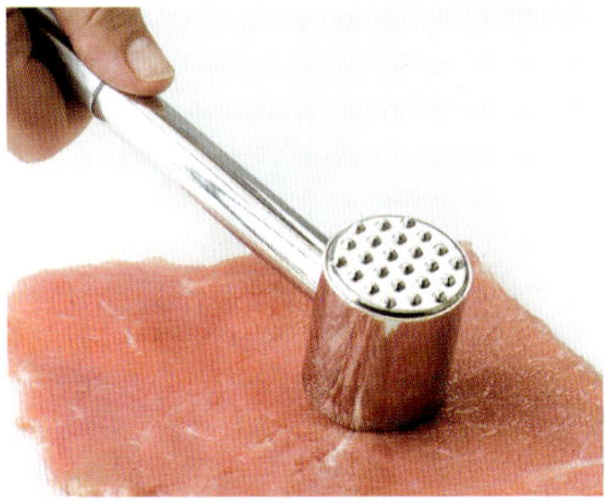

SCALOPPINE AL MARSALA
VEAL WITH MARSALA

The scaloppina is an integral part of every Italian kitchen. There are many versions: with wine, with herbs, with orange or lemon juice and grated rind, with vin santo, and lots of others. Here is the classic Marsala version from Piedmont.

SERVES 4

8 veal escalopes/US veal scallops, trimmed
15–30ml/2–3 tbsp plain/all-purpose flour
50g/2oz/$^{1}/_{4}$ cup unsalted butter
175ml/6fl oz/$^{3}/_{4}$ cup Marsala
sea salt and ground black pepper
mashed potatoes, to serve

1 Beat the meat carefully with a meat mallet or rolling pin until very thin. Put the flour on a plate and, just before you are ready to fry it, lightly coat the veal in the flour.

2 Heat the butter in a large frying pan and quickly fry the meat for 2 minutes on each side. Season with salt and pepper. Remove the meat from the pan and keep warm.

3 Pour the Marsala into the hot pan. Cook for 2 minutes over a high heat to allow the alcohol to evaporate, scraping the base of the pan to amalgamate the juices. Lower the heat a little, then cook, stirring to reduce the sauce slightly.

4 Serve the veal on top of mashed potatoes, with the sauce poured over.

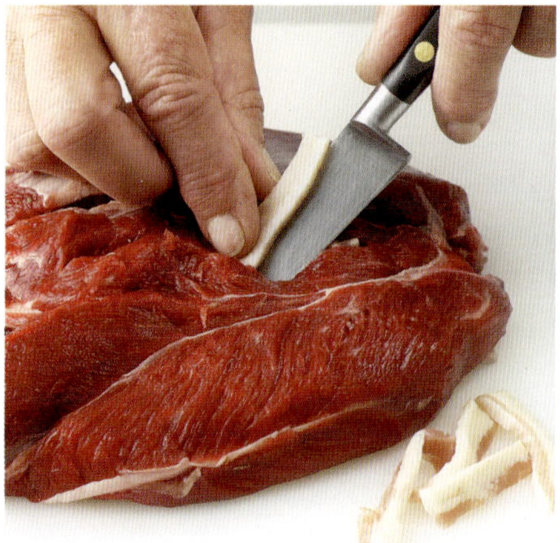

SERVES 6

- 2.5kg/5½lb beef stewing joint, such as brisket or shin/shank
- 50g/2oz pork fat, cut into strips
- 30ml/2 tbsp chopped fresh parsley
- 5ml/1 tsp chopped fresh sage
- 7.5ml/1½ tsp chopped fresh rosemary
- 2 garlic cloves, finely chopped
- pinch of grated nutmeg
- pinch of mixed/apple pie spice
- 75ml/5 tbsp plain/all-purpose flour
- 75ml/5 tbsp olive oil
- 15g/½oz/1 tbsp unsalted butter
- 1 onion, chopped
- 1 carrot, peeled and sliced
- 1 celery stick, sliced
- 2 bay leaves
- 3–4 small fresh parsley sprigs
- 750ml/1¼ pints/3 cups Barolo wine
- sea salt and ground black pepper
- polenta slices or mashed potatoes, to serve

BRASATO AL BAROLO
BRAISED BEEF IN BAROLO

This classic meat dish from Piedmont is often served with steaming-hot slabs of polenta. It is very satisfying and filling, and it allows all the flavour of the wine to shine through. It is not true that cooking wine can be of a lesser quality than the wine you choose to drink, especially when using a really good, carefully selected joint of beef. Barolo is famously expensive, but deservedly so. With this in mind, this dish could be reserved to impress your guests at a dinner party.

1 Pierce the joint all over with a sharp knife or thick skewer and insert the strips of pork fat into the meat.

2 Mix the chopped parsley, sage, rosemary and garlic together. Add plenty of salt and pepper and then stir in the nutmeg, mixed spice and half the flour.

3 Heat the oil and butter together in a large, heavy flameproof casserole until the butter is melted and foaming, then add the onion. Let the onion sizzle for a 3–4 minutes, stirring.

4 Meanwhile, roll the joint in the herb mixture. Lay it gently on top of the frying onion. Add the carrot, celery, bay leaves and parsley sprigs. Seal the meat all over, turning it several times until browned, then remove it from the casserole.

5 Carefully drain off any excess fat from the casserole, then add the remaining flour and stir into the juices, onions, carrots, celery and herbs that remain in the casserole to make a roux.

6 Pour in 350ml/12fl oz/1½ cups of red wine and stir together thoroughly. Cook for about 2 minutes to allow the alcohol to evaporate, then return the meat to the casserole. Turn it over several times, then add the rest of the wine and cover the casserole tightly with a lid. Lower the heat to the lowest setting and simmer as gently as possible for about 4 hours, turning the joint occasionally, until the meat is completely tender.

7 Remove the meat from the casserole and set aside. Remove and set aside a few chunks of carrot and celery, then push the sauce through a food mill or wide-meshed sieve or strainer. Season to taste, then put the vegetable chunks back into the sauce.

8 Slice the meat thickly, then serve on top of your chosen accompaniment, with the sauce poured over.

TARTRA' PIEMONTESE
PIEDMONTESE EGG AND CHEESE CUSTARD

A rich and delicious, smooth eggy custard – this is the sort of dish that is best served with lots of crunchy grissini, Piedmont's crisp breadsticks that are found in all the local bakeries. You could add chopped prosciutto or crumbled salame to this dish for an extra savoury note.

1 Preheat the oven to 200°C/400°F/Gas 6. Grease and flour an ovenproof dish. Heat the butter gently in a frying pan over a low-medium heat, add the onion and fry until golden brown.

2 Beat the eggs and egg yolks together in a bowl with the milk, cream, Parmesan cheese, chopped herbs, nutmeg, and salt and pepper. Add the cooked onion and combine.

3 Pour the mixture into the prepared ovenproof dish, then place the dish in a deep roasting pan. Put the pan in the oven and carefully pour just-boiled water into the roasting pan to come halfway up the sides of the ovenproof dish.

4 Bake for about 30 minutes, or until the custard is set in the middle and crisp and golden on top.

SERVES 4 TO 6

15g/½oz/1 tbsp unsalted butter, plus extra for greasing
flour, for dusting
1 onion, sliced
4 large eggs
2 egg yolks
500ml/17fl oz/2¼ cups full-fat/whole milk
250ml/8fl oz/1 cup double/heavy cream
45ml/3 tbsp freshly grated Parmesan cheese
30ml/2 tbsp mixed chopped fresh sage leaves and rosemary
a large pinch of grated nutmeg
sea salt and ground black pepper

SERVES 6 TO 8

2 or 3 salted anchovies
50g/2oz fresh flat leaf parsley, leaves removed
1 garlic clove
15ml/1 tbsp salted capers
75ml/5 tbsp soft white breadcrumbs
30ml/2 tbsp white wine vinegar
5ml/1 tsp tomato paste
2 hard-boiled eggs, shelled and halved
60ml/4 tbsp extra virgin olive oil
6–8 oven-baked salmon fillets

SALSA VERDE CON SAUMON
SALSA VERDE WITH SALMON

Originating in Piedmont, this sauce now exists in many different variations around the country. It adds a deliciously sharp tang to dishes like boiled meats or poached fish and is especially fabulous served with a classic bollito misto.

1 Wash and bone the anchovies. Chop the flat leaf parsley, garlic clove, anchovies and capers together very finely, then transfer to a mixing bowl.

2 Add the soft white breadcrumbs, white wine vinegar and tomato paste, and mix well together.

3 Remove the egg yolks from the halved hard-boiled eggs and chop them finely, then add to the anchovy mixture. Use the egg whites for something else.

4 Stir gradually, adding enough olive oil to create a smooth-textured, fairly thick sauce. Serve with the baked salmon fillets.

SERVES 6

15g/$^1/_2$oz/1 tbsp unsalted butter, softened, plus extra for greasing
6 large peaches
6 amaretti, crumbled finely
50g/2oz/$^1/_4$ cup caster/superfine sugar
25g/1oz/$^1/_4$ cup blanched almonds, chopped
150ml/$^1/_4$ pint/$^2/_3$ cup Marsala
12 squares unsweetened cooking chocolate

VARIATION

You could use other stone fruits for this simple yet elegant dessert. Nectarines and apricots are especially suitable, or you could try peeled, hollowed-out pears for something a bit different.

PESCHE AL FORNO
BAKED PEACHES

This simple peach dessert can be made very successfully with nectarines or even apricots, though it is especially good with the last of the season's peaches, which are slightly more woolly and therefore able to absorb the wine and the other flavours more easily (and aren't as pleasant to eat raw as earlier ones).

1 Preheat the oven to 190°C/375°F/Gas 5 and grease an ovenproof dish. Cut the peaches in half. Remove and discard the stones or pits. Scoop out half of the flesh and transfer to a bowl.

2 Mash the removed peach flesh with the crumbled amaretti and the butter, sugar and almonds. Moisten the mixture with a little of the Marsala – just enough so that the filling mixture has a sticky texture.

3 Position the halved peaches rounded-side down in an ovenproof dish into which they fit snugly, which will help prevent them from rolling around. Fill all the peaches evenly with the filling mixture and pour over the remaining Marsala.

4 Cover the dish loosely with foil and bake, basting occasionally, for 30 minutes, or until the peaches are tender.

5 Remove the foil and place a square of chocolate on top of each peach half. Increase the temperature of the oven to 220°C/425°F/ Gas 7 and bake the peaches for 5–10 minutes until the tops are lightly crisp and the chocolate has just melted. Alternatively, slide them under a hot grill or broiler for about 5 minutes. Serve the baked peaches hot or cold.

PERE COTTE NEL VINO ROSSO
PEARS POACHED IN RED WINE

In Piedmont and the Aosta Valley they'll tell you that the best possible pear for making this simple dessert is the highly sought-after martin sec variety. While this may be difficult to find outside of the area, what is essential is that the pears you use must be sweet and full of flavour, yet firm enough to keep their shape as they poach. Use the best red wine you can afford for maximum taste. Serve with cream, ice cream or mascarpone, if you like.

SERVES 6

6 firm pears, peeled, left whole with stalks on
½ cinnamon stick
75ml/5 tbsp caster/superfine sugar
750ml/1¼ pints/3 cups red wine
cream, ice cream or mascarpone, to serve (optional)

1 Cut a slice from the base of each pear so that they will stand up firmly.

2 Stand all the pears upright in a pan. Add the cinnamon and the sugar.

3 Pour over the red wine and bring to the boil, then reduce the heat to low and cover with a lid.

4 Simmer slowly until the pears are soft, turning them frequently so they become completely soaked and coloured by the red wine.

5 Transfer to a bowl and cool, turning frequently. Discard the cinnamon stick. If you like, you can serve the pears standing upright on serving plates.

SERVES 4

4 egg yolks
60ml/4 tbsp dessert wine, Marsala or sweet sherry
60ml/4 tbsp caster/superfine sugar
amaretti, to serve (optional)

ZABAGLIONE
ZABAGLIONE

This classic, world famous dessert is a true labour of love – a combination of fresh egg yolks, Marsala wine and sugar, beaten into a frothy mousse texture that is just warm. It is very light and delicious served with poached apples, amaretti, savoiardi biscuits or slices of panettone.

1 Whisk together the egg yolks, dessert wine or sherry and sugar in a large, round, heatproof bowl.

2 Place the bowl over a pan of very hot, but not boiling, water.

3 Whisk for 20 minutes (or 10 minutes if using an electric whisk), or until foaming, thick and shiny.

4 Pour the mixture into stemmed wine glasses and serve.

BUNET
PIEDMONTESE CHOCOLATE PUDDING

Chocolate, amaretti and coffee make a marvellous combination of flavours in this luxurious chilled pudding. It is very rich, so doesn't really need anything else to go with it, though you can serve it with cream for extra decadence.

SERVES 8

1 litre/1¾ pints/4 cups milk
250g/9oz amaretti
15ml/1 tbsp drinking chocolate powder
6 large/US extra large eggs, beaten
150g/5oz/¾ cup caster/superfine sugar
1 espresso (about 30ml/2 tbsp very strong black coffee)
90ml/6 tbsp granulated/white sugar
single/light cream, to serve (optional)

1 Preheat the oven to 160°C/325°F/Gas 3. Put the milk and the amaretti in a pan, bring to the boil, then immediately remove from the heat.

2 Break up the amaretti completely with a spoon. Stir in the drinking chocolate powder.

3 In a large bowl, beat the eggs and caster sugar together until pale and fluffy, then pour this mixture into the pan containing the milk and amaretti.

4 Using a large metal spoon, carefully fold in and amalgamate everything together, taking care not to knock out the air, then stir in the coffee.

5 Put the granulated sugar and 30ml/2 tbsp cold water into a pan and heat together without stirring, until the sugar has caramelised. Coat the base of a 1.5-litre/2½-pint loaf tin, pan or mould with the caramel.

6 Pour the egg mixture into the tin or mould and place it in a roasting pan. Pour enough boiling water around the tin or mould to come halfway up the side.

7 Place the roasting pan in the oven and bake for 30–40 minutes, or until a knife inserted into the middle comes out clean.

8 Remove from the oven, allow to cool, then chill slightly before turning out of the tin or mould and cutting into eight slices. Serve with cream, if you like.

COOK'S TIPS

- When baked in a loaf tin or pan, the pudding can be sliced into neat sections very easily.
- You can also use eight individual moulds. If you do so, reduce the cooking time to 20 minutes.

SERVES 8

1 litre/1$^{3}/_{4}$ pints/4 cups single/light cream
50g/2oz/$^{1}/_{2}$ cup icing/confectioners' sugar
3 or 4 sheets gelatine
60ml/4 tbsp granulated/white or caster/superfine sugar

COOK'S TIP

If you add a flavouring, do so at step 3, once you have whisked the two cream mixtures together. Try the grated rind of 1 lemon, 1 espresso (30ml/2 tbsp strong black coffee), 45ml/3 tbsp liqueur or brandy, or 10ml/2 tsp vanilla extract. Decorate before serving with grated lemon rind, fruit coulis or ground coffee beans.

PANNA COTTA
PANNA COTTA

This delicious Piedmontese speciality is gaining in popularity all over Italy and throughout the world. You can make it completely plain, if you like, or add flavourings such as crushed amaretti, coffee, chocolate, soft fruits, citrus rind or liqueur – the possibilities are almost endless. The skill of making this dessert lies in getting it to set without being rubbery, so just the right amount of sheet gelatine needs to be used. Trial and error will help you find out what works best for you, since different people prefer different textures.

1 Divide the cream in half and put it into two separate pans. Bring the cream in both pans to just under the boil over a low-medium heat. To one pan of cream add the icing sugar, and to the other add the sheets of gelatine.

2 Whisk the cream in both pans constantly until the sugar and gelatine have completely dissolved and the cream is very hot but not boiling. It might be a good idea to get someone to help you do the whisking, or you can whisk with both hands, if you can manage it.

3 Pour the cream from both pans into one bowl and whisk together. Allow the mixture to cool completely.

4 While the mixture is cooling, put the granulated or caster sugar into a small pan and melt over a low heat without stirring until caramelised to a light blond colour.

5 Coat the base of eight small metal moulds or ramekins with the caramel. (Alternatively, divide the sugar between the moulds and melt each over a low flame to lightly caramelise it.) Allow the caramel in the ramekins to cool.

6 Strain the cooled panna cotta into the moulds and put into the refrigerator to set for at least 4 hours but better overnight. When firmly set, dip the moulds into boiling water for 5 seconds and turn out on to cold plates.

IL MONTEBIANCO
CHESTNUT, CREAM, MERINGUE AND CHOCOLATE MOUNTAIN

A potato ricer, mouli or food mill will be required for this classic, luxurious Piedmontese recipe, which is a perfect dinner-party finale.

SERVES 10 TO 12

300g/11oz/generous $1\frac{1}{2}$ cups caster/superfine sugar
1kg/$2\frac{1}{4}$lb/9 cups fresh chestnuts, marrons if possible, peeled (see Cook's Tip) or 675g/$1\frac{1}{2}$lb/6 cups peeled chestnuts
pinch of salt
60ml/4 tbsp Strega liqueur (optional)
750ml/$1\frac{1}{4}$ pints/3 cups double/heavy or whipping cream
75ml/5 tbsp sifted icing/confectioners' sugar
5ml/1 tsp vanilla extract
6 large ready-made meringues, crushed
150g/5oz good-quality dark/bittersweet chocolate, with minimum 60 per cent cocoa solids
30ml/2 tbsp good-quality drinking chocolate powder
6 marrons glacés and 12 candied violets, to decorate

1 Put 120ml/4fl oz/$\frac{1}{2}$ cup cold water into a pan and add the sugar. Heat slowly until a syrup is formed at the thread stage (this is 107°C/225°F if you have a sugar thermometer; or when placed in cold water the syrup forms a fine, soft thread).

2 Add the peeled chestnuts to the syrup with a pinch of salt, and poach very gently for about 30 minutes.

3 Add the Strega, if using. Remove the chestnuts from the syrup using a slotted spoon and set aside. Reduce the syrup by about one-third over a medium heat, then add the chestnuts again. Set aside to cool.

4 Put the cream into a bowl with the icing sugar and the vanilla extract, and whip it until it forms stiff peaks. Divide the cream evenly into three separate bowls.

5 Mix three of the crushed meringues into one bowl of whipped cream. Divide the chocolate in half and melt one half in a heatproof bowl over a pan of simmering water. Mix the melted chocolate into the second bowl of whipped cream. Leave the third bowl plain. Chill all three bowls of cream until required.

6 Melt the remaining chocolate in a heatproof bowl over a pan of gently simmering water.

7 Push the chestnuts and syrup through a ricer or a food mill so that they fall in strands into the bottom of your serving bowls, reserving some for the top.

8 Cover the chestnut strands with a layer of chocolate cream, then a layer of meringue cream, then finally the plain cream. None of these layers need to be smooth and even – they can all overlap.

9 Crumble the remaining meringue on the top of the mound to symbolise the white peak, so that you can see still plenty of the plain white cream around it. Decorate the slopes of your Montebianco with the remaining chestnut strands. Drizzle with the melted chocolate and dust with a little drinking chocolate powder. Chill and serve within 8 hours.

10 Just before serving, arrange the marrons glacés and candied violets on top for decoration.

COOK'S TIP

To peel fresh chestnuts, preheat the oven to 200°C/400°F/Gas 6, then cut a cross-shaped slit into each one. Lay them on a baking sheet and cook for about 15 minutes, or until the skins begin to curl where they have been cut. Peel them while they are hot, holding them in a dish towel, then set them aside.

LIGURIA

Liguria in north-west Italy is famous for its lovely coastline, and is known as the Italian Riviera. As one of the country's smallest regions, it stretches in a narrow strip along the coast from France. Mountains separate it from Piedmont to the north, Emilia-Romagna to the east and Tuscany to the south. Liguria is divided into four provinces: Genova, the regional capital and only major city; Imperia; La Spezia and Savona.

The five little fishing villages of the Cinque Terre – a UNESCO World Heritage Site – as well as the stylish towns of Portofino and Santa Margherita Ligure, are on the eastern coast, known as the Riviera di Levante. The western coast, the Riviera di Ponente, is where you will find Sanremo – Italy's own gambling capital – a sun-dappled Mediterranean resort with a casino, a clutch of ostentatious villas and plenty of Riviera-style grandeur. Known colloquially as the City of Flowers for its famous summer blooms, in the 19th century the city became a magnet for regal European exiles, such as Tsar Nicholas II of Russia, who much favoured the balmy winters. There is even an onion-domed Russian Orthodox church, reminiscent of St Basil's Cathedral in Moscow, sitting rather bizarrely on the seafront.

The warm winters made it a special place for many other 19th-century northern Europeans, too, who often escaped to glorious villas with flower-filled terraced gardens built into the cliff faces that offer stunning views across the sea and tiny private swimming coves at the foot of the cliffs. I especially like the idea of Hans Christian Andersen wintering here and drawing some of his inspiration for his tales from this glorious landscape and lush vegetation. It was undoubtedly the gentle climate and the sparkling light that put this part of Italy firmly on the list of Grand Tour destinations.

Elsewhere in the region, Liguria is a land of contrasts, ranging from Italy's largest naval and commercial ports to seaside resort towns reminiscent of Cannes and Monaco, and from some of the most secluded stretches of Italy's coastline – featuring sandy strands, rocky coves and pebbly beaches where lush forests of lemon trees, herbs, flowers, almonds and pines fill the air with sweet-smelling breezes – to terraced hillsides that produce an olive oil considered much more delicate than that of neighbouring Tuscany, as well as fragrant white wines.

With no large flat areas of land available upon which usefully to grow crops in any great volume, this region's cuisine makes the most of absolutely everything that can grow in small spaces, most especially herbs, such as basil – which flourishes on every windowsill and in any sunny corner. This is then expertly transformed into the most important symbol of this sunny region's cuisine: the pine- and basil-scented, luscious, oily and much-adored condiment called pesto. According to some sources, the magic green stuff was originally created to be carried on board ships voyaging on the high seas, transporting such famous explorers as Cristoforo Colombo right across the world from the great port of Genova. Not only would this have been a welcome taste of home for the crew, but basil, being rich in vitamins A, C and B12, would probably have helped to ward off ailments such as scurvy and keep everyone healthy, and was presumably kept fresh by being sealed under a thick layer of olive oil.

The recipes of Liguria are connected to the sea, to the fishermen and sailors of this region, flavoured with herbs, dressed with the light, fragrant olive oil, with a little cheese and very little meat compared to other regions, especially those in the north. Although there has always been some cross-fertilization of ingredients and produce between Liguria and its neighbours – Piedmont, Tuscany and Emilia-Romagna – and other regions, if one looks closely, what really makes up the local dishes are fish and seafood, herbs, olive oil and olives, pine nuts, wine and salt.

A note about focaccia and pies

The great city of Naples is the place where pizza was born, but it is Recco on the Ligurian coast that first gave us focaccia. This bread, either made into a sandwich or eaten as it is, makes for a very portable form of food that requires no knives and forks – ideal for a population of sailors and fishermen. This theme continues when looking at the number of pies and open tarts that crop up on the Ligurian menu: delicious, nourishing and transportable fare that can easily be packed and forever contains the intense perfume and flavours of Liguria's famous olive oil and herbs as an evocative reminder of home.

FOCACCIA DI RECCO ALL'OLIO
RECCO'S OLIVE OIL FOCACCIA

Focaccia is widely associated with Ligurian cuisine and this focaccia from Recco is legendary. The story goes that during the 16th and 17th centuries, when Recco was an easy target for bandit attacks, men stayed behind to defend their lands while women left for the hinterland with the children and elders, taking with them little more than wheat, oil and salt. Once they felt safe, they kneaded the wheat with the stream water and bartered salt and oil for some cheese. Elders, who used to gather the wood and light up the fires, started leaning some slate over the burning coals to cook the mixture, and the focaccia was born. There are many versions of this famous bread in Recco and the fourth Sunday in May is the annual Recco Focaccia Festival.

1 Pour half the water into a small bowl and stir in the yeast. Leave in a warm place for 15 minutes, or until frothy.

2 Put the flour into a large bowl and add the olive oil and cooking salt. Pour in the yeast mixture and remaining water, and stir together well.

3 Knead the dough for 20 minutes, or until soft and stretchy. The dough should be quite wet, but it shouldn't feel sticky. Put the dough in a large, well-oiled bowl, cover loosely with clear film or plastic wrap and leave to rise in a warm place for about 1 hour.

4 Knock back or punch down the dough. Brush the base of a 40 x 60cm/16 x 24in tin or pan generously with olive oil and then flatten the dough out over the base to cover it completely.

5 Using your fingers, splash the surface of the dough with some water (or spray using an atomiser), then sprinkle over some coarse salt and drizzle with lots of olive oil (be generous with the oil). Using your fingertips, make lots of deep dimples all over the surface of the dough.

6 Leave the dough to rise in a warm, draught-free place for about 2 hours, or until it has doubled in volume. After 1¾ hours, preheat the oven to 200°C/400°F/Gas 6.

7 Bake the focaccia for 10 minutes in the preheated oven, during which time it will absorb all the olive oil on the surface. Drizzle over a little more olive oil, then bake for a further 20–25 minutes, or until the focaccia is golden in colour.

8 Immediately remove from the tin and allow it to cool slightly on a wire rack. Serve while still warm.

SERVES 4

350ml/12fl oz/1½ cups warm water
40g/1½oz fresh/compressed yeast
500g/1¼lb/5 cups unbleached strong white bread flour
30ml/2 tbsp extra virgin olive oil, plus extra for drizzling
10g/¼oz cooking salt
25g/1oz coarse salt

VARIATIONS

- For an onion focaccia, finely chop ½ red onion and add the onion to the mixture at step 2. Very finely slice the remaining onion and sprinkle over the top of the focaccia during the last 10–15 minutes of cooking time.
- For a rosemary focaccia, sprinkle a few sprigs of fresh rosemary over the top of the focaccia when you add the coarse salt and oil.
- For the classic focaccia al formaggio, divide the dough in half and spread the first half over the base of the tin. Cover with stracchino or crescenza cheese – a sour, stretched-curd cheese – then cover with the second sheet of dough, rolled out to fit over the first. Finish off as above.

PIZZA ALL'ANDREA
TOMATO AND ANCHOVY PIZZA

This type of pizza, which is similar to pissaladière from the South of France, is very popular throughout Liguria, but especially in Imperia, Diano Marino and Bordighera. It is also enjoyed in Sanremo, but here has been re-christened 'sardenea', or 'pizza with sardines'. The name is reputed to come from the name of Andrea Doria, 1466–1560, a celebrated local hero and ruler of Oneglia, who reputedly was very fond of this dish. You can make it with fresh little sardines instead of anchovies, if you prefer a slightly less salty flavour.

SERVES 6

600g/1lb 5oz/5$^1/_4$ cups strong white bread flour
about 300ml/$^1/_2$ pint/1$^1/_4$ cups lukewarm water
40g/1$^1/_2$oz fresh/compressed yeast
60ml/4 tbsp olive oil
large pinch of sea salt

FOR THE TOPPING

2 small onions, finely sliced
200ml/7fl oz/scant 1 cup olive oil, plus extra for drizzling
1kg/2$^1/_4$lb fresh ripe tomatoes, seeded
115g/4oz salted anchovies, rinsed and boned
leaves from 2 fresh basil sprigs
12 pitted black olives, or 30ml/2 tbsp salted capers, rinsed and dried
2 garlic cloves, thinly sliced

1 Pile the flour on to the work surface, make a hole in the middle using your fist and pour in enough lukewarm water to just fill the hollow. Crumble the yeast into the hollow and mix together gently then leave for a few minutes and mix again. Continue this gentle mixing and resting for 10 minutes, or until the dough is just fizzing and is soft.

2 Add the olive oil and salt, and knead together, adding more lukewarm water as required to create a soft, elastic ball of dough. Kneading will take at least 15 minutes in total.

3 Shape the dough into a ball and place it in a lightly oiled bowl. Cover loosely with clear film or plastic wrap or with a clean floured cloth. Leave to rise in a warm, draught-free place for 2–3 hours.

4 Meanwhile, make the topping. Fry the onions gently in a little olive oil until pale golden. Add the tomatoes and simmer for 30 minutes, until the sauce is glossy and thickened. Add the anchovies and simmer for a further 5–10 minutes, then remove from the heat.

5 Preheat the oven to 240°C/475°F/Gas 9. Generously oil one large or two small shallow baking trays.

6 Using your fingers, spread out the risen dough over the tray(s) so that it is 1cm/$^1/_2$in thick.

7 Spread the tomato sauce over the surface of the dough, then add the basil leaves, olives or capers and the sliced garlic. Drizzle a little oil over the top.

8 Bake for 30 minutes, or until the pizza is crisp and golden around the edges. Serve hot or cold, sliced into rectangular pieces.

INSALATA DI FRUTTI DI MARE ALLA LIGURE
LIGURIAN SEAFOOD SALAD

The shellfish and crustaceans used for this delicious salad can vary according to availability, as long as whatever you use is perfectly fresh and sweet to the taste. Razor shells, queen scallops, crab or small chunks of monkfish tail all work well.

SERVES 4

200g/7oz squid
1kg/2¼lb mussels
1kg/2¼lb baby clams
175g/6oz/1½ cups small raw prawns/shrimp
4 large raw prawns/shrimp
45ml/3 tbsp chopped flat leaf parsley, plus extra to garnish
juice of ½ lemon
90ml/6 tbsp extra virgin olive oil
sea salt and ground black pepper
lemon wedges, to serve

1 To prepare squid yourself, wash it carefully, rinsing off any ink that remains on the body. Holding the body firmly, pull away the head and tentacles. If the ink sac is still intact, remove it and discard. Pull out all the innards including the long transparent 'pen'. Peel off and discard the thin purple skin on the body, as well as the two small side fins. Slice across the head just under the eyes, reserving the tentacles. Discard the rest of the head. Squeeze the tentacles at the head end to push out the round beak in the middle and discard. Rinse the pouch and tentacles.

2 Cook the squid in a pan of boiling salted water for 25–30 minutes, or until tender.

3 Meanwhile, scrub the mussels and baby clams with a stiff brush and rinse well. Discard any mussels that remain open after being sharply tapped. Scrape off any barnacles and remove the 'beards' with a small knife. Rinse well.

4 Put the mussels and clams into a large pan. Cover and steam for 8 minutes. The shells will open; discard any that remain closed.

5 Put the small prawns in a pan and cover with cold water. Bring to the boil and cook for 1 minute. Drain and allow to cool, then remove their shells.

6 Remove the mussels from their shells and put them in a large bowl with the small prawns and squid. Mix together and set aside.

7 Cook the large prawns in a pan of boiling water for 2 minutes, then drain. Make a shallow cut down the middle of the curved back of each, pull out the black vein with a cocktail stick or toothpick or your fingers, then rinse and leave to cool.

8 Add the parsley to the seafood, squeeze over the lemon juice, then add the oil and some salt and pepper. Mix well and adjust the seasoning to taste.

9 Distribute between four plates, adding one large prawn to each. Serve sprinkled with extra parsley and with the lemon wedges.

COOK'S TIP

It is very important that you prepare seafood properly. Not only can it make you ill if you eat shellfish that hasn't opened during the cooking process, but any bits of grit or broken shell left on or inside the shells will spoil the whole dish. If in doubt, you could try asking your fishmonger to clean and prepare the produce for you.

CIUPPIN
SMOOTH LIGURIAN FISH SOUP

This is the easiest recipe for making a truly Italian-tasting velvety smooth fish soup. You can add whole cooked mussels or prawns if you wish, although the basic recipe as it appears here calls only for whole fish. The bread soaks up all the flavours and juices of the fish and is eaten at the end, once all the soup has been enjoyed. A lot of the flavour comes from the crushed bones of the fish, but you could bone the fish before using, if you prefer.

1 Heat the oil in a large, deep pan, add the finely chopped garlic, parsley and the tomatoes, and cook for 5 minutes.

2 Add all the fish and stir. Season with salt and pepper and pour over the fish stock.

3 Cover tightly with a lid and simmer very gently for 25 minutes.

4 Remove from the heat and cool slightly, then pass through a sieve or strainer or food mill. Return to the heat for 10 minutes, until reduced and thickened a little.

5 Rub the toasted bread with the whole garlic and place two slices in each bowl. Pour the soup over the bread and serve immediately, sprinkled with chopped parsley.

SERVES 6

120ml/4fl oz/$^1/_2$ cup olive oil
4 garlic cloves, finely chopped, and 1 garlic clove, peeled and left whole
60ml/4 tbsp roughly chopped fresh parsley
8 cherry tomatoes
1.5kg/3$^1/_4$lb whole fish, such as cod, monkfish, haddock, plaice or flounder, cleaned
about 200ml/7fl oz/scant 1 cup fish stock
12 slices ciabatta bread, toasted
sea salt and ground black pepper
30ml/2 tbsp chopped fresh parsley, to garnish

SERVES 4

- 250g/9oz potatoes, peeled and cut into 2.5cm/1in cubes
- 250g/9oz green beans, trimmed and cut into 2.5cm/1in lengths
- 300g/11oz trenette
- 300ml/½ pint/1¾ cups pesto (see page 60)
- 40g/1½oz pine nuts, lightly toasted
- sea salt
- grated Parmesan cheese, to serve

TRENETTE AL PESTO ALLA GENOVESE
GENOESE-STYLE TRENETTE WITH PESTO

For Ligurians, there are only two pasta shapes that, along with potato gnocchi, are acceptable for use when it comes to serving their green basil pesto, and these are trenette (long thin ribbons, often made with a little chopped borage blended into the dough) and trofie (the local, short corkscrew-shape). Pesto is traditionally made towards the end of the summer in large amounts, when the basil plants are flowering and at their most pungent, and it is then preserved for the winter months. Many different versions of the basic sauce exist; the recipes vary from household to household. This traditional way of enjoying the pasta together with pesto, potatoes and beans is typical of the city of Genoa.

1 Boil the potatoes for 10 minutes and steam the green beans for 7–8 minutes.

2 Bring a large pan of salted water to the boil, add the trenette and cook according to the packet instructions.

3 When there is 3 minutes of cooking time remaining, add the cooked potatoes and beans to heat them through.

4 Reserve 45ml/3 tbsp of the cooking liquid, then drain the pasta and vegetables in a colander. Add the reserved liquid to the pesto and stir to dilute.

5 Add the pasta and vegetables to the pesto and toss together well. Serve immediately, with the toasted pine nuts and a small amount of Parmesan cheese sprinkled over.

TONNO ALLA GENOVESE
GENOESE TUNA

The combination of tuna and mushrooms is quite unusual, but in this lovely light dish from Genoa, made with wild mushrooms picked in the woody hinterland, the two ingredients come together perfectly. The result is especially good when served with roasted cherry tomatoes and wedges of lemon.

SERVES 4

- 4 tuna steaks, about 600g/1lb 6oz total weight
- 1 small onion, finely chopped
- 1 large garlic clove, chopped
- 45ml/3 tbsp chopped fresh flat leaf parsley
- 135ml/9 tbsp extra virgin olive oil
- 175ml/6fl oz/$^{3}/_{4}$ cup dry white wine
- whole cherry tomatoes on the vine
- 300g/11oz wild mushrooms
- sea salt and ground black pepper
- lemon wedges, to serve

COOK'S TIP

You can use any wild mushrooms you like for this dish, depending upon availability. However, it would work almost as well with cultivated varieties such as button/white or oyster mushrooms, although they may not have quite so much flavour as their wild cousins.

1 Put the tuna steaks in a large shallow dish or bowl, and add the onion and garlic, half the parsley, and 90ml/6 tbsp olive oil. Season with plenty of ground black pepper.

2 Add about one-third of the wine and cover with clear film or plastic wrap. Leave to marinate in the refrigerator for about 3 hours.

3 Meanwhile, preheat the oven to 200°C/400°F/Gas 6 and line a baking sheet with foil.

4 Place the tomatoes on the baking sheet (you can leave them on the vine), drizzle them with a little of the olive oil and sprinkle with a little salt. Cook for 10 minutes.

5 Clean the mushrooms using a brush or a slightly damp cloth. Trim and slice them thinly.

6 Heat the remaining olive oil in a large frying pan, add the mushrooms and cook over a medium heat for 4–5 minutes until all the excess liquid from the mushrooms has evaporated. Season the mushrooms with salt and ground black pepper, then remove the pan from the heat.

7 Drain the tuna steaks from the marinade and blot them with kitchen paper. Put the pan with the mushrooms back on the heat, add the tuna steaks and the remaining white wine.

8 Cook the tuna steaks quickly over a high heat for 3 minutes on each side – the alcohol will evaporate during this fast cooking process. Remove the pan from the heat.

9 Season with salt and more ground black pepper, then sprinkle over the remaining parsley.

10 Serve immediately with lemon wedges and the roasted whole cherry tomatoes.

BIANCHETTI AL LIMONE
WHITEBAIT WITH LEMON

This Ligurian recipe for lemon-marinated whitebait is simplicity itself. The fish effectively 'cooks' in the citric acid of the lemon juice; there is no heat involved. Therefore, it is important to use fish that is absolutely fresh.

SERVES 4

500g/1¼lb very fresh whitebait
30ml/2 tbsp chopped fresh flat leaf parsley
juice of 2 lemons
90ml/6 tbsp extra virgin olive oil
sea salt
lemon wedges, to serve

1 Wash the fish thoroughly to rinse off any sand and salt water, then dry them well on kitchen paper. Arrange the whitebait on a large platter.

2 Sprinkle over the parsley and salt, then drizzle over the lemon juice and olive oil. Cover and leave to marinate for 2 hours, then serve with lemon wedges.

SERVES 4

1.2kg/2½lb baby squid, cleaned and tubes left whole
4 salted anchovies, boned
115g/4oz/2 cups soft white breadcrumbs
2 garlic cloves, chopped
30ml/2 tbsp chopped fresh flat leaf parsley
75ml/5 tbsp extra virgin olive oil, plus extra for greasing
sea salt
salad leaves and lemon wedges, to serve

SEPPIOLINE RIPIENE
STUFFED BABY SQUID

For this Ligurian dish, you need tender little squid that will hold their shape and look pretty once baked. Serve them on a bed of fresh salad leaves, such as peppery rocket, with lemon wedges for a lovely light meal.

1 Preheat the oven to 200°C/400°F/Gas 6. Thoroughly grease an ovenproof dish with a little olive oil.

2 Rinse the squid repeatedly in running cold water until they are pure white and no sand or grit remains inside the tubes.

3 Wash the anchovies then chop them finely. Mix the breadcrumbs, anchovies, garlic, parsley and salt together. Stir in one-third of the olive oil.

4 Fill the squid with the stuffing and seal the opening with a cocktail stick or toothpick. You may not use all of the stuffing.

5 Arrange the stuffed squid in the prepared ovenproof dish and sprinkle with any remaining filling. Drizzle over the remaining olive oil.

6 Bake the squid for 20 minutes, until they are golden. Serve on a bed of salad leaves, with lemon wedges.

ORATA CON PINOLI E OLIVE
SEA BREAM WITH PINE KERNELS AND OLIVES

In this flavoursome recipe from Liguria, succulent sea bream is baked on a bed of potatoes, olives and pine nuts. It is traditionally made with Taggiasca olives, which are grown in Liguria. However, if you cannot find them, you can use any other black olives instead – the dish will still taste delicious.

1 Preheat the oven to 180°C/350°F/Gas 4. Parboil the potatoes for 8 minutes, then drain and slice thinly. Meanwhile, season the bream inside with a little salt and pepper and add the fresh herb sprigs.

2 Grease an ovenproof dish large enough to take the fish with a little of the oil. Create a flat layer in the base of the dish using the potatoes, pine nuts and olives.

3 Lay the fish on top of the potatoes and drizzle with the remaining oil.

4 Cook for about 10 minutes, or until the oil begins to sizzle, then remove from the oven and pour the wine around the fish.

5 Return to the oven and continue cooking for a further 20 minutes, or until the fish is cooked through.

SERVES 4 TO 6

400g/14oz potatoes, peeled
2kg/4½lb sea bream, cleaned and small bones removed
1 sprig each of fresh rosemary, thyme and sage
90ml/6 tbsp extra virgin olive oil
25g/1oz pine nuts
175g/6oz Taggiasca olives
300ml/½ pint/1¼ cups dry white wine
sea salt and ground black pepper

SERVES 4

8 thinly sliced beef minute steaks or veal escalopes/US veal scallops
75ml/5 tbsp extra virgin olive oil
1 celery stick, chopped
1 carrot, chopped
1 small onion, chopped
175ml/6fl oz/¾ cup dry white wine
200g/7oz fresh or frozen peas
300ml/½ pint/1¼ cups vegetable stock

FOR THE FILLING
200g/7oz chard, steamed, drained and finely chopped
200g/7oz spinach, steamed, drained and finely chopped
50g/2oz/⅔ cup freshly grated Parmesan cheese
20g/¾oz/6 tbsp dried porcini mushrooms, soaked in warm water for 30 minutes, drained and chopped
10g/¼oz/1 tbsp toasted pine nuts
2 eggs, beaten
30ml/2 tbsp chopped fresh flat leaf parsley
a fresh marjoram sprig, leaves removed and chopped
1 garlic clove, chopped
sea salt

LE TOMAXÆLLE
TOMASELLE

This is a Ligurian interpretation of an ancient recipe, which could date back to the 15th century. It would have been a clever way of making scraps of cheap meat go further, by putting a filling inside, then cooking it in a sauce to make it tender.

1 Mix together all the ingredients for the filling and season to taste with salt. Beat the steaks with a meat mallet or rolling pin until they are almost transparent and each slice is about the same size as the palm of your hand.

2 Divide the filling between the meat slices, then roll each slice up, tucking in the ends. Tie securely with kitchen string or twine.

3 Pour the olive oil into a large frying pan and add the celery, carrot and onion. Fry gently for 5–10 minutes until just softened and browned.

4 Add the meat rolls and cook, turning them over frequently, until they are browned on all sides.

5 Pour in the dry white wine, then add the peas and continue to cook gently for about 1 hour, or until the meat rolls are cooked through, gradually adding vegetable stock throughout the cooking time as necessary to prevent the rolls from drying out.

6 Carefully remove the kitchen string from the meat rolls, transfer them to a serving dish and spoon over the peas and sauce. Serve immediately.

SERVES 4

12 sheets fresh lasagne
3 medium potatoes, peeled
50g/2oz/¼ cup unsalted butter
50g/2oz/½ cup plain/all-purpose flour
600ml/1 pint/2½ cups milk
60ml/4 tbsp pesto (see page 60)
115g/4oz/1¼ cups grated Parmesan cheese
sea salt and ground black pepper
small leaf basil or torn basil leaves, to garnish

COOK'S TIP

It is important not to boil the potatoes for too long or they will become so soft that you won't be able to slice them. They'll also taste watery.

LASAGNA AL PESTO CON LE PATATE
LASAGNA WITH PESTO AND POTATOES

The combination of potatoes and pesto is a classic one, and the addition of the pasta, cheese and creamy sauce here turns it all into a lovely dense, rich dish which makes a perfect vegetarian lunch or supper dish, especially during cold weather. Serve with a salad, if you like.

1 Blanch the pasta sheets in salted boiling water and drop them into cold water to prevent them sticking to each other. Lay them out ready to use. Do not let them overlap, or they will stick together.

2 Cook the potatoes in a large pan of salted boiling water for 10–15 minutes, until just soft. Drain and leave to cool slightly, then slice them thinly (this is easier to do once they are nearly cold). Preheat the oven to 190°C/375°F/Gas 5.

3 Melt the butter in a pan until it is foaming, add the flour and stir together vigorously until a smooth roux is formed.

4 Add the milk and stir together until smooth. Simmer gently, stirring frequently until the sauce is thickened enough to coat the back of a spoon.

5 Stir in half the pesto and season with salt and pepper. Add about half the Parmesan cheese and stir again.

6 Spread a layer of the sauce over the base of a shallow ovenproof dish. Cover with a layer of potatoes, then add a layer of sauce, and dot with some of the remaining pesto. Cover with lasagne sheets and another layer of sauce, then a few dots of pesto. Sprinkle with Parmesan.

7 Repeat the layering process, finishing off with a layer of sauce. Sprinkle the remaining Parmesan on top.

8 Bake for 20–30 minutes, until bubbling and golden. Serve immediately, sprinkled with basil and extra Parmesan.

LOMBARDY

North-western Lombardy has the largest population of any of Italy's regions – over ten million people live here, compared to just over half a million in Basilicata, and about six million in Lazio. Although landlocked, Lombardy compensates for not having a coastline with vast, crystal-clear lakes, such as Maggiore, Lugano, Como, Iseo and, largest of all, Garda; and its majestic rivers, such as the mighty Po to the south and the Ticino, which joins the Po near the city of Pavia. Twelve provinces make up this region: Bergamo, Brescia, Como, Cremona, Varese, Monza, Pavia, Sondrio, Lecco, Lodi, Mantova and the regional capital, Milan.

Lombardy is undisputedly the leading industrial and commercial region of Italy, with Milan being one of the largest industrial centres – producing iron and steel, cars and industrial vehicles, and machinery – as well as being a hub of banking and wholesale and retail trade. The other major cities and their provinces boast manufacturers of electrical appliances, textiles, furniture, processed foods, chemicals and leather goods.

Moreover, Lombardy is also Italy's leading agricultural area. The region's agriculture is centred on the fertile plains of the Po River valley, which produces wheat, maize, rice, sugar beet, and fodder crops for beef and dairy cattle. Cereals, vegetables, fruit trees and mulberries are grown on the higher plains, while the foothills of the Alps produce fruit, vines and olives, and afford excellent grazing for cattle, pigs and sheep.

The traditional cuisine of Lombardy has little to do with the tomato and garlic-based dishes that feature in central and southern Italy, nor durum-wheat pasta and bread, instead focusing on foods such as rice, for risotto; maize, for polenta; beef, veal and rich pork; plenty of butter; many different cakes; and numerous famous cheeses: Grana Padano – the first cousin of Parmigiano Reggiano; and of course Taleggio, Gorgonzola and many more. In many aspects, the cuisine has many things in common with the food of Austria and central Europe in general, yet it remains distinctive and varied within the region itself.

Milan is home to many culinary specialties. Of these, risotto alla Milanese, often served with braised veal shank – ossobuco – is one of the best known. There is also the wonderful cotoletta alla Milanese, a glorious, breadcrumb-coated veal chop or escalope and first cousin of the Austrian Wiener schnitzel, cooked in plenty of foaming butter. And then there is the rich pork stew known as cassoeula, whose origins are a part of the historical Spanish domination of this region.

The province of Como has traditionally produced a small quantity of olive oil along the lake's shoreline in the so-called 'valley of the oil' that, together with other areas around Lake Garda, make this the northernmost olive oil produced in the entire country. The recipes reflect the fish of the lake, served with polenta; worth a mention is 'toch', made with equal parts of maize flour, butter and cheese.

Brescia is where the rather alarming dish of polenta e uccelli (polenta with songbirds) hails from; there is even a sweet cake made to look like this dish, sold in all the local bakeries. Other specialities include the soup brofadei, in which thick fritters made of eggs, butter, milk, flour and salt are fried in butter, cut into squares and then cooked again in a rich beef broth; a frittata made with frog's legs; grilled goose; and grilled eel.

Cremona's culinary symbols have to be the wonderful torrone: nougat, which has been made here for centuries; and the all-important accompaniment to the Lombard version of bollito misto, the spicy and yet very sweet mostarda di Cremona, made of mixed candied fruits preserved in a mustard syrup.

Within the province of Pavia is the Lomellina, one of the main rice-growing areas of the region, so it is not surprising there are so many traditional risotto recipes. However, one cannot mention this province without a word about the famous zuppa alla Pavese, a simple broth with fried bread and eggs, which was apparently invented to feed the captive King Francis of France on 24 February 1525 after his defeat at the Battle of Pavia. This is also one of the richest wine-production areas of the region, including the very rare Barbarcarlo (beard of Charles) – with a production of only 10,000 bottles per year – as well as the curiously named Buttafuoco (spitfire) and Sangue di Giuda (Blood of Judas).

The province of Sondrio is where bresaola comes from, along with pizzoccheri: a cross between a soup and a stew made from buckwheat pancakes layered with broth, potatoes, cabbage and cheese.

IL MINESTRONE
MINESTRONE SOUP

This comforting, substantial soup is one of the great specialities of Lombardy. Made with a combination of vegetables and beans, it can be thickened with rice, pasta or semolina to turn it into the 'big soup'. In summer it is served cold or at room temperature, and hot or cold it is delicious when finished off with a drizzle of extra virgin olive oil and a dusting of freshly grated Parmesan. If using dried borlotti beans, you will need to soak them overnight before you begin.

1 If using dried beans, put the soaked beans in a pan and cover with cold water. Bring to the boil and boil for 5 minutes. Drain and rinse.

2 Put the fresh or boiled, dried beans in a large pan and cover generously with water or unsalted stock. Bring to the boil, then simmer for up to 30 minutes, adding more water or stock if too much of the liquid evaporates, until tender: the cooked beans should not be falling apart, and there should be about 550ml/18fl oz/$2\frac{1}{2}$ cups liquid left at the end of the cooking time.

3 Heat the oil in a large pan and fry the onion gently for 5 minutes, or until soft.

4 Strain the cooked beans, reserving the liquid. Add the beans to the onion and stir together well.

5 Add the parsley, the green vegetables, courgettes, potato and carrot. Fry together gently, adding about 45ml/3 tbsp liquor from the boiled beans to moisten.

6 Cook for 40 minutes, until the vegetables are starting to soften, then pour in the remaining bean liquor to cover, reduce the heat and simmer slowly for 30 minutes, stirring often, until the vegetables are soft. Add some extra water if necessary.

7 Season to taste and add the pasta or rice. Cook gently until the pasta or rice is cooked.

8 Remove from the heat, and allow to stand for 5–10 minutes.

9 Ladle into soup bowls and serve sprinkled with a little Parmesan cheese.

SERVES 6

- 200g/7oz fresh or dried borlotti beans, soaked overnight
- about 1 litre/$1\frac{3}{4}$ pints/4 cups water or unsalted stock
- 60ml/4 tbsp olive oil
- 1 onion, finely chopped
- 45ml/3 tbsp chopped fresh flat leaf parsley
- 300g/11oz green vegetables, such as spinach, cabbage, Swiss chard, lettuce leaves or spring greens/collards, chopped
- 2 courgettes/zucchini, chopped
- 1 potato, cubed
- 1 carrot, chopped
- 200g/7oz/$1\frac{3}{4}$ cups short stubby pasta, such as cannolicchi or Ave Marie, or 200g/7oz/1 cup long grain rice
- salt and ground black pepper
- 30–45ml/2–3 tbsp freshly grated Parmesan cheese, to serve

TROTA LESSA CON SALSA GONZAGA
TROUT WITH A GONZAGA-STYLE SAUCE

In 1509, Isabella d'Este, noble wife of Francesco Gonzaga, was Marchesa of Mantua and one of the leading women of the Italian Renaissance. In one of her famous letters, she begged her husband to hurry to Lake Garda from Mantova – the capital of their Duchy and less than 3 hours by road – to join her, to enjoy the local fish dishes. The original calls for pike, which are plentiful in Lake Garda, but I prefer trout, though any freshwater fish will work.

SERVES 4 AS AN APPETIZER OR 2 AS A MAIN COURSE

1 onion, peeled and quartered
1 celery stick, washed and halved
1 large carrot, washed and halved
1 garlic clove, peeled
2 bay leaves
100ml/3½fl oz/scant ½ cup plus 30ml/2 tbsp white wine vinegar
115ml/8 tbsp dry white wine
1kg/2¼lb fresh trout, gutted, washed inside and out and patted dry
30ml/2 tbsp salted capers, rinsed and dried
1 large red bell pepper, washed
a handful of fresh flat leaf parsley
3 canned anchovy fillets
30ml/2 tbsp extra virgin olive oil
grated zest of 1 small unwaxed lemon
sea salt and ground black pepper
grilled/broiled polenta (see page 204), to serve (optional)

1 Put the onion, celery, carrot, garlic, bay leaves, 30ml/2 tbsp vinegar, 90ml/6 tbsp of the wine and a pinch of salt into a fish kettle or wide pan. Place over a medium heat and bring to a gentle boil.

2 Allow to simmer for about 10 minutes, then slide in the fish and simmer very gently for a further 8–10 minutes. Remove from the liquid, drain and leave to cool completely.

3 Meanwhile, chop the capers, pepper and parsley together finely.

4 Gently fry the anchovy fillets and oil in a pan until the anchovy is melted, then add the capers, pepper and most of the parsley, reserving a little for the garnish. Stir until softened, then add the remaining vinegar and wine and simmer for 10 minutes, stirring occasionally. Season, set aside and keep warm.

5 Skin and fillet the fish and arrange on a platter, then sprinkle with the lemon zest. Cover with the sauce and sprinkle with parsley. Serve with slices of polenta, if liked.

SERVES 4

1 trout, about 1kg/2¼lb, cleaned and left whole
60ml/4 tbsp extra virgin olive oil
500ml/17fl oz/2¼ cups dry white wine
2 garlic cloves (1 left whole, and 1 crushed)
300ml/½ pint/1¼ cups passata/bottled strained tomatoes
45ml/3 tbsp chopped parsley
sea salt and ground black pepper
5ml/1 tsp dried oregano, to garnish
roast potatoes, to serve (optional)

TROTA ALLA DOGANA
TROUT DOGANA STYLE

On the outskirts of the town of Sirmione is an old building that was once an Austrian barracks during the days of the Hapsburg Empire. It later became the Ristorante Dogana and is famous all over the area for its simple cuisine, as epitomised by this tasty and colourful trout dish.

1 Rinse the cavity of the trout and pat it dry, then place it in a fish kettle. Add the oil, wine, whole garlic clove, 250ml/8fl oz/1 cup cold water, and salt and pepper, then set over a high heat and bring to the boil. Reduce the heat to low and cook the fish very gently for 30–40 minutes.

2 Carefully lift out the fish using slotted spoons or spatulas without breaking it up and transfer to an ovenproof serving dish.

3 Preheat the oven to 200°C/400°F/Gas 6. Simmer the passata for 5 minutes with the crushed garlic, parsley, and salt and pepper to taste.

4 Pour the tomato sauce over the fish in the serving dish, and place in the oven for 2–3 minutes, until heated through. Sprinkle lightly with oregano and serve with roast potatoes, if you like. For maximum effect, fillet the fish at the table.

SERVES 4

200g/7oz bresaola, thinly sliced
extra virgin olive oil, to drizzle
juice of ½ lemon or 10ml/2 tsp best-quality balsamic vinegar
75g/3oz rocket/arugula leaves
75g/3oz/1 cup Parmesan cheese, shaved
ground black pepper

COOK'S TIP

It is important to buy top-quality bresaola for this simple dish. Specialist Italian delicatessens – either ones you can visit or online – are usually the best places to buy this, or buy the best you can from a supermarket.

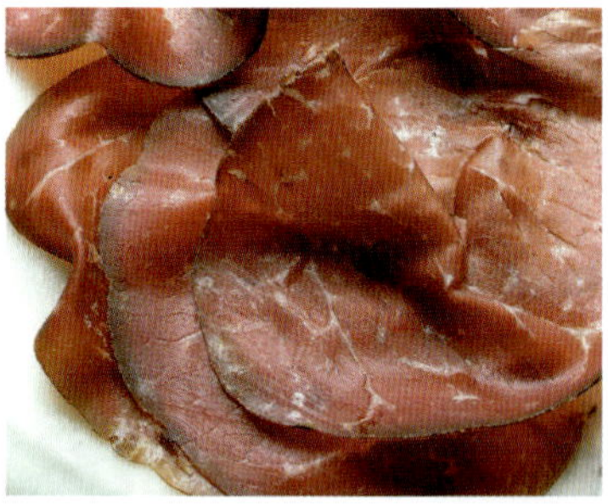

BRESAOLA CON PARMIGIANO E RUCOLA
BRESAOLA WITH PARMESAN AND ROCKET

Intensely and uniformly red in colour with a delicate, slightly salty aroma, bresaola is the only Italian cured meat made from selected beef haunches. The beef is seasoned with a special mixture of salt, pepper and other spices, then cured under controlled humidity and temperature conditions. The finished product is put inside pork gut casings and cured for a further period of between 1 and 3 months. The tradition of bresaola spans several centuries and is a product of the area of Lombardy called Valtellina. Once sliced, bresaola has a bright-red colouring and a well-defined flavour. Traditionally, it is served sliced paper thin, with a dressing of olive oil, lemon juice and pepper, and accompanied by some good bread.

1 Arrange the bresaola on a serving platter in a single layer, slightly overlapping the slices so they look attractive.

2 Drizzle with a little olive oil; not too much, however, just enough to give the meat a shiny appearance.

3 Drizzle with the lemon juice or balsamic vinegar, and sprinkle with black pepper.

4 Pile the rocket leaves in the middle and sprinkle over the Parmesan cheese shavings. Add a final drizzle of olive oil over the leaves and serve immediately.

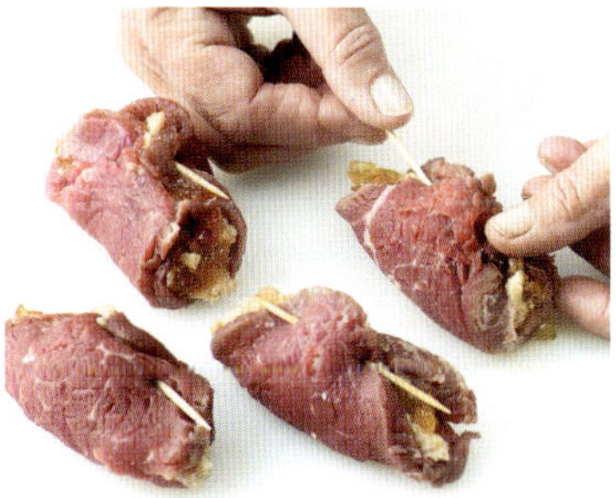

INVOLTINI ALLA MOSTARDA DI CREMONA
STEAK ROLLS WITH FRUIT MUSTARD

What makes this dish special is the use of mostarda di Cremona, the closest Italian cuisine comes to a kind of chutney. It is made with candied fruits, which are bathed in a heavy mustard syrup, and is usually served with cheese or robust and flavoursome meat dishes such as bollito misto.

SERVES 4

115g/4oz stale white bread, soaked in milk to cover until soft
200g/7oz Italian sausage meat/bulk sausage
2 egg yolks
30ml/2 tbsp freshly grated Parmesan cheese
1kg/2¼lb of fillet steak/beef tenderloin
300g/11oz fruit mustard (preferably mostarda di Cremona)
25g/1oz/2 tbsp unsalted butter
60ml/4 tbsp dry white wine
sea salt and ground black pepper

1 Squeeze the bread dry. In a bowl, mix together the sausage with the bread, egg yolks, Parmesan cheese, and salt and pepper to create a smooth mixture.

2 Slice the steak into 8 even portions. Beat the steaks with a meat mallet or rolling pin until 2cm/¾in thick.

3 Spread sausage mixture over the top of each steak. Take about a sixth of the fruit mustard and cut it up into small pieces. Spoon a little on to each steak. Roll up the steaks and secure with a cocktail stick, toothpick, kitchen string or twine.

4 Melt the butter in a large frying pan, add the steak rolls and cook for 8–10 minutes, turning often, until cooked evenly. Keep warm.

5 Keep the pan over a low heat, add the wine and 30ml/2 tbsp water, then increase the heat and boil the liquids quickly together, scraping the sides and base of the pan to incorporate any scraps.

6 Return the steak rolls to the pan and heat through for 3–4 minutes. Add water if needed to prevent them drying out. Serve immediately, with the sauce poured over and with the remaining fruit mustard.

OSSOBUCO IN UMIDO
STEWED OSSOBUCCO

The dish from Lombardy is traditionally served on a plain white or a saffron risotto, or on mashed potato, with gremolata – a piquant mixture of chopped flat leaf parsley and grated lemon rind – sprinkled on top.

1 Wipe the ossobucco or veal with kitchen paper to make sure there are no shards of bone. Put the oil, all the vegetables, and the garlic into a heavy frying pan that is large enough to take all the meat as well. Fry for 10 minutes, or until softened.

2 Remove the vegetables and set aside. Add the meat to the pan and brown carefully on both sides.

3 Add half the wine and boil over a high heat for 1 minute to evaporate the alcohol, then lower the heat and add the passata and the tomato paste.

4 Season to taste with salt and ground black pepper and cover. Simmer over a low heat for about 2 hours, stirring fairly frequently and adding the remaining wine, a little at a time to keep the meat moist, until it is very tender.

5 To make the gremolata, mix together the finely chopped parsley, lemon rind and some salt and ground black pepper in a small serving bowl.

6 Serve the stewed ossobucco on plain risotto, topped with some of the gremolata and with the remainder served alongside.

SERVES 6

1.5kg/3¼lb ossobucco or thick-cut veal shanks
60ml/4 tbsp olive oil
4 celery sticks, finely chopped
1 large onion, finely chopped
2 carrots, finely chopped
3 garlic cloves, finely chopped
750ml/1¼ pints/3 cups dry white wine
250ml/8fl oz/1 cup passata/ bottled strained tomatoes
30ml/2 tbsp tomato paste, diluted in 45ml/3 tbsp warm water
sea salt and ground black pepper
plain risotto, to serve

FOR THE GREMOLATA

30ml/2 tbsp finely chopped flat leaf parsley
grated rind of 1 lemon
sea salt and ground black pepper

SERVES 4

8 veal chops
600ml/1 pint/2½ cups milk
2 eggs, beaten
75g/3oz dried white breadcrumbs
115g/4oz/½ cup unsalted butter
sea salt and ground black pepper
steamed vegetables and lemon wedges, to serve

COOK'S TIP

A lighter version, known as cotolette, uses veal escalopes/US veal scallops. Fry these for 4 minutes on each side until crisp and golden. You can use turkey or chicken.

COSTOLETTA ALLA MILANESE
VEAL CHOP MILANESE STYLE

This is an incredibly rich dish, even though it contains only a few ingredients, due to the fact that a generous amount of butter is used to cook the chops. It shows off the flavour of the meat perfectly and needs just some steamed vegetables and lemon wedges as an accompaniment.

1 Beat the veal chops in a strong plastic bag with a meat mallet or rolling pin to about 2cm/¾in thickness. Soak them in the milk for 30 minutes.

2 Remove the veal chops from the milk and dip them into the beaten egg and then into the breadcrumbs, pressing the crumbs firmly and evenly on to the meat with the palm of your hand.

3 Melt the butter in a large frying pan over a medium heat, add the breaded chops and fry for 3 minutes on each side; turn them only once. The crust should be golden brown and the meat pink. You may need to fry the veal in batches.

4 Season to taste, then serve immediately with steamed vegetables, and lemon wedges for squeezing over.

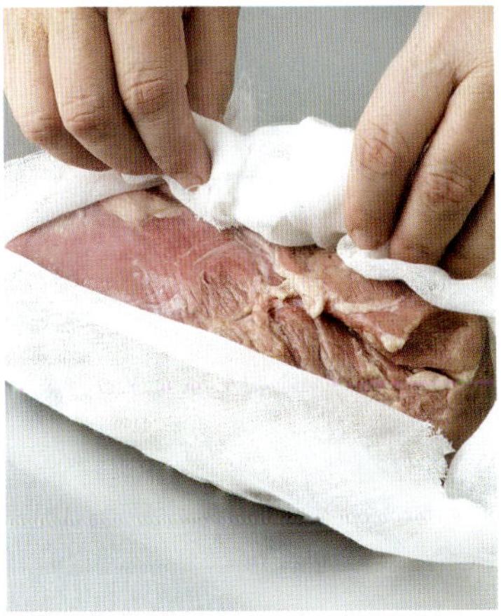

VITELLO TONNATO
COLD VEAL WITH TUNA MAYONNAISE

This is a real summer favourite all over Lombardy and other areas of north-west Italy, where you can always find this dish ready-made at good delicatessens when the weather gets hot. Although the combination of boiled meat and tuna mayonnaise might seem a little odd, when put together in this way it makes a very special dish. It needs only a green salad and some pickles to make a lovely meal. Don't serve the dish too cold or it will lose its delicate flavour. Start preparations the day before and allow it to come to room temperature.

SERVES 6

900g/2lb veal fillet joint
600ml/1 pint/2½ cups veal or chicken stock
green salad, capers, gherkins and lemon wedges, to serve
chopped parsley, to garnish

FOR THE MARINADE

750ml/1¼ pints/3 cups dry white wine
1 onion, sliced
1 carrot, sliced
4 cloves
3 bay leaves, chopped
salt and ground black pepper

FOR THE SAUCE

300g/11oz thick mayonnaise, (see Cook's Tip)
185g/6½oz canned tuna in olive oil, drained and finely flaked
200g/7oz capers preserved in salt or vinegar, rinsed, dried and finely chopped
sea salt and ground black pepper

1 First, make the marinade. Set aside 175ml/6fl oz/¾ cup of the white wine and pour the rest of the wine into a bowl. Add all the other marinade ingredients to the wine and mix together.

2 Lay the joint of veal in a deep bowl. Pour the marinade over the meat and leave it to stand in the refrigerator overnight.

3 The next day, lift the meat from the marinade (reserving the marinade) and wrap it in muslin or cheesecloth. Tie it up tightly using kitchen string or twine, then lay it in a deep pan.

4 Pour the marinade and the stock over the meat and boil it slowly for 1½ hours, or until the veal is completely cooked through. Leave the meat to cool in the marinade.

5 Take the meat out of the cold marinade and unwrap the muslin. Discard the marinade (or keep it to add to soup or gravy). Slice the meat thinly and arrange on a large platter.

6 To make the sauce, mix together the mayonnaise with the canned tuna, capers, and the reserved white wine, and season with salt and pepper. Drizzle the sauce over the sliced meat.

7 Serve immediately with green salad, capers, gherkins and lemon wedges on the side, and garnish with chopped parsley. Alternatively, chill until required, then garnish just before serving.

COOK'S TIP

To make mayonnaise, put 1 egg into a food processor and whizz until pale yellow. Mix 150ml/¼ pint/⅔ cup each of sunflower and extra virgin olive oil, then add to the egg in a very thin, slow, steady stream, keeping the motor running, until a thick sauce forms. Add the juice of ½ lemon, and season.

SERVES 8

600g/1lb 6oz cotechino
1 boiling fowl
8 peppercorns
2 large onions
8 cloves
2 large carrots
3 celery sticks
2 bay leaves
675g/1½lb veal breast
675g/1½lb beef shin/shank or skirt/flank
675g/1½lb veal silverside/pot roast
1 ready-to-cook tongue
sea salt
salsa verde (see page 103) and mustards, including mostarda di Cremona, to serve

BOLLITO MISTO
BOLLITO MISTO

This is one of Italy's great celebratory dishes, and a favourite to be served on special occasions. Although it involves separate cooking pans, it is actually a simple mixture of all kinds of meat, boiled together with vegetables. A boiling fowl is a rare thing these days (though not so much in Italy) however it is an older and usually much larger, tough bird that makes great stock. Of course, the secret to a delicious combination starts with high-quality ingredients, so that their flavours will stand out even after hours of simmering. It is important to serve the dish with various sauces, such as salsa verde and the ubiquitous accompaniment for bollito misto: mostarda di Cremona, which consists of glacé fruits preserved in a heavy mustard syrup.

1 Pierce the cotechino all over with the point of a knife and put into a large pan. Cover with cold water and leave to soak for 1 hour. Drain and cover with fresh water, then bring to the boil and simmer gently for 3 hours.

2 Put the boiling fowl into a second large pan and cover with cold water. Add 4 peppercorns, 1 onion stuck with 4 cloves, 1 carrot, 1 stick of celery, 1 bay leaf and a good pinch of salt. Bring to the boil and simmer gently for 3 hours.

3 Put the veal breast, the beef and the veal joint into a third large pan with the remaining peppercorns, onion stuck with cloves, carrot, celery sticks, bay leaf and a good pinch of salt. Cover with cold water and bring to the boil. Reduce the heat and simmer gently for 3 hours.

4 After 1 hour of cooking, put the tongue in a fourth pan with cold water to cover, and bring to the boil. Simmer for 2 hours.

5 When all the meat is cooked, transfer it all to a warmed casserole, discarding the studded onions, bay leaves and all the excess liquid.

6 Serve the bollito misto from the casserole, removing the various elements and carving them at the table on a large board. Each serving should contain a little of each type of meat and a slice each of carrot and celery for colour. Serve it piping hot, with salsa verde and a selection of mustards.

FRITTATA AL TALEGGIO CON PORRI E PATATE
POTATO AND LEEK FRITTATA WITH TALEGGIO

This frittata is substantial enough to serve as a one-pot meal on a hot summer day and is lovely at room temperature with a glass of refreshing white wine and some crisp green salad. Taleggio is a nutty, semi-soft cow's milk cheese that has been produced in Lombardy since the Middle Ages. It has a subtle truffle aroma, especially close to its rind, which imparts a unique taste to this dish. Taleggio might be difficult to find in smaller supermarkets, but you should be able to find it in good Italian delicatessens and most larger supermarkets.

SERVES 6

30ml/2 tbsp extra virgin olive oil
3 leeks, cut in half lengthways, and thinly sliced
1 large potato, peeled, quartered and thinly sliced
1 onion, thinly sliced
200g/7oz green beans, trimmed and cut into 5mm/¼in lengths
6 eggs
8 fresh basil leaves, torn
200g/7oz Taleggio cheese, rind removed and roughly cut into 1cm/½in cubes
sea salt and ground black pepper
green salad, to serve

1 Heat half the olive oil in a 30cm/12in non-stick frying pan over a medium heat. Add the leeks, potato, onion and beans. Season with salt and pepper. Cover with a tight-fitting lid and cook, stirring frequently, for 10 minutes.

2 Lower the heat to medium-low and cook, stirring frequently, uncovered, for 10 minutes more, or until the potato is tender and the mixture is fairly dry. Don't let it catch and burn or it will taste bitter.

3 Meanwhile, put the eggs into a large mixing bowl, add the basil and a pinch of salt and pepper, and beat to mix well.

4 Stir the hot potato and vegetable mixture into the bowl with the eggs, stirring constantly to avoid scrambling the eggs.

5 Pour the remaining olive oil into the frying pan and heat over a medium-high heat for 1 minute.

6 Pour in the egg and vegetable mixture, allow to cook for 1 minute, then sprinkle the cubes of Taleggio cheese over the top.

7 Shake the pan to flatten and even out the mixture, pulling the liquid egg into the middle as you work. Cook for about 8 minutes until the underside is browned and firm.

8 Turn the frittata over by covering the frying pan with a large lid or plate and overturning the frying pan on to it. Put the frying pan back down on to the heat and carefully slide the frittata, uncooked side down, back into the hot pan.

9 Cook the frittata again for about 5 minutes, until golden brown and firm on the underside.

10 Slide the frittata out on to a clean, flat plate and serve either hot or cold, sliced into chunky wedges, accompanied by a green salad.

SERVES 6

- ½ onion, finely chopped
- 115g/4oz/½ cup unsalted butter
- 40g/1½oz raw beef bone marrow, chopped (optional)
- 500g/1¼lb vialone gigante, or other risotto rice
- 1.5 litres/2½ pints/6¼ cups hot rich veal, beef, chicken or vegetable stock
- 1–2 sachets of saffron powder, or a small pinch of saffron threads
- 50g/2oz/⅔ cup freshly grated Parmesan cheese, plus extra to serve

RISOTTO ALLA MILANESE CLASSICO
CLASSIC MILANESE RISOTTO

The origins of this dish belong to an Italian legend about the master in charge of stained glass windows in Milan Cathedral, who employed a keen workman to paint the yellow robes of St Helen. The workman used saffron to colour the glass and he was so passionate about his saffron powder that he was named Zafferano (meaning 'saffron') by his colleagues, who claimed that one day he'd probably even add it to his risotto! And one day he did: on the occasion of the wedding of the master's daughter, he presented two tureens of the golden risotto, coloured and scented with saffron as a gift. This traditional recipe includes beef bone marrow but, if you prefer, use only butter instead.

1 Soak the onion in cold water for 10 minutes, then drain and squeeze dry in a napkin.

2 Heat half the butter in a pan, add the onion and fry very slowly with the beef marrow, if using, for 5 minutes or until soft. Add the rice. Stir and coat the grains thoroughly until the rice grains are crackling hot but not coloured.

3 Add a ladleful of the stock and stir constantly, allowing the liquid to be absorbed into the rice. Add another ladleful of stock and continue in this way, making sure that the rice always absorbs the stock before you add more.

4 After 10 minutes of cooking time, add the saffron powder or threads and stir through. Continue cooking the risotto, adding stock a ladleful at a time, and stirring constantly. The risotto will take about 20 minutes to cook: when it is creamy and velvety, but the rice grains are still firm to the bite, take it off the heat.

5 Stir in the remaining butter and the cheese. Cover and leave to rest for 2 minutes, then stir again and transfer to a warmed platter. Serve immediately, offering extra grated Parmesan cheese at the table, to sprinkle on top.

ZUCCHINE IN CARPIONE
COURGETTES WITH BREADCRUMBS

A Lombard recipe that mimics the fish recipe of the same name. The phrase 'in carpione' refers to food that is partially pickled by being cooked in vinegar, or at least has enough vinegar added to raise the level of acidity to the point when fermentation is naturally delayed. Many different kinds of food get treated in this way, not only in Lombardy, but in other areas of north-west Italy, and they reflect a time when refrigerators were not commonplace in every kitchen.

1 Trim and discard the ends from the courgettes, then cut them in half lengthways and remove the seeds using a spoon. Cut into chunks.

2 Heat the oil in a pan and cook the onions gently for 10 minutes, or until softened.

3 Add the courgettes to the pan and cook gently until completely soft.

4 Mix the breadcrumbs and vinegar together and stir this mixture through the vegetables. Cook for a further 10 minutes, then serve hot, with toasted bread.

SERVES 4

600g/1lb 6oz courgettes/zucchini
60ml/4 tbsp extra virgin olive oil
2 onions, finely sliced
75ml/5 tbsp soft white breadcrumbs
45ml/3 tbsp white wine vinegar
Italian bread, toasted, to serve

SERVES 6 TO 8

200g/7oz/scant 1 cup unsalted butter, melted, plus extra for greasing
150g/5oz/1¼ cups plain/all-purpose flour, plus extra for dusting
6 eggs, separated
90ml/6 tbsp caster/superfine sugar
50g/2oz/½ cup cornflour/cornstarch
5ml/1 tsp baking powder
7.5ml/1½ tsp grated lemon rind
pinch of salt
icing/confectioners' sugar, for dusting

LA TORTA MARGHERITA
DAISY CAKE

This classic cake is traditionally served at tea time for merenda (the snack that children have after their siesta). It is a plain sponge cake, usually covered with a thick layer of icing sugar, or split in half with a chocolate or jam filling. It tends to be rather dry, and is enjoyed dunked into a bowl of milk, hot chocolate or coffee, or a little dessert wine for adults. It is delightful by itself, and it is also an excellent base for making an Italian trifle, or any other Italian dessert that requires a plain cake base.

1 Preheat the oven to 180°C/350°F/Gas 4. Grease and flour a 25cm/10in cake tin or pan.

2 In a large bowl, beat the egg yolks with the sugar until pale yellow.

3 Sift the flour, cornflour and baking powder into a separate bowl, then gradually beat them into the egg mixture.

4 Gradually beat in the melted butter, lemon rind and salt.

5 Put the egg whites into a clean, grease-free bowl and whisk until they form stiff peaks. Fold into the cake batter.

6 Pour the cake batter into the tin and bake for 40 minutes, or until a knife inserted into the middle comes out clean.

7 Cool in the cake tin for 15 minutes, then turn out on to a wire rack to finish cooling. Dust with a thick layer of icing sugar just before serving.

TORTA DI MELE
ITALIAN APPLE CAKE

This is the simplest and most delicious of apple cakes. Make sure you use sweet and tasty eating apples rather than cooking ones. When in season, peaches, apricots, nectarines and plums all work well too.

SERVES 8

65g/2½oz/5 tbsp butter, cut into small pieces, plus extra for greasing
45ml/3 tbsp stale breadcrumbs
3 large/US extra large eggs
150g/5oz/¾ cup caster/superfine sugar, plus extra for dusting
200g/7oz/1¾ cups plain/all-purpose flour
150ml/¼ pint/⅔ cup milk
grated rind of ½ lemon
7.5ml/1½ tsp baking powder
1kg/2¼lb eating apples, peeled and thinly sliced
175g/6oz/1 cup blackberries
30ml/2 tbsp light brown sugar

1 Preheat the oven to 180°C/350°F/Gas 4. Grease a 25cm/10in cake tin or pan with butter, then dust with the breadcrumbs.

2 Beat the eggs in a large mixing bowl. Add the sugar gradually, beating until light and fluffy. Fold in the flour, milk, lemon rind and baking powder. The mixture should be quite liquid.

3 Turn the tin upside down to remove all the loose breadcrumbs. Discard them.

4 Add half the sliced apples and half the blackberries to the cake batter and stir through.

5 Pour the cake batter into the prepared tin and arrange the remaining sliced apples and blackberries on top.

6 Dot with butter, sprinkle with the light brown sugar and bake in the preheated oven for 55 minutes.

7 Take the cake out of the oven and leave to cool completely, then remove it from the tin. Serve sprinkled with extra sugar.

TORTA AL CIOCCOLATO
ITALIAN CHOCOLATE CAKE

Experienced cake makers will notice that the method for making this cake from Lombardy is quite unusual. Here, all the ingredients are added to beaten egg whites, not the other way around, which gives it quite a distinct texture.

SERVES 6 TO 8

- 130g/4½oz/generous ½ cup unsalted butter, cubed, plus extra for greasing
- 250g/9oz dark/bittersweet chocolate, chopped
- 5 large/US extra large eggs, separated
- 1 espresso (about 30ml/2 tbsp very strong black coffee)
- 200g/7oz/1 cup caster/superfine sugar
- 5ml/1 tsp baking powder
- 30ml/2 tbsp unsweetened cocoa powder
- 115g/4oz/1 cup plain/all-purpose flour
- 400g/14oz chocolate, melted, to cover

1 Preheat the oven to 180°C/350°F/Gas 4. Grease and line a 23cm/9in loose-based cake tin or pan with baking parchment.

2 Melt 250g/9oz of the chocolate in a heatproof bowl over a pan of gently simmering water. While the chocolate is melting, put the egg whites into a clean, grease-free bowl and whisk until they form stiff peaks. Remove the melted chocolate from the pan and stir in the butter, then add the coffee.

3 Carefully fold the sugar into the egg whites. Measure the baking powder with the cocoa powder and flour into a bowl. Stir the egg yolks into the melted chocolate mixture, then gently fold this mixture into the egg whites.

4 Sift over the baking powder, cocoa powder and flour mixture and gently fold in with a large metal spoon until the dry ingredients are completely incorporated, but taking care not to knock out too much air. Turn into the prepared tin.

5 Bake for 40 minutes, or until a skewer inserted into the middle comes out clean. Leave to cool in the cake tin.

6 Melt the remaining chocolate in a heatproof bowl over a pan of gently simmering water. Turn out the cooled cake and cover with melted chocolate. Leave to set before serving.

EMILIA-ROMAGNA

For many people, Emilia-Romagna represents the very best of Italian food. As the home of Parmesan cheese, prosciutto di Parma, traditional aged balsamic vinegar and fresh pasta in all its forms, there is certainly much for the region to be proud of.

Six other regions surround Emilia-Romagna, with the independent Republic of San Marino tucked away between the borders of Emilia-Romagna and Le Marche. Historically, its eight provinces have always been divided between the two separate areas of Emilia and Romagna: Piacenza, Parma, Reggio Emilia, Modena, Ferrara, and most of the regional capital Bologna are officially recognised as being part of Emilia; whereas Forli Cesena, Ravenna, the coastal resort of Rimini and the eastern communes of Bologna are part of Romagna.

In addition to being the regional capital, Bologna is also of enormous gastronomic and cultural importance, with an ancient history dating back to the Etruscans. The city later became a Gallic settlement called Boi, and then a Roman city called Bononia. It also boasts the oldest university in the world, which dates to the 11th century. Nicknamed 'Bologna La Dotta', meaning 'Bologna the Cultured One', it is a beautiful city filled with glorious Renaissance and medieval buildings and soaring towers, the most famous of these being the Torre degli Asinelli and the Torre Garisenda.

Modena, once the ancient Roman city of Mudina, has a tower of its own – the imposing bell tower of the city's cathedral called La Ghirlandina. Measuring more than 86m (282ft) in height, this is the symbol of Modena, visible from all directions outside the city. This is of course also the home of traditional balsamic vinegar, an ancient condiment – once used as a laxative and also according to local custom as part of a bride's dowry – the complete history of which remains shrouded in mystery and legend. It is made by ageing boiled wine must in the attics of Modena's houses, and its quality is protected not only by European and Italian law but also by its consortium of producers. The annual auction for the sale of traditional balsamic (which is distinct from cheaper, ordinary balsamic vinegar) takes place in the town of Spilamberto. It is amazing to reflect on the global explosion of this product, once a precious home-made ingredient and now synonymous with Italian food and a kitchen essential. It is also worth mentioning that the world-famous restaurant Osteria Francescana is located in Modena.

Ferrara is a graceful medieval city that was the seat of the noble d'Este family from 1200 to 1500, and it is also famous for its wonderful bread, which has a unique flavour and texture. Ravenna is known for its Romanesque architecture and glorious mosaics and for the flat bread called piadina; Parma for its Parma ham and Parmigiano Reggiano; and Reggio Emilia for being the place where the red, white and green flag of the Republic was first flown, in 1797. Comacchio, in the province of Ferrara, is a small town created out of 13 islets, separated by canals and a complicated network of bridges; and all along the Adriatic coast are the resorts of Rimini, Cesenatico, Cattolica and Riccione.

Every inch of this north-central region, geographically dominated by the great River Po, seems to reflect prosperity, with a cornucopia of fantastic food and internationally recognised specialities. The cuisine here is simple, yet full of strong, refined flavours with rich fresh egg pasta; sauces; cheeses; and myriad pork products that are still made according to tradition. Over the centuries, the marshes created by the Po have been transformed into some of the best farmland in Italy, and the region can boast more than 200 traditional products and 26 ingredients that hold a geographically protected status. It is no wonder that the region is considered by many to be the gastronomic heart of the country.

The one notable thing that Emilia-Romagna does not produce, however, is olive oil, at least in any notable quantity. The cuisine of a place or area can be defined by its cooking fat, and this one certainly excels in its use of butter and pork fat rather than oil.

A note about Lambrusco

The most famous wine of Emilia-Romagna is the sparkling wine Lambrusco, which is also the name of the grape from which it is made. For me, this is always a perfectly suited accompaniment to the rich, generous food of this region. Light, clean-tasting and fizzy, it helps the digestion and makes the experience even better when it comes to enjoying the traditional cuisine.

PROSCIUTTO E MELONE
CURED HAM AND MELON

This is the ultimate Italian antipasto and it remains a sure-fire winner every time it is served, as long as the melon is perfectly ripe and sweet, the figs are soft and a little sticky, and the ham is freshly and expertly sliced into paper-thin sheets. This refreshing yet toothsome combination was originally discovered in Emilia-Romagna, where this dish originates. Off-season, when the melons and figs are not available, the fruit of choice would be ripe pears. Serve it with fresh, crusty bread and chilled rosé on a sunny day.

1 Arrange the salad leaves on a large serving platter. Slice and seed the melon and arrange it on the salad leaves.

2 If the figs are firm, peel off their skins, otherwise leave the skin on.

3 Quarter the figs and arrange them alongside the melon slices.

4 Arrange the prosciutto slices in the middle of the dish, overlapping the melon slices and figs, then serve immediately.

SERVES 4

75g/3oz salad leaves
1 melon, about 1.2kg/$2\frac{1}{2}$lb, chilled
4 figs, either green or black, chilled
12 slices prosciutto crudo (prosciutto di Parma, prosciutto di San Daniele or prosciutto di Carpegna) or speck

SERVES 4

300g/11oz/4½ cups mixed mushrooms, such as button/ white, brown cap/cremini, chestnut, porcini and oyster, thinly sliced
200g/7oz mortadella, sliced and cut into sticks
115g/4oz/1¼ cups Parmesan cheese, shaved
juice of ½ lemon
15ml/1 tbsp chopped fresh mint
60ml/4 tbsp chopped flat leaf parsley
60ml/4 tbsp extra virgin olive oil
sea salt and ground black pepper

COOK'S TIP

For an elegant event, arrange the mushrooms in one layer on a pretty plate, then cover with a layer of mortadella, sprinkle on the dressing and finish off with the Parmesan cheese shavings.

MORTADELLA, FUNGHETTI E PARMIGIANO
MORTADELLA, MUSHROOMS AND PARMESAN

A large Italian sausage made of finely ground heat-cured pork, mortadella incorporates at least 15 per cent small cubes of pork fat (principally the hard fat from the neck). It is delicately flavoured with spices, including black pepper, myrtle, nutmeg, coriander and pistachio nuts and/or olives. Although other versions are made throughout Italy, mortadella originated in Bologna, the capital of Emilia-Romagna, and this is why the American version is given the name bologna or baloney sausage.

1 Put the mushrooms, mortadella and Parmesan cheese in a shallow bowl and mix together.

2 In a separate bowl mix together the lemon juice, mint and parsley, then season with salt and pepper.

3 Add the oil to the dressing mixture and whisk thoroughly until it thickens. Adjust the seasoning to taste.

4 Pour the dressing over the salad ingredients. Toss together gently, then divide among plates and serve immediately.

SERVES 6

400g/14oz/1¾ cups ricotta cheese
pinch of grated nutmeg
175g/6oz/2 cups freshly grated Parmesan cheese
6 eggs
250g/9oz/2¼ cups plain/all-purpose flour
200g/7oz/generous 1 cup fine semolina
1.5ml/¼ tsp olive oil
150g/5oz/10 tbsp unsalted butter
5 fresh sage leaves, rubbed gently between your palms to release their flavour
sea salt and ground black pepper

COOK'S TIP

Any scraps of pasta dough can be finely chopped and set aside to dry. They can be used in a clear broth to make a simple soup.

RAVIOLI CON RIPIENO DI RICOTTA
RICOTTA RAVIOLI

This is one of the simplest and most delicious of all the filled pasta recipes from Emilia-Romagna. Like a lot of classic Italian dishes, it relies on the absolute freshness and quality of ingredients, in this case, ricotta.

1 Put the ricotta cheese in a bowl and mix in the nutmeg, half the Parmesan cheese and season with salt and pepper. Add an egg and blend the mixture together. Set aside.

2 Put the flour and semolina on to the worktop and make a hollow in the middle using your fist. Break the remaining 5 eggs into the hole. Stir the eggs into the dry ingredients, then begin to knead together.

3 Add the olive oil and knead until you have a smooth, elastic dough. Rest the dough under a clean cloth or wrap in clear film or plastic wrap for 20 minutes.

4 Roll out the dough thinly using a rolling pin or pasta machine until fine, silky and cool. Divide it lengthways into 6cm/2½in-wide strips. Work on one strip at a time, covering the other with a slightly damp cloth.

5 Drop 5ml/1 tsp of the ricotta cheese mixture in heaps along one half of each strip, leaving a gap of two fingers between each one.

6 Fold the strip in half, over the filling, encasing the filling at one side. Using a pastry or cookie cutter or an upturned glass, cut around each section of filled pasta to make a crescent with a straight edge. Seal the curved edge of each crescent with the prongs of a fork. Continue in this way until all the dough has been cut.

7 Bring a large pan of salted water to a rolling boil. Drop the ravioli into the water and boil until they float on the surface and are tender. Remove the ravioli with a slotted spoon, and arrange in a warmed serving dish.

8 Meanwhile, melt the butter with the sage leaves in a small pan until warm and golden, but not browned.

9 When all the pasta is in the serving dish, pour over the melted butter and mix carefully to distribute without breaking up the ravioli. Sprinkle with the remaining Parmesan cheese and serve immediately.

RAVIOLI RIPIENI DI PESCE
ANCHOVY AND WHITE FISH RAVIOLI

Anchovies and tomato paste, combined with white fish, make this a special dish with an intense flavour, from Emilia-Romagna. The fragrant herb butter is the only dressing for these ravioli, complementing and not overpowering them.

SERVES 6

4 canned anchovy fillets, drained
a little milk
45ml/3 tbsp olive oil
1 onion, finely chopped
2 celery sticks, chopped
1 carrot, finely chopped
2 garlic cloves, chopped
45ml/3 tbsp chopped flat leaf parsley
60ml/4 tbsp tomato paste, diluted in 45ml/3 tbsp hot water
350g/12oz white fish fillets, such as cod, haddock, hake, plaice or flounder, boned and skinned
sea salt and ground black pepper

FOR THE PASTA

200g/7oz/1¾ cups plain/all-purpose flour
200g/7oz/generous 1 cup fine semolina
4 whole eggs

TO SERVE

300g/11oz/generous 1½ cups unsalted butter, melted
finely chopped parsley, chervil and a little tarragon

COOK'S TIPS

- Work fast while making the ravioli to prevent the sheets of dough from drying out. Keep the dough pliable at all times.
- You can open-freeze fresh pasta on trays, then transfer them to bags and freeze for up to 1 month.

1 Soak the anchovies in just enough milk to cover for 30 minutes, then rinse and dry on kitchen paper.

2 Heat the olive oil in a pan and add the anchovy fillets. Mash the anchovies to a pulp, using a fork, then add the onion, celery, carrot, garlic and parsley. Mix together and fry gently together for 10 minutes, or until soft.

3 Add the diluted tomato paste and simmer for 15 minutes. Add the fish. Mix again and cook until a thick sauce has formed and the fish has broken up. Season to taste, then take off the heat and set aside to cool completely.

4 To make the pasta, pile the flour and semolina on to the work surface and make a hollow in the middle with your fist. Break the eggs into a bowl and whisk together briefly. Pour into the hollow in the flour.

5 Using your fingers, mix the eggs roughly into the flour, then use both your hands to knead everything together thoroughly until you have a smooth, pliable ball of dough. Wrap the dough in clear film or plastic wrap and leave to rest for 20 minutes.

6 Roll the dough out as thinly as possible using a pasta machine or a rolling pin. Cut the dough into two even sheets.

7 Lay out one sheet of dough on the table and dot teaspoonfuls of the filling along the sheet in evenly spaced rows.

8 Lay the second sheet of dough on top and press around each covered mound of filling with the sides of your hands to press out all the air. Cut around each mound with a ravioli cutter or pastry or cookie cutter. They can be square or round, or even triangular. Leave them to dry until required.

9 Bring a large pan of salted water to a gentle boil. Drop in the ravioli and cook, in batches, for 3–4 minutes, or until they are floating on top of the water. Drain and transfer to a warmed serving dish. Serve immediately, with the melted butter spooned over and sprinkled with the chopped herbs.

TORTELLINI IN BRODO

TORTELLINI IN BROTH

This traditional dish is served on Christmas Eve, often after midnight Mass in many households of northern Italy. It is normal practice in Italy to ask people whether they prefer their tortellini with more or less brodo and to serve it accordingly.

1 To make the brodo, put the bird in a large pan with the vegetables, parsley, cold water and a little salt. Bring to the boil slowly and leave to simmer gently for about 2 hours. Leave to cool in the pan.

2 Remove the bird and reserve for another meal (see Cook's Tip). Strain the liquid through a fine sieve or strainer. Leave to stand, then remove any fat that forms on the surface and strain again. You will need 3 litres/5 pints/12½ cups.

3 To make the filling, melt the butter in a frying pan, add the the pork and turkey, and fry for 10 minutes, until cooked through. Mince the meat three times using a hand mincer, or process once in a food processor, together with the mortadella and prosciutto. Stir in the 2 eggs, Parmesan cheese, nutmeg and seasoning. Mix together thoroughly and set aside.

4 Pile the flour and semolina on a work surface and make a hollow in the middle using your fist. Pour in the 7 beaten eggs. Using your fingers, mix the eggs roughly into the flour, then use both hands to knead everything together until you have a smooth, pliable ball of dough. Rest the dough under a clean cloth or wrap in clear film or plastic wrap for 20 minutes.

5 Roll out the pasta very thinly using a pasta machine or rolling pin. Lay the sheet of pasta carefully on to a very lightly floured surface. You must work quickly to prevent it drying out.

6 Cut the dough into circles using a 4cm/1½in pastry or cookie cutter. Put 1.5ml/¼ tsp of filling in the middle. Fold in half and hold between your middle and index finger. Wrap the two extremities around the tip of your index finger.

7 Push the filled pasta pocket off your finger and turn it half inside out so that it looks like a little belly button. Press the ends together.

8 Bring the brodo to a very gentle boil and add the tortellini. Simmer for 8 minutes, or until the tortellini are cooked and float, then remove from the heat. Ladle the soup into individual bowls and serve, sprinkled with Parmesan cheese.

SERVES 10

350g/12oz/3 cups plain/all-purpose flour
350g/12oz/2 cups fine semolina
7 eggs, beaten
freshly grated Parmesan cheese, to serve

FOR THE BRODO

1 large boiling fowl or capon
3 carrots, trimmed
3 onions, halved
2 celery sticks, halved
2 tomatoes, halved
2 cabbage leaves
25g/1oz parsley
4 litres/7 pints/17 cups cold water
sea salt

FOR THE FILLING

50g/2oz/¼ cup unsalted butter
100g/3¾oz pork loin, cubed
50g/2oz turkey breast, cubed
100g/3¾oz mortadella, in one piece
115g/4oz prosciutto crudo, in one piece (preferably prosciutto di Parma)
2 eggs, beaten
175g/6oz/2 cups freshly grated Parmesan cheese
large pinch of grated nutmeg
sea salt and ground black pepper

COOK'S TIP

Try slicing the cooked fowl and using it for sandwiches or making a tasty salad.

RAGÙ CLASSICO ALLA BOLOGNESE
CLASSIC RAGÙ BOLOGNESE

A combination of several different kinds of meat, chopped with a heavy knife, is fundamental to this version of a classic pasta sauce, which uses only a tiny amount of tomato paste rather than canned tomatoes to give it sweetness and colour. Long cooking time over a very low heat is essential and this is one sauce that improves after being left for a day and then reheating. Serve it with tagliatelle for a truly authentic ragù alla Bolognese.

SERVES 4

115g/4oz pork loin, boned
115g/4oz beef steak, boned (rib-eye preferably)
115g/4oz prosciutto crudo
115g/4oz/$^{1}/_{2}$ cup unsalted butter
1 carrot, finely chopped
1 celery stick, finely chopped
1 onion, finely chopped
50g/2oz pancetta or streaky/fatty bacon, finely chopped
25ml/1$^{1}/_{2}$ tbsp tomato paste, diluted in 175ml/6fl oz/$^{3}/_{4}$ cup hot water
up to 175ml/6fl oz/$^{3}/_{4}$ cup hot broth or water
115g/4oz chicken livers, trimmed and finely chopped
90ml/6 tbsp double/heavy or single/light cream
1 small truffle, cleaned and thinly sliced (optional)
sea salt and ground black pepper
300–350g/11–12oz tagliatelle
freshly grated Parmesan cheese, to serve

1 Chop the meats together using a heavy knife until they resemble coarse minced or ground meat.

2 Melt half the butter in a frying pan and fry the vegetables and pancetta or bacon for 5–6 minutes, stirring all the time. Add the meats and stir together to seal all over.

3 Add the diluted tomato paste and season with salt and pepper. Stir thoroughly, then cover and leave to simmer very slowly for 2 hours, stirring frequently, until tender. Add a little hot water or broth as necessary to keep it moist.

4 Add the chopped chicken livers to the pan and simmer for 5 minutes, then stir in the cream, and the truffle, if using.

5 Leave the ragù to stand until required. You can, of course, use it immediately, but it does improve with standing and reheating.

6 Cook the tagliatelle according to the packet instructions until al dente. Serve with the ragù, sprinkled with Parmesan cheese.

RAGÙ BIANCO CON GARGANELLI
WHITE RAGÙ WITH GARGANELLI

Any white meat will work for this recipe, so turkey, rabbit or veal can all be used instead of chicken. Lamb can also be used, but the result is a different dish. The 'white' in the recipe title actually refers to the fact that no tomato is used. Garganelli are a kind of hand-made egg pasta shape, similar to penne, which are dried until hard. They are a speciality from Bologna. Normal dried penne or maccheroni, or even fresh tagliatelle, will also work well with this sauce.

SERVES 4

75g/3oz/6 tbsp unsalted butter
1 onion, chopped
1 celery stick, chopped
400g/14oz boned chicken, cubed
juice and grated rind of 1/2 lemon, plus extra grated rind, to garnish
250ml/8fl oz/1 cup dry white wine
250ml/8fl oz/1 cup chicken stock, plus extra if needed
400g/14oz garganelli
10ml/2 tsp chopped parsley
175ml/6fl oz/3/4 cup double/heavy cream
sea salt and ground black pepper
freshly grated Parmesan cheese, to serve

1 Heat half the butter in a frying pan, add the onion and celery, and fry together gently for 5 minutes, or until soft.

2 Add the chicken and cook, stirring, to brown the meat gently all over. Add the lemon rind and juice. Stir together and add the white wine.

3 Boil hard for 1–2 minutes to evaporate the alcohol, then reduce the heat.

4 Add the chicken stock, season and simmer, stirring frequently and adding extra stock if necessary, for 1 hour, until the meat is tender.

5 Meanwhile, cook the pasta in salted boiling water according to the packet instructions.

6 Take the sauce off the heat and stir in the remaining butter, the parsley and cream. Stir in the garganelli and serve, sprinkled with Parmesan cheese and lemon rind.

LASAGNA ALLA FERRARESE
LASAGNA IN THE FERRARA STYLE

This traditional lasagna recipe from the city of Ferrara uses lots of ingredients and a specific way of making the basic ragù. It is saved for special occasions.

SERVES 6 TO 8

300g/11oz spinach, rinsed
200g/7oz/1¾ cups plain/all-purpose flour
200g/7oz/generous 1 cup fine semolina
4 eggs, beaten
5ml/1 tsp olive oil
freshly grated Parmesan cheese, to serve

FOR THE RAGÙ

130g/4½oz/9 tbsp unsalted butter
115g/4oz pancetta, cubed
1 large carrot, finely chopped
1 large onion, finely chopped
2 celery sticks, finely chopped
200g/7oz pork loin, roughly chopped
200g/7oz beef steak (preferably rib-eye), roughly chopped
200g/7oz prosciutto crudo, chopped
60ml/4 tbsp tomato paste, stirred into 250ml/8fl oz/1 cup beef stock
250ml/8fl oz/1 cup dry red wine
115g/4oz peas
115g/4oz chicken livers, trimmed
90ml/6 tbsp double/heavy cream
sea salt and ground black pepper

FOR THE WHITE SAUCE

115g/4oz/½ cup unsalted butter
115g/4oz/1 cup plain/all-purpose flour
1 litre/1¾ pints/4 cups milk, warmed
pinch of salt
pinch of grated nutmeg
150g/5oz/1½ cups freshly grated Parmesan cheese

1 To make the ragù, heat 115g/4oz/½ cup butter in a frying pan and fry the pancetta, carrot, onion and celery until the vegetables are softened. Add the pork, beef and prosciutto and cook until browned. Add the tomato paste and stock mixture and stir, then add the wine. Boil for 1 minute, to evaporate the alcohol, then add the peas, season and reduce the heat. Cover and simmer for 1 hour, then remove from the heat.

2 Meanwhile, make the pasta. Put the rinsed spinach in a pan with just the water that clings to the leaves, cover and cook for 2 minutes. Drain. Squeeze the spinach as dry as possible. Chop to a purée.

3 Pile the flour and semolina on to the work surface and blend them together with your fingers. Make a hollow in the middle and pour in the eggs. Add the spinach and work the flour, spinach and eggs to make a smooth, elastic dough. Wrap in clear film or plastic wrap and leave it to rest for 20 minutes.

4 Meanwhile, make the white sauce. Melt the butter in a pan until foaming, add the flour and mix to a roux. Add the milk and whisk. Add salt and nutmeg. Simmer, stirring frequently, until smooth. Remove from the heat, stir in half the Parmesan, then cover the surface with a little cold water to prevent a skin forming.

5 Take apple-sized balls of pasta dough and work them through a pasta machine from the widest setting to the narrowest. Alternatively, roll it out as thinly as possible. Cut it into 7.5 x 15cm/3 x 6in rectangles.

6 Cook the lasagna sheets, four at a time, in a pan of salted boiling water for 1 minute. Using a slotted spoon, transfer to a bowl of cold water with the olive oil, to keep them soft and stop them sticking together.

7 In a separate pan, fry the chicken livers in the rest of the butter until browned, then stir into the ragù. Heat to a simmer, stir in the cream, then remove from the heat. Preheat the oven to 180°C/350°F/Gas 4.

8 Cover the base of a large, shallow ovenproof dish with a little white sauce. Add a layer of lasagna sheets. Add a layer of ragù, followed by a little Parmesan. Repeat with the remaining ingredients, finishing with white sauce and Parmesan. Bake for 30–40 minutes. Rest for 5 minutes, sprinkle with Parmesan and serve.

BRANZINO LESSO ALLA ROMAGNOLA
ROMAGNOLA-STYLE POACHED SEA BASS

As with all fish dishes, the real key to success is the absolute freshness of the fish, so that it can be cooked, dressed and served as simply as possible. You an use this simple method for other whole fish, such as a bream, or even freshwater fish, such as trout. If you eat fish regularly, it is worth buying a fish kettle.

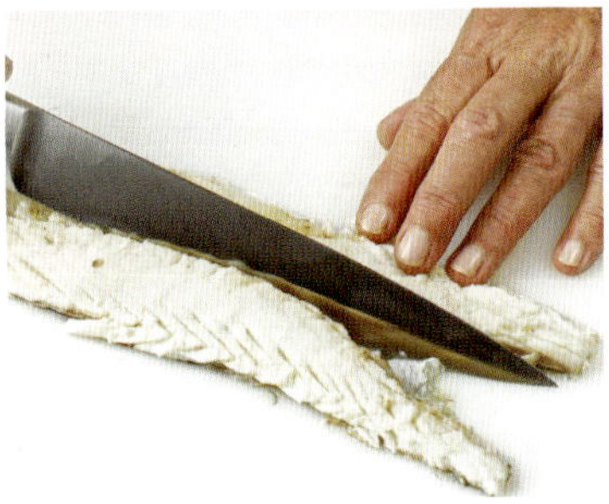

SERVES 4

1 sea bass, about 1.2kg/2½lb, scaled and cleaned
1 onion
1 celery stick
1 carrot
1 fresh parsley sprig
1 bay leaf
250ml/8fl oz/1 cup Trebbiano wine
30ml/2 tbsp white wine vinegar
sea salt and ground black pepper
olive oil, lemon juice, lemon wedges and chopped parsley, to serve

1 Wash the fish several times in cold running water and dry it inside and out. Season the fish on the inside with salt and ground black pepper.

2 Put the onion, celery, carrot, parsley sprig and bay leaf in a fish kettle with the wine and vinegar. Bring to the boil. Lay the seasoned fish in the fish kettle and return it to the boil, covered.

3 Remove from the heat and leave to stand for about 15 minutes, or until the fish is cooked through: the fish is perfectly cooked when the eyes become opaque.

4 Remove the fish from the fish kettle and fillet it carefully. Serve the fillets drizzled with olive oil and lemon juice, garnished with chopped parsley and with lemon wedges on the side.

SERVES 4

4 monkfish fillets, about 200g/7oz each
juice of 1 lemon
about 12 sage leaves, roughly chopped
75ml/5 tbsp sunflower oil
8 slices prosciutto crudo (preferably prosciutto di Parma)
sea salt and ground black pepper
lemon wedges, to serve

CODA DI ROSPO VESTITA AL PROSCIUTTO DI PARMA
MONKFISH WRAPPED IN PARMA HAM

This is a recipe from the coast of Emilia-Romagna, which combines the sweet meatiness of locally caught monkfish with the salty-yet-sweet delight of Parma ham, or prosciutto di Parma. This unmistakable cured ham, which is used to envelop the fish, give it extra flavour and keep it perfectly moist, is one of the region's most famous products and it is exported throughout the world. If you like, you can use another type of prosciutto crudo instead.

1 Put the fish in a dish or on a plate, sprinkle over lemon juice and season. Cover with clear film or plastic wrap and place in the refrigerator for 1 hour. Preheat the oven to 180°C/350°F/Gas 4.

2 Put the chopped sage in an ovenproof dish that is large enough to take the fish in a single layer. Drizzle over half the oil.

3 Wrap each fillet of fish in two slices of prosciutto crudo, then lay the fillets in the ovenproof dish containing the sage and the oil. Drizzle the remaining oil over the wrapped fish.

4 Bake in the preheated oven for about 30 minutes, or until cooked through, then serve with lemon wedges.

PETTO DI POLLO ALLA MODENESE
CHICKEN BREAST IN THE MODENESE STYLE

This is a dish from Modena, which uses local produce in the form of mortadella and Parmesan, finished off with indulgent cream for good measure! You might like to add a little shaving of black or white truffles just before serving.

SERVES 6

6 skinless chicken breast fillets
60ml/4 tbsp plain/all-purpose flour
75g/3oz/6 tbsp unsalted butter
6 slices mortadella
65g/2½oz/¾ cup freshly grated Parmesan cheese, plus extra to serve
90ml/6 tbsp double/heavy cream
sea salt and ground black pepper
green beans, to serve

1 Trim the chicken breast fillets and lay them between sheets of clear film or plastic wrap. Bash them lightly with a rolling pin to a thickness of 2cm/¾in to form escalopes. Toss them lightly in the flour, then season with salt and pepper.

2 Melt the butter in a large frying pan, add the floured chicken and cook for 4–5 minutes on each side, until golden and cooked through. You will probably need to cook two at a time.

3 Lay a slice of mortadella over the top of each chicken breast (while still in the frying pan) and distribute the grated Parmesan cheese over the top of each.

4 Pour the cream around the chicken, cover the pan and cook for 5 minutes, or until the cheese has melted. Serve the chicken with the cream spooned over, topped with a little extra grated Parmesan, and accompanied by green beans.

COSTOLETTE D'AGNELLO ALLA BOLOGNESE
BOLOGNESE LAMB CUTLETS

In this recipe, lamb cutlets are first coated in breadcrumbs and fried until crisp, then topped with mozzarella and prosciutto before being given a few moments in the oven to melt the cheese to a satisfying ooze. You could use tiny cutlets for a party dish that can be eaten with the fingers – just reduce the cooking time.

SERVES 6

12 lamb cutlets/US rib chops
20g/¾oz/3 tbsp plain/all-purpose flour
2 eggs, beaten
75ml/5 tbsp dried white breadcrumbs (preferably panagratto, or make your own from stale bread)
90ml/6 tbsp olive oil
115g/4oz prosciutto crudo, sliced thinly (preferably prosciutto di Parma)
150g/5oz mozzarella cheese, cut into 12 slices
sea salt and ground black pepper
roasted vegetables, to serve

1 Preheat the oven to 220°C/425°F/Gas 7. Trim the cutlets carefully and flatten them as much as possible with a meat mallet.

2 Put the flour on a plate and lightly coat the cutlets, then dip them in the egg, and finally in the breadcrumbs.

3 Heat the oil in a frying pan until sizzling, then fry the lamb cutlets on each side until golden brown and crisp.

4 Remove from the pan, and drain well on kitchen paper. Season to taste.

5 Arrange the cutlets on a baking tray, lay a slice of prosciutto and a slice of mozzarella cheese on each cutlet and bake in the oven for 5 minutes, or until the cheese begins to run.

6 Serve the lamb immediately, with some roasted vegetables.

SERVES 4 TO 6

6 large fennel bulbs (or 8 small ones)
185g/6½oz/generous ¾ cup unsalted butter, melted
185g/6½oz/generous 2 cups freshly grated Parmesan cheese, plus extra to serve
sea salt and ground black pepper

FINOCCHI ALLA PARMIGIANA
FENNEL WITH PARMESAN

Sliced fennel is layered with Parmesan cheese and drenched in butter in this dish from Emilia-Romagna. It's a lovely way to serve a very underrated vegetable and is particularly delicious served with fish or chicken.

1 Boil the whole fennel bulbs in a pan of salted water for 30 minutes, or until tender. Drain and cut them lengthways into finger-thick slices.

2 Preheat the oven to 180°C/350°F/Gas 4. Brush some of the melted butter over the base of an ovenproof dish.

3 Arrange half the fennel in a layer in the dish and cover with half the melted butter and Parmesan, then a sprinkling of salt and ground black pepper. Repeat with the rest of the ingredients.

4 Bake for 20 minutes, or until golden, and serve, sprinkled with extra Parmesan.

TORTA DI ZUCCHETTI
COURGETTE TART

This lovely recipe comes from the Modena province in Emilia-Romagna. The pretty and versatile lattice-topped tart is cut into squares and can be served either warm or cold. It makes a perfect appetizer and it can form part of an antipasti selection, accompanied by other savoury tarts or antipasti dishes. It could also be served simply as a light lunch, with nothing but some crisp salad leaves on the side and a glass of refreshing white wine to wash it down.

SERVES 4

200g/7oz/1¾ cups plain/all-purpose flour, plus extra for dusting
115g/4oz/½ cup ricotta cheese
115g/4oz/½ cup unsalted butter, softened and cubed, plus extra for greasing
1 egg yolk, beaten
sea salt and ground black pepper

FOR THE FILLING

500g/1¼lb courgettes/zucchini
40g/1½oz/3 tbsp unsalted butter, softened
2 eggs, beaten
200g/7oz mozzarella cheese, cut into small dice
75g/3oz/1 cup freshly grated Parmesan cheese

1 Put the flour into a bowl and make a hollow in the middle with your fist. Add the ricotta cheese, butter and a pinch of salt.

2 Rub the mixture together with your fingertips to make a soft ball of dough, adding a little water, if necessary. Cover the dough and chill for 30 minutes, or until required.

3 To make the filling, cut the courgettes into 1cm/½in discs. Put them in a pan of lightly salted water, bring to the boil and simmer for 5 minutes, until just soft but not disintegrating.

4 Drain the courgettes in a colander and return them to the same pan, but do not put it back on the heat. Add the butter to the pan and toss the courgettes in the butter until shiny, off the heat; the warmth from the pan and vegetables should be warm enough to melt the butter.

5 Preheat the oven to 180°C/350°F/Gas 4. Grease and flour a 24cm/9½in flan tin or pan.

6 Gently mix the courgettes with the beaten eggs, mozzarella and Parmesan cheese, and season with salt and ground black pepper.

7 Roll out the pastry on a floured surface to a thickness of about 3mm/⅛in and use to line the tin, reserving about one-quarter of the pastry for the topping. Pour the filling into the flan tin, spreading it out evenly with a fork.

8 Roll out the remaining pastry to a thickness of about 3mm/⅛in thick, then cut into 1cm/½in wide strips, long enough to cover the full length of the tin. Arrange the strips in a lattice on top of the filling and brush with the beaten egg yolk.

9 Put the tart into the preheated oven and bake for 40–45 minutes, or until set and golden brown. Remove from the oven and allow to cool to warm before cutting it into squares, or serve it cold.

NORTH-EAST ITALY

A MOUNTAINOUS REGION

The far north-eastern corner of Italy is known as Italia Nord-Orientale, a sub-region made up of Veneto, Friuli-Venezia Giulia and Trentino-Alto Adige, and is distinct from the rest of Italy. For the most part, locals speak their own languages, using Italian only with Italians from more southerly regions. In agriculture, cuisine and climate they are closer to Austria, Germany and Slovenia than to southern Italy, with a landscape of Alpine peaks and lakes.

A COOLER CLIMATE

The soaring mountain peaks that dominate most of north-eastern Italy mean cool summer temperatures and bitterly cold, often snowy winters. Only in the flat plains of the southern Veneto and along the Adriatic coast does the summer temperature and humidity rise. During the winter the cold air flows down the slopes of the Alps, the Dolomites and the Apennines and the mist rises up from the waterways of the plains. There is heavy snowfall both in the high mountains and on the lower hills, the air is often damp, the sun is rarely seen, and temperatures can barely rise above freezing for weeks on end.

This climatic pattern means that the crops grown here are very different from those usually associated with Italian food. This is not the area for tomatoes, bell peppers, aubergines/eggplants, melons, peaches and many of the other soft fruits and delicate vegetables one associates with an Italian market. Here, sturdy crops, such as cabbage, turnips, potatoes, rice, beans and maize reign supreme, and form the basis of the local cuisine.

BELOW *Veneto, Trentino-Alto Adige and Friuli-Venezia Giulia compose the far north-eastern corner of Italy. It is a largely mountainous region, with flatter plains towards the Adriatic coast.*

TOURISM AND AGRICULTURE IN THE VENETO

From the grandeur of Venice to the impressive mountains of the Dolomites, there are many sights to explore and the Veneto welcomes over 60 million tourists every year. The region is bound to the west by Lake Garda and to the north by the Dolomites. To the south-east, the region peters out in low-lying plains, river deltas and lagoons, which fringe the warm waters of the Adriatic.

The rich soil and damp climate are ideal for food production. Fields of maize and vegetables abound, as well as pasture for cattle, orchards and vineyards that grow the grapes for the delightful Prosecco wine. On the flat plains the weather can be humid in summer and cold in winter, with damp, foggy days that have become associated with the famous canals of Venice.

MOUNTAINS AND PLAINS IN FRIULI-VENEZIA GIULIA

To the far north-east of the country, the region of Friuli-Venezia Giulia borders the Veneto, Slovenia and Austria. The regional capital is Trieste, which lies in the far southern corner of the region on the Adriatic coast. Behind the Gulf of Trieste, erosion of the rocky mountains by wind and rain has created fascinating gorges, caves and underground rivers.

In northern Friuli-Venezia Giulia, the mountains rise towards the higher Alps, with precipitous passes leading into Austria and Slovenia. These high passes formed a major trading route from

THE BORA

The strong wind known as the Bora blows in violent gusts along the coastal areas of Friuli-Venezia Giulia, especially in the province of Trieste. Buildings in some towns and villages in these parts have stones permanently placed on their roofs to prevent roof tiles from being blown off. Chains and ropes are stretched along the sidewalks in downtown Trieste to help people to walk safely when the wind tries to lift them off their feet.

northern Europe to the Adriatic for hundreds of years. The region's economy is largely based on agriculture in the lower plains, with the main crops being maize, sugar beet, wheat and soy beans, as well as grapes for some wonderful, world-renowned wines. There are also many medium- and small-sized industries, making chemicals, textiles, paper and furniture.

REMOTE TRENTINO-ALTO ADIGE

This is a mountainous region, rich in rivers, streams and lakes, and divided neatly in two by the valley of the River Adige. To the west lie the remote glaciers of the Adamello-Presanella-Care Alto and Brenta mountain ranges. To the east the ranges of Lagorai, Latemar, the Dolomites of Fassa and the Pale di San Martino rise majestically. The biggest lake is the famous Lake Garda, just one of the 297 lakes in Trentino, most of which are hidden in the mountains at over 1,500m/5,000ft above sea level.

Extensive dark coniferous forests cover the slopes of the mountains, and three natural parks help to preserve the typical animals and vegetation of the Alpine environment, including the now rare wild bear. The pleasantly warm and green valleys nestling between the mountain peaks are ideal for growing orchard fruit and grapes for some world-class wines, such as a splendid Cabernet Sauvignon. The main industry here is tourism, with excellent winter ski resorts transforming themselves into centres for hiking in the beautiful countryside in the summer.

ABOVE *Horses roam on a grassy plateau in the province of Bolzano, overlooked by the beautiful Italian Dolomites.*

FAR LEFT *The beautiful Lake Garda is a world-famous tourist destination.*

A GLORIOUS HISTORY

The north-east of Italy contains many of the country's most precious treasures. It is a sumptuous area full of world-renowned natural beauty and man-made wonders, from the soaring peaks of the Dolomites and the lush flatlands of the southern Veneto to historic Verona and majestic Venice, the ultimate city of canals, gondolas and romance. Austrian-style buildings dot the mountainous northern landscape, contrasting with the more typical Roman ruins, which remind us of the centuries-long tug of war over control of these rich regions.

AN ANCIENT CULTURE

North-eastern Italy, from the Adriatic Sea to the eastern Alps, is situated in a strategic position at the main crossroads between the Mediterranean and northern Europe. It is known to have been inhabited before the first Bronze Age people settled there around 2000BCE. Later, the peaceful Veneto people began to cultivate the land. They lived beside the rivers in wooden dwellings similar to the present-day casoni of the Veneto lagoon, and were dedicated to farming, fishing, bronze-work and the breeding of horses.

THE ROMAN EMPIRE

Once Roman influence spread to north-eastern Italy, there followed a prosperous period of 300 years that favoured the arts and architecture, peaceful agriculture and trade. Unfortunately, however, after the fall of the Roman Empire in AD476, the region was invaded and plundered by barbarian hordes and much was lost. Ever resourceful, though, the people of the destroyed cities took refuge in the coastal lagoons and established new towns such as Venice, Chioggia, Caorle and Grado.

BELOW *Boats line the canals of the world-famous city of Venice.*

ABOVE LEFT *Austrian-style architecture is visible in the mountainous areas of northern Trentino-Alto Adige, serving as a reminder of the proximity and influence of Austria.*

ABOVE *The Lamberti Tower is just one of many graceful buildings in Verona, the construction of which was begun in 1172.*

THE RISE OF VENICE

Venice began its historical adventure on the seas, regularly having to defend itself against attacks from Franks, Slavs, Hungarians and Normans. Trade flourished between Constantinople (now Istanbul), Egypt, the Holy Land and northern Europe and ensured the city's prestige and riches. From 1500 to 1800, Venice was at the height of grandeur, though it was often attacked by other European states, jealous of its power and prosperity. Furthermore, there was an ongoing war against the Ottoman Empire, with whom the Venetians fought and traded at the same time.

The arts enjoyed a Golden Age during these years, and painting, architecture, literature and music all thrived. However, the city was in an inexorable and slow decline, which was largely concealed until the arrival of Napoleon, who put an end to the Venetian Republic, plundering it, then handing it over to Austria. For 60 years the Veneto remained under Austrian rule, but not without some epic battles, during which the Venetians fought valiantly to defend their beautiful city.

DECLINE AND REVIVAL

After 1866 the Veneto region became part of the Kingdom of Italy, but an economic crisis, followed by two World Wars, caused a serious depression in this mainly agricultural region. This was also the cause of the large-scale emigration, when so many Venetian people sought a better life in Argentina, Brazil, the USA, northern Europe, Canada, Australia and other countries of the world, where their hard-working ethic always stood them in good stead.

It was only in the 1960s that the Veneto really started to come alive again. Thanks to new commercial opportunities and the industriousness of its people, mainly in the sectors of machinery, wood, furniture, footwear, clothing, agriculture and wines, the Veneto has returned to being a commercially successful bridge between the Mediterranean and the rest of Europe.

VENICE'S NEIGHBOURING REGIONS

The adjoining region to the east, Friuli-Venezia Giulia, suffered most during the centuries of Venetian domination. The dangers of living in the Friulian plain, with great barbarian invasions passing through after the collapse of the Roman Empire, drove many people to seek shelter on the islands in the lagoons or in fortified hilltop villages, causing a general depopulation of the more fertile parts of the region and consequent impoverishment. For centuries, warring armies marched across the countryside and breeding animals were used to feed the soldiers. Venetian boat-builders also chopped down most of the trees that covered the Friulian plain to make bigger, better ships. Even after the Second World War, the region was unstable: much of the area was claimed by what was then Yugoslavia, and Friuli-Venezia Giulia was not incorporated as part of Italy until 1963. Many of its towns still bear the signs of both Austrian and Slovenian influence in lifestyle, language, folklore and cuisine.

To the north of Venice and the Veneto, Trentino-Alto Adige was more influenced by Austria and the Habsburg Empire, just on the other side of the mountains. This area has been conquered so many times that it feels as though it is part of both Italy and Austria at the same time; both languages are spoken, as well as local dialects. Today, particularly in the northern part of the region, Alto Adige (or Südtirol), there is still a northern European flavour, with street signs in German and Italian, Austrian architecture, and Austrian or German dishes on the menu in the restaurants.

A HEARTY CUISINE

The climate, landscape and history of the north-eastern corner of Italy have all contributed to create dishes that are very different to those of the Mediterranean south. Staples of the Italian menu, such as pasta, pizza, tomatoes and mozzarella, are very hard to find. Pasta is largely replaced by rice and polenta, and a great deal of meat is eaten, especially pork, game and poultry. The food tends to be creamy and rich, providing perfect warming sustenance for the population during the cold winters.

THE INFLUENCE OF NORTHERN EUROPE

German, Austrian, Slovenian and Hungarian influences are very evident in these regions, and ingredients such as paprika, horseradish, cumin and cinnamon are common. In the Veneto, Venice's tradition of trading with other nations around the world gives a cosmopolitan feel to the cuisine. One really notable difference between this area of Italy and regions further south is in the kind of bread baked for daily consumption. Here, bread tends to be dark and chewy, often made with rye, giving it a very Germanic flavour and texture. It looks and tastes extremely different from the famous light Italian breads, such as focaccia, or the full-flavoured crusty loaves that hail from Puglia and Tuscany.

THE RURAL FOOD OF THE VENETO

The low plains of the Po, Adige and Piave rivers supply livestock, rice for risotto and corn for polenta. Higher up, in the hills that rise towards the Alps around Lake Garda, game and wild mushrooms abound. These slopes have the perfect climate for curing prosciutto, salami and cheeses, and growers produce some splendid wine such as Bardolino, Valpolicella, Soave and Prosecco. The two best-known dishes of the Veneto region are risi e bisi, a creamy risotto with peas, Parmesan and pancetta; and pasta e fagioli, a very thick bean, pasta and vegetable soup.

Polenta, beans and rice form the solid basis of the local diet throughout the Veneto, rather than pasta. Inland, the main protein is meat, including beef, pork and game, which is often made into goulash, following the traditions of the Austro-Hungarian Empire. In the inland valleys, some of Italy's finest sharp cheeses are produced, such as Asiago and the lesser-known Monte Veronese.

Fish is also popular inland, far away from the coast, where there are traditional dishes using freshwater fish such as trout and eel, and also baccalà (salted white fish). Perhaps the most famous sweet cake of the Veneto region is the tall, star-shaped pandoro, which comes from the city of Verona, and makes a light alternative to the richer panettone from Lombardia.

BELOW *The marshy flatlands of the Po Delta are an excellent place to catch eels, as well as being an area of outstanding natural beauty.*

BELOW RIGHT *Grapes for some of Italy's finest wines are grown in north-eastern Italy.*

VENICE'S TRADING LEGACY

The traditional simple country cuisine of the Veneto is a far cry from the rich and varied dishes found in Venice, which has for centuries been able to use ingredients shipped here from many far-flung corners of the world. Trade with the Arabs led to the introduction of rice, which rapidly became a dominant element in the regional diet in the form of creamy risotto. Venetian traders also brought baccalà and stockfish from the chilly north to add to the vast range of food available in this cosmopolitan city.

ABOVE *White asparagus, a delicacy of Bassano, is displayed at markets throughout the Veneto.*

Fresh produce from the sea The region's proximity to the Adriatic means that fresh fish and shellfish are an important part of the Veneto diet, and all the treasures of the sea are available, from crabs such as moleche and spider crab to sardines and squid. The Venetian speciality, sarde in saor, is a sweet-and-sour dish of cooked, lightly pickled sardines. Another favourite is risotto al nero, a dramatic dish of black squid and soft risotto rice. Eels are extremely popular and abundant in the marshy areas of the Po Delta.

Local specialities Treviso is reputedly the place where the famous Italian dessert called tiramisù was first invented, but the town and province are also very well known for the prized radicchio Trevisano. This variety of red-leaved chicory has long, elegant leaves, and is used in many dishes, both sweet and savoury, even to flavour grappa. The region has been producing this sought-after vegetable for over a thousand years. Asparagus is also popular in its short season, particularly the white asparagus of Bassano in the Veneto.

FRIULI-VENEZIA GIULIA: GERMANIC FOOD

With Slovenia on its eastern border and Austria to the north, it is not surprising to see the influences of these countries in Friuli-Venezia Giulia. As a direct result of its long connection with the Austro-Hungarian Empire, the cuisine focuses on sauerkraut, potatoes, turnips, and savoury and sweet strudels, with an intriguing local boiled variation called strucolo. Friuli-Venezia Giulia boasts many other sweet cakes and desserts, including

LEFT *Alpine cows graze on the rugged mountain landscape of north-eastern Italy, the milk from which is used to make cheese.*

ABOVE *Dating back to the 12th-century, Toblino Castle is the most famous castle in Trentino-Alto Adige and is situated on the shores of Lake Toblino in the Sarca Valley, which also goes by the name 'Valley of Lakes'.*

gubana, a spicy sweet bread with grappa. Spices such as paprika, poppy seeds, cinnamon, cumin and horseradish are used daily, and rice or polenta feature instead of pasta. The local speciality, frico, is seasoned salty cheese, cut into pieces and fried in butter. This is sometimes served with polenta, but can also be eaten on its own.

Friuli-Venezia Giulia is well known for its barley fields, and the locals are fond of using this grain to make orzotto, which is similar to risotto. The chilly winter weather means that warming soups such as la jota are especially welcome, based on beans, greens and pork ribs, with some tasty pork fat. Another significant characteristic of the region is that tomatoes are rarely used, which radically changes the colour, texture and taste of the local food compared to that found in southern Italy.

Well-flavoured meat dishes The custom of lightly smoking cold cuts of meat, especially prosciutto, is common here but not in other parts of Italy.

SPECIALITIES FROM TRIESTE

Cooking in Trieste reflects the Venetian style, combined with strong Austrian and Slavic influences. The main specialities are the local brodetto, a fish soup, and mesta, a kind of polenta cooked in water and milk, also eaten with fish. Trieste has a tradition of delightful literary cafes; the last of these to survive is the famous San Marco cafe in Via Battisti.

There is an abundance of strong-flavoured wild game in the inland areas and some very good beef from the cattle raised on the plains bordering the Adriatic. Many delicious local sausages are made, as well as excellent cured ham from San Daniele, in the province of Udine, which rivals the best Parma ham in flavour and quality. Another favourite is the rich and tasty smoked ham called speck that is made both here and in neighbouring Trentino-Alto Adige.

Flowery white wines Friuli-Venezia Giulia produces some of the best Italian white wines, many of which are light and refreshing, and are made with Germanic grape varieties such as Riesling and Müller-Thurgau. One unusual speciality is Picolit, an extraordinary sweet wine developed in the 1700s as a substitute for the sought-after Hungarian wine, Tokay, which was prevented by war from reaching Europe's courts.

TRENTINO-ALTO ADIGE: WARMING FOOD

The landlocked region of Trentino-Alto Adige includes the lofty Dolomite Mountains in the north and east, and pleasantly undulating hills awash with vineyards and orchards in the south. Freshwater fish, pork, game, dairy produce, vegetables and fruit are basic elements of the simple local cuisine. Germanic and Hungarian influences are evident in the tasty dumplings, thick soups flavoured with caraway seeds, smoked ham, light pastry strudels of various kinds and the liberal use of sauerkraut. German-type sausages

LEFT *A variety of local wild mushrooms are sold at markets throughout north-eastern Italy.*

WILD PRODUCE FROM THE HILLS

The lively street market in Trento spills over with wonderful local produce, especially in the summer and autumn. Many of the 250 varieties of wild mushrooms found in the mountains and hills can be bought here in season. So important is the local passion for mushrooms that some policemen are trained to identify the different varieties, allowing uncertain foragers to get their precious findings checked by an expert.

are very popular, especially when served with beer and sauerkraut, or sweet fruity chutney. Big, hearty soups are made with barley and speck, and there is a tasty local version of a Swiss rösti, a crisp pancake of grated potatoes and chopped bacon. The emphasis of the cuisine is always on hearty, strong-tasting food made to sustain the population through the cold weather.

Polenta – the staple food The most fundamental element of the cuisine of Trentino is polenta, which consists of ground maize meal, boiled in salted water and stirred constantly until it has thickened into a kind of porridge/oatmeal. There are many different ways to enjoy polenta: it is often served warm and soft with local cheeses melting on top, or as an accompaniment to a meal such as game stew, baccalà (salted cod) or beans. It is traditionally cooked over an open fire, so that the burning wood adds a slightly smoky taste to the polenta bubbling in the pot. Basic polenta can take on another flavour altogether with the addition of some dark Saracen corn, and becomes polenta nera, black polenta.

Delicious dumplings Large dumplings called canederli are made out of stale bread, eggs, flour and milk, with the addition of chopped bacon, salami, liver and cabbage or spinach. These dumplings are simply boiled in a clear broth or water. A sweet version is made with the same basic bread and egg mixture, but with a prune in the middle, and the whole thing is dipped in breadcrumbs. Other dumpling-type dishes include small gnocchi flavoured with spinach, known as spinatspätzle, which are often served as an accompaniment to goulash.

Sweet treats Cakes and pastries play a key role in this cold climate. Favourites include strudel, which are often filled with apples and spiced with cinnamon, or zelten, which are similar pastries filled with walnuts and dried fruits. The wild berries that grow in the woods and meadows of the region are often used in the local desserts, as well as being turned into delicious liqueurs.

BELOW *Corn cobs dry out against a wall in Friuli-Venezia Giulia.*

FESTIVALS AND CELEBRATIONS

Across the north-east of Italy, a multitude of festivals take place each year that feature local food, wines or beers, or mark religious days in traditional fashion. These occur everywhere from small mountain villages and countryside towns to the large cities of Venice, Verona, Vicenza, Treviso and Padova. The origins of some of these traditions are buried in the distant past, but the one thing that they have in common is that they all provide an opportunity to celebrate with plenty of good food and wine.

THE CARNIVAL OF VENICE

Carnival time in Venice is a world-famous annual celebration that takes place every February and is still, after more than 900 years, one of the highlights of the Venetian calendar. At this time of year, with the early spring sunlight sparkling on the water after the damp and foggy winter, revellers enjoy sweet, sustaining snacks. This is when a range of deep-fried pastries and desserts really come into their own. They were traditionally served as street snacks for the carnival revellers and include deep-fried squares of custard, crema fritta, and many other delicious local specialities.

The tradition of wearing masks at carnival time in the city of Venice has ancient origins and has grown in popularity. At one time, masks were worn by the inhabitants of the city for many months of the year. They were sometimes used to conceal the faces of people picking pockets, gambling or begging on street corners, as well as those intent on more innocent escapades such as creeping into a lover's house. These masks are now sold in their millions as popular tourist souvenirs, and are still worn today in the narrow streets of Venice during carnival time.

BELOW *Traditional dancing takes place in San Daniele, in Friuli-Venezia Giulia, to celebrate the annual festival of the region's famous local ham.*

VINITALY

This is the annual international wine show in Verona, which takes place in April. Here, many Italian and international exhibitors gather to promote their best production in an overview of vine-growing and winemaking traditions.

THE VOGALONGA (HISTORICAL REGATTA)

This boat race, begun in the 1970s by a group of rowing enthusiasts, takes place each May, traditionally on Ascension Day, on the canals and lagoon of Venice, and is a key event on the Venetian calendar. It is a fun and non-competitive event in which any type of rowing boat is welcome and every entrant gets a prize.

SAN DANIELE PROSCIUTTO FESTIVAL

Each June, the town of San Daniele del Friuli in the region of Friuli-Venezia Giulia celebrates its famous prosciutto crudo. For 3 days, the streets are full of stalls where locals and visitors can sample the delights of the wonderful cured ham in a variety of local speciality dishes. There is a whole host of festivities, including traditional singing and dancing in the streets.

SAN VALENTINO FESTIVAL

The small village of San Valentino, near Trento, in Trentino-Alto Adige hosts a cheese-rolling contest each June to celebrate the local produce of this Alpine region. There is also a sausage-eating and beer-drinking competition, reflecting the Austrian influences of this area.

FESTA DEL REDENTORE

One of the most important summer festivals in Venice is the Festa del Redentore (Feast of the Redeemer), based on thanksgiving for the end of the bubonic plague in 1575, which killed tens of thousands of Venetian citizens. A week of celebrations leads up to the third Sunday in July, when there is a huge street party around the Franciscan church of the Redentore on the island of Giudecca, with church services, a regatta, bands, fireworks and feasting in the streets.

ABOVE *The beautiful masks of Venice are now a world-famous symbol of the February carnival celebrations.*

RISOTTO FESTIVAL

Just south of Verona, the village of Isola della Scala hosts an unmissable festival celebrating Veronese rice from mid-September to mid-October. During the festival, a multitude of delicious rice dishes are cooked and served, and there are tours of rice fields, events for children, concerts and gastronomic competitions.

MERANO INTERNATIONAL WINE FESTIVAL

Taking place every November in the province of Bolzano, this is the second-most important food and wine festival after Vinitaly. More than 400 winemakers and over 120 food producers gather together to show the very best of local produce.

FAMILY CELEBRATIONS

Although not as strictly Catholic as the south of Italy, baptisms, first communions and weddings are important celebrations for many in the north-eastern region. Vast sums are spent on lavish weddings with hundreds of guests, and the meal that is served is of the utmost importance. Each guest will receive a small gift with some sugared almonds attached, known as bomboniera.

CHRISTMAS MARKETS

Throughout this northern region, in the best Austrian tradition, delightful Christmas markets spring up in towns from early November, ending on Twelfth Night, 6 January. One of the most famous in the region is the market in Trento, which, like most of the others, features stalls selling all the local specialities, including delicious sweet pastries and cakes, such as trecchia mochèna, a braided pastry cake, as well as German-inspired stollen and lebkuchen.

VENETO

The Veneto was part of the powerful Venetian Republic for more than 1,000 years, between the 7th and 18th centuries, something that has given this region a very particular and rich identity. It is bordered to the east by Friuli-Venezia Giulia, to the south by Emilia-Romagna, to the west by Lombardy, to the north by Trentino-Alto Adige, and its most northern tip borders with Austria. The famous vineyards are fed by the mighty Adige River, which passes through the city of Verona as it winds its way south to empty itself into the Venetian lagoon: the enclosed bay of the Adriatic, featuring ponds, marshland and islands, and the city of Venice itself.

Suffice it to say that Venice is one of the most special places in the world. Made up of a web of more than 170 canals and waterways that link together the 120 little islands that comprise the city, La Serenissima is criss-crossed by more than 400 bridges and divided by the long, S-shaped Grand Canal with its glorious palaces and churches on either side.

At the heart of the city is the Piazza San Marco. If you get lost wandering around the back streets of Venice, which is probably inevitable, you can always find your way back to this square and re-orientate and refresh yourself at one of the many cafés, including the opulent Café Florian. Founded in 1724, this is supposed to be the oldest café in the world and, interestingly, was the only establishment of its time in the city that admitted women, which could potentially explain why it was so popular with the legendary Casanova.

The second-most important city of the region is Verona, where every summer since 1913 the greatest opera singers of the word have performed in its amphitheatre. This incredibly romantic place is the home of the deliciously light pandoro, first cousin to the panettone of Milan, both of which are served at Christmas time. This top hat-sized sweet bread, egg-yolk yellow and deliciously scented with vanilla, is star-shaped, fluffy and airy in texture, and completely plain, without the dried and candied fruit of panettone or similar cakes from other regions.

The stunningly varied, wide landscape of the Veneto is reflected in the region's diverse cuisine, and is also influenced in large part by the region's history and the lasting legacy of the most powerful maritime republic.

The food is a melting pot of country-style, rustic dishes blended with the many treasures of the east that poured into the port of Venice over the centuries: spices, coffee, stock fish, and many other riches.

The cuisine changes from one province to another, but all the traditional food is based on some common ingredients: rice: for risotto; very special vegetables, such as the beans of Lamon from the province of Belluno, the asparagus of Bassano del Grappa, and the bitter red radicchio of Treviso; and the ubiquitous polenta, mostly enjoyed with meat, fish or cheese.

Risotto holds a very special place in the hearts of all Venetians, grown for centuries in the rice fields in the flat lands, side by side with the maize used for polenta. Traditionally, the risotto is a bit wetter in texture compared to that made in the other great rice-growing areas of the north in Piedmont and Lombardy, partly due to the fact that the rice varieties grown here are different to those of the west, most notably the type called vialone nano. The most iconic risotto of the city of Venice itself is the soupy, sweet and delicious risi e bisi – rice and peas – but other local recipes include risotto made with radicchio, asparagus, seafood, beans and chicken, to name but a handful.

A complex and accepting place, Venice is home to many – fishermen and sailors, peasant and merchants, craftsmen, industry and tourism, and, of course: winemakers. This is the region that gives us Prosecco, Soave, Amarone di Valpolicella, Bardolino, Gambellara and many, many more.

A note about Grappa

Grappa is hugely popular in the Veneto. It's a very strong, clear spirit made from the pomace: grape skins, seeds and stalks that are left over after the winemaking process. These are put through a distillation process, which extracts all the remaining flavours before the waste is discarded. It can either be made from a mixture of pomaces from different wine-making sources, or from one grape variety, and can be aged in oak casks to turn it into a pale-yellow or tawny-coloured grappa known as Grappa Riserva. It is an extraordinarily effective digestif, served at the end of a meal, or added to a cup of espresso for a warming caffè corretto.

FRUTTI DI MARE GRATINATI
GRILLED MIXED SEAFOOD

A lovely, simple antipasto, this grilled dish makes the most of the delicious selection of seafood available from the fish markets of Venice, but it can be made anywhere. As with any seafood dish, it is the freshness of the raw material that makes all the difference. It is far better to reduce the number of shellfish varieties to one or two and eat them absolutely fresh, than to have lots of different types that may not be at their very best.

SERVES 4

16 mussels
8 oysters
4 scallops
20 large Venus clams
4 razor shells
60ml/4 tbsp fresh breadcrumbs
60ml/4 tbsp freshly grated Parmesan cheese
3 garlic cloves, finely chopped
45ml/3 tbsp chopped fresh parsley
75ml/5 tbsp olive oil
sea salt and ground black pepper

1 Scrub the mussels with a stiff brush and rinse under cold running water. Discard any that remain open after being sharply tapped. Scrape off any barnacles and remove the 'beards' with a small knife. Rinse well. Scrub the oysters, scallops and clams with a stiff brush to remove any sand. Gently scrub the razor shells.

2 Put the cleaned shellfish into a large pan – you do not need to add any water. Steam for 5–8 minutes over a medium heat, or until the shells open. Immediately, remove the pan from the heat and lift out the shellfish. Discard any that remain closed.

3 Preheat the grill or broiler to high. Remove one half of each shell and put all the shellfish in their half-shells into a wide, ovenproof dish or on a baking sheet.

4 Mix together the breadcrumbs, Parmesan cheese, garlic, parsley and seasoning. Cover the top of each shellfish with this mixture, then drizzle generously with the oil.

5 Put the dish or baking sheet under the grill for 5 minutes to brown, then serve immediately either on individual plates or a large serving platter.

ZUPPA DEI DOGI
DOGE'S SOUP

This warming, flavoursome dish is based on a very old recipe from the kitchens of the Doge's Palace in Venice. It is supposed to represent all the beauty and riches of the city, with the intense colours of precious stones reflected in the beetroot, carrot and courgette. The little golden rice balls represent Venice's great wealth, and especially that of the Doge's Palace, and are intended as a reminder of Venice in all her glory, with sunlight glinting off the water and the golden orbs of the churches.

SERVES 6

150g/5oz/⅔ cup long grain rice
50g/2oz fontina cheese, grated
1 egg, beaten
30ml/2 tbsp freshly grated Parmesan cheese
15ml/1 tbsp olive oil
1.5 litres/2½ pints/6¼ cups meat stock, strained
1 large beetroot/beet, boiled for 1 hour, peeled and cut into matchsticks
1 large carrot, boiled for 20 minutes and cut into matchsticks
1 large yellow potato, peeled, boiled for 20 minutes and cut into matchsticks
1 large dark green courgette/zucchini, boiled briefly, then cut into matchsticks
60–90ml/4–6 tbsp plain/all-purpose flour
vegetable oil, for deep-frying

1 Cook the rice in boiling water to cover for 10 minutes, or until still quite firm. Drain the rice and transfer to a bowl.

2 Add the fontina cheese to the rice and mix until well blended. Add the egg, Parmesan cheese and olive oil and mix thoroughly.

3 Shape into walnut-sized balls with dampened hands. Place the balls on a plate, cover with clear film or plastic wrap and chill until required.

4 Bring the meat stock to the boil in a pan and add the beetroot, carrot, potato and courgette matchsticks.

5 Simmer the vegetables for 5 minutes. Do not allow them to cook any longer or they will lose their shape.

6 Coat the chilled rice balls in flour. Heat the vegetable oil in a large, heavy pan until a cube of bread, dropped in the oil, browns in 45 seconds.

7 Deep-fry the rice balls, in batches, until they are crisp and golden. Lift out with a slotted spoon and drain on kitchen paper.

8 Put the rice balls into individual soup plates and ladle over the soup. Serve immediately or the rice balls will lose their crispness.

CANEDERLI
BREAD DUMPLINGS

In Trentino-Alto Adige these simple bread dumplings, floating in a meaty broth, are served as an antipasto, before a main course of meat with polenta. As with many recipes from this region, the cheapest of ingredients are turned into nourishing food. Brown bread is common in these parts, so it is likely that the breadcrumbs used would be wholemeal, although you can use any you have to hand. Many different versions of canederli exist, some with the addition of chopped bacon, or pork fat instead of butter.

1 Crumble or grate the bread finely. Transfer the crumbs to a mixing bowl and add the butter. Mix well.

2 Add the eggs, parsley, flour and nutmeg, and mix well. Season with salt. Stir in the warmed milk to make a fairly soft paste.

3 Leave to stand for 30 minutes to allow the bread to swell. With damp hands, shape the mixture into balls 5cm/2in in diameter.

4 Bring the stock to a gentle boil in a pan and add the balls. Simmer for 20 minutes, then serve sprinkled with extra parsley.

SERVES 4

350g/12oz dried bread
100g/3¾oz unsalted butter, softened
4 eggs, beaten
60ml/4 tbsp finely chopped fresh flat leaf parsley, plus extra to garnish
115g/4oz/1 cup plain/all-purpose or wholemeal/whole-wheat flour
1.5ml/¼ tsp freshly grated nutmeg
200ml/7fl oz/scant 1 cup full cream/whole milk, warmed
1.5 litres/2½ pints/6¼ cups rich meat stock
sea salt

SERVES 4

300g/11oz/1¾ cup dried beans, preferably lamon or borlotti, soaked overnight in cold water (alternatively, use 3 x 400g/14oz canned beans)
50ml/2fl oz/¼ cup olive oil or 50g/2oz pork fat
75g/3oz fatty pancetta
1 onion, chopped
1 carrot, chopped
1 celery stick, chopped
1 litre/1¾ pints/4 cups good meat stock
150g/5oz tiny pasta (rice-grain size)
sea salt and ground black pepper

PASTA E FAGIOLI
VENETIAN BEAN AND PASTA SOUP

Every region of Italy has a version of this old recipe containing the cheapest of ingredients: a handful of pasta, a few vegetables, a little fatty pork, beans and some good stock. It varies from one place to another, but is very much representative of the peasant style of cooking in the Veneto, which contrasts sharply with the elegant dishes of the aristocracy. Just as Tuscany favours the borlotto bean, the Veneto too has its favourite variety for this dish, the lamon bean, which may be hard to find outside of the region.

1 Drain the beans, put them into a large pan and cover with plenty of water. Boil rapidly for 5 minutes, then reduce the heat and simmer for 1 hour, or until tender. Drain.

2 Heat the olive oil or pork fat in a large pan and add the pancetta, onion, carrot and celery. Gently fry together over a medium heat for 5–10 minutes, until the vegetables are soft.

3 Add the drained beans to the pan and stir thoroughly. Add the stock and simmer slowly for 45–50 minutes, or until the beans are almost falling apart.

4 Add the pasta and cook for a further 10 minutes, or until the pasta is tender.

5 Season the soup to taste with salt and ground black pepper, and serve warm.

PANISSA
VENETIAN RICE AND BEAN SOUP

This much-loved and highly respected dish from the Veneto is one of those classic peasant dishes that have a real historical significance. It always strikes me how the inland countryside areas around the great cities of Venice and Verona reflect in their recipes a time of hardship and the need to nourish and warm many people, contrasting with the opulent and almost outrageous recipes designed to boast and impress graced the grandiose tables of the aristocracy. Yet, even for the former type the ingredients are specific, requiring care and detail to an otherwise simple dish. Note: the bean is absolutely key here!

SERVES 4

1 litre/1¾ pints/4 cups beef stock
300g/11oz fresh saluggia beans, podded (see Cook's Tip)
5cm/2in pork skin, hairs removed and well scraped and washed
75g/3oz lardo or pork fat, chopped
5–7.5cm/2–3in soft pork salame, skin removed, salame crumbled
1 large onion, thinly sliced
45ml/3 tbsp unsalted butter
45ml/3 tbsp olive oil
320g/11½oz/generous 1½ cups Vialone Nano rice
sea salt
cracked black peppercorns

1 Pour the beef stock into a large pan, then add 500ml/17fl oz/generous 2 cups of the water in which you boiled the dried borlotti beans the second time, along with the pre-cooked beans. If you are using fresh podded saluggia or borlotti beans, just add 500ml/17fl oz/generous 2 cups of water and the raw fresh beans. Add the pork skin.

2 Cover and simmer slowly for about 1 hour or until the beans are very soft.

3 In a separate pan, fry together the lardo or pork fat, the crumbled salame and the onion with the butter and oil.

4 When the onion is soft and transparent, add the rice and mix together with the other ingredients to coat and toast slightly, then add some of the water from the beans – enough to cover generously – and stir, allowing the rice to absorb the liquid.

5 Continue until the rice is cooked (not rice-pudding texture, but not chalky either), then add all the beans and sufficient water from the same pan to make a very thick soup or a very sloppy risotto.

6 Adjust the seasoning, finish with a little cracked black pepper, and serve.

COOK'S TIP

I appreciate these beans may be impossible to find outside of their very specific area of provenance – so I am going to suggest their nearest relative: fresh borlotti beans; or dried ones that have soaked overnight, boiled hard once, then rinsed and re-boiled slowly until just tender, then drained (reserve the water in which they are boiled the second time).

GNOCCHI CON LA FIORETTA
SOFT RICOTTA GNOCCHI

This traditional recipe in its original form comes from the city of Vicenza and calls for a very local cheese that is a close relative of ricotta. This is almost liquid in texture and is enjoyed in the Val Leogra as a drink. I have suggested a way to slacken ricotta to try to achieve a similar sloppy texture that can then be worked with flour and salt to create these delicate gnocchi.

SERVES 4

180g/6¼oz/generous 1½ cups 00 flour
400g/14oz Fioretta delle Valli Vicentine, or substitute with 400g/14oz soft ricotta cheese blended with enough skimmed milk to create a smooth, runny, drinkable texture
75g/3oz smoked pancetta
100g/3½oz/8 tbsp unsalted butter
12 fresh sage leaves
30g/1¼oz smoked Val Leogra ricotta, or substitute with 30g/1¼oz smoked hardened ricotta, or slightly less salted ricotta
50g/2oz/⅔ cup freshly grated Grana Padano
sea salt

1 Using a fork, blend the flour into the Fioretta delle Valli Vicentine or liquefied ricotta to make a smooth, thick batter. Chill in the refrigerator for 1 hour.

2 Cut the pancetta into small squares and fry these, tossing, in a hot non-stick pan until the fat runs and the pancetta becomes golden brown and crisp. Set aside and keep warm.

3 Bring a large pan of salted water to the boil, then turn down the heat to create a softly rolling boil.

4 Working in batches, use two large spoons to scoop the chilled ricotta mixture into egg-shaped gnocchi and drop these into the boiling water. Take care not to overcrowd the pan: cook just a few gnocchi at a time.

5 Scoop out the gnocchi with a slotted spoon when they bob up to the surface of the boiling water and keep hot in a separate warmed dish. Repeat until all of the gnocchi are cooked.

6 Meanwhile, in a very large frying pan that can hold all of the gnocchi at once (or use two smaller frying pans), melt the butter with the sage leaves until the butter is noisette (hazelnut) coloured.

7 Remove and reserve the sage, then tip the gnocchi into the hot butter, basting constantly.

8 When the gnocchi are coated in the butter, transfer to a serving dish. Sprinkle with the smoked ricotta, the reserved sage leaves, the grated Grana Padano and the reserved pancetta, then serve immediately.

LA POLENTA
BASIC POLENTA

Polenta is the basic staple starch eaten all over the north of Italy. Made from ground maize, it can be white or yellow, and comes in various different grades: fine, medium or coarse. The widely available quick-cook variety is frowned upon by purists who claim that only the real thing, which requires up to an hour of constant stirring, will have the correct flavour. Serve in a slab with some Gorgonzola on top, which melts over the hot polenta, or alongside a stew. It can also be served soft in a bowl with a stew, dressing, sauce or cheese on the top.

1 Put the water into a wide, heavy pan set over a high heat and bring back to the boil. Add a large pinch of salt.

2 Trickle the polenta flour into the boiling water in a fine rain with one hand, while whisking constantly with the other.

3 When all the polenta flour has been whisked into the water, reduce the heat to medium-low.

4 Stir with a long-handled wooden spoon until the polenta comes away from the sides of the pan. This will take 40–50 minutes.

5 Turn the polenta out on to a board and smooth it into a mound shape using spatulas. Leave it to rest for about 5 minutes.

6 Cut the polenta into six thick slabs. Evenly distribute the Gorgonzola over the top, if using. Serve immediately, while still hot.

SERVES 6

1.75 litres/3 pints/7½ cups boiling water
200–225g/7–8oz/scant 2 cups polenta flour
200g/7oz Gorgonzola dolce or piccante, sliced, for serving (optional)
sea salt

SERVES 4

300ml/½ pint/1¼ cups boiling water
300ml/½ pint/1¼ cups full-fat/whole milk
350g/12oz/3 cups medium-grade polenta flour
115g/4oz/½ cup unsalted butter
115g/4oz/1 cup grated Asiago cheese, or another cheese
150g/5oz/⅔ cup ricotta cheese
sea salt

COOK'S TIP

This polenta is much richer than the basic type shown opposite since it contains milk and copious amounts of butter and cheese – meaning it is best served as a dish in its own right rather than as an accompaniment.

POLENTA CONZATA
DRESSED POLENTA

Soft polenta is particularly tasty served this simple way. You can use any strong-tasting cheese to flavour the hot polenta, but in the Veneto they would use their local cheese, which is called Asiago. As polenta is relatively bland in taste, it can take on all kinds of different flavours. Make sure you keep the consistency quite soft, as it is served in shallow bowls and eaten with a spoon. You can use white or yellow polenta in this recipe – it is a matter of personal preference.

1 Put the water and milk into a large, heavy pan over high heat and bring to the boil. Add a good pinch of salt.

2 Trickle the polenta flour into the boiling liquid in a fine rain with one hand, while whisking constantly with the other.

3 When all the polenta flour has been whisked in, reduce the heat to medium-low.

4 Stir with a strong, long-handled wooden spoon until the polenta comes away from the sides of the pan, but is not stiff. This will take 40–50 minutes.

5 Melt the butter and stir it through the polenta. Divide the grated cheese and ricotta among four serving bowls, pour the buttered polenta on top of the cheese and serve immediately.

GNOCCHI DI POLENTA
POLENTA GNOCCHI

Here is a way of extending the use of any cold leftover polenta: by turning it, with the addition of a little egg and flour, into tasty boiled gnocchi that can be dressed in the style that is traditional in the Veneto – with smoked ricotta and sage butter or, as appears below, with shredded radicchio and Taleggio cheese. They are also sometimes served with game stews, specifically ones that are too highly spiced! These gnocchi really are very tasty stomach fillers, and can be made in any size or shape, although the guideline is about 3cm/1¼in. I love the fact that even in this simple recipe of what is fundamentally leftovers, the ingredients required are so specific in terms of their origin and variety.

SERVES 4

500–600g/1¼–⅓lb cooked, cold, set polenta (see page 204)
30ml/2 tbsp plain/all-purpose flour (or more if required)
1 large/US extra large egg
100ml/3½fl oz/scant ½ cup full-fat/whole milk
185g/6½oz Taleggio cheese
1 head of fresh radicchio – specifically the Variegato di Castelfranco if possible, but any radicchio will work in terms of the presentation and flavour
30–45ml/2–3 tbsp extra virgin olive oil (preferably from Lake Garda)
sea salt and ground black pepper

1 Blend the cold polenta with the flour and the egg to make a malleable texture, then shape the mixture into small (3cm/1¼in-long) gnocchi shapes and lay them out on a tray.

2 Put the milk and 130g/4½oz of the Taleggio in a heatproof bowl and place it over a pan of simmering water. Stir constantly until melted together. Cube the remaining cheese.

3 Wash and dry the radicchio, then shred it finely and set aside.

4 Bring a large pan of salted water to a gentle boil. Working in batches, drop in a few of the gnocchi at a time and cook them briefly until they bob up to the surface of the water.

5 Carefully remove the cooked gnocchi to a warmed bowl using a slotted spoon, then repeat the cooking process with further batches of gnocchi, until they are all cooked and in the warmed bowl.

6 Pour over the Taleggio sauce and gently mix everything together, taking care not to break up the delicate gnocchi.

7 Arrange the shredded radicchio on a platter and dress with the oil and a little salt and pepper.

8 Gently tip the dressed gnocchi over the radicchio salad, distribute the reserved Taleggio cubes over the top and serve immediately.

CROSTINI DI POLENTA CON FUNGHI
GRILLED POLENTA WITH MUSHROOMS

This is a quick and easy way to use up leftover polenta. It is a deliciously different appetizer that is filling and pretty to look at. You can vary the flavour by using fried onions instead of the mushrooms if you prefer, or make it really Venetian by adding some warm, braised radicchio leaves. Asiago is a local cheese of the Veneto and is prized on the cheese board as well as in cooking.

SERVES 4

1 quantity polenta, cut into 8 squares (see page 204)
45ml/3 tbsp olive oil
250g/9oz Asiago or fontina cheese, cubed
a little milk
400g/14oz/5½ cups mushrooms, sliced
2 garlic cloves, thinly sliced
45ml/3 tbsp finely chopped fresh flat leaf parsley, to garnish
sea salt and ground black pepper

1 Heat the grill or broiler and lightly oil the polenta squares. Put the cheese in a heatproof bowl and add milk to cover. Set it over a pan of simmering water and allow the cheese to melt and blend with the milk, stirring frequently.

2 Meanwhile, put the remaining oil in a frying pan over a medium heat and stir-fry the mushrooms and garlic for 10 minutes, until the mushrooms are cooked. Season.

3 When the cheese and milk have formed a smooth sauce, grill the polenta on both sides for a minute or two, until golden and crisp.

4 Arrange two squares of grilled polenta on each plate and cover with a spoonful of the melted cheese. Spoon the mushrooms evenly over the top, then sprinkle each portion with chopped flat leaf parsley and serve immediately.

COOK'S TIP

To make braised radicchio leaves to accompany the polenta, put shredded radicchio leaves and a pat of butter in a pan, then cook gently until soft, adding a little water as needed.

SERVES 4

- 250g/9oz/2¼ cups yellow polenta flour
- 600ml/1 pint/2½ cups beef or chicken stock
- 75g/3oz pork fat, finely minced/ground
- 2 Italian sausages, sliced into rounds
- 30ml/2 tbsp dried fine breadcrumbs
- 3 eggs, beaten
- 30–45ml/2–3 tbsp freshly grated Parmesan cheese
- 1 thick bacon rasher/strip or pancetta slice, weight 50g/2oz
- sea salt and ground black pepper
- salad leaves, to serve

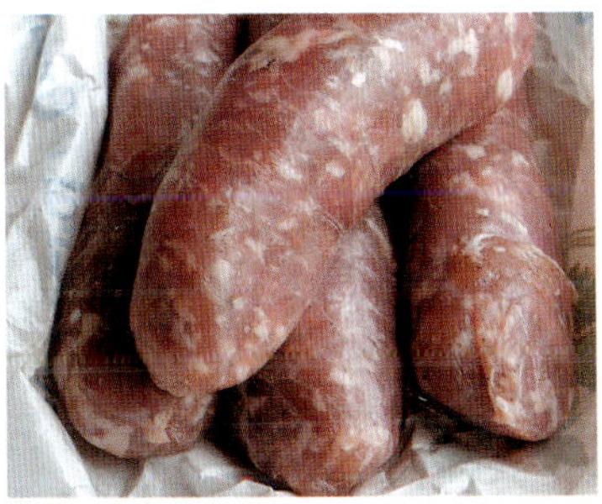

MACAFAM
SAVOURY POLENTA CAKE

This is a good example of a plain recipe that would have been eaten by the poorer population of the Veneto countryside rather than by the nobility of the grand households of Venice. It uses the basic starch maize meal, but instead of boiling it in water to make polenta, the flour is mixed with stock to make a smooth paste before it is combined with other ingredients and baked into a savoury cake. Note the use of the bacon for greasing, which reflects the fact that no butter or oil would have been available to those who once made this dish. You can, of course, use oil for greasing if you prefer.

1 Preheat the oven to 180°C/350°F/Gas 4. Pour the polenta flour into a bowl and add the cold stock, stirring gently and constantly to achieve a smooth paste.

2 Stir in the pork fat, sausages, breadcrumbs, beaten eggs and Parmesan cheese. Season with salt and pepper.

3 Use the bacon or pancetta to grease a 25cm/10in cake tin or pan. Pour in the polenta mixture and bake in the preheated oven for about 35 minutes, or until cooked through and golden brown.

4 Turn out of the tin and serve piping hot, with salad leaves.

SERVES 6

200g/7oz baby onions
2kg/4½lb fresh, tender peas
50g/2oz unsmoked pancetta
50g/2oz/¼ cup unsalted butter
30ml/2 tbsp chopped flat leaf parsley
sea salt and ground black pepper

BISI IN TECIA
VENETIAN STEWED PEAS

This simple recipe was created in the Veneto to enhance the special qualities of the local pea crop, grown on the foothills of the mountainous crag of Lumignano. Here, the effect of the sun's reflection against the rock creates the microclimate that allows this rich flourishing – so much earlier in the season than elsewhere that it used to be traditional to send the precious crops to Venice for the Feast of Saint Mark on 25 April. During the post-war period the production of these peas fell into decline but in recent years the cultivation of the 'Bisi di Lumignano' is once again celebrated and every weekend during the month of May the piazzas of the town of Lumignano celebrate their Sagra dei Bisi – the Festival of Peas.

1 Trim and peel the onions and put them into a bowl of cold water to soak.

2 Pod the peas and place these into another bowl of cold water to soak.

3 Finely chop the pancetta and put it into a pan with the butter. Place over a medium heat, melt the butter and fry the pancetta for about 5 minutes, until the fat is running, stirring frequently.

4 Drain both the onions and the peas and add them to the pan. Stir together, season with salt and pepper and simmer gently for about 30 minutes or until softened. Stir and baste occasionally with water during the cooking period, as required.

5 When the peas and onions are cooked through, remove from the heat, stir through the parsley, adjust the seasoning to taste, and serve immediately.

SERVES 4

- 2 litres/3½ pints/9 cups beef, veal, vegetable or chicken stock
- 1kg/2¼lb young fresh peas, in their pods, or 400g/14oz frozen petits pois/baby peas, thawed
- 60ml/4 tbsp extra virgin olive oil
- 50g/2oz/¼ cup unsalted butter
- ½ mild, sweet onion, finely chopped
- 50g/2oz pancetta, chopped
- 25g/1oz chopped fresh flat leaf parsley
- 300g/11oz short grain rice, preferably vialone nano gigante
- 100g/3¾oz/generous 1 cup freshly grated Parmesan cheese, plus extra to serve
- sea salt and ground black pepper

RISI E BISI

VENETIAN RICE AND PEAS

This is a typical Venetian recipe that is cooked in the old way of making risotto, without frying the rice in fat at the beginning. The end result is more like a very thick soup than a risotto. Not all recipes for rice and peas call for pancetta, but it adds flavour. The choice of rice variety is important, as the rice needs to become very soft while still keeping its shape. Bear in mind that this dish is served much wetter than other risottos, and should have a soupy texture.

1 Bring the stock to the boil in a large pan, then allow to simmer over a low-medium heat. If using peas in their pods, shell the peas and add the pods to the stock.

2 Put the olive oil and butter in a heavy pan, add the onion and pancetta, and fry gently for 10 minutes, or until the onion is softened. Stir in the parsley. Fry gently for 4 minutes more. Add the peas and stir well.

3 Add enough stock to barely cover the vegetables. Simmer slowly for 3–4 minutes until the peas are tender. Add the rice, stir and add a further two ladlefuls of stock.

4 Season and stir, then cook until the grains have almost completely absorbed the stock. Add another two ladlefuls of stock, keeping the mixture very moist.

5 Continue in this way, adding the stock two ladlefuls at a time and stirring constantly, until the rice is tender. Always allow the liquid to be absorbed before adding more.

6 When the rice is soft, remove from the heat and stir in the cheese. Cover and leave to rest for 3 minutes, then distribute evenly between shallow bowls to serve. Offer extra grated Parmesan to sprinkle on top.

RISO E LUGANEGA
RICE AND SAUSAGES

The luganega sausage is made in a long coil, and different versions appear in various parts of the country. Two theories exist in these parts regarding the name: one is that it is somehow connected to the city of Lugana in Switzerland. The other, more likely, is that the name is derived from the word for 'long', which in Italian is lungo. However, just to confuse things further, there is also a regional sausage with the same name that is short and slim, and not made in a continuous coil! This is a Venetian risotto and should be served quite wet and soupy.

SERVES 4

4 x 18cm/7in lengths of luganega sausage
75g/3oz/6 tbsp unsalted butter
30ml/2 tbsp olive oil
½ white onion, finely chopped
350g/12oz arborio rice
175ml/6fl oz/¾ cup dry white wine
1 litre/1¾ pints/4 cups rich beef stock, simmering
75ml/5 tbsp freshly grated Parmesan cheese
sea salt

1 Peel and crumble two of the sausages, leaving the other two whole.

2 Heat 40g/1½oz/3 tbsp butter and the oil in a large pan, add the onion and fry, stirring, until just golden. Add the crumbled sausages and fry, stirring frequently, until they are just cooked, but not browned.

3 Add the rice. Stir until well mixed. Add the wine and cook for 2 minutes to evaporate the alcohol. Add two ladlefuls of stock. Stir constantly until the liquid has almost all been absorbed, then add another two ladlefuls of stock and stir as before.

4 Continue adding the stock two ladlefuls at a time and stirring constantly, for 10 minutes.

5 Add the two whole sausages, then continue to add stock and cook as before until the rice is tender. It will take about 25 minutes for the rice to cook.

6 When the rice is tender, check the seasoning, and add salt only if necessary. Stir in the rest of the butter and half of the cheese. Remove the pan from the heat. Cover the pan and leave the rice to rest for 3 minutes.

7 Remove the sausages and slice them. Transfer the risotto to a serving platter and top with the sausages. Sprinkle over the remaining cheese.

COOK'S TIP

Venetian risottos are quite wet and liquid once cooked. If you run out of stock, use boiling water instead. Remember to allow all the liquid to be absorbed before adding more, and to keep the stock simmering.

RISOTTO CON LE TROTE
RISOTTO WITH TROUT

Lovely and creamy, this trout risotto uses lots of spices to add a real Venetian twist to the dish. You could also use other kinds of fish, but the delicate flavour of trout works especially well. Make sure the trout is really fresh for the best results and that the spices have not lost any of their pungency. This is especially delicious if served with a chilled Soave, the Veneto's best-known white wine. As with all fish-based rice or pasta recipes, no cheese is offered with this dish.

SERVES 4

1 bay leaf
5 black peppercorns
½ cinnamon stick
2 cloves
pinch of freshly grated nutmeg
pinch of ground ginger
pinch of ground allspice
60ml/4 tbsp chopped fresh flat leaf parsley, plus 30ml/2 tbsp chopped fresh flat leaf parsley, to garnish
2 or 3 small fresh trout, about 600g/1lb 5oz total weight, cleaned and gutted
75g/3oz/6 tbsp unsalted butter
30ml/2 tbsp olive oil
1 garlic clove, chopped
350g/12oz vialone nano rice
175ml/6fl oz/¾ cup dry white wine
sea salt

1 Put the bay leaf, spices and parsley into a pan large enough to take the fish, and cover with water. Simmer gently for 10 minutes, then lower the trout into the water.

2 Poach the trout for 5 minutes, then cover and remove from the heat. Leave the trout in the hot water until cooked through. The cooking time needed will depend on the size of each fish.

3 Remove the trout, then skin and fillet them. Strain the stock into a pan. Bring the stock to the boil then reduce the heat to a simmer.

4 Heat 40g/1½oz/3 tbsp butter and the oil in a heavy pan, add the garlic and cook until just softened. Add the rice and toast the grains well, then add the wine and cook for 2 minutes.

5 Add one ladleful of hot fish stock and cook, stirring constantly, until the liquid is absorbed. Continue in this way, adding the stock a ladleful at a time and stirring constantly. Always allow the liquid to be absorbed before adding more.

6 After the risotto has been cooking for 20 minutes or so, stir in the fish fillets, breaking them up as you stir them through.

7 When the rice is tender, remove the pan from the heat and stir in the remaining butter.

8 Cover and leave to rest for 2 minutes, then transfer to a platter. Sprinkle with the chopped parsley and serve immediately.

SERVES 4

50g/2oz/¼ cup unsalted butter
½ onion, finely chopped
500g/1¼lb skinless chicken, cubed
175ml/6fl oz/¾ cup dry white wine
350g/12oz vialone nano gigante or vialone nano rice
1 litre/1¾ pints/4 cups rich beef stock, simmering
60ml/4 tbsp freshly grated Parmesan cheese
sea salt and ground black pepper

RISOTTO ALLA SBIRRAGLIA
RISOTTO OF THE SERENE REPUBLIC GUARDS

This simple but rich chicken risotto is named after the men who guarded the treasures of Venice when it was known as La Serenissima, or the Serene Republic (the guards were called sbirraglia, or sbirri, and the latter term is still used as slang to refer to the police). The use of vialone rice reflects the importance that Italians place on their local ingredients. It is very hard-grained and is the rice most traditionally used in this region. The larger type, gigante, is hard to find outside of Italy or indeed the region itself, but fortunately vialone nano is easier to source, because it is widely exported.

1 Heat half the butter in a large pan, add the onion and fry until pale golden. Add the chicken cubes and cook gently, stirring frequently, until lightly browned.

2 Pour in the wine and cook for 2 minutes to allow the alcohol to evaporate, then add the rice. Stir thoroughly, then add one ladleful of stock and cook, stirring constantly, until the liquid is absorbed.

3 Continue adding stock a ladleful at a time and stirring constantly, for 25–30 minutes, until the rice is tender. Always allow the liquid to be absorbed before adding more.

4 Stir in the remaining butter and half the cheese. Add salt if needed, then remove from the heat. Cover, leave to rest for 3 minutes, then transfer to a platter. Sprinkle with pepper and the remaining cheese and serve.

ARINGHE MARINATE CON CIPOLLE
MARINATED HERRING WITH ONIONS

This is a typical fish dish of the Veneto region. The method, which involves leaving fish to marinate for at least 24 hours, is reminiscent of the kind of fish preparation carried out on board ships on long voyages. The dish is normally served cold, over hot polenta or with hot, buttered toast as an antipasto or snack. The flavour of the vinegar penetrates the whole dish, so it is essential to use one of a good quality for the best results.

SERVES 4

600ml/1 pint/2½ cups full-fat/ whole milk
600ml/1 pint/2½ cups water
4 whole herrings, gutted, scaled and washed
90ml/6 tbsp olive oil
2 large white onions, chopped
90ml/6 tbsp white wine vinegar
60ml/4 tbsp chopped fresh flat leaf parsley

1 In a large frying pan, bring the milk and water to the boil, then add the herrings. Cover and remove the pan from the heat. Allow the herrings to cook through in the residual heat for 5 minutes.

2 Remove the fish from the pan and place them on a rack over a bowl. Leave to drain and dry out for 30 minutes (alternatively, put them on a baking sheet in the oven heated to 200°C/400°F/Gas 6 to dry out for about 5 minutes).

3 Heat 45ml/3 tbsp oil in a pan, add the onions and fry until softened but not browned. Add the vinegar and boil for 2–3 minutes, then remove from the heat.

4 Fillet the herrings, then arrange them, the onions and parsley in layers in a deep bowl.

5 When all the ingredients have been layered, cover them with the remaining oil and leave to rest for at least 24 hours before serving.

SARDE IN SAOR
SWEET-AND-SOUR FRIED SARDINES

Sardines served this way make a traditional Venetian dish, and although the ingredients sound quite unusual, the final combination is delicious. You will find this on sale all over Venice, as it is extremely popular with the locals and there are lots of variations on the basic theme. Ideally, you should leave the dish to rest in the refrigerator for about 48 hours before eating it. Most important, however, is that the sardines are fat and meaty, and as fresh as possible.

1 Soak the sultanas in warm water to cover for 20 minutes, or until plump. Meanwhile, wash and dry the sardines, then toss them in flour to coat them all over.

2 Heat the oil in a large, heavy pan to 180°C/350°F, or until a small cube of bread dropped into the oil browns in 40 seconds. Fry the sardines until golden brown on both sides, then lift out and drain thoroughly on kitchen paper. Leave to cool.

3 Carefully transfer 15ml/1 tbsp of the oil to a separate pan, and fry the onions until just golden. Add the vinegar. Cook for 3 minutes more. Season and remove from the heat. Drain the sultanas.

4 Arrange the ingredients in layers in a serving dish as follows: a layer of fish, then onions, then sultanas and pine nuts, and so on, until all the ingredients have been used. Leave to chill for 24–48 hours before serving.

SERVES 4

100g/3¾oz sultanas/golden raisins
675g/1½lb fresh sardines, cleaned and heads removed
about 60ml/4 tbsp plain/all-purpose flour
1 litre/1¾ pints/4 cups sunflower oil, for deep-frying
675g/1½lb white onions, thinly sliced
30ml/2 tbsp red wine vinegar
115g/4oz/¾ cup pine nuts
sea salt and ground black pepper

COOK'S TIP

If you are preparing the sardines yourself, do be sure to remove the central bone carefully and gently so that you do not destroy the shape of the fish.

SERVES 6

1kg/2¼lb salt cod, soaked for 4 days with the water changed regularly
about 300ml/½ pint/1¼ cups extra virgin olive oil
60ml/4 tbsp finely chopped fresh flat leaf parsley, plus extra to garnish
2–4 garlic cloves, crushed
sea salt and ground black pepper
1 quantity polenta, cut into 12 squares (see page 204), to serve

BACCALÀ MANTECATO ALLA VENEZIANA
WHIPPED SALT COD IN THE VENETIAN STYLE

Baccalà is dried salted cod, which needs 4 days of soaking in fresh cold water to reconstitute it, changing the water two or three times each day. This is not an easy dish to make, but you may have eaten it at one of the many bars and street-food outlets in Venice, and wondered how it was made. Should you have difficulty in getting the fish going, you can put it in a bowl over a pan of simmering water and mash it with a fork to soften it enough to help you work with it. You could also make it using a food processor instead of a wooden spoon, but you will not achieve the same kind of lightness.

1 Rinse the fish, then put it in a large pan and cover with fresh water. Bring to the boil and skim off any scum. Boil for 15–20 minutes, or until tender (you may need to cook it for a little longer if it is still tough).

2 Drain and cool. Once cold enough to handle, remove the skin and bones. Transfer the fish to a bowl and break into flakes.

3 'Whip' the fish with a wooden spoon, gradually adding extra olive oil in a fine, steady stream.

4 Stop whipping when the fish is like whipped cream: white, and light and fluffy. The quantity of olive oil required will depend upon the greasiness of the fish and how good the oil is. Stir in the chopped parsley, garlic and pepper. Taste and add a little salt if necessary.

5 Grill/broil the polenta on both sides for a minute or two, until golden and crisp.

6 Serve chilled, sprinkled with parsley and accompanied by grilled polenta.

SERVES 4

45ml/3 tbsp plain/all-purpose flour
800g/1¾lb pre-soaked salt cod (see Cook's Tip)
50g/2oz/¼ cup unsalted butter
30ml/2 tbsp sunflower oil
250g/9oz onions, thinly sliced
750ml/1¼ pints/3 cups full-fat/whole milk
4 salted anchovies, boned, washed and dried
30ml/2 tbsp chopped fresh flat leaf parsley
1 garlic clove, chopped
45ml/3 tbsp extra virgin olive oil
sea salt

COOK'S TIP

Before you can make this recipe, the salt cod will need to soak in fresh cold water for 4 days, and you need to change the water two or three times each day.

BACCALÀ ALLA VICENTINA
SALT COD IN THE VICENZA STYLE

From the lovely city of Vicenza comes this famous dish, considered by many to be the very best way to enjoy the real pleasures of baccalà or salt cod. In some versions of this ancient recipe, raisins or currants are added to the dish with the onions, or they are mixed into the oil with the anchovies, garlic and parsley towards the end of cooking. Like many other dishes of its kind, baccalà cooked this way always tastes better when it is left to cool and then reheated at a later date, and is traditionally served on top of white polenta.

1 Put the flour on a plate. Wash and trim the soaked fish, removing any skin or bones. Cut the fish into chunks and toss lightly in the flour.

2 Heat the butter and sunflower oil in a large, heavy pan, add the onion slices and fry them gently until lightly browned.

3 Lay the floured fish in the pan and fry it gently on each side to brown it evenly.

4 Pour over the milk, then cover and simmer very gently for about 1½ hours.

5 Meanwhile, chop the anchovies finely and put into a bowl. Add the parsley, garlic and oil, and mix well. Season with salt if needed.

6 Stir the parsley and anchovy mixture into the fish mixture. Cover and cook for a further 30 minutes, or until cooked through. Serve piping hot.

SEPPIE COL NERO

SQUID COOKED IN ITS OWN INK

This dish never fails to create a sensation when it is served, because it is so dramatic in appearance, being mysteriously black in colour. In fact, the squid ink tastes much less strange than it looks – the flavour is not actually very strong. These days, it is increasingly hard to find squid with its ink sac intact within the body of the fish. If you can't find squid with its ink sac, you can buy the ink separately in small sachets, and this is perfectly fine to use for this recipe.

SERVES 4

800g/1¾lb very young, small whole squid
50ml/2fl oz/¼ cup extra virgin olive oil
2 garlic cloves, chopped
90ml/6 tbsp dry white wine
30ml/2 tbsp chopped fresh parsley
sea salt and ground black pepper

1 Wash the squid, rinsing off any ink. Holding the body firmly, pull away the head and tentacles. If the ink sac is still intact, remove it carefully and set it aside.

2 Pull out and discard all the innards including the long transparent 'pen'. Peel off and discard the skin on the body, but keep the two small side fins. Slice across the head just under the eyes, reserving the tentacles. Discard the rest of the head.

3 Squeeze the tentacles at the head end to push out the beak in the middle. Discard.

4 Rinse the squid pouch and tentacles well. Cut the squid into rings or strips.

5 Heat the olive oil in a frying pan over a medium heat and cook the garlic until softened. Add the squid pieces and cook to seal them on all sides.

6 Add the wine and simmer for 45 minutes. If the mixture appears dry, add a little water.

7 Add the ink from the sacs and cook for a further 45 minutes, or until tender. Season, sprinkle with the parsley and serve.

COOK'S TIPS

- You could ask a fishmonger to prepare the squid for you for speed or if you don't fancy doing it yourself.
- If you buy the squid ink separately, you will need three sachets for this quantity of squid in order to achieve the correct degree of darkness, but you can use a little more, if you like. Add it to the stew as above.

SEPPIE IN UMIDO
SPICED SQUID CASSEROLE

A typical Venetian dish, this deliciously spicy squid casserole makes full use of the traditional spices in the region, so is truly representative of Venice's centuries-long history as a major spice-trading port. Traditionally, the casserole would be generously spooned over a helping of hot, soft white polenta, but it could also be served with a portion of equally sustaining rice or mashed potatoes, if you prefer.

SERVES 6

60ml/4 tbsp sunflower oil
1 large onion, chopped
2 garlic cloves, chopped
1 fresh rosemary sprig, leaves finely chopped
1kg/2¼lb squid, cleaned (see page 221) and sliced
225g/8oz can tomatoes, seeds removed, chopped
5ml/1 tsp tomato paste
pinch of ground cinnamon
pinch of freshly grated nutmeg
pinch of ground ginger
sea salt and ground black pepper
polenta (see page 204), to serve

1 Heat the oil in a large pan over a medium heat, add the onion and garlic, and fry for 5 minutes, until softened but not browned.

2 Add the rosemary, then the squid, and mix. Pour over 500ml/17fl oz/2¼ cups water. Bring to the boil. Simmer for 45 minutes.

3 Add the tomatoes, tomato paste, salt, pepper and spices. Cover and simmer slowly for a further 45 minutes, or until the squid is tender and the sauce has thickened.

4 Serve the casserole hot over portions of soft polenta, if you like.

SERVES 4

16 large scallops
16 paper-thin slices of pancetta
16 radicchio leaves
30ml/2 tbsp extra virgin olive oil
 or melted pork fat
lemon wedges, to serve

COOK'S TIP

You can use frozen scallops for this dish instead of fresh, if you prefer. Make sure you defrost them thoroughly before cooking.

CAPESANTE IN CAMICIA
WRAPPED SCALLOPS

Scallops cooked this way taste wonderful, and are surprisingly simple to prepare. Their fresh sweetness is offset by the bitter flavour of the radicchio and the meatiness of the pancetta, and the finished dish looks very pretty too. It makes an excellent appetizer for eight people or a main course for four when served with some accompanying vegetables or salad. Serve the scallops with a chilled dry white wine such as the local Soave from around Verona in the Veneto region.

1 Wrap each scallop first in a slice of ham, then in a radicchio leaf, securing each one with a wooden cocktail stick or toothpick. Allow the pancetta to stick out slightly around the radicchio, if possible.

2 Brush each wrapped scallop lightly with a little extra virgin olive oil or melted pork fat.

3 Preheat the grill, broiler or a hot griddle (the griddle is hot when water splashed on to the surface evaporates instantly).

4 Cook for 5 minutes until the pancetta that is sticking out is crisp around the edges, turning twice or three times. Serve immediately, with lemon wedges.

SERVES 4

16 scallops with their shells, cleaned and prepared (see Cook's Tip)
175ml/6fl oz/¾ cup olive oil
3 garlic cloves, finely chopped
30ml/2 tbsp finely chopped fresh flat leaf parsley
25ml/1½ tbsp lemon juice
45ml/3 tbsp dry white wine
sea salt and ground black pepper
lemon wedges, to serve

COOK'S TIP

To prepare scallops in their shells, first scrub the shells in cold water. Cut the hinge muscles at the base using a knife, then carefully lift off the rounded shell. Scrape away the beard-like fringe. Remove the intestinal thread. Ease the scallop from the shell, then detach the orange coral from the scallop and set it aside.

CAPESANTE ALLA VENETA
SCALLOPS COOKED IN THE VENETIAN STYLE

In this recipe, fresh scallops are gently poached in their own juices with white wine, lemon juice and garlic, to make the simplest of dishes. The tender, sweet meatiness of the shellfish is beautifully offset by the other flavours. Scallops are popular in Venice and they feature in many rice and pasta dishes, or are served simply, as in this recipe. You can buy them cleaned and prepared from any good fishmonger – be sure to ask for the shells for serving the scallops. You could also serve it as an appetizer for eight people.

1 Scrub the scallop shells and put them into a low oven to warm. Heat the olive oil in a frying pan, then add the chopped garlic and the parsley. Fry everything together for 2–3 minutes.

2 Add the scallops (but not the corals) and lower the heat to the very lowest setting.

3 Season, add the lemon juice and wine, then simmer very gently for 8 minutes.

4 Add the corals and cook for 2 minutes more. The scallops should be just firm and white. Transfer the scallops back into their clean shells and serve immediately, with lemon wedges.

POLLO FRITTO ALLA VENETA
FRIED VENETIAN CHICKEN

Although fried chicken exists as a traditional dish in many parts of Italy, in the Veneto the chicken is first marinated in a sour mixture of lemon juice, parsley and salt to flavour it before coating it in egg and breadcrumbs for frying. The olive oil used in the northern regions tends not to be the intensely flavoured extra virgin that is used further south. Here, the much milder olive oil, from the second or third pressing, is used instead – and always more sparingly than in the south. Serve with a vegetable dish or salad.

SERVES 4

1 chicken, about 1.6kg/3½lb, boned and cut into large chunks
juice of 2 large lemons
60ml/4 tbsp chopped fresh parsley
2 eggs
75ml/5 tbsp fine dried breadcrumbs
200ml/7fl oz/scant 1 cup olive oil
1 large sage sprig
sea salt
lemon wedges and a salad, to serve

1 Put chicken in a bowl and set aside. Pour the lemon juice into a small bowl, add the parsley and a pinch of salt, and mix together.

2 Pour this mixture all over the chicken, stir well, then leave to marinate for 50 minutes, turning the pieces frequently.

3 Beat the eggs in another large bowl and stir in a pinch of salt.

4 Remove the chicken from the marinade and immerse in the egg. Leave for 10 minutes.

5 Put the breadcrumbs on a plate. Take each piece of chicken and dip it into the breadcrumbs to coat it thoroughly all over.

6 Heat the oil in a deep pan to 180°C/350°F, until a cube of bread, dropped into the oil, turns golden in 45 seconds. Add most of the sage, then fry the chicken, in batches, first over a very high heat to seal, then over a lower heat until cooked right through.

7 Serve, garnished with the reserved sage, with lemon wedges and a salad, if you like.

VARIATION

Although not traditional, sunflower or vegetable oil could be used in place of the olive oil, and would be less expensive.

POLASTRO IMBOTIO
VENETIAN STUFFED CHICKEN

In this recipe from the Veneto, a whole chicken is stuffed with a combination of bold tastes, including pancetta, rosemary, sage and onion, which permeate the flesh as it is cooked. Once it is juicy, tender and cooked all the way through, it is jointed and the stuffing ingredients are discarded. It is certainly worth splashing out on a good-quality free-range or organic chicken with lots of flavour for this simple but classic Venetian favourite.

SERVES 4

75g/3oz fatty pancetta or bacon, thinly sliced
1 oven-ready chicken, about 1.6kg/3½lb
7 fresh sage leaves
1 rosemary sprig
½ large onion, thickly sliced
30–45ml/2–3 tbsp olive oil
40g/1½oz/3 tbsp unsalted butter
250ml/8fl oz/1 cup warm chicken stock
sea salt

1 Preheat the oven to 200°C/400°F/Gas 6. Put the pancetta or bacon slices inside the cavity of the chicken with the sage, rosemary and onion. Add a pinch of salt and sew the chicken closed with kitchen string or twine.

2 Oil a roasting pan that the chicken will fit into snugly. Truss the chicken legs tightly together, crossing them over and tying them with kitchen string, then lay it in the roasting pan. Oil the chicken, then season with salt and dot with the butter.

3 Baste the chicken with 30–45ml/2–3 tbsp chicken stock, then place it in the oven to roast for 1 hour, or until cooked through. Test the chicken is cooked by piercing the thickest part with the point of a knife; the juices should run clear and the flesh should be white, not pink. Baste frequently throughout cooking.

4 Remove the string and joint the chicken, discarding the filling ingredients. Serve the chicken with the pan juices poured over.

COOK'S TIP

This is a great recipe for a leisurely lunch, since the chicken will sit quite happily, covered in foil, for up to about an hour. It will absorb some of the juices, making the flesh really tender.

SERVES 4

1kg/2¼lb boned pork loin, shoulder or leg, tied with kitchen string or twine
550ml/18fl oz/2¼ cups white wine
50g/2oz/¼ cup butter
5 sage leaves
5 tiny rosemary sprigs
1 litre/1¾ pints/4 cups full-fat/whole milk
sea salt and ground black pepper
braised radicchio and layered potatoes, to serve

MAIALE AL LATTE
PORK COOKED IN MILK

First marinated in wine, pork is stewed slowly in milk and herbs in this recipe. It is a popular cooking method in the whole of the north of Italy; certain cuts of veal are also often cooked in this way. The meat ends up tasting deliciously sweet and is perfectly tender, and the cooked milk gives the sauce a very unusual texture. The milk will have curdled quite dramatically by the time the meat is ready, but rest assured that this is quite normal.

1 Put the meat in a non-metallic bowl, cover with the wine and leave to marinate in the refrigerator for between 6 hours and 2 days.

2 Remove the meat from the wine and pat dry with kitchen paper. Discard the wine.

3 Heat the butter in a large frying pan. Add the herbs and fry the meat until browned all over. Season with salt and pepper.

4 Transfer the meat to a large flameproof casserole and pour over the milk. Simmer over a low heat, covered, for 3 hours or until the meat is cooked through.

5 Remove the lid for the last 5 minutes to allow the liquid to reduce. Transfer the meat to a warmed platter, slice thickly and pour the sauce over the slices. Serve with braised radicchio and layered potatoes, if you like.

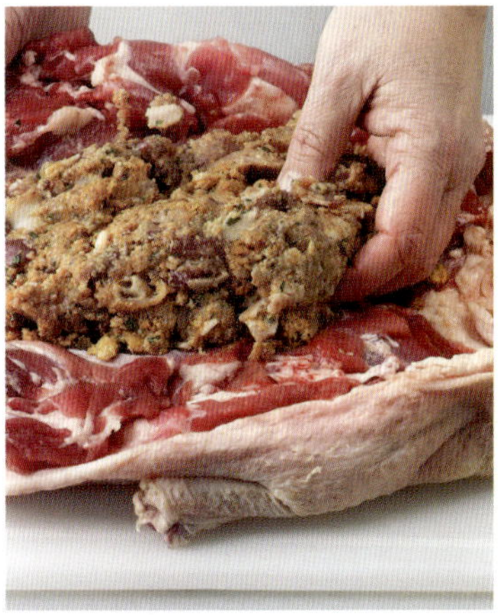

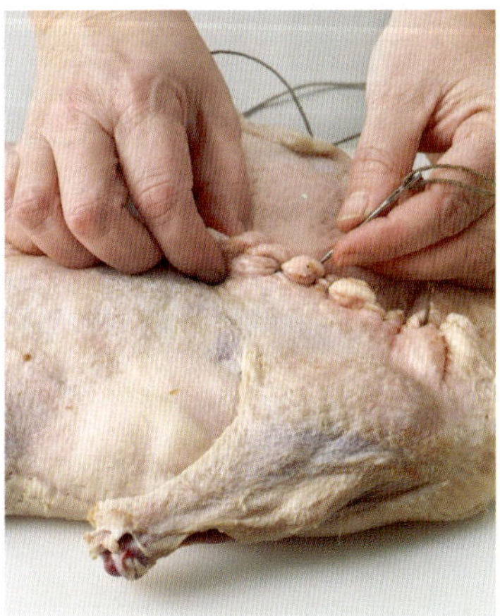

ANATRA COL PIEN
VENETIAN STUFFED DUCK

Sophisticated and elegant, this dish is one of the tastiest ways to serve duck. It is a very old recipe and one that makes the most of the wide variety of ingredients that have been available to the people of Venice for many centuries. The dish looks as good as it tastes, provided that the duck has been boned properly. If you are not confident about this yourself, ask your butcher to do it for you, or roast the duck whole and cook the stuffing separately (adjust the cooking time accordingly). Serve with Salsa Peverada, if you like.

SERVES 6

- 1 oven-ready duck, about 2kg/4½lb
- 115g/4oz veal escalope/US scallop or chicken breast fillet, minced/ground
- 115g/4oz, plus l rasher/strip, streaky/fatty bacon or pancetta, finely chopped
- 1 duck liver or 2 chicken livers, trimmed and chopped
- 75ml/5 tbsp olive oil, plus extra for greasing
- 60ml/4 tbsp chopped fresh parsley
- 1 stale white bread roll, crusts removed, grated
- 75ml/5 tbsp Marsala
- 4 amaretti or 2 macaroons, crumbled
- 15ml/1 tbsp freshly grated Parmesan cheese
- 30ml/2 tbsp candied mustard fruits (mostarda di frutta), chopped
- 1 egg yolk
- 2 rosemary sprigs, leaves chopped
- 750ml/1¼ pint/3 cups dry white or red wine
- sea salt and ground black pepper
- Salsa Peverada (see page 60) and cabbage, to serve (optional)

1 To bone the duck, first cut out the wishbone and the wing tips. Lay the duck breast-side down with the back facing up, then, using a sharp knife, cut along the backbone. Pull the flesh away from the bone as you cut between them on one side of the bird. Don't cut into the skin.

2 Cut through the wing and thigh joints and between the breast meat and ribcage. Turn the bird around and repeat on the other side. Cut off the flesh from the breastbone. Cut the tendons at the end of the thigh and wing bones and scrape off the flesh along the bone. Remove the bone. Set the boned duck aside.

3 Preheat the oven to 180°C/350°F/Gas 4. Mix together the minced veal or chicken, the 115g/4oz chopped bacon or pancetta (reserving the extra rasher), the duck or chicken livers, 30ml/2 tbsp olive oil, parsley and breadcrumbs.

4 Put the Marsala into a small bowl, add the amaretti or macaroons and stir until mushy. Add to the meat mixture. Stir in the Parmesan cheese and candied mustard fruits, and season to taste with salt and pepper. Stir in the egg yolk.

5 Lay the duck on a board, spoon this stuffing mixture into it and sew it closed with kitchen string or twine.

6 In a small bowl, blend together the remaining olive oil, a little salt, the chopped rosemary and the chopped bacon rasher.

7 Put the stuffed duck into an oiled roasting pan and spread the rosemary mixture over it. Baste the duck with 30–45ml/2–3 tbsp wine and put it in the oven. Roast the duck for 1½ hours, basting it frequently with the wine (it may not be necessary to use all of the wine), until cooked. Test by piercing with a knife – the juices should run clear.

8 Transfer the duck to a warmed platter and carve. Serve with Salsa Peverada and cabbage, if you like.

FARAONA AL VINO ROSSO
GUINEA FOWL IN RED WINE

The Veneto is the one Italian region where poultry seems to be particularly celebrated as an ingredient, and many recipes exist for cooking duck, chicken, guinea fowl, goose and turkey. The most famous red wine of north-eastern Italy is Amarone, and it comes from the Veneto. A variety of Valpolicella, which is a blended wine of several grape varieties, Amarone is arguably one of Italy's three great red wines, the others being Barolo and Brunello di Montalcino. Naturally, the better the red wine used for cooking a dish such as this one, the better the finished results will be, and Amarone would be an obvious choice. Serve the guinea fowl on a bed of steaming-hot polenta, for a warming winter supper.

SERVES 4

25g/1oz dried porcini mushrooms
1 large oven-ready guinea fowl, about 1kg/2¼lb
2 large onions, chopped
2 thick rashers/strips pancetta or bacon, chopped
1 Italian sausage, chopped
25g/1oz plain/all-purpose flour
500ml/17fl oz/2¼ cups full-bodied red wine, such as Amarone
50g/2oz/¼ cup unsalted butter
sea salt and ground black pepper
polenta (see page 204), to serve
finely chopped fresh flat leaf parsley, to garnish

1 Put the porcini mushrooms into a bowl. Cover them with hand-hot water, and leave to stand for 30 minutes, or until perfectly reconstituted and softened. Joint the guinea fowl into portions.

2 Cook the onions, pancetta and sausage together in a flameproof casserole over a medium heat for about 15 minutes, until the onions are golden brown.

3 Add the jointed guinea fowl, sprinkle with the flour and mix together until hot, then add three-quarters of the red wine. Season with salt and pepper and boil for about 2 minutes to evaporate the alcohol.

4 Drain the mushrooms and add them to the casserole, then cover with a lid, lower the heat and simmer very gently for about 40 minutes, or until the guinea fowl is cooked through.

5 Remove the guinea fowl joints from the casserole, set them aside and keep warm. Remove the casserole from the heat. Push the cooked mixture from the casserole through a food mill, or whizz it in a food processor and push it through a sieve or strainer if you don't have a food mill.

6 Return the mixture to the casserole and heat over a medium heat. Stir well, adding the butter and remaining red wine, then allow to reduce to make a smooth sauce.

7 Serve the guinea fowl on top of polenta, with the sauce poured all over it. Garnish with chopped fresh flat leaf parsley.

COOK'S TIP

You can reserve the soaking liquid from the porcini mushrooms to cook with in another recipe, if you like. Once softened, remove the soaked porcini from the bowl with a slotted spoon and allow the sediment in the bowl to resettle. Check over the mushrooms for grit before using, then strain the liquid left in the bowl carefully through a very fine sieve or strainer lined with kitchen paper, muslin or cheesecloth. Taste the liquid before using it to cook with, as it can sometimes be a little bitter.

PANADA D'AGNELLO E MAIALE
LAMB AND PORK PIE

This sustaining meaty pie from the Veneto countryside can be made with many different kinds of meat, ranging from kid – which is used together with artichokes, peas, ham and fresh herbs in the springtime – to chunks of horsemeat for a much richer and more substantial dish. In all cases, the meat tends to stay quite chewy, so make sure it is cut into quite small pieces before beginning to prepare the rest of the dish. It is also good served cold, and makes for an excellent addition to a picnic spread.

1 Trim the lamb and pork carefully, then cut into even dice-sized cubes.

2 Heat 30ml/2 tbsp of the oil in a wide pan and fry off the meat until it is well-browned all over. Remove from the heat and tip the meat into a sieve or strainer to drain until required.

3 Preheat the oven to 200°C/400°F/Gas 6.

4 Tip the flour on to a work surface, make a hollow in the middle with your fist and add the dripping or lard.

5 Gently knead together the flour and fat with your fingers to make a smooth ball of dough, adding a little tepid water if necessary. Wrap the dough in clear film or plastic wrap and leave it to rest for about 10 minutes in the refrigerator.

6 Cut off two-thirds of the dough and roll it out as thinly as possible on a floured surface. Use this to line a 25cm/10in shallow cake tin or pan or pie dish.

7 Put the browned-off meat in the lined dish, cover with the chopped tomatoes, garlic and parsley, season with salt and pepper, sprinkle with the remaining oil and cover with the remaining dough.

8 Seal the edges of the pie carefully, then pierce the top with a skewer here and there to let the steam escape during cooking.

9 Bake in the oven for about 90 minutes, then serve.

SERVES 8

500g/1¼lb lamb
200g/7oz pork
45ml/3 tbsp olive oil
300g/10oz/2½ cups plain/all-purpose white flour, plus extra for dusting
50g/2oz/¼ cup pork dripping or lard/white cooking fat
5 ripe fresh tomatoes, peeled and deseeded, chopped finely
1 garlic clove, peeled and chopped finely
45ml/3 tbsp chopped fresh flat leaf parsley
salt and ground black pepper

COOK'S TIPS

- If you can, use tender cuts of meat, such as fillet or tenderloin, rather than more sinuous parts of the animals.
- Beef dripping or lard/white cooking fat gives the pastry a lovely crumbly texture and a toothsome, savoury flavour, but if you prefer you could use butter instead.

PASTISSADA DE MANZO
VENETIAN BEEF STEW

This hearty dish originated on the peasant stoves of the Veneto. Although those dwelling in the coastal areas naturally preferred fish and shellfish as the major source of protein, inland meat would have occasionally graced the menus. A rich stew such as this one, on top of a mound of polenta, would have stretched a lot further and fed many more mouths. The idea of this quantity of meat feeding just four people would have seemed wildly extravagant only a century ago.

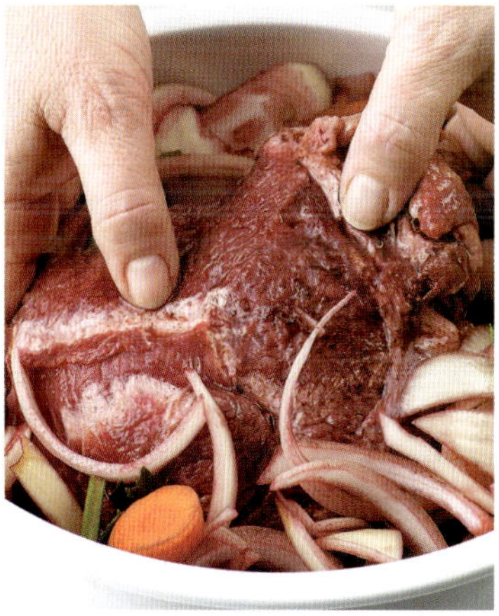

SERVES 4 TO 6

1kg/2¼lb stewing beef, trimmed
1 large onion, thickly sliced
1 large carrot, sliced
1 large celery stick, cut into chunks
750ml/1¼ pints/3 cups red wine
3 cloves
a large pinch of ground cinnamon
2.5ml/½ tsp lightly crushed black peppercorns
115g/4oz thinly sliced pancetta, lardons or streaky/fatty bacon, coarsely chopped
30ml/2 tbsp tomato paste
sea salt and ground black pepper
polenta (see page 204), to serve

COOK'S TIPS

- For a rich and deep flavour, use good-quality red wine.
- Remember to keep the meat barely simmering on a very low heat during the cooking process to ensure it remains extremely tender.

1 Put the whole piece of stewing beef in a large bowl. Add the onion, carrot, celery and red wine, then add the cloves, cinnamon and peppercorns.

2 Mix together, turning the meat in the marinade. Cover and chill for about 24 hours.

3 Remove the meat from the marinade, reserving the marinade. Blot away the excess liquid from the meat using kitchen paper.

4 Pierce the meat all over using the point of a sharp knife. Insert the pancetta, lardons or bacon into the holes using your fingers to help work them deep into the meat.

5 Pour the marinade into a flameproof casserole and bring it to the boil over a high heat, then add the marinated meat. Mix a ladleful of the marinade with the tomato paste and pour this back into the casserole. Stir to combine.

6 Cover the casserole with a lid and turn the heat down to the lowest setting, then simmer very gently for about 3 hours, or until the meat is falling apart. (Alternatively, transfer the casserole to the oven, preheated to 160°C/325°F/ Gas 3, for 3 hours.) Turn the meat in the marinade occasionally during the cooking process.

7 When the meat is cooked through and tender, remove it from the marinade and set it aside on a board or serving platter. Reserve the marinade remaining in the casserole.

8 Cook the contents of the casserole over a medium heat, uncovered, until the sauce is reduced and slightly thickened. Adjust the seasoning, adding salt and pepper to taste.

9 Carve the meat and place it on one big serving dish or distribute it between individual plates, accompanied by a mound of soft polenta. Pour the sauce over the meat and serve hot.

PAPARELE E FIGADINI
PAPARELE WITH CHICKEN LIVERS

Pastasciutta is the Italian word that refers to a dish of pasta that is drained, tossed with a sauce and served dry apart from the sauce. An alternative first course is a soup in which pasta has been cooked – this is a minestra or zuppa with pasta. This particular Venetian speciality is a cross between the two, and it relies heavily on the freshness and good quality of the chicken livers, and the dense richness of the stock. Although the pasta is called paparele, which is probably the dialect for pappardelle, these thumb-wide strips are not the same as the wide ribbons that are Tuscany's most traditional pasta shape. Unusually, the dough contains a little milk to make it even softer and more fragile.

1 Put the flour on to the work surface and make a hollow in the middle with your fist. Beat the eggs and milk together and pour into the hollow. Using your fingertips, bring the flour and liquid together, then knead until you have achieved a smooth, elastic ball of dough.

2 Roll out the dough thinly. Cut into 2cm/¾in strips and leave to dry on a floured surface for about 30 minutes.

3 To cook the livers, heat the butter in a large pan and fry the chicken livers for 3–5 minutes, or until well browned. Add the beef stock and sprinkle with salt. Keep warm until required.

4 Bring a large pot of salted water to the boil and add the pasta. Cook for 5 minutes, or until the pasta is al dente, drain and add to the chicken livers. Stir in the Parmesan cheese, taste and adjust the seasoning.

SERVES 4

300g/11oz/2¾ cups plain/all-purpose flour, plus extra for dusting
3 eggs
30ml/2 tbsp milk

FOR THE CHICKEN LIVERS

50g/2oz/¼ cup unsalted butter
175g/6oz chicken livers, washed and trimmed
1 litre/1¾ pints/4 cups beef stock
50g/2oz/⅔ cup freshly grated Parmesan cheese, plus extra to garnish
sea salt
chopped fresh parsley, to garnish

SERVES 4

500g/1¼lb calf's or lamb's liver, cut into very thin slices
750g/1lb 10oz red onions, very finely sliced
75ml/2½fl oz/⅓ cup vegetable oil
25g/1oz/2 tbsp unsalted butter
60ml/4 tbsp chopped fresh parsley, plus extra to garnish
175ml/6fl oz/¾ cup dry white wine
sea salt and ground black pepper
mashed potato or polenta (see page 204), to serve

FEGATO ALLA VENEZIANA
LIVER COOKED IN THE VENETIAN STYLE

Calf's liver cooked this way is a classic of Venetian meat cuisine. The quantity of onions used for the dish might seem enormous when raw, but they are cooked very slowly to become almost a sticky jam, which will be topped by the sautéed liver. It really is imperative that the calf's liver is as fresh as possible; it should be shiny and have no strong smell when raw. Serve with mounds of fluffy mashed potato or soft white polenta.

1 Trim the liver with care, pulling off the transparent, rind-like skin from around each slice. Rinse the onions in cold running water, then drain and pat dry.

2 Heat the oil and butter in a heavy frying pan over a very low heat and gently fry the onions and parsley, covered, for 1 hour, until shiny and soft. Stir frequently to avoid the mixture sticking or burning.

3 Increase the heat and add the liver to the onions in the pan. Brown the liver slices quickly on both sides and pour the wine over as it browns. The liver will cook in about 5 minutes. Season well with salt and ground black pepper.

4 Place a mound of potato or polenta on each plate, and top it with the onions and then the liver. Serve, sprinkled with parsley.

FRITTATA DI RISO AGLI ASPARAGI
RICE AND ASPARAGUS FRITTATA

The classic flat omelette, so popular in its various forms all over Italy, is an ideal way to make a few ingredients go further, and is also great for using up leftovers. This is a fairly sophisticated version of the dish, insofar as the risotto is made especially for the frittata, with delicious results. A similar version could also be made with leftover risotto that is mixed into beaten eggs. Serve with a salad and a light red wine, or make it a more substantial dish with some crusty bread.

SERVES 4

75g/3oz/6 tbsp butter
300g/11oz asparagus tips, roughly chopped
1 small onion, finely chopped
115g/4oz speck, chopped
115g/4oz/generous ½ cup risotto rice
about 600ml/1 pint/2½ cups vegetable stock
6 eggs
50g/2oz/⅔ cup freshly grated Parmesan cheese
sea salt and ground black pepper
salad leaves, to serve (optional)

1 Heat 65g/2½oz/5 tbsp butter in a large pan, add the asparagus, onion and speck, and fry together gently over a low-medium heat for 5–8 minutes, or until the onion is softened.

2 Add the risotto rice to the pan and mix together for about 5 minutes, or until the rice grains are crackling and well toasted.

3 Bring the stock to the boil in a separate pan and keep it at simmering point.

4 Add the stock to the rice, a ladleful at a time, and cook, stirring constantly, allowing each ladleful to be absorbed before adding the next.

5 After about 20 minutes the rice should be tender and cooked through. Remove the pan from the heat, season to taste and transfer to a bowl. Allow to cool, stirring frequently.

6 Whisk the eggs in a large bowl, then whisk in the Parmesan cheese. Add the cooked rice and mix thoroughly together.

7 Melt the remaining butter in a large non-stick frying pan and pour in the mixture. Shake the pan to flatten and even out the mixture, pulling the liquid egg into the middle as you work. Cook until the underside is browned and firm.

8 Turn over the frittata by covering the pan with a large lid or plate and then turning the pan over. Lift off the pan and put it back on the heat, then carefully slide the frittata (with the uncooked side underneath) back into the hot pan using both hands (carefully) to steady the process.

9 Continue to cook the frittata until golden brown and firm on the underside. This will take less time than the first side.

10 Slide the frittata out on to a clean platter and serve hot, accompanied by salad leaves, if you like.

VARIATION

If you cannot get hold of speck, you could use Parma ham instead.

FRITTATA DI RADICCHIO
RADICCHIO FRITTATA

The cream in this frittata softens the bitter taste of the radicchio leaves and enhances the texture of the finished dish by giving it density, and Parmesan cheese adds richness. The frittata is made in the traditional way: cooking the flat omelette on one side, then flipping it over and slipping it back into the hot pan to cook on the other side. It's lovely served as a flavoursome lunch with some thinly sliced fried potatoes, a side salad or some extra radicchio.

1 Whisk the cream with the Parmesan cheese and eggs, then season with salt and pepper.

2 Heat the oil and butter in a wide, non-stick pan. Mix the radicchio into the egg mixture, then pour it into the hot pan.

3 Shake the pan to flatten and even out the mixture, pulling the liquid egg into the middle as it cooks, and rocking the pan from side to side. Cook until the underside is browned and firm.

4 Turn over the frittata by covering the pan with a large lid or plate, then overturning the pan. Lift off the pan and put back on the heat, then slide the frittata (uncooked side underneath) back into the hot pan using both hands (carefully) to steady the process.

5 Continue to cook until golden brown and firm on the underside. This will take less time than the first side. Slide out on to a clean platter and serve hot, with some fried potatoes and extra radicchio, if you like.

SERVES 4

90ml/6 tbsp single/light cream
250g/9oz/3 cups freshly grated Parmesan cheese
5 eggs, beaten
45ml/3 tbsp olive oil
25g/1oz/2 tbsp unsalted butter
5 heads of radicchio Trevisano, sliced into strips, plus extra to serve
sea salt and ground black pepper
thinly sliced fried potatoes, a side salad or some extra radicchio, to serve

COOK'S TIP

- Use a non-stick pan for this recipe, as the cheese can cause the frittata to stick during cooking, which makes it difficult to keep it intact.
- Make sure you have a flat lid or plate larger than the pan ready before you begin.

SERVES 4

150g/5oz pork belly
500g/1¼lb fresh borlotti beans, podded
300g/11oz radicchio leaves, coarsely chopped
a drizzle of olive oil, to taste
sea salt and ground black pepper
4 slices of grilled/broiled yellow polenta (see page 204), to serve (optional)

COOK'S TIP

You can use dried borlotti beans instead of fresh, if you like. You will need 250g/9oz/1⅓ cups. Leave the beans to soak overnight, then rinse and boil them in fresh water for about 5 minutes. Drain, then rinse and use as above.

RADICCHIO E FAGIOLI
RADICCHIO WITH BEANS

This bitter, red-leafed vegetable is enormously popular all over the Veneto. Of the three most common varieties, radicchio di Chioggia is in the form of a tight ball; radicchio di Verona is floppy and lettuce-like; and radicchio Trevisano, perhaps the best-loved sort, has long, narrow leaves. Any of these can be used in this simple peasant recipe – a classic example of a dish where the protein is provided by a modest amount of meat, supplemented by beans. This makes the complete dish both cheaper and more healthy, while still being full of rich flavours. The radicchio needs barely any cooking and is simply allowed to wilt in the heat of the stew. It can be served on top of grilled or fried polenta, or alongside a meat dish, such as a roast or casserole.

1 Put the pork belly into a large pan with the beans and sufficient water to cover everything generously. Bring the water to the boil and cook gently over a low heat, uncovered, for about 40 minutes, or until the beans are soft. (There should be very little liquid left in the pan and it should not be necessary to drain it. If it seems watery, boil it for a little longer to reduce the liquid.) Add a pinch of salt.

2 Remove the pork belly from the pan, chop it coarsely and set it aside.

3 Mix the radicchio into the beans, crushing the beans with a fork. Return the chopped pork belly to the pan, and stir well. Add olive oil and season to taste.

4 Serve hot or cold, on a slice of yellow polenta, if you like.

RADICCHIO DI TREVISO ALLA VENETA
VENETIAN-STYLE TREVISO RADICCHIO

This dish is usually served alongside grilled meats. It is particularly good with a horsemeat steak, which is very popular locally, as the bitterness of the leaves and the sour tang of the vinegar act as a good foil for the sweet flavour of the meat. It is also good with fried calf's liver or with grilled cheese, for a lighter meal. This variety of radicchio is highly prized all over Italy and is used in a great many dishes, but another type of radicchio can be substituted if necessary.

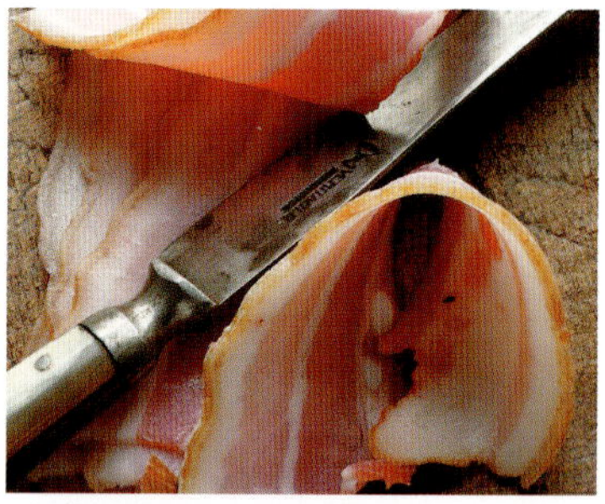

SERVES 4

60ml/4 tbsp olive oil
1 small onion, chopped
75g/3oz smoked pancetta, cut into thick, short strips
675g/1½lb radicchio Trevisano, leaves separated
30ml/2 tbsp red wine vinegar
sea salt and ground black pepper
polenta (see page 204), to serve (optional)

1 Heat the oil in a frying pan, add the onion and pancetta, and fry until the pancetta is brown and crispy.

2 Add the radicchio leaves, mix together and season with salt and pepper.

3 Add the vinegar, then cook gently, stirring frequently, for about 15 minutes, or until the radicchio is soft and wilted.

4 Serve hot, with some soft yellow polenta, or as an accompaniment to a meat dish.

SERVES 12

2kg/4½lb button/pearl onions, washed and unpeeled
250ml/8fl oz/1 cup olive oil
200g/7oz/1 cup sugar
500g/1¼lb canned tomatoes, seeded and chopped
50g/2oz dark/bittersweet cooking chocolate (minimum 70 per cent cocoa solids), grated coarsely
2 bay leaves
4 cloves
350ml/12fl oz/1½ cups dry white wine
sea salt and ground black pepper

COOK'S TIP

To preserve the onions, remove them from the roasting pan with a slotted spoon and transfer to hot, sterilised jars. Put the pan on the hob and boil rapidly to reduce the liquid, then pour in the jars to fill to the rim. Screw the lids on to the jars, then boil them in a pan of water for 15 minutes to further sterilise them. Remove and leave to cool, then store in the refrigerator. Use within 1 month.

CIPOLLINE ALLA VENETA
VENETIAN-STYLE STEWED BUTTON ONIONS

These little onions are served as an antipasto or as an accompanying vegetable with a simple meat dish such as a lightly fried calf's liver. They are traditionally made in great quantities and then preserved in sterilised jars and used as a chutney or accompaniment to cheese or cured meats. The flavours of the ingredients in this recipe blend together really well. Button onions are found at most greengrocers and market stalls in Italy, but pickling onions about the size of a walnut make a good substitute.

1 Bring a large pan of salted water to a rolling boil, add the onions and boil them hard for 5–10 minutes, or until tender.

2 Drain, cool and peel carefully, leaving them whole. Preheat the oven to 180°C/350°F/Gas 4.

3 Pour the oil into a roasting pan large enough to take all the onions, and set over medium heat. Heat gently for 5 minutes, then gently stir in the sugar and allow it to brown, stirring constantly over a low heat.

4 Dry the onions in a clean dish towel and add them to the oil and sugar. Mix carefully together to coat the onions completely, then add the tomatoes, chocolate, bay leaves, cloves and wine.

5 Stir and simmer for 5 minutes, then transfer to the oven and bake for 5 minutes more.

6 Take the roasting pan out of the oven, stir and season. The onions can be served hot or cold, or preserved in clean, sterilised jars for later use (see Cook's Tip).

SERVES 4

3 eggs
700g/1lb 9oz asparagus
5ml/1 tsp white wine vinegar
60ml/4 tbsp olive oil
sea salt and ground black pepper

ASPARAGI ALLA VENETA
ASPARAGUS IN THE VENETIAN STYLE

The area of Bassano del Grappa, in the Veneto, is famous for producing phenomenally good asparagus. This recipe makes a dish that is great for serving alongside cold poached fish or with meats such as thinly sliced roasted ham or rare roast beef. Try to pick asparagus spears that are not too thick, as they tend to have less flavour than those that have a firm stem of medium thickness. The olive oil needs to have a gentle taste without too much bite or pepperiness.

1 Add the eggs to a pan of boiling water and cook for 10 minutes. Drain the eggs and put them into a bowl of cold water to cool.

2 Snap off any woody ends from the asparagus at the point where they break easily. Tie into four bundles and boil upright in a tall pan of salted water for 8 minutes.

3 Meanwhile, peel the hard-boiled eggs and mash them in a small bowl. Add the vinegar, oil, salt and pepper, and mix together thoroughly.

4 Arrange the cooked asparagus in a serving dish, spoon over the dressing and serve immediately, while still hot.

FONDI DI CARCIOFI ALLA VENETA
VENETIAN-STYLE BRAISED ARTICHOKE HEARTS

The market at the Rialto in Venice has mountains of artichokes for sale when the season is right, and the market traders will happily prepare them for you, saving trouble and time. Frozen artichoke hearts are widely available and avoid a lot of work, but they simply don't have the same intense flavour of the fresh vegetable. Although learning to prepare them for cooking might be hard work the first few times you try, it soon becomes easy.

SERVES 4

12 globe artichokes
juice of 1 lemon
100ml/3½fl oz/scant ½ cup olive oil
60ml/4 tbsp finely chopped fresh flat leaf parsley
1 garlic clove, finely chopped
200ml/7fl oz/scant 1 cup chicken or vegetable stock
sea salt and ground black pepper

1 Prepare the artichokes by removing all the outer leaves and trimming right down to the heart. Scrape out the choke from the middle and leave just 1cm/½in of leaf stump around the edge.

2 Put the prepared artichokes in a bowl of water with the lemon juice.

3 Heat the oil in a large pan, then add the parsley and garlic and fry together, stirring frequently, for 5 minutes.

4 Add the artichokes, basting them with the oil, then pour over the stock. Season, cover tightly and simmer for 30 minutes, or until tender. Serve hot, with the pan juices.

CAVOLO ALLA VICENTINA
VICENZA-STYLE STEWED CABBAGE

This simple dish of stewed cabbage is a tasty accompaniment for any pork dish, including cooked Italian sausages. The variety of apple usually chosen for this recipe is similar to a russet but is known in Italy as a renetta. It is squat and rosy with a rough, brown crown around the stalk. The type of cabbage traditionally used is called cappuccio in Italy, and is not as coarse-leafed as a Savoy, although Savoy cabbage can also be used in the recipe.

SERVES 4

60ml/4 tbsp olive oil
25g/1oz/2 tbsp unsalted butter
1 large onion, chopped
1 garlic clove, chopped
115g/4oz pancetta, cubed
1.5kg/3¼lb green cabbage, cored and roughly chopped
1 eating apple, peeled, cored and sliced
sea salt and ground black pepper

1 Heat the oil and butter together in a large pan over medium heat and add the onion, garlic and pancetta. Fry for 5–8 minutes, or until the onion is softened and the pancetta is lightly browned.

2 Add the cabbage and apple, and mix everything together thoroughly. Season, cover tightly and simmer gently for about 45 minutes, or until the cabbage is tender, stirring occasionally. Serve hot.

SERVES 4 TO 6

400g/14oz aubergines/eggplants, cut into chunks
75g/3oz/6 tbsp unsalted butter
75ml/5 tbsp extra virgin olive oil
1 whole garlic clove, peeled
300g/11oz small onions, sliced
500g/1¼lb yellow and red bell peppers, cut into chunks
300g/11oz tomatoes, chopped
90ml/6 tbsp dry white wine
sea salt
chopped fresh flat leaf parsley, to garnish

PEPERONATA ALLA VENEZIANA
STEWED VENETIAN PEPPERS

This is the Venetian version of a dish that is made all over the country, especially at the start of the autumn, when the markets are filled with enormously juicy, brightly coloured peppers of every shape and size. The texture of the dish is soft and squashy, almost like jam. It is important to buy sweet peppers and to keep everything moist during the cooking process. This dish is fabulous as an accompaniment to chicken or fish, or served solo as part of an antipasto.

1 Put the aubergine chunks into a colander and sprinkle with salt. Put a small plate on top and weight it down with a can. Leave it for 30 minutes. Rinse and drain.

2 Heat the butter and oil in a large pan, add the garlic and fry until browned. Discard the garlic and add the onions.

3 Cook the onions until just soft, then add the aubergines, peppers, tomatoes, wine and salt to taste.

4 Cover and simmer gently over a low heat for 1 hour, stirring frequently. Serve the bell peppers hot or cold, garnished with some chopped fresh flat leaf parsley.

GRATIN POLESANO
POTATO AND CHEESE GRATIN

This recipe is for a complete supper dish, although it can also be served as a side dish for roast chicken or something similarly plain. Extra stock might be needed to cook the potatoes without them drying out, depending on the type of potatoes used and the thickness of the dish.

SERVES 4 TO 6

25g/1oz/2 tbsp unsalted butter
475ml/16fl oz/2 cups chicken or beef stock
1kg/2¼lb potatoes, peeled and very thinly sliced
300g/11oz fontina cheese, sliced
150g/5oz pancetta, thinly sliced
sea salt and ground black pepper

1 Butter the sides and base of a deep, flameproof and ovenproof dish using half the butter. Pour half the stock into the buttered dish and bring to the boil.

2 Remove from the heat and arrange half the potatoes in the dish, making sure they are covered by the stock. Return to the heat and cook gently for 10–15 minutes, until the stock has evaporated and potatoes are tender. Preheat the oven to 180°C/350°F/Gas 4.

3 Cover the potatoes with half the fontina and half the pancetta, season and cover with the remaining sliced potatoes. Pour over the remaining stock. Finish with the remaining fontina and pancetta, dot the top with the rest of the butter and sprinkle with salt and pepper.

4 Bake for 20 minutes, or until the potatoes are tender and the top is golden.

COOK'S TIPS

- Keep the sliced potatoes covered with cold water in a bowl until required to prevent them discolouring. This also washes off some of the starch from the potatoes' surface and prevents them from sticking together when they cook, allowing for a greater and more even distribution of flavours.
- Fontina cheese comes from Piedmont and is deliciously nutty and melts pefectly when cooked. Good substitutes could be Emmenthal or Gruyère, or even the main cheese of this region, Asiago – the wooden moulds for making it are shown in the photograph on the left.

FRITTELLE VENEZIANE
VENETIAN FRITTERS

These lovely, light and airy fritters have a gorgeous golden colour and are an important part of the street-food tradition connected to Carnevale. During this festival, fried goodies are available to warm and cheer all passing revellers. All over Italy, the art of deep-frying is highly respected. People usually do this sort of cooking either outdoors or on a balcony in order to prevent the house from being pervaded by the smell of frying. In Italy, the sounds and smells of the sizzling and bubbling of the frying process are often associated with the atmosphere of fun and partying. Serve these classic Venetian sweet treats with strong coffee, a chilled dessert wine or a helping of luscious ice cream.

MAKES ABOUT 28

40g/1½oz fresh yeast
50ml/2fl oz/¼ cup warm milk, plus 2–4 tbsp extra for kneading
130g/4½oz/scant 1 cup sultanas/golden raisins
25ml/1½ tbsp anise or rum
500g/1¼lb/5 cups plain/all-purpose flour, sifted
75g/3oz/6 tbsp caster/superfine sugar
pinch of salt
50g/2oz/½ cup pine nuts
50g/2oz/⅓ cup chopped mixed candied peel
grated rind of l lemon
sunflower oil, for deep-frying
icing/confectioners' sugar, for dusting

1 Put the yeast in a bowl and pour over the warm milk. Leave until frothy.

2 Put the sultanas in a small bowl and cover with the anise or rum. Leave to soak.

3 Put the flour and sugar in a large bowl and stir together. Make a well in the middle of the dry ingredients and pour in the yeast mixture.

4 Mix together thoroughly, adding as much milk as required to make a smooth, soft dough. Mix in the salt, pine nuts, candied peel and lemon rind.

5 Cover the bowl with clear film or plastic wrap and leave the dough to rise in a warm place for about 6 hours. The dough should be very sticky and stringy at this point.

6 Mix the dough again, adding a little more milk if necessary to make the dough slightly wet – you must be able to spoon it. Line a bowl with some sheets of kitchen paper.

7 Heat about 1 litre/1¾ pints/4 cups sunflower oil in a deep pan to 180°C/350°F, or until a small piece of bread dropped into the oil sizzles instantly and browns in about 45 seconds.

8 Fry tablespoonfuls of the fritter mixture in the hot oil, in batches. As soon as the fritters float to the surface, scoop them out of the pan using a slotted spoon and allow to drain on kitchen paper.

9 Dust the fritters with icing sugar and serve them piping hot, with coffee, if you like.

FORTI
VENETIAN SPICED BISCUITS

These typical Venetian biscuits are quite soft when first baked and harden as they cool and mature. As this happens, the molasses flavour intensifies and the colour darkens. Looking at this age-old recipe is like reading the list of available items from a 15th-century Venetian merchant! The word 'forti' means 'hard' or 'strong' in Italian, which you will discover is an apt name. The dough needs to be chilled in the refrigerator overnight, then baked the next day.

MAKES 40 TO 50 BISCUITS/COOKIES

250g/9oz/scant ¾ cup black treacle/molasses
250g/9oz/1¼ cups sugar
50g/2oz/¼ cup butter, softened and cubed, plus extra for greasing
2 eggs, beaten, plus 1 egg white
250g/9oz/2¼ cups almonds
90ml/6 tbsp sweet dessert wine
100q/3¾oz/scant ½ cup unsweetened cocoa powder
5ml/1 tsp ground cinnamon
5ml/1 tsp ground cloves
2.5ml/½ tsp ground ginger
2.5ml/½ tsp ground black pepper
5ml/1 tsp salt
15ml/1 tbsp warm milk
400–450g/14oz–1lb/3½–4 cups plain/all-purpose flour
30ml/2 tbsp icing/confectioners' sugar
30–60ml/2–4 tbsp sugar crystals

1 Whisk the black treacle, sugar, butter and beaten eggs together thoroughly.

2 Pound 200g/7oz/generous 1 cup of the almonds using a mortar and pestle, or process them in a food processor.

3 Stir the pounded almonds into the treacle mixture. Add the wine and cocoa powder, then stir in the ground cinnamon, cloves, ginger and black pepper. Stir the salt into the milk, then add this to the mixture.

4 Add enough flour to the mixture to make a stiff and kneadable dough, then wrap the dough in baking parchment and chill overnight in the refrigerator.

5 Preheat the oven to 180°C/350°F/Gas 4 and grease two baking sheets with butter.

6 Roll out the mixture into two 6cm/2½in thick tubes. Cut each into rounds about 2.5cm/1in thick. Push a hole in the middle of each with your thumb or a small pastry or cookie cutter. Arrange the rounds on the baking sheets, spacing them well apart.

7 Pound or process the remaining almonds with the icing sugar with a mortar and pestle or food processor.

8 Put the egg white into a clean, grease-free bowl and whisk until foaming. Combine it with the almond mixture, then use to brush over the forti.

9 Sprinkle with sugar crystals and bake the forti for 15 minutes, or until golden. They will still be soft after this time but will firm up as they cool. Leave them on the baking tray for 1 minute to allow them to firm slightly, then transfer to wire racks to cool. Store in airtight containers until required.

PEVARINI
VENETIAN BISCUITS

When making these very traditional Venetian treats, you will find you need to work with an extremely stiff, hard dough. If necessary, use a food processor to help you. Pevarini keep very well for up to 2 months in an airtight container. Many recipes from the Veneto region, and Venice in particular, seem to reflect the need for making foods that will store for a while, presumably with the idea of sea voyaging in mind. The marine shapes of these pevarini continue this theme.

MAKES 18 BISCUITS/COOKIES

300g/11oz/2¾ cups plain/all-purpose flour
5ml/1 tsp baking powder
25g/1oz/2 tbsp unsalted butter, lard/white cooking fat or vegetable oil
50g/2oz/4 tbsp soft dark brown sugar
15ml/1 tbsp mixed spices, including cinnamon, nutmeg and white pepper
ice cream or dessert wine, to serve

1 Preheat the oven to 190°C/375°F/Gas 5 and line a baking sheet with a piece of baking parchment.

2 Sift the flour on to a work surface with the baking powder.

3 Add the butter, lard or oil, the sugar, and the spices. Knead everything together thoroughly to combine. Roll the dough out to a thickness of 5mm/¼in.

4 With a sharp, pointed knife, cut biscuits out of the dough in your desired shapes (traditionally fish or seahorses).

5 Arrange on the prepared baking sheet and bake in the preheated oven for about 20 minutes, until golden brown.

6 Leave on the baking sheet for 5 minutes, then transfer to wire racks to cool. Serve with ice cream or dessert wine.

SERVES 6 TO 8

butter, for greasing
300g/11oz/2¾ cups blanched almonds
300g/11oz/generous 1½ cups sugar
300g/11oz/2¾ cups fine yellow polenta flour
grated rind of 1 lemon
3 egg yolks
90ml/6 tbsp single/light cream
pinch of salt
flaked/sliced almonds, to decorate
coffee or hot chocolate, to serve (optional)

TORTA SBRISULOTTA
POLENTA CAKE

As the name indicates (sbrisulotta means 'crumb-like'), this is a crumbly cake, which falls apart as soon as you bite into it. It has a wonderfully granular texture, and excellent flavour. Polenta flour, generally much more widely available in the region of the Veneto than wheat flour, has many culinary uses, including cake-making. Traditional recipes for this cake exist all over the region, but this is one of the richest because of the large quantity of almonds.

1 Preheat the oven to 180°C/350°F/Gas 4. Liberally grease a shallow 20cm/8in cake tin or pan with butter.

2 Grind the almonds finely using a mortar and pestle or in a food processor, then mix them with the sugar, polenta flour and the lemon rind in a large bowl.

3 Mix in the egg yolks and the cream to make a thick but wet dough. Stir in a pinch of salt.

4 Pour into the cake tin and bake for 20 minutes, until firm and crisp. Cool in the tin, then sprinkle with flaked almonds. Serve with coffee or hot chocolate, if liked.

TORTA DI ZUCCA
SOFT PUMPKIN CAKE

This rich, moist cake is excellent served warm with ice cream, mascarpone cheese or custard. Its texture will remain soft and squashy, making it more of a baked pudding than a cake. Traditionally, the knobbly, slightly blueish-skinned Barucca pumpkin from the Chioggia area is used to make this torta, but any kind of butternut squash or firm orange-fleshed winter squash will work, as long as it isn't too fibrous and stringy. What is special about this cake, apart from the flavour, is its glorious, bright orange colour.

SERVES 6 TO 8

- 50g/2oz/⅓ cup sultanas/golden raisins
- 45ml/3 tbsp grappa
- 600g/1lb 5oz pumpkin (preferably Barucca) or butternut squash, peeled and cubed
- 150g/5oz/10 tbsp unsalted butter
- 150g/5oz/¾ cup sugar
- 50g/2oz/½ cup coarsely ground almonds
- 50g/2oz/⅓ cup candied citron peel, chopped
- grated rind of 1 lemon
- 75g/3oz/⅔ cup plain/all-purpose flour
- 10ml/2 tsp baking powder
- 2 eggs, separated
- vegetable oil, for greasing
- icing/confectioners' sugar, for dusting
- sea salt

1 Preheat the oven to 180°C/350°F/Gas 4. Grease a 20cm/8in fairly shallow cake tin or pan and line it with baking parchment. Soak the sultanas in the grappa until swollen.

2 Put the pumpkin or butternut squash into a pan with the butter and cook over low heat until soft. Mash it thoroughly with a pinch of salt.

3 Stir the sugar into the pumpkin with the almonds, candied citron peel, grated lemon rind and the sultanas with the grappa. Beat together until thoroughly mixed.

4 Sift in the flour and baking powder, and stir to mix. Beat the egg yolks until light and foamy, then fold in.

5 In a grease-free bowl, whisk the egg whites until stiff. Fold them lightly into the mixture.

6 Pour the mixture into the prepared tin and bake for 1 hour, until a skewer inserted into the middle of the cake comes out clean.

7 Leave to cool in the tin for 10 minutes, then turn out on to a wire rack. Dust with icing sugar and serve cool.

TORTA DI PAPARELE ALLA VERONESE

VERONESE PASTA CAKE

This recipe comes from the beautiful city of Verona, which is famous for quite a few fabulous cakes. It may seem unusual to have pasta in a sweet recipe, but it works wonderfully. The end result should be moist and chewy. To save time, instead of making the pasta dough yourself, you could use ready-made, soft egg pasta cut into tiny ribbons, such as tagliolini, and then drizzle it with melted butter between the layers. Dried pasta cannot be used for this recipe.

SERVES 6 TO 8

350g/12oz/3 cups plain/ all-purpose flour
3 large/US extra large eggs
50g/2oz/¼ cup unsalted butter, melted, plus extra for greasing
pinch of salt
200g/7oz/1¾ cups almonds, finely chopped
200g/7oz/1 cup sugar
grated rind of 1 lemon
90ml/6 tbsp liqueur of your choice, traditionally Amaretto
30ml/2 tbsp lemon juice
200g/7oz cooking chocolate

1 Preheat the oven to 180°C/350°F/Gas 4. Put 300g/ 11oz/2⅔ cups flour on to the work surface. Make a hole in the middle and break in the eggs. Pour in the melted butter. Add a pinch of salt, then knead together to make a soft pasta dough.

2 Roll the dough out on a floured surface as thinly as possible.

3 Grease a 23cm/9in round cake tin or pan thoroughly with butter, then coat the inside with the rest of the flour.

4 In a small bowl mix together the almonds, sugar and lemon rind.

5 Cut the rolled-out pasta dough into narrow, even ribbons using a pasta wheel or sharp knife.

6 Arrange a layer of pasta ribbons in the base of the cake tin, then sprinkle with some of the almond mixture. Sprinkle with some of the liqueur and cover with another layer of pasta ribbons. Continue until you have used up all the ingredients, ending with pasta ribbons.

7 Cover the top of the pasta ribbons with a sheet of generously buttered baking parchment, then bake in the preheated oven for about 55 minutes, or until golden brown.

8 Remove the cake from the oven and immediately sprinkle the top with the lemon juice. Run a blunt knife around the edge of the cake, then carefully remove it from the tin and leave it to cool.

9 Melt the chocolate in a heatproof bowl over a pan of gently simmering water, then drizzle it over the cake. Serve warm or cold.

TRENTINO-ALTO ADIGE

Trentino-Alto Adige in northern Italy is known for its medieval castles, such as Castel Roncolo/Schloss Runkelstein, which dominates the city of Bolzano from its mountainous perch; Castel d'Appiano/Burg Hocheppan, which stands on precipitous crags above Missian; and Schloss Tirol, the ancestral seat of the Counts of Tyrol that gave the whole Tyrol region its name. Nowadays, you can visit the castle museum to learn all about the history of the Tyrol, from its early beginnings to its heyday during the Middle Ages.

Trento, the region's capital, boasts several beautiful Renaissance palaces with frescoed facades, and the vast Buonconsiglio castle, the largest and most important monumental building of the area, which was the residence of the prince-bishops of Trento from the 13th century to the end of the 18th century. The Council of Trent was held here (and also in Bologna) between 1545 and 1563, and is considered to be one of Roman Catholic Church's most important Ecumenical Councils, prompted by the Protestant Reformation.

This beautiful, largely unspoilt and very mountainous region, which covers a large part of the Dolomites and the southern Alps, is bordered to the east and north by Austria where the lowest pass across the Alps, the Brenner, is located; Switzerland to the north-west, Lombardy to the west and the Veneto to the south and south-east. It is made up of two provinces: Trentino in the south and South Tyrol or Alto Adige in the north. As their names suggest, Alto Adige, with its regional capital of Bolzano, remains more Austrian than Trentino and its regional capital of Trento, which is much more Italian. In South Tyrol, the main language is German, while most of the population of Trentino speaks Italian.

The area is home to aromatic pine forests, alpine lakes and vine-clad hills that lead down to the plains of the Veneto. The fortresses, castles and mountain dwellings are lasting symbols of the region's cultural autonomy and protectionist instincts. Travelling south through the valleys, the allegiance seems to almost visibly shift from Austrian to the culture of the Veneto, with its traditions of agriculture and farming. Moreover, like the people, geography and language, the cusine also splits in half: the north reflecting the traditions of Central Europe, while the south is reminiscent of dishes of the Veneto.

The only thing the two cuisines can be said to have in common is a genuine reliance on preserving food, which was vital during the long, hard mountain winters. So, everywhere you will come across smoked sausages and other preserved pork and game; delicious cheeses; fermented vegetables such as sauerkraut; countless jams, pickles and condiments; and bread that is designed to stay fresh for as long as possible, often made using grains such as rye and barley.

Leftover bread is used to make the large dumplings called canederli, flavoured with speck and combined with milk, egg and flour. These are gently poached in stock and served either in the stock as a kind of very filling soup, or drained and tossed with a sauce. Sometimes they are served alongside spicy goulash.

Speck is the region's most important cured meat. Often handmade by local farmers, the iconic product, just like prosciutto, is created from the haunch of a pig. The meat is smoked as slowly as possible to flavour and preserve it for months. Mortandela, not to be confused with mortadella, from the beautiful Val di Non, is another superb smoked pork sausage, frequently combined with sauerkraut or barley in the local soup tradition. Game is eaten throughout the entire region, often served with a woodland berry or apple sauce.

The Val di Non is reputed to have the perfect growing conditions for apple trees, and their fruits are prized throughout Italy. Wild woodland berries are also valued, and combine brilliantly with cream, custard or chocolate in many of the classic desserts of Alto Adige, although the most famous local one is undoubtedly the strudel, preferably made with a specific variety of apple grown in the Val di Non called rughetta rugginosa.

Grapes are another major crop, and this is one of the main regions for the production of the very popular Pinot Grigio and other highly prized crisp white wines. These are made from grape varieties that are resistant to the cold, such as Kerner, Veltliner and Rieslings, which make wines that are drier and more acidic than those produced elsewhere. When it comes to the reds, Lagrein and Schiava, both native grape varieties, produce low-tannin wines that perfectly match local foods, including the wonderful mountain cheeses, of which there are over 60 different types.

MINESTRA D'ORZO ALLA TRENTINA
TRENTINO BARLEY SOUP

This thick and creamy soup has lots of flavour with the added bonus of a meaty ham bone to make it really tasty and even more filling – perfect for a cold winter's day. The meat should fall off the bone and become a part of the soup as it cooks. This is a traditional and old-fashioned soup in Trentino, where thrifty barley is used in all kinds of different dishes. A similar soup can be made using beans or lentils instead of barley. Pork fat is the most common cooking fat used in the region, where olive oil is not produced.

SERVES 6

200g/7oz pearl barley, rinsed
30–45ml/2–3 tbsp pork fat or olive oil
1 large onion, chopped
1 large carrot, chopped
1 or 2 celery sticks, chopped
handful of fresh flat leaf parsley, leaves chopped
4 fresh sage leaves, chopped
1 fresh rosemary sprig, leaves chopped
4 fresh marjoram sprigs, leaves chopped
30ml/2 tbsp plain/all-purpose flour
2.25 litres/4 pints/10 cups meat stock
2 potatoes, peeled and chopped
1 meaty speck bone, or smoked ham bone
sea salt and ground black pepper
freshly grated Parmesan cheese, to serve

1 Put the barley in a large pan and cover it with plenty of cold water. Boil gently for 50 minutes, or until tender. Drain.

2 Put the pork fat or oil in a large pan and add the onion, carrot and celery, and most of the herbs. Set aside the remaining herbs for the garnish. Fry the vegetables and herbs gently until sizzling, then stir in the flour.

3 Add the barley, stock, potatoes and seasoning. Stir, then add the speck or ham bone and submerge in the liquid. Cover and simmer, stirring often, for 1 hour, until the meat has fallen off the bone and the vegetables are very soft.

4 Serve garnished with the reserved herbs, with Parmesan cheese offered separately.

SERVES 4

2 raw beetroot/beets
2 eggs, beaten
200g/7oz/1¾ cups wholemeal/ whole-wheat flour
45ml/3 tbsp sunflower oil
1.5ml/¼ tsp freshly grated nutmeg
sea salt
40g/1½oz/3 tbsp unsalted butter, cubed, plus extra for greasing
60ml/4 tbsp freshly grated Parmesan cheese

SPAETZLE DI RAPE ROSSE
BEETROOT DUMPLINGS

This is a traditional dish from the remote mountainous region of Trentino-Alto Adige where beetroot is used in many recipes. Locally, you can buy a special instrument for cutting the spaetzle dough to the correct shape and size, but a wide-holed ricer works reasonably well. Failing this, use two small spoons to form little dumplings that can be neatly dropped into the pan of boiling water. This recipe is from the northern part of the region, close to the Austrian border, where most people still speak German.

1 Put the beetroot in a pan of water, bring to the boil and cook for 45 minutes, or until tender. Leave to cool in the water, then drain, reserving the water. Peel.

2 Push the beetroot through a food mill into a mixing bowl to make a smooth purée. Add the eggs, 150ml/¼ pint/⅔ cup of the reserved cooking water, the flour, oil and nutmeg. Season with salt and leave to rest for about 20 minutes. Preheat the oven to 180°C/350°F/Gas 4.

3 Bring a wide pan of salted water to the boil and press the mixture into the boiling water through a wide-holed ricer, or use two small spoons to form little dumplings and drop them into the water. As soon as the dumplings rise to the surface of the water, scoop them out with a slotted spoon and arrange them in a buttered ovenproof dish.

4 Sprinkle with the butter cubes and the Parmesan cheese, then bake for 20 minutes, or until golden. Serve hot.

MAKES 6

300ml/½ pint/1¼ cups full-fat/ whole milk
25g/1oz fresh/compressed yeast
200g/7oz/2 cups porridge oats
10ml/2 tsp cumin seeds
400g/14oz wholemeal/ whole-wheat flour
vegetable oil, for greasing
sea salt

VARIATION

To lighten up these hearty rolls you could substitute half of the wholemeal/whole-wheat flour for strong white bread flour.

FILONCINI ALL'AVENA
WHOLEMEAL AND OAT ROLLS

These rolls, which are from Trentino-Alto Adige, use cumin, the most typical and memorable spice flavour of the north-east of the country. This spice is used to make everything from liqueurs to desserts and is also added to stews and soups. Served warm with plenty of unsalted butter, these rolls are delicious with a bowl of hearty bean soup or dipped into frothy hot chocolate on a cold day. Alternatively, split them open, top with cheese and toast until it melts.

1 Warm the milk until tepid and then put into a bowl and mix in the yeast. Leave to stand until frothy.

2 In a mortar, crush the oats and cumin seeds using a pestle. Transfer the mixture to a large bowl and add a pinch of salt and the flour. Turn out on to the work surface and make a hollow in the middle with your fist.

3 Pour the yeast and milk into the hollow, then begin to mix everything together with your hands. Use stronger pressure once you have achieved a ball of dough.

4 Knead for 15 minutes, then transfer to a floured bowl and cover with a floured cloth. Leave for 3 hours, or until doubled in size.

5 Punch down or knock back the dough, then divide into six balls. Lay them on a lightly oiled baking sheet, then leave to rise in a warm place for 2 hours, until doubled in size.

6 Preheat the oven to 200°C/400°F/Gas 6. Snip the balls twice on the top and bake for 20 minutes until light golden brown; they should sound hollow when tapped underneath. Cool on a wire rack.

GULASCH ALLA TIROLESE CON POLENTA
TYROLEAN GOULASH WITH POLENTA

There are countless versions of this classic Austro-Hungarian stew all over the north-east of Italy. The main ingredients, despite all the variations on the basic recipe, are the meat and the paprika, which gives the dish its deep brick-red colour. Naturally, paprika varies in intensity, so you may wish to add more or less depending on preference, but bear in mind that there needs to be enough for it to colour the dish, and that it is intended to be quite spicy. Serve over polenta.

SERVES 4

30–45ml/2–3 tbsp olive oil or 30ml/2 tbsp pork fat
2 onions, finely chopped
5–12½ml/1–2½ tsp paprika
1kg/2¼lb stewing steak, cut into large cubes
about 600ml/1 pint/2½ cups meat stock (optional)
1 garlic clove, finely chopped
2.5ml/½ tsp dried marjoram
2.5ml/½ tsp ground cumin
115g/4oz pancetta, cubed
sea salt
polenta (see page 204), to serve

1 Put the oil or pork fat in a large pan over a medium heat. Add the onions and cook for 10–12 minutes or until lightly browned.

2 Add the paprika and fry for 1 minute. Add the meat and brown all over. Add enough water or stock to just cover the meat, then cover and simmer gently for 2–3 hours, or until the meat is tender.

3 In a small bowl, mix together the garlic, marjoram and cumin. In a small pan, fry the pancetta cubes until crisp.

4 When the meat is cooked through, stir the spice mixture and the crisp pancetta into the stew. Adjust the seasoning, if necessary, by adding salt to taste. Serve immediately with soft polenta.

STOCCAFISSO ALLA TRENTINA
STOCKFISH IN THE TRENTINO STYLE

Similar to baccalà (salt cod), stoccafisso (stockfish) is dried cod, which was originally brought from much colder regions, such as the Scandinavian countries. The main difference between the two is that stoccafisso is dried by hanging it on special poles, then sometimes salted, whereas baccalà is cured by salting and is not previously air dried. Baccalà and stoccafisso are interchangeable for most recipes and it is generally a matter of personal preference which one is chosen to use in local dishes. The fish needs to be soaked overnight before use.

SERVES 6

500g/1¼lb stockfish, soaked (see Cook's Tip)
30ml/2 tbsp olive oil
1 onion, chopped
1 small celeriac, thickly sliced
500g/1¼lb potatoes, peeled and thickly sliced
2 garlic cloves, finely chopped
2 bay leaves
4 cloves
25g/1oz/2 tbsp unsalted butter
600ml/1 pint/2½ cups full-fat/whole milk
sea salt and ground black pepper

1 Drain and rinse the soaked stockfish. Bring a large pan of water to the boil, add the fish and cook it for 10 minutes over a medium heat.

2 Drain the fish, allow to cool then remove all the bones and skin completely. Cut the fish into small chunks and set it aside.

3 Heat the olive oil in a flameproof casserole, add the chopped onion and cook for 5–8 minutes, or until lightly browned.

4 Add the sliced celeriac to the casserole and turn it in the oil and onion until slightly browned, then add the potatoes. Stir everything together and season with salt and black pepper.

5 Add water to cover, cover the casserole with a lid and simmer gently over a low heat for about 15 minutes, or until half cooked. Meanwhile, preheat the oven to 180°C/350°F/Gas 4.

6 Remove the casserole from the heat and stir in the fish, garlic, bay leaves and cloves, then season with salt and black pepper.

7 Dot with the butter and pour over half the milk. Bake in the preheated oven for 15 minutes.

8 Remove the casserole from the oven and pour over the remaining milk. Return to the oven to bake for 20 minutes more, or until the milk has completely evaporated. Serve immediately.

COOK'S TIP

Soak the stockfish overnight in a bowl of half water and half milk, using enough to cover the fish completely in the liquid.

MANZO CON VINAIGRETTE DI SCALOGNO
BEEF WITH A SHALLOT VINAIGRETTE

Although this is a modern recipe from Trentino-Alto Adige, it reflects the regional tradition of boiling meat. If you prefer, you could flash-fry or grill the meat instead of immersing it in the boiling stock. The vinaigrette contains shallots and chives, which are both rare in southern Italian cuisine, and extra virgin olive oil (the area of Italy nearest to Trentino-Alto Adige that produces olive oil is around the shores of Lake Garda, in Lombardy).

1 To make the vinaigrette, mix the chopped shallots with the olive oil, chives, lemon juice and salt in a small bowl. Set aside.

2 Cut the beef fillet into eight equal slices. Bring the beef stock to a rolling boil in a shallow pan.

3 Immerse the beef slices in the boiling stock for 1 minute to just cook the outside.

4 Serve the hot beef slices on top of the salad leaves (a large handful for each serving), and divide the vinaigrette equally among the four portions. Serve immediately.

SERVES 4

400g/14oz beef fillet
250ml/8fl oz/1 cup beef stock
mixed salad leaves, to serve

FOR THE VINAIGRETTE

3 shallots, finely chopped
60ml/4 tbsp extra virgin olive oil
15ml/1 tbsp finely chopped chives
juice of 1 lemon
sea salt

SERVES 4

8 large potatoes, peeled (see Cook's Tip)
25g/1oz/¼ cup plain/all-purpose flour
90ml/6 tbsp full-fat/whole milk
60ml/4 tbsp freshly grated Parmesan cheese
200ml/7fl oz/scant 1 cup olive oil
sea salt

COOK'S TIP

It is preferable to use potatoes that are a few days old for this recipe, rather than fresh ones, as they will withstand the grating process better.

TORTEI DI PATATE
TRENTINO POTATO FRITTERS

This Trentino version of potato rösti is usually served piping hot with a platter of local cheeses and plenty of the local red wine, called Marzemino. Crisp on the outside and deliciously soft on the inside, the fritters are well flavoured with Parmesan cheese and incredibly moreish. They are equally tasty if you make them with different kinds of cheese, such as the sweet nutty types: fontina, Emmenthal or Gruyère. You can also use sunflower or rapeseed oil instead of the traditional olive oil for frying, if you prefer.

1 Grate the potatoes coarsely, then mix them with the flour, milk, Parmesan cheese and salt in a large bowl.

2 Heat the olive oil in a large frying pan. Shallow-fry spoonfuls of the potato mixture to make fritters.

3 Turn the fritters over once they are golden and crisp on the underside and finish cooking them on the other side.

4 Drain the fritters thoroughly on kitchen paper and sprinkle with a little salt before serving piping hot.

CROSTATA DI PERE E AMARETTI
PEAR AND AMARETTI TARTS

Crumbled amaretti cover the pastry case for these delectable little tarts, which are topped with pears and pine nuts. It is essential to use pears that are quite ripe, without being overripe, to ensure they cook to the perfect level of tenderness. Adding milk to the pastry near to the end of cooking makes it moist and crumbly and gives it a lovely golden sheen. Serve these tasty tarts warm, accompanied by a scoop of vanilla ice cream or mascarpone.

MAKES 6 INDIVIDUAL TARTS

250g/9oz/2¼ cups plain/all-purpose flour, plus extra for dusting
10ml/2 tsp baking powder, sifted
175g/6oz/scant 1 cup caster/superfine sugar
115g/4oz/½ cup unsalted butter, softened, plus extra for greasing
1 egg, plus 1 egg yolk
5ml/1 tsp vanilla extract
pinch of salt
breadcrumbs, for dusting
45ml/3 tbsp pear, peach or apricot conserve
75g/3oz amaretti, crumbled
6 small ripe pears, halved, peeled and cored
50g/2oz/½ cup pine nuts
45–60ml/3–4 tbsp full-fat/whole milk, for brushing
icing/confectioners' sugar, for dusting

1 Preheat the oven to 180°C/350°F/Gas 4. Sift the flour and baking powder in a pile on the work surface and make a hollow in the middle with your fist.

2 Add 115g/4oz/generous ½ cup of the caster sugar, the butter, egg and yolk, vanilla and salt, then knead together to make a soft ball of dough.

3 Remove one-third of the dough and roll it into a ball. Roll the remaining two-thirds into another ball and set both balls of dough aside until required.

4 Generously grease six individual tart tins or pans with butter, then dust each tin first with flour, then with breadcrumbs.

5 Roll out the larger ball of dough on a lightly floured work surface, to about 1cm/½in thick. Cut out circles of dough large enough to line each of the greased tins, then use to line them, pressing the pastry in carefully with your fingers.

6 Cover the base of each lined case with a layer of conserve, then arrange a thick layer of the amaretti crumbs on top.

7 Arrange the pears on top of the amaretti crumbs, cutting them to fit, then sprinkle over the pine nuts and remaining caster sugar.

8 Use the smaller ball of dough to first line the edges of the top of each tart carefully, and second, to create a lattice pattern for the top of each tart.

9 Bake the tarts in the preheated oven for about 20–30 minutes, or until browned. Remove the tarts from the oven, brush generously with milk, then bake for a further 8–10 minutes.

10 Remove the tarts from the tins and put each one on a serving plate. Dust with icing sugar, then serve while still warm.

COOK'S TIPS

- Although you won't get quite the same texture, you can use frozen sweet pastry, if you are very short of time.
- If you prefer, you can make one 30cm/12in tart with the same quantity of ingredients used in this recipe. Bake for 30–40 minutes, then add the milk glaze and bake for a further 8–10 minutes.

FRIULI-VENEZIA GIULIA

Friuli-Venezia Giulia is the easternmost of all the regions of Italy, with the beautiful city of Trieste, once part of the 19th-century Austro-Hungarian Empire, as its regional capital. It borders Slovenia to the east, Austria to the north, the Adriatic Sea to the west and the Veneto to the south. It is divided into four provinces, namely Gorizia, Pordenone, Trieste and Udine.

The region cherishes its cultural complexities and diversities, brought about by its history and also by its geography. This is a region of wild landscapes and remains a mix of Italian-Slovenian-Austrian and Croatian traditions. Whether it is snow-capped mountains you seek, or sandy beaches, tranquil lagoons teeming with wild water birds, remote alpine hamlets, Roman ruins, rocky coastal cliffs, busy seaports or charming fishing villages, you will find it all here, one of Italy's famously most versatile regions.

Trieste still feels rooted in its not-so-distant Austrian past, with its café culture and elegant architecture and menus featuring sauerkraut, strudel and goulash. Once under the domination of the Hapsburgs, the city was declared a free port and quickly became Mitteleuropa's gateway to the East. As a result, immigrants flocked here from all over the Mediterranean, giving this border city a cosmopolitan air matched only by Naples at the time. Today, its wide boulevards, handsome buildings and a faintly dowdy magnificence are reminiscent of a Vienna-by-the-Sea.

The province of Udine stretches from the Adriatic beaches of Lignano Sabbiadoro to the snowy mountaintops of the Alpine foothills, and the Carnic Alps and Julian Alps. Within this province is the town of San Daniele, where the famously sweet and pink cured ham of the same name is produced. Also worth trying is prosciutto di Sauris, which comes from the town of the same name in Carnia, where it is smoked and cured and where an annual festival is held in its honour every July. There is also the rarer prosciutto carsolino; and even more rare is the peta sausage from Valcellina, made with beef, goat, pork and game.

The food of Friuli-Venezia Giulia is made up of a variety of flavours, which help to unite the disparate cultures of the region. The local love of polenta comes from the Veneto and, when mixed with milk, vegetables, beans or cured meat or sausages, becomes a meal in itself. The Central European influence, meanwhile, is evident in the omnipresence of soups and dumplings rather than pasta. This is a region in which you will commonly find thick barley soups, dumplings made with plums, and a type of dumpling with raisins and breadcrumbs.

There are a number of traditional Friulian cured meats that are certainly worth seeking out. The aforementioned prosciutto di San Daniele DOP is perhaps the most well known and is much sought after, rivalling Parma ham in terms of excellence. Muset is a typical sausage made from pork shin, snout and skin and is often paired with horseradish, or the local pickled turnip dish called brovada, which is very similar to sauerkraut. Cevapcici is a traditional Slavic dish of grilled pork, beef and lamb. Goose, almost unused elsewhere in Italy, is employed here to make salumi and sausages, and the breast and thigh are sometimes smoked. Frico, a famous local savoury cheese crisp, is made using only Montasio, which is the most important regional cheese.

With Austria directly to the north, this area's desserts are mainly interpretations of the great Austrian classics, and make full use of spices such as cinnamon, cumin, cloves and caraway. Grado, known as the Golden island, is famous for its array of fish and seafood dishes, including spider crab and the famous local fish stew called boreto, which is served here with white polenta.

It would be impossible to think of Friuli-Venezia Giulia without mentioning its remarkable white wines, mostly made from the Friulano and Pinot Grigio grape varieties, as well as sparkling wines made from the local grape called Glera. It produces the highest proportion of white wine of any region, and in terms of terroir, the most important influence is the vineyards' unique position between the Alps and the Adriatic.

For a tiny region that is largely off the beaten track in terms of mass tourism, Friuli-Venezia Giulia has so much to offer, even though at times it is hard to feel that one is truly in Italy, with few of the mainstays such as olive oil or tomatoes featuring on the menu. For me, though, part of what makes Italian food so fascinating is just these differences between one region and another.

LA JOTA TRIESTINA
THE JOTA OF TRIESTE

This tremendously sustaining, rib-sticking soup is the pride of the city of Trieste and exists in various versions, although the basic principle of beans and cabbage remains the same. La jota must be very thick once cooked and is generally thought to be much more delicious the day after it has been made, left to rest overnight and then gently reheated. It is sometimes served as an accompaniment to local meat dishes rather than as an appetizer.

SERVES 6

- 675g/1½lb/3¾ cups dried borlotti beans, soaked overnight in cold water (alternatively, use 6 x 400g/14oz canned beans)
- 90ml/6 tbsp olive oil or 50g/2oz/¼ cup unsalted butter
- 2 garlic cloves, chopped
- 115g/4oz smoked pancetta, cubed
- 3 potatoes, peeled and cubed
- 400g/14oz sauerkraut
- 5ml/1 tsp ground cumin
- 1 bay leaf
- 25ml/1½ tbsp plain/all-purpose flour
- sea salt and ground black pepper

1 Drain the beans, then rinse thoroughly and transfer to a pan with fresh water to cover. Bring to the boil and boil rapidly for 5 minutes, then drain and rinse.

2 Heat half the oil or butter in a large pan and fry the garlic, pancetta and potatoes for 5 minutes. Add the beans. Stir, then add 1 litre/1¾ pints/4 cups water and cover. Bring to the boil, then simmer gently, stirring occasionally, for 1½ hours, or until the beans are tender. Add more water if necessary.

3 Put the sauerkraut, cumin and bay leaf in a pan and cover with water. Bring to the boil. Cook until the water has almost evaporated.

4 Heat the remaining oil or butter in a large frying pan. Add the flour and cook it until it is nutty brown. Add the cooked sauerkraut to the frying pan and stir together, then add half the bean mixture.

5 Push the remaining half of the bean mixture through a food mill into the soup. Alternatively, if you do not have a food mill, you could process the remaining half of the bean mixture in a food processor or blender, then add it to the soup.

6 Stir the soup well and season to taste, then cover and simmer for a further 30 minutes before serving.

RAVIOLONI ROSA
GIANT BEETROOT AND MASCARPONE RAVIOLI

This dish always looks so beautiful with the brilliant heliotrope pink of the beetroot against the white of the pasta, sitting in a little pool of melted butter studded with poppy seeds. This unusual pasta dish comes from the Trieste area, and really does taste as good as it looks. Make sure the pasta isn't too thin, so that the filling doesn't bleed through too much, as it would spoil the surprise of cutting the ravioli open once it is on the plate.

SERVES 4

400g/14oz/3½ cups plain/all-purpose flour
4 large/US extra large eggs, beaten
2.5ml/½ tsp extra virgin olive oil
sea salt

FOR THE FILLING

2 large beetroot/beets
150g/5oz/⅔ cup mascarpone
30ml/2 tbsp freshly grated Parmesan cheese, plus extra to serve
large pinch of ground cumin
sea salt and ground black pepper

FOR THE DRESSING

115g/4oz/½ cup unsalted butter
7.5ml/1½ tsp poppy seeds

1 To make the filling, cook the beetroot in a large pan of water for 1 hour. Remove from the heat and leave to cool in the water until just warm. Drain, peel and cut into cubes. Process or blend until smooth.

2 Add the mascarpone to the beetroot to make a smooth, fairly thick paste. Stir in the Parmesan cheese and the cumin, then season to taste with salt and pepper. Chill until required.

3 Pile the flour in a mound on the work top, make a hollow in the middle and pour the eggs into it.

4 Mix the eggs into the flour with your fingertips, then knead the dough with both hands for at least 10 minutes, gradually adding the oil as you work.

5 Roll out the dough thinly. (If you have a pasta machine, roll it out to the penultimate thickness.)

6 Cut the rolled-out dough into eight sheets approximately 10cm/4in wide and 24cm/9½in long. Drop four 15ml/1 tbsp heaps of filling evenly spaced along four of the sheets, leaving even gaps all the way around the filling.

7 Lay the remaining four sheets on top and, with a pastry wheel, cut each strip into four across the width, then trim around the edges, well away from the filling. Make sure you seal the edges very thoroughly as you cut. This will make a total of four ravioli per sheet, for a total of 16 ravioli; four per portion.

8 For the dressing, melt the butter in a small pan until brown. Remove from the heat, stir in the poppy seeds and leave to stand for 15 minutes. Meanwhile, bring a large pan of salted water to the boil.

9 Slide the ravioli into the gently boiling water and cook for 4–5 minutes, or until they float on the surface and the pasta is just tender. Scoop out with a slotted spoon and arrange four ravioli on each of four warmed plates. Spoon over the warm butter. Serve immediately, with Parmesan offered separately.

COOK'S TIPS

- It is important to use raw and not pickled beetroot/beets, because the vinegary flavour would completely overpower everything else.
- If you prefer, you can cook the ravioli in a light stock.

FALSA GRANCEOLA ALLA TRIESTINA
MOCK SPIDER CRAB IN THE TRIESTE STYLE

One of the greatest Venetian dishes is boiled freshly caught spider crab, locally known as granceola or grancevola, served in its shell and simply, but effectively, dressed with olive oil, lemon juice, seasoning and parsley. In Trieste, the capital of neighbouring Friuli-Venezia Giulia, the recipe given here is also traditionally served in the half-crab shell to give the impression that you are eating that Venetian dish made with the rare spider crab. It can be served in shells, ramekins or other ovenproof dishes, depending upon what you have to hand.

SERVES 4

2 eggs
115g/4oz canned tuna in olive oil, drained and oil reserved
60ml/4 tbsp chopped fresh flat leaf parsley
½ garlic clove, finely chopped
juice of ½ lemon
75ml/5 tbsp fine dry breadcrumbs
30ml/2 tbsp olive oil
sea salt and ground black pepper

1 Add the eggs to a pan of boiling water and cook for 10 minutes. Drain, then put them into a bowl of cold water to cool. Peel and chop.

2 Flake the tuna and mix with the hard-boiled eggs, parsley and garlic. Stir in the lemon juice and enough of the reserved oil from the tuna to form a thick paste. Season with salt and pepper.

3 Preheat the grill or broiler to medium. Arrange the tuna mixture in half-crab shells, or in other suitable shells, small ramekins or ovenproof dishes.

4 Cover the fish with breadcrumbs and drizzle with the olive oil.

5 Slide under the grill and brown gently for 10–15 minutes.

SERVES 4

4 soles, filleted (to make 16 fillets)
16 thin slices of speck or prosciutto crudo
1 bunch rocket/arugula leaves, stalks removed, coarsely chopped, plus extra whole leaves, to serve
45ml/3 tbsp olive oil
sea salt and ground white pepper

BOCCONCINI DI SOGLIOLA
PARCELS OF SOLE AND ROCKET

This light and delicious recipe is from Friuli-Venezia Giulia, which is where speck comes from. Speck is a smoked ham that has been made in this region for centuries, using aromatic local wood in the smoking process. Here, the smoky speck, the peppery rocket and the delicate fish combine to form a tasty dish. You could also use plaice fillets, or thin slices of monkfish tail. The speck is important, but if it is impossible to find, you can use prosciutto crudo instead.

1 Preheat the oven to 220°C/425°F/Gas 7. Lay the sole fillets out on a board. Line each one with a slice of speck, then season and sprinkle with the chopped rocket.

2 Roll up the fillets and secure with kitchen string, twine, cocktail sticks or toothpicks.

3 Arrange the parcels in oiled ovenproof dishes, drizzle with the remaining oil and bake for 15 minutes, or until cooked through.

4 Remove the string or cocktail sticks and serve the parcels hot, accompanied by extra whole rocket leaves.

POLENTA CON POMODORI
POLENTA WITH TOMATOES

This is a relatively modern way of preparing polenta and is a recipe from Friuli-Venezia Giulia. In this region, white polenta is preferred to the yellow variety, as it is considered to have a much more delicate flavour, best suited to the local dishes. Although tomatoes and olive oil are not a major part of the cuisine of this area, they all work well together in this dish. It makes a very tasty lunch or supper, to which other ingredients, such as sliced salami, could be added.

SERVES 4

- 4 large ripe tomatoes, sliced
- 750ml/1¼ pints/3 cups boiling water
- 200g/7oz/1¾ cups medium-grade white polenta flour
- 45ml/3 tbsp extra virgin olive oil
- 1 fresh thyme sprig, leaves chopped
- 1 fresh marjoram sprig, leaves chopped
- 50g/2oz freshly grated pecorino cheese
- sea salt and ground black pepper
- vegetable oil, for greasing

VARIATION

You can swap the tomatoes for roasted red bell pepper, or other roasted summer vegetables of your choice, such as aubergine/eggplant, courgette/zucchini or, in the winter when fresh vegetables are not at their best, bottled roasted bell peppers.

1 Sprinkle the tomatoes with salt and lay them in a colander to drain for about 30 minutes. Preheat the oven to 200°C/400°F/Gas 6 and cover a baking sheet with baking parchment.

2 Drain the tomatoes and spread them out cut-side up on the prepared baking parchment, then sprinkle with ground pepper. Bake in the hot oven for 4 minutes.

3 Put the water into a wide, heavy pan over a high heat and return to the boil. Add a good pinch of salt, then trickle the polenta flour into the boiling water in a fine rain with one hand, while whisking constantly with the other.

4 When all the polenta flour has been whisked into the water, reduce the heat to medium-low and stir with a strong, long-handled wooden spoon until the polenta comes away from the sides of the pan. This will take 40–50 minutes.

5 Remove from the heat and stir in 30ml/2 tbsp olive oil and a good grinding of pepper. Spread it evenly into a greased 20 x 30cm/8 x 12in ovenproof dish.

6 Arrange the tomato slices on top and sprinkle with the chopped herbs, the Pecorino cheese and the remaining olive oil. Bake for 10 minutes, or until the cheese has melted and browned. Serve.

INSALATA TIEPIDA DI CALAMARI ALLA RUCOLA
WARM CUTTLEFISH SALAD WITH ROCKET

Warm seafood salads are popular all along the Adriatic coast of Italy. This one, from Friuli-Venezia Giulia, is made especially tasty by the addition of anchovy paste and garlic, and has a finishing touch of rocket to add pepperiness to the dish. You could make the same salad using different types of seafood, such as octopus, squid, prawns or a mixture of fish and shellfish, including mussels and chunks of firm white fish. If the cuttlefish are small and tender, it is better to leave them whole rather than chopping them.

SERVES 4

600g/1lb 5oz prepared cuttlefish (ask your fishmonger to do this for you)
5ml/1 tsp black peppercorns
handful of fresh flat leaf parsley
1 bay leaf
175ml/6fl oz/¾ cup dry white wine
5ml/1 tsp anchovy paste
1 garlic clove, chopped
juice of ½ lemon
60ml/4 tbsp olive oil
1 bunch rocket/arugula, about 3 handfuls
sea salt

1 Clean the prepared cuttlefish and cut them into rings and tentacles.

2 Bring a large pan of salted water to the boil and add the peppercorns, half the parsley, the bay leaf and the wine.

3 Add the cuttlefish to the pan and cook at a gentle boil for 35–40 minutes, or until tender; the cooking time will depend on how large the cuttlefish rings and tentacles are.

4 Meanwhile, chop the remaining parsley and mix with the anchovy paste, garlic, lemon juice and oil, and season with salt.

5 Drain and chop the cuttlefish coarsely, then distribute between four plates.

6 Pour over the oil and herb mixture, cover with a layer of rocket and serve immediately.

RAMBASICI
STUFFED SAVOY CABBAGE BUNDLES

This recipe from Friuli-Venezia Giulia has a dialect name that means 'escaped birds', as the swollen cabbage leaves are supposed to look like little birds hiding away from hunters' guns. You'll need only the green leaves from the cabbage, some of which will be large enough to cut in half, or even into quarters, once you have blanched them all. This makes a satisfying winter dish, and needs only a warm potato salad and some good red wine to make it into a delicious supper.

SERVES 4

- 1 large Savoy cabbage
- 300g/11oz/scant 1½ cups lean minced/ground pork
- 300g/11oz/scant 1½ cups lean minced/ground beef
- 50g/2oz parsley, leaves chopped
- 2 garlic cloves, finely chopped
- 2 hard-boiled eggs, peeled and finely chopped
- 2 slices brown bread, cut into very small cubes
- 3 slices salami, cut into small squares
- 90ml/6 tbsp vegetable oil or 50g/2oz/¼ cup unsalted butter
- 1 large onion, sliced
- 300ml/½ pint/1¼ cups meat stock
- 30ml/2 tbsp olive oil
- 30ml/2 tbsp dry breadcrumbs
- 30ml/2 tbsp freshly grated Parmesan cheese
- sea salt and ground black pepper

VARIATION

You can omit the fried breadcrumbs, if you prefer, and instead lightly coat the finished cabbage rolls with a little tomato sauce for a healthier take on this dish.

1 Select 12 of the unblemished outer leaves of the cabbage with care, blanch them for 1 minute in salted boiling water, then arrange them flat on a work surface, ready to fill. Set aside while you make the filling.

2 Mix together the minced pork and beef, parsley, garlic, hard-boiled eggs, bread and salami in a small bowl. Divide the mixture among the cabbage leaves – there should be about 15ml/1 tbsp of filling in each.

3 Roll up each cabbage leaf around the filling, carefully seal closed with two cocktail sticks or toothpicks and set aside.

4 Heat the vegetable oil or butter in a wide shallow pan and fry the sliced onion for 5–8 minutes over a medium-high heat, until well browned.

5 Remove the onion from the pan and set aside. Put the cabbage rolls, in a single layer, into the pan in which you cooked the onion. Cover with half the stock, bring to the boil, then reduce to a simmer and cook for 15 minutes.

6 Add the remaining stock to the pan and cook for a further 15 minutes.

7 Heat the olive oil in a separate pan and fry the breadcrumbs and Parmesan cheese until crisp.

8 Arrange all the rambasici on a warmed platter, sprinkle them with the fried breadcrumb mixture and serve immediately.

CHIFELINI
POTATO FRITTERS

These little fritters are a traditional sweet treat of the port city of Trieste. They are sometimes called chifeletti. They are also found all over the region of Friuli-Venezia Giulia and in neighbouring Trentino-Alto Adige. They are especially delicious when served at the end of a meal with a small glass of chilled sweet dessert wine, or as an afternoon snack with a cup of warming hot chocolate. Whatever you accompany them with, make sure they are served piping hot.

1 Boil the potatoes in a large pan of water for about 15 minutes or until they are tender. Drain the potatoes well and leave to cool just enough so that you can handle them, then remove the skins. Immediately push them through a food mill into a large mixing bowl; they need to be fairly hot or they will become gluey in texture when you do this.

2 Stir the flour into the mashed potatoes with the sugar, eggs, salt and melted butter.

3 Using a little at a time, shape the mixture into tiny crescent shapes, using extra flour to stop them sticking to your hands or the work surface.

4 Heat the oil in a pan to 180°C/350°F, or until a cube of bread sizzles instantly and browns in about 45 seconds.

5 Fry the crescents, in batches, until they are crisp and golden. Drain them thoroughly on kitchen paper.

6 Serve the fritters hot, dusted with the icing sugar and cinnamon, with cups of hot chocolate or a glass of dessert wine, if you like.

SERVES 4

1kg/2¼lb floury potatoes, unpeeled
200g/7oz/1¾ cups plain/all-purpose flour, plus extra for dusting
115g/4oz/generous ½ cup caster/superfine sugar
2 eggs, beaten
pinch of salt
20g/¾oz/1½ tbsp unsalted butter, melted
1 litre/1¾ pints/4 cups sunflower oil, for deep frying
30ml/2 tbsp icing/confectioners' sugar, sifted, for dusting
5ml/1 tsp ground cinnamon, for dusting

COOK'S TIP

The dough can be made in advance. Cover and put in the refrigerator, then form into crescent shapes and deep fry when needed.

GUBANA
CANDIED FRUIT AND NUT ROLL

This is a traditional cake of Trieste, in the far north-east of Italy, which for centuries has been one of the most important Adriatic ports. Trieste is famous for its cafés and patisseries, which celebrate the culinary talents and ingredients of the Austro-Hungarian Empire. This spiral-shaped bread is filled with nuts and candied fruit, scented with grappa and enriched with butter, eggs and sugar. It's wonderful with coffee or hot chocolate, or at the end of a meal with dessert wine.

SERVES 8

30g/1¼oz fresh/compressed yeast
675g/1½lb/6 cups plain/all-purpose flour, plus extra for dusting
5 eggs
150g/5oz/¾ cup sugar
150g/5oz/10 tbsp unsalted butter, softened, plus extra for greasing
30ml/2 tbsp grappa
grated rind of 1 lemon
90–105ml/6–7 tbsp milk
75g/3oz/½ cup sultanas/golden raisins
60ml/4 tbsp dessert wine
75ml/5 tbsp unblanched almonds
90ml/6 tbsp shelled walnuts
40g/1½oz/¼ cup mixed/candied peel
40g/1½oz/¼ cup candied orange peel
30ml/2 tbsp pine nuts
grated rind of 1 orange
15ml/1 tbsp dried fine breadcrumbs
sea salt

1 Put the yeast in a bowl and mix in 75–90ml/5–6 tbsp tepid water. Stir in 115g/4oz/1 cup flour, then leave to stand for about 20 minutes.

2 Beat 3 eggs. Put them into a large bowl with the remaining flour, 115g/4oz/generous ½ cup sugar, 115g/4oz/½ cup butter, 15ml/1 tbsp grappa, a pinch of salt and the lemon rind.

3 Add the yeast and flour mixture and knead together. Remove from the bowl and knead to form a soft dough, adding the milk to the mixture, a little at a time. You may not need to add all the milk.

4 Put the dough back into the bowl, cover with a dampened dish towel and leave to rise in a warm place for 2 hours, or until doubled in size. Meanwhile, put the sultanas into a bowl and pour over the wine to cover. Leave to swell.

5 Put the almonds and walnuts into a bowl and pour over enough boiling water to cover. Leave to stand for 2–3 minutes, then peel off the skins. Chop the blanched nuts and the candied peels, then put them into a bowl with the pine nuts and grated orange rind. Drain the sultanas and add, along with the remaining grappa. Mix well.

6 Heat 15g/½oz/1 tbsp butter in a frying pan, add the breadcrumbs and fry until crispy. Add to the fruit.

7 Preheat the oven to 190°C/375°F/Gas 5. Grease and flour a baking sheet. Separate 1 egg. Beat the yolk and set aside. Put the white into a clean, grease-free bowl and whisk until stiff. Mix the remaining egg into the fruit mixture, then fold in the egg white.

8 Knock back or punch down the dough on a floured surface and roll out to 2cm/¾in thick. Spread the filling over the dough, then roll it up to make a spiral. Transfer to the baking sheet and brush with the egg yolk. Sprinkle with the remaining sugar and dot with the remaining butter. Bake for 45 minutes, or until golden brown and cooked through.

TUSCANY, UMBRIA & LE MARCHE

A DIVERSE LANDSCAPE

Breathtakingly stunning coastlines, verdant green plains awash with vineyards, precipitous snow-clad mountains, rolling hills topped by ancient towns, and swathes of olive groves – Tuscany, Umbria and Le Marche are unparalleled in their charm. Three of the four regions that make up the beautiful territory of Central Italy (the fourth region, Lazio, lies further south), these regions are geographically close, nestling together around the splendid Apennine mountain range. They share a glorious landscape dotted with hill-top medieval towns, but there are subtle differences in landscape, climate and agriculture, which makes their respective cuisines quite distinctive. Despite these differences, their traditional dishes all share a rustic simplicity and demonstrate a sincere, unassuming joy of food.

TUSCANY – A GREEN AND GENTLE LANDSCAPE

One of the largest regions of Italy, Tuscany is blessed with exceptional beauty and has long been one of Italy's most loved regions. It stretches along the north-western coast of Italy, bound inland by mountains to the north and east. Much of the landscape is green and fertile – ideal for agriculture; the two most renowned crops, olives and grapes, flourish on these warm, gentle hills.

The Arno is the region's major river, flowing down from the Apennines to provide plentiful irrigation for crops in the fields from Florence to the coast. The cities of Florence and Pisa are both built on this majestic waterway. Just off the coast lies a cluster of coastal islands, including the island of Elba (site of Napoleon's first period of exile), where the delicious dessert wine Aleatico is produced.

Generally, the climate in Tuscany is mild all year round. A cold snap is rare, though much feared since it can cause untold damage to the region's precious olive trees and vineyards. In spring and autumn Tuscany remains mostly dry and sunny, but there is sufficient rain to give the crops a good soaking. Winter brings pleasantly mild days near the coast, though it can get very cold at night. The temperature high in the mountains often falls below freezing, with enough snowfall for skiing to be enjoyed at resorts such as Abetone, north of Florence.

BELOW *Tuscany, Umbria and Le Marche stretch across the middle of Italy.*

UMBRIA – FERTILE HILLSIDES

The region of Umbria, though less well-known than that of Tuscany, is no less beautiful. The towns that dot the hillsides are steeped in history. Umbria falls roughly into two distinct landscapes. To the east, the Apennine mountains march proudly down from the north; in the lower-lying west, the mountains give way to gentle rolling hills that are much more conducive to farming. Agriculture remains the chief occupation of the area. The olive oil produced here is sweet, and considered by many to be the finest in Italy; the vineyards make delightful wines; and the wheat crop is made into the best-quality pasta.

The highest mountain in the Umbrian Apennines is Monte Vettore. Snow-capped for much of the year, it dominates the intriguing landscape of the Piano Grande, a flat area ringed by high mountains. This dried-up lake bed still floods, creating large shallow ponds, with vegetation submerged under a layer of water. Some of the ground is cultivated, though much of it is effectively a huge natural hay meadow, with flocks of sheep roaming the slopes, tended by shepherds with their dogs. In April, the snow retreats and the flat grassland glows with pale-purple crocuses, some of which are harvested to produce saffron.

The Umbrian climate runs to extremes, as it has no sea breezes to cool and refresh the atmosphere. There is roasting heat in summer, deep snow in winter, and violent storms can occur at any time.

LE MARCHE – UNDISCOVERED MOUNTAINS

The peaceful region of Le Marche, on the eastern coast of Central Italy, has seen an influx of foreign tourists in the last decade, thanks to its beautiful coastlines and idyllic countryside; one of the things that makes this region so attractive is its breathtakingly unspoilt vista.

The landscape is characterised by a rugged and mountainous hinterland that gently rolls towards the Adriatic Sea to the east, and this unforgiving terrain forces most of the population to live near the coast. The sparsely populated inland areas are home to remote mountain gorges, waterfalls and caves. The Adriatic coast has many beach resorts and fishing towns, such as Recanati, where people flock to enjoy delicious fish and shellfish dishes at the local seafront restaurants.

Snow falls as early as autumn on the peaks of the Sibillini Mountains, to the south of the region, and remains on the mountain tops until the end of May. Spring weather is quite unpredictable, though tender plants such as tomatoes and bell peppers are planted out in early May. Summers are hot and dry, and there is usually very little rain until late September. Autumn in Le Marche is beautiful and full of colour, with the woods and forests vibrant with yellow, orange, red and russet-brown leaves. There are many wild mushrooms to be found in the forests, as well as the elusive and rare white truffles, which are sought by eager truffle hunters during the autumnal months.

ABOVE *Vines flourish on the hills of the picturesque Chianti region in Tuscany.*

BELOW *Wild horses graze the lush pasture on the slopes of Monte Vettore in the Umbrian Apennines.*

AN ANCIENT HISTORY

The central area of Italy has its own distinct character, which sets it apart from the hot, passionate south and the cool, cosmopolitan north. Treasured traditions are alive and well within the age-old walls of the rural medieval villages and world-famous Renaissance towns. The superb cuisines of Tuscany, Umbria and Le Marche are based on a cornucopia of local ingredients, which are meticulously and lovingly prepared according to cooking methods handed down over generations, some even dating back to pre-Roman times.

TUSCAN WEALTH

The original inhabitants of Tuscany, along with Umbria and some other parts of Italy, were the Etruscans, about whom little is known. They inhabited the area from around 700BCE to 100BCE, when they succumbed to the Romans, who established many towns. Archaeological evidence shows it may have been the Etruscans who first enjoyed cooking and eating pasta.

The Middle Ages saw the cities of Pisa, Siena, Arezzo, Pistoia, Lucca, and especially Florence become wealthy thanks to textile manufacture, trade, banking and agriculture. By the 12th century, Florence was beginning to overshadow all its neighbouring cities. It was ruled by an oligarchy of wealthy aristocrats, most importantly the Medici family who became dominant in the 15th century. Under the patronage of these wealthy families, arts and literature flourished as nowhere else in Europe.

The skill of cooking and presenting elaborate dishes was first recognised as a real art form at around this time. Great care and attention was given to the preparation of dishes in the kitchens of the aristocracy to impress friends and rivals, and thus Tuscan cuisine developed and prospered alongside sculpture, painting and music. There was also a wealth of new ingredients available for the first time, thanks to the Medici family's connections with rulers from far-flung countries.

Such was the quality of Tuscan cooking that some even claim that France owes its culinary skill to Italy, and Florence in particular, through the marriage of Catherine de' Medici to Henry, second son of King Francis I of France, in 1533. Upon her marriage, Catherine was followed to France by her kitchen staff, armed with her favourite recipes, and the cooks of Florence taught the cooks of France to prepare dishes fit for a royal court.

Today, gourmets and wine connoisseurs descend on Tuscany to enjoy the wonderful cuisine and high-quality wines. The historical and artistic heritage, and its sheer number of fascinating towns and beautiful landscapes, is awe-inspiring: the more you know the region, the more extraordinary Tuscany seems.

BELOW *The splendid grandeur of the Piano Grande is enhanced by a display of wildflowers.*

BELOW RIGHT *The Ducal Palace nestles within the walled city of Urbino, demonstrating the stunning Renaissance architecture of Le Marche.*

ABOVE *The imposing duomo dominates the skyline of Florence to this day – a jewel in the heart of this wonderful city.*

UMBRIAN SPIRITUALITY

This landlocked region of Central Italy is named after the Umbri tribe, who settled in the region during the 6th century BCE. Invasions by the Etruscans and then the Romans followed. Nearly a millennium later, like other areas of Italy, Umbria suffered hardship with the fall of the Roman Empire. The struggle between barbarians and Byzantines created a power vacuum that began to be filled by Christianity, and by the 4th century, Christian bishops became the cultural and spiritual figureheads of the region. This is the home of St Francis of Assisi, St Scholastica and many other holy men and women. The area became a centre of learning, due to the number of Franciscan and Benedictine monasteries, and the respected University of Perugia was established in 1308.

Umbria is affectionately known as the green heart of Italy. Its cuisine has not generally been influenced by neighbouring regions or nations, and remains based around local ingredients, such as game, fresh and cured pork, lentils and spelt flour, freshwater fish from Lake Trasimeno, and, of course, precious truffles.

LE MARCHE TRADITION

Although Le Marche borders Umbria, and is within easy reach of Tuscany and the capital city of Rome, it maintains a very strong sense of its own identity. People have lived on this fertile landscape since at least 6000BCE, thousands of years before the Etruscans. Via the port of Ancona, they established links with the Ancient Greeks, and later the Gauls. Two-and-a-half millennia later, a Gallic influence is still apparent in the dialects spoken in the north.

Ancona became the gateway through which Christianity entered Italy, paving the way for battles for control of the region during the Renaissance. This era saw huge fluctuations in power between the ruling families.

Historically, the region of Le Marche formed a natural boundary between the Papal and Imperial lands. Napoleon temporarily interrupted the Papal rule of Le Marche but it was resumed until the battle of Castelfiardo in 1860, when the Piedmontese army of the House of Savoy defeated the Papal army. Le Marche was thereafter absorbed into the new nation of Italy, in November 1861.

Le Marche history lives and breathes in the rich tapestry of art and architecture of the walled cities, in the taste of the centuries-old classic cuisine and excellent wines, and in the many ancient pagan and religious festivals that are still celebrated today. Changing times have left their mark on the region, but all the important traditions remain.

A TIMELESS CUISINE

Throughout Italy, there is a great sense of respect for all the different elements that make a region's cuisine unique, and a delight in promoting local dishes and ingredients. The varied histories and landscapes of Tuscany, Umbria and Le Marche have created distinctive regional cuisines that are celebrated around the world. Recipes that derive from medieval kitchens or Renaissance banquets have survived the passage of time and are still found today, perhaps with minor adaptations, in the restaurants and homes of Central Italy.

HISTORICAL FOODS

Although the three regions of Tuscany, Umbria and Le Marche have their own very individual recipes, ingredients, culinary traditions and habits, they do share one common factor: all have a set of recipes that were historically created for the wealthy, and another set eaten by the poor. Only the nobility or the clergy would have been able to afford expensive ingredients such as salt, sugar, fine flour or spices from faraway lands, exotic fruit and vegetables, the best cuts of meat, and the most valuable fish or shellfish. The poorer people, mainly peasant farmers or simple craftsmen, would have lived off a completely different fare, eating a basic and more repetitive diet. Both types of recipes survive today.

The temperate climate and fertile landscape mean that a diverse range of foods are produced in the region. In Central Italy, summers are hotter and longer than those in the north. Consequently, soft fruit and vegetables such as tomatoes flourish, and there are plenty of tomato-based dishes to be found. However, unlike the south, the winters can be extremely cold, especially inland, making it also possible to grow green leafy vegetables that require a sharp frost to develop the best flavour. These nutritious vegetables, along with carbohydrates such as pasta, bread, grains and pulses, are used to make hearty, rib-sticking soups and stews that pepper the traditional menu amid the more familiar pasta dishes, risottos, salads and antipasti.

BELOW *Bread, such as these loaves made with a thrifty mixture of chestnut and wheat flour called la marocca di Casola from Lunigiana, is a staple food in Tuscany.*

ABOVE LEFT *Olives are harvested in the traditional way throughout Tuscany for their precious oil.*

ABOVE *Chestnuts, which are used to make flour for bread, pasta and cakes, litter the forest floor in the hills of Tuscany.*

THE CUISINE OF TUSCANY

It is the basic peasant dishes that have defined the traditional cuisine of Tuscany most clearly. Fragrant local olive oil, for example, has always been chosen as the main cooking fat instead of the more expensive options of butter or pork fat. Along the coast, full use has always been made of the daily fish and shellfish catch, with the port city of Livorno leading the way with its fantastic fish soup, cacciucco. What is still evident throughout Tuscany is the historical continuity and respect for the classic dishes, with each area maintaining its unique specialities and local culinary traditions.

Bread – the basic ingredient Next to olive oil, bread is the most fundamental part of Tuscan cuisine. Different breads are made all over the region and come in a multitude of forms and flavours: long, flattish loaves, unsalted bread, crown-shaped loaves, bitesized crostini, schiacciata all'olio (a type of focaccia), fragrant rosemary rolls, not to mention a fabulous variety of sweet breads, such as buccellato from Lucca, or the Florentine schiacciata all'uva, which is prepared only during the grape harvest.

The absence of salt in Tuscany's traditional bread is a reminder of a time when, for many, salt would have been simply too expensive to add to the dough. Many of the region's most characteristic recipes are created with bread as the main ingredient.

More unusual bread is made from chestnut flour. In the Tuscan mountains, chestnuts are harvested, dried and then milled into flour for making bread, as well as for use in pasta, griddle cakes known as necci, and the delicious cake called castagnaccio.

FAMOUS TUSCAN BREAD DISHES

- La panzanella, made with hard bread that is soaked in water, squeezed dry, and then mixed with fresh vegetables and dressed with oil and vinegar.
- Pappa al pomodoro, a deliciously thick soup made with bread, tomatoes and basil.
- Ribollita, meaning 'boiled again', a reheated vegetable and pulse soup, to which bread is added the second time round to make the soup stretch a bit further.

ABOVE *Grapes are grown in great abundance in Tuscany and are used to make the world-famous wines of the region.*

Local specialities from Tuscany Many of the region's towns are known for specific dishes. Florence, for example, has the huge Fiorentina steak; nearby Prato is where the much-loved dunking biscuits, cantucci, were created; Pisa is dominated by the truffles of nearby San Miniato, as well as locally caught eels and a dried salted cod, or stoccafisso.

In the Maremma, a flat marshy land, the most celebrated local dish is named acquacotta, 'cooked water'. This very basic peasant dish would originally have been made with nothing more than bread, water and a little olive oil, with a sprinkling of the sharp local pecorino cheese, although nowadays a number of other ingredients are added as toppings.

THE CUISINE OF UMBRIA

Umbrian cooking is hearty and filling. Anchovies, olives, artichokes and capers are the primary ingredients, along with pork, pigeon and an assortment of wild game.

Umbrian cooks use ancient spit-roasting techniques to cook game. A local wood pigeon or other game bird is turned slowly on the spit while being brushed with la ghiotta, a traditional game marinade made of red wine, olive oil, pancetta, capers, vinegar, olives, anchovies, onion, garlic, juniper berries or cloves, sage leaves and lemon juice – a recipe that has remained unchanged for hundreds of years.

Delicacies from the forests The most prized ingredient of this region is the black truffle, tartufo nero. Black truffles ripen during the winter and are sniffed out from underground by specially trained dogs. The truffles are a highly valued find, their whereabouts a closely held secret passed from generation to generation. With their pungent, earthy taste and musty aroma, truffles are unmatched in flavour when shaved over freshly made thin ribbons of pasta, or sprinkled over an egg fried in butter, or added to savoury sauces.

In springtime, locals roam through fields and woods foraging for the elusive stalks of the local wild asparagus, asparagi selvatici. The stalks are pencil-thin, delicate and tender, and make a delicious accompaniment to game and pork.

Local specialities from Umbria Perugian cuisine is perhaps the most typical of the whole region. The olive oil produced here is of tremendously high quality. Norcia is noted for its butchered and cured pork meat, and the production of world-class salumeria (cold meats). There is even a word used to define this special skill: norcineria.

The people of Terni, further south, enjoy a diet rich in meat, especially game. The area is also famous for its unsalted bread. Baked in a wood-fired oven, this delicious, crusty bread is perfect with the local cured pork meats, or sliced and toasted on a grill or broiler set over glowing wood embers, rubbed with garlic, drizzled with olive oil and served with stews or topped with truffle slices.

Freshwater fish dishes are popular in this inland region. The fish is roasted over an open wood flame to char it on the outside. It is then skinned and cleaned, filleted and dressed with plenty of extra virgin olive oil, and a little salt, pepper and chopped garlic.

THE CUISINE OF LE MARCHE

The food and cooking of Le Marche makes the most of the bounty of the sea as well as produce from the land. The port of Ancona has traded in exotic ingredients from countries to the east for centuries. There is always something joyous about the preparation and consumption of food in this region, a sense of tremendous happiness and pleasure derived from making and eating the traditional dishes. The huge number of farms testifies to the area's rich agricultural heritage.

Meat and fish recipes The local cuisine is dominated by the strong flavours of many meat recipes – principally the rich roasted pork dish known as porchetta. Favourite meats in this region also include veal, rabbit, game birds such as guinea fowl, pigeon and quail, as well as chicken and goose. Both meat and fish are usually cooked with fennel, garlic and rosemary, or in the potacchio style, with onion, tomato, rosemary and white wine. Also worth a very special mention is the delicious naturally-aged cured ham, prosciutto di Carpegna, which, like Parma ham, is traditionally cured in a small area blessed by a microclimate that ensures uniquely tasty results.

The local fish soup, actually more of a stew, is called brodetto. This is the most famous fish dish of the Adriatic coast and recipes vary from one coastal town to another. Brodetto traditionally includes red and grey mullet, cuttlefish or squid, oil, garlic and saffron, and is usually served on fried or toasted bread. There are many other popular recipes using locally caught sole, bream, clams and mussels from the port of Ancona, as well as stoccafisso (dried cod), but brodetto remains the most symbolic and defining fish dish of Le Marche.

Local specialities from Le Marche A typical speciality is the large juicy olives, which are stuffed with meat, rolled in flour, egg and breadcrumbs, and then deep-fried in hot oil. The Romans and Carthaginians are thought to have enjoyed these unique extra-large green olives centuries ago.

Pecorino, especially the softer, young pecorino, made from local ewe's milk, is the favourite cheese. Desserts in this region are not usually overwhelmingly sweet and are often based on pale, soft cheeses such as ricotta.

FAR LEFT *Black truffles, one of the most valuable delicacies in Italy, are sniffed out by trained dogs in Umbria's forests.*

LEFT *Traditional fishing boats and nets are used to catch eel and several types of freshwater fish from the waters of Lake Trasimeno, Umbria.*

FESTIVALS AND CELEBRATIONS

Italians love an excuse for a party. As well as an array of religious celebrations, there is a vast number of small local festivals that take place all over the country, especially during the summer. These celebrate anything and everything: the mushroom crop, pasta dishes, the local saint's day or a political affiliation. Anyone is welcome to join in the festivities, which usually include food, wine and music, and a wonderful sense of fun. Small local celebrations such as these are often advertised at the roadside, via a hand-painted sign, and are really worth a detour.

CHRISTMAS

All over Italy, the solemn rituals of Christmas Eve (in Italian, Vigilia – meaning 'keeping watch') are celebrated. The traditional Vigilia feast involves fish, and is made up of seven dishes to represent the seven sacraments, with simple pasta dishes that do not contain any meat, at least until after the celebration of the midnight Mass. Some people like to eat a light meal before the Mass, followed by a huge celebratory feast afterwards, featuring fresh pasta, roasted meat, guinea fowl, and traditional cakes and pastries. After all this feasting, Christmas Day and St Stephen's Day (Boxing Day) tend to be much quieter days, largely devoted to visiting family and friends.

Traditional Tuscan dishes include crostini neri (liver pâté on bread) and pollo in galentino, a broth made by boiling a sort of chicken sausage made by stuffing chicken skin with a mixture of chicken meat and other flavourings. The by-product is a boiled chicken meatloaf that is served on Santo Stefano (26 December).

EPIPHANY

Traditionally, Epiphany is the day when gifts are exchanged and there is a parade in honour of the Three Wise Men in Florence. La Befana, the warty old witch, comes to visit on her broomstick, bringing presents for the good children and a lump of coal for those who have been naughty. Special cakes are prepared in honour of this day, sometimes baked in the embers of the fire for Befana to find when she comes down the chimney.

CARNIVAL

The most important day of Carnival is Martedi Grasso, the last day before Ash Wednesday, which marks the beginning of Lent and the long quiet period of self-denial. Martedi Grasso (Fat Tuesday) is a wild day of feasting before Lent, a final thrilling moment of pure indulgence. In Tuscany, traditional parades bring plenty of noisy fun. During Carnival, the custom is to fry great batches of sweet frappe, simple sugared pastry strips flavoured with a little wine.

BELOW *As well as religious celebrations, Italy's villages host a variety of unusual festivals, such as this chestnut festival in Le Marche.*

BELOW RIGHT *The great Tuscan tradition of the Befana parade, taking place on the streets of Florence during Epiphany.*

EASTER

In the past, meat was never eaten on Good Friday. Although this is no longer an official Church rule, it is still respected by some religious households. For this reason, fish and vegetables, usually simply cooked, are served on this day, which for many is a time of quiet reflection.

In some Italian homes a variety of flat omelettes, called frittatas, along with an assortment of sausages and other meats, are served on Holy Saturday with pane di Pasqua or Easter bread. Easter Sunday is celebrated with special breads and pastries, as well as the main Easter feast, with the agnello Pasquale (Easter lamb) as the centrepiece of the meal.

One of the most joyous of Italian traditions, Easter Monday (Pasquetta) is the unofficial start of spring and a chance to get reacquainted with family, friends, and the great outdoors. Italian Catholics know it as the day to remember the women of the sepulchre, including Mary Magdalene. However, for most Italians, Pasquetta is a secular holiday, and a day of picnics. Families and friends go out in droves to the mountains or the beaches and set up camp with packed lunches or portable barbecues. They eat frittatas or hard-boiled eggs and an assortment of grilled meats. 'Natale con i tuoi, Pasqua con chi vuoi', goes the Italian saying, which translates as, 'Christmas with your family, Easter with the friends of your choice'.

FRITELLE FESTIVAL

This festival takes place in the beautiful walled village of Montefioralle on the Sunday following St Joseph's Day in March. Fritelle, fried rice cakes, are made in a big cauldron of oil and everyone shares in the eating.

TARTUFO FESTIVAL

This is the black truffle festival, which takes place in the medieval Umbrian town of Norcia on the last weekend of February. Although not as highly prized as white truffles, the black truffles from this region are some of the finest in Italy.

PORCINO MUSHROOM FESTIVAL

The most famous Italian mushroom is celebrated in the town of Ronta in Tuscany at the end of the summer, where an entire menu based on porcini mushrooms is cooked and eaten.

THE PALIO

This famous horse race occurs twice a year in Siena, Tuscany, on the 2nd July and 16th August. Ten horseriders compete in the race, representing the various contrades, or districts, of Siena. Festivities begin 3 days prior to the horse race, however, with banquets and parades for each contrade competing.

ABOVE *Flags are flown in support of the different riders for each of various contrades or areas of Siena during the Palio horse race.*

BAPTISMS

This is a very important occasion for all Catholic Italians. The church ceremony is solemn, but it is followed by a joyful gathering of family and friends and an enormous feast where the baby, parents and godparents are the special guests.

WEDDINGS

Individual traditions attached to weddings vary tremendously from one place to another in Italy, but the occasion is always as grand as possible and no expense is spared. Wedding feasts often involve many hours of celebratory dining at the table with a long succession of antipasti, pasta, meat and fish courses, desserts, and finally the wedding cake. All of this is washed down with copious quantities of wine and many opportunities to raise a glass to the happy couple with a brindisi (toast). Guests always expect to go home with a bomboniera, a little package of sugared almonds with a small present attached – there is usually one for each person.

TUSCANY

My home region of Tuscany remains one of the most popular and well-known destinations for global tourism, and its excellent food and wine certainly help to maintain its enduring reputation as one of the most attractive areas in the whole of Italy.

Tuscany's diverse landscape encompasses the rugged Apennine Mountains, the islands of the Tuscan Archipelago, the Tyrrhenian coastline, and countless mesmerising, beautifully cared-for olive groves and vineyards. Then there are the cities of Florence, Siena, Pisa, Lucca, Volterra, Arezzo and many other ancient towns and villages, which together timelessly preserve Tuscany's incomparable cultural legacy. This is the birthplace of the Renaissance, and is synonymous with many important figures that have been so influential in the history of art and science. One cannot underestimate the great impact that this region has had on European culture in the course of its history. Petrarch, Dante, Botticelli, Michelangelo, Leonardo da Vinci, Galileo, Vespucci, Boccaccio, Machiavelli and Puccini … these are all Tuscans.

In Tuscany, history, culture and art seem to be the basis of everything, not just something you devote time to when you can by visiting a museum or an art gallery, although there are certainly plenty of those. Here, it is constantly all around you, embracing and seducing you at every turn, but it somehow never feels elitist; it's never boring, just somehow a part of everyday life.

Tuscans spend a lot of time thinking and talking about food, and it is perhaps for this reason that other Italians consider the Tuscan dinner guest to be one of the trickiest to satisfy. As instinctive and uncompromising connoisseurs of good food, they can always tell if something has been overcooked, undercooked, incorrectly seasoned or is simply not up to the diner's exacting standard, and they don't shirk when it comes to saying so!

With such an exacting palate and keen eye for quality and detail, you'd be forgiven for imagining perhaps that their cuisine is somehow packed with sophisticated, complicated recipes that are hard to replicate, but in fact the opposite is true. This is a cuisine that celebrates the treasures of its fertile land and sea with great simplicity and a delicious, agreeable rusticity.

The rest of the country has always referred to the Tuscans as the 'mangiafagioli', the 'bean eaters', because so many traditional recipes use beans, mainly borlotti and cannellini. During the Renaissance, cooking was elevated to the level of an art form in the Medici kitchens of Florence, and those carefully recorded recipes, which have stood the test of time to become international favourites, were first created here alongside the paintings, frescoes and sculptures. However, the dishes that have survived are homely and uncomplicated, perfectly celebrating the bounty of the region.

For me, the iconic pasta shape of the area – the big, wide ribbons called pappardelle – is one of the best ways of illustrating the cuisine of Tuscany and encapsulates its characteristics. Unashamedly big and bold, this glorious, onomatopoetically named pasta is usually served with rich ragù made with meat such as wild boar, or other game. Essentially, Tuscany, and its food specialities, manages to combine fierce pride and an eye for detail with unpretentious, uncomplicated, down-to-earth manners and plenty of style.

Siena is the centre for Tuscan sweetmeats, such as the hard, nutty panforte, or the light and chewy almond ricciarelli as well as the hard cantuccini biscuits that are dipped into a glass of sweet, amber-coloured vin santo at the end of a Tuscan feast. This dessert wine, which once was reserved as a gift to the church, specifically for the celebration of Holy Communion, is made at the end of the main wine harvest with a proportion of the grapes deliberately left on the vines to over-ripen. They are then pressed and aged for five years to create this honey-sweet drink.

My beautiful home region holds a very special place in my heart. My particular corner is the area around Lucca, travelling north towards the seaside region known as La Versilia. These beaches, and the inland parts of La Garfagnana and next-door Lunigiana, will always be my natural habitat. Whenever I visit, I make a beeline for the local speciality of testaroli, big sheets of dough that are cooked in the embers of a chestnut-wood fire in special flat, lidded terracotta pans, then cut into strips and served with pesto from neighbouring Liguria, or a meaty ragù, creating what is apparently one of the earliest forms of pasta. And then, I know I am really home.

ZUPPA DEI MORI
TUSCAN COLD SUMMER SOUP

The origins of this classic, elegant cold soup date back to the Medici court, and it is believed to have been created for banquets honouring guests from North Africa, hence the name Mori, which translates as Moors. Before the invention of the food processor, the vegetables would have been chopped into tiny pieces, then pounded into a rough purée using a large mortar and pestle. Cooling and delicious, this soup is perfect for serving on hot summer days.

1 Place the cucumber, slices of fennel, chopped celery, lettuce, tomatoes, carrots, lemon, garlic, chilli and basil in the bowl of a food processor, and gradually process all ingredients until well mixed; alternatively, use a blender and blend until smooth.

2 Add 250ml/8fl oz/1 cup water and the extra virgin olive oil, then season with salt and black pepper to taste.

3 Ladle into a serving bowl and chill until required. Serve with croûtons, if you like.

SERVES 6

½ cucumber, peeled and cubed
1 fennel bulb, thinly sliced
1 celery heart, chopped
1 lettuce, chopped
4 tomatoes, peeled (see Cook's Tip), seeded and chopped
3 carrots, quartered
1 lemon, peeled and thinly sliced
3 garlic cloves, chopped
1 dried red chilli, finely chopped
1 bunch fresh basil
75ml/2½fl oz/⅓ cup extra virgin olive oil
sea salt and ground black pepper
croûtons, to serve (optional)

COOK'S TIP

To peel tomatoes, place them in a bowl, cover with boiling water and leave for 30 seconds. Refresh under cold water and the the skins will peel off easily.

SERVES 6

1.5 litres/2½ pints/6¼ cups vegetable, chicken or meat stock
1 large onion, chopped
1.2kg/2½lb very ripe tomatoes, coarsely chopped
120ml/4fl oz/½ cup extra virgin olive oil
400g/14oz stale ciabatta, crusts removed, thinly sliced
3 garlic cloves, crushed
a large handful of fresh basil leaves, chopped
sea salt and ground black pepper

COOK'S TIP

Pushing the soup through a food mill (a mouli) or a wide-meshed sieve or strainer is essential to get the right texture. Do not be tempted to blitz it in a food processor, or it will be too smooth.

PAPPA AL POMODORO
TOMATO AND BREAD SOUP

This is a very thick, almost solid, soup, which makes the best of the glut of overripe tomatoes at the end of summer. These are combined with that ever-present standby ingredient: stale bread. It is marvellous served lukewarm with plenty of basil and extra olive oil to drizzle over it. It became especially famous during the 1960s when a pop song, sung by Rita Pavone, described how wonderful this soup was. It remains a traditional part of the classic Tuscan menu.

1 Heat the stock in a large pan. Meanwhile, put the onion, tomatoes and half the oil in a separate pan and fry together over a gentle heat for 10 minutes, or until softened.

2 Push the onion and tomato mixture through a food mill, sieve or strainer and add it to the hot stock. Stir thoroughly.

3 Add the bread, garlic and most of the basil, and season to taste.

4 Cover and simmer gently for 45 minutes, until thick and creamy, stirring occasionally. Stir in the remaining oil, adjust the seasoning if necessary, and add the rest of the basil to taste. Serve hot or at room temperature.

ZUPPA DI FARRO
TUSCAN SPELT SOUP

This hearty soup exists in many forms and is especially common in the Garfagnana region, the mountainous area north-west of Lucca, but it is popular in the rest of Tuscany as well, including along the Umbrian border. Spelt is an ancient grain, and is reminiscent of an era when wheat was simply not available in these parts. Recently, it has become fashionable all over the country, and is used in soups such as this one, or boiled, drained, cooled and turned into delicious salads.

SERVES 4 TO 6

200g/7oz whole spelt grain
75g/3oz pancetta (smoked if possible), coarsely chopped
75ml/5 tbsp extra virgin olive oil
a few thyme sprigs
1 onion, finely sliced
2 garlic cloves, left whole
1.8kg/4lb ripe plum tomatoes, seeded and chopped, or 400g/14oz canned chopped tomatoes (with juice)
a handful of fresh flat leaf parsley leaves, chopped
a handful of fresh basil leaves, torn into small pieces
about 1 litre/1¾ pints/4 cups hot vegetable, chicken or meat stock
sea salt and ground black pepper
freshly grated pecorino or Parmesan cheese, to serve

1 Wash the spelt well, picking over the grains to remove chaff, pebbles or bad grains, then soak it overnight in cold water. Rinse the soaked spelt repeatedly until the water runs clear.

2 Fry the pancetta gently in half the olive oil, until the fat runs, then add the thyme, onion and garlic. Cook for 5 minutes, or until the onion has softened.

3 Remove and discard the garlic. Stir in the chopped tomatoes, parsley and basil. Cook for 3 minutes.

4 Stir in the hot stock and bring back to the boil. Add the spelt.

5 Cook the soup over a low heat, stirring often, for about 2 hours, or until the spelt is cooked (test by tasting one grain: it should be tender).

6 Adjust the seasoning. Remove from the heat and leave the soup for 1 hour to serve it just warm, with the remaining olive oil drizzled over.

7 Offer around some grated cheese for each person to add to their own portion.

LA RIBOLLITA
TUSCAN BEAN AND CABBAGE SOUP

An absolutely classic Tuscan recipe, la ribollita is typical of the big, wholesome soups of this region. When in season, cavolo nero, the narrow-leafed black cabbage of Tuscany, is used for this dish, but in fact any kind of cabbage will work just as well. At the table, offer around olive oil so that people can drizzle it over their individual portions, as they wish – this is known as blessing your soup in Tuscany. You can also offer freshly grated Parmesan or aged pecorino cheese.

SERVES 4 TO 6

- 3 carrots, coarsely chopped
- 2 medium potatoes, peeled and cubed
- 2 garlic cloves, finely chopped
- 2 onions, finely sliced
- 1 small cabbage, shredded
- 2–3 handfuls of any other leaf vegetables of your choice, such as spinach or chard, washed and dried, then shredded coarsely
- 4 Italian pork or wild boar sausages
- about 1.2 litres/2 pints/5 cups cold water
- 250g/9oz stale country-style white or brown bread: the staler the better
- 30ml/2 tbsp olive oil, plus extra to serve
- 150g/5oz/1 cup cooked cannellini beans, drained
- sea salt and ground black pepper
- freshly grated Parmesan or aged pecorino cheese, to serve (optional)

1 Put all the vegetables and the sausages into a large pan and cover with the cold water. Season with salt and pepper and cover with a lid.

2 Bring to the boil, then reduce the heat and simmer for 1½ hours, stirring occasionally and adding water if required.

3 Slice the stale bread and season it with salt and pepper. Brush it thoroughly on either side with the olive oil. If you wish, you can toast it at this stage to make it crisper.

4 Use the bread to line a soup tureen or large bowl. You can either place the bread on the bottom of the bowl, so it soaks up the liquid in the soup, or you can tuck the slice of bread into the side of the bowl and dip it in as you eat the soup.

5 Remove the sausages from the pan and keep warm. Stir the beans into the soup and simmer for a further 10 minutes.

6 Adjust the seasoning to taste, then pour the soup over the prepared bread in the tureen or bowl. Arrange the sausages on top, then cover and leave to rest for about 10 minutes before serving.

7 Arrange the sausages on top, then cover and leave to rest for about 10 minutes before serving with a jug or pitcher of olive oil to drizzle over the soup, and freshly grated Parmesan or pecorino cheese, if you like.

CROSTINI
TUSCAN LIVER PÂTÉ

Some say that this is the original, 15th-century recipe for pâté from the Medici kitchens, and that it was then exported to France along with various other classic recipes, such as onion soup and ice cream. It is a delicious way to sharpen the appetite at the start of a meal. In Tuscany the word crostini traditionally refers to this pâté, as opposed to toasted bread with various toppings, which is what the word has come to mean in more recent times.

1 Put the olive oil and half the butter in a large pan and fry the vegetables over a medium heat for 15 minutes, or until soft.

2 Add the parsley, and the chicken and calf's livers. Stir well and add the dry white wine. Cook for 2 minutes, stirring, then add the diluted tomato paste.

3 Season to taste, then add 30ml/2 tbsp water, cover and simmer for 20 minutes, or until the livers are cooked.

4 Remove the pan from the heat, lift the livers out of the sauce and chop finely or process them in a food processor or blender until quite smooth.

5 Return the semi-puréed livers to the pan. Stir in the remaining butter and the capers. Heat through and remove from the heat, but keep warm.

6 Spread the bread generously with the liver topping and serve.

SERVES 4

45ml/3 tbsp olive oil
40g/1½oz unsalted butter
½ onion, finely chopped
1 carrot, finely chopped
1 celery stick, finely chopped
15ml/1 tbsp finely chopped parsley
1 chicken liver, trimmed
115g/4oz calf's liver, trimmed
30ml/2 tbsp dry white wine
25ml/1½ tbsp tomato paste, diluted in 60ml/4 tbsp hot water or stock
25g/1oz salted capers, rinsed and finely chopped
4 large or 8 small thin slices crusty white or brown bread
sea salt and ground black pepper

SERVES 4

8 slices casareccio-type bread or ciabatta, stale
4 beefsteak tomatoes, chopped
1 large red onion, chopped
1 large cucumber, chopped
a handful of fresh basil leaves, torn into pieces
extra virgin olive oil, to taste
red wine vinegar, to taste
sea salt and ground black pepper

LA PANZANELLA
TUSCAN BREAD AND TOMATO SALAD

This famous Tuscan salad has a substantial bread base with the addition of juicy ripe tomatoes, onions, cucumbers and basil to give it flavour and freshness. Served elegantly, in a pretty bowl or on a flat platter, this makes a wonderful appetizer and can be enlarged with the addition of flaked canned tuna in olive oil or cooked fish fillets to make a more filling meal. It is a rustic dish, perfect for hot summer days, and is a useful way of using up precious leftover bread, which needs to be coarse and crusty for this classic recipe.

1 Soak the bread in cold water for about 15 minutes, then squeeze the bread dry in a clean dish towel.

2 Mix the damp bread with the tomatoes, onion, cucumber and basil.

3 Dress the salad with with olive oil, vinegar and salt and pepper to taste.

4 Toss the salad ingredients together thoroughly and leave it to stand for about 30 minutes before serving.

FICATTOLE
TUSCAN BREAD FRITTERS

These simple and delicious little bread-dough fritters appear all over Tuscany under various different names, but the basic principle is always the same: just flour, salt, water and yeast are needed to make them, and plenty of hot olive oil for deep-frying them until they are crispy and golden brown. Perfect as a little snack, they are usually served with an antipasto platter as an alternative to ordinary bread. You might also come across them under the name of panzanelle, frittelle di pane, crescentine or many other locally used names. In some parts of Tuscany cooks add herbs such as fresh basil to the dough to add extra flavour. Serve them piping hot with cured meats such as salami, mortadella or prosciutto.

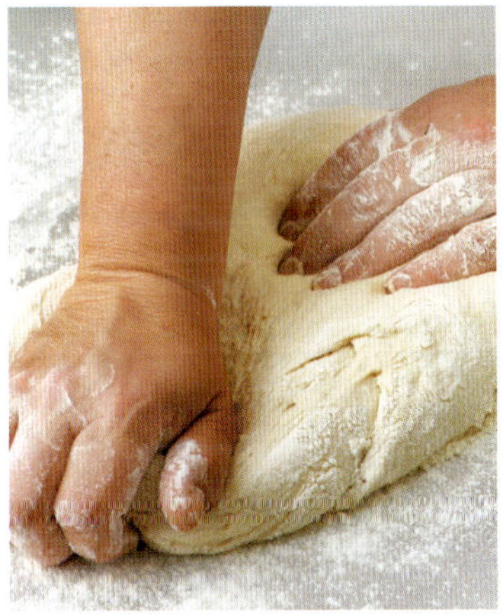

SERVES 4

300g/11oz/2⅔ cups plain/ all-purpose flour, plus extra for dusting
30g/1¼oz fresh/compressed yeast
120ml/4fl oz/½ cup warm water
300ml/½ pint/1¼ cups cold water
olive oil and sunflower oil mixed, for deep-frying (see Cook's Tips)
sea salt

COOK'S TIPS

- Do make sure the oil is really hot before you start to deep-fry the fritters or they won't cook properly and will be fairly stodgy and very oily once cooked.
- On this occasion the perfect oil for deep-frying is olive oil (but not extra virgin olive oil), mixed approximately half and half with a seed oil such as sunflower. Alternatively you could just use whichever vegetable oil you have, such as rapeseed/canola oil.

1 Put the flour on to the work surface in a mound and make a hollow in the middle with your fist.

2 Mix the yeast with the warm water and a pinch of salt in a small bowl and stir until dissolved.

3 Pour the yeast mixture into the hollow and work it into the flour, adding enough of the cold water as necessary to produce a smooth dough.

4 Knead the dough for 10 minutes, or until it is soft and spongy. Put the ball of dough into a lightly oiled bowl and cover with oiled clear film or plastic wrap.

5 Leave the dough to rise in a warm place for about 1 hour, or until it has doubled in size.

6 Knock back or punch down the dough and roll it out on a floured surface until it is about 2.5cm/1in thick. Cut into finger-sized strips.

7 Heat the olive and sunflower oils in a deep-fryer or large, deep pan until a small piece of dough, dropped into the oil, sizzles instantly.

8 Fry the fritters, in batches, for 2–3 minutes, or until they are golden brown.

9 Remove the fritters carefully from the oil using a slotted spoon. Drain them well on kitchen paper and sprinkle with salt. Serve immediately.

MALTAGLIATI AL SUGO DI CINGHIALE ALL'ARETINA

WILD BOAR MALTAGLIATI IN THE AREZZO STYLE

Tuscany can stake a claim to just two different pasta shapes: pappardelle and maltagliati. Neighbouring Emilia Romagna is the most important region in the entire country when it comes to fresh pasta and its traditions, notably tagliatelle, ravioli and tortellini. In a gesture of typical Tuscan defiance, making pasta that is so obviously big and substantial, devoid of unnecessary ornament and, in the case of the maltagliati, cut roughly into rectangles, is testament to the ongoing feuding between the two areas. When it comes to food, Tuscany has to make a point of showing off. Cinghiale (wild boar) is one of the most iconic of all the Tuscan specialities, and has a wonderful flavour.

SERVES 6

60ml/4 tbsp olive oil
1 onion, finely chopped
1 carrot, finely chopped
1 celery stick, finely chopped
115g/4oz prosciutto crudo, coarsely chopped
450g/1lb wild boar stewing meat, cubed
300ml/½ pint/1¼ cups full-bodied red wine
75ml/5 tbsp tomato paste diluted with 90ml/6 tbsp hot game or beef stock
275g/10oz canned tomatoes, strained
large pinch of fennel seeds
small pinch of ground cumin or cumin seed
450g/1lb maltagliati
sea salt and ground black pepper
freshly grated Parmesan cheese, to serve (optional)

1 Put the olive oil in a pan and fry the vegetables and prosciutto gently for 5 minutes, or until the onion is translucent.

2 Add the cubes of boar. Cook until browned all over, then pour over the wine and add seasoning. Cover and simmer for 1 hour.

3 Add half the diluted tomato paste and half the strained canned tomatoes to the meat and vegetable mixture. Cook for 1 hour more.

4 Add the remaining tomato paste and tomatoes. When the meat is falling apart, stir in the fennel seeds and cumin. Cover and simmer for a further 1 hour. Adjust the seasoning to taste as necessary.

5 Bring a large pan of salted water to the boil, add the maltagliati, stir and then return to the boil. Cook the pasta according to the packet instructions, until it is al dente. Drain and return it to the pan.

6 Add the wild boar sauce to the pasta. Mix it through gently and transfer to a serving platter or individual plates to serve. Offer Parmesan cheese separately.

SERVES 6

1kg/2¼lb dried chickpeas, soaked overnight and drained
2 celery sticks
2 carrots
2 onions, peeled and halved
4 garlic cloves
2 x 15cm/6in sprigs fresh rosemary
450g/1lb short ribbed pasta, such as ditalini
sea salt and ground black pepper
extra virgin olive oil, to serve

PASTA E CECI
PASTA AND CHICKPEAS

This simple, thick pasta soup, comprised of the very cheapest of ingredients, is made all over Italy with few variations on the central theme. It is intended to be a satisfying, cheap, nourishing and tasty soup that relies on the addition of other available ingredients to enrich and improve on the basic recipe. You could easily, for example, use rich chicken or meat stock instead of water if you like, or add some meaty bones to the simmering soup, or you could may choose to include other vegetables, such as shredded cabbage, ripe tomatoes or chopped courgettes, towards the end of cooking. Very much the same recipe can be used and adapted if you are making a basic pasta e fagioli (pasta and beans) or pasta e lenticchie (pasta and lentils).

1 Rinse the drained chickpeas. Put them in a large pan and cover with plenty of cold water. Bring to the boil and boil hard for 5 minutes, then drain and rinse again.

2 Return the chickpeas to the pan, cover with fresh water and add the vegetables and rosemary sprigs. Bring to the boil and simmer gently for 45 minutes. Remove and discard the vegetables.

3 Whiz one-third of the chickpeas until smooth, then return to the pan. Stir, season and simmer for 20 minutes.

4 Cook the pasta in a pan of salted boiling water until almost tender. Drain, stir it into the chickpeas, then boil everything for about a minute, stirring gently. Adjust the seasoning, and serve. Offer olive oil to diners to drizzle over their soup.

GNOCCHI DI POLENTA
POLENTA GNOCCHI

This is a tremendously substantial dish, which is perfect for cold, damp winter Tuscan days. It is a real rib-sticker, so if you decide to serve it make sure the next course is light. Polenta, like pasta, is hearty and sustaining, and it is an inexpensive way to satisfy hungry stomachs. The pork and porcini sauce can also be used to dress pasta or even as a risotto base.

SERVES 4

50g/2oz/1 cup dried porcini mushrooms
1 large onion, thinly sliced
115g/4oz/½ cup unsalted butter, plus extra for greasing
50ml/2fl oz/¼ cup olive oil
275g/10oz stewing pork, cubed
15ml/1 tbsp tomato paste
300ml/½ pint/1¼ cups pork or chicken stock
450g/1lb polenta flour
75ml/5 tbsp freshly grated Parmesan cheese
sea salt

1 Put the mushrooms in a bowl and cover with warm water. Allow them to soak for about 15 minutes. Meanwhile, fry the onion in half the butter and the oil for 5 minutes, or until softened.

2 Add the stewing pork and stir thoroughly to brown the meat all over. Stir the tomato paste into the stock, then pour into the pan. Drain the mushrooms and chop them coarsely. Add them to the pan, stir and simmer for 20 minutes.

3 Meanwhile, bring 2 litres/3½ pints/9 cups water in a pan to the boil and add a pinch of salt. Trickle the polenta flour into the water in a steady stream, whisking constantly.

4 Turn the heat to medium-low. Using a strong wooden spoon, stir the polenta constantly for 45 minutes, until it comes away from the sides of the pan. Turn out on to a board and leave to cool enough to set slightly.

5 Preheat the oven to 190°C/375°C/Gas 5. Butter a large ovenproof dish. Using a tablespoon dipped into cold water, scoop the polenta into balls and use to line the base of the dish. Cover with a little of the pork, dot with some of the butter and sprinkle with Parmesan.

6 Continue layering the polenta, meat, butter and cheese. Finish with polenta coated in butter and cheese. Bake for 20 minutes. Serve.

MALFATTI
SPINACH AND BREAD GNOCCHI

The word malfatti means 'badly made', so in other words they can look quite roughly shaped, without too much concern for elegant presentation. There is another version of this dish, which uses ricotta cheese as an ingredient as well as the spinach, but the version given here is reputedly the much older recipe from the Medici kitchens. Malfatti are traditionally served simply with melted, warm, unsalted butter, but they can also be accompanied by a basic tomato sauce. The recipe, in very similar forms, exists in various parts of the country, including the Veneto, but this is the most classically Tuscan version.

SERVES 6

1.3kg/3lb fresh spinach
2 eggs, beaten
2 egg yolks
30ml/2 tbsp single/light cream
150g/5oz stale bread, soaked in milk to cover for ½ hour
150g/5oz/1½ cups freshly grated Parmesan cheese
1.5ml/¼ tsp freshly grated nutmeg
up to 75ml/5 tbsp plain/all-purpose flour
115g/4oz/10 tbsp unsalted butter, melted
sea salt and ground black pepper

1 Steam or boil the spinach for 1–2 minutes until soft. Drain and leave to cool. Squeeze out the water, then chop finely.

2 Put the spinach in a large bowl and stir in the eggs and egg yolks, then the cream.

3 Squeeze the bread dry with your hands, then mix it into the spinach with half the Parmesan. Season to taste with nutmeg, salt and pepper. Bring a large pan of water to the boil.

4 Using your fingers and a very light touch (see Cook's Tip), form the mixture into small dumplings, using a small amount of flour to prevent sticking.

5 Transfer the dumplings carefully, in small batches, into the boiling water. Cook the gnocchi for no more than 2–3 minutes – they will be ready when they float freely on the surface of the water.

6 Carefully remove the cooked gnocchi from the water using a slotted spoon and arrange them on a warmed serving dish. Continue in this way, with the remaining batches, until all the gnocchi are cooked.

7 Smother the gnocchi with the melted butter, sprinkle over the remaining Parmesan cheese and serve immediately.

COOK'S TIP

One way to achieve lightness when shaping the gnocchi, is to roll each ball of dough around a glass tumbler, dusted inside with flour. This way, you will prevent the gnocchi from becoming too solid and avoid squashing the air out.

RISOTTO AL CHIANTI
RISOTTO WITH CHIANTI

Although risotto is not a typical dish of this region, there is a small area of rice production near the small town of Pontedera – where the world-famous factory of Piaggio is situated, home of the Vespa scooter and the remarkable three-wheeled Ape agricultural vehicle – so a few rice recipes do exist. This one is for a classic risotto, and uses the red wine of the Chianti area to reiterate its Tuscan authenticity. Sage is the herb of choice, but since rosemary is a common herb of this region, you could use that instead if you like.

1 Fry the red onion and celery with half the butter and the sage for 5 minutes, or until soft and translucent.

2 Add the rice and stir until all the grains are toasted, opaque and crackling hot. Do not let the rice or vegetables brown. Add about 150ml/¼ pint/⅗ cup red wine. Stir for 2 minutes, or until the wine has been absorbed and the alcohol has evaporated (the smell will change when this has occurred). Gradually add the rest of the wine, stirring constantly.

3 Start adding the hot stock, a ladleful at a time, stirring constantly and allowing the liquid to be absorbed before adding more.

4 When the risotto is creamy and velvety, but the rice grains are still firm to the bite, remove the pan from the heat and stir in the remaining butter and the Parmesan cheese. Season to taste and cover with a lid.

5 Leave to stand for 3–4 minutes, then stir once more and transfer to a warmed platter to serve.

SERVES 4

- 1 red onion, finely chopped
- ½ celery stick, finely chopped
- 75g/3oz/6 tbsp unsalted butter
- 3 fresh sage leaves, finely chopped
- 200g/7oz/1 cup arborio rice
- 750ml/1¼ pints/3 cups full-bodied Chianti red wine
- about 550ml/18fl oz/2½ cups simmering beef, chicken or vegetable stock
- 50g/2oz/⅔ cup freshly grated Parmesan cheese
- sea salt and ground black pepper

COOK'S TIP

Keep an eye on your risotto in the last stages of cooking, since arborio rice has a tendency to overcook extremely quickly, and become mushy in a flash.

SERVES 6

½ onion
12 small red mullet, scaled, cleaned and gutted
30–45ml/2–3 tbsp plain/all-purpose flour
75ml/5 tbsp olive oil
250ml/8fl oz/1 cup dry white wine
1 garlic clove, chopped
1 bay leaf
a handful of fresh flat leaf parsley leaves, chopped
400g/14oz canned tomatoes, strained and chopped
sea salt and ground black pepper

TRIGLIE ALLA LIVORNESE

RED MULLET IN THE STYLE OF LIVORNO

The ancient port city of Livorno – Leghorn in English – is renowned for two fish specialities. One of these is the dense fish stew or soup called cacciucco, the other is this recipe for cooking sweet red mullet. The smaller the mullet, the better the flavour, but they are quite bony, so some people prefer to use large fillets rather than the whole fish – although the purists will claim that the flavour is nowhere near as delicious. It is particularly tasty if the fish is freshly caught.

1 Finely chop the onion. Dry the fish with kitchen paper and coat them with flour.

2 Heat the oil in a frying pan and fry the mullet for about 4 minutes.

3 Turn the fish over carefully, without breaking them, then add the wine, chopped onion, garlic, bay leaf, parsley and a little salt and pepper.

4 Shake the pan, then spoon the flavouring ingredients over the fish.

5 Allow the alcohol from the wine to evaporate for 1–2 minutes, then add the canned tomatoes.

6 Cover the pan with a lid and simmer the liquid gently for a further 5 minutes, until the fish is cooked. Serve immediately.

SERVES 4

2–3 stale crusty white bread rolls, crusts removed
about 120ml/4fl oz/½ cup milk
40 fresh sardines or large anchovies, scaled and filleted
3 eggs, beaten
45ml/3 tbsp freshly grated Parmesan cheese
2 garlic cloves, chopped
a handful of fresh flat leaf parsley, leaves chopped
1 dried red chilli
about 90ml/6 tbsp plain/all-purpose flour
about 2 litres/3½ pints/9 cups sunflower oil, for deep-frying
sea salt

SARDINE RIPIENE
STUFFED SARDINES

This delicious Tuscan recipe for fresh sardines or plump, overgrown anchovies could not be simpler and relies very much on the fish being freshly caught. Like many recipes from this region, the ingredients are quite generous and call for about 10 fish per person, although you may prefer to reduce the quantities slightly. Once the fish have been filleted, any that have been damaged in the process are added to the bread filling. To remove the scales without them flying all over the kitchen, local cooks use a piece of newspaper – or yellow kitchen paper as found locally – soaked in water, to rub vigorously over the fish. They can be served just as they are, with a wedge of lemon, or with a basic tomato sauce flavoured with a pinch of ground fennel seeds.

1 Soak the bread in the milk to cover, then squeeze dry. Use any damaged fish fillets for the filling. Put all the perfectly shaped fillets to one side.

2 Mix the bread with the damaged fish, half the beaten eggs, the grated Parmesan cheese, garlic, parsley, chilli and a pinch of salt. Blend it all together to make a firm paste with your hands or a fork.

3 Sandwich two fillets together with a generous spoonful of the filling in the middle, then gently coat in the remaining beaten egg and then the flour. Repeat for the remaining fillets.

4 Heat the oil in large pan until sizzling, then fry the fish, in batches, until crisp and golden brown; about 2 minutes. Drain on kitchen paper and serve.

SGOMBRI AL FINOCCHIELLO
MACKEREL WITH WILD FENNEL

Le Marche is a coastal region and fish plays an important part of the daily diet in the towns and villages that dot the shoreline. Fishermen and their families generally eat their smaller catch, often salted to preserve it for longer, and sell the larger and more profitable fish. Although mackerel isn't considered to be a much sought-after fish, it tastes superb when cooked with care and with some thoughtfully chosen ingredients, such as fennel.

SERVES 4

1.2kg/2½lb fresh mackerel, cleaned
45ml/3 tbsp olive oil
6 small onions or shallots, chopped
4 carrots, chopped
1 large celery stick, chopped
a small handful of wild fennel fronds, chopped (see Cook's Tips)
a small bunch of fresh flat leaf parsley, leaves chopped
1 garlic clove, chopped
5cm/2in piece of unwaxed orange peel, chopped
juice of ½ orange
15ml/1 tbsp tomato paste diluted with 15ml/1 tbsp hot water or stock (see Cook's Tips)
sea salt and ground black pepper

1 Boil the mackerel in lightly salted water until cooked through (see Cook's Tips). Gently remove the cooked fish from the pan and fillet them carefully. Discard the bones, head and skin.

2 Put the oil in a large pan and gently fry the onions or shallots, carrots, celery, fennel, parsley, garlic and orange peel for about 10 minutes. Season with salt and pepper.

3 Add the orange juice. Stir and reduce the heat to low. Simmer, stirring frequently, for 15 minutes.

4 Stir in the tomato paste. Cook for a further 15 minutes, until the sauce has thickened.

5 Arrange the fish on a serving platter and pour over the sauce. Serve immediately, or chill to serve cold.

COOK'S TIPS

- To calculate the cooking time for boiling the fish, measure the thickest part and calculate 10 minutes per 2.5cm/1in.
- Save some of the water in which the mackerel was cooked to use as fish stock for diluting the tomato paste.

CACCIUCCO
TUSCAN FISH STEW

The story behind this Tuscan fish stew from Livorno concerns a fisherman's wife whose husband was lost at sea during a storm. Left alone with many children to feed, she spent the little money she had to buy fish for a soup called cacciucco, adding to the fish the few basic ingredients she had in her kitchen. So successful was the recipe that she managed to find work as a cook. To commemorate her, the soup is kept simple. Although it may vary slightly, it must contain at least five varieties of fresh fish, one for each of the 'C's in the recipe's name.

SERVES 6 TO 8

1.8kg/4lb assorted fish in varying sizes including some of the following: hake, monkfish, whiting, scorpion fish, moray eel, conger eel, John Dory, cleaned and gutted
450g/1lb octopus and cuttlefish or squid, cleaned
150ml/¼ pint/⅔ cup extra virgin olive oil
1 onion, chopped
1 carrot, chopped
1 celery stick, chopped
a handful of fresh flat leaf parsley leaves, finely chopped
1 dried red chilli, finely chopped
4 garlic cloves, 3 chopped and 1 halved
250ml/8fl oz/1 cup dry white wine
900g/2lb ripe tomatoes, peeled (see page 304), seeded and coarsely chopped
12 large raw prawns/shrimp, peeled and deveined
15 small, thin slices crusty bread
sea salt and ground black pepper
about 1 litre/1¾ pints/4 cups simmering fish or vegetable stock, for basting and diluting

1 Cut the larger fish into generous pieces and leave the smaller ones whole. Keep all the heads, if removed, and set them aside. Cut the octopus and cuttlefish or squid into large pieces.

2 Put the oil in a large frying pan and fry the onion, carrot, celery, parsley, chilli and chopped garlic for 10 minutes, or until lightly golden.

3 Add the octopus and squid to the pan and cook for 2–3 minutes, or until they have released their fluid and it has been evaporated. Pour over the white wine. Cook for 2 minutes, until the alcohol has evaporated, then add the tomatoes. Stir and cover.

4 Simmer for 45 minutes, or until the squid and octopus are tender, then remove them and set aside. Add the fish heads and smaller fish to the pan and stir. Cook for about 25 minutes, basting occasionally with a little hot water or stock.

5 Pass the sauce and fish through the medium blade of a food mill (mouli) and return to the pan. You should have a smooth, thick sauce. If it is too thick, dilute with a little hot water or stock.

6 Add the larger whole fish and pieces of fish to the pan and stir gently to coat with the sauce. Simmer together very gently for about 20 minutes.

7 Return the octopus and squid to the pan, and stir into the sauce. Add the prawns and cover with sauce, using more stock if necessary. Cook for about 15 minutes, until all the seafood is tender.

8 Toast the bread and rub with the halved garlic clove. Line the sides of a large bowl with the toast.

9 Raise the heat under the pan and stir the fish and sauce together while it returns to the boil. Season to taste with salt and pepper. Immediately, remove the pan from the heat and transfer the cacciucco to the bowl lined with toasted bread. Serve immediately.

SCAVECCIO
MARINATED EELS

In the many ditches, rivers and slow-moving streams of the Tuscan plains, eels are caught and turned into delicious, simple dishes for the table. This is a very old recipe from the Pisa area, and is served cold as part of an antipasto. After 48 hours in the marinade, the strong, slightly muddy flavour of the eel is much reduced and the vinegar acts as a good foil to the natural oiliness of the fish.

1 Clean the outside of the eels carefully to remove all trace of slime, using coarse sea salt or gritty wood ash. Split and gut them, then wash and dry them all over. Cut them into finger-length chunks.

2 Heat the oil in a frying pan and fry the eel chunks until golden brown all over. Remove them with a slotted spoon and drain on kitchen paper. Place in a bowl to cool.

3 Using the same oil, fry the garlic, chilli, sage and rosemary together for 3 minutes.

4 Add the white wine vinegar to the frying pan and then boil to reduce by about one-third. Season with salt.

5 Pour this marinade over the eels and cover the bowl. Leave to marinate for about 48 hours before serving.

SERVES 4

900g/2lb very fresh eels
coarse sea salt, for cleaning
150ml/¼ pint/⅔ cup extra virgin olive oil
3 garlic cloves
1 dried red chilli
3 fresh sage leaves
1 rosemary sprig
300ml/½ pint/1¼ cups white wine vinegar
sea salt

SERVES 6

800g/1¾lb tiny octopuses or squid
100ml/3½fl oz/scant ½ cup extra virgin olive oil
2 garlic cloves, chopped
a handful of fresh flat leaf parsley leaves, chopped
sea salt and ground black pepper

POLPO IN GALERA
JAILED OCTOPUS

The deliciously sweet taste of octopus makes it a much sought-after ingredient and there are countless recipes all over Italy for this cephalopod. The name of this recipe has arisen because the octopus is traditionally cooked in a tightly sealed pot until tender and moist – the lid of the pot is never removed to stir the dish while it is cooking. It is important to use small octopuses or, if you can find them, small squid, as they are much less tough than larger specimens and will tenderise more quickly without needing to be bashed before cooking.

1 Clean the octopuses or squid carefully, removing eyes, beaks and bladders. Wash thoroughly in salted water. Peel and cut into small chunks.

2 Put the oil in a large pan and fry the garlic over a low heat for 5 minutes, or until soft.

3 Add the octopuses or squid. Season with salt and pepper, and cover with a lid.

4 Simmer for 30 minutes, or until tender, shaking the pan from time to time to prevent sticking. Add the fresh parsley and serve piping hot.

SERVES 4

1.5kg/3¼lb beef brisket in a single piece
2–3 garlic cloves, cut into long strips
50g/2oz fatty pancetta, chopped
75g/3oz/6 tbsp unsalted butter
1 onion, chopped
1 carrot, chopped
1 celery stick, chopped
1 litre/1¾ pints/4 cups simmering beef stock
15ml/1 tbsp tomato paste
sea salt and ground black pepper

STRACOTTO ALLA TOSCANA
TUSCAN POT ROAST

This hearty pot roast is delicious served with plenty of red wine, and is often brought to the table with polenta or mashed potatoes as an accompaniment. It is cooked over an extremely low heat for about 6 hours, which gives wonderfully tender beef and a rich stock with which to make a thick and tasty sauce.

1 Pierce the meat all over with the point of a sharp knife and insert strips of garlic to taste, depending on how much you like garlic or the size of the cloves.

2 Put a large flameproof casserole over medium heat and add the pancetta, butter, onion, carrot and celery. Fry together for about 8 minutes, stirring constantly.

3 Add the meat and seal it on all sides.

4 Pour over about 300ml/½ pint/1¼ cups stock, season with salt and pepper and stir in the tomato paste.

5 Cover and simmer over a very low heat for about 6 hours, adding more stock occasionally to prevent it from drying out.

6 When the meat is tender and cooked through, remove it from the casserole and set it aside to keep warm.

7 Rub the vegetables and stock left in the casserole through a sieve or strainer or food mill, and season to taste.

8 Slice the meat thickly and arrange it on a warmed platter. Pour over the smooth sauce and serve.

BISTECCA ALLA FIORENTINA
FLORENTINE T-BONE STEAK

This recipe is an iconic symbol of Florentine gastronomy. A huge, luscious, rare and tender steak of Chianina beef, grilled over a scented wood fire and dressed simply with oil, rosemary, garlic and salt and pepper (unless you are a real purist, see below), the fire and the wood used to cook this superb meat is actually one of the most important ingredients for the success of the dish. Many people gasp at the sight of the thickness and size of the steaks, but they are meant to be for sharing, and accompanied with just a green salad and some Tuscan bread. Once washed down with a good bottle of Chianti, the beauty of this very Tuscan eating experience becomes obvious.

SERVES 2

3–4 rosemary sprigs
3–4 garlic cloves
30–45ml/2–3 tbsp extra virgin olive oil
1 T-bone steak, about 675g/1½lb
sea salt and ground black pepper
salad and bread, to serve

1 Combine the picked leaves from the rosemary, the garlic, a good pinch of salt and pepper and the oil in a bowl.

2 Place the steak in a flat dish, then add the marinade ingredients. Stir to mix, then leave to marinate for 24–48 hours.

3 Light the barbecue and, when the flames have died down, position a griddle rack over the hot coals. Cook the steak to taste. Alternatively, preheat a griddle pan on a stove set to high, until it is smoking hot, then cook the steak to taste. Serve with salad and bread.

COOK'S TIP

Traditionally, the plain steak would be cooked in front of a fire on a long fork with its end stuck in the ground, so all the fat from the meat would run down the fork. It would then be served very, very rare and just seasoned to taste with salt and ground black pepper.

SALSICCE ALL'UVA
PORK SAUSAGES WITH GRAPES

In the early autumn, when grapes are plentiful, they make a delicious combination of flavours when fried in a pan with rich pork sausages. If the pig has been recently killed for the celebration of a local festivity, as well as to put away cured meat for the cold winter ahead, the sausages will be fresh and tender. Big, sweet, thick-skinned and firm, white grapes are best for this dish, which is like the hot-weather version of sausages with beans or lentils. However, a mixture of white and red grapes will add colour, so choose which you'd prefer. Serve with roast potatoes and a green salad, if you like.

SERVES 4

8 plump Italian sausages
10ml/2 tsp olive oil
30ml/2 tbsp water
8 handfuls firm grapes
roast potatoes and a green salad, to serve (optional)

1 Prick the sausages all over with a knife to allow the fat to run and the heat to permeate the sausage.

2 Put the oil and water in a large frying pan over a medium heat for 2 minutes.

3 Lay the sausages in the pan. Cook gently, turning frequently, for 10 minutes, or until cooked through.

4 Add the grapes. Cook until slightly caramelised, then serve.

SERVES 6

30–45ml/2–3 tbsp fresh rosemary leaves, chopped, or 25ml/ 1½ tbsp dried rosemary
6 large garlic cloves, finely chopped
10ml/2 tsp ground black pepper
1.3kg/3lb pork loin, boned
45–60ml/3–4 tbsp olive oil
500ml/17fl oz/2¼ cups white wine
sea salt
peas and onions, to serve

COOK'S TIP

Although you can use dried rosemary for convenience, fresh rosemary leaves work better for this dish, as you can achieve a softer texture once the meat is cooked.

ARISTA DI MAIALE ALLA FIORENTINA
FLORENTINE ROAST PORK LOIN

This simple roast pork dish has a wonderful story behind it. It is an ancient Medici court recipe, from a banquet held in honour of the Greek Bishops who were journeying to Florence for the Ecumenical Council. As this was the first time the Greeks had journeyed this far, nobody was quite sure when they would arrive, so a dish had to be created that would last a few days and taste good either hot or cold. Lots of pepper, salt and garlic were used to preserve the meat as much as possible, while sweet-smelling rosemary was abundantly applied to add fragrance. When the Greeks arrived, they pronounced the meat 'Aristos!' which in ancient Greek means 'excellent', and so this tasty pork roast became known as arista for evermore and is still enjoyed on a regular basis.

1 Preheat the oven to 160°C/325°F/Gas 3. Mix the rosemary with the chopped garlic. Season with salt and the black pepper.

2 Take a skewer and make lots of deep holes in the joint of meat. Insert the rosemary mixture into the holes, pushing it inside the flesh. Tie the joint securely with kitchen string or twine and put it into a roasting pan.

3 Rub the meat all over with oil and season well. Roast, basting frequently with the pan juices and with the white wine, for about 2 hours, or until cooked through. Turn the meat over each time you baste.

4 Traditionally, the joint is served cold, but is equally good hot, with the pan juices and accompanied by peas and onions.

CINGHIALE ALLA CACCIATORA
WILD BOAR CACCIATORA

Cinghiale, or wild boar, is synonymous with Tuscan cuisine. In the forests and mountains of the entire region, this wild animal, closely related to the domestic pig but much stronger in flavour, has long been prized for its excellent meat. The hunting season opens in late October or early November, and the local hunters, accompanied by packs of special dogs, take great pride in seeking out these intelligent, fast-moving beasts. Serve with greens, such as spinach.

SERVES 6

45ml/3 tbsp extra virgin olive oil
2 onions, thickly sliced
2 celery sticks, thickly sliced
2 carrots, thickly sliced
900g/2lb wild boar meat
about 500ml/17fl oz/2¼ cups dry red wine
1 large rosemary sprig
wilted spinach, to serve (optional)

FOR THE CACCIATORA SAUCE

75ml/5 tbsp extra virgin olive oil
1 garlic clove, crushed
½ large onion, chopped
1 dried red chilli
300ml/½ pint/1¼ cups basic tomato sauce (see page 20)
sea salt

COOK'S TIP

The cooking time for the meat will largely depend upon the age of the wild boar – the older the animal, the tougher and stringier the meat will be and the longer it will need to be cooked.

1 Put the oil in a large pan and fry the onions, celery and carrots for 10–15 minutes, or until well browned.

2 Meanwhile, cut the wild boar into large chunks and place in a deep bowl.

3 Pour in the wine and add the rosemary and then the vegetables. The wine should cover the meat completely; add more wine if necessary and mix everything together with your hands. Leave to marinate overnight.

4 Drain and dry the meat, reserving the marinade. In a wide, preferably non-stick, pan, brown all the meat so that it releases its juices.

5 Once the meat has released its liquid, remove and set it aside. Discard the liquid left in the pan.

6 To make the cacciatora sauce, add the oil to the pan with the garlic, onion and chilli. Fry together for 5 minutes, stirring, then pour over the tomato sauce. Season with salt and simmer gently for 10 minutes.

7 Add the meat and the marinade vegetables to the sauce. Lower the heat, cover and simmer, stirring occasionally, for 1 hour, until tender. Add more of the marinade if the meat appears to be drying out.

8 Serve with wilted spinach, if you like.

CONIGLIO ALLA TOSCANA
TUSCAN RABBIT CASSEROLE

Rabbit is a much-loved and respected meat in most parts of Italy, but perhaps especially in Tuscany, where every smallholding, farm or country home will have a few chickens and some rabbits kept for eating purposes in the back garden. Rabbit is lean and tasty, and at least 50 or so well-known recipes exist that are frequently and lovingly cooked in order to enjoy this delicious meat. This is a truly ancient recipe, apparently dating back to the time of the Etruscans, and is a thoroughly tried-and-tested way of cooking rabbit, although the method also works with jointed chicken. Serve with polenta or roast potatoes.

1 Put the rabbit joints into a bowl. Mix the wine vinegar with 600ml/1 pint/2½ cups water and pour over the rabbit. Soak for 1 hour.

2 Drain the rabbit joints and dry them carefully on kitchen paper. Chop half the garlic cloves and one rosemary sprig and mix them with the salt and pepper. Rub this mixture all over the rabbit joints.

3 Chop the remaining garlic. Heat the oil in a large pan and add the garlic and remaining rosemary. Fry the rabbit joints all over until brown. Add the red wine gradually, so that it simmers constantly.

4 Stir in the tomato paste and 300ml/½ pint/1¼ cups hot water. Cover and simmer gently for 45 minutes, or until cooked through. Serve.

SERVES 8 TO 10

- 2 rabbits, about 900g/2lb each, each cut into five pieces
- 90ml/6 tbsp strong red or white wine vinegar
- 6 garlic cloves
- 3 large rosemary sprigs
- 2.5ml/½ tsp sea salt
- 2.5ml/½ tsp ground black pepper
- 75ml/2½fl oz/⅓ cup olive oil
- 750ml/1¼ pints/3 cups red wine
- 15ml/1 tbsp tomato paste
- polenta (see page 204) or roast potatoes, to serve

SERVES 4

1.2kg/2½lb fresh peas in their pods, or 450g/1lb shelled peas
100ml/3½fl oz/scant ½ cup olive oil
1 onion, thinly sliced
2.5ml/½ tsp caster/superfine sugar
sea salt and ground black pepper

VARIATION

Fry a little chopped pancetta or fatty prosciutto crudo with the onion, if you like.

PISELLI ALL'OLIO
PEAS COOKED IN OLIVE OIL

Peas cooked in this way can be added to a delicious frittata, or mixed with a little warmed cream to dress pasta, with just a sprinkling of freshly grated Parmesan cheese and black pepper to finish it off. The peas are soaked first, which means that they soften without cooking, and their natural sweetness develops perfectly. If you use an attractive pan you can serve the peas in it.

1 Soak the peas in cold water for 1 hour.

2 Meanwhile, put the oil in a flameproof casserole or heavy pan and add the sliced onion. Fry the onion over a low heat for about 10 minutes, or until it has softened and turned golden brown in colour.

3 Drain the peas and add to the onion. Add the sugar, season with salt and pepper, then cover and cook gently until soft and cooked through. The timing will depend on how large or small the peas are: tiny ones will take about 4 minutes; larger, fat peas with tougher skins could take up to 15 minutes.

SERVES 4

45–60ml/3–4 tbsp olive oil
3 cloves garlic, crushed
2 or 3 leaves fresh sage
400g/14oz can cannellini beans, drained
200g/7oz canned tomatoes, strained
sea salt and ground black pepper

FAGIOLI ALL'UCCELLETTO
STEWED BEANS

Tuscans love their beans, and this recipe is a real classic, one you will find all year all over the region, but especially in and around Florence. Delicious hot or cold, this recipe can be served on its own or as part of another dish, for example on top of toasted bread as crostini or alongside meat or fish dishes. It is a very adaptable bean dish that can be made with canned or dried beans, or fresh beans when they are in season. If using dried beans, soak them overnight in cold water, boil hard in fresh water for 5 minutes, then rinse and use as fresh. Sometimes fagioli all'uccelletto is made with rosemary instead of sage, though the sage gives a more subtle flavour.

1 Put the oil in a pan and gently fry the garlic and sage.

2 When the oil is golden brown, add the beans and season with a pinch of ground black pepper.

3 Stir the mixture together thoroughly, then add the strained tomatoes. Simmer gently for a further 20 minutes.

4 Check and adjust the seasoning to taste, then serve.

SERVES 4

7.5ml/1½ tsp fennel seeds
450g/1lb green beans, trimmed
75ml/5 tbsp olive oil
1 large red onion, thinly sliced
20ml/4 tsp tomato paste diluted in 60ml/4 tbsp hot water
sea salt and ground black pepper

FAGIOLINI ALLA FIORENTINA
GREEN BEANS IN THE FLORENTINE STYLE

This is a sure-fire way to liven up green beans. Even frozen green beans, which are rarely tasty, take on a new lease of life with this very simple Florentine recipe. For this dish, Florentine cooks use the dried fennel seed that is so popular in local recipes and in many culinary specialities, including the huge soft salame known locally as finocchiona, which is so soft that it is almost spreadable, and has a strong fennel flavour. Like so many of these kinds of stewed vegetable dishes that are popular all over Italy, the beans are allowed to cook until they are really soft and have absorbed as much as possible of the surrounding flavours – the perfect accompaniment to some sausages or meat.

1 Crush the fennel seeds to a powder in a spice grinder or using a mortar and pestle.

2 Boil the beans in a pan of lightly salted water until tender. Meanwhile, heat the oil in a large frying pan, add the onion and fry until soft.

3 Stir in the diluted tomato paste and the crushed fennel seeds.

4 Drain the beans thoroughly and toss them into the pan. Mix well and season to taste. Cover the pan and cook through for 10–15 minutes more, then serve.

ZUCCHINI FRITTI
DEEP-FRIED COURGETTES

This is a recipe from Tuscany, although other versions of the same dish exist more or less all over the country. It can be made with courgette flowers, if they are available, but using thin slices of courgette is much simpler and tastes delicious. If you do choose to use flowers, check them on the inside for insects before proceeding, and remove the pistil, which will taste bitter.

1 Cut the courgettes into thin strips with a vegetable peeler or mandolin.

2 In a bowl, beat together the egg yolk, flour and milk, or mixed milk and water, to make a smooth paste. Put the egg white into a clean, grease-free bowl and whisk until stiff. Gently fold into the batter.

3 Carefully dip the courgettes into the batter to coat thoroughly.

4 Heat the oil in a wide, deep pan until a cube of bread dropped into it sizzles at once.

5 Carefully lower the courgette strips into the hot oil and deep-fry for 4 minutes, or until crisp and golden all over, turning frequently. (If they take longer than this then the oil is not hot enough.)

6 Drain well on kitchen paper, sprinkle with a little salt and serve immediately.

SERVES 4

2 courgettes/zucchini
1 egg, separated
40g/1½oz/⅓ cup plain/all-purpose flour
150ml/¼ pint/⅔ cup milk, or milk mixed with water
600ml/1 pint/2½ cups sunflower oil, for deep-frying
sea salt

VARIATIONS

If using courgettes/zucchini flowers, you could try filling them before frying:

- For a punchy flavour, push a small piece of anchovy and a cube of mozzarella cheese into the middle of the flower.
- For a smooth, sweet taste that contrasts brilliantly with the crispy fried flower, use a spoonful of ricotta cheese.

SERVES 4

500g/1¼lb mixed wild or cultivated mushrooms
200g/7oz Parmesan cheese
a large handful of fresh flat leaf parsley leaves, finely chopped
juice of ½ lemon
extra virgin olive oil, to drizzle
sea salt and ground black pepper

INSALATA DI FUNGHI CRUDI
WILD MUSHROOM SALAD

This delicately flavoured salad makes the most of the special taste of raw mushrooms, and is traditionally made in Tuscany using fresh porcini or other wild mushrooms foraged locally. If you are picking wild mushrooms to make this salad, you must make sure that the mushrooms are edible, and also that they are safe to eat raw as some varieties do require cooking. You can also make the salad using cultivated mushrooms or field mushrooms, but the important thing to remember is that they need to be sliced as thinly as possible. The salad should be eaten soon after preparation, within half an hour at the most, so that the mushrooms don't shrivel up.

1 Clean and trim the mushrooms carefully. Do not wash them, but use a brush to clean off any traces of soil.

2 Once clean, slice the mushrooms very thinly. Shave the Parmesan cheese as thinly as possible.

3 Arrange the sliced mushrooms on a large platter, then sprinkle the chopped parsley and Parmesan shavings over the top.

4 Sprinkle the mushrooms with lemon juice, drizzle with oil and season. Serve within half an hour.

COOK'S TIP

Choose a mildly flavoured olive oil for drizzling over this salad, so that you do not overpower the mushrooms.

ZUCCOTTO
TUSCAN CREAM AND CHOCOLATE PUDDING

This delicious iced pudding is intended to look like the traditional helmet of a Tuscan mercenary going into battle, which in turn was named after a small, rounded pumpkin. It's not difficult to make; the most fiddly part is the stencilling at the end. If you prefer, just dust the whole thing with icing sugar, then lightly dust with cocoa powder. This is a great dessert to keep as a standby in the freezer. Divide the mixture in half and make two smaller bowls if you wish.

SERVES 6 TO 8

75g/3oz/½ cup hazelnuts
115g/4oz unsweetened cooking chocolate
ready-made basic sponge cake, preferably 25cm/10in
90ml/6 tbsp brandy
60ml/4 tbsp Amaretto di Saronno
1 litre/1¾ pints/4 cups double/heavy cream
75g/3oz/½ cup blanched almonds, coarsely chopped
30ml/2 tbsp plain/semisweet chocolate drops
30ml/2 tbsp chopped mixed crystallised/candied peel or glacé/candied fruits
150g/5oz/1¼ cups icing/confectioners' sugar, sifted, plus extra for dusting
30ml/2 tbsp unsweetened cocoa powder, for dusting

1 Lay the hazelnuts out on a baking sheet and toast them under a hot grill or broiler, turning occasionally, for about 5 minutes, or until golden. Hold a few hazelnuts at a time in a dish towel and rub off their skins. Cool and chop, then set aside.

2 Melt the cooking chocolate in a heatproof bowl over a pan of simmering water. Remove the bowl from the pan.

3 Take a large bowl and draw a circle slightly larger than its circumference on a sheet of stiff paper. Cut out the circle and set it aside. Line the bowl with foil.

4 Slice the cake into strips about 4cm/1½in wide, dip each strip in brandy, then in Amaretto, and press the strips against the sides of the bowl to line it. Set aside.

5 In a large bowl, whip the cream until stiff peaks form. Fold the hazelnuts, almonds, chocolate, mixed peel or glacé fruits, and sugar into the cream.

6 Transfer half the cream mixture to another bowl. Stir the melted chocolate into one half of the cream.

7 Spoon the white cream over the base and sides of the cake-lined bowl, then use the chocolate cream to fill the hollow in the middle. Level the top with a spatula. Place in the freezer for at least 3 hours.

8 Meanwhile, fold the circle of paper into eight and cut out four alternate sections.

9 Shortly before serving, turn the zuccotto out on to a platter. Remove the foil carefully, and, using a sieve or strainer, dust with the remaining icing sugar.

10 Lay the cut-out circle of paper on top of the zuccotto. Carefully hold it in place and dust it with the cocoa powder. Remove the paper carefully. You should now have alternate segments of brown and white, which is the traditional design. Serve the dessert immediately.

I CAVALLUCCI
TUSCAN HONEY COOKIES

The Italian name of these little cookies literally translates as 'little horses', as they were once made for the riders and stablehands of the famous horse race, known as Palio, which is run in Siena twice a year. Over the years, the cookies gradually became so popular that they are now almost as well known, and certainly as typical, as the famous panforte di Siena, the hard, spicy, fruit-laden flat cake that also originates from the town. These cookies are wonderfully chewy and strongly flavoured with aniseed, and are traditionally eaten around Christmas time. They are especially delicious served with strong coffee.

SERVES 8

115g/4oz/⅔ cup almonds
200g/7oz/1 cup caster/superfine sugar
115g/4oz/½ cup acacia honey
450g/1lb/4 cups plain/all-purpose flour, plus extra for dusting
115g/4oz/½ cup crystallised/candied citrus fruits, finely chopped
30ml/2 tbsp fennel seeds
a pinch each of ground cinnamon, freshly grated nutmeg and ground coriander
1.5ml/¼ tsp bicarbonate of soda/baking soda, or ammonium carbonate, if available
oil, for greasing

1 Blanch the almonds by soaking them in hot water for about 1 minute, then removing the skins. Alternatively, use ready-blanched almonds.

2 Lay the almonds out on a baking sheet and toast them under a hot grill or broiler, turning occasionally, for about 5 minutes, or until golden. Keep checking the almonds regularly as they burn easily. Chop the almonds coarsely.

3 Put the sugar and honey into a large, heavy pan and melt them together very slowly over a low heat, stirring occasionally.

4 When the mixture is hot enough to form a string as you lift up the spoon, very gradually mix in the flour, then the crystallised citrus fruits, fennel seeds, blanched almonds and spices. Stir in the bicarbonate of soda or ammonium carbonate.

5 Flour a work surface of baking sheet well, then spread the cookie dough mixture out on the floured surface to a thickness of about 1cm/½in, using a spatula dipped in water to help you spread it easily without sticking.

6 Leave the cookie mixture to cool completely. Once it is nearly cool, preheat the oven to 180°C/350°F/Gas 4.

7 Cut the cold cookie dough into rectangles and lay them carefully on a well-oiled baking sheet. Bake the cookies for 20 minutes, or until golden.

8 Remove from the oven, then cool the cookies on a wire rack. Store them in an airtight container for up to 1 week.

VARIATION

Although it is traditional to use acacia honey in this recipe, you could use another variety.

I RICCIARELLI
SOFT ALMOND SWEETMEATS

These delicately flavoured Tuscan soft almond sweetmeats can be bought in all good Italian food stores and are traditionally eaten at Christmas time. The bought versions are perfectly shaped, like large lozenges, and pure white in colour. This recipe for home-made ricciarelli gives you slightly less aesthetically faultless results, but they are delicious nonetheless and perfect with a glass of chilled, sweet, amber-coloured vin santo. It is customary to bake these on a host – a small piece of edible paper that forms the base and is eaten with the sweetmeat – but they can also be cooked directly on a sheet of baking parchment.

MAKES ABOUT 12

200g/7oz/generous 1 cup blanched almonds
115g/4oz/⅔ cup pine nuts
200g/7oz/1 cup caster/superfine sugar
5ml/1 tsp vanilla extract
2 egg whites
grated rind of ½ small unwaxed orange
115g/4oz/1 cup icing/confectioners' sugar, sifted

1 Pound the blanched almonds and the pine nuts together to make a fine powder using a mortar and pestle, or alternatively, pulse in a food processor.

2 Transfer into a bowl and add the caster sugar and vanilla. Mix thoroughly.

3 Put the egg whites into a clean, grease-free bowl and whisk into stiff peaks – you should be able to turn the bowl upside down and the egg whites remain inside.

4 Carefully fold the orange rind into the egg whites, then fold in the almond mixture.

5 Line a baking sheet with some baking parchment, then put heaped tablespoonfuls of the mixture on to the parchment, set well apart. Chill for about 6 hours.

6 Preheat the oven to 150°C/300°F/Gas 2. Bake the sweetmeats for 15 minutes. Cool on a wire rack and sprinkle generously with icing sugar before serving.

SERVES 8 TO 10

oil, for greasing
225g/8oz/1⅓ cups almonds
1kg/2¼lb plain/all-purpose flour, sifted
8 eggs, beaten
1kg/2¼lb/generous 5 cups caster/superfine sugar
10ml/2 tsp ammonium carbonate (see Cook's Tip)
pinch of salt

COOK'S TIP

The traditional raising agent is ammonium carbonate, but it is sometimes difficult to obtain. Bicarbonate of soda/baking soda will also work, giving the cookies just enough of a lift during baking.

CANTUCCI
TUSCAN HARD DUNKING COOKIES

Italians love to dunk things, and these cookies are made for being dunked into a glass of vin santo, Tuscany's favourite sweet dessert wine, or a cup of dark and fragrant espresso coffee, to make a simple but very satisfying dessert. Recently, these tasty little cookies have become hugely popular all over the world and a host of recipes exist for them, using all kinds of weird and wonderful ingredients, from pink peppercorns to hazelnut liqueur. This, however, is the more simple classic, much-loved recipe from their native Tuscany.

1 Preheat the oven to 150°C/300°F/Gas 2. Oil two baking sheets. Blanch the almonds by soaking them in hot water for about 1 minute, then removing the skins.

2 Lay the almonds out on a baking sheet and toast them under a hot grill or broiler, turning occasionally, for about 5 minutes, or until golden. Chop coarsely.

3 Put the flour on to a work surface and use your fist to make a hollow in the middle. Pour the eggs into the hollow. Add the sugar, ammonium carbonate or bicarbonate of soda, and salt. Mix together, then add the almonds.

4 Knead everything together thoroughly and shape the dough with your hands into several thick strips about 7.5cm/3in long, 6cm/2½in wide and 2.5cm/1in thick.

5 Slide the strips of dough on to the baking sheets and bake in the preheated oven for 10 minutes, or until golden.

6 Cut the strips into cookie-sized lengths, on the diagonal. Return them to the oven for a further 6 minutes, to crisp them.

7 Transfer the cookies to a wire rack and leave to cool. Store in an airtight container for up to 3 months.

LA TORTA DI RISO
SOFT TUSCAN RICE CAKE

It is the rich, eggy and sticky quality of this cake that makes it the traditional Tuscan children's cake – despite containing a little brandy. Delicious and incredibly filling, it is like a home-made version of those little oval rice cakes you can buy at all Tuscan cafés and pâtisseries, called simply budino, which literally translates as 'pudding'. All Tuscans know that budino contains rice, but the name is always guaranteed to confuse anybody who does not come from the region. This is the classic version of the recipe, but you can vary the cake by adding nuts or candied fruits, if you like.

MAKES 1 CAKE

150g/5oz/⅔ cup short grain rice
1.2 litres/2 pints/5 cups milk
butter, for greasing
30ml/2 tbsp semolina
9 eggs
225g/8oz/generous 1 cup caster/superfine sugar
45ml/3 tbsp brandy
grated rind of 1 unwaxed lemon

1 Put the rice and 750ml/1¼ pints/3 cups of the milk into a pan. Boil for 10 minutes, then drain, reserving the milk, which will have absorbed some of the starch from the rice. Set aside to cool slightly.

2 Preheat the oven to 180°C/350°F/Gas 4. Butter a 25cm/10in fixed-base cake tin or pan, thoroughly, and then sprinkle with the semolina. (Do not use a loose-based one, or it will leak.) Turn the cake tin upside down and shake to remove any loose semolina.

3 Using an electric whisk, beat the eggs in a large bowl until foaming and pale yellow. Add the sugar gradually, beating constantly, then add the brandy and lemon rind. Stir well.

4 Add the rice and remaining milk (including the reserved milk). Pour into the cake tin.

5 Bake for 50 minutes, or until a skewer inserted into the middle comes out clean. The cake should be well set and golden brown. Serve warm or cold.

COOK'S TIP

Don't worry about how runny the mixture seems when you pour it into the tin/pan; the finished cake should remain very moist and sticky when baked, and just be firm enough to slice into portions.

PANFORTE
TUSCAN CANDIED FRUIT-AND-NUT HARD CAKE

Panforte is an old-fashioned sweetmeat, which dates back to the Renaissance and was reputedly first created in Siena. It is widely available to buy ready-made in all Italian food stores. Making it at home is a sticky but enjoyable process, and the end result, although a lot less perfect-looking than the ready-made version, tastes absolutely wonderful. You can normally buy the edible rice paper from good confectioners and many supermarkets, but otherwise simply line the baking tin with baking parchment and then remove it before eating the cake. Serve the flat, shallow cake sliced into thin strips. It is especially delicious with some black coffee or dessert wine.

MAKES 1 CAKE

rice paper
200g/7oz/generous 1 cup unblanched almonds
225g/8oz/1 cup mixed/candied peel, chopped
50g/2oz/¼ cup crystallised/candied orange peel
130g/4½oz/generous ⅔ cup shelled walnuts
200g/7oz/1¾ cups plain/all-purpose flour
5ml/1 tsp ground cinnamon
2.5ml/½ tsp ground allspice
2.5ml/½ tsp ground coriander
350g/12oz/1¾ cups caster/superfine sugar
30ml/2 tbsp clear honey
15ml/1 tbsp each ground cinnamon and icing/confectioners' sugar, sifted together, for dusting

1 Preheat the oven to 150°C/300°F/Gas 2 and line a 25cm/10in a round shallow cake tin or pan with rice paper or baking parchment.

2 Blanch 150g/5oz almonds by soaking them in hot water for about 1 minute, then removing the skins. Lay the almonds out on a baking sheet and toast them under a hot grill or broiler, turning occasionally, for about 5 minutes, or until golden. Chop them coarsely.

3 Put the chopped almonds into a food processor or blender with the chopped peel, the crystallised orange peel and the walnuts. Whiz until it forms a rough mass. (Alternatively, chop very finely using a sharp knife.) Put the mixture on to a work surface.

4 Combine the nut and peel mixture with the remaining unblanched almonds and the flour and spices.

5 In a small pan, melt the sugar and honey together and boil until it reaches the 'soft ball stage' (119°C/238°F – see Cook's Tip).

6 Pour the hot sugar and honey mixture over the dry ingredients and mix well with a spatula and, when cooler, using your hands.

7 Press the mixture into the tin and level the surface using a spatula. Bake the panforte in the oven for 30 minutes, or until golden.

8 Remove from the oven and on a wire rack. Dust with the icing sugar and cinnamon mixture. Store it in an airtight container – it will keep for up to 1 year.

COOK'S TIP

A sugar thermometer is a good way to measure the temperature of the sugar accurately. However, you can always use the old-fashioned method: drop a tiny amount into a small cup of cold water. It is ready if it forms a perfect ball when you roll it between your thumb and index finger.

IL BUCCELLATO
THE TRADITIONAL SWEET BREAD OF LUCCA

The older, most elegant part of the city of Lucca, in north-western Tuscany, is surrounded by the old restored Renaissance city walls, so that it is possible to walk or cycle around the entire circumference and enjoy the view from the top of the wall. To make the experience even more pleasurable, each of the four principal sides is lined with a different kind of tree. This sweet bread, which is famously typical of this attractive town, is presented annually there for blessing as part of a special Mass in the city's cathedral.

SERVES 10

450g/1lb/4 cups plain/all-purpose flour
20g/¾oz fresh/compressed yeast
about 250ml/8fl oz/1 cup tepid water
15ml/1 tbsp fennel seeds
175g/6oz caster/superfine sugar
50g/2oz/¼ cup unsalted butter, melted
2 eggs, beaten
5ml/1 tsp bicarbonate of soda/baking soda
70g/2¾oz/½ cup mixed/candied peel and sultanas/golden raisins
grated rind of ½ unwaxed lemon
oil, for greasing
flour, for dusting
1 egg white
icing/confectioners' sugar, for dusting

1 Put a handful of flour in a small bowl and crumble in the fresh yeast. Stirring constantly, trickle in enough tepid water to make a thick paste.

2 Cover the top of the bowl with clear film or plastic wrap and place the bowl in a warm place for about 45 minutes, or until the flour has reacted with the yeast and the mixture has begun to expand.

3 Grease and flour a 20cm/8in ring mould. Preheat the oven to 150°C/300°F/Gas 2. Crush the fennel seeds to a powder in a spice grinder or using a mortar and pestle.

4 Put the remaining flour on to a work surface and use your fist to make a hollow in the middle.

5 Pour the sugar into the hollow, then add the butter, eggs, bicarbonate of soda, fennel seeds, peel, sultanas and lemon rind.

6 Put the yeasted flour starter into the hollow and roughly work all the ingredients together. Pour most of the remaining water into the hollow and begin to knead the ingredients together until you have an even, elastic dough, adding more water if required. Knead steadily for 10–15 minutes.

7 Roll out the dough into a cylinder, then turn it into a crown shape by joining the two ends together to form a circle.

8 Transfer the dough into the prepared ring mould. Mark the surface of the dough by cutting through it with a sharp knife all the way around the circle.

9 Cover with oiled clear film and leave to rise in a warm place for 1 hour, until doubled in size.

10 Lightly beat the egg white and brush it over the surface, then sprinkle with the icing sugar. Bake for 40 minutes, until light golden. Allow to cool slightly on a wire rack. Serve warm or cold.

SCHIACCIATA D'UVA
TUSCAN GRAPE-HARVEST FOCACCIA

This type of sweet bread is made around the time of the wine harvest – vendemmia – when there is a bountiful supply of fresh, sweet grapes around. You need to squash the grapes down well into the top of the focaccia base, using plenty of sugar to bring out the flavour of the fruit; the amount of sugar you need will depend on the sweetness of the grapes. The end result looks beautiful and tastes delicious. During the vendemmia, all the smartest cafes in Florence and the surrounding areas will be selling slices of this traditional focaccia to celebrate the arrival of the new wine.

1 Preheat the oven to 220°C/425°F/Gas 7. Oil two baking sheets generously and dust with semolina or polenta flour.

2 Divide the dough into six portions. On a floured work surface, roll them in to 1cm/½in-thick circles and place on the baking sheets.

3 Drizzle the surface of each schiacciata with a little oil, then cover each one with grapes.

4 Press the grapes down into the dough with the flat of your hand. Sprinkle with the sugar and bake for 15–20 minutes, or until cooked through. Serve warm or cold.

MAKES 6

extra virgin olive oil, for greasing and drizzling
semolina or polenta flour, for dusting
450g/1lb ready-made, risen Basic Bread Dough (see page 61)
plain/all-purpose flour, for dusting
450g/1lb fresh black or white grapes, seedless
15–30ml/1–2 tbsp caster/superfine sugar

MAKES 14 SMALL ROLLS

- 30ml/2 tbsp sultanas/golden raisins
- 60ml/4 tbsp good-quality extra virgin olive oil, plus extra for greasing
- 450g/1lb ready-made, risen basic bread dough (see page 61)
- 1 rosemary sprig, leaves coarsely chopped

PANINI AL RAMERINO
ROSEMARY AND SULTANA ROLLS

These fragrant little rolls, slightly sweetened with dried fruit, are a perfect teatime treat and are popular with children. Served warm, with olive oil, butter or a sour cheese such as a Stracchino, they are wonderful with a fresh glass of milk or hot chocolate. Alternatively, try them with salami, olives, prosciutto crudo or mortadella as an antipasto. However they are served, the intense rosemary perfume, released as their crusts are broken, will transport you to Tuscany in an instant.

1 Soak the sultanas in warm water for 10 minutes, then drain and dry on kitchen paper. Grease a large baking sheet.

2 Put the bread dough on a work surface and make a hollow in the middle.

3 Heat the oil (do not allow it to sizzle) in a small pan with the rosemary leaves for 10 minutes. Cool completely, then pour the oil into the hollow in the dough.

4 Knead for 10 minutes, then roll the dough into a ball and put it in an oiled bowl.

5 Cover with oiled clear film or plastic wrap and put in a warm place to rise for 1 hour.

6 Knead the sultanas into the dough. With oiled hands, shape the dough into 14 small rounded rolls.

7 Place on the baking sheet, cover with oiled clear film and leave to rise for 45 minutes, or until doubled in size. Preheat the oven to 200°C/400°F/Gas 6.

8 Bake the rolls for 10 minutes, or until crisp and golden. Serve warm or cold.

UMBRIA & LE MARCHE

Umbria, in Central Italy, is the only Italian region that has neither a coastline nor a shared border with another country, although Lazio, Tuscany and Le Marche surround it. Containing only two provinces, Perugia and Terni, it is crossed by the great River Tiber, and is home to huge Lake Trasimeno. The beautiful hilltop medieval regional capital is Perugia, which has for centuries been an important hub of knowledge and learning – one of Italy's oldest universities is here, dating back to 1308. It is Assisi, however, that is probably the most visited town in Umbria, being the birthplace of two significant saints in Italian history: Saint Francis and Saint Clare, a fact that makes the city one of the main destinations for pilgrims.

Despite its small size, Umbria is well known for its landscape, traditions, history, culinary delights, wines, artistic legacy, and its influence on culture, but at the time of writing it has also tragically become famous for a series of terrible earthquakes in 2016, which caused untold damage to property and people.

Like much of Italy, over half of the Umbrian landscape is made up of hills or high plateaux. Temperate in climate, this is a region that is primarily agricultural, and is most especially proud of its olive oil, which is thought by many to be the very best in Italy. It also boasts some impressive red wines, the most iconic of which is the very tannic Sagrantino, a contraction of the original name of the wine: 'Sacro Vino' or sacred wine, which indicates it was a wine reserved for Communion or religious ceremonies, and which is perfect for drinking with the local specialities involving tasty wild boar. The other most important agricultural products of this region are tobacco and sunflowers, and of course the incredible, revered and liberally-used black truffle.

The food of Umbria centres around pulses, especially the prized lentil from the town of Castelluccio; pecorino cheese; wild boar; and the aforementioned olive oil, red wine, and black truffle. This is also the region of Italy most famous for its legendary talent for butchery. 'Norcineria' is the special word for this skill, and is named after little town of Norcia. It is also produces Bacio Perugina chocolate, whose silver wrappers each contain a love message; very appropriate for the region that is supposed to be the birthplace of St Valentine.

Neighbouring Le Marche is bordered by Emilia-Romagna, the tiny republic of San Marino, Tuscany, Abruzzo and Lazio, and the Adriatic Sea to the east. This is a mainly hilly region, except for the river valleys and its narrow coastal strip, and is divided into the provinces of Macerata, Pesaro and Urbino, Fermo, the regional capital Ascoli Piceno, and port of Ancona.

This is very much a rural region, and its food is a mixture of seafood from the long coastline and rustic country cooking from the inland areas, based on locally-grown produce. Brodetto is the famous Marchigian dish of fish stew from the Adriatic coast, the recipe for which varies hugely depending on the customs and traditions of each coastal town, but that usually includes red and grey mullet, cuttlefish or squid (or both), oil, garlic and saffron, and is served on either fried or toasted bread.

The area of Acqualagna, in the province of Pesaro and Urbino, is one of the most important truffle-producing areas in Italy and boasts four types of truffle. The most famous and expensive of these is the white truffle, which is harvested between October and December, whereas the less-expensive black truffle is harvested from the first of December until mid-March.

The region produces a much-prized traditional salame called ciauscolo, which is not unlike the 'nduja of Calabria, although without the chilli. This is a smoked and dry-cured sausage, made from pork meat and fat and spiced with black pepper and garlic, sometimes with vincotto, or wine must, added to the mix. Also worth a mention is prosciutto di Carpegna, a cured ham that comes from Montefeltro in the province of Pesaro and Urbino. This area is characterised by a microclimate that benefits from the combination of the proximity of the sea and a moderate altitude, which has been proved to spell ham-curing perfection.

Other highlights include olive all'Ascolana – giant, deep-fried, breadcrumb-coated stuffed green olives; the region's sumptuous version of lasagna, called vincisgrassi after the Austrian General Windisch-Graetz; and crema fritta (literally, fried custard), which makes a somewhat unusual appearance in the local version of fritto misto. Vernaccia, a sparkling red wine unique to the village of Serrapetrona, makes a refreshing accompaniment to this feast of fried food.

CIPOLLATA IN TAZZA
THICK ONION SOUP IN A CUP

The point of this simple soup is that it celebrates the famous onion of the little town of Cannara, a town and comune on the Topino River in the floodplain of central Umbria, in the province of Perugia. Its importance is celebrated every year since 1981 by a 2-week long onion festival. The local cultivation of this unique onion has a long history and its special properties are put down to the soil of this area, which is rich in potassium and clay, with plenty of water. The producers are small family farmers, who pass the secrets and techniques from father to son, sometimes for four or more generations. A Consortium dedicated to the onion was created in 2003 to protect and promote the producers of the Cannara onion. This very simple, rustic soup is thick, tasty and nourishing and does work well with any kind of onion.

SERVES 6

45–60ml/3–4 tbsp extra virgin olive oil
75g/3oz lardo, chopped finely
1.6kg/3½lb Cannara or other onions, peeled and thinly sliced
a handful of fresh basil leaves, torn into small pieces
500g/1¼lb tomatoes, blanched, peeled, deseeded and chopped
1 litre/1¾ pints/4 cups water
3 eggs, beaten
75ml/5 tbsp freshly grated pecorino cheese
sea salt and ground black pepper
toasted bread croûtons, to serve (optional)

1 In a deep pan, heat the oil with the chopped lardo over a medium-high heat until sizzling, then add the sliced onions, the basil and seasoning.

2 Stir, cover and cook very slowly for about 1 hour: the onions must not brown at all. If necessary, add a little hot water during the cooking process.

3 When the onions are almost falling apart, add the tomatoes and water, stir, and adjust seasoning. Simmer for a further 1 hour.

4 Remove from the heat and stir vigorously as you trickle in the beaten eggs and the freshly grated pecorino cheese.

5 Serve piping hot in big, wide cups, as is traditional, with toasted bread croûtons, if you like.

BRODETTO ALL'ANCONETANA
ANCONA FISH SOUP

Although the diminutive name used locally to describe this dish would make you think you were getting a simple soup, it is actually a chunky and substantial stew. Traditionally, 13 different varieties of fish are used in brodetto, which is symbolic of the great port of Ancona. Among these you would always find scorpion fish, gurnard, eel, sea cricket and red mullet. Because the fish are added whole, bones and all, you need plenty of time to leisurely wade through the process of removing the fish from the bone, then enjoy the fish juices with some crusty bread. There are no other ingredients of any note, so the freshness and variety of the fish is the most important part of the dish.

SERVES 4 TO 6

60ml/4 tbsp extra virgin olive oil
1 onion, chopped
1 garlic clove, chopped
90ml/6 tbsp white or red wine vinegar
300g/11oz canned tomatoes, strained or coarsely chopped
900g/2lb mixed whole fish, such as small monkfish, red mullet, whiting or scorpion fish
sea salt and ground black pepper
crusty bread, to serve

1 Put the oil in a very large pan, add the onion and garlic, and fry over medium heat for 10 minutes, or until soft.

2 Gradually add the vinegar to the pan, stirring constantly, until the sharp vinegar smell has disappeared.

3 Add the strained tomatoes, stir and simmer for 10 minutes. Gradually add the fish, one at a time, starting with the largest.

4 Cook, stirring gently, for 30 minutes, until the fish is cooked through. Season and serve with some crusty bread.

SERVES 4 TO 6

275g/10oz stale, hard bread, finely grated
150g/5oz freshly grated Parmesan cheese
8 eggs
grated rind of 1 unwaxed lemon
freshly grated nutmeg
a little milk, as required
about 2 litres/3½ pints/9 cups strong chicken stock
sea salt and ground black pepper

PASSATELLI IN BRODO
CLEAR CHICKEN SOUP WITH PASSATELLI

This is one of the oldest and most traditional of all the dishes of Le Marche and it belongs both to this region and to certain parts of Emilia Romagna, although the recipe does vary slightly. The word 'passatelli' comes from the verb 'passare', meaning to pass, which refers to the mixture being forced through the widest holes of the food mill or ricer, thus 'passing' into the soup itself. A specific tool for this job does exist, but is only available for purchase in local stores.

1 Put the finely grated bread and Parmesan cheese, eggs and lemon rind in a bowl and mix together with your hands to form a thick paste.

2 Season with nutmeg, salt and pepper. If the mixture is too crumbly, dampen with a little milk. Leave to rest in the refrigerator, covered, for 1 hour.

3 Bring the stock to a gentle boil in a large pan. Using a ricer or food mill with large holes, push the bread mixture, a small amount at a time, into the hot stock, cutting off the strands to drop into the soup when they are about 10cm/4in long.

4 Cook for 5–6 minutes, until the passatelli are cooked, then serve hot.

MINESTRA DI CECI E MAIALE
CHICKPEA AND PORK SOUP

This dish, which originates from Le Marche, is one of those robust cold-weather soups that are designed to fill hungry stomachs in the depths of a bitter winter, where the only heating comes from the kitchen fireplace. Guaranteed to provide much sustenance and comfort, it is filling and satisfying, as well as wonderfully warming. Made with a variety of the most basic of local ingredients that are available to even the poorest of families, this soup, and many others like it, relies on long, gentle cooking to draw out the depth and mixture of flavours and to keep the meat from becoming stringy and tough.

SERVES 4 TO 6

275g/10oz/1½ cups dried chickpeas, soaked overnight and drained
45–60ml/3–4 tbsp extra virgin olive oil, plus extra to serve
200g/7oz prosciutto crudo, diced
2 garlic cloves, chopped
1 large onion, chopped
a large handful of fresh parsley leaves, chopped
3 pork ribs
200g/7oz escarole or bitter leaves, such as endive/US chicory
3 celery sticks, coarsely chopped
225g/8oz passata/bottled strained tomatoes
sea salt and ground black pepper
freshly grated pecorino cheese and toasted crusty bread, thinly sliced, to serve

1 Rinse the chickpeas. Put them in a large pan and cover them plenty of water. Bring to the boil and boil hard for 5 minutes, then drain and rinse again.

2 Return the chickpeas to the pan and cover with fresh water. Bring to the boil and boil gently for 15 minutes.

3 Meanwhile, put the olive oil in a large pan or flameproof casserole and fry the prosciutto, garlic and onion until soft. Add the fresh parsley and cook for 5 minutes.

4 Drain the chickpeas and add them to the pan. Stir well to allow the chickpeas to combine, then add 2 litres/3½ pints/9 cups water and simmer, covered, for about 1 hour.

5 Cut the meat from the pork ribs, and then cut it into rough chunks.

6 Bring the soup back to the boil and, as soon as it reaches boiling point, add the bitter leaves, celery, pork meat and bones to the pan. Stir, then add the passata and season to taste. Stir once more and cover tightly with a lid.

7 Leave the soup to simmer over the lowest possible heat for about 3 hours, stirring occasionally.

8 Adjust the seasoning to taste and serve with freshly grated pecorino cheese, a drizzle of extra virgin olive oil and toasted bread.

COOK'S TIPS

- This soup is even more delicious if it is served reheated the following day.
- You can use canned chickpeas, although the flavour will not be as intense.

OLIVE ALL'ASCOLANA
STUFFED DEEP-FRIED GIANT OLIVES

These stuffed olives are one of Le Marche's most famous and traditional recipes. They are usually served either as part of an antipasto or alongside a meat recipe as a delicious side dish. They are best served just warm, but are also good cold. The key to this recipe is to find olives that are large enough to stuff successfully without them splitting. The recipe is named after the town of Ascoli Piceno, which is surrounded on three sides by the mountains of two vast national parks: Parco Nazionale dei Monti Sibillini on the north-western flank and Parco Nazionale dei Monti della Laga to the south.

SERVES 6

60 giant green olives, preserved in brine
115g/4oz pork fat
60ml/4 tbsp extra virgin olive oil
150g/5oz/⅔ cup minced/ground pork
115g/4oz/½ cup minced/ground beef
15ml/1 tbsp tomato paste, diluted in 15ml/1 tbsp cold water
3 chicken livers, trimmed and chopped
45ml/3 tbsp fresh white breadcrumbs
45ml/3 tbsp beef stock
1 egg, beaten
50g/2oz/⅔ cup freshly grated Parmesan cheese
pinch freshly grated nutmeg
75ml/5 tbsp plain/all-purpose flour
2 eggs beaten with 15ml/1 tbsp milk
45–60ml/3–4 tbsp fine dry breadcrumbs
vegetable oil, for deep-frying
sea salt and ground black pepper
lemon wedges, to serve

1 Pit all the olives carefully using an olive pitter, cherry stoner, apple corer or long, thin-bladed knife. It is important to keep them whole and as tidy as possible. Discard the pits.

2 In a frying pan, heat the pork fat with the oil, then add the minced pork and beef, and cook for about 5 minutes until the meat is all well browned. Add the tomato paste mixture to the pan. Mix well, and cook for about 20 minutes, stirring occasionally. Add the chicken livers and cook for a further 10 minutes.

3 Allow the mixture to cool, then chop the liver and mince mixture finely using a heavy knife. Alternatively, put the liver and mince mixture into a food processor or blender and blend until smooth.

4 Add the breadcrumbs, stock, beaten egg and Parmesan cheese to the mixture. Add the nutmeg and season with salt and pepper.

5 Carefully, using your fingers, fill each olive with a little of the meat mixture. Roll the olives in the flour, then in the beaten egg and milk, and then in the dry breadcrumbs.

6 Half fill a heavy pan with oil. If using a deep-fryer, fill it to the level recommended in the instruction book. Heat the oil to 180°C/350°F or until a cube of bread, added to the oil, turns golden in about 45 seconds.

7 Add the olives, in batches, to the hot oil and deep-fry until golden brown. Drain the olives on kitchen paper and serve hot or cold with the lemon wedges.

PIZZA DI PASQUA AL FORMAGGIO
UMBRIAN EASTER BREAD

This is not a pizza as such, but is called a pizza since the word is sometimes used to describe a savoury bread, or a simple cake. It is actually very rich and labour-intensive, which is typical of the traditional dishes that mark the feasting for important religious festivities. In Italy, Easter Monday is often the day when family and friends head into the countryside for a picnic, and this bread would be exactly the kind of food that is suitable for taking along to share on such an occasion. Serve with cured meats, olives and cheeses.

MAKES 2 OR 3 LARGE LOAVES

- 225g/5lb 6oz ready-made, risen basic bread dough (see page 61)
- about 725g/1lb 9oz/6¼ cups strong white bread flour
- warm water, as needed
- 115g/4oz pork dripping
- 4 eggs, beaten
- 10g/¼oz fresh/compressed yeast mixed with 75ml/5 tbsp warm water
- 275g/10oz/1⅔ cups freshly grated pecorino cheese
- 45–60ml/3–4 tbsp extra virgin olive oil
- sea salt and ground black pepper
- unsalted butter, for greasing
- plain/all-purpose flour, for dusting

1 Knead the bread dough with 500g/1¼lb/5 cups of the flour and enough warm water to achieve a very soft dough.

2 Turn this dough into a lightly oiled bowl and cover with lightly oiled clear film or plastic wrap. Leave in a warm place to rise for about 1 hour, or until doubled in size.

3 Knead the pork dripping, eggs, yeast mixture, pecorino cheese, olive oil and salt and pepper into the dough.

4 Knead thoroughly, using the remaining 225g/8oz/2 cups strong white bread flour, to achieve a dough that is not too sticky.

5 Butter and flour two or three large loaf tins or pans. Divide the dough among the tins. Leave in a warm place to rise for 2 hours.

6 Preheat the oven to 200°C/400°F/Gas 6 and bake the bread for 50 minutes, until the top of the loaves are golden brown and crisp. Cool completely before removing them from the tins.

RAVIOLI PESARESI
RAVIOLI IN THE PESARO STYLE

Ravioli with a ricotta cheese and spinach filling exist in most parts of Italy where fresh pasta is featured. There are many variations on this recipe – meat or other kinds of cheese can be added to the filling mixture, and instead of spinach, Swiss chard can be used, or it could even be substituted by fresh young nettles. In Le Marche, it is the addition of lots of tangy lemon rind that gives a fresh boost to the flavour. Lemons grown in the coastal areas of Italy always have an especially recognizable intensity of perfume and taste.

SERVES 6

about 400g/14oz/3½ cups plain/all-purpose flour
50g/2oz/2 tbsp fine semolina, plus extra for dusting
4 eggs
1 egg yolk
350g/12oz fresh ricotta cheese
500g/1¼lb spinach, cooked and finely chopped
grated rind of 1 large unwaxed lemon
115g/4oz/1¼ cups freshly grated mild pecorino cheese
sea salt and ground black pepper
tomato sauce (see page 20) or melted butter, to serve

1 Mix together the flour and semolina and place the mixture on a work surface in a mound. Use your fist to make a hollow in the middle.

2 Beat the eggs and egg yolk together and pour the mixture into the hollow in the flour. Work the flour and eggs together with your fingertips until you have a pliable ball of dough that is neither too sticky or too dry – add more flour as required.

3 Knead the ball of dough until it is smooth and elastic. Cover with a clean cloth or wrap in clear film or plastic wrap, and leave to rest for about 30 minutes while you make the filling for the ravioli.

4 In a large bowl, mix together the ricotta cheese, chopped spinach and grated lemon rind. Season to taste with salt and pepper.

5 Roll out the pasta into a long, thin rectangle as finely and as evenly as possible. Drop the filling, in a neat row, along half the sheet, a scant tablespoon at a time, leaving 2.5cm/1in between the mounds of filling. Fold the sheet over to cover the filling.

6 With your fingers, press down firmly between the mounds of filling so that the pasta sticks together and closes up. Cut out the ravioli with a serrated pasta cutter or knife and press round the edges again to make sure each is perfectly sealed.

7 Dust a wide baking sheet with semolina and lay the ravioli over it, taking care not to overlap them or lay them on top of one another.

8 Bring a large pan of water to the boil and drop in the ravioli. Cook for 3–4 minutes, in batches. They should rise to the surface when cooked. Scoop out the ravioli using a large slotted spoon as soon as they are cooked and transfer them to a warmed bowl.

9 Dress the ravioli with tomato sauce or melted butter and sprinkle with grated pecorino cheese.

COOK'S TIP

The best place to make, knead and roll out pasta is on a wooden kitchen table or a warm work surface. Marble is not suitable.

SERVES 6

60ml/4 tbsp olive oil
2 garlic cloves, peeled and left whole
900g/2lb fresh wild asparagus, fine local asparagus or sprue, cut into short sections
450g/1lb ripe tomatoes, peeled, seeded and chopped
450g/1lb spaghetti
sea salt and ground black pepper
freshly grated Parmesan cheese, to serve

SPAGHETTI CON ASPARAGI DI CAMPO
SPAGHETTI WITH WILD ASPARAGUS

The secret of this recipe is in the simplicity of just a few carefully selected ingredients. All along the mountains and hillsides that cross Umbria you can find small wild asparagus that is famous for its amazingly bright green colour and its intense flavour. This delicious wild vegetable, which the local people go out to pick on warm spring days when it is in season, is used to make this local speciality. Good-quality, fresh asparagus, or sprue, which are the first pickings and have thinner stems, can of course be used in the place of the famous wild Umbrian asparagus – just choose fine stems if you can.

1 Heat the olive oil in a pan and fry the garlic gently until golden brown. Discard the garlic. Add the asparagus to the garlic-flavoured oil. Stir and cook gently for about 5 minutes, until tender.

2 Add the tomatoes to the asparagus and stir together. Season to taste.

3 Cook the spaghetti in a large pan of salted boiling water, until al dente. Drain and return to the pan.

4 Pour the asparagus sauce over the pasta and mix together gently. Transfer to a warm serving dish and serve immediately, with the Parmesan cheese offered separately.

TAGLIATELLE CON CALAMARI E MOLECHE
TAGLIATELLE WITH CUTTLEFISH AND SHRIMP

The tails of the local shrimps are called moleche or molecche in the coastal areas of Le Marche, and are much sought after and greatly appreciated for their delicious sweetness. This is a very simple combination of tastes and textures, put together to create a sumptuous pasta dish. Using empty, clean scallop shells – known locally as scrigno di Venere (Venus's casket) – is one way in which pasta dishes such as this one often get served in Le Marche and also further south along the same coastline in the Abbruzzi. It looks pretty, and the pasta stays wonderfully hot, but of course you can serve it in a standard bowl.

SERVES 4

120ml/4fl oz/½ cup olive oil
1 garlic clove, peeled
a pinch of crushed chilli flakes
450g/1lb cuttlefish, cleaned and cut into small cubes
275g/10oz raw shrimp tails or prawns/shrimp, peeled and cut into small cubes
175ml/6fl oz/¾ cup dry white wine
3 ripe tomatoes, peeled, seeded and diced
350g/12oz fresh tagliatelle
sea salt
a handful of fresh flat leaf parsley, leaves chopped, to garnish

1 Put the olive oil, garlic clove and chilli flakes into a pan and fry gently until the garlic is golden brown.

2 Add the cuttlefish and shrimp tails or prawns, and stir together.

3 Add the white wine, bring to the boil and cook for 1–2 minutes.

4 Add the diced tomatoes and stir well. Simmer for 5 minutes and season with salt.

5 Meanwhile, cook the tagliatelle in a large pan of salted boiling water until al dente.

6 Drain the pasta and return it to the pan. Add the sauce and mix together gently. Serve immediately, sprinkled with parsley.

VINCISGRASSI
MARCHE BAKED PASTA

This wonderful dish is related distantly to the lasagna dish of Emilia Romagna, but it was created locally in honour of General Wiensgratz, the ruler of this area during the Austro-Hungarian domination of these northern provinces. The original recipe is more intricate, contains no tomato sauce and uses pigeon breasts, and the pasta dough in the classic recipe uses Marsala mixed into the flour with the eggs, giving it a strange colour and quite a different taste. Here is a more modern – yet just as special – version of the recipe, where arguably the most essential ingredient is still very much present: fresh black truffle.

1 Mix together the flour and semolina, and pile on a work surface in a mound. Make a hollow in the middle.

2 Beat the eggs with the oil and salt. Pour into the hollow in the flour, then work the flour and egg mixture together with your fingertips to form a pliable dough. Knead until springy, then wrap in clear film or plastic wrap and leave to rest for 30 minutes.

3 Roll out the pasta dough using a rolling pin or pasta machine, and cut it into 18–20cm/7–8in squares or into rectangles. Drop into salted boiling water in batches and cook until soft, then drain on damp dish towels, taking care not to overlap the pieces of pasta.

4 To make the ragù, put the oil in a pan and gently fry three-quarters of the onion with the carrot, celery and marjoram for 10 minutes, until the vegetables are softened but not coloured. Add the veal, prosciutto and mushrooms, and sauté until browned.

5 Stir in the flour. Increase the heat, add the wine and stir over a high heat for 1–2 minutes, or until the alcohol has evaporated from the wine. Lower the heat and season with salt, pepper and nutmeg. Stir in the passata. Cover and simmer for 50 minutes, stirring occasionally. Meanwhile, prepare the white sauce if you haven't already.

6 Sauté the chicken livers with 15g/½oz/1 tbsp of the butter and the remaining onion until just browned. Slice thinly. Add the livers and the truffle to the ragù. Preheat the oven to 180°C/350°F/Gas 4.

7 Butter an ovenproof dish and cover the base with the pasta. Cover with the ragù, then a layer of white sauce. Continue until you have used up all the ingredients, finishing with a layer of pasta. Cover with Parmesan cheese and dot with the remaining butter.

8 Bake for 30–40 minutes, until golden and bubbling. Leave to stand for at least 5 minutes before serving.

SERVES 6 TO 8

200g/7oz/1¾ cups plain/all-purpose flour
115g/4oz semolina
5 eggs
15ml/1 tbsp olive oil
a pinch of salt
600ml/1 pint/2½ cups white sauce (see page 20)
150g/5oz/1½ cups freshly grated Parmesan cheese

FOR THE RAGÙ

45ml/3 tbsp olive oil
1 large onion, finely chopped
1 carrot, finely chopped
1 celery stick, finely chopped
a pinch of dried marjoram
225g/8oz stewing veal, coarsely minced/ground or fairly finely chopped
50g/2oz prosciutto crudo or pancetta, chopped
25g/1oz/½ cup dried porcini mushrooms, soaked for about 30 minutes in boiling water until softened, then drained and chopped
15ml/1 tbsp plain/all-purpose flour
250ml/8fl oz/1 cup red wine
1.5ml/¼ tsp freshly grated nutmeg
200ml/7fl oz/scant 1 cup thick passata/bottled strained tomatoes
115g/4oz chicken livers, trimmed
65g/2½oz unsalted butter, plus extra for greasing
1 fresh black truffle, brushed clean and thinly sliced
sea salt and ground black pepper

POLENTA E FAGIOLI
POLENTA AND BEANS

Polenta and beans, a peasant-food staple, is eaten in all three regions, although this is an Umbrian recipe. This dish is made with standard polenta – cornmeal boiled in salted water until thick and porridge-like in consistency – to which some beans, enriched with tomato sauce, are added. The incorporation of the stewed beans and their sauce into the polenta makes for a really tasty dish. It is traditionally served with a good sprinkling of freshly grated pecorino cheese.

SERVES 6

400g/14oz/2⅔ cups dried borlotti or cannellini beans, soaked overnight and drained
50g/2oz/⅓ cup lard, white cooking fat or fatty pancetta, cubed
1 carrot, finely chopped
1 celery stick, finely chopped
1 onion, finely chopped
450g/1lb ripe tomatoes, peeled, seeded and coarsely chopped
300g/11oz/2⅓ cups coarse or medium-grade polenta flour
sea salt and ground black pepper
freshly grated pecorino cheese and extra virgin olive oil, to serve

COOK'S TIP

Although for convenience you could use canned beans for this recipe, you will get a better flavour if you use dried beans.

1 Rinse the soaked borlotti or cannellini beans. Put them in a large pan and cover with plenty of water. Bring to the boil and boil hard for 5 minutes, then drain and rinse again.

2 Return the beans to the pan, cover with fresh water, bring to the boil, and boil gently for 45 minutes, or until the beans are softened. Drain away most of the cooking water, reserving just a spoonful or two.

3 In a separate pan, fry the lard, cooking fat or pancetta together with the carrot, celery and onion for 10 minutes, until softened.

4 Add the tomatoes and stir together. Simmer until the mixture is thickened and glossy, then season to taste with salt and ground black pepper.

5 Add the boiled beans and the remaining water, stir to mix, and simmer over a very low heat while you cook the polenta, stirring occasionally to prevent it from catching on the bottom of the pan.

6 Bring 2 litres/3½ pints/9 cups water to the boil in a large pan. Add a large pinch of salt, then trickle the polenta flour into the boiling water in a steady stream, whisking constantly.

7 Turn the heat to medium-low. Using a strong wooden spoon, stir the polenta constantly for about 40 minutes.

8 Add the beans and their sauce, reserving a little to serve separately, if you wish, and continue to stir and cook for a further 10 minutes.

9 Serve sprinkled with pecorino cheese and a drizzle of olive oil.

SERVES 2

- 2 medium sized trout, cleaned and gutted
- 120ml/8 tbsp soft breadcrumbs
- juice of 1 lemon
- 150ml/10 tbsp extra virgin olive oil, plus extra for brushing
- 30ml/2 tbsp chopped fresh flat leaf parsley
- sea salt and ground black pepper

TROTA AI FERRI
UMBRIAN STUFFED GRILLED TROUT

This is a very simple Umbrian recipe for trout. The region, being landlocked, relies on either freshwater fish from the rivers and lakes, or on preserved fish such as baccalà (salted cod) or canned fish. In Umbria, the trout caught in the river Nera are highly prized and much sought after. This recipe serves two people, so to feed more people you'll need a large barbecue.

1 Light the barbecue and wait until you have a heap of hot, even red embers. Position the grill or broiler rack. Rinse the trout under cold running water inside and out. Pat dry with kitchen paper.

2 In a small bowl, mix the breadcrumbs with the lemon juice, half the olive oil and the parsley and season to taste.

3 Stuff the inside of each trout with this mixture. Score each trout lightly on each side through the skin, and rub the remaining oil all over the fish.

4 Lay the fish on a grill and cook for about 10 minutes on each side, until the trout is cooked through, brushing with more oil during the cooking process.

FRITTELLE DI BACCALÀ
SALT COD FRITTERS

As the region of Umbria has no coastline, the only fresh fish recipes found here will be those using the fish caught in the rivers, streams or lakes. Recipes for freshwater fish abound in the villages and towns surrounding Lake Trasimeno, for example. However, the ancient way of preserving fish in salt also has a place on the menu in this region, and these simple crispy fritters are one of the many ways in which baccalà (salted cod) is used in Umbrian cooking. Try to buy fish that has already been soaked for 3 days to make sure that is has softened thoroughly, or you could soak it yourself, if you have the time.

SERVES 6

- 1.25kg/2¾lb salted cod, soaked for 3 days, changing water frequently
- 1 egg
- about 45ml/3 tbsp plain/all-purpose flour
- about 350ml/12fl oz/1½ cups cold water
- about 2 litres/3½ pints/9 cups sunflower oil, for deep-frying
- lemon wedges, to serve

1 Drain the fish, pat dry with kitchen paper and remove any bones and skin. Cut into small fillets.

2 Mix together the egg, flour and enough cold water to make a thick coating batter. Use the batter to cover the fish completely.

3 Heat the oil until sizzling, then fry the fish in batches until golden brown.

4 Drain the fried fish on kitchen paper to remove the excess oil, then serve the fish fritters piping hot with lemon wedges for squeezing over.

FARAONA IN PIRAMIDE
GUINEA FOWL IN A PYRAMID

Called faraona in Italian, guinea fowl were introduced to Italy from Egypt, and in Le Marche they were considered to be a mark of distinction, enjoyed by only the aristocrats and wealthy farmers, who would serve them at wedding feasts and for other special occasions. This recipe was created by the composer Rossini's cook, for the banquet held in celebration of the première of his famous opera *Mosè in Egitto* (Moses in Egypt), which took place on 20 November 1842. The guinea fowl was theatrically unwrapped at the table when served, alongside a small hammer, which was provided to crack the hard salt crust.

1 Preheat the oven to 180°C/350°F/Gas 4. Clean and wash the guinea fowl. Put the herbs, juniper berries and the peeled cloves of garlic inside the bird's cavity. Season.

2 Rub a long strip of muslin or cheesecloth with the halved garlic clove and wrap the bird in the cloth.

3 Line the base of a high-sided ovenproof dish with 300g/11oz of the sea salt and put the wrapped guinea fowl in the middle.

4 Mix the remaining salt with the flour and, using your hands, mix in the whisked egg white to make a sticky paste.

5 Use the salt-and-flour paste to create a pyramid shape over the guinea fowl, covering it completely. Place into the preheated oven and roast for 3 hours.

6 Crack open the salt crust and carefully take the bird out. Unwrap the muslin, and carve the fowl. Serve.

COOK'S TIP

The dish was originally served with couscous shaped to look like sand dunes.

SERVES 4

1 plump, oven-ready guinea fowl
1 thyme sprig
1 sage sprig
1 bay leaf
2 juniper berries, lightly crushed
4 garlic cloves, peeled and left whole, plus 1 garlic clove, halved
900g/2lb coarse sea salt
45ml/3 tbsp plain/all-purpose flour
1 egg white, whisked until frothy
sea salt and ground black pepper

SERVES 2

2 plump quails or wood pigeons, cleaned, rinsed, dried and ready to cook
9 fresh sage leaves
2 slices prosciutto
60ml/4 tbsp olive oil
500ml/17fl oz/2¼ cups dry red wine
2 garlic cloves, peeled and left whole
½ onion, sliced
115g/4oz pancetta, cubed
45ml/3 tbsp pitted black olives, roughly chopped
15ml/1 tbsp capers, rinsed and roughly chopped
sea salt and ground black pepper
4 slices farmhouse bread, such as ciabatta, toasted, to serve

QUAGLIA ALLA MANIERA DI TODI
QUAIL IN THE TODI STYLE

This is a traditional Umbrian way of cooking quail, which works well with small pheasant or other small game birds too, particularly wood pigeon. One of the most famous hunting regions of Italy, Umbria is home to many wild animals, and game has long played a crucial role in traditional Umbrian cuisine. Todi is a very pretty town in the province of the regional capital Perugia. It sits perched on a tall, two-crested hill overlooking the east bank of the river Tiber.

1 Preheat the oven to 180°C/350°F/Gas 4. Wrap each quail or wood pigeon in 3 sage leaves and a slice of prosciutto.

2 Put the quail into a roasting pan and roast for about 10 minutes, or until half-cooked.

3 Remove from the oven and take the meat off the carcass in large chunks, but leave the legs intact. Chop the remaining sage leaves.

4 In a pan, fry together the oil, wine, garlic, onion, pancetta, olives, capers, and remaining sage leaves for about 5 minutes.

5 Add the chunks of meat. Season with salt and pepper and cover. Leave to simmer for 1 hour, or until tender.

6 Serve the meat atop the toasted bread, with the sauce poured over.

SERVES 4 TO 6

200g/7oz chicken giblets
15g/½oz/1 tbsp unsalted butter
90ml/6 tbsp extra virgin olive oil
1 oven-ready free-range chicken, about 3kg/6lb 9oz
chicken stock, as needed
3 eggs, beaten
juice and grated rind of ½ large, unwaxed lemon
sea salt
handful chopped fresh flat leaf parsley and lemon slices, to garnish

POLLO ALLA MACERATESE
CHICKEN IN THE STYLE OF MACERATA

This recipe of slow-cooked chicken and livers is named after the city of Macerata, although similar versions appear on the menu in other parts of the region. Macerata is the capital of the province of the same name in Le Marche. The old centre of the city is located on a hill between the Chienti and Potenza rivers and is connected to the sprawling modern town by an elevator. After 2 hours of cooking, the chicken is wonderfully moist, tender and full of flavour.

1 Clean and trim all the giblets and chop them coarsely. Put them in a deep pan with a lid over a medium heat and add the butter and olive oil. Cook together for 5 minutes. Lay the chicken in the pan and cook briefly on all sides to seal.

2 Pour in an even mixture of water and chicken stock to come about three-quarters of the way up the pan. Add salt and cover tightly, then simmer gently for about 1½–2 hours, or until the chicken is completely cooked through.

3 The liquid in the pan should have almost completely evaporated. Take the chicken out of the pan and carve it into portions. Arrange the carved chicken on a warmed serving dish.

4 Whisk the eggs and the juice and rind of the lemon, then add to the juices left in the pan. Beat until the eggs thicken slightly.

5 Pour this sauce over the chicken portions, sprinkle with parsley and serve immediately, garnished with lemon slices.

GALLINA 'MBRIACA
DRUNKEN CHICKEN

SERVES 4 TO 6

- 1 oven-ready free-range chicken, about 3kg/6lb 9oz
- 1.75 litres/3 pints/7½ cups dry white wine, preferably Verdicchio dei Castelli di Iesi
- 5 garlic cloves, chopped
- 1 onion, sliced
- 1 large rosemary sprig
- 5 fresh sage leaves
- 2 celery sticks, coarsely chopped
- 2 carrots, coarsely chopped
- a handful of fresh flat leaf parsley leaves, chopped
- 1 dried red chilli, chopped
- 10 cherry tomatoes, peeled and seeded
- sea salt and ground black pepper

COOK'S TIP

It's important not to move the chicken or lift the lid during the entire cooking time.

This recipe for chicken cooked in lots of dry, aromatic white wine comes from the region of Le Marche, where cooking and eating are always approached with joy and generosity. The wine used for this recipe would have to be the region's most famous white wine: Verdicchio dei Castelli di Iesi, which has been carefully made in the same way for decades. Verdicchio can only be produced in a specific area of Le Marche, known as Castelli di Iesi, where the terroir, climate and constant ventilation provided by the sea breezes allow the grapes to develop in a very special way. This pale, straw-coloured wine with greenish tones is delicate and flowery, with a hint of almonds and a clean, slightly bitter finish.

1 Rinse the chicken with about 600ml/1 pint/2½ cups of the wine, then cover it all over, inside and out, with garlic, salt and pepper. Cover and chill for at least 8 hours.

2 Joint the chicken and put it into a large bowl. Cover it with the remaining white wine and add the onion, rosemary, sage, celery, carrots, parsley, chilli and tomatoes. Mix all the ingredients together with your hands. Cover and chill overnight.

3 The next day, transfer everything to a flameproof glazed terracotta casserole or enamel pan that has a heavy, tight-fitting lid.

4 Cover the surface of the chicken with a double sheet of baking parchment, put the lid on top, and place a heatproof weight on the lid to press down as much as possible.

5 Simmer for about 4 hours, until very tender, without lifting the lid. Serve.

AGNELLO AL TARTUFO NERO
LAMB WITH BLACK TRUFFLE

This rich and delicious dish of roasted lamb flavoured with mushrooms and truffle really shows off the very best of the cuisine of Umbria. This is without doubt a grand recipe of the upper-class kitchens of the region, and is a sharp contrast to the simple, basic recipes of the neighbouring peasant and shepherd communities. If fresh truffle is not available, it is always better to use a truffle butter rather than truffle oil, which is sometimes so full of chemical ingredients that it can be a long way from the real taste of precious Italian black truffle.

1 Preheat the oven to 180°C/350°F/Gas 4. Open out the boned leg of lamb and carefully check the meat for any bone splinters. Remove any excess fat from the lamb. (You could use the removed bone to make the lamb stock, if you like.)

2 Mix the minced meats with the truffle, kidneys, mushrooms, four of the juniper berries and 15ml/1 tbsp of the extra virgin olive oil. Season with salt and black pepper. Spoon this stuffing mixture on to the inside of the opened-out lamb leg.

3 Carefully close up the lamb leg and tie it tightly and securely into shape using kitchen string or twine. Transfer it into a roasting pan. Season again on the outside with salt and black pepper, and rub it all over with the remaining olive oil.

4 Roast the lamb for about 40 minutes, turning and basting from time to time, until cooked through. When it is cooked, transfer the meat to a board and leave it to rest.

5 Meanwhile, place the roasting pan over a medium heat. Pour the red wine into the pan and boil to remove the acidity while scraping the sediment from the base of the pan.

6 Mix the stock with the potato starch or flour and stir into the roasting pan. Add the remaining juniper berries and cook, stirring, to form a reduced and thickened gravy.

7 Carve the lamb and serve with the gravy.

SERVES 8

1.8kg/4lb leg of lamb, boned
200g/7oz minced/ground veal
200g/7oz minced/ground pork
50g/2oz black truffle, chopped
2 lamb kidneys, trimmed and chopped
600g/1lb 6oz/8½ cups mushrooms, finely chopped
6 juniper berries, lightly crushed
45–60ml/3–4 tbsp extra virgin olive oil
250ml/8fl oz/1 cup dry red wine
about 450ml/¾ pint/scant 2 cups stock (made with the removed lamb bone, if you like)
15ml/1 tbsp potato starch or potato flour
sea salt and ground black pepper

COOK'S TIP

A dish of tender artichokes, braised with garlic and mint, is the usual accompaniment to serve alongside the lamb.

FRITTATA CON LE ERBETTE ODOROSE
FRITTATA WITH FRESH HERBS

A frittata, made with all the wild herbs one can possibly find, is typical of the Easter period, when the first spring shoots are plentiful. Everything goes into the mixture, such as wild asparagus or cultivated thin asparagus, wild garlic leaves, wild hops, borage, chicory and many more. These are combined with whatever is available in the vegetable garden, such as pea shoots, broad bean shoots, broccoli or rocket flowers, the new season's tiny artichokes, and so on; there is no limit to the possible combinations. This is a typical recipe from Umbria, where wild edible plants are available all over the countryside in the springtime. Serve the frittata either hot or cold with salad, if you like.

SERVES 4

about 45ml/3 tbsp extra virgin olive oil
1 garlic bulb, cloves chopped
5 small spring onions/scallions, chopped
a small bunch of fresh mint leaves, chopped
a small handful of fresh lemon balm leaves, chopped
a small handful of fresh flat leaf parsley leaves, chopped
a small handful of fresh chervil leaves, chopped
8 eggs
sea salt and ground black pepper
salad leaves, to serve (optional)

1 Put the oil in a non-stick frying pan and add 45ml/3 tbsp cold water. Add the garlic, spring onions, mint, lemon balm, flat leaf parsley and chervil, and cook for 5 minutes, or until softened.

2 Beat the eggs together in a small bowl, then season with salt and pepper.

3 Pour the beaten eggs into the frying pan with the herb mixture and stir gently with a wooden spoon to combine.

4 As the egg begins to set, rock the pan slightly from side to side and pull the outer edge of the frittata towards the middle, making sure the underneath of the frittata sets completely, without burning.

5 Cover the frittata with a plate that is larger than the pan. Turn it over in one smooth movement, so that it lands safely on the plate.

6 If the pan looks completely dry, add a little more oil, then slide the frittata back into the hot pan, starting at the opposite side of the pan and drawing the plate back towards you.

7 Shake the frittata into position, flatten it gently with a spatula, and continue to cook it until it is golden brown underneath.

8 Slide the frittata out on to a serving platter and serve it hot or cold, cut into wedges, with a green salad alongside, if you like.

FRITTATA AL TARTUFO
BLACK TRUFFLE FRITTATA

This recipe is made with the black truffle of Umbria, which is liberally used in many dishes throughout the region. These elusive fungi grow under the trees in the local woods and forests and are sought out by specially trained dogs, then dug up by the truffle hunters. Although neither as expensive nor as intensely flavoured as the white Piedmontese truffle of Alba, black truffles taste unique, and are highly prized both within the region and throughout the world. The international black truffle festival of Umbria always takes place over the last weekend of February in the lovely medieval town of Spoleto. The flavours of truffles and eggs marry together beautifully, so this frittata has a taste that is really very special, making it ideal for a celebration.

1 Beat the eggs in a small bowl, then season them and stir in the sliced truffles.

2 Heat the oil in a large frying pan and swirl it around to coat it thoroughly. Pour the egg and truffle mixture into the frying pan.

3 As the egg begins to set, rock the pan from side to side and pull the outer edge of the frittata towards the middle, making sure the underneath sets, without burning.

4 Cover the frittata with a plate that is larger than the pan.

5 Turn the frittata over in one movement, so that it lands on the plate.

6 If the pan looks completely dry, add a little more olive oil, then slide the frittata back into the hot pan, starting at the opposite side of the pan and drawing the plate back towards you.

7 Shake the frittata into position, flatten gently with a spatula, and cook until golden brown underneath. Sprinkle with the wine, slide out on to a platter and serve immediately, piping hot.

SERVES 4

9 eggs
115g/4oz sliced fresh black truffles or sliced truffles preserved in oil (tartufata)
about 45ml/3 tbsp extra virgin olive oil
45ml/3 tbsp dry white wine
sea salt and ground black pepper

COOK'S TIP

If using a fresh truffle, you'll need to brush it clean with a special little brush, or a brand-new nailbrush. Never wash them! To slice, use a special truffle slicer or a mandolin to get the slices extremely thin.

SERVES 4

450g/1lb ripe tomatoes
45ml/3 tbsp extra virgin olive oil
1 onion, sliced
450g/1lb red bell peppers, seeded and sliced
sea salt

LA BANDIERA
THE FLAG

This Umbrian bell pepper stew is almost a purée by the time it has been cooked gently for almost 40 minutes, but it is really delicious either as a side dish with meat or as part of an antipasto. It can even be added to beaten eggs and turned into the most flavoursome frittata, and is also good with cheese melted on top of it. The name of the dish is thought to refer to the brightness of the colour: bright and strident like a red flag.

1 First, peel the tomatoes. Place them in a large heatproof bowl and cover them with boiling water. Leave for about 30 seconds, then carefully drain them. The skins should peel off easily. Chop the flesh, discarding the seeds.

2 Put the oil in a pan and fry the sliced onion for 10 minutes, or until it is softened but not browned.

3 Add the sliced bell peppers, stir, and cook for 10 minutes.

4 Add the chopped tomatoes, season with salt and stir well.

5 Simmer the mixture gently over a low heat, stirring frequently, for 30 minutes, or until the peppers and tomatoes have softened completely.

SERVES 6

200g/7oz ready-to-cook spelt
4 potatoes, quartered
4 courgettes/zucchini, halved
115g/4oz green beans
200g/7oz fresh haricot/navy or cannellini beans
275g/10oz cabbage leaves, shredded
3 carrots (or similar quantity of other vegetables of your choice)
115g/4oz thinly sliced pancetta
3 garlic cloves, peeled
15ml/1 tbsp extra virgin olive oil, plus extra for drizzling
1 dried red chilli, chopped
sea salt
toasted bread rubbed with a garlic clove, to serve (optional)

COOK'S TIP

Serve as an accompaniment to grilled or broiled meats.

FARRO E VERDURA
SPELT WITH VEGETABLES

Spelt is a species of wheat grain. It was an important staple food in various parts of Europe from the Bronze Age to medieval times, but has survived as part of the daily diet in various parts of Italy, including Tuscany, Umbria and Le Marche. More recently, it has found a new market as a health food and as a substitute for common wheat for those with a gluten intolerance or allergy. Nutty and delicious, spelt is used in soups, salads or casseroles, or is ground to a flour for bread and pasta making. This recipe is from Le Marche.

1 Boil the spelt in plenty of lightly salted water for 50 minutes–1 hour, until tender.

2 Meanwhile, boil the potatoes in a separate pan for 10 minutes, then add the courgettes, two types of beans, cabbage leaves and carrots and cook for a further 10–15 minutes, until tender.

3 Drain both the cooked spelt and the cooked vegetables.

4 In a large frying pan, fry the pancetta and garlic in the olive oil until the garlic is softened and the pancetta is crispy. Discard the garlic.

5 Add the spelt and all the vegetables to the frying pan. Mix well and season with salt and the dried red chilli. Stir-fry everything together for 5 minutes to heat through, then serve. If you wish, serve on a slice of toasted bread and drizzled with oil.

CAVOLINA IN INSALATA
WARM SPRING CABBAGE SALAD

A very simple recipe for a warm cabbage salad from Le Marche, this dish is perfect served alongside the many pork or chicken dishes from this region. The recipe does call for fresh, crisp, spring cabbage as opposed to the coarser, heavier-leaved cabbages such as Savoy or the Tuscan cavolo nero. As with all recipes that rely on very few, basic ingredients, it is important that the flavourings, in this case the red wine vinegar, should be of the best possible quality – in other words, strong and tasty as well as sharp and sour, but not too astringent or acidic; it is worth buying a decent bottle.

COOK'S TIP

You could save the hard outer leaves of the cabbage to add to other vegetables for vegetable stock, or use them for a soup such as minestrone, rather than composting them or throwing them away.

SERVES 4

1 large spring cabbage
300ml/½ pint/1¼ cups extra virgin olive oil
100ml/3½fl oz/scant ½ cup red wine vinegar
3 garlic cloves, lightly crushed
sea salt and ground black pepper

1 Remove the hard outer leaves of the cabbage. Shred the rest of the cabbage finely and put it into a colander. Rinse it well several times, then drain thoroughly.

2 Put the oil, vinegar and garlic into a pan over a medium heat. Heat until sizzling.

3 Transfer the shredded cabbage to a salad bowl, then pour over the hot garlic oil. Toss the mixture together thoroughly.

4 Season with salt and pepper, toss again and cover with a plate to allow it to steam for about 2–3 minutes. Serve.

FRAPPE
CARNIVAL FRITTERS

During Carnival, people have always celebrated out on the streets, especially on Shrove Tuesday and the Thursday after Ash Wednesday, or Giovedi Grasso in Italian. This is the last important opportunity for a lot of noise and fun before the rigours of Lent really set in. Many types of street food, or at least food that was once cooked on the streets, are attached in some way to this period, most of them sweet and deep-fried in oil according to tradition. This particular recipe is from Le Marche, but frappe are made in various ways all over Italy. They are as much a part of the Carnival spirit as the masks and costumes, the endless practical jokes and street parading that happens in towns and cities throughout the country at this time of the year.

SERVES 8

450g/1lb/4 cups plain/all-purpose flour, plus extra for dusting
50g/2oz/¼ cup unsalted butter, lard or white cooking fat
2 egg yolks
1 egg
15ml/1 tbsp caster/superfine sugar
pinch of salt
a few drops of lemon juice
30ml/2 tbsp Mistra liqueur (optional)
dry white wine, if needed
sunflower oil, for deep-frying
icing/confectioners' sugar, for dusting
Alchermes liqueur, for sprinkling (optional)

1 In a large bowl, mix together the flour, butter, lard or white cooking fat, egg yolks and whole egg, sugar, salt, lemon juice and Mistra, if using.

2 Gently knead to make a soft ball of dough. If dry, add a little dry white wine. Leave the dough to rest, covered with a clean dish towel, for about 30 minutes.

3 Put the dough on a lightly floured surface and roll it out thinly, then cut it into long, wide ribbons, using a pastry wheel or knife.

4 Heat the oil in a large pan until a small cube of bread dropped into it sizzles instantly. Carefully drop a few frappe into the oil, about six or seven in every batch.

5 As soon as the frappe are golden and puffed up and are floating on the surface of the oil, scoop them out with a slotted spoon and drain thoroughly on kitchen paper.

6 Dust the frappe with icing sugar, sprinkle with Alchermes, if using, and serve warm with chilled dessert wine.

COOK'S TIP

You can omit the Mistra and Alchermes liqueurs if you are planning to serve these fritters to children.

SERVES 4

300g/11oz/2¾ cups short pasta, such as penne, tortiglione or maccheroni
150g/5oz/scant 1 cup walnuts, broken
50g/2oz/¼ cup sugar
grated rind of 1 large unwaxed lemon
5ml/1 tsp ground cinnamon
5ml/1 tsp unsweetened cocoa powder (optional)
25g/1oz/2 tbsp unsalted butter
pinch of sea salt

NOCIATA
PASTA WITH SWEET WALNUT SAUCE

Most people do not associate pasta with desserts, but this unusual recipe is very much a part of the Umbrian culinary tradition, and the texture of pasta works perfectly with the sweet, nutty sauce. It was created to be a part of the Vigilia (Christmas Eve) feast, in times when this special festive meal had a formal, ceremonial atmosphere. All over Italy, the main Christmas meal takes place on Christmas Eve, either after midnight mass or before the mass, depending on the regional custom. It is usually served cold.

1 Bring 3 litres/5¼ pints/12½ cups salted water to the boil in a large pan. Add the pasta, cover and return to the boil. Cook according to the pack instructions until just tender; do not overcook.

2 Put the walnuts into a food processor. Using the blade attachment, process to a fine mass with the sugar, lemon, cinnamon and cocoa, if using. Reserve a little lemon rind to garnish. (Alternatively, pound the walnuts in a mortar and pestle, and stir in the sugar, lemon, cinnamon and cocoa.)

3 Transfer the walnut mixture to a large serving dish. Remove a ladleful of the boiling water from the pasta and stir into the walnut mixture.

4 Drain the pasta and add to the walnut mixture. Add the butter, then toss all the ingredients together well to distribute the sauce evenly.

5 Leave to stand for 5 minutes, then serve, sprinkled with the reserved lemon rind. Alternatively, leave to cool and serve cold.

SERPENTONE
SNAKE-SHAPED CAKE

Apples and dried fruit, nuts and sugar are the main ingredients for this classic Umbrian cake. The pastry is quite unusual: made with olive oil, flour, sugar and water, it has quite a different texture to butter pastry. The decoration of the cake is where the cook's imagination takes flight – all kinds of expressions on the 'snake's' face can be created using a few carefully placed ingredients. Some local cooks also add small coloured sweets to the snake, to represent scales. The cake is quite sweet, so should be served thinly sliced, with some chilled, fairly dry dessert wine or some strong coffee.

SERVES 6 TO 8

115g/4oz/⅔ cup sultanas/golden raisins
225g/8oz/2 cups plain/all-purpose flour, plus extra for dusting
115g/4oz/generous ½ cup caster/superfine sugar
60ml/4 tbsp extra virgin olive oil, plus extra for greasing
pinch of salt
100–150ml/3½fl oz–¼ pint/scant ½ cup–⅔ cup warm water
50g/2oz/⅓ cup blanched almonds, coarsely chopped
8 walnuts, coarsely chopped
3 large eating apples, peeled and sliced
5 dried figs, chopped
5 ready-to-eat prunes, stoned/pitted and chopped
30–45ml/2–3 tbsp icing/confectioners' sugar

FOR THE DECORATION

2 glacé/candied cherries or 2 coffee beans
1 blanched almond
10–20ml/2–4 tsp caster/superfine sugar

1 Soak the sultanas in a small bowl of warm water for about 20 minutes, until they are plump and softened.

2 Put the flour and caster sugar on to the work surface and add the oil and the salt. Add a little warm water, then knead gently to make a fairly solid pastry dough.

3 Cover the dough with a clean dish towel and leave to rest for about 20 minutes.

4 Preheat the oven to 180°C/350°F/Gas 4. Grease and flour a baking sheet.

5 Roll out the pastry on a floured surface as thinly as possible. Sprinkle the blanched, chopped almonds over the sheet of dough.

6 Drain the sultanas and pat them dry with kitchen paper. Spread them over the almonds, with the walnuts, apples, figs and prunes.

7 Sprinkle with the icing sugar and carefully roll the dough up on itself, to form a long cylinder. Twist the cylinder around to form a coiled snake shape and transfer on to the baking sheet.

8 To make the decoration, press the glacé cherries or coffee beans into place to represent the snake's eyes, and then press in the almond to represent the snake's tongue. Sprinkle with sugar.

9 Bake the cake for 40 minutes, or until golden. Cool on a wire rack before serving.

PANPEPATO
SPICED UMBRIAN CAKE

The Umbrian recipe for this Christmas speciality originates in the small town of Terni and its surrounding area. The Italian name literally translates as 'peppered bread', referring to the spices, which include some ground black pepper. The recipe has medieval roots and is typical of the kind of recipes attributed to that period of history, when spices and other expensive ingredients were used in generous quantities for special-occasion dishes. Several versions of a similar recipe, with exactly the same name, exist in various parts of Central Italy.

MAKES 4 TO 6 CAKES

oil, for greasing
300g/11oz/scant 2 cups almonds
300g/11oz/scant 2 cups hazelnuts
1.5kg/3¼lb/8½ cups walnuts
300g/11oz/1½ cups honey
40–60ml/3–4 tbsp strongest possible espresso coffee
about 400ml/14fl oz/1⅔ cups boiled wine must (see Cook's Tip)
400g/14oz/scant 2 cups currants or sultanas/golden raisins, soaked in water for 20 minutes, or until plump and softened
300g/11oz/1⅓ cups crystallised/candied citrus fruit, chopped
grated rind of 1 unwaxed orange
1.5ml/¼ tsp freshly grated nutmeg
1.5ml/¼ tsp ground black pepper
225g/8oz/2 cups pine nuts
700g/1lb 9oz dark/bittersweet cooking chocolate, chopped
115g/4oz/1 cup unsweetened cocoa powder
200g/7oz/1 cup caster/superfine sugar
about 200g/7oz/1¾ cups plain/all-purpose flour
icing/confectioners' sugar, for dusting

1 Preheat the oven to 180°C/350°F/Gas 4. Grease and flour a baking sheet.

2 Blanch the almonds by soaking them in a bowl of hot water for about 1 minute, then draining them and removing the skins.

3 Lay the hazelnuts and the walnuts out on a baking sheet and toast them under a hot grill or broiler, turning occasionally, for about 5 minutes, or until golden. Keep a close eye on them. Hold a few hazelnuts and walnuts at a time in a dish towel and rub off their skins. Repeat with all the remaining nuts. Chop them coarsely.

4 Put the honey into a pan and add the coffee and the wine must, stir together and warm gently over a low heat.

5 Drain the currants or sultanas and pat them dry with kitchen paper. Pile them on to a work surface. Add the chopped citrus fruit, the grated orange rind, nutmeg and pepper, as well as the pine nuts, chocolate, cocoa powder and sugar.

6 Mix all these dry ingredients together with your hands, adding the warm honey mixture a little at a time. Gradually add the flour until you have achieved a manageable dough. (Add more flour or wine must as required.)

7 Form this mixture into 4–6 small loaf shapes and lay them on the prepared baking sheet. Bake them in the preheated oven for about 10 minutes, or until golden brown.

8 Remove the cakes from the oven and allow to cool on a wire rack. Panpepato should be allowed to rest for 2–3 days after baking before it is eaten. To serve, dust the cakes with icing sugar and cut into slices.

COOK'S TIP

Boiled wine must is fermented grape juice, which has been reduced and sweetened. You can also use a sweet red wine if you prefer.

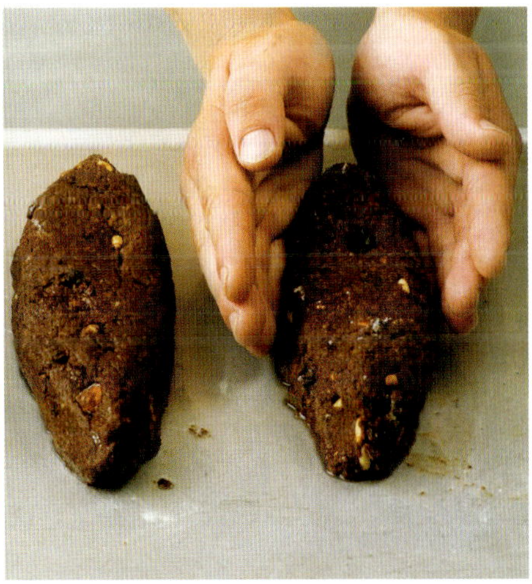

CENTRAL ITALY & SARDINIA

A STUNNING LANDSCAPE

The central regions of Italy, comprising Lazio, Campania, Abruzzo and Molise, as well as the charming island of Sardinia, are linked by beautiful countryside and thriving cities. At the very heart of Lazio lies Rome, the Eternal City. With its breathtaking atmosphere, vibrant food culture and diverse population, there is no wonder this ancient city attracts millions of tourists each year. To the south and east, the mountainous Abruzzo and Molise regions have a peaceful agricultural focus. Still further south is Naples, a populous and sprawling metropolis, where many of the best-known Italian dishes – especially pizza – were first created. In startling contrast, the lovely island of Sardinia has its own intriguing, unique and well-preserved traditions of food and farming.

BELOW *Lazio, Campania, Abruzzo and Molise make up the heart of mainland Italy, with the large, autonomous island of Sardinia set across the Tyrrhenian Sea quite far from mainland Italy.*

BELOW RIGHT *The colourful island of Procida, off Naples, sits in the sparkling waters of the Mediterranean Sea and is a magnet for tourists.*

ROME AND THE LAZIO REGION

Although the allure of Rome is very strong, Lazio offers an extraordinary variety of landscapes to delight the visitor: wide beaches, pine woods, mountains, gentle hills and expansive plains dotted with picturesque monasteries and ancient villages.

The Lazio region experiences the typical Mediterranean climate that is characteristic of the western coast of Italy, with hot summers and temperate spring and autumn weather, giving a long growing season that is ideal for farming. Even tender crops such as citrus fruits can be grown in the south of the region, although la tramontana, the cold winter wind that blows from the mountains, can cast a chill over the whole area.

Like most regions that were once Papal States, Lazio was historically poor, with little economic development until recent times. Now, however, Lazio contributes 10 per cent of Italy's national wealth from tourism, agriculture and industry.

NAPLES AND THE CAMPANIA REGION

It is hard to begin to describe the extraordinary, chaotic, exciting and resolutely southern city of Naples – it is totally distinct from the rest of Italy. Staunchly Catholic, Naples is rich in historical, artistic and cultural traditions, and has its own distinct cuisine. Pizza, the iconic Italian dish, originated here, and it is eaten, like so many other local foods, out on the street. Neapolitan is a language in its own right and you'll hear the dialect everywhere at full volume. Naples has some beautiful architecture, a thriving port area, and fantastic restaurants and bars serving fresh food.

Running along the gulf of Naples and Sorrento, Campania is home to picturesque towns and strong cultural traditions. The volcano Vesuvius looms on the skyline and the preserved Roman towns of Pompeii and Herculaneum act as a reminder of the damage it caused when it erupted in AD79. The climate is mild, with many hours of sunshine.

REMOTE ABRUZZO AND MOLISE

The climate of the Abruzzo region is typically Mediterranean near the coast, where the land levels out. However, high up in the Apennines, which dominate the region with their snowy tops, there are very cold winters and hot summers. These high mountains have become popular for walking and skiing. The landscape in the hills and lower mountains is full of green meadows, sparkling rivers and lakes.

The difficult terrain and contrasting temperatures mean that farming is not easy. The hills allow for the cultivation of figs, carrots and grapes, while down on the plains, farmers can grow wheat, potatoes, beetroot and tobacco. Two rarer specialities of the Abruzzo region are liquorice and saffron, and shepherds tend sheep on the uneven grassy hillsides.

Molise, to the south of Abruzzo, offers some of the most pristine natural areas in all of Europe, with fragrant green forests, expansive plains and snow-topped mountains. Nestling in the landscape are well-preserved medieval castles and hamlets, and fascinating ancient ruins that date back to the 4th century BCE.

A BEAUTIFUL COASTLINE

The beauty of Campania has long caught the attention of artists and poets alike. During the times of the ancient Greeks, Campania was home to Homer's sirens. Later, during the Roman period, the region was a hot spot among the rich, who built breathtaking villas by the sea. The Amalfi Coast, claimed by many to be the most beautiful stretch of coastline in Europe, has lemon groves sloping down to the blue sea, with brightly coloured houses climbing the hillside.

THE RUGGED ISLAND OF SARDINIA

The second-largest island in the Mediterranean Sea (after Sicily), Sardinia is hot and dry in summer, while spring and autumn are pleasant. Winters are mild and humid with the occasional hot day. The island is surrounded by the Mediterranean and its long coastline sees plenty of sun. The terrain is not easy for farmers, with high hills and mountains inland. Agriculture tends to focus on livestock and growing tender crops, such as olives, citrus fruits and grapes. Fish is also plentiful in the surrounding waters and forms an important part of the diet.

Sardinia is one of two Italian regions whose inhabitants have been recognised as a popolo (a distinct people) by a local statute; the other region is the Veneto. The people here, unusually, have more in common genetically with Bosnia and Croatia than they do with the rest of Italy.

ABOVE *Abruzzo and Molise have retained a largely pastoral landscape and a strong history of farming.*

A POWERFUL HISTORY

The central regions of Italy have a colourful history that dates as far back as the Bronze Age, if not further. From the legend of Romulus and Remus to the spread of the Roman Empire, the story of central Italy, with Rome at the heart, is universally known. The influence of this glorious city was felt not only in the surrounding area of what is now Italy, but also far and wide across the world due to the spread of the all-powerful Roman Empire. After the decline of the Empire, the region was controlled by other powers, which led to many new dishes and ingredients being incorporated into the local cuisine. Sardinia's isolated position, meanwhile, has created a unique history that is illustrated in its architecture and food culture.

BELOW *Rome displays a wealth of fabulously preserved architecture and art from many periods of history, such as the awe-inspiring St. Peter's Basilica at the heart of Vatican City.*

ROME AND LAZIO: A CENTRE OF POWER

The founding of Rome goes back to the very early days of civilization. Kings first governed Rome, but after a short time, the citizens took power and ruled themselves for nearly 500 years, followed by the Roman Empire under many emperors for a further 500 years.

The Roman Empire had collapsed by the year AD476. In the succeeding years, invaders came and went, leaving behind their own artistic and culinary traditions, and the fabric of Rome was left in very poor shape. Gradually Roman pride reasserted itself, but it was not until the 19th century that the structure of modern Italy, with Rome as the capital, was fully established. Some of the world's most important art and architecture resides here, and Rome also contains Vatican City, a city-state and the centre of the Catholic Church, within its boundaries.

The region that is now known as Lazio, right in the centre of Italy, has been home to agricultural populations since the early Bronze Age. People settled in this pleasant, equable climate, raising crops and keeping animals for food. From the Middle Ages to the 18th century, Lazio served as an important hub for all forms of artistic and scientific creation and development, keeping the flame of culture alive through multiple invasions. Its decline in the lean years of the 18th and 19th centuries has been reversed at last, and in the 21st century, mainly because of successful Rome, Lazio has regained its reputation as a forward-thinking area with plenty of entrepreneurial spirit.

NAPLES AND CAMPANIA: GRECO-ROMAN UNITY

The bustling, energetic, sometimes lawless city of Naples is still regarded as the capital of the south of Italy. Naples was probably founded by the Greeks in the 8th century BCE, a few kilometres from the older town of Partenope, when Campania was part of the Magna Græcia. This new town or 'neapolis' (from where it got its name) has been absorbing the influences of its settlers and invaders ever since.

Campania was part of the Roman Empire by the 4th century AD, although its inhabitants still spoke Greek; it was a centre of Greco-Roman culture. Its fertile landscape and elegant Greek architecture made it an important region. Campania changed hands many times in the next few centuries, and became part of Italy as we know it in October 1860.

Today, Naples is most famous for its rich, simple dishes that have transcended international borders, including the basic pizza, made of just a few ingredients, but of very good quality.

ABOVE *A shepherd leads his flock over the mountain grasslands of Campo Imperatore in the L'Aquila province of Abruzzo.*

ABRUZZO AND MOLISE

Many different tribes populated this part of Italy in ancient times, living a predominantly pastoral life, caring for their animals and growing food. People inhabited the few low-lying areas along the Adriatic seashore and beside the rivers in the green, fertile valleys. During the Augustan era (27BCE to AD14), the whole region was subdued and incorporated into the Roman Empire, after much fierce resistance from the local people.

Between the 6th and 19th centuries, the area underwent numerous changes of government due to its position as a wedge between the north and south of Italy. Garibaldi's campaign to unify Italy brought all the regions together in 1860, but this was no unqualified blessing – Molise and Abruzzo suffered from their relatively poor development during the centuries of constant fighting, and there was a spate of migration, both abroad and to other parts of the country. It was not until 1963 that Molise was recognised as a separate region from Abruzzo, with its own proud traditions.

SARDINIA: AN ANCIENT LAND

The island dates back to the Cambrian period, 570 million years ago. With the periodic fluctuation of sea level, Sardinia has at times been linked physically to the rest of Italy, and people and animals crossed the land bridge to and from Tuscany.

The scant population that lived in Sardinia from around AD1800 to 200BCE built the strange conical towers that are still a characteristic feature of the landscape. This population was mainly a pastoral people and their basic traditions of farming have been maintained in Sardinia for over 3,000 years, right up to the present day. It is still common to see peasant farmers travelling around by donkey and, up to just a few years ago, you could occasionally witness the tilling of the land with an ox-drawn wooden plough.

Throughout its history, Sardinia fell prey to invaders and marauders, due to its position in the Mediterranean Sea. It is no wonder, therefore, that most of the main cities are set inland, and well protected. The highest mountain peak, Monte Moro, is so called because it provided a lookout against the Moors. On the coast, older cottages are tucked away where they could not be seen from the sea. Moreover, Sardinia lacks a fishing history – the sea was a dangerous place – and today's fishermen tend to be descendants of migrants from the Pontine Islands, close to the mainland, rather than islanders.

A WORLD-FAMOUS CUISINE

To many people outside of Italy, 'Italian cuisine' is basically Neapolitan cooking, and most especially pizza. This is partly because many of the Italian immigrants all around the world came from the city of Naples and its environs. When these ambitious migrants opened restaurants in their new countries, they naturally served the style of food they loved and knew best: the cooking of Naples and Campania. However, there is much more to the central region than Naples. Lazio, Abruzzo, Molise and the island of Sardinia all have their own traditions of making delicious dishes using local ingredients, including tender lamb from the sheep trails of Abruzzo, fresh fish from the Campania coastline, gutsy pasta sauces and offal from Rome, and speciality Sardinian desserts.

THE CUISINE OF ROME AND LAZIO

Traditional cooking in Lazio reflects the simple, sustaining meals of shepherds and farmers. It's no surprise that tender, milk-fed lamb is a favourite dish, usually roasted and served with seasonal vegetables. The cuisine is a savoury tapestry, incorporating the farming traditions of the region with an amalgam of ingredients from outlying areas, including Umbria. The vegetables found in the markets are of exceptional quality, perhaps because of the sun-drenched volcanic soil of the region.

Fish is an integral part of Roman cuisine, and features most frequently in Rome as salt cod – baccalà. Offal is also key, and although it has been ousted from many of the more refined city-centre

ROMAN PASTA

Although all sorts of pasta shapes are served in Roman restaurants, spaghetti and the local specialities bucatini or tonnarelli (thick-cut spaghetti) are the favourite shapes. These chunky strips of pasta stand up well to the coarse, rich sauces the Romans prefer, such as a very simple, strong-tasting aglio e olio (garlic and oil), cacio e pepe (Pecorino cheese and ground black pepper), alla carbonara (with beaten eggs, cubes of pan-fried pork or bacon, and Pecorino or Parmesan cheese), and alle vongole (with fresh baby clams).

RIGHT *The wonderful market of Campo de Fiori in Rome is awash with the vibrant colours of various types of fresh fruit and vegetables each day.*

restaurants, it still appears on the menus of more traditional eateries, especially those in the Testaccio area. More conventional meat dishes include abbacchio (milk-fed lamb roasted to melting tenderness with rosemary, sage and garlic), scottadito (grilled or broiled lamb chops eaten with the fingers) and saltimbocca alla Romana (thin slices of veal cooked with a slice of prosciutto, mozzarella cheese and sage on top). Artichokes are the quintessential Roman vegetable, served alla Romana (stuffed with garlic and mint) and in all their unadulterated glory, alla Giudia (flattened and fried in olive oil, Jewish-style).

No description of the gastronomy of Rome would be complete without a mention of the city's countless bars, cafés and restaurants, where Romans can be found morning, noon and night, sipping their daily cappuccinos, or eating and drinking with family and friends.

ABOVE *Pizza remains the iconic Neapolitan dish and is cooked and eaten with delight throughout the city, and elsewhere in Italy.*

NEAPOLITAN STREET FOOD

Food in Naples is a joyful experience to be shared with friends and family. There are all kinds of fast foods available, from friggi e mangia ('fry and eat'), or the products of the local rosticceria (delicatessen), to various passatempi ('fill-time'), little treats of shellfish, small pizzas, tarts or fritters which are offered at kiosks and street stalls and are eaten at any hungry moment throughout the day. In these traditional foods, Naples extravagantly displays its legendary culinary heritage for all to admire.

NAPLES AND THE CAMPANIA REGION

This is a region in which peasant and noble cuisines have grown up alongside each other, using the same produce. Superb fruits and vegetables are grown here, particularly tomatoes and aubergines or eggplants. Other favourite ingredients include the mild mozzarella cheese that is made from water buffalo milk, which is often served with tomatoes as a salad called la Caprese.

As in Rome, the most common pasta shape is spaghetti, frequently served with shellfish and meatless marinara tomato sauce. Fish and shellfish are brought in from the Mediterranean as a principal protein source and they are far more widely eaten than red meat, which is usually reserved for major feast days.

The pizza, the most famous creation of the region's cuisine, is one of the most representative dishes of Naples. Resplendent with its tomato topping, sizzling and cheerful, pizza became extremely popular among the masses in the 18th

ABOVE *Creamy buffalo mozzarella is made by hand in Campania.*

ABOVE RIGHT *Campania is famous for its fruit and vegetables, in particular the lemons of the Amalfi coast and the region's distinctive tomatoes.*

century, but also with barons and princes: it was a main feature at the grand receptions of the Bourbons. The pizza-maker Raffaele Esposito created a patriotic tri-colour pizza for Queen Margherita of Savoie in 1889. The three colours of the Italian flag, white, red and green, became a topping of mozzarella, tomato and basil. There are numerous varieties of pizza, including quattro formaggi (four cheeses), frutti di mare (shellfish), and alla marinara (tomato and garlic), but the presence of tomato sauce, at least in Naples, is always guaranteed.

Other glories of Neapolitan cuisine include recipes based on the magnificent vegetables of the Campania countryside, such as parmigiana di melanzane (aubergines/eggplants baked with tomato and cheese) or stuffed bell peppers. The fruits of the sea feature in many classic dishes, such as polpi alla Luciana (octopus Luciana style), which originates from the working-class quarter of Santa Lucia; it is cooked with hot chilli peppers and the ever-present tomatoes. Dairy products, particularly cheeses such as provolone, scamorza, caciocavallo and ricotta, are also an important part of the cuisine. The queen of the cheeses, however, is mozzarella, a fresh, soft, white cheese with a stringy texture, made from buffalo milk.

Pasta was not invented in Naples, but here it has reached the highest levels of perfection. Local pasta dishes are extraordinary for the care with which the pasta is cooked – it must be al dente. From the pummarola (tomato sauce), through a range of more elaborate sauces based on vegetables or shellfish, right up to the apotheosis of slow-cooked ragù meat sauce, the creativity of the area is in real evidence in pasta dishes.

The cakes and desserts of Naples are a delicious, rich treat: ice creams, babas, spumoni, sfogliatelle, taralli and the magnificent pastiera, the cake eaten from Epiphany to Easter, made with ricotta cheese, orange flower water, cinnamon and candied fruit.

TOMATOES

At the heart of Neapolitan cuisine there is an ingredient which merits a mention in its own right: the tomato. It was brought to Italy from South America in the 16th century, but it was only around the beginning of the 19th century that it became a common ingredient in many Italian recipes. It is now one of the most important and iconic of all the crops grown in Campania.

THE CUISINE OF ABRUZZO AND MOLISE

Rugged mountains (the highest peaks in the Apennines), palm-lined beaches and charming hill towns combine to make Abruzzo one of Italy's most beautiful and geographically diverse regions. It is a place where ancient agricultural traditions are still handed down from one generation to the next. The region is famous for its livestock and farming, including crops of the highly prized spice saffron, and for the fish and shellfish caught along the coast of the Adriatic Sea.

Pasta, vegetables and meat (especially lamb and pork) are the staples of Abruzzo cuisine. Many lamb dishes and subtly aromatic cheeses, such as pecorino (from sheep's milk) and scamorza (from cow's milk, often smoked), are rooted in pasture farming and the everyday life of the region's shepherds, although their numbers are now in decline. The legendary panarda, a colossal thanksgiving banquet of up to 30 courses that dates back hundreds of years, and is occasionally held today, is symbolic of the region's devotion to good eating.

Very little meat is eaten in Molise, a result of a tradition called la transumanza, when the townspeople walked their sheep to Puglia to be sold. Because people were travelling a lot, many Molisani dishes reflect simplicity and a quick preparation time, and meat was considered a luxury. Today in Molise, vegetables and cheese dominate, along with pasta, grains and fresh fruits. Like their neighbours in Abruzzo, the people of Molise love the hot chilli pepper, affectionately known as diavolino, or little devil, adding it to nearly every savoury dish.

THE ANCIENT TRADITIONS OF SARDINIA

Sardinian cuisine is a celebration of products that come mainly from the land. Rather oddly, given that it is an island, this cuisine is not widely represented by the bounty of the sea. The flavours of the island's natural and traditional ingredients such as lamb, suckling pig and the huge variety of vegetables that flourish here are all profoundly enriched by the unmistakable aromas of Sardinia and the abundance of Mediterranean herbs and plants.

Among the many celebrated meat dishes, the most well-known is porceddu (suckling pig cooked on a spit or in a hole in the ground, using the aromatic wood of the Mediterranean scrubland). However, there are numerous other meat dishes, such as rabbit a succhittu, served in a sauce made from the liver, wine, capers and tomatoes; wild boar in Cannonau wine; or chicken wrapped in myrtle leaves. These days, fish and shellfish dishes are of course widely present on the Sardinian menu, but most of these are much more recent additions compared to the truly historical dishes of the island, when everything that came from or out of the sea seemed to represent danger and caused the original inhabitants of the island to genuinely fear it. Bottarga (salted or dried mullet or tuna eggs) is a favourite along the island's south-west coast, and is often considered to be the caviar of Sardinia.

The Romans called Sardinia 'the granary of Rome'. Each region boasts its own bread, made with special techniques according to ancient recipes. One of the most famous of these is pane carasau, wafer-thin sheets of toasted bread. This is typical of the Barbagia region and was a staple for shepherds.

Sardinian desserts are justly famous throughout Italy. Round, sweet ravioli called sebardas, filled with cheese, are fried and then covered in sweet, sticky honey. Also popular are the special cookies known as sospiri, which translates as 'sighs', as well as nougat and other confections made from almonds and sweet cheeses.

BELOW LEFT *A variety of local breads have been typically made by hand in Sardinia for centuries.*

BELOW *Local women collect crocus flowers in Abruzzo, ready to prepare the highly-prized saffron.*

FESTIVALS AND CELEBRATIONS

Many regions of Italy maintain the generations-old tradition of putting on local festivals to celebrate not only religious holidays but also the arrival of the new season's crops. It is a matter of pride, particularly in this agricultural central area of Italy, that a rich vegetable harvest, a prolific haul from the sea or the careful husbandry of animals for meat or dairy products should be celebrated with a feast. Festivals bring whole villages or towns together, year after year, with traditional rituals, songs and dancing, as well as a wealth of regional foods being cooked and served to festival-goers. The Italians love an excuse for a party, and from the large religious ceremonies to the smallest, most unusual festivals, these celebrations are well worth a visit.

FESTIVALS OF LAZIO AND ROME

In April, the Matticella Artichoke Festival in Velletri uses the matticelle, the long vine shoots that are kept and left to dry after the vines have been pruned, to fuel the fires for cooking artichokes, which are served to everyone who passes by.

Summer festivals in Lazio include the Laina e Fasuri Festival in Sant'Ambrogio sul Garigliano – only in Italy would a simple dish of home-made pasta served with beans qualify for its own festival. It is eaten by everyone in the town at this time of year. Another local speciality is enjoyed at the Marzoline Festival in Esperia in August, which celebrates a goat's milk cheese made in the mountains of the Monti Aurinci Natural Park. Tradition demands that it is left to mature for a few days on wooden racks and then aged for several months in glass jars.

BELOW *Chestnuts are roasted on the streets of Rome during the Christmas period.*

CHRISTMAS IN ROME

In November and December, the Piazza Navona Christmas market takes place in this spectacular square in Rome, and runs right through to Twelfth Night, when La Befana, the Christmas witch, calls to bring presents to the children. Christmas cribs and other decorations glow alongside stalls selling sweets, chestnuts, sugared apples, the famous torrone (nougat) and liquorice.

FESTIVALS OF NAPLES AND CAMPANIA

In early summer, at the Lemon Festival at Massa Lubrense, the local crop of these special lemons is celebrated with a delightful festival of food and fun. Here you can sample the classic Caprese salad with lemon, or for a cooling sweet treat, lemon ice cream and lemon granita. This is also the place for a glass of the famous limoncello in its area of origin.

The PizzaFest in Naples takes pride of place on the culinary calendar in September. This world-famous Neapolitan dish stars at PizzaFest, and the visitor can taste pizzas of many types and shapes, as well as other Neapolitan foods. There is a feast for the eyes and ears too, as pizza-makers show off their dough-throwing skills and everyone dances to live music.

At Christmas in Naples, the Christmas markets in the Spanish Quarter burst into life. Although the main focus is the delightfully carved Christmas nativity scenes, or presepi, stallholders will not lose the opportunity to sell hot snacks to the passerby, such as individual pizzas or deep-fried slices of aubergine/eggplant.

FESTIVALS OF ABRUZZO AND MOLISE

Spring festivals in Molise include the Scurpelle Festival in Fossalto, which celebrates this local speciality, a kind of savoury fritter made with flour, eggs, salt and yeast, and fried in very hot oil.

The Scattone Festival in Gildone in August focuses on a special kind of pasta dough, which is cooked in boiling water to which wine is added according to taste, along with a spoonful of sugar and a pinch of peppercorns or crushed chilli pepper. Apparently, this fierce pasta dish is very good for curing colds. Whether or not this is true, it is likely to clear your nose!

FESTIVALS OF SARDINIA

In early spring, the Sardinian carnival season, with its strange and ancient rituals, starts on the night of the feast of Sant'Antonio Abate in January, with bonfires lighting up towns and villages. In the Barbagia region the carnival unfolds with processions made up of people in sombre masks, who move with rhythmical step to the haunting sound of bells, recalling ancient rural rites.

The important religious festival of Easter is celebrated with numerous solemn ceremonies. In Castelsardo, all the people of the town join together for a meal at lunchtime, before a candlelit procession and chanting choirs lead the way round the town in the dark.

Summer brings more food-related festivals in Sardinia. In June, the remote rural area of Meana Sardo, in the middle of Sardinia, celebrates the local sheep's cheese, pecorino, and other local dairy products. This pecorino cheese tastes delicious grilled or broiled and spread on thin toasted sheets of Sardinian bread, pane carasau.

The Honey Festival of Montevecchio is held in the Geo-Mineral Sardinian Park, an area well suited to the production of arbutus blossom honey. And in September, the Su Succu Festival at Busachi makes a centrepiece of the local recipe for angel-hair noodles dropped into a delicious meat soup.

ABOVE *Sa Sartiglia is a unique, ritualised 3-day festival that takes place in Orsitano, the region's capital, and features masked jousts, music and of course, food, including favata (broad/fava bean soup), zippole (deep-fried sugar-dusted enriched dough), and ravioli filled with custard, jam or ground almonds.*

A GRAND REUNION

The International Chefs' Festival takes place every year at Sangro in Abruzzo on the second Sunday of October. The Val di Sangro, a mountain valley in the province of Chieti, is renowned for producing generations of chefs who have turned Abruzzo's simple yet sophisticated regional foods into culinary wonders. In celebration, this festival draws chefs home from all over the world to share their expertise and sample the delicacies of local restaurants from special stands lined up along the village's main street.

LAZIO

Lazio is the centre of Italian political life due to the presence of the government and parliament in Rome – the region's and country's glorious capital city – and the home of Catholicism, Vatican City, a city-state in Rome. The region is divided into five provinces: Frosinone, Latina, Rieti and Viterbo, though more than half of the population lives in or around Rome itself.

With Rome being such a draw, it is not surprising that so much of Lazio often gets overlooked, especially when it comes to tourism, yet this is a place that is not only stunningly beautiful, but is also littered with cultural treasures: innumerable historical sites and monuments of both the ancient Roman civilization and, to the north, the Etruscans. Moreover, it is a rich landscape that is green and hilly to the north, becoming more parched and rugged to the south. Until the late 19th century, much of the lowland area was marshy and dangerously malarial. However, the vast reclamation works in the Maremma, the Campagna Romana and the Pontine Marshes that began in the early 20th century resulted in the drainage and repopulation of the plain, which totally transformed the region's agriculture.

Viterbo, to the north, is an historic town with a well-preserved medieval centre. Its province offers a wealth of attractions, such as the lovely Lakes Vico and Bolsena, the splendid formal gardens in Bagnaia at the Villa Lante, the grand palace of Caprarola, the Etruscan remains at Tarquinia and Vulci, and the wine called Est! Est!! Est!!! at Montefiascone near Lake Bolsena.

The Province of Latina runs for 100km (62 miles) along the coast, between Rome and Campania, and includes long stretches of sandy beach featuring resorts such as Sperlonga, and the lovely Pontine Islands. Frosinone is an inland town, and within this province is its most well-known tourist destination: Fiuggi, a large spa resort with ancient thermal springs.

Roman food is really big on offal, which appears on the menu in many a dish – from coda alla vaccinara (braised oxtail) to pagliata, a dish of calf or lamb innards, removed from the animal immediately after slaughter and still full of mother's milk, then cooked and served with pasta – not for the faint of heart... This type of cooking is known as la cucina del quinto quarto – cuisine of the 5th Quarter – and refers to a tradition whereby while the Pope, Cardinals and nobility could afford the best cuts of meat, the working-class people would gather the scraps from the main slaughterhouse of Testaccio and then transform them into dishes that have since become ingrained in the culture of the city.

Continuing this carnivorous theme, Lazio is the region for the enjoyment of very young, un-weaned lamb known as abbacchio. This is usually chopped into fist-sized chunks, then roasted with garlic, oil, rosemary and anchovy paste and basted liberally with white wine; or the tiniest cutlets – called scottadito or 'finger burning' – which are served simply roasted with oil and salt and pepper, to be eaten strictly without cutlery. This is also where whole pigs and piglets are roasted on spits, served in thick slabs tucked into crusty bread rolls; and for the deeply satisfying guanciale – the bacon made from the jowls or cheeks of the pig that is considered essential for at least one of the region's most important pasta dishes – spaghetti alla carbonara – and is also contested as an essential part of the wonderful pasta all'amatriciana, though some say it should be pancetta.

The traditional flavours of Rome, and of the region as a whole, are made up of ingredients that are strong-tasting and can largely be described as unsubtle, but always delicious, featuring anchovies (the legacy of the Ancient Roman condiment of garum, made with salt and fermented fish), plenty of pungent garlic and onions, and intensely perfumed herbs such as mint. This is food that is somehow virile and lusty; food that is brave and warrior-like, chunky, filling and always honest.

A note about Est! Est!! Est!!!

The story behind this white wine goes like this: there was once a German Cardinal called Defuck, who was on his way either to or from the Vatican, and came by the town of Montefiascone. Here, he sent his servant Martino ahead to check out which of the inns served the best wine. Whenever Martino found one, he would write 'EST!' on the door with a piece of chalk, to let the Cardinal know which inn to choose once he had caught up. At one, Martino found the wine so exceptional that he chalked 'EST! EST!! EST!!!' on the door. His master clearly agreed, since he promptly died of overindulgence in the village and is buried there in the graveyard.

LA STRACCIATELLA ALLA ROMANA
ROMAN EGG AND CHEESE SOUP

This light soup is much more difficult to make than it would first appear. The skill lies in making sure the delicate strands of beaten egg and cheese separate and disperse into the hot soup, rather than forming one or several large, unsightly lumps. Make the soup with a richly flavoured, clear chicken stock and ensure it is really hot, and that you pour in the egg mixture gently and with constant whisking. This is intended to be the best first course of a long Roman feast.

1 Put the eggs in a bowl and whisk until blended, then add the Parmesan cheese and season the mixture with some salt and ground black pepper. Stir in the nutmeg or lemon rind.

2 About 10 minutes before you want to serve the soup, bring the stock to the boil.

3 As soon as it boils, take it off the heat. Pour in the egg mixture, whisking for about 3 minutes, until the eggs have cooked enough to hold their irregularly shaped strands, floating in the broth.

4 Ladle into bowls and serve immediately, sprinkled with chopped parsley.

SERVES 6

6 eggs
75g/3oz/1 cup freshly grated Parmesan cheese
freshly grated nutmeg or grated lemon rind, to taste
1.5 litres/2½ pints/6¼ cups rich, clear chicken stock
sea salt and ground black pepper
fresh flat leaf parsley, finely chopped, to garnish

SERVES 4

- 1kg/2¼lb (unshelled weight) fresh broad/fava beans
- 50g/2oz/¼ cup lard or white cooking fat
- 1 large onion
- 30ml/2 tbsp tomato paste
- 300ml/½ pint/1¼ cups hot water
- 200g/7oz/1 cup short grain rice
- 25g/1oz unsalted butter
- 1 litre/1¾ pints/4 cups boiling water
- sea salt and ground black pepper
- 115g/4oz/1¼ cups freshly grated pecorino cheese, to serve

MINESTRA DI RISO E FAVE
RICE AND BROAD BEAN SOUP

From springtime onwards, broad or fava beans are sold at roadside kiosks, which sporadically line the route from the airport into the heart of Rome. One of the most perfect flavour combinations in the world has got to be these fresh, tender beans coupled with soft and crumbly, incredibly strong-tasting pecorino cheese. Both reach their peak at the same time, when the ewes have plenty of milk available for their spring lambs, and extra for cheesemaking.

1 First, shell the broad beans, then skin them by putting them in a bowl and pouring over boiling water to cover. Leave for 1–2 minutes, then refresh in cold water. Push the beans out of their skins using your fingers.

2 Chop the lard and the onion together to make a blended mass (this is called battuto in Italian). Fry this slowly in a large pan until the onion is soft. Add the beans.

3 Stir the tomato paste into the hot water and pour into the pan, then season with salt and pepper. Stir and simmer for 10 minutes.

4 Stir the rice into the soup, then stir in the butter. Gradually add the boiling water, stirring constantly and keeping it at a slow rolling boil. Cook for about 15 minutes, until the rice is tender. Season to taste and serve with grated pecorino.

MINESTRA ALLA VITERBESE
VEGETABLE SOUP WITH SEMOLINA

This is a typical country summertime soup, prepared when all the vegetables are at their peak of luscious ripeness. This recipe is from the pretty town of Viterbo, which has a few age-old culinary specialities that have passed the test of time.

SERVES 4

- 1 large, very ripe tomato
- 1 large courgette/zucchini, sliced into thin matchstick strips
- 1 large onion, sliced into rings
- 1 large garlic clove, finely chopped
- 1 large celery stick, finely chopped
- 1 large potato, grated
- 1 large carrot, grated
- 8 parsley sprigs, finely chopped
- 9 fresh basil leaves, finely chopped
- 1.2 litres/2 pints/5 cups cold water
- 50g/2oz/$^1/_3$ cup semolina
- 25g/1oz/2 tbsp unsalted butter, plus extra to serve
- 50g/2oz/$^2/_3$ cup freshly grated Parmesan cheese, plus extra to serve

1 Plunge the tomato into a bowl of boiling water for 30 seconds, then refresh in cold water. Remove the skin and seeds, and chop the flesh.

2 Put the tomato, courgette, onion, garlic, celery, potato, carrot and herbs into a large pan. Add the cold water. Bring to the boil, cover and simmer over a medium heat for 15 minutes.

3 Trickle the semolina into the simmering soup in a very fine stream, stirring constantly with a strong wooden spoon. Simmer the soup for a further 15 minutes, stirring occasionally, until thickened.

4 Remove from the heat and stir in the butter and the cheese. Allow to cool slightly before serving with extra Parmesan and butter on top.

UOVA AL TEGAMINO CON POMODORO
BAKED EGGS WITH TOMATOES

This really is a delightfully simple, nutritious and colourful dish, which comes from Lazio. Serve it with plenty of crusty bread and a dressed green salad. If you like, you can add some chopped canned anchovy fillets or capers to the tomato sauce after straining, which will give a more robust-tasting dish. Alternatively, you could sprinkle the finished dish with a generous pinch of dried oregano or torn fresh basil leaves. This recipe will make enough to feed four people, but if you are serving it as an appetizer, it will stretch to eight people.

SERVES 4

500g/1¼lb/2½ cups canned tomatoes, seeded and chopped
45ml/3 tbsp olive oil
8 eggs
sea salt and ground black pepper
green salad, to serve (optional)

1 Preheat the oven to 200°C/400°F/Gas 6. Put the tomatoes into a pan with 30ml/2 tbsp water and 2 pinches of salt. Cover the pan and simmer slowly for 30 minutes, stirring occasionally.

2 Push the tomato sauce through a sieve or strainer using the back of a spoon.

3 Pour the oil into an ovenproof dish and pour the sauce on top of the oil. Crack the eggs on top of the sauce carefully, so you don't break the yolks, and dust with pepper.

4 Bake for 5 minutes, or until the eggs are just set but the yolks are still runny. Serve immediately, with a green salad, if you like.

MOZZARELLA IN CARROZZA
DEEP-FRIED MOZZARELLA SANDWICHES

The word carrozza means carriage, and these deep-fried sandwiches are the perfect vessel to carry luxurious mozzarella. It is quite a heavy dish, so when served as an antipasto it should be followed by a light main course, although often it is served as a stand-alone snack instead.

SERVES 4

8 slices white bread, crusts removed
7.5ml/1½ tsp anchovy paste
250g/9oz mozzarella, cut into 8 thick slices
3 eggs, beaten
sunflower oil, for deep-frying
ground black pepper
tomato salad or tomato sauce (see page 20), to serve (optional)

1 Trim the bread to slightly larger than the mozzarella slices. Lay 4 slices of bread on a board and spread each with anchovy paste.

2 Cover the anchovy paste with 2 slices of mozzarella. Season to taste with black pepper, and cover with the other slices of bread. Squash together very firmly.

3 Put the beaten eggs into a shallow bowl. Slide the sandwiches into the eggs and leave to soak for 15 minutes.

4 Meanwhile, pour enough sunflower oil into a wide, deep frying pan to a depth of about 7.5cm/3in. Heat until a small cube of bread, dropped into the oil, sizzles instantly.

5 Fry all the sandwiches in the hot oil until crisp and golden on both sides, remove with a metal spatula and drain thoroughly on kitchen paper.

6 Serve piping hot, with tomato salad or tomato sauce offered separately, if you like.

SERVES 4

115g/4oz/1 cup finely cubed Gruyère cheese
75g/3oz/3/4 cup chopped prosciutto crudo
25ml/1 1/2 tbsp freshly grated Parmesan cheese
1 egg, beaten
300g/11oz/2 2/3 cups plain/all-purpose flour
50g/2oz/1/4 cup unsalted butter, cubed
2 egg yolks
1 egg white, lightly beaten
sunflower oil, for deep-frying
sea salt and ground black pepper

PANZEROTTI ALLA ROMANA
ROMAN CHEESE AND HAM FRITTERS

Probably one of the earliest recipes from the culinary history of the great city of Rome, these rich and savoury dough fritters would traditionally be served as an antipasto or a snack; at some time in their history they were probably cooked as street food and sold from sizzling cauldrons of boiling oil to hungry passers-by. You can vary the contents of the filling according to personal taste; for example, mozzarella or scamorza can be used instead of the Gruyère, and salami or cooked ham could be used instead of the prosciutto crudo.

1 Mix the cubed cheese with the prosciutto, Parmesan cheese and the beaten whole egg. Season with a little salt and ground black pepper, and set aside until required.

2 Put the flour in a mound on the work surface. Plunge your fist into the middle to make a hollow. Put a pinch of salt, the butter and the egg yolks into the hollow. Blend together with your fingertips, adding 30–45ml/2–3 tbsp cold water, if necessary.

3 When you have achieved a smooth ball of dough, roll it out as thinly as possible.

4 Use a 5cm/2in pastry or cookie cutter or inverted tumbler to cut out circles of dough.

5 Put a spoonful of the cheese mixture on to each circle and fold in half. Brush the edges with a little beaten egg white, and seal the panzerotti closed.

6 Heat the oil for deep-frying in a deep pan until a small piece of the pastry, dropped into the oil, sizzles instantly. Fry the panzerotti for 5 minutes, or until golden brown and puffy. Drain on kitchen paper and serve hot.

SPIEDINI DI PROVATURA
CHEESE SKEWERS WITH ANCHOVY SAUCE

Provatura is basically a Roman version of mozzarella. It tends to be slightly more solid and less creamy than mozzarella. If you can't get hold of it, you can instead use scamorza (matured and sometimes smoked mozzarella) or fresh mozzarella that has been allowed to harden slightly over 3 or 4 days. In fact, this is a useful recipe for using up any mozzarella that is past its best. It's perfect cooked over a barbecue, but can be cooked under a grill too. You could offer the anchovy sauce separately, if you prefer.

1 Soak four wooden skewers in water for 30 minutes. Cut the cheese and bread into equal-sized pieces about 2cm/¾in thick.

2 Thread the cheese and bread alternately on to the skewers, making sure that they are packed together as tightly as possible.

3 Cook the skewers on a barbecue or under a a grill or broiler until the cheese is just running and the bread is crisp.

4 Meanwhile, put the butter and anchovies into a small pan and warm over a low heat (you can do this on a corner of the barbecue), stirring constantly until the anchovies have been reduced to a smooth cream.

5 Stir in the milk as the mixture begins to amalgamate. Season with black pepper.

6 Arrange the skewers on a serving platter, cover with the anchovy sauce and serve hot.

SERVES 4

- 300g/11oz provatura or scamorza cheese
- 1 small loaf of crusty bread or sliced white bread
- 150g/5oz/10 tbsp unsalted butter
- 2 large salted anchovies, boned, rinsed and patted dry on kitchen paper
- 30ml/2 tbsp milk
- ground black pepper

SERVES 4

45ml/3 tbsp extra virgin olive oil, plus extra for greasing
4 slices slightly stale white bread
45ml/3 tbsp milk
2 scamorza, thinly sliced
sea salt and ground black pepper

VARIATION

Try adding some chopped anchovy fillets, or topping with prosciutto crudo.

CROSTINI CON LA SCAMORZA
SCAMORZA CROSTINI

An often underrated cheese, scamorza is made by allowing mozzarella to dry out so that it forms a thin rind on the outside. It is sometimes smoked, giving it a light brown skin and slightly woody flavour, which becomes more pronounced when it melts in the oven or under the grill.

1 Preheat the oven to 180°C/350°F/Gas 4. Grease a shallow baking tray with oil.

2 Lay the slices of bread on the baking tray. Drizzle the bread with enough of the milk to moisten it.

3 Cover the bread with the sliced scamorza and sprinkle with the oil. Season generously.

4 Bake for 10 minutes, until the bread is crisp and the cheese is melted and bubbling. Serve immediately.

SERVES 4

400g/14oz spaghetti or spaghettini
175ml/6fl oz/$^{3}/_{4}$ cup extra virgin olive oil
3 garlic cloves, crushed
30ml/2 tbsp chopped fresh flat leaf parsley
sea salt and ground black pepper

COOK'S TIP

Featuring so few ingredients, this dish really does taste best if you use really good-quality spaghetti and cook it carefully so it is just al dente.

SPAGHETTI AJO E OJO
SPAGHETTI WITH OIL AND GARLIC

Lots of versions of this classic Roman recipe exist, but this is a traditional one. It is reputedly very good for preventing a hangover when consumed last thing at night. Another version, ajo ojo e peperoncino, includes chilli, which can be added in varying amounts depending upon personal preference.

1 Bring a large pan of lightly salted water to a rolling boil. Add the pasta and stir. Return to the boil and cook the pasta according to the pack instructions until al dente.

2 Meanwhile, heat the oil and garlic together until the garlic turns black. Discard the garlic and keep the oil hot. Timing is crucial, as the oil must not burn; although it must be hot.

3 Drain the cooked pasta and return it to the hot pan. Pour over the flavoured oil and mix together to thoroughly coat the pasta in the oil.

4 Season with plenty of ground black pepper and mix in the chopped parsley.

5 Transfer to a warmed serving platter and serve immediately.

LA PUTTANESCA
PUTTANESCA PASTA

This sauce is named after the famous Roman 'ladies of the night', who are as strident, garish and obvious as the bold flavours of this sauce. The key here is that all the ingredients should sing out so that you can taste each one individually, as well as blending beautifully to create the overall taste of the sauce. It is crucial not to add the olives until the end of cooking, and not to omit the dried oregano, which is absolutely essential for the flavour.

SERVES 4

- 120ml/4fl oz/½ cup extra virgin olive oil
- 1–3 garlic cloves, peeled and lightly crushed
- 3 anchovy fillets (either salted or canned in oil), rinsed and patted dry on kitchen paper
- 1–3 small dried red chillies, according to taste, finely chopped
- 25ml/1½ tbsp salted capers, rinsed, dried and chopped
- 300g/11oz passata/bottled strained tomatoes or canned chopped tomatoes
- 5ml/1 tsp dried oregano
- 90ml/6 tbsp dry white wine
- 400g/14oz penne or spaghetti
- a handful of pitted black olives
- 30ml/2 tbsp chopped fresh flat leaf parsley
- sea salt and ground black pepper

1 Heat half the oil in a pan and fry the garlic with the anchovy fillets and dried chillies, until the anchovies disintegrate.

2 Add the capers and passata or canned tomatoes, and stir together. Simmer for 5 minutes, then add the oregano, salt and pepper, and wine. Stir, then simmer gently for at least 15 minutes, or up to 30 minutes if you have time.

3 Meanwhile, bring a large pan of lightly salted water to a rolling boil. Add the pasta and stir. Return to the boil and cook according to the pack instructions until al dente. Drain and return to the pan.

4 Add the olives to the sauce and stir through. Pour the sauce over the pasta and add the remaining olive oil and the parsley. Toss together and serve.

RIGATONI AL POMODORO E RICOTTA
RIGATONI WITH TOMATO AND RICOTTA

With its broad shape and fine ridges, rigatoni is the most perfect pasta to suit this particular sauce of clingy ricotta cheese and tomato. It is a superbly simple dish, but very filling and satisfying – a real family favourite for many Italians.

SERVES 6

45ml/3 tbsp extra virgin olive oil
3 garlic cloves, chopped
900g/2lb canned Italian plum tomatoes, chopped and juice reserved
450g/1lb rigatoni
250g/9oz ricotta cheese
30ml/2 tbsp torn fresh basil
45ml/3 tbsp freshly grated Parmesan cheese
sea salt and ground black pepper

1 Pour the oil into a medium pan. Add the garlic and heat for about 3 minutes, or until it is just translucent.

2 Add the tomatoes and their juice, and simmer over a low heat for 50 minutes, or until the liquid has evaporated.

3 Bring a large pan of lightly salted water to a rolling boil. Add the pasta and stir. Return to the boil and cook according to the pack instructions until al dente.

4 Meanwhile, put the ricotta cheese into a heatproof bowl and crumble it with a fork. Set the bowl in a pan of hot water and leave to heat the cheese.

5 Add the basil to the tomato sauce and season. Stir. Drain the pasta and transfer it to a warm serving bowl.

6 Add the tomato sauce and half the ricotta. Toss gently. Cover with the remaining ricotta, sprinkle with Parmesan, and serve.

SERVES 4

400g/14oz bucatini or spaghetti
200g/7oz pancetta, guanciale or best-quality streaky/fatty bacon, cubed
3 eggs, beaten
75ml/5 tbsp freshly grated pecorino or Parmesan cheese, plus extra to serve
sea salt and ground black pepper

COOK'S TIP

Timing is critical when cooking pasta carbonara, so take care not to cook the egg for too long. It should also be served immediately, since the beaten egg will keep cooking in the heat of the pan and the other ingredients: have bowls at the ready before you start.

PASTA ALLA CARBONARA
PASTA CARBONARA

This dish has two different stories relating to its origins. The first tells us of the carbonari, or charcoal burners, living on the banks of rivers like the Tiber. These families lived with just a few basics: a sheep for milk and cheese, hens for eggs, and a pig for fresh and cured meats. Their lives were dusted with black charcoal flakes and the ever-present smoke. So the recipe honours these people, by putting together the cheese, eggs and pancetta, and the ground black pepper represents the flakes of charcoal. Some think it was a more recent invention, created for the American GIs at the end of the Second World War because they constantly demanded 'ham and eggs', and the locals obliged with this creation!

1 Bring a large pan of lightly salted water to a rolling boil. Add the pasta and stir. Return to the boil and cook according to the pack instructions until al dente.

2 While the pasta is cooking, dry-fry the pancetta, guanciale or bacon in a very hot frying pan until crisp and the fat has run.

3 Beat the eggs in a bowl with the cheese and plenty of freshly ground black pepper.

4 When the pasta is cooked, drain it and return it to the pan, then turn off the heat.

5 Immediately pour the egg mixture and the pancetta into the pan, and stir together so that the eggs scramble very lightly and bring the other ingredients together. The fat from the pancetta should sizzle as it mingles with the pasta.

6 Serve sprinkled with cheese and pepper.

SERVES 4

45ml/3 tbsp extra virgin olive oil
300g/11oz pancetta, cubed
1 onion, finely chopped
3 garlic cloves, chopped
$^{1}/_{2}$–2 dried red chillies, seeded and finely chopped
400g/14oz can chopped tomatoes
400g/14oz bucatini or other chunky dried durum-wheat pasta
75g/3oz/1 cup freshly grated pecorino or Parmesan cheese
sea salt and ground black pepper

BUCATINI ALL'AMATRICIANA
BUCATINI WITH AMATRICIANA SAUCE

From the little town of Amatrice, in Lazio, comes this classic sauce. It has many fans, and is one of those recipes that cause a great deal of argument and discussion among aficionados: Should the bacon be pancetta or guanciale? Is it right to use both onion and garlic? Should it not be one or the other? How much chilli, and what kind of chilli, makes this sauce just right? There are no clear answers to these questions, and the sauce remains one of those that can be tinkered with until it is exactly as you like it.

1 Heat the oil in a pan and fry the cubed pancetta until the fat is transparent and running freely.

2 Add the onion, garlic and chillies to the pan and fry together gently until the onion is translucent and soft. Add the tomatoes.

3 Cover and simmer for 20 minutes, stirring frequently until the sauce is nice and thick and glossy.

4 Bring a large pan of lightly salted water to a rolling boil. Add the pasta and stir. Return to the boil and cook the pasta according to the pack instructions until al dente.

5 Drain the pasta thoroughly and return to the pan, then pour in the sauce and mix together.

6 Serve sprinkled with the cheese and a little black pepper.

RISOTTO CON LE SEPPIE
SQUID RISOTTO

This is not the black and inky risotto associated with Venice, but the strong and garlicky chilli-and-tomato version of the Lazio coastline. Sweet-tasting squid is a perfect backdrop for the intense flavours that typify the cuisine of the region, and it appears frequently on Lazio menus.

SERVES 4

500g/1¼lb squid, cleaned and sliced into rings, the tentacles cut into sections (see page 221)
50ml/2fl oz/¼ cup olive oil
4 garlic cloves, crushed
1 salted anchovy, boned, rinsed and patted dry on kitchen paper
45ml/3 tbsp tomato paste
45ml/3 tbsp chopped fresh parsley
350g/13oz/1¾ cups risotto rice
½ dried red chilli, or to taste, crushed
sea salt

1 Dry the squid on kitchen paper. Heat the olive oil in a large pan and fry the garlic and anchovy together, stirring frequently, for 3 minutes, or until the garlic is just soft.

2 Add the tomato paste and the squid. Stir everything together, then simmer for 5 minutes.

3 Add enough cold water to cover generously. Do not add salt at this stage because it will turn the squid rubbery. Cover and simmer very slowly for about 2 hours, adding more water if necessary.

4 When the squid is completely tender, add the chopped parsley and the rice. Stir and continue to cook, stirring continuously, until the rice has absorbed the water.

5 Add a ladleful of boiling water and cook, stirring, as before. Add more boiling water, a ladleful at a time, only when the liquid in the pan has been absorbed into the rice. Continue until the rice is cooked – it should be tender with a little bite in the middle.

6 Stir in salt and crushed chilli pepper to taste. Transfer to a platter to serve.

GNOCCHI ALLA ROMANA
ROMAN SEMOLINA GNOCCHI

This is a really soothing example of ultimate Roman comfort food. Circles of cooked semolina are luxuriously coated with butter and Parmesan cheese, then baked until golden. It makes a perfect supper dish for children, as it is delicate in flavour and sustaining. Alternatively, it can be served as a simple primo when preceding a very spicy or full-flavoured main course. Semolina gnocchi is also tasty served with a punchy green salad as a lunch dish.

SERVES 6

1 litre/1¾ pints/4 cups milk
250g/9oz/1⅓ cups semolina
2 egg yolks
100g/3¾oz/scant 1¼ cups freshly grated Parmesan cheese
100g/3¾oz/scant ½ cup unsalted butter, plus extra for greasing
a pinch of freshly grated nutmeg
sea salt and ground black pepper

1 Preheat the oven to 220°C/425°F/Gas 7 and grease a shallow, ovenproof dish.

2 Put the milk in a large pan and bring to the boil. Sprinkle in the semolina with one hand while whisking constantly with the other to prevent lumps forming.

3 Continue whisking until the mixture begins to thicken, then use a strong wooden spoon to stir constantly for about 10 minutes, or until the mixture begins to come away from the sides and the base of the pan, and forms a soft, rounded ball.

4 Remove the pan from the heat and stir in the egg yolks, half the Parmesan cheese and half the butter. Season to taste with nutmeg, salt and black pepper.

5 Dampen a work surface lightly with cold water and pour out the semolina. Spread it out flat to a thickness of about 1cm/½in using a palette knife or metal spatula dipped in cold water.

6 Cut all the semolina into even circles using a 5cm/2in pastry or cookie cutter or inverted tumbler.

7 Break up the scraps of left-over semolina and arrange them in a layer over the base of the dish – this means that none will be wasted.

8 Set aside about 25g/1oz/2 tbsp of the butter for melting at the end, then cover the semolina scraps with a few dots of butter and a sprinkling of grated Parmesan cheese.

9 Arrange a layer of slightly overlapping semolina circles on top of the semolina scraps, and cover these with a sprinkling of cheese and a few dots of butter as before. Continue in this way until all of the ingredients have been used up, except for the reserved butter.

10 Melt the reserved butter and trickle it over the top. Bake in the preheated oven for 15 minutes, or until golden. Serve immediately.

VARIATION

You can ring the changes and spice up this basic dish with the addition of extra ingredients. Try adding saffron, flaked cooked fish, chopped prosciutto, salami or Gorgonzola.

ACQUA PAZZA
CRAZY WATER

On the island of Ponza in the Tyrrhenian Sea, the fishermen call any dish that is cooked in a lot of water 'all'acqua pazza' – 'crazy water'. Nobody really knows why, but the name has stuck, and cooking this way with lots of intense flavourings keeps the delicious taste of the fish intact.

1 Pour 1.5 litres/2½ pints/6¼ cups cold water into a large pan. Add the olive oil, tomatoes, garlic, herbs, chilli and salt. Stir well and bring to the boil.

2 Cover and simmer for 20 minutes.

3 Add the fish and cook for 5–10 minutes more, or until the fish is cooked through. This will depend on the size of the fillets.

4 Distribute among warmed dishes and serve, with crusty bread, if you like.

SERVES 4 TO 6

75ml/5 tbsp olive oil
1kg/2¼lb/4 cups canned tomatoes, drained, seeded and chopped
2 garlic cloves, chopped
60ml/4 tbsp chopped fresh parsley
10ml/2 tsp dried oregano
1 tiny dried, hot red chilli
5ml/1 tsp sea salt
1.5kg/3¼lb white fish fillets and/or steaks, such as cod or haddock
crusty bread, to serve (optional)

SERVES 4

1kg/2¼lb very young, tender lamb on the bone
50ml/2fl oz/¼ cup olive oil
a knob/pat of butter
1 lamb's kidney, cubed
250ml/8fl oz/1 cup water
350ml/12fl oz/1½ cups dry white wine or water
2 x 6cm/2½in rosemary sprigs
2 large preserved, salted anchovies, or 5 canned anchovy fillets in oil, drained
4 garlic cloves, peeled
60–75ml/4–5 tbsp red wine vinegar
sea salt and ground black pepper
steamed broccoli, to serve (optional)

ABBACCHIO ALLA ROMANA
ROMAN ROAST LAMB

The unexpected ingredients of salty anchovies and sour vinegar cut the sweetness of lamb to perfection in this springtime Roman speciality. With a hint of garlic and rosemary, it's the most delicious way to serve tender young lamb.

1 Wipe the meat carefully all over in case any bone shards remain, then cut into rough chunks about 7.5cm/3in square.

2 Set a wide, deep frying pan with a heavy base over a low heat. Add the oil and butter, and heat together for 5 minutes.

3 Add the kidney and meat chunks to the hot fat, browning them thoroughly all over. Season generously with salt and pepper, add the water, then lower the heat.

4 Cover and simmer for 45 minutes, occasionally adding a little water or wine and turning the meat from time to time.

5 Pound the leaves from the rosemary sprigs with the anchovies and garlic using a mortar and pestle. Stir in the vinegar and pour this mixture all over the meat. Stir well.

6 Simmer for 5 minutes. Serve immediately, with a green vegetable such as broccoli, if you like.

SERVES 4

8 thin veal escalopes/US scallops, about 115g/4oz each, trimmed
250g/9oz mozzarella
8 slices prosciutto crudo
16 fresh sage leaves
15ml/1 tbsp plain/all-purpose flour
30ml/2 tbsp unsalted butter
120ml/4fl oz/$^1/_2$ cup dry white wine
sea salt and ground black pepper

COOK'S TIP

Rose veal can be used instead of standard veal for this dish. This is a flavoursome product that makes use of the meat from male bullocks, who are not required for dairy herds.

SALTIMBOCCA ALLA ROMANA
VEAL WITH SAGE, PROSCIUTTO AND MOZZARELLA

Although veal for saltimbocca is sometimes served rolled up, like a beef olive, the original recipe from Rome calls for it to be flat, with mozzarella melting on top, sealed in by a lightly fried slice of prosciutto. Fresh and fragrant sage tucked between the layers and added to the butter for frying is an essential part of the dish, as is the generous glug of dry white wine. Use Frascati, if you can get hold of it, to continue the authentic Roman theme. Chicken or turkey breast escalopes can be cooked in this way too.

1 Put the escalopes between two sheets of clear film, plastic wrap or baking parchment and beat with a meat mallet or rolling pin until about 3mm/⅛in thick.

2 Cover each slice of meat with a slice of mozzarella and prosciutto, slipping a sage leaf between the meat and the mozzarella. Dredge the underneath of each saltimbocca in flour to just coat.

3 Melt the butter in a large frying pan with the remaining sage leaves. Lay the meat, covered side down, in the pan to seal the prosciutto to the meat with the cheese.

4 Turn and fry the other side until opaque, making sure the butter does not colour and burn. Season to taste.

5 Cover the pan and cook gently for 1–2 minutes, until the cheese is oozing out and the saltimbocca is cooked through. Transfer to a serving platter and keep warm.

6 Pour the wine into the pan and boil quickly, stirring and scraping the juices from the base of the pan, for 3 minutes to create the sauce.

7 Pour the sauce over the meat and serve.

ROGNONE IN UMIDO
ROMAN STEWED KIDNEYS

Offal is an important aspect of Roman cuisine, and it crops up in many different recipes. It is important to wash the kidneys carefully in several changes of cold water before using, in order to remove any trace of ammonia flavour.

SERVES 4 TO 6

500g/1¼lb calf's kidneys, trimmed
500g/1¼lb ripe tomatoes
15ml/1 tbsp lard/white cooking fat
1 large onion, finely sliced
45ml/3 tbsp dry red wine
sea salt and ground black pepper
30ml/2 tbsp chopped fresh parsley, to garnish

1 Slice the kidneys and put them into a pan over a low heat. Cover with a lid and cook for 10 minutes to remove the bitter water.

2 Remove the kidneys and transfer to a sieve or strainer set over the sink. Leave to drain for at least 20 minutes.

3 Meanwhile, plunge the tomatoes into boiling water for 30 seconds, then tip them into a strainer and refresh in cold water. Peel away the skins and remove the seeds. Chop them roughly.

4 In a large pan, melt the lard or fat and gently fry the onion in it for 10 minutes, until soft. Add the tomatoes. Simmer, covered, for 15 minutes, until the tomatoes start to fall apart.

5 Add the kidneys and stir together, then add the wine and cook for 1 minute to evaporate the alcohol. Add salt and pepper and stir again.

6 Simmer for 5 minutes, then transfer to a warm serving dish and sprinkle with parsley.

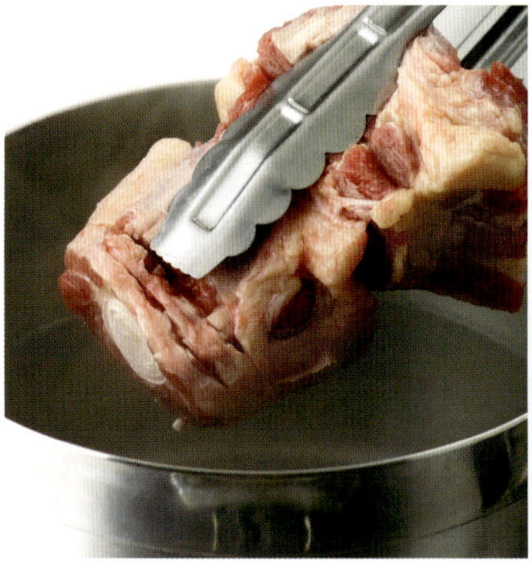

CODA ALLA VACCINARA
ROMAN BRAISED OXTAIL

For thousands of years, until the Second World War, teams of oxen ploughed fields and pulled loads in the countryside around Rome. When they could no longer work, they were slaughtered and their skins became leather, their horns a variety of accessories and their meat was cooked in stews. The people whose jobs were to slaughter, butcher and skin the oxen were paid with skins, unwanted offal and other parts of the animal – including the oxtails. This created a style of cooking that is closely associated with the Roman neighbourhood where the slaughterhouse and tanneries were located – Testaccio. Nowadays, it is a trendy area, but the traditions remain, and the local restaurants still serve these old Roman dishes, using the humblest meats.

SERVES 6

- 1 oxtail and 1 ox cheek, 2.5kg/5½lb total weight, cut into large chunks
- 200g/7oz pork belly or bacon, finely chopped
- 1 large carrot, very finely chopped
- 1 celery stick, very finely chopped, plus 5 celery sticks, diced
- 1 onion, very finely chopped
- 2 garlic cloves, very finely chopped
- a large pinch of crushed dried red chilli
- 250ml/8fl oz/1 cup dry white wine
- 45ml/3 tbsp tomato paste diluted in 500ml/17fl oz/generous 2 cups warm water
- sea salt and ground black pepper

1 Bring a large pan of water to the boil and add the chunks of oxtail and cheek. As soon as the water comes back to the boil, remove the meat using a slotted spoon or kitchen tongs. Set it aside to cool.

2 Put the pork belly or bacon into a separate pan with the carrot, celery stick, onion and garlic. Fry gently together for 10 minutes, stirring frequently.

3 Add the oxtail and cheek, and brown it thoroughly all over. Season with salt and a generous pinch of crushed dried red chilli.

4 Add half the wine and cook for 1 minute to evaporate the alcohol. Pour in the diluted tomato paste and stir. Cover and simmer for 1 hour.

5 Add the remaining wine and cook, uncovered, for 2–3 minutes to evaporate the alcohol. Cover and simmer for 3 hours more.

6 Stir in the diced celery and cook slowly for a further 30 minutes. Transfer the finished dish to a platter and serve immediately.

BIGNE' DI SAN GIUSEPPE
ST JOSEPH'S DAY CHOUX BUNS

The story goes that St Joseph, husband to the Virgin Mary and, in Italy, the patron saint of fathers, was a carpenter and so always had enough leftover wood to build a fire to cook on. According to the story, many carpenters of that time had a sideline in selling fried street food as a way of supplementing their income, and would offer simple food to passers-by, such as the famous bigne'. These buns are traditionally eaten on St Joseph's Day, which is also Father's Day in Italy.

1 Put the butter in a pan with the water. Heat until the butter has melted and then bring to the boil. Add the flour all at once and stir constantly with a wooden spoon.

2 Cook for 2 minutes, or until the mixture pulls away from the sides of the pan, forming a ball.

3 Remove from the heat and allow to cool. Wrap in clear film or plastic wrap and chill for 30 minutes.

4 Transfer the dough to a bowl. Using a wooden spoon or the paddle attachment of a food processor or mixer, mix the dough for 1–2 minutes.

5 Slowly add the eggs, mixing the dough until smooth each time and scraping down the sides. The dough should be soft and glossy, but able to hold its shape.

6 Heat the oil in a large pan or deep-fryer until a cube of bread, dropped into the oil, sizzles instantly. Using two teaspoons, scoop balls of the mixture into the hot oil.

7 Cook until they are puffy and golden. Remove with a slotted spoon and drain on kitchen paper.

8 Lightly toss in caster or icing sugar, or a mixture of cornflour and cinnamon, and serve warm.

MAKES ABOUT 24 BUNS

130g/4½oz/generous ½ cup unsalted butter
250ml/8fl oz/1 cup cold water
150g/5oz/1¼ cups plain/all-purpose flour
4 eggs, beaten
sunflower oil, for deep-frying
caster/superfine sugar, icing/confectioners' sugar, or a mixture of cornflour/cornstarch and cinnamon, for dusting

VARIATION

Carefully snip open the base of the buns with scissors and, using a clean piping bag, fill them with confectioners' custard, zabaglione, whipped cream or melted chocolate. You could also drizzle melted chocolate over the top.

SERVES 6

250g/9oz/1¼ cups Arborio rice
1 litre/1¾ pints/4 cups full-fat/whole milk
45ml/3 tbsp water
a pinch of salt
3 whole eggs, plus 3 chilled egg whites
150g/5oz/1¼ cups plain/all-purpose flour
150g/5oz/¾ cup caster/superfine sugar
150g/5oz/1 cup sultanas/golden raisins, soaked in enough white wine to cover for about 30 minutes
2.5ml/½ tsp ground cinnamon
grated zest of 1 lemon or orange
10ml/2 tsp vanilla extract
45ml/3 tbsp rum
5ml/1 tsp baking powder
1 litre/1¾ pints/4 cups sunflower oil, for deep-frying
icing/confectioners' sugar, for dusting

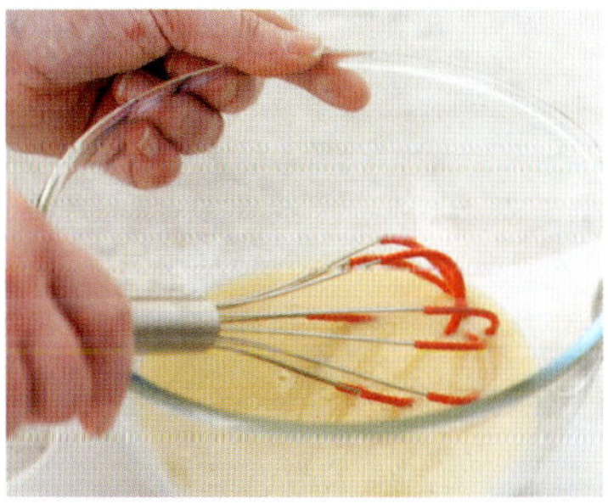

FRITTELLE DI RISO DI SAN GIUSEPPE VITERBESI

VITERBO ST JOSEPH'S DAY RICE FRITTERS

The city of Viterbo, in the region of Lazio, is where this delicious recipe was first officially created in the 1830s. It lies in the land of Tuscia, which covers an area from the walls of Rome, across the province of Viterbo and all the way to parts of Tuscany and Umbria as far as the sea. It is a historical region of Italy that comprised all the territories under Etruscan influence and Tuscia was the name adopted for Etruria after the Roman conquest. These crispy, deliciously sweet fritters – like bigne' di San Giuseppe – are traditionally prepared to celebrate the feast of St Joseph on 19 March.

1 Put the rice, milk, water and salt in a large pan and boil until soft, then strain, reserving the milk.

2 In a bowl, whisk the whole eggs with the flour, sugar and the strained milk from cooking the rice. Add the sultanas, cinnamon, zest, vanilla, rum and finally the baking powder and whisk together.

3 Whisk the egg whites until they form stiff peaks, then fold this into the sugar and flour mixture using a metal spoon.

4 Gently stir in the boiled rice until you have a thick batter. Leave to rest for 1 hour.

5 Heat the oil in a large, deep pan suitable for deep-frying until sizzling hot, then drop the batter into the oil in egg-sized scoops using 2 spoons. Take care not to overcrowd the pan: work in batches if necessary.

6 Fry the fritters until golden brown and crisp, then remove with a slotted spoon and drain on kitchen paper. Dust with icing sugar and serve piping hot.

SARDINIA

Sardinia is the second largest island in the entire Mediterranean Sea and is also an autonomous region of Italy. At least five local indigenous languages are spoken here, all of which are respected under Italian law. This incredibly beautiful island, with white sandy beaches and turquoise waters has, over the course of history, seen its fair share of invaders come and go due to its strategic position, and tragically has suffered many famines and has had its fair share of unwelcome invasions.

The island is home to nearly 4 million sheep, which makes this one of the areas of the world boasting the highest density, along with some parts of the UK and New Zealand. It is and always has been an island of shepherds, not sailors.

The shallow, stony, infertile soil of this island, and the general shortage of water, somewhat surprisingly produces some notable crops, famously the early season violet artichoke, and of course olive trees and vineyards. In recent years, the island wine production has really expanded, and Sardinian wine is now gaining ground in both quality and renown. The wider lowlands make it possible to grow barley, durum wheat and oats. The paddy fields in the Arborea district make this a prolific area for rice production, although, despite this, rice and risotto appear extremely rarely on the menu.

Sardinia has an ancient tradition of horse breeding, inherited since the Aragonese domination, though never for eating as in other parts of the country. The Spanish relied upon the equine heritage of the island to strengthen their own army or to make a gift of a Sardinian-bred horse to other European sovereigns. The island boasts the highest number of wild horse herds in Italy, and horse riding is still very important.

Whilst I understand the psychological and historical reasons behind it, it always strikes me as odd, somehow, that such a beautiful island in the middle of the Mediterranean should have so little gastronomic connection to the sea, apart from their inordinate passion for fish roe – bottarga, which is so loved by Sardinians and is grated over pasta to add its own very intensely fishy flavour. But these gentle island shepherds never really fought back against the marauding invaders who swarmed up their beaches, nor did they feel any desire to go out into the sea – after all, everything they knew of as bad or frightening came out of it, so an introverted, inland-facing culture developed. Is it any wonder, therefore, that their iconic, most famous of island specialities should be the fantastic porcheddu, a tiny suckling pig traditionally cooked in a fire pit underground, with only a wisp of escaping smoke to give away its location; or the local version of grappa, called filu 'e ferru, which translates as iron wire, which is also aged underground with just the tip of the piece of wire wound into the cork top sticking out above the soil to indicate where the bottles were hidden. To me, these reflect a culinary culture that speaks of fear, a need to take cover and keep away from trouble.

And yet, in sharp contrast to these examples and to all the many very rustic lamb dishes, many of which feature all kinds of challenging offal – quite literally nose to tail eating – often combined together in the same dish, there is also the extraordinary range of Sardinian pastries. These reveal a passion and a skill for baking and cake decorating that is hard to beat anywhere. It is difficult to believe that such delicate, intricate, lacy works of art belong to the same cuisine as the kebabs of heart, lung, kidney and sweetbreads, which are then wrapped in abdominal perineum before being grilled (a highly prized dish called Trattalia!). The pastries – with delightful names like Gueffus, Candelaus, Pabassinos, Copulettas, Orilletas, Pardulas, Amarettos and Casadinas – are a riot of icing, coloured sugar strands, silver balls and dried fruit and nuts, are a feast for the eyes and so delicious to eat, an absolute revelation and such a vital part of the island's culinary culture.

A note about bread

The high-quality wheat grown on the island, although limited in quantity, makes bread that is full of flavour and with a fantastic texture, and it comes in many different guises. The island's expert and varied bread tradition can be traced back to the time when Sardinia supplied wheat for bread to the Carthaginians, and many of the bread varieties appear to have survived through the centuries.

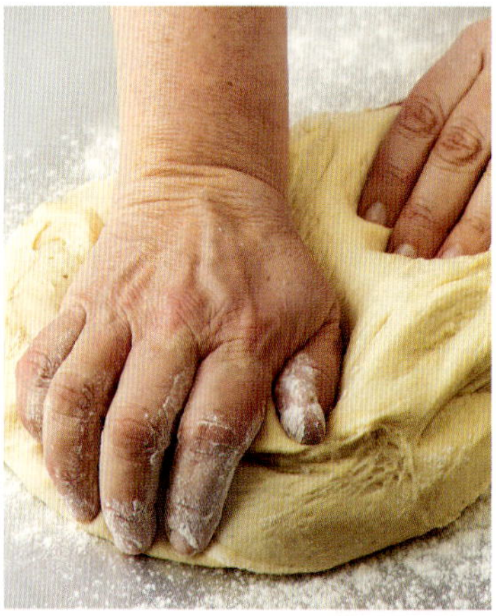

'NFIGGHIULATA
SARDINIAN FOCACCIA TWIST

This lovely sticky loaf made with ricotta and salami is delicious eaten simply on its own (perhaps with a glass of local wine), but it is especially good when served as part of an antipasto selection with olives, cured meats and strong-flavoured Sardinian pecorino cheese. It has a bit of a kick as it contains a good pinch of potent dried chilli flakes, but you can, of course, vary the heat by increasing or decreasing the amount of chilli added according to your own taste.

1 Put the flour on to the work surface and make a hollow in the middle. In a small bowl, mix the yeast and warm water together. Mix in the sugar and about 30ml/2 tbsp of the flour.

2 Put the yeast mixture in a warm place to activate for 30 minutes, or until the froth begins to appear on the surface.

3 When the yeast mixture is fizzing gently, add it to the hollow in the flour. Combine it together, then knead it energetically into the remaining flour, adding a little more water if necessary.

4 Add the salt and the oil, and knead the dough well for about 10 minutes until soft, elastic and slightly shiny. Transfer the dough to a large, floured bowl.

5 Oil the underside of a piece of clear film or plastic wrap to prevent it sticking against the rising dough, and use it to cover the bowl. Put the bowl in a warm place and leave it to rise for about 2 hours, or until doubled in size.

6 Preheat the oven to 220°C/425°F/Gas 7 and oil a baking sheet. Roll out the risen dough thinly and brush the surface generously with oil.

7 Cover half the dough with the ricotta and salami, and add a sprinkling of chilli.

8 Fold the dough in half to cover the filling, then roll the focaccia up on itself, brushing the dough's surface generously with oil on each turn.

9 Transfer the focaccia to the baking sheet and bake in the preheated oven for 30–35 minutes, or until it is lightly golden.

10 Remove the focaccia from the oven, cover loosely with foil and leave to cool.

11 Serve, sliced, either at room temperature or while still slightly warm.

SERVES 6

450g/1lb/4 cups strong white bread flour
30g/1¼oz fresh/compressed yeast
about 300ml/½ pint/1¼ cups warm water
pinch of sugar
sea salt
90–120ml/6–8 tbsp extra virgin olive oil, plus extra for greasing
350g/12oz fresh ricotta cheese, drained overnight in a colander
300g/11oz salami, chopped
large pinch coarsely ground dried chilli flakes

VARIATION

If you like, you could add chopped garlic, sliced raw onion or chopped fresh tomatoes to the basic filling, with or without the salami.

RISOTTO SARDO ALLO ZAFFERANO
SARDINIAN SAFFRON RISOTTO

This unusual risotto is from Sardinia, where small quantities of rice are grown, which means that risotto should form part of the local menu, however it does not usually appear, despite this very traditional recipe. Saffron also grows on this beautiful island, although, disappointingly, it seldom appears in the island's repertoire of recipes. On the occasions that it does, such as in this intensely flavoured and coloured dish, it really is superb. This is the only region of Italy that I know of where saffron is used in threads instead of powder.

SERVES 6

300g/11oz ripe tomatoes
75g/3oz pork dripping, lard or white cooking fat or pork belly
1 large onion, finely chopped
300g/11oz pork, such as hand or shoulder, finely cubed
90ml/6 tbsp dry white wine
a pinch of saffron threads, soaked in a little warm water
1.5 litres/2½ pints/6¼ cups pork stock, simmering
500g/1¼lb/scant 3 cups risotto rice, such as arborio, carnaroli or vialone nano
50g/2oz/⅔ cup freshly grated pecorino cheese, plus extra to serve
sea salt and ground black pepper

1 Plunge the tomatoes into a bowl of boiling water for 30 seconds, then refresh them in cold water. Peel away the skins and chop them roughly. Set aside.

2 Heat the pork dripping, lard or white cooking fat or pork belly in a pan, add the chopped onion and fry over a low heat for 10 minutes or until soft.

3 Add the pork cubes. Cook together for 10 minutes, adding the wine a little at a time, until the pork is browned all over. Add the peeled, chopped tomatoes to the pan and mix everything together thoroughly. Pour in the saffron and its soaking water. Continue to simmer gently, adding a little stock from time to time as necessary to keep it moist, for 20–30 minutes, or until the pork is falling into shreds.

4 Add the rice and stir until all the grains are coated with the liquid and are very hot. Add a ladleful of stock and cook, stirring constantly, until the liquid has been absorbed into the rice.

5 Add more hot stock, a ladleful at a time, stirring continuously and allowing each ladleful of liquid to be absorbed before adding more each time. Continue in this way until the rice is cooked – it should be creamy and velvety, but the grains of rice should still be firm to the bite.

6 Season the risotto with salt and ground black pepper, then remove the pan from the heat. Stir in the pecorino cheese and cover the pan with a lid. Allow the risotto to rest, covered, for 2–3 minutes, then stir it again. Serve the risotto immediately, in warmed bowls, sprinkled with extra pecorino cheese and some ground black pepper.

TONNO AL ALGHERESE
TUNA IN THE STYLE OF ALGHERO

This is an unusual way of cooking a tuna loin, which is soaked then baked and served thickly sliced. The soaking keeps it extra moist. It is perfect to serve as an alternative to a meat joint, with roasted or boiled potatoes and a green vegetable.

1 Put the tuna into a large, deep bowl of cold water and add the vinegar. Leave to soak for 2 hours. Drain and pat dry on kitchen paper.

2 Heat the oil in a large, heavy frying pan, add the onion, celery and bay leaves. Fry gently for 10 minutes, until the onion is soft.

3 Add the tuna loin to the pan and cook gently, turning frequently, for 20 minutes.

4 Add the dry white wine to the pan and cook for 1–2 minutes to allow the alcohol to evaporate.

5 Add the olives and season with salt, then cover and simmer over a low heat for a further 10 minutes.

6 Thickly slice the tuna loin, then serve it on a warmed platter, with the sauce from the pan drizzled over.

SERVES 4 TO 6

1kg/2¼lb fresh tuna loin
100ml/3½fl oz/scant ½ cup white wine vinegar
100ml/3½fl oz/scant ½ cup extra virgin olive oil
1 onion, finely chopped
1 small celery stick, finely chopped
3 dried bay leaves
200ml/7fl oz/scant 1 cup dry white wine
30g/1¼oz/generous ¼ cup pitted black olives
sea salt

SERVES 4

150ml/$^1/_4$ pint/$^2/_3$ cup extra virgin olive oil
1 onion, finely chopped
30ml/2 tbsp chopped fresh flat leaf parsley
4 medium sea bass, cleaned and scaled
175g/6oz/1 cup pitted black olives, roughly chopped
250ml/8fl oz/1 cup dry white wine, such as Vernaccia di Oristano
lemon wedges and boiled potatoes, to serve (optional)

ARANGIOLA A S'ORISTANESA
SEA BASS IN THE ORISTANO STYLE

Black olives, onions and white wine are cooked with fresh sea bass in this lovely dish from Oristano in Sardinia. The wine traditionally used, Vernaccia di Oristano, is from this area, but any good dry white wine will work equally well.

1 In a frying pan large enough to hold all the fish, heat half the oil. Add the onion and parsley and fry over a medium heat until the onion is soft and golden.

2 Add the sea bass to the pan and baste them with the oil. Add the olives and wine.

3 Cook over a high heat for 1–2 minutes to evaporate the alcohol. Cover and cook for 5–10 minutes over a medium heat, until the fish is cooked through.

4 Spoon the olive mixture over the fish. Serve with lemon wedges and potatoes, if liked.

BRANZINO AL SALE
SEA BASS IN A SALT CRUST

This has evolved into a recipe that has become something of a national Italian dish, but my version is the one I learned to make on the beautiful island of Sardinia, and it has never let me down.

SERVES 2

- 1 sea bass, weighing about 800g/1¾lb
- 6 fresh sage leaves
- 6 fresh thyme sprigs
- a handful of fresh parsley
- 2 or 3 fresh chervil sprigs
- 4 bay leaves
- 3 fresh rosemary sprigs
- 1 lemon, zested
- 2 garlic cloves, finely chopped
- 4 egg whites
- 1kg/2¼lb sea salt
- 1kg/2¼lb coarse sea salt
- boiled or roasted potatoes, lightly dressed with olive oil, salt and chopped herbs, and wedges of lemon, to serve

1 Preheat the oven to 180°C/350°F/Gas 4. Prepare the fish by gutting and scaling it, then rinse it thoroughly and pat it dry inside and outside.

2 Chop all the herbs finely and divide them in half. Mix one half with the lemon zest and the garlic.

3 Whisk the egg whites until stiff, then fold in the remaining herbs, then the salts.

4 Lay a sheet of baking parchment over a shallow baking tray and spread a thin layer of the salt mixture across it, about 1.5cm/¾in deep, roughly the size of the fish.

5 Put the reserved mixture of herbs, lemon zest and garlic inside the fish, then lay it on top of the salt bed. Cover the fish with the rest of the salt paste, pressing to help it to stick and shaping it around the fish.

6 Bake for about 40 minutes (if you are using 2 smaller fish of about half the weight each, reduce the time to 20–25 minutes).

7 Remove from the oven and let it stand for about 2 minutes, then crack the crust with a small hammer or heavy object (I use the pestle from my mortar and pestle). Skin and fillet the fish. Serve with the dressed potatoes and wedges of lemon.

CASSOLA
SARDINIAN FISH STEW

All over Italy in all the small ports along the long coastline and on the islands, there are many recipes for creating sumptuous fish stews, soups and casseroles. This fish stew is a traditional recipe from the island of Sardinia and, like all the recipes for similar dishes, it relies on a wide selection of different kinds of fish and a few very simple ingredients to turn it into a memorable gastronomic experience. Here, dried and fresh red chilli gives the finished dish plenty of punch.

SERVES 4

- 120ml/4fl oz/½ cup extra virgin olive oil
- 1 onion, finely chopped
- 1 garlic clove, finely chopped, plus 1 garlic clove, halved
- 30ml/2 tbsp chopped fresh parsley
- 500g/1¼lb canned tomatoes, strained
- 1 dried red chilli, chopped
- 1.5kg/3¼lb mixed fish, cut into even chunks, and a small whole raw lobster (optional)
- 4 thick slices coarse, crusty bread
- 1 fresh red chilli, whole
- sea salt and ground black pepper

1 Heat the oil in a large pan, add the onion, the garlic clove and the parsley, and fry for 10 minutes, until softened but not browned.

2 Add the tomatoes, a pinch of salt and the chopped chilli. Simmer for about 10 minutes, stirring gently.

3 Add the chunks of fish, starting with the thickest pieces and ending with the whole lobster, if using, basting with the sauce as you add each type of fish.

4 Add 200ml/7fl oz/scant 1 cup boiling water to the pan, cover and simmer over the lowest heat for about 1 hour.

5 Rub the slices of bread with the fresh chilli and the remaining garlic, then toast under a grill or broiler for 1–2 minutes on each side, until golden and crispy.

6 Arrange the bread in a large serving bowl, and pour the fish stew over it, placing the lobster on top, if using. Serve immediately.

COOK'S TIP

If using a cooked whole lobster, or a defrosted frozen cooked lobster, reduce the cooking time in step 4 to 30 minutes.

FREGOLA SARDA CON COZZE E VONGOLE
FREGOLA WITH MUSSELS AND CLAMS

Rough, grainy-textured fregola pasta is a little like couscous and is becoming a popular choice in restaurants. It consists of fine beads of durum-wheat pasta. Fregola is made by combining durum-wheat flour and water – sometimes with the addition of saffron. It is then rolled, and the little balls of pasta are lightly toasted, which gives it a wonderful, nutty flavour. In this dish it is served with mussels and clams in a rich tomato sauce.

SERVES 6 TO 8

1kg/2$\frac{1}{4}$lb mussels
1kg/2$\frac{1}{4}$lb clams
3 garlic cloves, chopped
$\frac{1}{2}$ dried red chilli, chopped
60ml/4 tbsp chopped fresh flat leaf parsley
60ml/4 tbsp olive oil
1kg/2$\frac{1}{4}$lb canned chopped tomatoes
250ml/8fl oz/1 cup dry white wine
1kg/2$\frac{1}{4}$lb fregola
sea salt

1 Keeping the clams and mussels in separate bowls, scrub them thoroughly in several changes of fresh water until the water is completely clear. Scrape off any barnacles and pull off the 'beards' from the mussels. Drain. Discard any clams or mussels that do not close tightly when tapped against a work surface.

2 In a large pan over a low heat, fry the garlic, chilli and half the parsley in the oil for 3 minutes. Add the mussels and cover the pan.

3 Cook for 8 minutes, or until the mussels open. Remove the pan from the heat. Discard any mussels that remain closed. Remove the mussels from their shells, and strain and reserve both the shelled mussels and the cooking liquid.

4 Return the mussel liquid to the pan. Add the canned tomatoes, stir and lower the heat to simmer gently for 15 minutes. Add the wine and season with salt. Cook for a further 5 minutes, until the liquid has reduced slightly.

5 Put the clams into a wide pan. Cover and cook them over a medium heat until they open. Discard any that remain closed.

6 Strain the cooking liquid and add it to the pan with the mussel juices and tomatoes. Shell most of the clams, leaving a few in their shells, and add them to the pan together with the reserved shelled mussels. Cook for a further 5 minutes, until the sauce is thick and glossy. Remove from the heat.

7 In another pan, boil the fregola in salted water for 8 minutes, or according to the pack instructions, then drain and add to the sauce with the remaining parsley. Stir well, then cover with a lid and leave to rest for 3 minutes before serving.

SERVES 4

400g/14oz spaghetti
90g/3½oz bottarga, in a solid piece
75ml/5 tbsp olive oil
1 garlic clove, halved
30ml/2 tbsp chopped fresh flat leaf parsley
ground black pepper

SPAGHETTI CON LA BOTTARGA
SPAGHETTI WITH DRIED FISH ROE

Bottarga is one of Sardinia's most important ingredients. It consists of tightly packed dried fish roe, which can be red mullet, grey mullet, tuna or other fish. The bottarga is often sliced in transparent shavings over the finished dish with the same ceremony that is afforded to truffles in other regions of Italy. Cheaper, ready-grated bottarga is also available and can be bought in jars or sachets.

1 Bring a large pan of lightly salted water to a rolling boil. Add the spaghetti and stir. Return to the boil and cook for 8 minutes or according to the pack instructions until al dente. Drain and return to the pan, reserving some pasta water.

2 Grate the bottarga finely. Heat the oil in a large pan and fry the garlic for 5 minutes, or until golden, then take the pan off the heat.

3 Discard the garlic. Add two-thirds of the bottarga to the pan with 25ml/1½ tbsp parsley.

4 Add pepper and a ladleful of reserved water from the pasta pan, then stir to reduce the contents of the pan to a smooth cream.

5 Transfer the spaghetti to the pan with the bottarga sauce. Mix together thoroughly, adding a little more of the pasta water if the mixture appears to be drying out.

6 Divide the dressed pasta among four warmed plates, sprinkle with the remaining grated bottarga and chopped parsley, and serve immediately.

GALLINA COL MIRTO
CHICKEN STEEPED IN MYRTLE

Using myrtle as a flavouring is common throughout the whole of Sardinian cuisine. It is a plant that produces small purple berries, which are harvested from November to January, and has fragrant leaves that are used in the preparation of many savoury meat and fish dishes. Myrtle is also made into the island's favourite liqueur, mirto. It may be difficult to get hold of outside of Sardinia, so try specialist Italian food stores. You will need a heatproof lidded container, such as a casserole or chicken brick.

SERVES 4 TO 6

1 large onion, halved
1 large carrot, halved
1 large celery stick, halved
a small bunch of flat leaf parsley
1 medium oven-ready chicken, about 2.5kg/$5^1/_2$lb
a large bunch of myrtle
sea salt

1 Put the onion in a deep pan with the carrot, celery and parsley, and cover with water. Season with salt. Cover and bring to the boil.

2 Once the stock is boiling, add the chicken. Cover and simmer for 1½ hours, or until the chicken is cooked through.

3 Line a large casserole or chicken brick with myrtle.

4 Remove the chicken from the pan and transfer it to the container. Cover the chicken with more myrtle, put the lid on the top and leave the chicken to steam, off the heat, absorbing the flavour of the myrtle.

5 Leave the chicken in the myrtle-lined container until the next day, then remove it from the casserole, carve the meat and serve cold.

IMPANADAS DI FUNGHI E CARNI MISTE
MUSHROOM AND MEAT SARDINIAN IMPANADAS

This is a typical recipe from Sardinia, and is not to be confused with the well-known Argentinian dish called empañadas. Pastry fritters are filled with cooked meat, porcini mushrooms, sun-dried tomatoes, peas, onion and garlic, then deep-fried. The fritters can be made in a variety of different sizes, and using all kinds of ingredients, including grated pecorino cheese, cured meats, or fresh fish – they work particularly well with small eels.

SERVES 6

200g/7oz/scant 1 cup butter, cubed
400g/14oz plain/all-purpose flour, plus extra for dusting
1 small egg, beaten
vegetable oil, for deep-frying
sea salt and ground black pepper

FOR THE FILLING

50g/2oz/1 cup dried porcini mushrooms
25g/1oz/2 tbsp unsalted butter
1 large onion, finely chopped
3 garlic cloves, finely chopped
45ml/3 tbsp fresh or frozen peas, thawed if frozen
5 sun-dried tomatoes, chopped
200g/7oz cooked meat (beef, lamb, pork or veal), finely chopped

1 First, make the pastry. Rub the butter into the flour, with 1.5ml/¼ tsp salt, using your fingers or a pastry or cookie cutter until it resembles fine breadcrumbs.

2 Sprinkle over 45ml/3 tbsp cold water. Using a fork, stir to just bind the dough together, adding more water as necessary, 15ml/1 tbsp at a time.

3 Using your hands, gather it together into a ball and put into a plastic bag or wrap it in clear film or plastic wrap. Chill the pastry for 30 minutes.

4 Place the porcini mushrooms in a small bowl and cover with warm water. Leave to soak for 30 minutes, then drain and rinse them well.

5 Melt the unsalted butter in a large pan and add the chopped onion, garlic, drained mushrooms, peas and sun-dried tomatoes. Cook for 10 minutes over a medium heat, or until the peas are tender.

6 Stir in the chopped meat and mix together. Season with salt and pepper, and allow the mixture to cool.

7 Roll out the pastry thinly on a floured surface and cut into circles using a 10cm/4in pastry cutter.

8 Put a spoonful of the filling mixture in the middle of half the pastry circles. Use the other half of the circles (that don't have filling in them) to place on top, forming a lid. Seal the edges with your fingers, using a little beaten egg to make it stick.

9 Heat the oil until a small piece of the pastry, dropped into the oil, sizzles instantly. Fry the impanadas in batches until crisp and golden.

10 Carefully remove the impanadas using a slotted spoon and drain them on kitchen paper. Serve them piping hot.

COOK'S TIP

If you have not got time to make your own shortcrust pastry, you can use 500g/1¼lb ready-made shortcrust pastry, thawed if frozen. Begin the recipe at step 4.

SEBADAS
SARDINIAN HONEY FRITTERS

These sticky and sweet ravioli fritters are called sebadas and are a classic dessert from the unique and beautiful island of Sardinia. They are traditionally filled with local creamy sheep's milk cheese (but any cream cheese can be used instead) and drizzled with fragrant orange blossom honey. They are one of the typical sweet recipes of the mountainous, sparsely populated area of Barbagia, which is located just south of the central part of the island.

SERVES 8

500g/1¼lb plain/all-purpose flour, plus extra for dusting
45ml/3 tbsp lard or white cooking fat
a pinch of salt
sunflower oil, for deep-frying
60ml/4 tbsp clear honey
grated rind of 1 lemon

FOR THE FILLING

500g/1¼lb/5 cups cream cheese
250ml/8fl oz/1 cup boiling water
a pinch of salt
grated rind of 1 lemon
30ml/2 tbsp fine semolina

1 To make the filling, put the cream cheese in a small pan and mix with the boiling water, salt and lemon rind. Simmer gently, stirring with a whisk, until the mixture is smooth and creamy.

2 Add the semolina and whisk until it has become a thick paste. Remove from the heat and leave to cool.

3 Dip your hands in cold water and shape the mixture into little flat pancakes about 6cm/2½in in diameter and about 1cm/½in thick.

4 Line a baking tray with baking parchment. Lay the pancakes out in one layer on the tray, well spaced out. Use a clean dish cloth to dab any excess moisture off them. You can lay a sheet of baking parchment over the pancakes and arrange another layer of pancakes on top, if you are short of space.

5 To make the pastry, pile all the flour on to the work surface and make a hole in the middle. Add the lard and salt. Knead together, adding enough tepid water to make a smooth, elastic dough.

6 Put the dough in a plastic bag and rest it in the refrigerator for about 15 minutes.

7 Divide the dough in half. On a floured surface, roll out each piece very thinly to make two even sheets. Lay the sebadas on one sheet of dough, evenly spaced and side-by-side in rows.

8 Lay the other sheet of dough on top and gently roll the rolling pin around the edges to seal. Using a pastry wheel or a 7.5cm/3in pastry cutter, cut around each pancake, leaving a narrow edge of pastry.

9 Heat the sunflower oil in a large pan or deep-fryer until a small cube of bread, dropped in the oil, sizzles instantly. Fry the pastries in batches until golden.

10 Remove the pastries using a slotted spoon, and drain on kitchen paper. Serve hot, drizzled with honey and sprinkled with lemon rind.

PAPASSINAS
SARDINIAN ICED COOKIES

These deliciously nutty, fruity little cookies are another speciality of picturesque Sardinia and go perfectly with a glass or two of local Moscato wine or some strong black coffee. They contain a tasty mix of walnuts, almonds, pine nuts, raisins and candied peel, and are traditionally coated with pure white icing, topped with pretty coloured sugar sprinkles. Throughout Sardinia you will find these local sweet treats on sale in all good bakeries and cake stores.

SERVES 10 TO 12

- 500g/1¼lb/4¼ cups plain/all-purpose flour
- 5ml/1 tsp baking powder
- 4 eggs, beaten
- 150g/5oz caster/superfine sugar
- 200g/7oz/generous 1 cup lard or white cooking fat, softened
- 250g/9oz/2¼ cups chopped walnuts
- 250g/9oz/2¼ cups blanched chopped almonds
- 250g/9oz/scant 2 cups raisins or sultanas/golden raisins, soaked for 20 minutes in warm water and drained
- 200g/7oz/scant 2 cups pine nuts
- 115g/4oz/⅔ cup finely chopped candied orange peel

FOR THE ICING

- 300g/11oz/generous 1½ cups caster/superfine sugar
- 2 egg whites
- 15ml/1 tbsp coloured sugar sprinkles

1 First, begin to make the icing. Place the caster sugar in a heatproof bowl with 45ml/3 tbsp cold water, and set the bowl over a pan of simmering water. Stir continuously until the sugar has dissolved completely, then remove the bowl from the simmering water and set aside to cool a little.

2 Preheat the oven to 180°C/350°F/Gas 4, and line a baking sheet with baking parchment.

3 Sift the flour and baking powder into a large bowl and stir in the eggs and the sugar with a wooden spoon until smooth.

4 Gradually mix in the lard or white cooking fat, nuts, soaked raisins or sultanas, pine nuts and candied orange peel. Work this dough with your hands until it is compact and even.

5 Shape the dough into sticks 1cm/½in wide and 6cm/2½in long and arrange them on the prepared baking sheet.

6 Bake the cookies for 10 minutes, or until they are lightly golden. Transfer them to a cooling rack while you finish the icing.

7 Put the egg whites into a clean, grease-free bowl and whisk until they form stiff peaks. Gently fold them into the cooled sugar syrup until you have created a shiny, glassy icing.

8 When the baked cookies are cooled, brush them with the icing, then sprinkle them with the coloured sugar sprinkles. Allow the icing to set, then serve.

CAMPANIA

Campania, dominated by its glorious Thyrennian coastline and the gloomy majesty of Vesuvius, is one of the most densely populated regions in the whole of Italy, especially in and around the regional capital: the bustling, noisy city of Naples. The five provinces of the region are Benevento, Avellino, Salerno, Caserta and Naples. The stunningly beautiful islands of Ischia, Procida and Capri lie in the Gulf of Naples.

Campania is mountainous and hilly, the Neapolitan Apennines in the extreme east giving way to the lower uplands of the Matese and Picentini mountains, with the Cilento mountains extending to the coast in the south. The main farming areas are the fertile coastal lowlands, particularly those of the Terra di Lavoro, an area in the north that spreads into southern Lazio and western Molise; and the volcanic plains around Vesuvius. The farming in these parts is intensive, the plots of land producing cereals and grains on the ground, fruit on the trees along the edges of the plots, and grapes from vines trailing between the trees. The chief crops of the region are fruit (apricots, apples, peaches, nuts, citrus, and grapes), early vegetables (the famous and much sought-after primizie), flowers, and industrial crops such as tobacco and hemp, not forgetting the ubiquitous tomato – the red gold of Campania that so richly and famously flourishes under the hot sun.

Some of the best dried durum-wheat pasta, buffalo-milk mozzarella, tomatoes, pizza and amazing pastries are among the most important specialities of this fertile region. Pasta was first commercially made here as long ago as the 1800s, with the first factories established at Torre Annunziata, Torre del Greco and Castellammare di Stabia, where the sea breezes helped to dry the pasta perfectly. The original pasta shape was ziti – long, hollow tubes that would then be broken into shorter sections for cooking and eating. It is amazing to think that from those humble beginnings there are now over 650 different shapes of dried pasta on the market. Like pizza, pasta used to be a basic street food in Naples, served with a simple tomato sauce, barely cooked at all to preserve all its fragrance and sweetness.

According to historical records, buffalo mozzarella has been produced in Sardinia, particularly in the areas around Caserta and Salerno, as far back as the 12th century. The introduction of the water buffalo is still not clearly defined, but some historians say it happened as far back as the year 1,000 and was brought by the Normans from Sicily, where it had been first established during the Arab domination, while others say it was Goths who brought these beasts to the area during the late Middle Ages. Either way, the milk of the water buffalo produces a soft, pure-white cheese that is very special and that has held a DOP status since 1993 and has been protected under European law since 1996.

The bright-yellow liqueur called limoncello – which started out as way of using up the unused lemons that grow all along the coastline around Sorrento and Amalfi – was once only made at home, but has now become something of a worldwide phenomenon and joined the long list of iconic products of this region. Another liqueur is the famous Strega, made in Benevento since 1860. The area around the city was once famous for its reputation for witchcraft, dating back to the time of the Lombard invasion; the word 'Strega' means 'witch' in Italian, and so the name was chosen. It is made yellow by the addition of saffron, along with 70 other herbs and spices and, like limoncello, is considered a digestif, and is an essential ingredient for flavouring torta Caprese.

The pastry chefs of Campania almost rival those of Sicily when it comes to the creation of delicious and inventive cakes and sweetmeats. Take for example the wonderfully boozy and soft baba, soaked in its syrup of rum and sugar; the sweet cake of wheat grains, ricotta and candied peel called la pastiera; and the intricate, crisp, light sfogliatelle, shaped like a seashell and filled to bursting with sweet ricotta.

I think that one of the things that makes the recipes of this region so popular is that they are created using very simple ingredients such as grains and vegetables, combined with fresh cheeses, fish and seafood, and fragrant olive oil. The locals refer to their cuisine as being 'food of the people', food that is as cheerful and exuberant as the natural personality of the inhabitants. It is colourful, attractive and mostly quick and simple to prepare, as exemplified by the ubiquitous insalata Caprese – just perfect tomatoes, fresh mozzarella, basil leaves and a drizzle of extra virgin olive oil.

CALZONE CON SALSA AL POMODORO
CALZONE WITH TOMATO SAUCE

The word calzone means 'stocking' or 'trouser' in Italian (with the plural calzoni translating as 'trousers'), as the folded pastry is supposed to look like a folded pair of pantaloons! Here the calzoni are filled with tomato, ricotta cheese and salami, but you can vary the filling according to your personal taste or the season – try experimenting with whatever ingredients you happen to have in your refrigerator. This recipe is from the bustling city of Naples and is now a worldwide classic, featuring on many Italian restaurant menus.

SERVES 4

extra virgin olive oil, for greasing and drizzling
semolina, for dusting
1 quantity pizza dough (see page 61)
30ml/2 tbsp fresh ricotta cheese
3 slices salami, coarsely chopped
2 sun-dried tomatoes in olive oil, drained and chopped
15ml/1 tbsp chopped fresh flat leaf parsley
sea salt and ground black pepper

FOR THE SAUCE

30ml/2 tbsp extra virgin olive oil
2 garlic cloves, finely chopped
400g/14oz can chopped tomatoes
30ml/2 tbsp chopped fresh flat leaf parsley

1 To make the tomato sauce, heat the olive oil in a pan over a low heat and fry the garlic for 5 minutes without browning. Add the tomatoes and stir together.

2 Bring the tomato sauce to the boil and simmer for 15 minutes. Add salt and pepper to taste, then stir in the chopped parsley.

3 Preheat the oven to 200°C/400°C/Gas 6. Lightly oil a baking sheet and sprinkle it lightly with semolina.

4 Cut the pizza dough into four equal pieces, then roll each portion into a circle measuring about 20cm/8in in diameter.

5 Spread the ricotta cheese over one half of each circle of dough, keeping the edges clear so that you can fold it in half and seal it. Sprinkle the salami, sun-dried tomatoes and parsley on top of the ricotta cheese. Drizzle with a little olive oil and season lightly with salt and pepper.

6 Using a metal spatula, lift each calzone on to the baking sheet. Fold each calzone in half and seal the open edge firmly with the back of a fork.

7 Bake in the preheated oven for 15 minutes, or until they are golden, then serve with the tomato sauce offered separately.

VARIATIONS

- You can also make two large calzoni. They will take 20–25 minutes to bake.
- Alternatively, make eight mini calzoni: divide the dough into eight equal pieces, fill and seal, then deep-fry them in sunflower oil until golden.

LA PIZZA NAPOLETANA
PIZZA NAPOLETANA

Although pizzas can be topped with all kinds of savouries, the Napoletana is the much-loved classic recipe – the first pizza ever created, and named after the city where it is believed to have first been made: Naples. It is interesting that although the original recipe, and the concept of this Italian speciality, have become a global phenomenon over the years, the name of the baker or cook who first created it has seemingly been forgotten.

MAKES 6 SINGLE PIZZAS

1 quantity pizza dough (see page 61)
30ml/2 tbsp passata/bottled strained tomatoes or chopped fresh tomatoes
4 garlic cloves, finely chopped
7.5ml/1½ tsp dried oregano
60ml/4 tbsp olive oil, plus extra for greasing
18 fresh basil leaves
sea salt and ground black pepper
green salad, to serve (optional)

1 Preheat the oven to 220°C/425°F/Gas 7 and lightly oil two baking sheets. Divide the dough into six equal pieces. Roll or press out each piece thinly and transfer to the baking sheets.

2 Cover thinly with the passata or chopped tomatoes, leaving a border of 2.5cm/1in around the edges.

3 Sprinkle each pizza with the garlic, oregano, olive oil, basil and a little salt and ground black pepper.

4 Bake for 5–10 minutes until the border is crisp and well cooked and the pizzas are dry underneath (lift up one edge to check). Serve immediately, with some salad leaves on the side, if you like.

SERVES 6

- 2.5ml/½ tsp sea salt
- 4 thick slices of crusty, rustic bread, such as casareccio
- 4 large, ripe tomatoes, chopped
- 1 garlic clove, finely chopped
- 10ml/2 tsp dried oregano
- 300ml/½ pint/1¼ cups extra virgin olive oil

ACQUA SALE
MOLISAN BREAD AND TOMATO SALAD

The simple, but delicious, fresh tomato salad from the tiny region of Molise has a soft bread base, making it similar in principle to the Tuscan salad panzanella. Don't skimp on the dried oregano – the one herb that is always much more delicious when used dried instead of fresh – as this will bring the salad vibrantly to life. Lots of good-quality olive oil is used to give the salad extra richness. Choose the sweetest and ripest tomatoes you can find, while they are in season.

1 Dissolve the salt in 500ml/17fl oz/generous 2 cups water. Dampen the slices of crusty bread with the salted water and lay them out on a platter.

2 Arrange the tomatoes on top. Sprinkle with the garlic and the dried oregano. Drizzle with the olive oil and leave to stand for an hour before serving.

SERVES 6

1kg/2¼lb unpeeled floury potatoes, scrubbed
65g/2½oz/3 tbsp unsalted butter, melted
60ml/4 tbsp freshly grated Parmesan cheese
30ml/2 tbsp finely chopped fresh parsley
2 eggs, separated
75g/3oz/⅔ cup plain/all-purpose flour, for coating
75g/3oz/generous 1 cup fine dried breadcrumbs
1 litre/1¾ pints/4 cups sunflower oil, for deep-frying
sea salt and ground black pepper

CROCCHÈ DI PATATE
POTATO CROQUETTES

These crisp little potato patties are hugely popular in Naples as a snack or as part of an antipasto course. They are a legacy of the French chefs who, in the late 1800s and early 1900s, were employed to cook in the large houses of the grand aristocracy; the wealthy southern Italian families believed that the presence of a French chef raised their profile. In the same way that the word croquette was corrupted to a much more Italian-sounding crocchè, the name for the household French chef became Monsu, as opposed to Monsieur.

1 Put the potatoes in a large pan, cover with cold water and boil until softened. Drain and peel while they are hot, and then push them through a food mill with large holes several times. If you do not have a food mill, mash them thoroughly or push them through a ricer. Mix and blend the potatoes until smooth.

2 Add the butter, Parmesan and parsley, then season with salt and pepper. Gradually blend in the egg yolks, one at a time.

3 Work the mixture with your hands until well mixed, then shape it into croquettes.

4 Put the flour on a plate. Put the egg whites in a bowl, and whisk until foaming. Put the breadcrumbs on another plate.

5 Dip each croquette in the flour until coated all over, then dip it into the egg whites, and finally coat in the breadcrumbs.

6 Heat the oil in a large pan to 180°C/350°F, or until a small cube of bread browns in 40 seconds.

7 Fry the croquettes until crisp and golden, then drain on kitchen paper and serve them piping hot.

LA CAPRESE
TOMATO, MOZZARELLA AND BASIL SALAD

This classic, simple summer salad of tomatoes and mozzarella comes from the beautiful island of Capri. The juice from the ripe tomatoes and the whey from the cheese will seep out to create liquid around the salad – this is delicious soaked up with plenty of crusty bread. The cheese should be perfectly fresh and juicy, whether it is made from buffalo milk or not. The basil leaves must always be torn, and never cut with a knife or scissors, because this alters the flavour and blackens the leaves, which looks unattractive.

SERVES 4

2 very large, firm tomatoes (about the same size as the mozzarella balls)
2 x 125g mozzarella balls, drained
90ml/6 tbsp extra virgin olive oil
about 24 fresh basil leaves, torn into small pieces
sea salt and ground black pepper

1 Slice the tomatoes and the mozzarella into even slices, cubes or chunks.

2 Put them into a salad bowl and mix them together with your hands.

3 Sprinkle with the oil and mix together again with a spoon. Add the basil.

4 Season to taste, and mix again. Leave to stand for 15 minutes before serving.

COOK'S TIP

Don't add too much salt to the salad, as the mozzarella may already be quite salty.

PASTA ALLA CAPRESE
PASTA WITH TOMATOES AND MOZZARELLA

Ripe tomatoes and mozzarella cheese, with the pungent flavouring of oregano, is a classic combination found in so many dishes of Capri. One thing to note is that pasta in Campania is served extremely al dente, which can be a bit of a shock for tourists! You can cook it a little more if you like.

SERVES 4

- 450g/1lb fusilli lunghi or spaghetti
- 2 large tomatoes, diced
- 2 x 125g/4$^{1}/_{2}$oz mozzarella balls, cubed
- 60ml/4 tbsp extra virgin olive oil
- 5ml/1 tsp dried oregano
- 4 fresh basil leaves
- sea salt and ground black pepper

1 Bring a large pan of lightly salted water to a rolling boil. Put the pasta into the water and stir. Return to the boil and cook the pasta for 8 minutes, or according to pack instructions, until al dente. Reserve the pasta cooking water.

2 Meanwhile, mix the tomatoes and mozzarella in a large bowl.

3 Add the olive oil and oregano to the tomatoes and mozzarella. Season with salt and pepper, then tear the basil leaves and add to the bowl.

4 When the pasta is ready, add it to the bowl with about 120ml/4fl oz/$^{1}/_{2}$ cup of the pasta water. Mix well to combine and serve immediately.

COOK'S TIP

Use good-quality extra virgin olive oil to achieve the most authentic flavour for this simple, tasty dish.

SERVES 4

600g/1lb 5oz ripe tomatoes
1 garlic clove, crushed
45ml/3 tbsp olive oil
10 fresh basil leaves, torn into small shreds
30ml/2 tbsp chopped fresh parsley
5ml/1 tsp dried oregano
½ onion, very finely chopped
1 celery stick, very finely chopped
400g/14oz maccheroni
salt and ground black pepper

MACCHERONI AI SETTE ODORI
MACCHERONI WITH SEVEN FLAVOURS

This is the most famous dish from the lovely village of Positano. Few things are more inspiring and beautiful than the views from the top of the cliff there, or the incredible winding road that takes you out of the chaos of Naples into the bright sunlight and greenery of the coastline. The sauce for this dish is best made the day before, although you can also make it about 3 hours in advance. Ripe, soft and fresh tomatoes are essential to accompany the seven flavours of garlic, olive oil, basil, parsley, oregano, onion and celery. In Campania, maccheroni is often a generic term for pasta, so you can use any other pasta shape for this dish. As the sauce is served cold, the dish will be lukewarm.

1 Plunge the tomatoes into boiling water for 30 seconds, then refresh in cold water. Peel away the skins. Cut in half and remove the seeds. Quarter and place in a colander, set over a bowl, to drain for 30 minutes.

2 When the tomatoes are drained, discard their juice and transfer them to a bowl. Add the garlic, olive oil, basil, parsley, oregano, onion and celery, and stir carefully into the tomatoes.

3 Season with salt and pepper, and leave to stand overnight or for at least 2 hours.

4 When you are ready to serve, bring a large pan of lightly salted water to a rolling boil. Add the maccheroni and stir. Return to the boil and cook for 8 minutes or according to the pack instructions until al dente.

5 Drain and return to the pan. Pour over the sauce and stir together. Serve immediately.

SPAGHETTI ALLE VONGOLE
SPAGHETTI WITH CLAMS

This is an absolute classic of southern Italian cooking, and depends on the careful preparation of really fresh clams for the best result, as well as good-quality pasta. As with all recipes using clams, do make sure that they are as clean as possible before you cook them to avoid an unpleasant muddy taste or a gritty sensation between your teeth. Rinse them in several changes of water until the water runs clear. Many different versions of this traditional dish exist all over the country, but this one is from Campania.

1 Scrub the clams thoroughly in several changes of fresh water to make sure you have removed all traces of sand or mud. When the water is completely clear, the clams are clean. Discard any clams that do not close when sharply tapped on a work surface.

2 Drain the clams and put them into a wide, fairly deep frying pan with 30ml/2 tbsp of the oil. Cover the pan and put it over a high heat.

3 When the pan is hot, shake it regularly over the heat for 6–7 minutes, to open the clams up. Discard any clams that remain closed after this time.

4 Meanwhile bring a large pan of salted water to the boil for the pasta.

5 Drain the clams and reserve the liquid. Set the clams and their liquid aside.

6 In the same pan, heat the remaining olive oil with the garlic over a low heat for 3 minutes, then add the clams and strain the reserved liquid over.

7 Mix everything together and bring to the boil, then cover and take off the heat.

8 Add the pasta to the pan of salted boiling water and stir. Return to the boil and cook according to the pack instructions until al dente.

9 Drain the pasta and return it to the pan.

10 Pour the clams and liquid over the pasta and toss everything together. Add the parsley and plenty of freshly ground black pepper. Toss again and transfer to a warmed platter or bowl. Serve immediately.

SERVES 4

1.5kg/3¼lb fresh baby clams
90ml/6 tbsp extra virgin olive oil
3 garlic cloves, finely chopped
400g/14oz spaghetti or vermicelli
45ml/3 tbsp chopped fresh flat leaf parsley
sea salt and ground black pepper

VARIATION

This classic recipe can also be made with a tomato-based sauce, though it does make for a very different kind of dish. Use the same ingredients as here, but shell the clams and add a 400g/14oz can of tomatoes or passata/bottled strained tomatoes to give the sauce a deep, sweet richness.

SERVES 4 TO 6

- 1.5kg/3¼lb fresh clams, preferably carpet shell clams (see Cook's Tip)
- 50ml/2fl oz/¼ cup extra virgin olive oil
- 5 garlic cloves, chopped, plus 1 clove, halved
- 6 parsley sprigs, coarsely chopped
- ½–1 dried red chilli, coarsely chopped
- 150ml/¼ pint/⅔ cup dry white wine
- 4–6 slices crusty bread
- sea salt and ground black pepper

COOK'S TIP

If possible, soak the clams overnight in several changes of salted water before cleaning them.

SARTÙ DI VONGOLE
SAUTÉED CLAMS

From Naples and Campania comes this simple and most delicious way to enjoy perfectly fresh clams. This style of cooking – superbly quick and easy, and using only a few top-quality, fresh ingredients – is absolutely typical of the cuisine of the area. The clams traditionally used for this classic dish are vongole veraci, known as carpet shell clams in English. They tend to be larger and juicier than the other varieties, but if you cannot get hold of them, any other clams are fine to use instead – just adjust the cooking time accordingly.

1 Scrub the clams in several changes of fresh water until the water is completely clear. Drain and set aside. Discard any clams that do not close tightly when tapped against a work surface.

2 Heat the olive oil in a pan that is large enough to take all the clams in one go, and add the chopped garlic, parsley and chilli. Fry for 3 minutes, then add the clams, wine and seasoning.

3 Stir everything together thoroughly, then cover and leave to simmer, shaking the pan occasionally, for 6 minutes, or until the clams have opened up.

4 Meanwhile, toast the bread and rub one side of each slice with the halved clove of garlic. Remove the pan from the heat and discard any clams that remain closed. Pour the hot clams and their juices over the toasted garlic bread and serve.

IMPEPATA DI COZZE
PEPPERED MUSSELS

This traditional way of serving mussels – bathed in garlic and olive oil – is from Naples. It is easy to prepare and very tasty, whether as an appetizer or main course. In the past, mussels were consumed only in the poorer south, but today they are celebrated as an important part of the menu.

SERVES 4 TO 6

60ml/4 tbsp extra virgin olive oil
2 garlic cloves, lightly crushed
1kg/2¼lb fresh mussels, cleaned (see page 443)
ground black pepper
wedges of lemon and slices of toasted, crusty Italian bread, to serve

1 Heat the oil and garlic in a large pan until hot and sizzling, then add the mussels and cover with a lid. Cook for 8 minutes, or until the mussels open. Shake the pan regularly during cooking. Discard any mussels that remain closed.

2 Take the pan off the heat and grind plenty of black pepper over the mussels (it should be obviously visible).

3 Serve the mussels with lemon wedges and toasted crusty bread.

FRITTO MISTO
MIXED FRY-UP

Any variation of ingredients, in any quantity and in any combination, is perfectly acceptable for the classic Campanian dish fritto misto, but it's essential to have a range of different ingredients, and they should be as fresh as possible. This recipe uses a mixture of small fish, sliced vegetables and chunks of Italian cheeses, deep-fried in a simple batter. You will need either two deep-fryers or a large pan and a wok to cook this selection, and it is a good idea to make sure that your kitchen is well aired while you work.

SERVES 8

675g/1½lb small fish (such as whitebait) mixed with large raw prawns/shrimp
1kg/2¼lb mixed vegetables, such as globe artichokes, very firm tomatoes, bell peppers, courgettes/zucchini and fennel, cut into even pieces about 4–6cm/1½–2½in
6 basil sprigs
6 sage sprigs
150g/5oz mozzarella, cut into even chunks
150g/5oz firm ricotta cheese, cut into even chunks
vegetable oil, for deep-frying
sea salt
4 lemons cut into wedges, to serve

FOR THE BATTER

5 eggs
50g/2oz/½ cup plain/all-purpose flour
pinch of salt
750ml/1¼ pints/3 cups milk

1 To make the batter, beat the eggs in a large bowl with a balloon whisk until well blended and smooth. Gradually add the flour and salt, beating constantly, then gradually pour in the milk, still beating. When you have a completely smooth batter, leave it to stand until required.

2 Make sure that all of the ingredients for deep-frying (the fish, vegetables, herbs and cheese) are as dry as possible by patting them with kitchen paper if necessary.

3 Divide the batter equally into three large bowls. Put the fish into one, the vegetables into another and the herbs and cheese in the third. Submerge all of the ingredients in the batter and leave them to stand for about 30 minutes.

4 Pour the oil into two deep-fryers, deep pans or a pan and a wok. Lay out several layers of kitchen paper on to a large serving platter and place the platter over a large pan of simmering water to keep everything warm once cooked without allowing the food to go soggy.

5 Heat the oil until a small cube of bread, dropped into the oil, sizzles instantly. The fish will be deep-fried in one pan, and all the other ingredients will be deep-fried in the second pan.

6 Quickly deep-fry the battered ingredients by lowering them into the oil, in batches, turning them over in the oil after about 2 minutes and lifting them out with a slotted spoon as soon as they are golden and crisp. It is best to work quickly, in small batches to keep the oil at maximum heat, so that everything can cook as fast as possible.

7 Transfer the ingredients directly to the kitchen paper to drain, and sprinkle with a little salt.

8 Serve immediately on a warm platter with the lemon wedges for squeezing over.

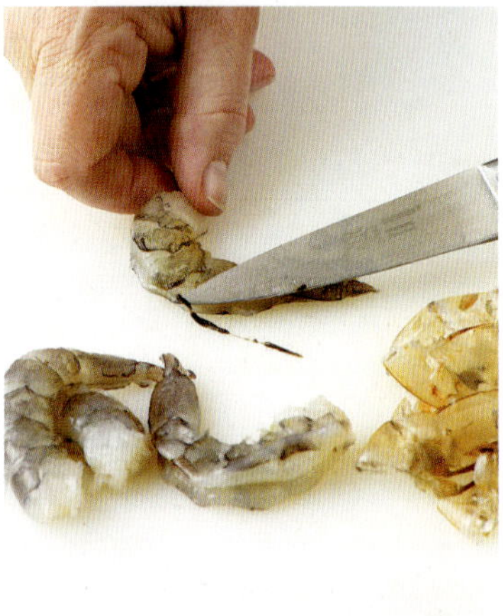

TURBANTE DI RISO CON GAMBERI
RICE RING MOULD WITH PRAWNS

Fresh prawns are cooked in two ways and served with a rice ring and a creamy sauce that's full of the flavour of these tasty shellfish. It's the perfect dish for an impressive dinner-party main course. This recipe is from Campania, but it has a somewhat classic French style. This is typical of the recipes imported to the grand households of the area by the 19th-century French chefs who introduced their customs and traditions to the kitchens of the southern Italian aristocracy.

SERVES 10

2.25kg/5lb large raw prawns/shrimp, with shells
1.5 litres/2½ pints/6¼ cups water
1 bouquet garni
175ml/6fl oz/¾ cup dry white wine
1.5ml/¼ tsp sea salt, plus extra to taste
30ml/2 tbsp olive oil
115g/4oz/½ cup unsalted butter, plus extra for greasing
1 onion, finely chopped
1 garlic clove, chopped
45ml/3 tbsp chopped fresh parsley
45ml/3 tbsp cognac
150g/5oz/1¼ cups plain/all-purpose flour
5ml/1 tsp paprika, plus extra to serve
250ml/8fl oz/1 cup single/light cream
800g/1¾lb/4 cups long grain rice, cooked in salted boiling water until just tender

1 Set aside 30 prawns. Remove and reserve the shells from the others, then devein them (see Cook's Tip). Rinse. Put the shells into a pan with the water, bouquet garni, 30ml/2 tbsp wine and the salt. Simmer, covered, for 20 minutes. Strain into a clean pan, return to a simmer, and put the shells to one side.

2 Drop the prawns into the stock. Blanch for 1 minute, remove with a slotted spoon and set aside. Simmer the stock for 10 minutes, then strain it again through a fine sieve or strainer. Process all the cooked shells with a little of the stock, to a purée. Strain through muslin or cheesecloth and set aside. Keep the stock hot.

3 Heat the olive oil and one-third of the butter in a large pan. Fry the onion and garlic for 10 minutes, gradually adding the remaining wine. Stir in half the parsley. Cook for 2 minutes, then add the 30 unshelled prawns. Fry over a high heat for 4 minutes, stirring. Transfer the prawns to a clean pan and place over a high heat. Pour over the cognac, ignite it, then immediately remove from the heat. Sprinkle the prawns with salt.

4 Add half the remaining butter to the pan in which the unshelled prawns were cooked. Heat it until it foams, then add the flour. Whisk, then gradually add the stock, stirring. Simmer, stirring, until smooth and thick. Sieve the sauce and return it to a low heat. Stir in the prawn-shell cream, half the paprika, cream and remaining parsley. Pour half of this over the shelled prawns and stir over a low heat.

5 Keep everything warm while you prepare the rice. Preheat the oven to 140°C/275°F/Gas 1. Lay a clean dish towel on a baking sheet. Spread the rice on top. Place in the oven for 10 minutes, then transfer to a bowl. Stir in the remaining butter. Grease the mould. Transfer the rice to the mould and bake for 5 minutes.

6 Turn out on to a serving dish. Put the prawns in the sauce in the middle. Arrange the unshelled prawns around the edges. Sprinkle with the remaining paprika. Serve with the rest of the sauce.

COOK'S TIP

To devein the prawns, make a shallow cut down the centre of the curved back of each shelled prawn. Pull out the vein with a cocktail stick or toothpick or your fingers.

POLLO ALLA CACCIATORA
CHICKEN CACCIATORA

Chicken cooked with tomatoes is a real classic among the best-loved Italian dishes. There are dozens of versions of the recipe for 'hunter's chicken', but this is the original one from Campania, flavoured with porcini mushrooms, wine and juniper berries. The variations on the basic recipe are very wide indeed. For some cooks this dish is just a plain chicken stewed in tomatoes with a little wine; others add olives or prawns, and some use completely different ingredients altogether. Try out several for yourself and see which you prefer.

1 Drain and chop the soaked porcini mushrooms. Set aside. Heat the oil in a large pan and gently sauté the carrot, celery, onion and garlic for 15–20 minutes, or until tender, but not crisp.

2 Add the chicken, salt and pepper, bay leaf and juniper berries, and allow the chicken to brown over a high heat.

3 Add the wine, cook until it has evaporated, then add the mushrooms, tomatoes and stock.

4 Half-cover with a lid, then simmer for 45 minutes over a medium heat. When cooked through, remove from the heat, add the chopped parsley and arrange on a warm platter to serve.

SERVES 6

50g/2oz dried porcini mushrooms, soaked in hot water for about 20 minutes
90ml/6 tbsp olive oil
1 small carrot, chopped
1 celery stick, chopped
1 onion, chopped
1 garlic clove, chopped
1.2kg/$2\frac{1}{2}$lb chicken joints
1 bay leaf
5 juniper berries
175ml/6fl oz/$\frac{3}{4}$ cup dry white wine
450g/1lb tomatoes, or 600g/1lb 6oz canned
750ml/$1\frac{1}{4}$ pints/3 cups chicken stock
15ml/1 tbsp chopped fresh flat leaf parsley
sea salt and ground black pepper

SERVES 4 TO 6

2kg/4½lb brown onions, sliced
1 celery stick, chopped
200ml/7fl oz/scant 1 cup extra virgin olive oil
30ml/2 tbsp unsalted butter
1.5kg/3¼lb stewing veal in one single piece, tied into shape with kitchen string or twine to fit the pan
sea salt
large pasta shapes, such as sciaffettoni, and grated Parmesan cheese, to serve

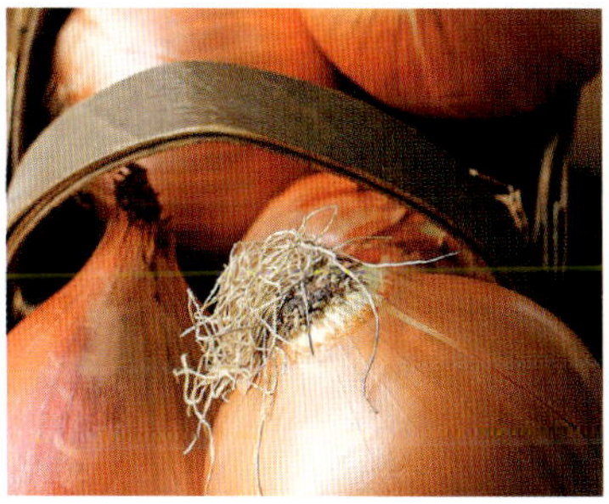

SALSA GENOVESE ALLA NAPOLETANA
GENOVESE ONION SAUCE

The origin of this Neapolitan dish is still a mystery. It is a purée of the sweetest onions, cooked until browned and very soft, and flavoured with meat. One legend links the sauce to the chefs of the Genovese merchants living in Naples during the 16th century. When the merchants returned to Genoa, some of their chefs remained in Naples, selling food to the public. The sauce that was to become known as la Genovese was their speciality. The meat should be served as a second course, with a little of the sauce, after the pasta dish with the onion sauce. Sometimes the meat is omitted from the recipe, and pasta served with the sauce made only with the onions is called a finta Genovese (fake Genovese).

1 Put the onions and celery into a deep pan, large enough to take the piece of meat. Add the oil and butter, and season with salt.

2 Lay the meat in the pan, add water to cover, then bring to the boil. Reduce the heat and simmer slowly for 4 hours, stirring often and adding more water as required.

3 After this time, the meat should be very tender, and the onions should be completely brown and very soft.

4 Serve most of the onion sauce over large pasta shapes as a primo, sprinkled with Parmesan cheese. Serve the meat as a second course, sliced thinly with just a little of the sauce.

SERVES 4

300g/11oz/1$^2/_3$ cups dried cannellini beans, soaked overnight
1 celery stick, quartered
500g/1$^1/_4$lb ripe tomatoes
30ml/2 tbsp chopped fresh parsley, plus extra to garnish
2–3 garlic cloves, chopped
135ml/9 tbsp olive oil
2.5ml/$^1/_2$ tsp dried oregano
8 thin slices stale ciabatta
sea salt and ground black pepper

COOK'S TIPS

- If using fresh cannellini beans in their pods, you will need 1.2kg/2$^1/_2$lb. Soak them overnight as for dried beans, then cook for 20 minutes, until soft, at step 2.
- The cooked beans should be mushy; the dish will be like a thick soup. If needed, add a little boiling water.

FAGIOLI ALLA MARUZZARA
STEWED BEANS WITH BREAD

In Campania, this dish uses fresh white cannellini beans, but they are sometimes difficult to get hold of outside Italy. Dried beans, as used here, will work equally well, but remember that they will need to be soaked overnight before they are cooked.

1 Drain and rinse the beans, then place in a pan. Cover with water and bring to the boil. Boil for 5 minutes, then drain and rinse well.

2 Return to the pan and cover with plenty of water. Bring to the boil. Cover and simmer slowly for 10 minutes. Add the celery and continue to simmer for a further 30 minutes.

3 Meanwhile, plunge the tomatoes into boiling water for 30 seconds, then refresh in cold water.

4 Peel the skins from the tomatoes and discard them. Halve the tomatoes, and remove and discard the seeds. Chop the flesh coarsely.

5 Add the tomatoes to the pan with the parsley, garlic, oil and oregano. Season well and cook for a further 15 minutes; the beans should be mushy.

6 Divide the ciabatta among four soup plates and pour the beans over the bread. Serve, sprinkled with chopped parsley.

MELANZANE ALLA PARMIGIANA
AUBERGINES WITH TOMATO AND MOZZARELLA

Many versions of this classic recipe exist all over the south of Italy, but the principle is always the same: layers of cooked aubergine with a rich tomato sauce, some peppery basil and creamy melting cheese, baked in the oven. It's a hearty dish, which tastes even better the next day.

SERVES 4

3 long aubergines/eggplants, cut into circles
45ml/3 tbsp extra virgin olive oil, plus extra for greasing
250ml/8fl oz/1 cup passata/ bottled strained tomatoes
115g/4oz mozzarella, sliced
200g/7oz Parmesan cheese, grated
15 fresh basil leaves, torn into shreds
sea salt and ground black pepper

1 Sprinkle the aubergine with salt and lay in a colander. Put a plate on top and weight it down. Stand the colander in the sink for 1 hour to allow the bitter juices of the aubergines to drain away.

2 Rinse and pat the aubergine slices dry, then brush them lightly with oil. Use the extra oil to lightly grease four medium ramekins.

3 Heat the grill or broiler to high and grill the aubergine slices until soft and lightly browned, turning them once.

4 Preheat the oven to 180°C/350°F/Gas 4. Put a little passata across the bottom of an ovenproof dish. Cover with a layer of aubergine slices.

5 Cover with a layer of mozzarella, a layer of passata, a little Parmesan and a few torn basil leaves.

6 Repeat until the ingredients are used up, finishing with a layer of passata, topped with Parmesan and basil. Bake for 40 minutes, until golden. Leave to stand for 10 minutes, then serve.

VARIATION

The aubergines can also be shallow-fried in oil instead of being grilled or broiled, and then used as above, from step 4.

ZUCCHINE ALLA BELLA NAPOLI
COURGETTES WITH TOMATO AND MOZZARELLA

In this dish, sliced courgettes are dusted in flour then fried before being layered with tomato and mozzarella, and then baked. Although it is fairly labour intensive, the end result is delicious and the dish is lovely served hot or cold.

1 Arrange the courgettes on a platter, sprinkle with salt and stand it in the sink. Lift it up at one end so that the platter remains on a slant and allows the juices to seep out into the sink. Leave for 1 hour.

2 Meanwhile, heat the dripping or white cooking fat and olive oil in a large pan and fry the onion for about 10 minutes, until soft. Add the tomatoes, basil and oregano. Season with salt, then cover and simmer for 45 minutes.

3 Push the tomato sauce through a sieve or strainer using the back of a spoon. Preheat the oven to 180°C/350°F/Gas 4.

4 Rinse and dry the courgettes on kitchen paper. Heat the sunflower oil in a large pan until a small piece of bread, dropped into the oil, sizzles instantly.

5 Dust the courgette slices lightly in flour, then fry them carefully in hot oil, in batches, until lightly golden. Remove them with a slotted spoon and drain on kitchen paper. Set aside.

6 Layer the courgettes, sauce and mozzarella in a shallow ovenproof dish, finishing with a layer of tomato sauce.

7 Bake for 20 minutes and serve hot or cold.

SERVES 4

6 courgettes/zucchini, thinly sliced lengthways
50g/2oz dripping or white cooking fat
45ml/3 tbsp olive oil
1 very small onion, finely sliced
500g/1¼lb ripe tomatoes, quartered and seeds removed
5 fresh basil leaves
2.5ml/½ tsp dried oregano
sunflower oil, for deep-frying
30ml/2 tbsp plain/all-purpose flour
300g/11oz mozzarella, finely sliced
sea salt

SERVES 8

250g/9oz/generous 1 cup unsalted butter, plus extra for greasing
6 eggs, separated
250g/9oz/1$\frac{1}{4}$ cups caster/superfine sugar
60ml/4 tbsp limoncello
400g/14oz/2$\frac{1}{3}$ cups blanched almonds, finely chopped
300g/11oz plain/semisweet chocolate, grated
icing/confectioners' sugar, for dusting

TORTA CAPRESE
CAPRESE CAKE

This delicious chocolate and almond cake is sticky and moreish, but light at the same time. You can alter the flavour by using a different liqueur, such as Maraschino, though limoncello is the most traditional liqueur to use.

1 Preheat the oven to 180°C/350°F/Gas 4. Grease a 20cm/8in cake tin or pan, then line with baking parchment. Melt the butter in a heatproof bowl set over a pan of simmering water. Remove from the heat. Leave to cool.

2 Whisk the egg yolks and sugar together with the limoncello until light and fluffy. Fold in the melted butter and the chopped almonds and chocolate.

3 Put the egg whites into a clean, grease-free bowl and whisk until they form stiff peaks. Fold into the cake mixture.

4 Transfer to the tin and bake for about 50 minutes, or until a knife inserted into the middle of the cake comes out clean.

5 Leave to cool on a wire rack, and then dust with icing sugar to serve.

LA PASTIERA
NEAPOLITAN EASTER CAKE

This time-honoured cake originates in the city of Naples and the surrounding region of Campania, and dates back many centuries to ancient Rome. It was traditionally made to symbolise fertility and was always baked to celebrate the beginning of spring. Today it is an essential part of the Easter feast for all Neapolitans. It is quite an unusual recipe as it is made with cooked wheat grain. You should be able to find this in specialist delicatessens or health food stores, but if not you can substitute it (see Cook's Tip).

SERVES 8 TO 12

400g/14oz cooked wheat grain (see Cook's Tip)
100ml/3½fl oz/scant ½ cup milk
30g/1¼oz unsalted butter, plus extra for greasing
grated rind of 1 lemon
675g/1½lb/3 cups ricotta cheese
600g/1lb 5oz/3 cups caster/superfine sugar
5 eggs, plus 3 egg yolks
10ml/2 tsp vanilla extract
15ml/1 tbsp orange flower water
a pinch of ground cinnamon
50g/2oz glacé/candied citron, chopped
50g/2oz candied orange peel, chopped
50g/2oz mixed glacé/candied fruit, chopped
1kg/2¼lb shortcrust pastry
plain/all-purpose flour, for dusting
icing/confectioners' sugar, for dusting

COOK'S TIP

Canned wheat grain is sold in Italian stores. Alternatively, soak raw wheat grain in cold water for 2 days, changing the water twice a day, then simmer for up to an hour, until softened. You can also substitute wheat grain with pearl barley (soaked overnight in cold water then drained and boiled in fresh water for 30 minutes) or boiled pudding rice (cooked for 20 minutes in water).

1 Preheat the oven to 180°C/350°F/Gas 4 and generously grease a 30cm/12in diameter flan tin or pan with butter.

2 Put the wheat grain into a pan and add the milk, butter and grated lemon rind. Simmer slowly over a low heat for about 10 minutes, or until creamy.

3 In a mixing bowl, whisk together the ricotta cheese, sugar, the 5 eggs and 2 of the egg yolks, the vanilla, orange flower water and cinnamon.

4 Work this mixture together until smooth, then mix in the glacé fruit and candied peel, and the creamy grains.

5 Roll out the pastry on a floured surface to about 5mm/¼in thick and use to line the flan tin. Cut all the excess pastry into 1cm/½in-wide 30cm/12in-long strips to make the lattice topping of your pastiera. Set aside.

6 Beat the remaining egg yolk. Pour the ricotta and grain mixture into the tart case and arrange the strips of pastry over the top in a lattice pattern.

7 Brush the pastry with the beaten egg yolk. Bake for 1½ hours, or until golden brown. Remove from the oven and leave to cool.

8 Sprinkle the pastiera with icing sugar just before serving. Once baked, the pastiera can be kept in the refrigerator for 3 days, during which time it will improve daily.

ABRUZZO & MOLISE

Abruzzo lies east of the region of Lazio and is as close as you get to real mountain conditions so close to Rome and so far south. For skiers, there are even some well-equipped resorts such as Campo Felice, and also the largest glacier in southern Europe: the Calderone.

The regional capital is L'Aquila, which means 'the eagle'. For centuries, this city has sat proudly upon a hillside in the middle of a narrow valley with the tall snow-capped mountains of the Gran Sasso flanking it. It is a city shrouded in history, important religious events and mystique, where the terrible earthquake of 2009, which caused so much tragic devastation, is still all too fresh in the minds of the citizens.

The tiny region itself is divided into the provinces of Teramo, Pescara, Chieti and L'Aquila. The landscape of the Province of Teramo is dominated to the east by the coastline and sandy beaches of the Adriatic, and by the tallest peaks of the Apennine Mountains to the west. This province is famous for its production of liquorice, a local crop destined for the pharmaceutical market as well as confectionery.

Pescara, also on the coast, is the most densely populated and perhaps most dynamic of all the towns in the region, its suburban sprawl gradually creeping to merge with the outskirts of the city of Chieti.

The town of Chieti, reputedly founded by Achilles in 1181BCE and named after his mother Thetis, lies on a crest alongside the Pescara River, just a few kilometres from the coast. It is famous for its Easter procession on Good Friday, one of the oldest and most important events surrounding the Easter traditions in all of Italy that is attended by more than 40,000 people annually.

Traditionally, this has always been a region of sheep farmers and wool traders. In L'Aquila, vast fortunes have been made off the backs of countless sheep flocks. The city stands as the northern destination for the ancient sheep trails, the traturri that wend their way all the way down the eastern coast, traversing Molise and the length of Puglia to finally end close to Lecce. It is no wonder, therefore, that lamb and mutton feature so vividly on the menu here, where ingredients and cooking customs have migrated with the sheep and shepherds between the regions of Abruzzo, Molise and Puglia over centuries of deeply ingrained tradition.

Until 1963 Molise, formed part of the region of Abruzzi e Molise. The split, which did not become effective until 1970, makes Molise the youngest region in Italy. It is very small and sparsely populated, with only 312,00 inhabitants; the region has always suffered greatly from emigration, especially during the 19th century. It is divided into two provinces: Isernia and Campobasso, which is also the regional capital and is known for its mountain-top Monforte Castle and many Romanesque churches.

Lying between the Apennine ridge and the Adriatic Sea, nature, history, art, age-old traditions and rustic good food are the treasures of this largely undiscovered and tiny region, which is almost completely covered with mountains, including the areas closest to the coast. Despite the cold winters, agriculture remains a thriving industry. In addition to wine, olives, wheat, corn and tobacco are all grown here.

Molise was first occupied by the ancient tribe of the Sanniti, and was then taken over by the Romans. The history of the area then largely mirrors that of Abruzzo and during the course of history has been dominated in turn by the Lombards, the Franks and then by the Normans, who gave the region its name. It was also once under the rule of Sicily and the enduring Sicilian influence is still evident in the gastronomic culture: sheep and sheep products are an important element of the regional economy, as in many other regions in southern Italy. The local lamb dishes are very similar to those found in Abruzzo, but in Molise, pork skin, fatty and dense, is often used to make delicious sauces to dress superb pasta, the types of which resemble what you find in neighbouring regions.

Other influences include Puglia, which manifests itself in the regional custom of pairing cheese and fish, as in the traditional recipe for stuffed mussels. The local cheeses, as may be expected in a sheep-dominated area, are primarily made from sheep's milk and include pecorino, scamorza, caciocavallo and provolone.

Ventricina, the pork sausage typically found in Abruzzo, is also produced in Molise, but here it is liberally seasoned with fennel seeds and chilli. The local olive oil is also intensely flavoured and features in the regional cakes and biscuits.

SCRIPPELLE IN BRODO
PANCAKES IN CHICKEN BROTH

This filling dish is deliciously warming on snowy evenings. Its success rests heavily on using a chicken stock that is really bursting with flavour. This is a classic and very typical recipe from the region of Abruzzo.

SERVES 4

4 eggs, beaten
30ml/2 tbsp milk
45ml/3 tbsp chopped fresh parsley
75g/3oz/1 cup freshly grated Parmesan cheese, plus extra to serve
1.5ml/$^1/_4$ tsp sea salt
1.5ml/$^1/_4$ tsp freshly grated nutmeg
45ml/3 tbsp plain/all-purpose flour
1.5 litres/2$^1/_2$ pints/6$^1/_4$ cups chicken stock
30ml/2 tbsp lard or white cooking fat

1 Put the eggs and milk in a bowl, and add the parsley, 15ml/1 tbsp of the Parmesan cheese, salt and nutmeg. Beat thoroughly, then gradually beat in the flour.

2 Dilute the mixture with 30–45ml/2–3 tbsp cold water to make a batter; it should have a dropping consistency.

3 Heat the stock to boiling point and keep it simmering. Grease a 20cm/8in frying pan with lard and heat until sizzling hot.

4 Fry a small amount of the batter in the pan to make a thin pancake. Using a spatula, turn it over and cook the other side. Remove it from the pan and roll it up, then keep it warm while you make the others. Continue until all the batter has been used up.

5 Arrange two or three rolled pancakes in each person's bowl and sprinkle generously with the remaining Parmesan cheese. Pour over the stock to cover, Serve immediately, with extra Parmesan, if you like.

SERVES 4

4 large oranges
8 small anchovy fillets, canned in olive oil, drained
45ml/3 tbsp extra virgin olive oil
sea salt and ground black pepper

ANTIPASTO DI ARANCE
ORANGE ANTIPASTO

Anchovies go surprisingly well with orange in this very simple salad from the Abruzzo region. The fresh and zingy citrus flavour, enhanced by the salty anchovies, is guaranteed to sharpen the tastebuds.

1 Place each orange on a plate and cut off the peel and pith in strips using a sharp knife. Cut the remaining peel and pith from each end of the oranges.

2 Slice the oranges and arrange on a platter.

3 Arrange the anchovy fillets on top of the slices of orange.

4 Drizzle with the extra virgin olive oil. Season with salt and ground black pepper, and serve.

Capri

CALZONCINI ABRUZZESI
RICOTTA FRITTERS

These hearty little fritters from Abruzzo can be served as part of an antipasti selection or as a tasty cheesy snack at any time of day. Traditionally, they would be part of a great mound of deep-fried goodies such as artichoke hearts, scamorza cheese, cauliflower florets and many other delicious bits and pieces. This would be followed by the pasta course, the main course and then the desserts. Perhaps it is not surprising, therefore, that feasts in the Abruzzo can begin at one o'clock and not finish until seven o'clock in the evening!

SERVES 6

300g/11oz/generous $1^{1}/_{4}$ cups ricotta cheese
2 egg yolks
115g/4oz prosciutto crudo, finely chopped
115g/4oz/1 cup coarsely grated provolone cheese
50g/2oz/1 cup chopped fresh parsley
vegetable oil, for deep-frying
sea salt and ground black pepper

FOR THE PASTRY

400g/14oz/$3^{1}/_{2}$ cups plain/all-purpose flour, plus extra for dusting
2 eggs
115g/4oz/$^{2}/_{3}$ cup lard or white cooking fat
juice of 1 lemon
salt

1 Put the ricotta cheese in a bowl and mix with the egg yolks, prosciutto, provolone and parsley, and season with salt and black pepper. Stir until the mixture has a smooth, even consistency. Set aside while you make the pastry.

2 To make the pastry, put the flour on to the work surface. Make a hole in the middle and break in the eggs. Add the lard, lemon juice and a pinch of salt.

3 Knead it all together until you have a smooth ball of dough.

4 Roll the dough out thinly on a lightly floured surface and cut into 7.5cm/3in circles using a pastry or cookie cutter.

5 Put a teaspoonful of the filling on one half of each circle, fold in half and seal tightly by pressing the prongs of a fork all the way around the open edge.

6 Heat the vegetable oil in a large pan or deep-fryer until a small piece of the pastry, dropped into the oil, sizzles instantly.

7 Slide the calzoncini into the oil, about four at a time, and fry them until puffy and golden.

8 Remove the calzoncini using a slotted spoon, drain on kitchen paper and keep them warm while you cook the rest. Serve them piping hot.

SERVES 4

150ml/$^{1}/_{4}$ pint/$^{2}/_{3}$ cup olive oil
1 large onion, very thinly sliced
3 thick slices prosciutto crudo, cubed
1 garlic clove, chopped
1 hot dried red chilli
400g/14oz tagliolini
15ml/1 tbsp chopped fresh parsley
sea salt

TAGLIOLINI ALLA MOLISANA
TAGLIOLINI WITH HAM, ONION AND CHILLI

The ancient tradition of excellence in pasta making has made the region of Molise famous all over the world. Although the good old-fashioned, hand-made pasta is still lovingly prepared in many households, Molise also makes top-quality industrially prepared pasta, with brands such as La Molisana and Guacci showing off their expertise. You can choose from the huge variety of local factory-made durum-wheat pasta available: zite, zitoni, canneroncini, conchiglie and many other shapes – use whichever takes your fancy.

1 Heat the oil gently in a large, wide frying pan. Add the onion, prosciutto, garlic and dried chilli. Mix together and simmer slowly over a low heat for 20 minutes, until the onion is completely soft and translucent.

2 Bring a large pan of lightly salted water to a rolling boil. Add the pasta and stir.

3 Return to the boil and cook according to the pack instructions until the pasta is al dente. Drain. Transfer to the frying pan with the onion mixture.

4 Stir everything together over the heat for 2 minutes, sprinkle with the parsley and serve immediately.

SERVES 6

60ml/4 tbsp extra virgin olive oil
3 garlic cloves, finely chopped
$^1/_2$ onion, chopped
30ml/2 tbsp chopped basil, plus some extra basil leaves to serve
30ml/2 tbsp chopped fresh parsley
1 green bell pepper, cut into cubes
1kg/2$^1/_4$lb raw prawns/shrimp, with shells
120ml/4fl oz/$^1/_2$ cup Cognac
120ml/4fl oz/$^1/_2$ cup cold water

GAMBERONI UBRIACHI
DRUNKEN PRAWNS

The region of Molise has few recipes to offer, but this is a delicious way of serving plump, juicy prawns, flavoured with basil, green pepper, garlic and Cognac. It has to be eaten with the fingers for maximum enjoyment, so do supply finger bowls and plenty of napkins for guests to clean their hands.

1 Heat the olive oil in a large pan, add the chopped garlic, onion, basil, parsley and green pepper, and fry over a medium heat, stirring frequently, for 10 minutes or until the pepper has softened.

2 Add the prawns and baste them with the oil. Cook until they are bright pink, then add the Cognac and water. Simmer for 5 minutes, then serve, sprinkled with a few extra basil leaves.

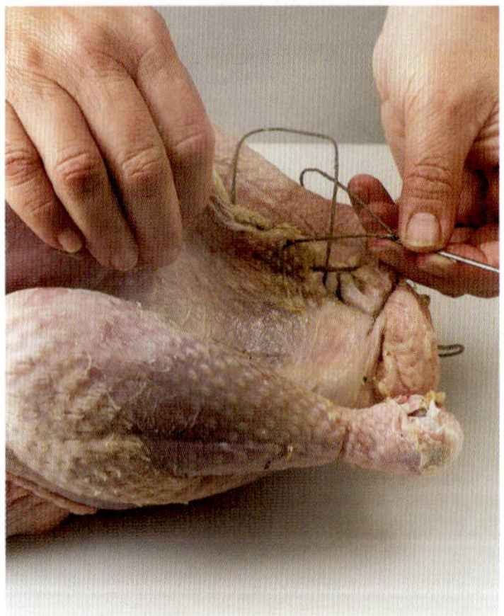

TACCHINO RIPIENO ALLA MOLISANA
STUFFED ROAST TURKEY IN THE MOLISE STYLE

This is a superb recipe for a stuffed turkey from the little-known region of Molise. The food here has many similarities with its northern neighbour Abruzzo, although Molise also shares some culinary traditions with Campania and Apulia – blending different Italian cooking traditions with its own local rustic ingredients. Classic accompaniments for the roast turkey include cabbage, braised onions, carrots or other seasonal vegetables. The same stuffing can also be used for chicken or game birds such as pheasant.

1 Preheat the oven to 180°C/350°F/Gas 4. Pat the turkey dry with kitchen paper.

2 Trim and chop the giblets and put them into a pan with 15ml/1 tbsp olive oil and the chopped onion. Discard the neck.

3 Fry gently until the onion is soft and the meat is browned. Transfer to a bowl and leave to cool.

4 When cool, add the breadcrumbs, eggs, cheese, pine nuts, currants, parsley and nutmeg. Mix it all together very thoroughly and season to taste with salt and ground black pepper.

5 Add 15ml/1 tbsp olive oil, mix again and then use this mixture to stuff the turkey. Sew the neck of the turkey closed tightly, using cook's string, once you have finished stuffing it. Grease a roasting pan with about half the remaining oil.

6 Mix the garlic and rosemary into the remaining oil. Stir in the peppercorns and season with salt. Stir the sage leaves into the oil and add the white wine, then use about half of this mixture to brush all over the turkey. Reserve the rest of it to baste the turkey as it cooks.

7 Roast the turkey, basting frequently, for 3½ hours, or until the juices from the thickest part of the leg run clear and the bird is crisp and golden brown.

8 Carve the turkey and serve it with the stuffing mixture and some stewed lentils or cannellini beans.

SERVES 8

4.5kg/10lb oven-ready turkey, with giblets
120ml/4fl oz/½ cup olive oil
½ onion, chopped
115g/4oz/2 cups fresh white breadcrumbs
2 eggs, beaten
45ml/3 tbsp freshly grated pecorino cheese
30ml/2 tbsp pine nuts
30ml/2 tbsp currants, soaked in warm water for 15 minutes, then drained thoroughly
30ml/2 tbsp chopped fresh parsley
1.5ml/¼ tsp freshly grated nutmeg
2 garlic cloves, crushed
15ml/1 tbsp finely chopped fresh rosemary leaves
15ml/1 tbsp black peppercorns
3 fresh sage leaves, chopped
75ml/5 tbsp dry white wine
sea salt and ground black pepper
stewed lentils or cannellini beans, to serve (see Cook's Tip)

COOK'S TIP

To make tasty stewed pulses, sauté a clove of crushed garlic with a little olive oil until pungent, then add 900g/2lb lentils, cannellini beans or other pulses (canned, or soaked and boiled until tender) and cook for 2–3 minutes. Add stock or water to cover and simmer until soft. Season with salt and pepper before serving.

AGNELLO CACIO E UOVA
LAMB WITH CHEESE AND EGG

In this recipe from the region of the Abruzzo, cheese and eggs are beaten together with lemon juice to create a rich sauce to accompany the lamb. It is often served as part of the Easter feast in some parts of the south, and the ingredients are chosen as symbols of this important time in the Christian calendar. The primary ingredients are lamb, symbolic of the sacrifice of God's son; eggs, representing rebirth and the resurrection of Jesus; and vegetables, celebrating the return of the fertility of spring.

SERVES 4 TO 6

1 medium leg of lamb, about 2.25kg/5lb, boned
75ml/5 tbsp extra virgin olive oil
3 garlic cloves, coarsely chopped
a sprig of rosemary
250ml/8fl oz/1 cup dry white wine
90ml/6 tbsp freshly grated pecorino cheese
4 eggs, beaten
juice of 1 lemon
30ml/2 tbsp chopped fresh flat leaf parsley
sea salt and ground black pepper
boiled potatoes and roasted red bell peppers, to serve (optional)

1 Cut the lamb into 2.5cm/1in chunks. Heat the oil in a large pan and add the garlic and the rosemary. Add the lamb and brown it all over in the oil, then gradually add the white wine and use it to baste the meat and prevent it sticking.

2 Cover and simmer gently for 15 minutes, or until the lamb is cooked through. Remove the pan from the heat and discard the rosemary.

3 Beat the cheese and eggs together and add the lemon juice. Season with salt and pepper and pour this mixture over the lamb.

4 Return the pan to the heat and cook over a medium heat for 8 minutes, or until the eggs have set.

5 Sprinkle with a little chopped parsley and serve, accompanied by boiled potatoes and roasted red peppers, if you like.

SERVES 4

4 large potatoes, peeled
25ml/1½ tbsp dried oregano
135ml/9 tbsp olive oil, plus extra for greasing
60ml/4 tbsp fresh white breadcrumbs
3 very large, ripe tomatoes, such as beefsteak or marmande, sliced
3 red onions, thinly sliced into rings
sea salt and ground black pepper

TERRINA DI PATATE, CIPOLLE E POMODORO
POTATO, ONION AND TOMATO BAKE

The humble potato is sliced and layered with onion, tomato and breadcrumbs to make a very easy dish from Abruzzo that is full of flavour. It's ideal for a light lunch, served with a big salad and some crusty, warm garlic bread.

1 Boil the potatoes for 4 minutes, then drain and slice into thin discs.

2 Grease a shallow ovenproof dish (large enough to hold all the vegetables) with olive oil.

3 Arrange a layer of potatoes on the bottom of the dish. Sprinkle with oregano, a little olive oil and a few pinches of breadcrumbs, then season with salt and pepper.

4 Cover with a layer of tomatoes and a layer of onions, topped with seasoning, oil and breadcrumbs as before.

5 Repeat until all the vegetables have been used up, finishing with a generous coating of breadcrumbs. Leave to stand while you preheat the oven to 180°C/350°F/Gas 4.

6 Bake for 30 minutes, or until the top is browned and crisp. Serve warm.

SERVES 4

150g/5oz/$^2/_3$ cup brown or green lentils
75ml/5 tbsp olive oil
1 celery stick, coarsely chopped
1 large carrot, chopped
1 large onion, chopped
2 garlic cloves, chopped
3 rashers/strips pancetta, or streaky/fatty bacon, chopped (optional)
10cm/4in rosemary sprig
4 or 5 medium potatoes, cubed
250ml/8fl oz/1 cup chicken or meat stock
sea salt and ground black pepper
tomato salad, to serve (optional)

COOK'S TIP

This dish is also excellent served cold, with salad, cheese and bread.

PATATE E LENTICCHIE
POTATOES WITH LENTILS

Here is a typical, simple rustic dish from the Abruzzo region that is bursting with flavour. A good helping of olive oil gives richness to the combination of lentils and vegetables – and you can also add some pancetta or bacon. Serve this as an accompaniment to a game stew or chicken casserole, or enjoy it on its own with some crusty bread and a good bottle of red wine. Some types of lentils need to be soaked before they are cooked, so ensure you check the instructions.

1 Rinse the lentils, then put them in a pan of water to cover. Bring to the boil and cook for 5 minutes. Drain and rinse again.

2 Return the lentils to the pan, and add fresh cold water to just cover. Simmer for 15 minutes. Set aside.

3 Heat the oil in a separate pan, and gently fry the celery, carrot, onion, garlic, pancetta or bacon, if using, and rosemary, until softened and the fat in the meat starts to run.

4 Add the lentils with their cooking liquid and stir thoroughly. Season generously with salt and pepper. Cover and simmer slowly for 30 minutes, stirring frequently.

5 Add the potatoes and stock and continue to cook, uncovered, until the potatoes are tender all the way through.

6 Adjust the seasoning to taste as necessary and serve immediately, with a tomato salad, if you like.

PEPERONI IN TEGLIA ALLA NAPOLETANA
YELLOW PEPPERS WITH CAPERS

This is one of those dishes that brings together the colours, flavours and textures of the food of southern Italy absolutely perfectly. It is best eaten at room temperature, with green salad, bread and chilled white wine.

SERVES 4

4 yellow bell peppers
60ml/4 tbsp olive oil
2 garlic cloves, sliced
15ml/1 tbsp tomato paste
7.5ml/1½ tsp salted capers, rinsed and chopped
3 anchovy fillets, preserved in oil, drained and chopped
sea salt
salad and bread, to serve (optional)

1 Halve the bell peppers and remove the seeds and membranes. Cut each one into four pieces.

2 Heat the oil in a pan and fry the garlic until browned. Add the peppers. Dilute the tomato paste with 45ml/3 tbsp water and pour over the peppers.

3 Season, then stir. Cover and simmer for 25 minutes, until the peppers are soft.

4 Mix the capers and anchovies together, then stir them into the peppers. Cover and leave to stand for 3 minutes before serving warm with salad and bread. Alternatively, serve cold.

CAUCIUNI DI NATALE
CHRISTMAS CHICKPEA PASTRIES

This Christmas Eve speciality from Molise is from an ancient recipe for little fried pastries with a sweet chocolate and citrus filling, the origin of which is lost in historical rituals. There are two particular Molisan customs connected with making cauciuni. First, the chickpeas are soaked out of doors overnight, preferably on a frosty night. Second, when testing whether or not the oil for frying the pastries is hot enough, it is traditional to make a wish for the coming year while you watch the first small piece of pastry sizzle in the pan.

MAKES ABOUT 30

500g/1¼lb plain/all-purpose flour, sifted
90ml/6 tbsp olive oil
1.5ml/¼ tsp salt
10ml/2 tsp vanilla extract
60ml/4 tbsp dry white wine
sunflower oil, for deep-frying
45ml/3 tbsp icing/confectioners' sugar
7.5ml/1½ tsp ground cinnamon

FOR THE FILLING

500g/1¼lb dried chickpeas, soaked overnight and drained
45ml/3 tbsp unsweetened cocoa powder
45ml/3 tbsp caster/superfine sugar
200g/7oz/generous 1 cup chopped candied citrus peel
45ml/3 tbsp clear honey
30ml/2 tbsp sweet liqueur of your choice, Amaretto or Maraschino

1 To make the filling, rinse the soaked chickpeas, then boil them rapidly for 5 minutes in some fresh water. Drain them and rinse once again, then cover with fresh water and simmer slowly for about 3 hours, or until completely tender and almost pulpy.

2 Drain the chickpeas and push them through a food mill or a sieve or strainer to create a purée.

3 In a large mixing bowl, mix the chickpea purée with the cocoa powder, caster sugar, citrus peel, honey and liqueur, using a wooden spoon, to make a smooth filling. Set the filling aside while you make the pastry, to allow the flavours to develop.

4 To make the pastry, pile all the flour on to the work surface and make a hole in the middle with your fist. Pour the oil into the well with the salt, vanilla extract and half the wine.

5 Knead the ingredients into the flour, adding the remaining wine, a little at a time, until you have a very smooth, shiny and elastic dough. You may not need all of the wine.

6 Roll the dough out very thinly and cut it into 7.5cm/3in circles using a pastry or cookie cutter.

7 Put a spoonful of filling on one half of each circle, fold in half and seal using the prongs of a fork.

8 Heat the sunflower oil in a large pan or deep-fryer until a small piece of the pastry, dropped into the oil, sizzles and browns almost immediately.

9 Fry the cauciuni in batches of four or five at a time. As soon as they are puffy and golden brown, remove them from the hot oil using a slotted spoon. Drain carefully on kitchen paper and keep them warm while you cook the rest.

10 Dust generously with icing sugar and cinnamon, and serve piping hot.

PARROZZO ABRUZZESE
CHOCOLATE-COVERED ALMOND CAKE

The name of this cake derives from 'pan rozzo', a bread made by Abruzzese shepherds from ground corn, water and olive oil. In 1920, a baker called Luigi D'Amico, from the coastal town of Pescara, took this rather characterless example of cucina povera (or 'the poor kitchen'), and elevated it by adding ground sweet almonds from Abruzzo's abundant almond groves and coating it with chocolate. Its popularity spread beyond Pescara, and parrozzo is now one of the region's iconic sweets. In fact, the Pescaran poet and writer Gabriel D'Annunzio was so inspired by its flavours that he composed a poem about it, 'Song of the Parrozzo'.

SERVES 6 TO 8

75g/3oz/$^{1}/_{2}$ cup blanched almonds
130g/4$^{1}/_{2}$oz/scant $^{3}/_{4}$ cup caster/superfine sugar
75g/3oz/6 tbsp unsalted butter, plus extra for greasing
5 eggs, separated
50g/2oz/$^{1}/_{2}$ cup plain/all-purpose flour
50g/2oz/$^{1}/_{2}$ cup cornflour/cornstarch
150g/5oz cooking chocolate

1 Preheat the oven to 180°C/350°F/Gas 4 and grease a 23cm/9in cake tin or pan. Put the almonds and 40g/1$^{1}/_{2}$oz sugar in a mortar and pound with a pestle into a fine powder. Alternatively, you can use a food processor.

2 Melt the butter in a heatproof bowl set over a pan of simmering water, then leave it to cool without letting it harden.

3 Put the egg yolks in a large bowl and whisk, gradually adding the remaining sugar, until light and fluffy. Gradually add the almond mixture alternately with the flour, cornflour and butter, stirring constantly.

4 Put the egg whites into a clean, grease-free bowl and whisk until they form stiff peaks. Fold them gently into the mixture.

5 Pour the cake mixture into the tin and bake for 40 minutes, or until a knife inserted into the middle comes out clean. Allow to cool in the tin for 15 minutes. Turn out on to a wire rack to cool completely.

6 Melt the chocolate in a heatproof bowl set over a pan of simmering water, then use it to cover the top of the cake, spreading it evenly with a metal spatula. Allow the chocolate to harden, then serve.

SERVES 6 TO 8

- 115g/4oz/generous ½ cup caster/superfine sugar
- 100ml/3½fl oz/scant ½ cup red wine
- 100ml/3½fl oz/scant ½ cup olive oil
- about 250g/9oz/2¼ cups plain/all-purpose flour
- 15ml/1 tbsp lard or white cooking fat

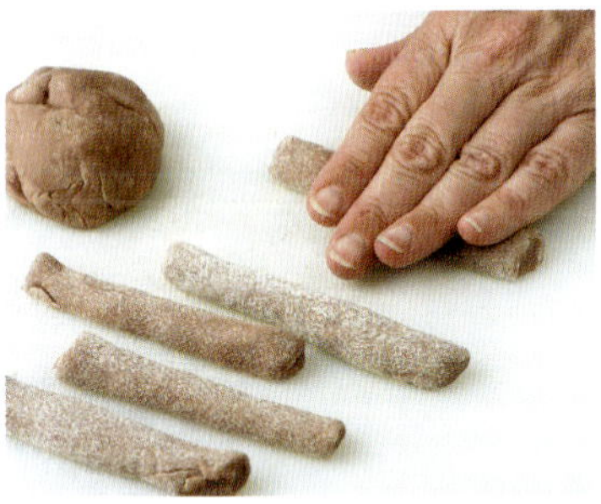

CIAMBELLINE ABRUZZESI
ABRUZZESE RING COOKIES

Designed specifically to be dunked, these unusual wine-flavoured ring-shaped biscuits are hard in texture so that they won't disintegrate when they are dipped into wine at the end of a meal. They are especially delicious with frothy, milky coffee or hot chocolate for breakfast.

1 In a large bowl, mix together the sugar, wine and oil using a whisk.

2 Gradually beat in the flour until you have a pliable, kneadable dough. You may not need all of the flour so just add it a little at a time.

3 Transfer the ball of dough to a bowl, cover with a cloth, and leave to rest in the refrigerator for at least 30 minutes.

4 Preheat the oven to 160°C/325°F/Gas 3 and grease a baking sheet with the lard or white cooking fat.

5 Roll the rested dough into 10cm/4in-long sausage shapes on a floured surface. Bend them to form rings. Arrange on the baking sheet, spaced well apart.

6 Bake for 20 minutes, then cool on a wire rack. Serve with coffee, if you like.

SICILY & SOUTHERN ITALY

A SUN-BAKED LANDSCAPE

The hot and arid regions of Sicily, Calabria, Basilicata and Puglia lie in the sun-drenched south of Italy, and are part of the Mezzogiorno, which also includes Molise and Campania. Long expanses of coastline plunge into the temperate waters of the Mediterranean, but inland, mysterious forests, rugged mountains and ancient villages provide startling natural beauty too. On a map, Italy resembles a boot kicking a ball. With this in mind, the four regions of southern Italy are easy to identify: Puglia is the heel, Basilicata is the instep, Calabria is the toe and Sicily is the ball. The whole of southern Italy is rich in history, culture, art and gastronomy, but it is so different from the industrial north that it is sometimes hard to believe it is part of the same country.

The south of Italy has a typical Mediterranean climate, with short, mild, wet winters and long, hot, dry summers with only occasional rain and thunderstorms. Summers are mainly influenced by the Sirocco, a hot wind from the North African coast. The scorching temperatures are the dominating feature, especially during the summer, when the ground turns into parched dust, though it can also become extremely cold in winter in the mountains. Despite the heat and aridity, these regions produce legendary wines, wonderful fruit and vegetables, and golden durum wheat for making world-famous pasta and delicious bread.

SICILY – AN ISLAND OF NATURAL BEAUTY

A truly amazing island, Sicily is set like a jewel in the blue waters of three seas: the Tyrrhenian, Mediterranean and Ionian Seas. It is a place of breathtaking natural beauty, with rugged hills, rocky inlets, wide sandy beaches and Etna, the stupendous volcano that dominates the land. The architectural and agricultural legacy of the various nations who have ruled here, from the Phoenicians, Greeks and Romans to the Arabs and Spanish, still remain.

The warm climate and an almost total absence of frost allows Sicilian farmers to grow tender crops. Never-ending groves of citrus fruits and olives and sprawling vines bearing watermelons and grapes are visible at every turn. The best weather is usually found near the coast – inland and in the larger cities it can be unbearably hot. The southern and western coasts are, however, close to Africa and therefore susceptible to higher temperatures and the Sirocco wind.

CALABRIA – A MOUNTAINOUS REGION

Across the Strait of Messina, where the narrowest strip of sea between Sicily and the mainland is only 3.2km/2 miles wide, lies the region of

BELOW *Sicily, Calabria, Basilicata and Puglia are set at the very south of Italy, in the warm waters of the Mediterranean and close to the North African coast, so the region has a hot, dry climate.*

BELOW RIGHT *The sparkling blue waters of the Tyrrhenian Sea provide a dazzling backdrop to the Calabrian coastline.*

Calabria. Two deep furrows running east to west divide the landscape into three mountainous sections. This natural formation tends to isolate the towns and cities from each other.

The Pollino Mountains in the north of the region form a natural barrier separating Calabria from the rest of Italy. Some parts are heavily wooded, while others are windswept plateaux with little vegetation or agriculture. La Sila, in the middle, is a vast mountainous plateau about 1,200m/4,000ft above sea level, which boasts numerous lakes and dense coniferous forests, and is famous for the production of cheeses. The southern Aspromonte range overlooks the Straits of Messina. The rare bergamot, a lemony-yellow fruit used in perfumes and to flavour Earl Grey tea, flourishes here, but agriculture in Calabria is mainly limited to the level areas near the coast, where citrus fruits, vegetables, vines and olives grow profusely, and tender, valuable crops such as sugar beet, tobacco, flowers and oranges abound, as well as fig and almond trees. Sheep farming, though very traditional all over this region, is sadly in decline.

BASILICATA – A RUGGED TERRAIN

The 'instep' of the Italian 'boot', Basilicata has little coastline compared to the other southern regions – it has one short coastline on the Tyrrhenian Sea to the west and another on the Gulf of Taranto to the south-east. Set at the southern end of the Apennine mountain range, which runs down the spine of Italy, the region is almost entirely mountainous and the harsh terrain has always made communications difficult. This is a land of farmers and shepherds, who tend their hardy flocks on the stony slopes of the mountains. Until very recent times Basilicata was one of the least developed provinces of Italy, and one of its poorest regions, but the area has become significantly richer over the past years, largely thanks to the recent discovery of oil under the rocks.

PUGLIA – THE LOWLANDS

This region, known as Apulia in English, is located in the eastern tip of the Italian peninsula. It has the longest continuous stretch of coastline of any region of Italy, and near the beautiful resort area of the Gargano are Italy's largest coastal lakes – Lesina and Varano. The landscape of the region consists of flat plains and soft hills, which are ideal for food production in the warm climate. Puglia is more economically developed than other southern regions, and a range of crops are grown here, including durum wheat, figs, tobacco and sugar beet. The fields also contain rows of lettuce, peppers, fennel, artichokes, grapes, almonds and olives. Pugliese olive oil is famous the world over, and is reputed to have been Cleopatra's favourite oil. Sheep farming is a long-standing tradition, and fishing thrives along the length of the coastline.

ABOVE *The wonderfully preserved ancient Greek theatre in Taormina on the east coast of Sicily sits in a remarkably picturesque location, with views over Mount Etna.*

A TURBULENT HISTORY

The south of Italy followed a different historical path from the north. After hundreds of years of Roman domination, the southern regions were fought over in constant battles between the Greeks, Lombards and Caliphs, to name a few. The area became part of Spain until Duke Victor Amadeus II of Sardinia took Sicily in 1713. The south was eventually conquered by Giuseppe Garibaldi and the Redshirts in 1861 and, with the north, formed the modern State of Italy. The landscape of the south is rich with evidence of a turbulent, diverse and fascinating history – it is dotted with ancient Greek temples and amphitheatres, beautiful Roman mosaics, enduring Byzantine architecture and splendid Norman churches.

SICILY – PLAYTHING OF FOREIGN POWERS

Colonised by the Greeks from the 8th century BCE, Sicily was included as part of Magna Graecia. However, by 242BCE, Sicily was in Roman hands, becoming Rome's first province outside the Italian peninsula. For the next six centuries Sicily remained something of a rural backwater, prized chiefly for its golden fields of grain, which were a mainstay of the food supply for the Roman population.

In AD826, an Islamic army of Arabs, Berbers, Spaniards, Cretans and Persians was sent to Sicily. The conquest took more than a century to be completed, with Syracuse holding out for a long time, but the island was finally conquered in AD965. During this period, new kinds of crops, such as oranges, lemons, pistachios and sugar cane, were brought to Sicily from North Africa.

Over the next millennium, Sicily was continuously fought over by the Normans, Lombards, French, Spanish and various other royal houses of Europe. Even when Italy as a country was finally unified, Sicily, and much of southern Italy, was the object of harsh repression by the Italian army. The Sicilian economy did not adapt easily to unification, and competition with northern industrial giants made industrialization in the south very difficult.

CALABRIA – A GROWING ECONOMY

Like Sicily, Calabria was part of the rich and powerful Magna Graecia, until the Romans conquered it. Throughout the millennium that followed the fall of the Roman Empire, Calabria too was occupied by invading forces. During these periods the population, plagued by malaria epidemics as well as violent raids by the Saracens and the Turks along the coast, withdrew to the mountains. This phenomenon created an internal and external isolation, with the population of each valley often unable to visit the next because of impassable roads during the winter. When Italy was unified in 1861, Calabria had only one road that crossed it from the north coast to Reggio in the south, and there was no railway.

BELOW *Crops such as pistachios were brought to Sicily by the Islamic army around 1,200 years ago, and have since featured in the cakes and pastries made in the area.*

BELOW RIGHT *The medieval church of Santa Maria dell'Isola in Tropea sits on its own rocky island off the coast of Calabria and is one of many tourist attractions in the area.*

THE STONE CAVES OR 'I SASSI' OF MATERA

This extraordinary city in Basilicata began as a group of three small Neolithic villages, grouped around a water source. These remained the region's only human settlement until two of the villages were abandoned and all the inhabitants moved into the third. There, people continued to develop and build into the rockface until 1860, with rule passing from the Longobards to the Byzantines, to the Normans, and the Saracens – who sacked and destroyed the city – before it finally became a Piedmontese province. The population of Matera began to swell at this point, since under Piedmontese rule much of the farmed land outside the city was sold off and local agriculture was destroyed, changing the time-honoured way of life completely. As a result, largely out of despair and fear, the population crowded into the ancient city of caves and narrow streets, which is built out of the chalky rock with one home on top of another, like a human anthill, above a deep ravine called the Gravina of Matera that divides the territory into two areas.

Matera was originally built to be hidden, but this made it difficult for the inhabitants to receive water. Early dwellers thus invested much energy in building enormous cisterns and intricate systems of water channels. In the 8th and 9th centuries, hermits and monks came to live in the caves and built 117 churches and several convents and monasteries. The paintings and decorations in these contain elements of Byzantine and Latin art styles, and reflect other unknown influences redolent of the city's long history.

In 1993 the town was made a UNESCO World Heritage site, for being: 'the most outstanding, intact example of a troglodyte settlement in the Mediterranean region, perfectly adapted to its terrain and ecosystem', but in the 1950s the local government – in the face of rising local crime and problems with sanitation, malaria and overcrowding, which became a national scandal – took the decision to turn all the residents out of the town and rebuilt a second, new Matera on a nearby plateau. For 30 years, the city was abandoned, as various international bodies studied this extraordinary and unique spontaneous urban development. Plans were commissioned, drawn up and failed, until at last, by the late 1980s the city was finally carefully restored and readied to receive its citizens. Although most of the original population had by then established themselves in their new city and had no desire to return to the cave dwellings of the ancient city, it has since become a worthy tourist destination and many people seeking an alternative lifestyle have moved back into some of the caves.

conditions have changed radically. Thanks to tourism, coastal towns have sprung up, packed with restaurants serving regional specialities.

BASILICATA – A NEGLECTED REGION

In Roman times Basilicata was known as Lucania, after the Lucani people who were the first known invaders of the region before the Greeks invaded during the 7th century BCE. The area was under Roman rule by the 2nd century BCE and under the government of Rome it fell into decay. Cities on the coast became depopulated, and malaria began to gain the upper hand. The few towns of the interior were of little importance. A large part of the land was given over to pasture, and the mountains were covered with forests, which were full of wild boar, bears and wolves. In more recent times, the discovery of oil within the harsh mountainous landscape has meant the region has started to regenerate and has begun to promote its emerging tourist industry.

PUGLIA – A TREASURED FOOD STORE

One of the richest areas in Italy in terms of archaeology, this region was inhabited from the 1st millennium BCE, and like most of the south, it formed part of the Magna Graecia. Later, the Romans captured the ports of Brindisi and Taranto, and established their domination. During Roman occupation, Puglia was renowned for its grain and olive oil, becoming the most important exporter of these ingredients to the eastern provinces. Top-quality durum wheat, which makes delicious bread and pasta, remains its main crop to this day.

After the fall of Rome, Puglia was held successively by the Goths, the Lombards and, from the 6th century onward, the Byzantines. From AD800 the region was mostly under Byzantine authority, and subsequently, like much of the south, it was controlled by different European powers whose various influences can be seen in the architecture. In 1861 the region of Puglia finally joined the State of Italy.

COPING WITH ORGANISED CRIME

Government neglect in the 19th century ultimately enabled the establishment of an organised crime network commonly known as La Mafia, with influence in many areas of Sicilian culture, not least in food production and restaurants. Efforts to eradicate it in Italy and the USA continue to this day.

A VIBRANT CUISINE

The differences between the south of Italy, especially the far south, and the north are highlighted in its food traditions. Pasta here means dried pasta, as opposed to the fresh home-made pasta and hearty polenta of the northern regions, and meat and cheese are eaten only in small quantities. A hot climate with relentless sunshine, slow industrialization and myriad historical influences has led to the cuisine of the south being mostly earthy and peasant-like with exotic twists of taste. Compared to the north, the flavours are somewhat stronger and the combinations of ingredients are bolder, which mirrors the extremes of the climate and landscape, and perhaps also the hot-blooded nature of the people.

BELOW *Sicily is famous for its citrus fruits, which grow in abundance in the hot conditions and are used in many local dishes as well as being exported around the world.*

THE CUISINE OF SICILY

This small island off Italy's south-western coast is a living celebration of family, food and culture. The landscape, a mosaic of golden coastlines and wheat fields, fruit orchards, forests, flourishing vineyards and brilliant wild flowers, has inspired works of art in writing, painting and cuisine. The legacy of the island's many invaders throughout history – Romans, Byzantines, Arabs, Normans and Spaniards – has fostered a fascinating multicultural cuisine full of exotic and aromatic dishes. A culinary tour of Sicily is always a joy.

Savoury delights A Sicilian meal might start with caponata, an appetizer made of aubergine, pine nuts, celery, olives and capers. The recipe varies, sometimes including artichokes and even chocolate. To the west, in Palermo, the aroma of Arab-inspired vegetable couscous and roast lamb made wafts from the town's open-air markets. Down by the southern coast, fish, mussels and clams, which have been plucked from the Mediterranean, are for sale on the quayside. The region's most famous cheese is caciocavallo, which is made from curdled cow's milk.

Sweet treats Ice cream is almost a Sicilian obsession. An abundance of flavours and varieties is available, including the very special granita al caffè con panna, a slushy iced coffee topped with whipped cream.

Among the vast array of sweetmeats in a Sicilian pastry store window, the place of honour definitely goes to the cassata. Made of a mixture of sponge cake, chocolate, sweetened ricotta cheese, candied fruit and nuts, it is usually decorated with thick icing or marzipan and covered with more brightly coloured candied fruits. The ever-popular cannoli, deep-fried pastry cylinders filled with a rich combination of sweetened ricotta, chocolate and candied fruit, were once a treat only at carnival time, but are now enjoyed all year round.

ABOVE LEFT *Fresh fish, such as these beautiful red mullet, are enjoyed in local dishes along the southern coast.*

ABOVE *Ice cream and other iced treats are a big deal in Sicily, and are sold in a wide range of flavours at seaside shacks, parlours, cafés and restaurants all over the island.*

Centuries ago, a delicious sweet wine was created in the western Sicilian town of Marsala to challenge the Portuguese and Spanish monopoly on fortified wines such as Madeira and sherry. Today, Marsala is used all over the world to enhance the flavour of a dish, as part of a sauce, or to be sipped as a dessert wine.

THE CUISINE OF CALABRIA

Although it is neither as refined nor as rich in ingredients, the cuisine of Calabria is very substantial and infused with the intense flavours of chilli peppers, mint, garlic, tomatoes, sweet bell peppers, aubergines and the famous red onions of Tropea. Durum-wheat pasta, pork and bread, as well as fish in the coastal areas, are the foods enjoyed by Calabrians. The region boasts a strong, frugal peasant tradition that combines simple ingredients to make lively, tasty foods.

THE MEDITERRANEAN DIET

Researchers have discovered that people in the countries bordering the Mediterranean Sea, especially southern Italy, exhibit strikingly low rates of heart disease compared with Americans or Northern Europeans. Meals mostly consist of grains, fruits, pulses and vegetables, with just a little meat, cheese and fish. The main fat is olive oil, which is used in lavish quantities instead of butter. The garlic that appears in many dishes may help prevent blood clots, lower cholesterol and protect against cancer. The diet also includes moderate amounts of red wine, which may help protect the heart.

Inventiveness and thrift One of the dishes that sums up the Calabrian philosophy of food is caviale dei poveri (poor people's caviar), made by packing herring roe in oil and flavouring it with hot chilli peppers. Bottarga, or preserved tuna roe, is another local speciality and features prominently in many traditional dishes.

The sheep that scramble over the rocks are the source of delicious lamb dishes and many different cheeses made with ewe's milk. Vegetables of all kinds abound, and fiery chilli peppers are used to spice up everything from cured meats to pasta. Particularly famous are the Calabrian soft chilli-flavoured sausages, 'nduja, which are served as appetizers or in sandwiches.

Figs, chestnuts and almonds are mainly used in desserts such as fichi ripieni (stuffed figs), a speciality of Cosenza that tops dried figs with unsweetened cocoa powder, almonds and other nuts. These few sweet ingredients are essential to local cooking and form the basis of many dishes.

ABOVE *A farmer in Basilicata begins to harvest the golden fields of durum wheat.*

PRESERVING FOOD

Calabrians have traditionally placed a great emphasis on preserving their foods, partly because the dry, hot climate of the mountains inland makes crop failures a possibility. For this reason, the Calabrian people plan ahead, bottling vegetables and meats in oil, salting meat and, along the coast, curing fish, especially swordfish and tuna.

THE CUISINE OF BASILICATA

With little coastline and a mountainous interior, Basilicata is a rural farming region, so pork, pasta (made from durum wheat and water), bread and vegetables are the stars of the table. The flavours of the local food are always robust, sharp and intense. Desserts are also good, especially those sweetened with the flavoursome local honey.

A peasant cuisine Pork is the fundamental staple food. A pig can be reared in any kind of terrain and every bit can be used, even its blood, which is used for making a well-known local dessert called sanguinaccio. These pigs are generally muscular, and yield a ham that is dry, sinewy and full of flavour, especially when cured with wonderful spices.

The famous pork sausage is made using only top-quality pork seasoned with fennel seeds, salt and pepper, or peperoncino. It has a strong taste, and is eaten fresh, roasted, fried, smoked and left to dry, or preserved in oil. Other local sausages include soppressata, a dry-cured salami, and the typical pezzente (beggar), a sausage composed of meat scraps chopped up into tiny pieces and flavoured with generous quantities of black pepper and garlic. Another very typical dish of the Basilicata region is lamb, mutton or kid cooked in a pignata, or deep earthenware pot.

Bread made with durum wheat is vital to the cuisine of Basilicata, and appears not only as an accompaniment to meals, but also as a basis for many dishes, sitting at the bottom of a bowl of salad or soup, for example, to provide bulk.

Pasta shapes of all kinds are also made using durum-wheat flour, along with water and salt, which are kneaded and shaped by hand to produce dough that is much thicker than industrially-made dry pasta. The most common dressing for pasta in Basilicata is a tomato and meat sauce with small pieces of mutton or lamb, which have been sliced with a knife, rather than minced or ground. On top of the meat sauce, there will be a sprinkling of strong cheese as well as chilli pepper fried in oil. Bright and fragrant, this is a substantial pasta dish.

CHILLI PEPPERS

Beneath the tranquil surface of Basilicata's quiet exterior lies a cuisine that rages with the heat of the peperoncino, the fiery chilli pepper that is found in all sorts of shapes and sizes at the local markets. The 'little red devil' is used in such generous quantities in Basilicata that the unsuspecting tourist, as well as the uninitiated Italian, may find themselves gasping for breath and reaching for a cooling drink.

THE CUISINE OF PUGLIA

Puglia overflows with the fruits of both land and sea. It has golden wheat fields, plentiful olive groves, famous vineyards, and good fishing grounds in the Adriatic and Ionian Sea. The dry, hot climate makes it ideal for growing top-quality durum wheat – accounting for the superior, irresistible taste of its bread and pasta – and producing world-renowned olive oil. With good cheer and hospitality, delicious food and wine, a Pugliese feast is always a memorable experience.

Simple tastes of the countryside Puglia cultivates most types of wheat, but durum wheat is the main crop. The density of this wheat, combined with its high protein content and gluten strength, make it the best choice for producing fantastic pasta and bread. For instance, pane di Altamura is a wonderful sourdough bread, made only with durum-wheat flour from the Alta Murgia near Bari, plus natural yeast, water and salt. It is shaped into enormous round loaves and baked in ovens fired by oak wood. When fresh, it is soft on the inside with a crunchy coat, becoming firmer over time.

Shellfish is very popular in this area, especially in the area around Bari where the locals love to eat it raw, freshly plucked from the sea. Broad beans, tomatoes, aubergine, broccoli and courgettes are just a few of the exquisite vegetables cultivated in the region's rich, fertile soil.

Most of the cakes and desserts found in Puglia are very sweet, based on almonds, sugar and sometimes honey as well. There is a tradition of making desserts for special occasions, and these tend to be wonderfully elaborate confections in comparison to the simpler everyday sweetmeats, cakes and cookies.

OLIVE OIL

The different varieties of olive oil produced in Puglia are regarded as some of the finest in the world. For a simple taste of Puglia, tear off a generous piece of local rustic bread, such as pane di Altamura, and dip it into one of the many provincial varieties of olive oil to enjoy the splendid range and intensity of flavour.

BELOW LEFT *Fiery chilli peppers are hung out to dry in the scorching Basilicata sun to both preserve them and intensify their potency.*

BELOW *The durum-wheat flour that is produced in such abundance in the area is used to make wonderful large loaves of bread as well as many different types of pasta.*

FESTIVALS AND CELEBRATIONS

One of the best ways to get to know a country is through its festivals. While this often means braving crowds of boisterous people, especially in the south, it also means enjoying the food and drink of the region at its flamboyant best. In southern Italy it seems as if there is always some town or village in the region that is in party mode, with saint's days, celebrations of particular seasonal foods or dishes, sporting events and much more.

BELOW *One of the many events in Sicily is the Flower Festival of Caltagirone, which sees the famous Staircase of Santa Maria del Monte, which is decorated with thousands of beautiful tiles, also adorned with blooms as a tribute to the city's patron, Our Lady of Conadomini.*

BELOW RIGHT *Musicians perform at the Sagra del Mandorlo in Fiore, a celebration of folk dance and music, where Sicilian farmers promote local products each spring.*

FAMILY CELEBRATIONS

Baptisms, first communions and weddings are among the most important celebrations for families in southern Italy. No expense is spared, from the clothes to the venue and menu. These enormous feasts, to which hundreds of family members and friends are invited, are opportunities for people to show off their wealth and generosity. It is considered dishonourable to provide anything less than a huge banquet, however much it costs.

CHRISTMAS AND EPIPHANY

In southern Italy, Christmas is traditionally celebrated right through from 24 December, Christmas Eve, to 6 January, Epiphany. This Christian festival was originally based on the pagan season that started with Saturnalia, a winter solstice festival, and ended on the Roman New Year, the Calends. Traditional Christmas food includes a selection of fish dishes on Christmas Eve, when meat is shunned, and a long lunch of several courses on Christmas Day. For sweet treats, southern Italians love panettone and cookies served with figs and plenty of sugar.

As is the case elsewhere in Italy, although Babbo Natale (Father Christmas) and Christmas presents are becoming more common, the tradition of La Befana is still a big part of Christmas celebrations. This is the tale of a white-haired witch who arrives on her broomstick during the night of 5 January and proceeds to fill the children's stockings with toys and sweets for the well-behaved and lumps of coal for the naughty ones.

NEW YEAR

La Festa di San Silvestro is celebrated on 31 December, New Year's Eve. As with most Italian festivals, food plays a major role, and families and friends get together for a feast. The star of the

dinner is a dish of lentils, representing money and good fortune. Traditionally, the dinner also includes cotechino, a large spiced sausage, or zampone, which are stuffed pig's trotters. These symbolise the richness of life that is wished for the coming year.

Most towns have huge midnight firework displays in a central square. Parties will often last until dawn so that the guests can watch the first sunrise of the newborn year together.

A custom that is still followed in some southern towns is to throw old possessions, ranging from china to furniture, out of the window to symbolise one's readiness to embrace the coming new year with a fresh start.

FESTIVAL OF SAINT AGATHA

This celebration takes place during 3–5 February in Catania, Sicily, to honour the life of Saint Agatha of Sicily. Among other things, she is the patron saint of bakers, whose loaves are blessed on the feast day.

CARNIVAL

This is a huge winter festival all over Italy, which is celebrated with parades, masquerade balls, entertainments, music, food and parties. Children throw confetti at each other, and mischief and pranks are common around this time, hence the saying: 'a carnevale ogni scherzo vale' (anything goes at carnival).

Carnival has its roots in pagan traditions and, as is often the case with traditional festivals, was adapted to fit into Catholic rituals. Some carnival traditions in Sicily date back to the 17th century, including the construction of the first papier-mâché chariot in Palermo in 1601, which represented Neptune surrounded by mermaids. This art form was then adopted by other towns in Sicily with great enthusiasm. The food tends to be rich and fatty, with pork being the favourite meat. Carnival is followed by a period of self-restraint in Lent.

LENT

Catholics traditionally abstain from consuming certain rich foods for the 40 days before Easter, both as penance for their sins, and to reflect on Jesus' crucifixion and resurrection. Today, many Italians still make sacrifices or changes to their lives during Lent. The most well-known rule is meatless Fridays, when people eat stick to fish and vegetables. Indeed, some Italian Catholics refrain from eating meat on Fridays all year round, but this is a personal choice and no longer a Church rule.

ABOVE *Sicilian Easter bread reveals the island's Greek religious roots, being topped with hard-boiled eggs in the same way as those from Greece.*

EASTER

Solemn processions are held in many towns on the Friday or Saturday before Easter and sometimes also on Easter Sunday. Olive branches and palm fronds are waved and used to decorate the churches. Among the sweet treats eaten during the Easter period, the most traditional is scarcedda from Basilicata. This has a pastry base filled with ricotta cheese, and hidden inside is a peeled hard-boiled egg. Whoever finds the egg (or a piece of it) in their slice will have a lucky year.

FEAST OF SAN PAOLO

This feast is celebrated in the town of Palazzolo Acreide, Sicily, 27–29 June. On the feast day, large, doughnut-shaped loaves of bread are offered to the saint, as well as being sold to festival goers, to celebrate the harvest of a good wheat crop.

AUTUMN FESTIVAL

The slaughtering of a pig in November has become a ceremony in the region that is tied to legends, customs and traditions. The climax of the festival occurs at the dinner table, where an exceptionally rich meal of pork is served. The remaining pig is made into sausages and cured meats to last the next few months.

SICILY

Sicily is the largest island in the Mediterranean, and has nine provinces. The regional capital is Palermo, with its crumbling grandiose architecture and huge, colourful, bustling markets: Il Capo, La Vucciria and Ballarò. Here, in just a few minutes' walk, you can take in Norman palace walls, Arab domes and arches, and Byzantine mosaics. There is so much to say about this intriguing island and its cuisine and food traditions: every corner of Sicily is a feast for the eyes as well as the stomach.

Historically, this island has always been something of a Mediterranean crossroads; the remains of many ancient cultures are buried here, including those of the Phoenicians, Carthaginians, Romans, Greeks, Arabs, Normans and Spanish. It is said that the early Greeks introduced the cultivation of both the olive tree and the vine here, while the 200-year Arab domination of Sicily that began in the 7th century gave the island ingredients such as rice; spices such as nutmeg, saffron, cloves, pepper and cinnamon; pine nuts; and fruit like melons, apricots, lemons, bergamot and oranges as well as raisins and sultanas/golden raisins. The Spanish brought more ingredients from the New World, including cocoa, maize, tomatoes and bell peppers, and the Normans and medieval German kings influenced the preponderance of meat recipes.

The list of culinary influences is vast and creates a wonderfully delicious potted history of the island's history. Put all these influences together with natural ingredients of exceptional quality, and you have one of the most interesting and seductive cuisines to be found in Italy. Nonetheless, it still relies on its key ingredients: pasta, bread, citrus fruits, aubergines or eggplants, almonds, ricotta, pistachios, swordfish, tuna, almonds, and the famous capers of the neighbouring island of Pantelleria. There is also an almost universal liking for sweet-and-sour flavour combinations as well as for cuscuscu or couscous – both of which are probably culinary trends adopted from North Africa.

The Arab influence is very clear in Sicily's most famous dessert, cassata – the incredibly sweet and very popular confection made out of a sponge cake filled with sweetened ricotta, traditionally turned out so that it resembles a dome, and then smoothly covered with a coating of pale-green or white icing and candied fruits.

Marzipan also came from the Arabs, and is still widely used in Sicily, notably in very life-like shaped and coloured fruits called frutta alla Martorana, and in other delicacies cheekily named minni di vergini (virgins' breasts) or chiappe del cancelliere (chancellor's buttocks). The Arabs also invented ice cream here, using snow from the peak of Etna as the base ingredient, and taught Sicilians their great skill of deep-frying.

I always tell people that if you don't like aubergines, then it is probably true to say that the cuisine of Sicily might not be for you, since it is very hard to ignore them. The number of recipes using this vegetable are truly legion, each one more imaginative and intriguing than the next. The local version of parmigiana di melanzane, for example, is quite a different dish on this island compared to the gooey, mozzarella-rich version of Campania, and one of the most iconic pasta dishes of Sicily is the delightful recipe from Catania for pasta alla norma, which also features aubergines. In the past, during times of hardship, these vegetables all but replaced meat or fish on the menu for many poorer families.

Arancini di riso, now so universally popular, are just one of Sicily's many street-food specialities. These little balls of cooked rice are mixed according to local custom with either peas, mushrooms and ham, or with a rich ragù. The name means 'little oranges', which is what they are supposed to look like, and it is worth mentioning that many dishes from the island have this curious habit of being named for what they are supposed to look like, rather than what they contain. This peculiarity is almost unique to Sicilian cooking, and is repeated in pasta dishes such as the aforementioned pasta alla norma: supposed to be Etna in full eruption; vegetables dishes like fegato ai sette cannoll – the pumpkin dish that is meant to represent a liver; and the cheese dish that represents a steak, not to mention many of the famous sweet dishes.

Sicily does not stint on its wine production, and is most famous for full-bodied reds like Nero d'Avola, Frappato and Primitivo, classic dessert wines such as Marsala, Malvasia and the gorgeously named Zibibbo, One of my own favourites is the dry white wine called Grillo, which means 'grasshopper' or 'cricket'.

SFINCIUNI
SICILIAN ONION AND TOMATO PIZZA

This dish has ancient roots and is sometimes called schiavazza or rianata. One of the most famous versions was prepared by the nuns of the San Vito and Sfinciuni di Santu is still famous in the city of Palermo in Sicily. Unlike the thin and crispy pizzas usually associated with Italy, this simple Sicilian classic is sometimes half as deep as it is wide, and it has a soft and spongy texture.

1 Spoon 75ml/5 tbsp hand-hot water into a small bowl. Crumble in the yeast, stir and set aside. Pile the flour on a clean work surface and make a hollow in the middle. Add 2.5ml/½ tsp each of salt and pepper to the hollow, then spoon in one-third of the cheese.

2 Pour 45ml/3 tbsp of the oil into a pan and add the lemon juice. Warm until hand-hot, pour into the hollow, then add the yeast mixture. Stir, incorporating the surrounding flour. Add more warm water if needed and knead to a smooth, elastic dough. Knead the dough for 10–15 minutes more, then roll it into a ball and place it in a large bowl. Cut a cross in the top of the ball. Cover with a cloth, clear film or plastic wrap. Leave to rise for 2 hours in a warm place.

3 Meanwhile, put the tomatoes in a bowl of boiling water for 1–2 minutes. Remove and peel. Halve them, remove the seeds and chop the flesh.

4 Heat 60ml/4 tbsp olive oil in a pan and fry the onion for 4–5 minutes, until transparent. Add the tomatoes. Season. Simmer for 1 hour, stirring occasionally.

5 Grease an 18cm/7in square cake tin or pan at least 10cm/4in deep (see Cook's Tip) with oil. Knock back or punch down the dough, then knead for 10 minutes. Pat it out to the shape of the tin. Cover and leave to rise again in a warm place for 30 minutes.

6 Meanwhile, mix the parsley, half the anchovies and half the remaining cheese into the tomato sauce.

7 Preheat the oven to 200°C/400°F/Gas 6. When the dough has risen, press a finger deeply into it at 5cm/2in intervals. Reserving a little, fill the hollows with the sauce, spreading some over the surface.

8 Bake for 25 minutes. Meanwhile, heat 45ml/3 tbsp of the remaining oil in a small frying pan and fry the breadcrumbs until crisp. Take the pizza out of the oven, spread the surface with the reserved tomato sauce, top with the remaining anchovies and cheese, then sprinkle with breadcrumbs. Drizzle with olive oil and return to the oven for 10 minutes more. Serve.

MAKES ONE 18CM/7IN PIZZA

- 35g/1¼oz fresh/compressed yeast
- 250g/9oz//2⅓ cups plain/all-purpose flour, plus extra for dusting and kneading
- 75g/3oz/¾ cup freshly grated pecorino or caciocavallo cheese
- 250ml/8fl oz/1 cup olive oil
- juice of 1 lemon
- 500g/1¼lb ripe tomatoes
- 1 small onion, thinly sliced
- 50g/2oz/1 cup fresh parsley, finely chopped
- 5 large salted anchovies, rinsed, boned and chopped
- 15–30ml/1–2 tbsp coarse white breadcrumbs
- sea salt and ground black pepper

VARIATION

In Sicily, sausage meat/bulk sausage is sometimes spread over the dough with a little of the tomato sauce, topped with a second layer of the dough, then baked.

COOK'S TIP

Use a spring-release or a loose-bottomed tin or pan to make this pizza. If you don't have one, use a regular cake tin, but line it first with a wide strip of baking parchment. The parchment strip should be long enough to extend beyond the rim of the tin on both sides, giving you 'handles' for lifting out the pizza.

SERVES 4

500g/1¼lb large potatoes
1 slice cooked ham, about 25g/1oz
25g/1oz/1 cup fresh parsley leaves
25g/1oz/¼ cup coarsely grated caciocavallo or provolone cheese
2 eggs, separated
25g/1oz/¼ cup freshly grated pecorino cheese
25g/1oz/2 tbsp unsalted butter
25g/1oz/¼ cup plain/all-purpose flour
60ml/4 tbsp stale white breadcrumbs
sunflower oil, for deep-frying
sea salt and ground black pepper

COOK'S TIP

Use a skewer to check that the potatoes are tender. To produce really fine and creamy mashed potatoes, put the cooked potatoes through a food mill or ricer.

CAZZILLI
SICILIAN FRIED POTATO ROLLS

These traditional croquettes are popular all over Sicily, and can be bought, piping hot and crisp, from markets, or made at home. When times were hard, meat was a luxury afforded only by the few, so vegetables, which could be grown with relative ease, were often combined with basic ingredients to create main-course dishes to feed the family.

1 Put the unpeeled potatoes in a large pan of salted water and bring to the boil. Lower the heat, cover the pan and simmer for 30 minutes.

2 Meanwhile, chop the ham and the parsley together and set the mixture aside.

3 When the potatoes are really tender, drain them, steam dry for a minute, then peel and mash them as finely as possible.

4 Scrape the mash into a bowl and stir in the ham and parsley. Add the cheeses, egg yolks and butter. Mix well, season with salt and pepper and leave to cool. Lightly beat the egg whites.

5 Put the flour, egg whites and breadcrumbs in three separate shallow bowls.

6 Mould the potato mixture into sausage shapes by rolling spoonfuls between the palms of your hands. Coat them in flour, then in beaten egg white and finally in breadcrumbs, to cover completely.

7 Heat the oil for deep-frying until a small piece of bread dropped into it sizzles instantly. Add the cazzilli, in batches, and fry them for 2–3 minutes until crisp and golden all over.

8 Drain the cazzilli carefully on kitchen paper and serve piping hot.

MELANZANE AL FORNO CON MOZZARELLA
BAKED AUBERGINES WITH MOZZARELLA

In various parts of Europe, eating aubergines was once alleged to cause madness, leprosy, cancer and bad breath, and these superstitions led to its being used largely as a decorative plant. It wasn't until the 18th century that the vegetables were established as a food in Italy and France. Sicilians love aubergines, as this delicious dish shows.

SERVES 4 TO 6

500g/1¼lb aubergines/eggplants, sliced into 2cm/¾in rounds
2 eggs
plain/all-purpose white flour, for coating
350ml/12fl oz/1½ cups olive oil
150g/5oz mozzarella cheese, thinly sliced
4 salted anchovies, washed and boned, then chopped finely
60ml/4 tbsp stale white breadcrumbs
sea salt and ground black pepper

1 Spread the aubergine slices out in a colander and sprinkle generously with salt. Stand the colander in the sink, fit a plate inside, put a weight on top and drain for 1–2 hours.

2 Meanwhile, put the eggs in a bowl. Season and beat them lightly.

3 Rinse the aubergines to remove the excess salt, drain well, then pat dry with kitchen paper. Coat the slices lightly in flour.

4 Heat the oil in a large frying pan. When it sizzles, add the aubergine, in batches if necessary, and fry for 3 minutes on each side, until crisp and golden.

5 Remove the aubergine slices from the frying pan with a slotted spoon and allow to drain on kitchen paper.

6 Preheat the oven to 200°C/400°F/Gas 6. Arrange half the slices in a roasting pan. Top each one with a slice of mozzarella and a few pieces of anchovy.

7 Cover the mozzarella with the remaining fried aubergine slices to form small sandwiches. Press these tightly together to prevent them from falling apart.

8 Season with a little salt, sprinkle evenly with the breadcrumbs and bake for about 10 minutes. Serve immediately.

COOK'S TIP

This is delicious with rocket/arugula salad or a garlicky roasted bell pepper salad as part of an antipasto.

ARANCINI DI RISO
SICILIAN RICE FRITTERS

These delicious rice balls are on sale at every café in Sicily, and are eaten as a quick snack. Few dishes say as much about the various nationalities who have contributed to the island over the centuries: the rice came from the Arabs; the cheese (traditionally canestrato fresco but here replaced with mozzarella) was contributed by the Greeks; the ragù derives from the French ragoût, and the tomato dipping sauce came from the Spanish. Arancini di riso are the pride of every rotisserie or Tavola Calda.

MAKES ABOUT 20

FOR THE RISOTTO

1.5 litres/2½ pints/6 cups hot chicken, meat or vegetable stock
75g/3oz/6 tbsp unsalted butter
1 onion, finely chopped
600g/1lb 6oz/2½ cups risotto rice, preferably vialone nano
90–105ml/6–7 tbsp freshly grated Parmesan cheese

FOR THE FRITTERS

15g/½ oz/1 tbsp butter
50g/2oz/½ cup mushrooms, sliced
100g/3½oz/scant 1 cup cooked peas
80g/3¼oz mozzarella cheese, diced
50g/2oz prosciutto, finely chopped
45ml/3 tbsp plain/all-purpose flour
3 eggs, beaten
90ml/6 tbsp white dried breadcrumbs
1 quantity ragù (see page 21; optional)
sea salt and ground black pepper
sunflower oil, for deep-frying
tomato sauce (see Cook's Tip), for dipping (optional)

COOK'S TIP

To make a tomato sauce for dipping, finely chop 1 onion, 1 celery stick and 1 carrot and gently fry in 60ml/4 tbsp olive oil in a pan until soft. Do not let the onion brown. Add 500g/1¼lb fresh or canned tomatoes, cover and simmer for 30 minutes, stirring often. Season to taste.

1 Pour the stock into a pan and heat to simmering point. Keep it simmering while you cook the risotto.

2 Melt half the butter in a large heavy pan and add the onion. Cook over a very low heat for 10 minutes, until the onion is soft but not coloured.

3 Stir the rice into the onion mixture and toast the grains thoroughly on all sides, so that they are opaque but not coloured. Add a ladleful of hot stock and stir it in until it has been absorbed.

4 Add a further two ladlefuls of hot stock and stir constantly so that the rice absorbs the liquid and all its flavour. Continue in this fashion, adding more stock only when the spoon draws a clear wake behind it as you draw it through the cooking rice.

5 After about 20 minutes, when the rice is soft and creamy, take the pan off the heat and stir in the grated Parmesan cheese and the rest of the butter. Adjust the seasoning to taste and set aside to cool.

6 Put the cold risotto into a bowl. Melt the butter in a pan and sauté the mushrooms lightly. Add them to the risotto, with the peas, mozzarella and prosciutto.

7 Place the flour, beaten eggs and breadcrumbs in separate shallow bowls.

8 Shape the rice mixture into balls, about the size of tangerines. If you want to fill them with ragù, make an indentation in each ball, spoon in 5ml/1 tsp of ragù, then reshape so that the ragù is enclosed.

9 Roll the balls in the flour, then the eggs and finally the dried breadcrumbs.

10 Heat the oil in a large pan to 180°C/350°F, or until a cube of bread, dropped into the oil, browns in about 45 seconds. Fry the balls, in batches, for 6–8 minutes until golden. Drain on kitchen paper. Serve hot, with the tomato sauce for dipping, if you like.

POLPETTE DI FUNGHI
SICILIAN MUSHROOM FRITTERS

These little fritters make a wonderful canapé or antipasto dish. They taste especially delicious when handed around with a garlicky dip, possibly with a yogurt or sour cream base, or with traditional l'arrabbiata. Whichever type of mushrooms you choose, make sure they have a soft texture.

MAKES 24

500g/1¼lb/8 cups mushrooms
2 eggs, beaten
3 garlic cloves, very finely chopped
45ml/3 tbsp chopped fresh parsley
45ml/3 tbsp grated pecorino cheese
45ml/3 tbsp fresh white breadcrumbs
sunflower oil, for deep-frying
sea salt and ground black pepper

1 Fill the base of a steamer (or a pan fitted with a steamer basket) with water and bring to the boil. Put the mushrooms in the steamer or steamer basket and steam until just cooked.

2 Squeeze the mushrooms to remove some of the moisture and then chop them very finely in a food processor or with a heavy-bladed knife.

3 Put the chopped mushrooms in a bowl and add the eggs, garlic, parsley, cheese and breadcrumbs. Season with salt and plenty of ground black pepper. Mix well.

4 Shape the mixture into 24 balls and flatten these to make round fritters.

5 Heat the oil for deep-frying to 180°C/350°F or until a small piece of bread, dropped into the oil, browns in about 45 seconds.

6 Fry the fritters, in batches if necessary, for 2–3 minutes until they rise to the surface and are crisp and golden.

7 Remove with a slotted spoon, drain on kitchen paper and keep hot while cooking successive batches. When all the fritters are cooked, serve them immediately.

SERVES 4

60ml/4 tbsp olive oil
3 garlic cloves, chopped
225g/8oz fresh, ripe tomatoes, quartered and seeded
10 fresh basil leaves, torn into shreds
115g/4oz/1 cup coarse dried breadcrumbs
30–45ml/2–3 tbsp grated pecorino or Parmesan cheese
60ml/4 tbsp chopped fresh flat leaf parsley
450g/1lb/4 cups anelli or other pasta shapes
sea salt

COOK'S TIPS

- Instead of anelli, you could use maccheroncelli (a thin tubular shape, slightly thinner than a pencil) or pennette (short, thin penne).
- Use sweet, sun-ripened tomatoes so the sauce has no trace of the sour flavour that unripe tomatoes tend to impart.

ANELLI AMMUDDICATI
ANELLI WITH BREADCRUMBS

In southern Italy, especially Sicily and Calabria, fine, stale breadcrumbs are often used instead of grated cheese on pasta. This is either because there is simply no cheese available, or a hangover from the days when there was no money for cheese. Sometimes the breadcrumbs are fried for extra texture.

1 Pour the oil into a large pan and add the garlic. Fry for 2–3 minutes, until the garlic is transparent, then add the tomatoes and basil. Stir in salt to taste, then cover and simmer the mixture for 20 minutes on a medium heat. Add water if the sauce becomes too thick.

2 Bring a large pan of salted water to the boil. Meanwhile, put the breadcrumbs in a small bowl and add the cheese and parsley.

3 When the tomato sauce is almost ready, add the pasta to the boiling water. Bring it back to the boil, then cook the pasta for 12–14 minutes, until just tender, then drain and return to the pan.

4 Pour the tomato sauce over the drained pasta and toss well to combine. Divide the mixture among four bowls, sprinkle each portion generously with the breadcrumb mixture and serve immediately.

PASTA CON LE SARDE
PASTA WITH FRESH SARDINES

The ingredient that gives this dish its unique aniseed flavour is wild fennel. It is not only used in the sauce, but also flavours the pasta, which is boiled in the water in which the fennel was cooked. Saffron and fresh sardines complete the palette of flavours, unique to this most Sicilian of pasta dishes.

1 Put the sultanas in a bowl. Pour over warm water to cover and set aside for 15 minutes.

2 Put the saffron in a separate bowl and stir in 45ml/3 tbsp cold water.

3 Meanwhile, put the fennel in a large pan with the salt and the measured water. Bring to the boil, lower the heat and cover the pan. Simmer for 10 minutes.

4 Remove the fennel with a slotted spoon and put it in a strainer until cool enough to handle. Squeeze the fennel in your hands over a bowl to remove the moisture, then put it on to a board and chop it very finely. Set the pan with the cooking water aside.

5 Put the onion in a large pan and cover generously with water. Bring to the boil, then simmer for about 10 minutes or until the onion is soft.

6 Add half the olive oil, the saffron with its soaking water, and the pine nuts to the cooked onion. Drain the sultanas and stir them into the pan. Simmer, stirring frequently, for 10 minutes.

7 Stir in the chopped fennel and the prepared sardines. Cover the pan and cook over a very low heat, turning the fish frequently, for 4–5 minutes, until the sardines are cooked through.

8 Meanwhile, in a separate pan, cook the anchovies for 2–3 minutes in the remaining olive oil, mashing them into a smooth purée.

9 When the sardines are cooked, stir in the anchovy purée. Mix well and season to taste with salt and black pepper. Keep the mixture warm.

10 Return the pan used for cooking the fennel to the heat. Taste and add salt if necessary. Bring to the boil, add the pasta and stir. Cook fresh pasta for about 4 minutes; dried pasta for 12–14 minutes.

11 When the pasta is tender, drain it well, transfer it into a warmed bowl and pour over the sauce. Toss thoroughly and serve.

SERVES 4 TO 6

30ml/2 tbsp sultanas/golden raisins
1 sachet saffron powder
150g/5oz wild fennel (leaves and stalks), washed and trimmed
10ml/2 tsp fine salt
2 litres/3½ pints/8 cups cold water
1 large onion, chopped
90ml/6 tbsp olive oil
25g/1oz/⅓ cup pine nuts
275g/10oz fresh or thawed frozen sardines, cleaned, boned and with heads removed
2 whole salted anchovies, boned and washed
400g/14oz fresh or dried bucatini, thick perciatelli or other pasta shapes
sea salt and ground black pepper

COOK'S TIP

If wild fennel proves hard to find, buy some leafy fennel bulbs instead. Cut off all the feathery leaves, then use the harder outer leaves and the stalks to make up the weight. This is a good way of using parts that might otherwise be discarded, but which give excellent flavour to the dish.

VERMICELLI AL NERO DI SEPPIE
VERMICELLI WITH SQUID INK

Using really fresh squid is key here, as this will ensure the sweetest and most fragrant finished dish. The truly authentic recipe calls for strattu, an amazingly tasty sun-dried tomato paste, which is available in all good food stores and market stalls on the island of Sicily, but is less easy to find anywhere else. Good-quality concentrated tomato paste is the best substitute.

SERVES 4 TO 6

whole fresh squid with ink sac (around 500g/1¼lb)
60ml/4 tbsp olive oil
2–3 whole garlic cloves, bruised
45ml/3 tbsp chopped fresh parsley
100ml/3½fl oz/scant ½ cup dry white wine
15ml/1 tbsp strattu or 45ml/3 tbsp concentrated tomato paste
400g/14oz vermicelli
sea salt and ground black pepper

1 Rinse the squid thoroughly. Holding one firmly, grasp the tentacles at the base and pull the head and entrails away from the body. Cut off the tentacles from the head and set them aside. Discard the head with the hard 'beak' but retain the ink sac, which looks like a black vein. Peel the membrane from the body, then pull out and discard the 'quill'.

2 Cut the body of the squid into small cubes. Chop the tentacles finely. Repeat with the rest of the squid. Rinse and dry all the squid well.

3 Heat the olive oil over a medium heat in a large pan. Add the garlic cloves, fry until brown, then remove with a slotted spoon and discard.

4 Add the squid to the garlic-flavoured oil. Stir in the parsley and plenty of pepper. Cover and simmer the mixture for 45 minutes.

5 Pour over the white wine and add the strattu or tomato paste. Stir well and continue to simmer, uncovered, for 20 minutes.

6 Lower the heat, cover the pan again and cook for a further 30 minutes, adding a little hot water as and when needed to dilute the sauce.

7 About 15–17 minutes before serving, bring a large pan of salted water to the boil. Add the pasta, stir and cook for 10–12 minutes over a medium heat until just tender.

8 Meanwhile, add the ink sacs to the sauce and stir to mix.

9 Drain the pasta thoroughly and return it to the pan. Pour over the sauce and mix well to combine. Cover the pan and leave the pasta to stand for 5 minutes, then turn out on to a platter and serve immediately.

COOK'S TIP

If you cannot find fresh, whole squid, use ready-to-use squid and buy the ink separately in a sachet or jar from a fishmonger or Italian food shop. Take care when handling the ink sacs, as squid ink stains clothing and turns fingernails black.

SPAGHETTI ALLA SIRACUSANA

SPAGHETTI WITH CAPERS AND YELLOW PEPPER

This simple recipe from the ancient and atmospheric city of Siracusa makes for a delicious and very attractive pasta dish. Only the sweetest, juiciest yellow peppers, such as those that grow in rich profusion all over Sicily, should be used to achieve the right intensity of sweet, slightly peppery flavour.

1 Roast the bell pepper over a naked flame or under a hot grill or broiler, turning it frequently until the skin blisters and is blackened all over. Put the pepper in a bowl, cover the bowl with clear film or plastic wrap and set aside.

2 Heat the oil in a pan and add the garlic. As soon as the garlic turns brown, lift it out with a slotted spoon and discard.

3 Add the anchovies to the flavoured oil and cook for 2–3 minutes, mashing them with a wooden spoon until they form a smooth purée.

4 Pull off the skin from the pepper, removing any stubborn pieces with a sharp knife. Cut in half, remove the seeds and membranes and chop the flesh into small squares. Add these to the anchovy mixture with the aubergine and tomatoes.

5 Stir in the olives, basil and capers, with a little salt, if needed, to taste. Cover the pan and simmer until the vegetables are soft.

6 Bring a large pan of salted water to the boil. Add the spaghetti and cook for 12–14 minutes until just tender. Drain the pasta and put it into a warmed bowl. Pour over the sauce, toss to mix, and serve.

SERVES 4

1 large yellow bell pepper
120ml/4fl oz/½ cup olive oil
2 garlic cloves, lightly crushed
3 large, salted anchovies, washed, dried and boned
1 large aubergine/eggplant, peeled and cubed
275g/10oz ripe tomatoes, peeled, seeded and cut in quarters
4 black olives, pitted and chopped
4 green olives, pitted and chopped
8 fresh basil leaves, torn into shreds
15–20ml/3–4 tsp salted capers, rinsed, dried and chopped
400g/14oz dried spaghetti
sea salt (optional)

SARDE A BECCAFICO
BAKED STUFFED SARDINES

Beccafico, literally translated from the Italian as 'pecker of figs', are little birds that like to hang by their feet from ripe figs and peck away at the sweet flesh of the fruits. You might (or might not!) see a resemblance between them and the stuffed sardines, with their rounded bellies and beak-like tails. This particular recipe comes from the eastern side of Sicily.

SERVES 4

- 800g/1¾lb fresh sardines or thawed frozen sardines
- 50g/2oz/⅓ cup sultanas/golden raisins, soaked in warm water for 15 minutes
- 120ml/4fl oz/½ cup olive oil
- 60ml/4 tbsp fresh white breadcrumbs
- 50g/2oz/⅔ cup pine nuts
- 30ml/2 tbsp chopped fresh parsley
- sea salt and ground black pepper
- 6 salted anchovies, rinsed, dried and boned
- 3–4 dried bay leaves

COOK'S TIP

This is best made with really fresh sardines, ideally straight from the sea, but you can use thawed frozen fish if you can't get fresh fish.

1 Preheat the oven to 180°C/350°F/Gas 4. If using fresh sardines, slit them along the belly and remove the innards while holding them under running water.

2 Place each sardine flat on its back, tail pointing towards you. Twist off the head by pulling it towards you so that it comes away with the spine and other bones, leaving the tail intact.

3 Drain the sultanas and pat them dry with kitchen paper. Put half the oil into a pan and add 15ml/1 tbsp of the breadcrumbs. Heat, stirring gently, so that the crumbs absorb the oil.

4 Remove the breadcrumbs from the heat and stir in the sultanas, pine nuts and parsley. Season the stuffing with pepper, then chop the anchovies finely and stir them into the mixture. Add salt if needed.

5 Using half the remaining oil, liberally grease a baking dish that is large enough to hold all the fish in a single layer.

6 Insert the stuffing into each of the fish. Depending upon the size of the sardines, you can either put the stuffing into the belly or wrap the flattened fish around the filling and roll them up. Secure with a cocktail stick or toothpick.

7 Arrange the stuffed sardines in the dish with their tails pointing upwards and the bay leaves tucked in between the fish. Drizzle with the remaining oil and sprinkle over the remaining breadcrumbs.

8 Bake for 30 minutes and serve immediately or allow to cool. Sardines cooked this way are delicious hot or cold.

CUSCUSU DI TRAPANI
TRAPANI FISH COUSCOUS

This dish comes from Trapani, where the salt flats of Sicily glisten under the sun. Couscous was introduced to the island centuries ago and was adopted so enthusiastically that it is now synonymous with Sicilian food. It is particularly popular in the west and on the outlying islets. Cooks often make couscous from scratch, using a bowl called a maffaradda to roll the damp semolina into tiny balls. This is a time-consuming task, so it is easier to use ready-made couscous.

SERVES 8

- 3 sachets powdered saffron, or a large pinch of saffron threads
- 120ml/4fl oz/½ cup hot water
- 400g/14oz/2⅓ cups coarse couscous
- 90ml/6 tbsp olive oil
- 60ml/4 tbsp chopped fresh parsley
- 3 garlic cloves, chopped
- 1 onion, thinly sliced
- 1 dried bay leaf
- 1 tomato, peeled, seeded and quartered
- 1.2kg/2½lb mixed fish fillets, such as cod, eel, red mullet and John Dory
- 1.5ml/¼ tsp ground cinnamon
- pinch of freshly grated nutmeg
- sea salt and ground black pepper

1 Put the saffron in a bowl and pour over the hot water. Leave to stand for about 10 minutes.

2 Put the couscous into a large bowl. Strain in the saffron liquid, then mix together. Spread out on a large tray and leave to dry while you cook the fish.

3 Heat half the olive oil in a large, deep pan. Add the parsley and garlic. Fry gently for 5 minutes, then add the onion and bay leaf. Fry for 5 minutes more, then add the tomato. Level the mixture in the pan and lay the fish fillets on top, in a single layer.

4 Season and pour over water to cover. Simmer over low heat for 20 minutes or until the fish flakes easily when tested with the tip of a knife.

5 Using a slotted spoon, transfer the fish fillets to a board. When cool enough to handle, remove the skin and any remaining bones. Set the fish aside.

6 Strain the liquid into a bowl. Pour 475ml/15fl oz/2 cups into a measuring jug or cup and set aside. If you have any left over, take note of the amount, pour it into a pan and top up with water to make 2 litres/3½ pints/8 cups. If no stock remains, just use water.

7 Place a strainer over the pan containing the stock or water. Plug any gaps to prevent steam from escaping (see Cook's Tip). Add the couscous.

8 Stir the remaining 45ml/3 tbsp oil into the couscous. Cover the pan with a lid and then lay a thick, heavy cloth over the lid. Place over low heat and steam for about 40 minutes, or until the couscous is fluffy.

9 Reheat the reserved stock. Transfer the couscous to a bowl and stir in half the hot fish stock. Cover with a lid, then wrap the bowl and the lid in the heavy cloth. Leave to stand while you gently reheat the fish in a separate pan with the remaining stock.

10 Unwrap the couscous. Stir in the cinnamon, nutmeg, salt and pepper. Serve with the fish on top.

COOK'S TIP

If your strainer is narrower than the pan it sits upon, use a damp, clean dish towel to plug any gaps. It is important that no steam escapes during the cooking process.

TRUSCELLO DI MESSINA
MEATBALL AND RICOTTA BAKE

Truscello is a delicious, very light dish made up of tiny balls of clove-scented ricotta and beef, layered in a dish, bathed in stock and poached in the oven. The preparation is a bit fiddly but well worth the effort. It comes from Messina, which is the third-largest city on the island of Sicily.

SERVES 4 TO 6

275g/10oz/1¼ cups very lean minced/ground beef
115g/4oz/1⅓ cups freshly grated Parmesan cheese, plus extra if needed
115g/4oz/2 cups stale white breadcrumbs, plus extra if needed
45ml/3 tbsp chopped fresh parsley
5 eggs
500ml/17fl oz/generous 2 cups strongly-flavoured beef stock
275g/10oz drained fresh ricotta cheese
1.5ml/¼ tsp ground cloves
sea salt and ground black pepper

1 Put the beef in a large bowl. Season well with salt and pepper, then add 30ml/2 tbsp of the Parmesan cheese with the breadcrumbs and parsley. Beat 2 of the eggs lightly and add them to the bowl.

2 Using wet, clean hands, mix the ingredients together. Add a little stock if necessary, to bind the mixture, but not too much as it should be firm, not sloppy.

3 Pinch off small pieces of the mixture and roll into tiny meatballs, no larger than big olives.

4 Pour the stock into a large pan and bring to the boil. Lower the heat to a simmer and then add the meatballs. Simmer for no more than 3 minutes.

5 Lift the meatballs out with a slotted spoon and put them on a dish. Set aside to cool. Leave the stock over a low heat. Preheat the oven to 200°C/400°F/Gas 6.

6 Put the ricotta in a bowl and add the remaining Parmesan cheese. Beat the remaining eggs lightly and add them to the bowl with the ground cloves. Season.

7 Shape the ricotta mixture into balls the same size as the meatballs. The ricotta needs to be really dry and stiff – if the mixture is too sloppy, add more breadcrumbs and Parmesan until you can shape it into balls with ease.

8 Pour a little of the hot stock into a 1.5-litre/2½-pint/6-cup baking dish. Cover with a layer of ricotta balls, then with a layer of meatballs.

9 Pour over stock to just cover, then layer the ricotta balls and meatballs on top. Continue in this way until the final layer of meatballs has been added. Pour over the remaining stock.

10 Bake for 5–10 minutes, so that the meat and cheese balls heat through but the ricotta does not melt. Serve immediately.

COOK'S TIP

To prevent the meat and ricotta balls from falling apart, and the dish from becoming sloppy, use crumbs from bread that is at least a day old, ricotta cheese that is really dry and crumbly, and very lean beef.

INVOLTINI CON CARCIOFI
BEEF ROLLS WITH ARTICHOKES

This luxurious, somewhat time-consuming recipe has something very French about it, and was probably introduced by one of the French chefs employed by the Sicilian aristocracy during the early 20th century. It was de rigueur for every noble household to have a French chef or a monsù (an Italian corruption of Monsieur) and the influence on Sicilian cooking is still evident.

1 Fill a heatproof bowl with boiling water and add the lemon juice.

2 Clean the artichokes and trim them thoroughly, removing all the sharp points and hard leaves. Drop them carefully into the bowl of acidulated water and leave to soak for about 10 minutes.

3 Meanwhile, put the chopped prosciutto in a bowl and add half the butter. Stir until the mixture forms a rough paste.

4 Lift the artichokes out of the water and stand them upside down on a board to drain. When they are cold, cut them into quarters and remove the choke from each section. Cut each quarter in half again to give 16 segments.

5 Flatten the meat slices by beating them with a meat mallet or rolling pin until they are as thin and flat as possible.

6 Spread a slice of meat with an eighth of the butter and prosciutto mixture and lay 2 pieces of artichoke on top. Season with salt and ground black pepper.

7 Roll up the package neatly and tie with kitchen string or twine. Make seven more in the same way, then coat all the rolls in flour.

8 Heat the remaining butter with the oil in a large frying pan. Add the onion and fry for 5 minutes until softened but not browned.

9 Push the onion to one side and add the meat rolls to the pan. Brown them over a medium to high heat, then lower the heat and mix the onions with the meat rolls.

10 Reduce the heat to the lowest setting, cover the pan and simmer slowly, basting the meat rolls occasionally with the juices in the pan, for 20 minutes or until the meat is tender.

11 Arrange on a heated platter and serve immediately.

SERVES 4

juice of 1 lemon
2 artichokes
50g/2oz prosciutto crudo, finely chopped
75g/3oz/6 tbsp butter, softened
8 thin slices of veal or beef, total weight 400g/14oz
45ml/3 tbsp plain/all-purpose flour
30ml/2 tbsp vegetable oil
1 onion, thinly sliced
sea salt and ground black pepper

COOK'S TIP

If you place the meat slices between sheets of clear film or plastic wrap before flattening them, they will be less likely to tear.

RISO E MELANZANE ALLA PALERMITANA
RICE AND AUBERGINE BAKE

The shiny aubergine is the most popular vegetable in Sicily and has been ever since the Arabs introduced it to the island. It is used in everything from antipasti to desserts. This recipe may seem slightly long-winded, but it is definitely worth all the effort as the finished result looks and tastes spectacular.

SERVES 8

3 large aubergines/eggplants
2 onions
50g/2oz/¼ cup unsalted butter
90ml/6 tbsp olive oil, plus extra for greasing
30ml/2 tbsp chopped fresh parsley
8 fresh basil leaves, torn into shreds
275g/10oz tomatoes, peeled, seeded and cut in quarters
275g/10oz/1½ cups risotto rice
600ml/1 pint/2½ cups hot chicken or vegetable stock
45ml/3 tbsp plain/all-purpose flour
sunflower oil, for shallow frying
115g/4oz/1 cup freshly grated caciocavallo cheese (see Variations)
sea salt and ground black pepper

VARIATIONS

- Use freshly grated provolone or mozzarella cheese instead of caciocavallo, if necessary.
- This tastes just as good served cold the next day.

1 Trim the aubergines and slice into rounds 2cm/¾in thick. Spread them out in a colander or strainer and sprinkle generously with salt. Stand the colander or strainer in the sink, fit a plate inside, put a weight on top and leave to drain for 1–2 hours.

2 Meanwhile, peel the onions and put them in a pan. Cover with water, bring to the boil and cook for 10 minutes. Drain. Cool for 4–5 minutes, then slice thinly.

3 Melt the butter with half the oil in a pan. Add half the onion and fry for 4–5 minutes until softened. Stir in the parsley and basil. Cook for 5 minutes, then stir in the tomatoes. Season, cover and simmer for 20 minutes, stirring occasionally.

4 Preheat the oven to 190°C/375°F/Gas 5. Heat the rest of the oil in a flameproof casserole. Add the rest of the onion and fry for 4 minutes until transparent.

5 Stir in the rice until shiny and coated in oil, then stir in the stock. Cover the casserole with a lid or foil and put it in the oven. Bake for 15 minutes.

6 Meanwhile, rinse the aubergine slices and pat dry with kitchen paper. Dust them lightly with flour. Heat the sunflower oil in a frying pan until sizzling. Fry the slices in batches for 3 minutes on each side or until golden brown. Add more oil to the pan as needed between batches. Lift out the slices with a slotted spoon and drain on kitchen paper.

7 Take the rice mixture out of the oven and stir in 30–45ml/2–3 tbsp grated caciocavallo cheese.

8 Grease a 1.2kg/2½lb round mould with oil, then line the base and sides with aubergine slices. Cover with a layer of the tomato sauce, then with a layer of rice, and then a generous sprinkling of grated caciocavallo. Continue in this way until the mould is full, banging it down firmly on the work surface every now and again to settle the ingredients. Finish with a sprinkling of cheese.

9 Bake for 10 minutes, then remove from the oven and turn out on to a platter. Serve immediately.

MAKES ABOUT 12

115g/8oz/½ cup unsalted butter, softened
200g/7oz/1 cup caster/superfine sugar, plus extra for sprinkling
1 whole egg or 2 egg yolks, well beaten
15ml/1 tbsp milk
2.5ml/½ tsp vanilla extract
250g/9oz/generous 2 cups plain/all-purpose flour
5ml/1 tsp baking powder
1.5ml/¼ tsp salt

FOR THE SWEETMEAT

450g/1lb/2⅔ cups hard dried figs
450g/1lb/2⅔ cups sultanas/golden raisins or raisins
115g/4oz/1 cup shelled walnuts
115g/4oz/1 cup blanched almonds
finely grated rind of 1 unwaxed lemon
finely grated rind of 1 unwaxed orange
300ml/½ pint/1¼ cups sweet dessert wine or sherry

COOK'S TIPS

- You may need to chop the nuts roughly with a knife before processing them.
- The sweetmeat will keep in the refrigerator for up to 1 year if 5ml/1 tsp dessert wine or sherry is stirred in once a month to keep it moist and lightly fermented.

CUCCIDATI
SICILIAN FIG PASTRIES

The sticky, nutty, Sicilian sweetmeat that forms the middle of these pastries is also wonderful on its own or with salty pecorino cheese. About one-tenth of the sweetmeat will be used to fill the pastries in this recipe, but there is no point making it in small batches as it keeps extremely well for up to a year, so store the rest in your refrigerator. The flavour develops and changes over the months, as the mixture ferments gently with the monthly addition of the dessert wine.

1 First make the sweetmeat. Put the figs and sultanas or raisins in a bowl with water to cover. Soak for 30 minutes. Drain and transfer to a pan. Pour over fresh water to cover. Bring to simmering point and cook for 2–3 minutes to soften. Allow to cool.

2 Chop the nuts finely in a food processor or with a knife, transfer to a large bowl and set aside. Drain the softened dried fruit and place in a food processor with the lemon and orange zest. With the motor running, add half the wine or sherry through the feeder tube and process in bursts until reasonably smooth.

3 Scrape the mixture into the large bowl containing the nuts, stir to combine, then add more wine or sherry as needed to create a medium to dry consistency.

4 Set aside 45ml/3 tbsp of the mixture and spoon the rest into a plastic container, close the lid securely and store in the refrigerator (see Cook's Tips). Preheat the oven to 180°C/350°F/Gas 4. Grease 2 baking sheets.

5 Put the butter in a bowl and beat it with a spoon or whisk until creamed. Beat in the sugar, egg or egg yolks, milk and vanilla extract, adding a little flour if the mixture shows signs of curdling. Sift in the flour, baking powder and salt. Mix to a soft dough. Cover and chill for at least 1 hour.

6 Scoop up a teaspoon of the mixture. Roll it into a ball and place it on a baking sheet, then flatten it to a round. Repeat with the remaining mixture, leaving room for spreading. Spoon a little of the sweetmeat on to each round and pull up the edges to partially cover the filling.

7 Bake for 10 minutes or until golden. Leave on the baking sheets for 5 minutes, then transfer to wire racks and sprinkle with sugar. Leave to cool.

GELO D'AGRUMI
SICILIAN ORANGE JELLY

Sicilians love the silky coolness of jelly on a hot summer's day and make it with all sorts of flavourings, including spices such as cinnamon or the creamy milk of fresh almonds. For this version, use freshly squeezed orange juice if you have the time and facilities to squeeze it and serve the dessert in pretty stemmed glasses so that the light can shine through the gorgeous golden colours of the jelly under the scattering of deep-green mint.

1 Put the orange juice in a pan. Soak the gelatine in a small bowl of cold water for 5 minutes or until floppy, then drain, squeeze and add it to the juice.

2 Add the sugar. Stir vigorously over low heat until the sugar has dissolved and the gelatine has melted completely.

3 Pour into a shallow square or rectangular mould. Chill until firm.

4 Remove the set jelly from the refrigerator, and cut into rough cubes.

5 Arrange in four glasses, scatter with the mint leaves and drizzle with limoncello.

SERVES 4

750ml/1¼ pints/3 cups fresh orange juice
10 sheets leaf gelatine
50g/2oz/¼ cup sugar
handful of fresh mint leaves, chopped
limoncello liqueur, for drizzling

COOK'S TIP

The orange juice should be freshly squeezed if possible. If you can't freshly squeeze your own orange juice, do try and buy the best quality version you can.

SERVES 6 TO 8

500g/1¼lb watermelon, seeded and skinned
275g/10oz/1¼ cups caster/superfine sugar
30ml/2 tbsp jasmine flower water or 10ml/2 tsp orange blossom water
115g/4oz dark/bittersweet chocolate, diced
40g/1½oz/3 tbsp hulled and skinned pistachio nuts, chopped
115g/4oz/⅔ cup candied pumpkin, diced
5ml/1 tsp ground cinnamon

COOK'S TIP

Candied pumpkin is available in good Italian food stores. A suitable alternative would be candied pear as this has a similar texture and appearance.

GELATO DI COCOMERO
SICILIAN WATERMELON ICE

Nowhere in the world will you taste ice creams and water ices quite like those produced in Sicily, and the following recipe, with its intense perfume and flavour, is a superb example. Do make sure you use a really sweet, ripe watermelon; in Sicily their perfume wafts on the breeze throughout the summer.

1 Press the watermelon through a sieve or strainer into a bowl.

2 Add half the sugar and stir until dissolved, then mix in the jasmine flower or orange blossom water.

3 Scrape the mixture into a mould or freezerproof bowl and freeze it, stirring vigorously with a fork every 10 minutes or so to break up the ice crystals.

4 When the mixture is thick and slushy, stir in the remaining sugar, then the chocolate, nuts, pumpkin and cinnamon.

5 Return the mould or bowl to the freezer and continue to freeze until the mixture is solid, stirring occasionally.

6 To serve, dip the mould briefly into hot water to loosen the edges. Spoon into serving dishes.

LA CASSATA SICILIANA
SICILIAN CASSATA

This rich and sumptuous Sicilian classic is traditionally made in springtime. Its origins lie deep in Sicily's culinary history, and it takes its name from an Arab word meaning big round bowl. The dessert – not the ice-cream version – used to be made and sold by the nuns of Palermo's convents. The story goes that the business became so successful, and the Holy Sisters so absorbed in making cassata, that they began to neglect their prayers and holy duties. Eventually they received an official reprimand from the Archbishop.

SERVES 4

500g/1¼lb/2½ cups very fresh ricotta cheese
300g/11oz/scant 3 cups icing/confectioners' sugar, sifted
5ml/1 tsp vanilla extract
45ml/3 tbsp rum or liqueur
50g/2oz dark/bittersweet chocolate, grated or shaved
50g/2oz/⅓ cup chopped mixed candied peel
300g/11oz sponge or pound cake, cut in thin slices
90ml/6 tbsp custard
chocolate flakes, candied and glacé fruit, silver balls, sugared almonds, pistachio halves, coloured dragées/candies and rice paper flowers, to decorate

FOR THE FONDANT ICING

450g/1lb/2 cups caster/superfine sugar
150ml/¼ pint/⅔ cup water
2.5ml/½ tsp cream of tartar

1 Press the ricotta cheese through a sieve or strainer into a bowl. Gradually mix in the sugar until the mixture has the consistency of lightly whipped cream.

2 Flavour the ricotta mixture with the vanilla extract and rum or liqueur, then stir in the grated or shaved chocolate and the candied peel.

3 Line a 15cm/6in bowl with clear film or plastic wrap, making sure there is plenty of overhang. Line the base and sides with slices of sponge or pound cake, using the custard to cement the slices together securely.

4 Fill with the ricotta mixture and level the top carefully. Bring the surplus film over the cassata to cover the surface. Put a plate on the top, fitting it inside the bowl, press it down, then chill the dessert in the refrigerator for 2–3 hours.

5 Meanwhile, make the fondant icing. Dissolve the sugar in the water in a large, heavy pan over low heat. Wipe down the sides of the pan with a clean brush dipped in cold water to prevent crystals from forming.

6 Dissolve the cream of tartar in a little water, then stir into the syrup in the pan. Bring to the boil and boil steadily until the syrup registers 115°C/242°F on a sugar thermometer, or when a drop of icing forms a soft ball when dropped into a small bowl of cold water.

7 Slowly pour the syrup into a heatproof bowl and set aside until a skin forms on the surface. Beat it until opaque and firm. When cool enough to handle, knead it until smooth. Cover and set aside.

8 Remove the plate, unfold the film and invert a plate on top. Turn the plate and dessert over and lift off the bowl. Remove the film.

9 Ice the dessert with the fondant icing. Decorate it with chocolate flakes, candied and glacé fruit, silver balls, sugared almonds, pistachio halves, dragées and rice paper flowers. Chill until served.

PUGLIA & BASILICATA

Puglia is the heel of Italy's boot, bordered by Molise, Campania and Basilicata, and facing Croatia, Greece, Bosnia-Herzegovina, Albania and Montenegro across the Adriatic. It has the longest coastline of any of Italy's regions, and is famous for its white-washed towns, conical trulli and centuries-old farmlands. Stretching for 400km (250 miles) from north to south, for centuries this area held a strong strategic position, and as such was colonised, invaded and conquered by just about every major power of the day, from the Greeks to the Spanish.

Puglia has plenty sights of architectural interest, as each ruling dynasty left its own distinctive mark on the landscape; the Romans bequeathed their agricultural schemes and the feudal lords their fortified medieval towns. Perhaps most distinctive are the Kasbah-like quarters of many towns and cities, a reminder of the Saracen conquest of the 9th century. The Norman domination gave Puglia splendidly ornate cathedrals, while the Baroque exuberance of towns like Lecce and Martina Franca are a living testament to the region's ancient Spanish legacy.

Puglia is synonymous with sheep farming and the ancient tradition of the 'transumanza' – moving flocks of sheep from the Abruzzo to Puglia twice a year, always following the climate and the best pastures. So, when it comes to meat, lamb reigns supreme. With so many sheep, cheese is generally made from ewe's milk and Puglia's pecorino and ricotta are legendary. Not to be missed is burrata d'andria, a soft type of mozzarella that has to be eaten within hours of being produced.

Puglia's long coastline and age-old fishing traditions bring large quantities of fish and seafood to the table. Red mullet, anchovies, bream, sea bass, mussels, squid and cuttlefish are featured in numerous local recipes and the many seafront restaurants in coastal towns such as Gallipoli, Otranto, Brindisi and Taranto.

At the heart of the cooking is its extraordinary olive oil, the production of which has been a part of this area since ancient times and made fortunes for many noble families between the 17th and 18th centuries. The most traditional pasta shape here is orecchiette, meaning 'little ears' because of its shape. Dense and slightly spongy, it partners well with bitter greens in the region's most iconic pasta dish, orecchiette alle cime di rapa.

The remote mountainous region of Basilicata lies in the instep of the boot of Italy. An arid, underpopulated place that has for centuries existed in almost complete isolation, the only stretch of fairly fertile land lies to the north, where the ashes of the extinguished volcano, now the mountain of Vulture, have left the soil rich in natural minerals. The lower slopes are covered in vineyards and olive groves, but as you climb higher these give way to oak, ash and horse chestnut trees. This region was once densely wooded, but over history they have been stripped, leaving behind an arid, stony landscape that suffers from torrential flooding in the winter and breathtakingly hot summers. Perhaps for this reason, there are more Basilicatans living in other parts of the world than there are in the region itself.

The region divides into the two provinces of Potenza and Matera. Potenza is the highest regional capital in Italy, sitting in the Apennines to the east of Salerno. Within the province is the delightful seaside town of Maratea, the region's only town on the Tyrrhenian coast, which is known as 'The Pearl of the Tyrrhenian' or, because of its numerous churches and chapels, 'the town of 44 churches'. The region has another, longer coastline on the Ionian in the Matera province, with beach resorts such as Metaponto.

Elsewhere, the region is most famous for 'I Sassi' or the ancient city of Matera, one of the oldest inhabited cities in the world and a UNESCO World Heritage Site, the European Capital of Culture in 2019.

In such an inhospitable landscape with just a short coastline, staples such as wheat, vegetables and pork are the primary ingredients, and the cuisine is a somewhat robust and rustic one. That is not to say the food isn't tasty, however – many local dishes are spiked with fiery chilli, which is used freely as a condiment or as a dressing (a legacy of the spice's link with the cholera, malaria and plague epidemics of the past, when it was thought to be a curative) – and the bread is excellent, carrying an IGP certification. This is still made using locally grown wheat grains that give it its characteristic yellow colour and unique texture and flavour. Many traditional recipes have been developed for the leftover or stale bread, a cunning way to use every scrap of this precious commodity.

SERVES 4

500g/1¼lb potatoes
450g/1lb rocket/arugula leaves, trimmed
8 thick slices stale crusty bread
90ml/6 tbsp olive oil
4 garlic cloves, lightly crushed
1 small dried red chilli
sea salt

COOK'S TIP

When flavouring the oil, do not let the garlic burn or the oil will taste bitter. Lift out and discard the chilli and garlic as soon as you can smell the garlic strongly.

PANCOTTO CON RUCOLA E PATATE
BREAD SOUP WITH POTATOES AND ROCKET

This recipe is typical of la cucina povera; making something tasty out of practically nothing at all. Pancotto means 'cooked bread' and dishes with this title always have bread added for bulk, texture and flavour. There are many different versions of this sustaining yet delicious dish in Italy, all of which arose from the need to feed the family in times of hardship.

1 Fill a large pan with cold water and add a pinch of salt. Peel the potatoes and slice them thickly. Immediately add them to the water and bring it to the boil.

2 Lower the heat and simmer the potatoes for 7 minutes.

3 Add the rocket and continue to cook until the potato slices are tender and have begun to disintegrate.

4 Add the bread, without breaking it up or removing the crusts, and mix thoroughly.

5 In a separate frying pan, heat the oil with the garlic and chilli. Cook for 2–3 minutes, to flavour the oil.

6 Pour the soup into a large heated bowl. Pour over the hot oil, holding back (and later discarding) the chilli and garlic, and stir to combine. Serve immediately.

MINESTRA DI FAVE BIANCHE
WHITE BROAD BEAN SOUP

Purity of ingredients and utter simplicity sum up this nourishing winter recipe. In Puglia, where it originated, cooked rice or pastina (tiny pasta for soups) is often added to a finished soup to make it more sustaining. This dish is similar to the highly traditional, thick bean purée maccu di fave, the recipe for which is given on page 544. This soup, however, is topped with olive oil and a delicate sprinkling of freshly chopped chives.

SERVES 4

500g/1¼lb/3 cups dried white broad/fava beans (see Variation)
2 litres/3½ pints/8 cups water
90ml/6 tbsp olive oil
sea salt and ground black pepper
chives, finely chopped, to garnish

1 Put the dried white beans in a large, heavy pan and pour over the water. Cover the pan and leave the beans to soak for at least 24 hours.

2 Transfer the pan containing the beans and soaking liquid to the hob and bring to the boil over a medium heat.

3 Lower the heat and simmer for about 45–55 minutes, stiring frequently. Add more water if the purée appears to be drying out too much.

4 When the beans have disintegrated and are smooth and creamy, season to taste, stir in the oil and sprinkle with chives.

VARIATION

Dried white broad/fava beans are characteristic of the Puglia region famed for this dish, but dried butter/lima beans or dried green broad beans can be used instead.

MACCU DI FAVE
BROAD BEAN PURÉE

'Fave' is the Italian name for the broad bean, but in Puglia, where this recipe comes from, the word is also used to describe this dense, oily mash based on broad beans and potatoes. Along with orecchiette, the ear-shaped pasta peculiar to the region, fave is a staple food. It is usually eaten as a first main course (primo piatto), as an alternative to pasta or risotto. Traditionally, it is topped with boiled bitter greens, creating a wonderful combination of textures and flavours as well as being extremely nutritious and cheap to make.

SERVES 4 TO 5

225g/8oz/1¼ cups dried broad/fava beans
400g/14oz potatoes
about 2 large handfuls greens, such as cabbage or kale
100ml/3½fl oz/scant ½ cup extra virgin olive oil
sea salt

1 Put the beans in a large pan or flameproof earthenware pot and cover generously with cold water. Bring to the boil, lower the heat and simmer gently for 2 hours.

2 Meanwhile, peel the potatoes, cut them into 2.5cm/1in slices and put them in a bowl of cold water. Leave to soak until the beans are ready.

3 After 2 hours, the pan of beans will have developed a foamy scum. Skim this off, then pour away most of the water by tilting the pan carefully over the sink.

4 Drain the potato slices and spread them over the semi-drained broad beans, then top up to the level of the potatoes with fresh water. Add a pinch of salt and return the pan to the heat for a further 30–40 minutes.

5 Meanwhile, boil the greens in salted water for 10–20 minutes, until tender.

6 Adjust the seasoning to taste, then serve the purée in heated shallow bowls, with a generous swirl of olive oil on top of each portion and a topping of greens.

COOK'S TIP

This is delicious with rocket/arugula salad or a garlicky roasted bell pepper salad as part of an antipasto

SERVES 4

3 large, strong-tasting onions
60ml/4 tbsp olive oil
15ml/1 tbsp chopped fresh mint
115g/4oz/¾ cup salted capers, rinsed and chopped
2–3 dried chillies, finely crushed
sea salt

CIPOLLE FRITTE CON CAPPERI
FRIED ONIONS WITH CAPERS AND CHILLI

The flavours in this dish assault the senses and tingle the tastebuds. The recipe comes from the Basilicata region, where even the bread has a distinctive potency, though it is neither peppery nor particularly salty. This combination of onions, capers and chilli is perfect served as part of an antipasto with generous slices of strong Italian cheese and perhaps some bread.

1 Slice the onions thinly. Gently heat the olive oil in a frying pan over a low heat.

2 Add the sliced onions and fry them gently for about 10 minutes until they are softened, but not coloured.

3 Raise the heat and stir the onions constantly for 3 minutes until golden.

4 Remove the pan from the heat. Stir in the mint and capers. Season with salt and stir in dried chillies to taste. Cool before serving.

STRANGOLAPRETI FRITTI
FRIED PRIEST STRANGLERS

There are many explanations for how this recipe from Basilicata got its name; almost as many as there are versions of the dish itself. It can be a pasta, a dessert or, as here, a platter of tiny fritters to be served as an antipasto. The story (and the recipe) varies depending upon where you are in Italy, but one of the best tales concerns a cook who took revenge upon a notoriously greedy priest by preparing this speciality in his honour. The fritters were so tasty and the priest so greedy that the cook just somehow knew he would stuff himself with them until he choked. Which he did.

SERVES 6 TO 10

300g/11oz/2¾ cups fine pasta flour or fine-milled plain/all-purpose white flour
3 eggs
1.5ml/¼ tsp salt
grated rind of 1 lemon
olive oil, for deep-frying

1 Put the flour on to a clean work surface and make a hollow in the middle.

2 Break the eggs into the hollow in the flour and add the salt and the lemon rind. Mix the eggs, gradually incorporating the surrounding flour to make a dough. Knead the dough energetically; it should be dense and tight. Wrap it in clear film or plastic wrap and leave to rest for 10 minutes.

3 Unwrap the dough and divide it into 10–12 pieces. Shape each piece into a sausage and roll on the work surface to lengthen and thin the dough until the each piece is the same size and shape as grissini (breadsticks). Cut each thin roll into 2.5cm/1in lengths.

4 Press each piece of dough against the back of a curved cheese grater so that it becomes concave on one side and marked with the grooves of the grater on the other. Lay the shaped pieces on a lightly floured work surface or clean dish towel.

5 Heat the oil for deep-frying to 180°C/350°F or until a small piece of bread, dropped into the oil, browns in about 45 seconds. Fry the dough shapes, in batches, for 2–4 minutes or until the fritters have risen to the surface of the oil and are puffy and golden.

6 Drain the fritters on kitchen paper and keep them hot while cooking successive batches until all of the dough has been cooked. Serve immediately.

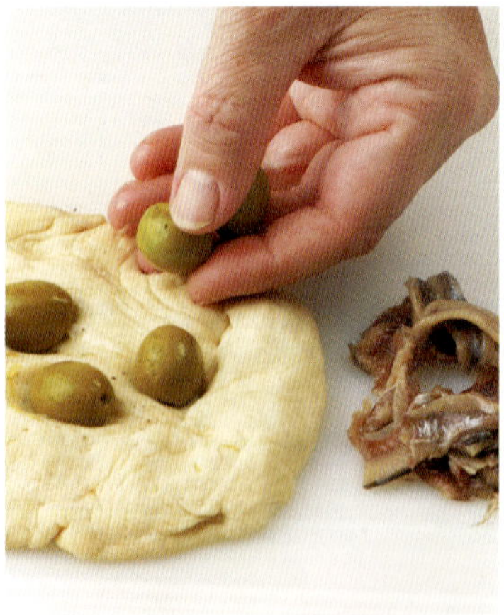

SFOGLIATA CON OLIVE E ACCIUGHE
OLIVE AND ANCHOVY BREAD

This is a light loaf from Puglia with lots of flavour and a lovely texture. To prepare the dough the traditional way you really need on-the-spot training from a local baker, but this recipe is a good start and will produce something quite delicious. Serve the bread as part of an antipasto course, with a richly dressed tomato salad and some chilli-spiked salami and sliced prosciutto, or with a selection of seafood dressed with olive oil, chilli and garlic. Serve warm or cold.

SERVES 4 TO 6

400g/14oz/3½ cups strong white bread flour
15g/½oz fresh/compressed yeast
20 marinated green olives, pitted
7 or 8 salted anchovies, rinsed, boned and chopped
175ml/6fl oz/¾ cup olive oil
ground black pepper

1 Pile the flour on a clean work surface and plunge your fist in the top of the flour to make a hollow all the way through.

2 Mash the yeast in a small bowl with just enough water to make a thick liquid. Pour this into the hollow, add about one-third of the olive oil and knead together very thoroughly with your hands for at least 10 minutes to make a dough that is as pliable and elastic as possible.

3 When the dough comes away easily from your hands and is no longer sticky, divide it into smallish lumps and roll each lump out to a disc that is about the size of a side plate.

4 Place each dough disc on a separate plate (so they don't stick), cover with clean dish cloths and leave in a warm place to rise until doubled in bulk. This should take about 30 minutes.

5 Preheat the oven to 180°C/350°F/Gas 4. Brush an oval baking dish, about 18cm/7in in length, with some of the remaining oil.

6 Knock back or punch down each of the discs of dough and flatten them using your hands. Sprinkle each disc with a few olives, a few pieces of anchovy and a little olive oil.

7 Roll a disc up loosely to make a tube shape about 2.5–3cm/1–1¼in thick, then stand it on end and push it down from the top to squash it slightly. Repeat for the remaining discs.

8 Stand all the squashed tubes side by side in the greased baking dish. Push them up tight against one another to make one big loaf. Brush the surface with oil.

9 Bake for 40 minutes, until the loaf is well risen and is golden brown. Remove from the dish and cool on a wire rack.

LAGANE E CECI
HOME-MADE PASTA WITH CHICKPEAS

This is one of those very simple, yet tasty, dishes that was born out of the poverty that the people of Basilicata have endured throughout history. In this remote area, ingredients have always been extremely limited – what could not be cultivated or bred in the severe climate simply did not exist. Even today, unusual ingredients are hard to come by and local cooks continue to prepare the traditional dishes that have been handed down by previous generations.

SERVES 4

500g/1¼lb/3 cups dried chickpeas
500g/1¼lb/5 cups plain/ all-purpose white flour
500ml/18fl oz/generous 2 cups water
75ml/5 tbsp olive oil
2 garlic cloves, finely chopped
½ onion, sliced
sea salt
dried red chilli, to garnish (optional)

COOK'S TIPS

- Getting the pasta dough to the correct texture so that it can be rolled to a fine sheet takes time and considerable energy. The best way to learn is by observing an experienced cook; if this isn't possible, persevere until you develop the knack.
- A good way to dry the strips of pasta is to place a clean dish towel over the back of a kitchen chair, then carefully drape the pasta over this.

1 Put the chickpeas in a large bowl and cover with plenty of cold water. Cover the bowl and leave the chickpeas to soak overnight.

2 Drain the chickpeas and put them in a large pan. Pour in cold water to cover, bring to the boil and boil hard over a high heat for 5 minutes.

3 Drain the chickpeas again, rinse them thoroughly and return them to the pan. Cover with fresh water. Bring to the boil, reduce the heat and simmer for about 2 hours over a low heat, or until the chickpeas are soft and tender. Top up the water as needed during the cooking time.

4 Once the chickpeas have been cooking for 2 hours, check the water levels, top up if necessary and cook for a further hour while you make the pasta.

5 Put the flour on to a clean work surface. Make a hollow in the middle and add a little salt. Pour about a quarter of the measured water into the hollow. Gradually incorporate the surrounding flour, adding more water as needed, to make a dough. Knead until smooth and elastic.

6 Roll the dough out on a floured surface to a very thin sheet. Using a pastry wheel, cut it into 2.5cm/1in strips. Leave these to dry for 15 minutes.

7 When the chickpeas have been cooking for 3 hours in total, drain any remaining liquid and season them with salt. Keep them warm

8 Heat the oil in a pan and fry the garlic and onion gently for about 10 minutes, until soft and golden.

9 Bring a large pan of salted water to the boil. Add the pasta and cook for about 5 minutes or until tender.

10 Drain the pasta and transfer to a large warmed bowl. Add the chickpeas and the fried onion and garlic, toss everything together and serve. Garnish with a dried chilli, if you like.

ORECCHIETTE CON AGLIO E PEPERONCINO
ORECCHIETTE WITH GARLIC AND CHILLI

All pasta shapes work well in this incredibly fiery pasta dish, but orecchiette are particularly suitable, since their blandness and chewy texture act as a perfect foil for the hot sauce. The region that created this recipe, Basilicata, is famous for its use of chilli (known locally as il diavolino or 'the little devil'), which locals eat in large quantities and intensity without any obvious ill-effects.

SERVES 4

150ml/¼ pint/⅔ cup olive oil
3 garlic cloves
4 whole dried red chillies
60ml/4 tbsp tomato paste
400g/14oz dried orecchiette

1 Bring a large pan of salted water to the boil over a high heat.

2 Heat the oil in another very large pan. Add the garlic and chillies and fry over low to medium heat for 3–4 minutes, until the garlic is soft and golden brown and the chillies are very shiny and swollen. Do not let either burn.

3 Scoop the garlic and chillies out of the oil with a slotted spoon.

4 Put the garlic and chillies in a food processor or blender and add the tomato paste. Process until smooth, then stir back into the oil remaining in the pan.

5 Add the pasta to the boiling water. Cook for 12–14 minutes until just tender, then drain.

6 Transfer the pasta into the pan containing the garlic and chilli mixture. Toss over the heat until the pasta is coated with the sauce, then serve.

ORECCHIETTE CON IL CAVOLFIORE
ORECCHIETTE WITH CAULIFLOWER

Orecchiette means 'little ears' and that's exactly what these dense, hard pasta shapes look like. Made from just flour and water, they require skill and patience to make by hand, as well as plenty of time and lots of effort, so many cooks prefer to simply buy a packet of dried orecchiette. This dish is from Puglia.

SERVES 4

115g/4oz bacon lardons or pancetta, cubed
1kg/2¼lb green cauliflower florets
400g/14oz fresh orecchiette
115g/4oz/1⅓ cups grated pecorino cheese
sea salt and ground black pepper

1 Place the lardons or cubed pancetta in a cold frying pan. Heat gently until the fat runs, then cook without browning for about 10 minutes.

2 Meanwhile, bring a large pan of salted water to the boil. Add the cauliflower florets and cook them for 5–7 minutes.

3 Add the orecchiette to the pan, stir once and cook for 2–3 minutes, or until the pasta shapes rise to the surface of the water.

4 Drain the cauliflower and the orecchiette, and transfer the mixture into a warmed serving bowl.

5 Add the fried lardons or pancetta and the grated pecorino cheese to the orecchiette and cauliflower mixture.

6 Add a generous grinding of black pepper to the orecchiette mixture, toss well to mix all of the ingredients together thoroughly and serve immediately.

VARIATIONS

- You can use streaky/fatty bacon instead of pancetta or lardons, but fry it until crisp before adding it to the pasta.
- You can use dried pasta if you add the cauliflower to the pan towards the end of the pasta's cooking time.

PASTA AL RAGÙ POTENTINO
PASTA WITH POTENZA RAGÙ

Potenza, the regional capital of Basilicata, is famous for having the most extreme temperatures in Italy. When the weather is icy, a one-pot dish like this one is ideal. The sauce is cooked with a large piece of flattened pork or beef in it to impart a rich flavour. In Potenza, the pasta and the sauce would be served as a substantial, nourishing first course and the meat then served as a flavoursome second course, or it can even be cooled and reserved for a separate meal.

SERVES 6

50g/2oz pecorino cheese, plus extra to serve (optional)
2 garlic cloves, chopped
45ml/3 tbsp chopped fresh parsley
1.5ml/¼ tsp chilli powder
1.5ml/¼ tsp freshly grated nutmeg
1 large slice pork or beef, about 600g/1lb 6oz (see Cook's Tips)
75g/3oz finely sliced pancetta
30ml/2 tbsp lard, white cooking fat or dripping
45ml/3 tbsp olive oil
75ml/5 tbsp dry white wine
2 x 400g/14oz cans chopped tomatoes, drained and seeded
500g/1lb 6oz fresh pasta
sea salt

1 Cut half the pecorino cheese into small cubes. Grate the remaining cheese. Mix together the grated and cubed cheese in a bowl.

2 Add the garlic and parsley, then stir in the chilli powder and nutmeg.

3 Lay the meat on a board and cover it with clear film or plastic wrap, tucking the film under the board to secure it. Using a meat mallet, flatten the meat as much as possible, taking care not to tear it.

4 Unwrap the meat and trim off any fat or gristle. The piece of meat should be fairly even, relatively thin and capable of being rolled.

5 Cover the flattened meat completely with pancetta slices, top with the cheese mixture, sprinkle with salt and carefully roll it up. Secure the roll with kitchen string or twine.

6 Heat the lard or dripping with the olive oil in a deep frying pan or casserole. Add the meat roll and sear it on all sides, then pour in the wine. Cook for 3 minutes, turning the meat frequently, to boil off the alcohol.

7 Add the tomatoes to the pan, sprinkle with a little salt and cover the pan or casserole tightly. Simmer very slowly for about 3 hours, adding a little water occasionally as necessary.

8 Bring a large pan of lightly salted water to the boil. Add the pasta and return to the boil. Cook for 2–3 minutes until the pasta has risen to the surface of the water and is just tender. Drain well.

9 Remove the meat roll from the sauce and either keep it hot to serve as a second course, or allow it cool for serving as part of a separate meal.

10 Add the pasta to the sauce, toss well together, then transfer to a heated platter and serve, sprinkled with extra grated pecorino, if you like.

COOK'S TIPS

- This dish works best when the meat is in one piece. Beef skirt is excellent for this purpose, or use a skinned and boned shoulder of pork.
- The meat roll is also delicious served cold.

PASTA CON LE COZZE
PASTA WITH MUSSELS

This is one of the easiest ways to enjoy the delicious combination of pasta with shellfish. The recipe is a famous speciality of Campomarino, a seaside resort on the Ionian coast in the province of Salento in Puglia. Mussels are extremely popular in the area, and the locals like to eat them raw with just a squeeze of lemon juice. In this recipe, they are flavoured almost as simply, with oil, garlic and parsley, and cooked briefly in a frying pan.

SERVES 4

500g/1¼lb live mussels or cooked mussels in their shells
350g/12oz dried maccheroncini or spaghetti
60ml/4 tbsp olive oil
2 garlic cloves, finely chopped
45ml/3 tbsp chopped fresh parsley
400g/14oz chopped and seeded ripe tomatoes, drained
sea salt and ground black pepper

1 If using fresh mussels, check them and discard any that are not tightly closed, or that do not snap shut when tapped on the work surface. Scrub all the mussels carefully and rinse them thoroughly.

2 Place the cleaned mussels in a wide frying pan. Cover the pan and place over medium-high heat for 5–6 minutes, shaking the pan frequently, until the mussels have opened. Any mussels that have not opened after this time should be discarded.

3 Remove all the mussels from the open shells, wipe off any traces of sand or sediment, and set them aside. Discard the shells.

4 Bring a large pan of lightly salted water to the boil and add the dried pasta. Stir, return to the boil and cook for 12–14 minutes or until just tender.

5 Meanwhile, heat the olive oil in a large frying pan and add the garlic and parsley. Fry for about 5 minutes, then add the tomatoes.

6 Season well, stir, and cook over a high heat for about 8 minutes. Stir in the mussels.

7 Drain the cooked pasta and add it to the pan containing the mussels and tomatoes. Stir to coat the pasta in the sauce, then serve in warmed bowls.

TIMBALLO DI RISO E CARCIOFI
RICE AND ARTICHOKE TIMBALE

This rather elegant dish is a recipe I discovered in Puglia, though I suspect its origins are possibly Sicilian. Either way, it is very simple to make, although the longest preparation is doubtless the rather tedious preparation of the artichokes themselves. They need to be stripped right back, leaf by leaf, and then carefully trimmed down to the bases, removing every trace of the furry choke itself.

SERVES 4 TO 6

juice of ½ lemon
12 medium artichokes
75ml/5 tbsp olive oil
1 garlic clove
175ml/6fl oz/¾ cup dry white wine
350g/12oz/1⅔ cups arborio rice
2 sachets powdered saffron or 1 pinch saffron threads, soaked in 45ml/3 tbsp hot water
200g/7oz thick-cut prosciutto crudo, cubed
2 eggs
100g/3½oz/scant 1 cup grated pecorino cheese
sea salt and ground black pepper

FOR THE BESCIAMELLA (BÉCHAMEL) SAUCE

75g/3oz/6 tbsp unsalted butter
50ml/4 tbsp plain/all-purpose flour
600ml/1 pint/2½ cups milk
pinch of freshly grated nutmeg
pinch of sea salt

1 To make the besciamella sauce, melt the butter in a pan and stir in the flour until a yellow paste forms. Gradually add the milk, whisking constantly to prevent lumps forming. Stir in the nutmeg and salt to taste and simmer for 15 minutes, stirring constantly, until the sauce is thick enough to coat the back of a spoon.

2 Remove the pan from the heat and cover the surface of the sauce with a little cold water to prevent a skin from forming. Set aside.

3 Fill a bowl with water and add the lemon juice. Clean and trim the artichokes (see page 603) and wash them in the acidulated water, then thinly slice.

4 Heat the olive oil in a pan and add the garlic. Fry for about 3 minutes, then add the sliced artichokes and fry for 5 minutes, turning them as they cook.

5 Add the wine and season with salt and pepper. Simmer for about 30 minutes, adding water as necessary if the artichokes appear to be drying out too much. They need to become very soft.

6 Meanwhile, bring a pan of lightly salted water to the boil. Add the rice. Cook over a medium heat for 10 minutes, then add the saffron. Cook for a further 2 minutes or so, until the rice is just tender. Drain the rice and spread it out in a large bowl to cool. Stir in the ham, eggs, cheese and sauce.

7 Line a 1.5-litre/2½-pint baking dish with baking parchment. Preheat the oven to 200°C/400°F/Gas 6. Spoon the rice and the artichokes in even layers in the baking dish, finishing with a layer of the rice. Level the surface and bake for about 30 minutes, allow to stand for 5 minutes and then serve straight from the dish.

8 Or alternatively, cover the sides of a lightly greased ovenproof mould with two-thirds of the rice and spoon all the artichokes into the centre. Use the remaining rice to seal the top and then level the surface with the back of a spoon. Bake as above, then turn it out of the mould to serve.

COOK'S TIPS

- To save time, artichokes are available ready to use in frozen form in all good supermarkets, but don't be tempted to use the canned or bottled versions as the results will be disappointing.
- The ham needs to be cut thicker than normal, but not so thickly that the end result is too chewy.

TRIGLIE AL CARTOCCIO
RED MULLET IN A PARCEL

Baking fresh fish in a parcel of baking parchment or foil is a cooking method used to great effect all over Italy. It has the benefit of retaining all the wonderful flavour of the fish and preventing it from drying out during the cooking process. This is a recipe from Puglia, and like most dishes from this region, it uses very few ingredients. Mullet is quite bony, but it is so delicious cooked in this way that it is worth braving the bones for the magnificent meaty flavour.

SERVES 4

4 even-sized red mullet, total weight about 1kg/2¼lb, scaled and cleaned
20ml/4 tsp dried oregano
120ml/4fl oz/½ cup extra virgin olive oil
30ml/2 tbsp chopped fresh parsley
16 black olives, pitted and halved
salt and ground black pepper

1 Preheat the oven to 200°C/400°F/Gas 6. Rinse the mullet thoroughly and pat them dry with kitchen paper. Season generously inside and out, and sprinkle 5ml/1 tsp oregano inside each fish.

2 Liberally oil four large squares of baking parchment or foil. Place a fish on each and sprinkle with the parsley. Arrange 8 olive halves on each fish.

3 Sprinkle with the remaining olive oil. Bring up the sides of the foil or parchment and twist or fold to enclose the fish completely.

4 Place the parcels in a large roasting pan. Bake for 30 minutes.

5 Place each parchment or foil parcel on a suitable plate for unwrapping at the table, and serve immediately.

SERVES 4

1 large gilthead bream, cleaned and scaled, about 1kg/2¼lb
500g/1¼lb potatoes
150ml/¼ pint/⅔ cup extra virgin olive oil, plus extra for basting
a handful of fresh flat leaf parsley, chopped
4 garlic cloves, finely chopped
75g/3oz pecorino cheese, grated
sea salt and ground black pepper

VARIATION

Although traditionally this dish uses a gilthead or emperor bream, any large, thick fish could be used instead, provided it will cook in more or less the same time as the potatoes.

ORATA ALLA PUGLIESE
PUGLIESE BAKED BREAM

The fish for this dish is cooked on a base of sliced potatoes that has been flavoured with garlic, fresh parsley and grated pecorino. The cheese needs to be really pungent and peppery so it stands up to the fish, so choose one that is mature and full of flavour. Serve this dish with a crisp green salad and some slow-roasted tomatoes for a fantastic meal.

1 Preheat the oven to 200°C/400°F/Gas 6. Rinse the fish thoroughly and pat it dry.

2 Peel the potatoes, slice them about 1cm/½in thick and place them in a bowl of cold water. Leave to soak until required.

3 Use half of the oil to coat the fish generously, both inside and out. Season with salt and pepper and tuck half the parsley and garlic into the cavity.

4 Drain the potatoes and rub the slices dry in a clean cloth.

5 Put the potatoes into a baking dish that is large enough to hold the fish. Add the rest of the oil with the remaining parsley and garlic. Mix well. Spread the potatoes evenly in the dish, season them with salt and pepper, then sprinkle with the cheese.

6 Lay the fish on top of the potatoes. Bake for about 40 minutes or until the potatoes are tender and the fish is cooked through, basting occasionally with a little olive oil.

7 Serve the fish and potatoes immediately, straight from the baking dish.

SERVES 8

1.3kg/3lb prepared seafood, such as a mixture of huss and cod (cut into chunks), small whole red mullet, squid, raw unshelled prawns/shrimp, mussels, razor clams and Venus clams
120ml/4fl oz/½ cup olive oil
3 garlic cloves, chopped
45ml/3 tbsp chopped fresh parsley
10 ripe tomatoes, peeled, seeded and sliced into strips
8 thick slices ciabatta
sea salt and ground black pepper

COOK'S TIPS

- Shellfish such as mussels and clams must be tightly closed when you start to cook them, and should open naturally when cooked. Never force a cooked mussel or clam open to eat it.
- Provide lemon slices, finger bowls and paper towels for guests as well as empty bowls for shells and bones.

ZUPPA DI PESCE PUGLIESE
PUGLIESE FISH STEW

This is a speciality of the large coastal city of Taranto, in Puglia. This important Italian port is home to wonderful seafood markets, which are filled with a remarkable array of fresh fish and shellfish. With so many varieties to choose from, local cooks will adapt the ingredients according to what is available at the time. This is the sort of dish that requires plenty of time to enjoy, as the seafood is only partially prepared and diners need to remove bones and shells at the table.

1 Put the chunks of fish, whole small fish, squid and prawns in a large colander. Wash thoroughly under cold running water, then drain well.

2 Scrub the remaining shellfish and pull off the beards from the mussels. Discard any clams or mussels with broken shells or which gape open and do not close when tapped on the work top. Put the mussels and clams in separate bowls. Pour cold salted water over both. Leave to soak.

3 Heat half the oil in a large pan. Add the garlic, half the parsley and half the tomatoes. Fry for 5 minutes, then add the fish from the colander. Add 30–45ml/2–3 tbsp cold water and season. Lower the heat, cover and cook for 6–8 minutes.

4 Put all the mussels into a large shallow pan. Cover tightly and shake the pan over the heat for 6 minutes, or until all the mussels have opened. Discard any that have not opened. Strain the liquid from the mussels over the cooked fish. Put the mussels into a bowl.

5 Put the remaining oil into a large, heavy pan. Add the remaining parsley and tomatoes and fry gently for 5 minutes. Add the clams, stir, season, cover and cook for 6 minutes or until the shells have opened. Discard any that remain shut.

6 Toast the ciabatta slices until golden and place a slice in each of eight soup bowls. Divide the cooked fish, with the liquid, among the bowls, then scatter over the mussels, with their liquid, then the clams. Serve.

SEPPIE RIPIENE
STUFFED SQUID

Elaborate recipes are rare in Puglia, where the tendency is to use just a few basic, but good-quality, ingredients. The squid for this delectable dish must be fresh and carefully cleaned, and the tomatoes need to be juicy and sweet.

SERVES 4

60ml/4 tbsp olive oil
1 garlic clove, crushed
9 tomatoes, peeled and seeded
4 large squid, cleaned and ready to cook (see Cook's Tip)
60ml/4 tbsp dry breadcrumbs
60ml/4 tbsp grated pecorino cheese
1 egg, beaten
sea salt and ground black pepper
chopped fresh parsley, to garnish
green salad, to serve (optional)

COOK'S TIP

To prepare a squid yourself, rinse it, then holding it firmly, grasp the tentacles and pull the head and entrails away from the body. Cut off the tentacles and set them aside. Discard the head, with the hard 'beak' and the ink sac. Peel the membrane from the body. Pull out and discard the 'quill'. Wash the body under cold running water, drain and dry it.

1 Heat the olive oil in a wide, shallow pan that is large enough to hold all the squid in one layer. Add the garlic and fry over a medium heat for 5 minutes. Do not let it burn or it will taste bitter.

2 Chop the tomatoes, then add them to the pan. Season to taste. Bring to the boil, then lower the heat and simmer for 30 minutes, stirring frequently and adding a little water if the sauce becomes dry.

3 Chop the tentacles and add them to the sauce. Remove from the heat and set aside.

4 Put the breadcrumbs in a bowl and add the cheese and enough of the beaten egg to bind the mixture. Mix the stuffing well.

5 Spoon the stuffing into the squid, dividing it evenly among them. The mixture will swell during cooking, so do not overfill the squid.

6 Either sew the stuffed squid closed using a darning needle threaded with fine kitchen string or twine, or secure them with wooden cocktail sticks or toothpicks.

7 Lower the stuffed squid into the sauce, cover the pan and simmer very gently for about 1½ hours over a low heat or until the squid are very tender, adding more water as required.

8 Season with salt and pepper, then serve either hot or cold, garnished with parsley, with crusty bread and a fresh green salad, if you like.

SERVES 6

800g/1¾lb salt cod
75ml/5 tbsp extra virgin olive oil
275g/10oz bottled roasted red bell peppers, drained
3 garlic cloves, chopped
3 dried red chillies, chopped
a handful of fresh flat leaf parsley, chopped
sea salt (optional)

VARIATIONS

• Fresh fish can be used for this dish, but because it has a much more delicate taste than salt cod, the quantity of chilli should be reduced or it may be overpowering. Fresh fish doesn't require soaking before use.
• Reconstituted dried red bell peppers can be used instead of bottled roasted ones, if you like.

BACCALÀ E PEPERONI
SALT COD WITH RED PEPPERS

Fiery and full of flavour, this winter dish comes from Basilicata, and was created for that time of year when there is a shortage of fresh vegetables and rough seas mean fish is in short supply. Salt fish needs to be soaked before cooking, so allow for this when planning the dish.

1 Soak the salt cod in enough cold water to cover the fish for 24 hours, changing the water often. Drain well.

2 Trim the fish, removing any obvious bones, and put it in a pan. Pour over cold water to cover and heat to simmering. Cook for about 8 minutes until the fish is soft.

3 Drain well and remove the skin. Flake the cod, removing any remaining bones.

4 Heat the olive oil in a wide pan and add the roasted peppers, garlic, chillies and parsley. Fry over a medium heat for about 10 minutes, stirring frequently. Add a little water if necessary.

5 Add the flaked salt cod to the pan and mix well. Taste and add salt if necessary, although the fish may already be salty enough. Cook for 1–2 minutes to heat through. Serve in a warm bowl.

SERVES 4

45ml/3 tbsp extra virgin olive oil
1 large onion, peeled and thinly sliced
1 medium chicken, jointed
250ml/8fl oz/1 cup dry white wine
2 small dried chilli peppers, chopped
400g/14oz tomatoes, blanched, peeled, deseeded and quartered
handful fresh basil leaves, torn into small pieces
sea salt and ground black pepper

POLLO IN SALSA PICCANTE ALLA LUCANA
CHICKEN IN A LUCANIAN SPICY SAUCE

This very simple, fresh-tasting and light chicken casserole recipe comes from the region of Basilicata, where the chilli pepper reigns supreme. Lucania is the historical name for this region, named for the ancient people known as Lucani who once populated this area in the deep south of Italy.

1 Heat the oil in a casserole or large, heavy, lidded pan over a medium heat, then add the onion. Fry gently for 10 minutes, until softened, then add the chicken joints and brown them all over, turning frequently.

2 Pour over the wine and allow it to boil for about 2 minutes. Chop the chillies, then stir in with the tomatoes, basil, and seasoning.

3 Cover the casserole or pan tightly with a lid and simmer gently over a low heat for about 1 hour, basting occasionally with a little extra white wine and turning the chicken joints from time to time.

4 Serve the chicken directly from the casserole or pan or transfer it to a warmed serving dish and serve piping hot.

LAKRUAR
LUCANIAN CHICKEN PIE

Lucania was the ancient region of southern Italy that now comprises Basilicata. Nobody is sure of the origin of this ancient recipe. There is something vaguely North African about its composition, so maybe it was inspired by a Moroccan pastilla. Whatever its source, though, the combination of ingredients makes for a delectable pie that is a little different.

SERVES 4 TO 6

500g/1¼lb/5 cups plain/ all-purpose flour
pinch of salt
2 eggs, beaten
90ml/6 tbsp dry white wine
90ml/6 tbsp extra virgin olive oil
green salad, to serve (optional)

FOR THE FILLING

1 Italian sausage
275g/10oz cooked chicken, preferably boiled or steamed
275g/10oz soft tumma cheese
2 eggs
large pinch of ground cinnamon, plus extra for sprinkling
pinch of salt

VARIATION

Tumma is a cheese local to the south of Italy, and may be difficult to find. Made from sheep's milk, this stretched-curd cheese is useful for cooking because it melts slowly. A good alternative is unsmoked scamorza. Mozzarella can also be used, but the flavour will be much milder.

1 Put the flour and salt in a large bowl and make a well in the middle. Mix together the eggs, wine and oil in a jug or pitcher.

2 Add the mixture to the well in the flour with about 30ml/2 tbsp warm water. Mix with your hands, gradually incorporating the surrounding flour and adding more water as needed, to make a smooth, elastic dough. Cover the bowl and leave the dough to rest while you prepare the filling.

3 Skin the sausage and crumble the sausage meat into a bowl.

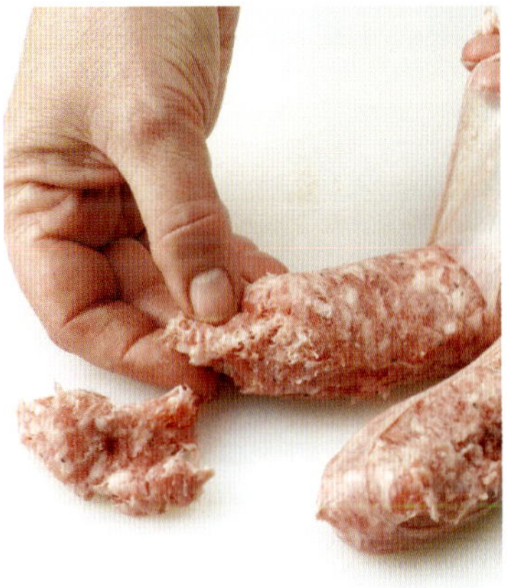

4 Cut the chicken and cheese into small pieces. Add these to the sausage meat, then add the eggs and flavour with the cinnamon and a pinch of salt. Stir to combine thoroughly.

5 Preheat the oven to 200°C/400°F/Gas 6. Grease a shallow 20cm/8in pie dish.

6 On a lightly floured surface, roll out the pastry thinly and then cut out two rounds, the first one large enough to line the baking dish and the other, slightly smaller, for the top crust.

7 Use the first piece of pastry to line the dish and trim the edges with a small, sharp knife.

8 Fill the lined dish with the chicken mixture and cover with the pastry lid. Seal the edges securely by pressing down on the rim with the prongs of a fork. Trim away any excess pastry.

9 Using a sharp knife or metal skewer, pierce the surface of the pie in several places to let the steam escape during cooking. Sprinkle with cinnamon.

10 Bake for about 30 minutes, until the crust is crisp and golden. Serve the pie hot or cold, with a green salad, if you like.

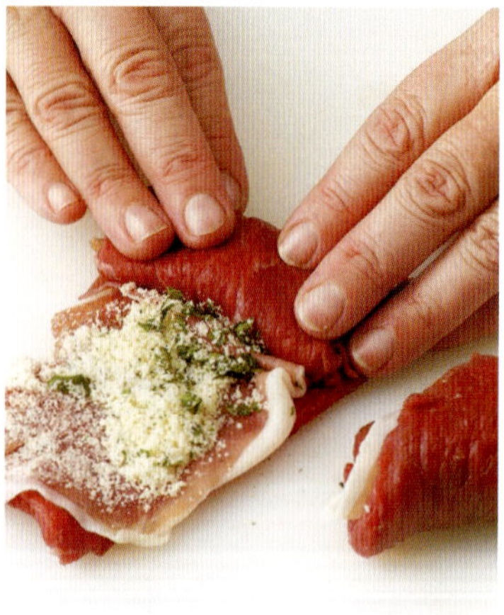

BRACIOLINE
PUGLIESE BEEF ROLLS

This traditional dish from Puglia consists of stuffed beef rolls stewed in a flavoursome tomato sauce. It is generally served over pasta, although the rolls can also be served as a main course accompanied by potatoes and vegetables.

1 Make the tomato sauce. Heat 60ml/4 tbsp of the oil in a heavy pan and add the chopped onion, celery and carrot. Fry over a low heat for 10 minutes until all of the vegetables are soft and the onion is transparent. Add the tomatoes and stir well. Cover and simmer for 30 minutes, stirring often.

2 Meanwhile, lay one of the meat slices on a board and cover it with clear film or plastic wrap, tucking the film under the board. Using a meat mallet or a rolling pin, beat the meat until really thin, being careful not to tear it.

3 Remove the clear film and place a slice of prosciutto over the flattened beef slice. Add a sprinkling of parsley, a little black pepper and an eighth of the grated cheese.

4 Roll the meat up tightly to enclose the filling and secure the roll with a wooden cocktail stick or toothpick, or a piece of kitchen string or twine. Make the remaining rolls in the same way.

5 Heat the remaining oil in a large frying pan. When it sizzles, add the rolls. Fry until browned all over, then lift out and drain in a colander.

6 Season the tomato sauce, then add the beef rolls and spoon the sauce over them. Continue to simmer gently for about 30 minutes, adding a little water as necessary to prevent the sauce from getting too thick.

7 Serve the meat rolls with vegetables or with pasta, if you like.

SERVES 4 TO 6

135ml/9 tbsp extra virgin olive oil
1 medium onion, finely chopped
1 large celery stick, with leaves if possible, chopped
1 large carrot, finely chopped
500g/1¼lb fresh tomatoes, peeled and chopped, drained canned tomatoes or passata/bottled strained tomatoes
8 thin slices of lean beef, such as minute steak
8 slices prosciutto crudo
45ml/3 tbsp finely chopped fresh flat leaf parsley
75ml/5 tbsp grated pecorino cheese
sea salt and ground black pepper
vegetables or pasta, to serve (optional)

VARIATIONS

- Add sultanas/golden raisins and pine nuts to the sauce if you like. This variation comes from Foggia, a city in Puglia, and echoes a similar recipe from Naples.
- Substitute pork or chicken escalopes/US scallops instead of beef, if you like.

CUTTURIEDDE
PUGLIA LAMB CASSEROLE

This is one of the oldest recipes still current in southern Italy, and comes from Puglia, an area famous for its sheep trails. These run the length of the region, from the Abruzzi to Lecce. The container in which the lamb is cooked is quite important if you want the dish to be really authentic. In Puglia they traditionally use a deep, copper pot with a narrow mouth to retain maximum flavour, but any deep casserole or even an ovenproof tagine will work well.

SERVES 4 TO 6

- 1kg/2¼lb lamb, any cut, cut into big chunks
- 1 head of celery, roughly chopped
- 115g/4oz soft pecorino cheese, cut into small pieces
- 150g/5oz small tomatoes, lightly crushed
- 1 large onion, sliced
- 7–8 dried bay leaves
- a small handful of fresh flat leaf parsley, chopped
- 1 dried hot red chilli, chopped
- sea salt
- roast potatoes, to serve (optional)

VARIATION

The taste of bay leaves is very prominent; it is intended to be so in this dish. For a less pungent flavour, use fewer leaves.

1 Preheat the oven to 160°C/320°F/Gas 3. Pat dry the chunks of lamb, checking for any shards of bone.

2 Put the lamb in a big bowl and add the celery, cheese, tomatoes, onion slices, herbs and chilli. Season with salt. Mix well using clean hands.

3 Pack the mixture tightly into a casserole. Cover with a sheet of baking parchment and a heavy, tight-fitting lid.

4 Bake in the oven for about 3 hours, or until the lamb is so tender that it has begun to fall apart. Serve with roast potatoes, if you like.

AGNELLO ALLA GENZANESE
GENZANO BAKED LAMB

Genzano di Lucania is a town and commune in the province of Potenza, which is in the southern region of Basilicata. The citizens of this small town are called Genzanesi, which explains the name of this interesting, and very hearty, one-pot lamb dish. You can use any cut of lamb you prefer, so long as it is not too fatty and has been boned as much as possible by your butcher.

SERVES 8

250g/8oz/5 cups soft white breadcrumbs
10ml/2 tsp dried oregano
60ml/4 tbsp finely chopped fresh flat leaf parsley
4 garlic cloves, finely chopped
250ml/8fl oz/1 cup extra virgin olive oil
2kg/4½lb yellow-fleshed potatoes
2kg/4½lb lamb (any cut), boned and cut into chunks
sea salt

1 Preheat the oven to 180°C/350°F/Gas 4. Put the breadcrumbs into a bowl and mix in the oregano, 2.5ml/½ tsp sea salt, parsley and garlic, using your hands.

2 Drizzle over half the olive oil and mix gently until the breadcrumbs stick together to form a clumpy mixture that resembles a crumble topping.

3 Peel the potatoes and slice them thickly and evenly. Use a little of the remaining oil to grease a baking dish that will hold all the meat and potatoes snugly.

4 Spread out the potatoes in an even layer on the base of the prepared baking dish, then drizzle with a little oil. Lay the lamb chunks evenly over the top.

5 Top with the breadcrumb mixture, then sprinkle over the remaining oil. Season lightly with salt. Drizzle over a little water to moisten.

6 Cover with foil or baking parchment and bake for 1¼–1½ hours, until the meat and potatoes are tender and the topping is brown and crisp. Serve immediately.

COOK'S TIP

If the topping has not browned sufficiently, remove the foil or paper and place the dish under a hot grill or broiler for a few minutes.

FRITTATA COL PEPERONCINO
CHILLI FRITTATA

The Italian flat omelette, known as a frittata, can be made with all sorts of fillings, from cooked vegetables to leftover pasta. In Basilicata, spicy red chillies are often included, with the addition of pecorino cheese for extra piquancy. Chillies are used liberally in the cooking of this region and are somewhat revered by the locals – a custom that dates from the times when it was believed that they offered protection from epidemic diseases such as the plague and cholera.

SERVES 4

45ml/3 tbsp olive oil, plus extra if needed
1 very hot dried red chilli, sliced into rounds
5 eggs
1 medium hot dried red chilli, finely chopped
75g/3oz/¾ cup grated pecorino cheese
sea salt (optional)
crisp salad, to serve (optional)

1 Heat the olive oil in a wide frying pan. Add the sliced hot chilli and fry over medium heat for 3 minutes. Strain into a large bowl, discarding the chilli and any seeds, and leave the chilli-flavoured oil to cool. Do not wipe the pan clean.

2 Break the eggs into the bowl with the chilli oil. Whisk lightly, then add the chopped red chilli and the pecorino cheese. Beat well. Season with salt if necessary, but check the cheese first as pecorino can be salty.

3 Reheat the frying pan, adding a little more olive oil if needed. When it is very hot, pour in the egg mixture. Shiver the pan so the mixture spreads evenly to the edges.

4 Cook for about 5 minutes over medium heat, occasionally lifting the edges of the frittata and tilting the pan so that liquid mixture flows underneath and sets. Do not let the base of the frittata burn.

5 Invert the frittata on to a large plate. The easiest way to do this is to place a large plate upside down on top of the frittata, covering it completely. Then, holding plate and pan firmly together, quickly turn both over. Slide the frittata back into the pan.

6 Return the pan to the heat and cook the frittata for a further 2–3 minutes, until the base is golden brown. Slide out on to a clean, flat platter and serve hot or cold, with a crisp salad, if you like.

COOK'S TIPS

- Since making a frittata is a skill that takes a little practice, you could start by making individual ones, using a small frying pan to make turning it easier.
- If the frittata sticks to the pan, slide a palette knife or slim spatula underneath to free it before inverting it on the plate.

PEPERONI RIPIENI ALLA PUGLIESE

STUFFED BAKED PEPPERS PUGLIESE-STYLE

Served with a salad, this makes a wonderful vegetarian main course or antipasto dish. The countryside of Puglia is incredibly fertile, producing abundant grain, tomatoes, grapes, artichokes, lettuces, fennel, bell peppers and onions, as well as fine olive oil. Local cooks have a simple dictum that translates as: 'There's no need to complicate things: just combine the best local ingredients and delicious dishes will practically create themselves.'

1 Using a sharp knife, slice the top off each bell pepper to form a lid. Set the lids aside. Keeping the peppers intact, carefully remove the core and seeds from each. Rinse out the cavities, then stand the peppers upside down on kitchen paper to drain.

2 Peel the potatoes and cut them into large cubes. Bring a pan of lightly salted water to the boil, add the potato cubes and parboil them for 5 minutes. Drain.

3 Preheat the oven to 180°C/350°F/Gas 4. Oil a deep baking dish that is large enough to hold the 4 peppers comfortably.

4 Put the potatoes into the dish and level the surface. Dot with the cherry tomatoes, then sprinkle over the onion slices, and half the garlic and parsley.

5 Top with half the pecorino and season with salt and pepper. Moisten with a little water and drizzle with about half the oil.

6 Put the eggs in a bowl. Add the breadcrumbs, then add the remaining pecorino cheese, as well as the remaining parsley and garlic. Stir in the Parmesan cheese. Season with salt and pepper. Mix well, then stir in half the remaining olive oil.

7 Using a spoon, fill the hollow peppers three-quarters full with the egg and breadcrumb mixture, then replace the lids.

8 Stand the stuffed peppers upright on the bed of vegetables in the baking dish. Use the potato cubes as wedges, if necessary, to prevent the peppers from falling over.

9 Season with salt and pepper, drizzle over the remaining olive oil and bake the peppers for 1 hour, stirring the vegetable mixture gently from time to time. Cover the baking dish loosely with foil if the top seems to be browning too much during cooking. Take care not to overbalance the peppers. This dish can be served hot or cold.

SERVES 4

4 large yellow bell peppers
800g/1¾lb potatoes
200ml/7fl oz/scant 1 cup extra virgin olive oil, plus extra for greasing
8 cherry tomatoes, sliced in half
1 large onion, sliced
2 garlic cloves, sliced
2 large fresh flat leaf parsley sprigs, roughly chopped
75g/3oz/¾ cup freshly grated pecorino cheese
3 eggs
40g/1½oz/¾ cup fresh white breadcrumbs
40g/1½oz/½ cup grated Parmesan cheese
sea salt and ground black pepper

COOK'S TIP

If the vegetables seem to dry out too much during cooking, pour a little water into the base of the baking dish to keep them moist.

INSALATA DI SPINACI E BASILICO
SPINACH SALAD WITH BASIL

This deliciously crunchy and refreshing green salad from Basilicata owes its pungent flavour to fresh basil. The herb grows best in hot, dry conditions, so is very well suited to the climate of southern Italy.

SERVES 6

450g/1lb fresh spinach leaves
2 small green bell peppers, halved, seeded and roughly chopped
1 onion, thinly sliced
about 8 fresh basil leaves
20ml/4 tsp lemon juice
60ml/4 tbsp extra virgin olive oil
sea salt and ground black pepper

1 Remove and discard the stalks from the spinach, then wash the leaves and dry them thoroughly on kitchen paper.

2 Place the spinach in a salad bowl and add the peppers, sliced onion and basil leaves.

3 Pour the lemon juice into a separate bowl. Whisk in the oil and season with salt and pepper.

4 Pour the dressing over the salad, toss thoroughly and serve immediately.

COOK'S TIP

This salad should be fresh and crisp so dress the salad only a few minutes before serving. If you dress it in advance the leaves will wilt.

SERVES 4 TO 6

- 8 medium courgettes/zucchini, trimmed
- 250ml/8fl oz/1 cup olive oil
- 12 fresh mint leaves, roughly chopped
- 150ml/¼ pint/⅔ cup light red wine vinegar
- 2 large garlic cloves, chopped
- sea salt

ZUCCHINE ALLA POVERELLA
POOR WOMAN'S COURGETTES

This traditional way of preparing courgettes comes from Basilicata, and gets its name from the fact that all its ingredients are cheap and readily available. Most people who cultivate their own courgettes will also have garlic and mint growing in the garden, and oil and vinegar in the kitchen.

1 Using a peeler, slice the courgettes lengthways into thin strips.

2 Heat the oil in a shallow pan. When it is very hot, add the courgette strips, in batches, and fry for about 4 minutes on each side or until softened and golden.

3 Lift out the strips with a slotted spoon and drain on kitchen paper.

4 Layer the courgettes in a heatproof dish, sprinkling each layer with a little salt and chopped mint. Set aside.

5 Pour the wine vinegar into a pan and add a pinch of salt. Stir in the garlic and the remaining mint. Boil for 5 minutes, then pour all over the courgettes. Leave to stand until cold, then cover and place in the refrigerator. Serve lightly chilled.

SERVES 4

2 large aubergines/eggplants
2 large tomatoes
300ml/½ pint/1¼ cups extra virgin olive oil
3 large onions, sliced into thin rings
2 large yellow bell peppers, cored, seeded and cut in thick strips
a handful of fresh parsley
a handful of fresh basil leaves
2 garlic cloves, peeled
sea salt and ground black pepper
toasted ciabatta, to serve

PIATTO DI VERDURE ALLA LUCANA
LUCANIAN VEGETABLE CASSEROLE

Lucania is the old name for Basilicata. The name is said to derive from the Latin 'lucus non lucendo' (a dark grove with no light), since the area was covered with dense forests. Many regional recipes, customs and traditions are still referred to as Lucanian, including this ancient recipe for a fragrant vegetable casserole.

1 Cut the aubergines into cubes. Spread the cubes out in a colander and sprinkle them generously with salt. Stand the colander in the sink. Fit a plate over the aubergines, put a weight on top and leave them to drain for about 1 hour.

2 Meanwhile, blanch the tomatoes. Cut a cross in the base of each one, put them in a heatproof bowl and pour over boiling water to cover. Leave for 30 seconds or until the skin starts to peel back from the crosses. Drain the tomatoes, peel them, cut them into cubes and discard the seeds.

3 Heat the oil in a large, shallow pan. Add the onions and fry for 6–8 minutes until just starting to soften but not browned.

4 Rinse the aubergine cubes, pat them dry with kitchen paper, then add them to the onions. Cook, stirring often, for 5 minutes, then stir in the bell peppers and tomatoes. Season and simmer for 10 minutes.

5 Chop the parsley and basil with the garlic. Add the mixture to the pan and stir to mix. Cook, uncovered, for about 45 minutes, until the mixture is thick and flavoursome.

6 Serve hot or cold with toasted ciabatta.

MUSTAZZUELI
PUGLIESE ALMOND COOKIES

These simple almond cookies from Puglia seem incredibly hard when you first attempt to bite into them, but once in your mouth they crumble very satisfactorily, and can also be dunked in dessert wine. A similar style of biscuit or cookie is made in the Cosenza area of Calabria, where they are known as mostaccioli. The Calabrian recipe adds a little aniseed liqueur and some grated orange rind to the mixture, and the resulting texture is lighter.

MAKES ABOUT 25

250g/9oz/2¼ cups whole blanched almonds
250g/9oz/generous 1 cup sugar
75ml/5 tbsp cold water
350g/12oz/3 cups plain/all-purpose white flour, sifted twice

COOK'S TIP

Keep a close eye on the almonds while toasting them in the oven, as they scorch readily. They could also be toasted under the grill or broiler, or in a hot, dry pan, but since the oven is required for baking, it does make sense to use it.

1 Preheat the oven to 200°C/400°F/Gas 6. Spread out the almonds evenly over one or two baking sheets and toast for 5 minutes, or until golden brown. Take the almonds out of the oven, but leave the oven switched on.

2 Put the sugar into a small pan. Add the water and stir over a low heat until the sugar has dissolved and the mixture has formed a smooth syrup. Remove from the heat and leave to cool slightly.

3 Grind the almonds to a fine powder in a food processor or nut mill.

4 Put three-quarters of the flour on to a clean work surface. Make a hollow in the middle. Pour the ground almonds into the hollow and add the syrup.

5 Mix the syrup into the flour and almonds with your hands, working quickly to achieve a smooth and elastic dough.

6 Sprinkle half the remaining flour on the work surface. Shape the dough into a cylinder with a diameter of about 4cm/1½in.

7 Using a knife, cut the cylinder into about 20 even discs, then flatten each one with the palm of your hand, lightly floured, so that you reduce its thickness to about 5mm/¼in.

8 Cut each dough disc into a roughly square shape using a 4cm/1½in cookie cutter, and re-shape the excess dough.

9 Use the remaining flour to dust one or more baking sheets. Arrange the cookies on them in rows. Bake for 10–15 minutes, until golden.

10 Remove from the oven and leave the cookies on the baking sheets for 1–2 minutes to firm up, then, using a spatula, transfer them to wire racks to cool completely. Stored in airtight containers, the mustazzueli will keep for up to 1 month.

CALABRIA

Here, in the toe of the boot of Italy, is where the heady red wines of the region and the liberal use of chillies combine to create a deliciously stupefying effect on the dinner table. Here is where Italy points her toe towards Sicily to push her out into the Mediterranean, separated at the narrowest point by the narrow Straits of Messina.

Known as Bruttium in antiquity, this region is made up of the provinces of Catanzaro, which is also the regional capital, and Reggio Calabria, Cosenza, Crotone and Vibo Valentia. The region has a fine coastline, with many splendid resorts such as Pizzo and Tropea; mountains like the Aspromonte and the Sila; and plenty of fertile plains of reclaimed marshland, used for the cultivation of the famous red onion of Tropea and many other crops, including strawberries, liquorice, luscious bell peppers and the intensely perfumed bergamot.

In terms of meat, the pig reigns supreme, traditionally big and black, slaughtered in November and turned into a wide range of cured pork products and plump sausages, often liberally flavoured with the ubiquitous chilli to see families through the cold winter months.

The olive oil produced here is rich and deep green. The wines, mostly red, are full bodied and strong, and there is a regional passion for the art of preserving, almost as if the region's hard history of poverty and hunger has somehow left the inhabitants with an inbuilt need to put things away for the winter or for lean times. Tomatoes and bell peppers get sun dried and hung on strings. Aubergines/eggplants, mushrooms foraged in the mountain forests, courgettes/zucchini, onions, and many other vegetables are either pickled or preserved in oil. Fish of many varieties – from baby octopus and the tiny newborn fish called nunnata, to anchovies, stoccafisso and baccala – is preserved with great zeal, even though the sea almost surrounds the region. Sausages are preserved in jars of lard or extra virgin olive oil, or allowed to dry out and become salame, and all the while there is the hit of chilli, adding fire and spice to almost every mouthful. Swordfish and tuna are also very much a part of the diet, having for centuries swum the waters of the Straits of Messina.

For me, there is always something faintly baffling about some of the traditional dishes of this region, almost as if they are somehow linked to history or legend, part of a bigger picture in some way. This is cuisine that has always a reputation for being quite heavy on the digestion; a very traditional kind of focaccia, made from unleavened bread lined with pork fat, is a good example of this. But there are signs of welcome change in some parts of Calabria and many new restaurants and delis, while respecting and celebrating the local mainstay ingredients, have given their dishes a new twist that makes the food somehow lighter, fresher and much more visually appealing. In the mountains behind the Lamezia Terme coastline, where I have spent many happy summers, several little restaurants, agriturismi and trattorie spring up every year, breathing new life into the recipes and traditional ingredients of this stunningly beautiful region with its extraordinarily varied landcape.

A note about 'nduja

In recent times, the world at large has discovered 'nduja, a pork sausage made out of various parts of the pig – such as the shoulder and head, as well as belly, offal and tripe – chilli peppers and a mixture of spices and flavourings that is traditionally made in and around the town of Spilinga, in the province of Vibo Valentia. This very spicy and sweet, spreadable sausage has a name that is hard to pronounce, but a flavour that is utterly impossible to resist and has rightfully become famous and much sought after outside Italy.

The name 'nduja is apparently connected in some way to the French Andouille, although I am delighted to say that it is absolutely nothing like its French quasi namesake! The name actually derives from the Latin 'inducere', meaning 'to lead', 'introduce' or 'bring in'. In Calabria, it is mainly served with slices of toasted bread or with strong pecorino cheese, or as a contrast to sweet and clean-tasting burrata cheese from the Sila. However, its amazing and unique flavour makes it a suitable ingredient for a huge variety of dishes, including as an addition to a simple tomato sauce for pasta; mixed with crab to make a simple non-cook pasta dressing or topping for crostini; warmed and brushed over fish or meat before grilling; with fried or scrambled eggs; or melted and whisked into oil and vinegar for a smoky, spicy vinaigrette.

SERVES 4

1 Savoy cabbage
2.5 litres/4½ pints/10 cups best beef stock
115g/4oz/1 cup freshly grated pecorino cheese
8 thin slices toasted ciabatta
sea salt

COOK'S TIP

Make the stock with marrow bones for the best flavour, and spread the cooked marrow from the bones over the toasted ciabatta.

MINESTRA DI CAVOLO VERDE
GREEN CABBAGE SOUP

This simple, healthy Calabrian recipe proves that as long as you use top-quality ingredients – in this case, first-class beef stock and crisp, flavoursome cabbage – you can transform a basic dish into something special. The pecorino is intrinsic to the flavour of this dish. Make sure it is hard and very mature, and add a generous sprinkling to each portion to lend body as well as taste.

1 Trim the cabbage, remove the core and all the hard spines. Discard any really hard leaves, shred the remaining cabbage very finely and put it in a large pan. Pour over cold salted water to cover. Bring to the boil and cook for 5 minutes, then drain and set aside.

2 Pour the stock into the clean pan and bring it to the boil. Toss in the cabbage and cook it again for 10 minutes.

3 Spoon into a large bowl and serve. Offer the cheese and toasted ciabatta separately.

SERVES 4 TO 6

450g/1lb aubergine/eggplant skins
135ml/9 tbsp olive oil
30ml/2 tbsp red wine vinegar
3 garlic cloves, chopped
8 fresh mint leaves, chopped
7.5ml/1½ tsp dried oregano
sea salt and ground black pepper
crusty bread, to serve

INSALATA DI BUCCE DI MELANZANE
AUBERGINE SKIN SALAD

Thrifty Calabresi cooks make salads out of everything edible. Aubergines are often peeled when they are added to pasta sauces and casseroles, so this is a canny way of using them up the skin, which would otherwise go to waste. The dish makes a lovely antipasto, gutsy and quite filling. It is delicious with salami or soppressata, or robust, aged pecorino cheese.

1 Bring a large pan of salted water to the boil, add the aubergine skins and cook over a medium heat for 8 minutes.

2 Drain the skins and cut them into neat strips, no more than 2cm/¾in wide.

3 Put the warm strips in a salad bowl and stir in the oil to coat. Add the vinegar in the same way, then add the garlic and herbs. Season with salt and pepper and toss well. Leave to stand for 5 minutes before serving with crusty bread.

CRISPEDDI A LICI
ANCHOVY FRITTERS

To make the batter for this recipe in the traditional Calabrian style, you need a bavanu, a classic terracotta bowl with a glazed lining. Whichever bowl you use, make sure it is a large one and be sure to use only your hands to beat the batter for the full 30 minutes in order to make it really tacky and light. The fritters make a lovely tasty snack, especially when served with plenty of dry white wine.

1 Put the flour into a bowl and make a well in the middle.

2 Pour the water into a cup and crumble in the yeast. Pour this mixture into the well in the flour. Using your hands, mix the water into the flour, adding more water if required to make a sticky, stringy mass. Be careful not to add too much liquid.

3 Knead the batter by beating with your hands in a circular motion for about 30 minutes. Beat in the salt. Cover the bowl with a cloth and leave the batter to rise at warm room temperature for 3–4 hours. Meanwhile, roughly chop the anchovies.

4 Heat the oil in a large pan to 180°C/350°F or until a small cube of bread, dropped into the oil, browns in about 45 seconds.

5 Using your hand, scoop up about a tablespoon of batter and stretch it slightly with your fingers. Tuck a piece of anchovy inside and drop the dough into the hot oil. Add more pieces of dough in the same way but do not overcrowd the pan.

6 Fry the fritters, in batches, for 4–6 minutes until they rise to the surface of the oil and turn crisp and golden, then lift out with a slotted spoon and drain on kitchen paper. Serve immediately – the hotter the better.

SERVES 12

- 1kg/2¼lb/9 cups plain/all-purpose flour
- 120ml/4fl oz/½ cup hand-hot water
- 50g/2oz fresh/compressed yeast
- 1.5ml/¼ tsp salt
- 300g/11oz salted anchovies, rinsed, boned and dried
- sunflower oil or light olive oil, for deep-frying

COOK'S TIP

Rinse the anchovies very well, to remove the surplus salt, and take care to remove the bones. Dry them with pieces of kitchen paper before chopping them.

SERVES 4

25g/1oz/2 tbsp unsalted butter
1 onion, finely chopped
1.5 litres/2½ pints/6 cups fish stock (preferably made with trimmings from the dried fish)
500g/1¼lb stockfish or dried salt cod, soaked, washed and flaked
175ml/6fl oz/¾ cup dry white wine
350g/12oz/1⅔ cups risotto rice
30ml/2 tbsp extra virgin olive oil
a handful of fresh flat leaf parsley, finely chopped

RISOTTO CON LO STOCCO
RISOTTO WITH STOCKFISH

Stocco is dried stockfish: a medium-size cod that has been hung on wooden scaffolding to dry in the sun, then expertly salted and air dried. To transform this hard, unappetizing product into something edible, the fish must be cleaned and soaked in good-quality tap water. The water that flows from the Apennine springs in the area of Mammola is said to be perfect for the task, and this, together with the skill of the local craftsmen, has given Calabrian stocco the reputation of being the finest in Italy.

1 Melt the butter in a large heavy pan, add the onion and fry over a medium heat for 15 minutes or until golden brown. Meanwhile, set the stock simmering in a separate pan.

2 Stir the flaked stockfish into the onion, then add the wine and stir over the heat until the alcohol evaporates. Add the rice and toast the grains for 2–3 minutes, stirring constantly to prevent them from scorching.

3 When the rice is crackling hot, start adding the hot stock, one or two ladlefuls at a time. Stir constantly and do not ladle in more stock until the previous amount has been absorbed.

4 After about 20 minutes, when the rice grains are soft and plump, stir in the oil and the parsley. Take the pan off the heat, cover it with a lid and set aside for 3–4 minutes, then stir again gently and serve.

SERVES 4

4 thick swordfish steaks, about 175g/6oz each
225g/8oz/4 cups soft white breadcrumbs
150g/5oz pecorino cheese, grated
45ml/3 tbsp finely chopped fresh flat leaf parsley
90ml/6 tbsp extra virgin olive oil
juice of 1 lemon
sea salt and ground black pepper

VARIATIONS

- Use tuna steaks instead of swordfish, adjusting the cooking times if necessary, depending upon the thickness of the fish.
- Flavour the breadcrumb topping by adding some chopped olives and rinsed and chopped capers.

PESCE SPADA ARRAGANATO
CALABRIAN BAKED SWORDFISH

The perfect accompaniment for this delicious swordfish dish is a platter of grilled vegetables such as bell peppers, courgettes, carrots, red onions and aubergines. For baking the fish, use a dish that will hold all the steaks snugly side by side, and ensure they're completely sandwiched in the breadcrumb mixture, as this will help to keep the swordfish moist.

1 Rinse and dry the swordfish steaks. Preheat the oven to 180°C/350°F/Gas 4.

2 Put the breadcrumbs in a bowl and add the grated cheese and parsley. Season with salt and pepper to taste and mix well to combine everything.

3 Use a little of the olive oil to grease a baking dish that is just large enough to hold the steaks snugly in one layer. Brush the steaks with oil on both sides.

4 Spread half the breadcrumb mixture over the base of the dish, the lay the swordfish steaks on top. Season the fish with salt and ground black pepper.

5 Cover with the rest of the breadcrumb mixture, then drizzle with the remaining oil.

6 Bake for 10 minutes, then remove from the oven, pour the lemon juice over the crumb topping and return to the oven for 10 minutes more. Serve immediately.

TONNO ALLA CALABRESE
CALABRIAN TUNA STEAKS

This recipe typifies Calabrian cuisine and brings together many of the ingredients that are most closely identified with the region. The flavours work very well, making the most of the taste of fresh tuna and creating a satisfying dish, with just enough chilli to add a hint of fire.

SERVES 4

4 even-sized fresh tuna steaks, total weight about 800g/1¾lb
60ml/4 tbsp olive oil
30ml/2 tbsp plain/all-purpose flour
60ml/4 tbsp dry white wine
50g/2oz pancetta, chopped
1 large garlic clove, chopped
1 onion, chopped
30ml/2 tbsp chopped fresh parsley
4 anchovy fillets in oil, drained and boned
400g/14oz can chopped tomatoes, drained
½ dried red chilli, chopped
sea salt and ground black pepper

1 Pat dry the tuna steaks using kitchen paper. Season the steaks thoroughly on both sides with salt and pepper.

2 Heat half the olive oil in a frying pan that is large enough to hold the tuna steaks in a single layer. Coat the tuna steaks lightly in flour, add them to the pan of hot oil and fry them over a medium heat for 3 minutes on each side.

3 Sprinkle with the wine and allow the alcohol to boil off for 1 minute.

4 Using a spatula, lift out the fish and drain on kitchen paper. Place on a plate and spoon over the pan juices.

5 Heat the remaining olive oil in the pan. Add the pancetta, garlic, onion and half the parsley. Fry gently for 5 minutes, stirring from time to time.

6 Add the anchovy fillets and mash them into the hot mixture with a fork. After 1 minute, stir in the tomatoes. Add the chilli and simmer over low heat for 15 minutes.

7 Slide the tuna steaks back into the pan and spoon some of the tomato mixture over them. Heat through thoroughly for about 8 minutes, turning them over gently once.

8 Serve immediately topped with the sauce and sprinkled with the remaining parsley.

COZZE RIPIENE AL SUGO
STUFFED MUSSELS WITH TOMATO SAUCE

This is a very tasty way to enjoy fresh mussels. Use the biggest shellfish you can find, as the preparation – which involves tying shut the mussels – is more fiddly if the mussels are small. Clean them carefully, as any trace of grit or splinter of barnacle will spoil the effect of the whole dish.

1 Check the mussels, discarding any with damaged shells and any which are open and fail to close when tapped on the work surface.

2 Spread out the mussels in a wide frying pan. Cover the pan and place it over a fairly high heat. Shake the pan frequently. After about 6 minutes, all the mussels should have opened and yielded their liquid. Discard any that remain closed.

3 Drain the mussels, reserving the liquid in the pan, and set them aside.

4 Heat the oil in a medium pan. Peel 2 garlic cloves and add them, whole, to the oil. Fry the garlic until it turns brown, then lift the cloves out with a slotted spoon and discard them.

5 Stir the passata or strained tomatoes into the garlic-flavoured oil and season. Bring to the boil, then lower the heat, cover the pan and simmer the mixture for 20 minutes.

6 Meanwhile, make the stuffing. Chop the remaining garlic clove finely and put it in a bowl. Add the eggs, parsley and soft white breadcrumbs. Season with salt and pepper.

7 Fill the empty half shell of each mussel with the stuffing, then close the shells around the mussels. Tie each one with a loop of kitchen string or twine to keep the stuffing securely inside.

8 Strain the reserved liquid from the mussels and add it to the tomato sauce, with the basil.

9 Stir to mix, then add the mussels to the pan and spoon the sauce over them. Cover the pan tightly and simmer for 10 minutes.

10 Remove and discard the string from the mussels and transfer them, with the sauce, to a heated platter. Serve immediately.

SERVES 4

1kg/2¼lb live mussels, scrubbed and debearded
75ml/5 tbsp olive oil
3 garlic cloves
600ml/l pint/2½ cups passata/ bottled strained tomatoes or strained canned tomatoes
2 eggs, beaten
30ml/2 tbsp chopped fresh parsley
120ml/8 tbsp soft white breadcrumbs
a small handful of fresh basil, leaves torn into shreds
sea salt and ground black pepper

POLPETTE DI STOCCO
CALABRIAN FISH PATTIES

These are the Calabrian version of fishcakes – hot and spicy with plenty of garlic and some grated goat's cheese for extra pungency. The fish that is traditionally used is stocco, or stockfish, which is a member of the cod family. It is dried and then salted, as opposed to baccalà, which is salted without being dried first. Stockfish from Mammola in Calabria is recommended for this recipe, but another type of fish could be used instead, as long as it is robust enough to withstand the other flavours in the dish.

SERVES 4 TO 6

1kg/2¼lb stockfish, preferably stocco di Mammola, soaked in water until soft
115g/4oz/2 cups soft white breadcrumbs
75g/3oz hard goat's cheese, grated
45ml/3 tbsp chopped fresh flat leaf parsley
1 dried red chilli, chopped
3 garlic cloves, finely chopped
2 eggs, beaten
60ml/4 tbsp olive oil
400g/14oz can chopped tomatoes
sea salt

1 Drain the soaked stockfish, clean and trim it, then flake and chop it finely, removing any bones. Put it in a large bowl.

2 Add the breadcrumbs, cheese, parsley, chilli and half the garlic. Stir in the beaten eggs, mixing well.

3 Divide the mixture into 8–12 portions and shape into patties. Set aside.

4 Heat the olive oil in a large frying pan and add the remaining garlic. Fry over gentle heat for about 3 minutes. As soon as the garlic begins to brown, stir in the canned tomatoes. Simmer the sauce for 10 minutes.

5 Season with salt to taste, then add the stockfish patties and spoon the sauce over to coat. Cover the pan and simmer for 10–15 minutes until cooked, then serve hot.

COOK'S TIPS

- You may not need to add all the egg. Stir in enough to bind the mixture. It should be firm enough to shape into patties.
- Shaping the patties is easier if the mixture is lightly chilled, so put it into the refrigerator for 30 minutes, if you have time.
- For a less spicy mixture, do not use the seeds from the dried chilli.

SERVES 4

600g/1lb 6oz thin turkey steaks
10ml/2 tsp dried oregano
3 ripe limes, 2 juiced and 1 sliced into wedges
75ml/5 tbsp extra virgin olive oil
1 garlic clove
sea salt and ground black pepper

VARIATIONS

- Orange or lemon juice could be used instead of lime juice.
- Instead of turkey steaks, try escalopes/US scallops of chicken or veal, or thin slices of monkfish.
- Add finely grated lime rind to the marinade for an extra flavour boost.

FESA DI TACCHINO AL CEDRO
CALABRIAN TURKEY STEAKS WITH LIME

Citrus fruits such as limes, bergamots and grapefruit grow profusely all over Calabria. Limes are an important feature of this simple, summery dish, which is delicious with a potato salad. For colour, serve it with some sliced tomatoes, dressed with oil, salt and torn basil leaves.

1 Place the turkey steaks between sheets of clear film or plastic wrap and beat them with a meat mallet or rolling pin until they are as thin as possible.

2 Spread out the flattened turkey steaks in a shallow dish and sprinkle with the oregano. Drizzle with the lime juice and half the olive oil and season with salt and pepper. Cover and leave to marinate at room temperature for about 1 hour.

3 Lift out the turkey slices and pat them dry with kitchen paper.

4 Pour the remaining olive oil into a frying pan. Add the garlic and heat over a high heat. When it sizzles, add as many of the turkey slices as the pan will hold in a single layer. Fry quickly, for only 1–2 minutes on each side, until cooked through.

5 Transfer the turkey to heated plates and keep hot while cooking the remaining slices.

6 Divide the juices remaining in the pan among the turkey slices, spooning them over the top. Garnish with the lime wedges and serve.

POLPETTE IN AGRODOLCE
CALABRIAN SWEET-AND-SOUR MEATBALLS

There is plenty of texture and flavour in this wonderful Calabrian dish, which is capable of infinite variety. Although it usually consists of little meatballs, the mixture can also be made as one large meatloaf and cooked for much longer. The proportion of pork and beef can be altered, or just one type of meat can be used. The cheese, too, can be varied. The tomato sauce is delicious, but it can be omitted, and the meatballs simply fried, covered with wine must, spiked with almonds and served with some boiled potatoes.

SERVES 4 TO 6

- 2 slices day-old bread, total weight about 115g/4oz
- 120ml/4fl oz/½ cup extra virgin olive oil
- ½ onion, chopped
- 1 garlic clove, chopped
- 400g/14oz passata/bottled strained tomatoes
- 200g/7oz/scant 1 cup minced/ground pork
- 200g/7oz/scant 1 cup minced/ground beef
- 2 eggs, beaten
- 30ml/2 tbsp chopped fresh flat leaf parsley
- 50g/2oz/½ cup grated pecorino cheese
- 30–45ml/2–3 tbsp wine must or sweet balsamic vinegar (see Cook's Tip)
- 75g/3oz/¾ cup flaked/sliced almonds
- sea salt and ground black pepper

1 Soak the bread in water until soft. Heat about a quarter of the olive oil in a large pan and fry the onion and garlic for 3–4 minutes until the onion has softened.

2 Pour in the passata, mix well, season with salt and pepper and leave to simmer while you prepare the meatballs.

3 Put the pork and beef in a bowl and mix well, preferably with your hands. Add the eggs.

4 Drain the bread, squeeze it dry and mix the bread and eggs with the meat. Add the parsley and grated cheese, with salt and pepper to taste.

5 Work the mixture with your hands until all the ingredients are well distributed. Shape this mixture into little balls.

6 Heat the remaining oil in a large frying pan and shallow-fry the meatballs for about 5 minutes, until browned all over. Using tongs or a slotted spoon, transfer them to the tomato sauce and continue to cook for 10 minutes.

7 Remove the pan from the heat. Pour over the wine must. Leave to stand for 2–3 minutes.

8 Spoon the meatballs and sauce on to a heated serving platter and slip a few almond flakes into each meatball before serving.

COOK'S TIP

Wine must is wine that has just begun to ferment. If you can't find it, use good-quality, sweet balsamic vinegar instead. To make regular balsamic vinegar sweet and sticky, boil it fast in a wide pan for 15 minutes, or until sticky and reduced by about half. Cool and return to the bottle to use as normal.

CONIGLIO AI PEPERONI ALLA CALABRESE
CALABRIAN RABBIT AND RED PEPPER STEW

This simple rabbit recipe comes from the region of Calabria, the 'toe' of Italy's famous boot shape. It is a long, slow-cooked dish flavoured with rich red wine and deliciously sweet red peppers. In Calabria the rabbit used would probably be wild as they are readily available in this region as throughout the rest of Italy, and therefore the meat would be quite gamey in flavour. Farmed rabbit, on the other hand, has a much milder taste. You can use either.

SERVES 4

1 large rabbit, jointed
2 bay leaves
3 celery sticks, chopped
a handful of fresh parsley, chopped
5ml/1 tsp dried oregano
a handful of fresh basil leaves, lightly bruised
10 crushed peppercorns
350ml/12fl oz/1½ cups red wine
4 red bell peppers
90ml/6 tbsp olive oil
1 onion, thinly sliced
1 garlic clove, sliced
sea salt

1 Clean the rabbit carefully, rinse it and pat the pieces dry with kitchen paper. Place these in a deep bowl, then add the bay leaves, celery, parsley, oregano, basil leaves and peppercorns.

2 Pour over the wine, cover the bowl and leave to stand for 2–3 hours at cool room temperature, or overnight in the refrigerator.

3 Using a slotted spoon, lift the pieces of rabbit out of the marinade and put them in a colander. Drain for 30 minutes, reserving the marinade.

4 Halve the bell peppers, remove the seeds and cut the flesh into large square pieces.

5 Heat the oil in a flameproof casserole over a medium heat. Add the onion and garlic and fry for 2 minutes. Add the rabbit and fry, turning the pieces of rabbit occasionally, for 6–8 minutes, until the rabbit and onion have browned.

6 Pour in the marinade and add the peppers. Season with salt, stir, then cover tightly.

7 Simmer over a very low heat for about 50 minutes, or until the rabbit starts to fall off the bone and the peppers have cooked down to a thin purée. Serve in heated bowls.

COOK'S TIP

If the casserole is a bit watery at the end of the cooking time, simply remove the pieces of rabbit, raise the heat under the pan and boil the sauce, uncovered, until reduced and thickened. Return the rabbit to the pan and serve.

SERVES 4 TO 6

800g/1¾lb yellow pumpkin, peeled and seeded
60ml/4 tbsp coarse salt
sunflower oil for deep-frying
150ml/¼ pint/⅔ cup olive oil
60ml/4 tbsp red wine vinegar
45ml/3 tbsp salted capers, rinsed and finely chopped
5 garlic cloves, very thinly sliced
75ml/5 tbsp chopped fresh mint
120ml/8 tbsp fresh white breadcrumbs

COOK'S TIP

The red wine vinegar should be really strongly flavoured. This will give the dish plenty of sharpness, which cuts the sweetness of the pumpkin.

ZUCCA GIALLA ALLA CALABRESE
YELLOW PUMPKIN WITH MINT AND CAPERS

This colourful, tasty vegetable dish is almost a salad, and is good served with cold meats, especially roast beef. Pumpkins originated in Central America and would have found their way to Italy along with tomatoes, potatoes and tobacco, with New World explorers. This recipe calls for the yellow-fleshed pumpkin that holds its shape when fried, rather than disintegrating into mush.

1 Cut the pumpkin into neat, even slices. Spread these out in a colander and sprinkle with salt. Cover with a plate, put a weight on top and stand the colander in the sink. Leave it to drain for 1 hour.

2 Rinse the pumpkin to remove the excess salt. Drain well, then pat the pieces dry with kitchen paper.

3 Heat the sunflower oil in a wide pan until a small piece of bread, dropped into the oil, sizzles instantly.

4 Fry the pumpkin, in batches, for 4 minutes on each side, then lift them out with a slotted spoon and drain on kitchen paper.

5 In a bowl, mix together the oil, vinegar, capers, garlic, mint and half the breadcrumbs.

6 Spread out half the pumpkin in a shallow dish and spoon over half the dressing. Cover with the rest of the pumpkin, then the remaining dressing. Press down firmly and coat with the remaining breadcrumbs. Leave to stand for 1 hour before serving.

COSTE AL SUGO
CELERY IN TOMATO SAUCE

Celery and onion, which, along with carrot, are the constituent ingredients of the French mirepoix, are equally popular in Italian cooking as in French, forming the background flavouring for many savoury dishes. Stocks, stews, soups and sauces almost always contain celery, and in the south the leaves are often added for extra flavour, much as a herb might be.

SERVES 4

1 head of white celery, separated into sticks, leaves reserved
45ml/3 tbsp olive oil
3 garlic cloves, chopped
1 onion, chopped
2 x 400g/14oz cans plum tomatoes, drained and strained
sea salt and ground black pepper

1 Using a sharp knife, trim the celery sticks, removing any tough strings. Cut into chunks and place in a bowl. Chop the leaves finely; set them aside in a separate bowl.

2 Heat the olive oil in a large pan and add the garlic and onion. Cook for 6–8 minutes, until the onion has almost softened but not browned.

3 Stir in the prepared celery chunks. Cook for 5 minutes. Pour in the tomatoes, stir and season to taste. Cover the pan and simmer the mixture for about 15 minutes or until the celery is soft.

4 Stir in the chopped celery leaves, spoon the mixture into a heated dish and serve it hot or warm.

COOK'S TIP

Stringing the celery sticks is important, as the strings will not break down during the cooking process and if left, would spoil the dish.

TORTIERA DI CARCIOFI
SAVOURY ARTICHOKE CAKE

This lovely artichoke recipe comes from Calabria. Artichokes have been cultivated in Sicily since the time of the Greeks, who called them kaktos. It is thought that they were introduced to France, along with other Italian ingredients, by Catherine de' Medici. It is recorded in the journal of Pierre de L'Estoile on 19 June 1576, that at the wedding of two courtiers, Queen Catherine de' Medici 'ate so much that she thought she would die, and was very ill... They said it was from eating too many artichoke bottoms'. This is delicious served warm with a selection of salads.

SERVES 4

6 large artichokes
juice of ½ lemon
1 lemon, cut in half
120ml/8 tbsp olive oil
45ml/3 tbsp soft white breadcrumbs
2 garlic cloves, very finely chopped
45ml/3 tbsp chopped fresh parsley
50g/2oz/½ cup freshly grated pecorino cheese
4 medium to large potatoes
50g/2oz/⅓ cup capers, rinsed and roughly chopped
sea salt

COOK'S TIP

This savoury cake is delicious served just warm, accompanied by a selection of salads, such as a simple green salad and a tomato and red onion salad.

1 Before preparing the artichokes, fill a bowl with water and add the lemon juice. Remove the hard, outer leaves from the artichokes and cut off the stalks. Snip off the sharp tips with a pair of scissors. Halve the artichokes and cut out and discard the furry chokes. Rub all the pieces of artichoke with the cut lemon to prevent discoloration. Slice in half again, then slice each quarter into three segments. Drop the pieces of artichoke into the acidulated water and leave to soak for 30 minutes.

2 Preheat the oven to 160°C/325°F/Gas 3. Use a little of the olive oil to generously grease a 20cm/8in cake tin or pan that is at least 2cm/¾in deep. Add a quarter of the breadcrumbs to the tin. Turn and shake the tin to coat the sides and base with crumbs.

3 Put the remaining breadcrumbs in a bowl and add the garlic, parsley and pecorino cheese. Add a pinch of salt and about 15ml/1 tbsp of the olive oil.

4 Peel the potatoes and cut them in 2cm/¾in slices. Arrange a layer of potato slices on the base of the tin, taking care not to disturb the crumb lining. Sprinkle some of the capers and a little of the breadcrumbs over the potatoes.

5 Drain and dry the artichokes and arrange a layer of them over the breadcrumb mixture. Drizzle with olive oil. Repeat these layers until all the ingredients have been used, saving some oil to drizzle over the top. Press down to compress the layers. Fit a lid or heavy ovenproof plate inside the tin to keep the layers compressed. Bake for 50 minutes.

6 Turn the tin upside down so the lid or plate is underneath. Stand it in a roasting pan. Reduce the oven to 140°C/275°F/Gas 1. Bake for 30 minutes more.

7 Remove the tin from the oven and leave it to stand for 10 minutes before inverting the cake on to a platter. Serve warm or at room temperature.

PETRALI
CALABRIAN PASTRIES

To make these traditional pastries, the filling must be left for 12 hours before baking to allow the flavours to develop. Versions of these simple yet extremely rich pastries are found all over Calabria. It is quite likely that they were originally created in convents, where the nuns would busy themselves by preparing vast quantities to sell to the locals. In some parts of the region they are a traditional Christmas treat, but petrali are also made to celebrate St Martin's Day in summer, when they are known as pitte di San Martino.

MAKES ABOUT 20

500g/1lb/ 2½ cups plain/ all-purpose white flour
2 small/US medium egg yolks
75g/2oz/¼ cup lard or white cooking fat/shortening, diced
100g/4oz/scant ½ cup sugar
scant 40ml/2½ tbsp sweet vermouth
3½ml/¾ tsp baking powder
7.5ml/1½ tsp olive oil
icing/confectioners' sugar, for dusting

FOR THE FILLING

400g/14oz/2⅓ cups dried figs
400g/14oz/2⅓ cups whole blanched almonds
400g/14oz/2⅓ cups walnut halves
400g/14oz/1¾ cups clear honey
2.5ml/½ tsp ground cinnamon
2.5ml/½ tsp ground cloves
50ml/2fl oz/¼ cup sweet dessert wine

FOR THE ICING (OPTIONAL)

135ml/9 tbsp icing/ confectioners' sugar
multicoloured sugar strands

1 Start by making the filling. Cut the dried figs into quarters and put them in a pan. Slice the almonds in half and add them to the pan with the walnut halves, honey, spices and wine. Stir over a low heat for 10 minutes.

2 Remove the pan from the heat, cover and set aside for 12 hours.

3 To make the dough, put the flour on to a clean work top and make a hollow in the middle with your fist.

4 Put the egg yolks, lard or cooking fat, sugar, vermouth, baking powder and olive oil into the hollow. Mix together, gradually incorporating all of the surrounding flour to make a dough.

5 Knead the dough until smooth and elastic, but do not overwork it. Cover with clear film or plastic wrap and leave to rest for 30 minutes.

6 Roll out the dough on a lightly floured board to a thickness of 5mm/¼in. Using a 10–12cm/4–5in pastry cutter or upturned glass, cut it into rounds.

7 Spoon a little of the fig and nut mixture over one half of each round and fold over to make miniature pasties. Seal the edges carefully by pressing them together with the prongs of a fork. Alternatively, top the round with the fruit and nut mixture, leaving the pastry rim clear, and cover with a pastry lattice.

8 Preheat the oven to 180°C/350°F/Gas 4. Arrange the petrali on lightly oiled baking sheets. Bake them for 10–15 minutes, until pale golden.

9 Transfer them on to wire racks to cool completely.

10 Sprinkle the petrali with icing sugar. Alternatively, mix the icing sugar with enough water to make a thick, spreadable paste and spread the icing over the petrali. If you like you could also sprinkle them with multicoloured sugar strands before the icing sets.

ZEPPOLE A VENTO
HONEY-COATED FRITTERS

The ingredients for this very sticky, honey-coated Calabrian sweet could not be simpler, yet the skill of the local cooks transforms them into something that is pretty to look at and delicious to eat. Zeppole are traditionally made on La Festa di San Giuseppe (Saint Joseph's Day) on 19 March. In Rome, Naples and Sicily, these little pastries are sometimes sold on street corners and are given away as gifts. In certain parts of Calabria, savoury anchovy zeppole are eaten on New Year's Eve and New Year's Day.

MAKES ABOUT 30

500ml/17fl oz/generous 2 cups cold water
500g/1¼lb/5 cups very fine plain/all-purpose white flour or cake flour, sifted twice
light olive oil, for deep-frying
90ml/6 tbsp clear honey

1 Pour the water into a heavy pan and bring it to the boil. Gradually trickle in the flour, stirring constantly. Continue to stir until the mixture forms a dough and comes away from the sides of the pan. Turn the dough into a bowl and leave to cool completely.

2 Pinch off small pieces of dough and roll them into small sausage shapes about 5cm/2in long and 5mm/¼in wide. Squeeze each sausage in the middle to make a bow shape.

3 Heat the oil in a large pan until a cube of bread dropped into it sizzles instantly.

4 Add the dough shapes, in batches, and fry until they rise to the surface of the oil and turn golden and crisp.

5 As each batch cooks, lift the bows out with a slotted spoon and drain on kitchen paper. Place them on a warmed heatproof platter and keep them warm while cooking the remaining shapes.

6 Heat the honey in a small pan. When it bubbles, pour it all over the fritters. Allow the fritters to cool slightly, then serve them while warm.

COOK'S TIP

It is important to stir constantly while the flour mixture cooks, as this will prevent lumps from forming. The paste must be smooth. Serve the fritters with a dish of orange wedges, which will cut through the intense sweetness of the honey.

CROSTATA ALLA CREMA DI LIMONE
CALABRIAN LEMON TART

Citrus fruits come into their own under the baking-hot Calabrian sun. This tangy lemon tart uses freshly grated rind for an intense flavour. It is made with pre-prepared custard so is quick and easy to make – but you can make your own (see page 611). Serve with a small glass of limoncello for a delicious grown-up dessert.

1 Put the flour in a bowl. Add the chopped butter and rub it in with your fingers until the mixture resembles fine breadcrumbs.

2 Stir in the sugar and add the egg and egg yolk. Mix to a soft dough. Knead lightly in the bowl until it is just smooth, then wrap the dough in clear film or plastic wrap and chill for about 30 minutes.

3 While the pastry is resting, make the filling. Heat the custard in a pan and stir in the sugar and lemon rind until the sugar is dissolved. Cover the surface of the lemony custard with baking parchment and leave it to cool.

4 Preheat the oven to 180°C/350°F/Gas 4. Grease a 20cm/8in tart tin or pan with butter. Beat the ricotta into the custard, then add the beaten egg. Mix thoroughly until well combined.

5 On a large sheet of baking parchment, thinly roll out the pastry using a lightly floured rolling pin. Line the tart tin, pressing the pastry into the ridges, and trim the edges.

6 Pour the lemon filling into the tart case and bake in the oven for 30 minutes, until the filling is just set. Leave to cool, then dust with icing sugar. Serve at room temperature or cold.

SERVES 6

250g/9oz/2¼ cups plain/all-purpose flour, plus extra for dusting
125g/4¼oz/generous ½ cup cold unsalted butter, chopped, plus softened butter for greasing
115g/4oz/½ cup caster/superfine sugar
1 egg, plus 1 egg yolk
icing/confectioners' sugar, for dusting

FOR THE FILLING

250ml/8fl oz/generous 1 cup ready-made custard
115g/4oz/½ cup sugar
finely grated rind of 3–4 unwaxed lemons
250g/9oz/generous 1 cup ricotta cheese
1 egg, beaten

COOK'S TIP

When lining the tin or pan, take care not to stretch the pastry or it will shrink when it is baked.

SOSPIRI DI MONACA
NUN'S SIGHS

These sweet little buns are a traditional speciality of the town of Bagnara Calabra in the province of Reggio Calabria. They are made out of sponge cake, sandwiched together with custard and glazed with white icing, finished off with a halved red glacé cherry placed rather provocatively in the middle, which is why they are sometimes called tette di monaca, or nun's breasts!!

SERVES 8

FOR THE SPONGE
5 eggs
75g/3oz/6 tbsp caster/superfine sugar
150g/5oz/1¼ cups plain/all-purpose flour

FOR THE CUSTARD
1 litre/1¾ pints/4 cups full-fat/whole milk
8 egg yolks
200g/7oz/1 cup sugar
50g/2oz/½ cup plain/all-purpose flour
grated zest of 1 unwaxed lemon

FOR THE ICING
2 egg whites
300g/11oz/2⅔ cups icing/confectioners' sugar
few drops of lemon juice
red glacé/candied cherries, halved, to decorate

1 Preheat the oven to 180°C/350°F/Gas 4. Grease 8 muffin cases and place in a muffin tin or pan.

2 First make the sponge for the buns. Beat the eggs in a large bowl with a balloon or electric whisk until thick and pale, gradually adding the sugar. Sift in the flour very slowly, folding it into the mixture a little at a time.

3 Pour the mixture into the muffin cases and bake for 15–20 minutes. Cool in the muffin cases while you make the custard.

4 Pour the milk into a pan and heat until it is just below boiling point.

5 Beat the eggs and sugar together in a second pan until thickened, then gradually sift in the flour. Gradually add the hot milk, whisking constantly.

6 Add the grated lemon zest and keep stirring until the custard thickens and comes to a slow boil. Allow to boil gently for about 3 minutes, then remove from the heat and pour into a bowl to cool.

7 For the icing, whisk the egg whites until foaming and thick but not stiff. Gradually sift in the icing sugar and fold through the egg white. Stir in the lemon juice and stir until the icing forms a continuous ribbon when you lift up the spoon, then set aside.

8 Remove the buns from their muffin cases and split them in half, then sandwich them back together with the cooled custard.

9 Cover the buns smoothly with the icing and place a halved cherry in the middle of each one before serving.

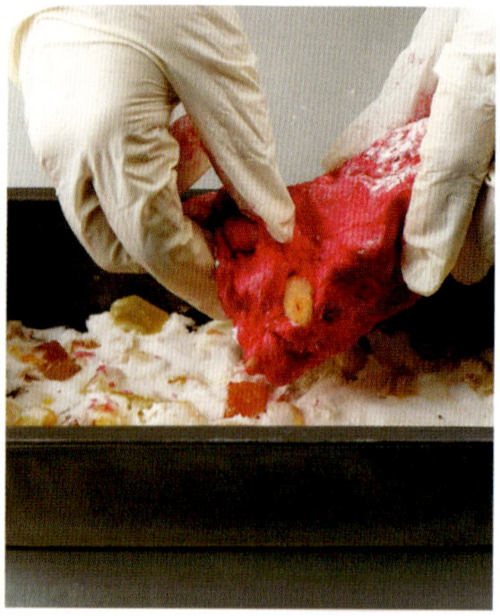

TORRONE GELATO

CALABRIAN FROZEN NOUGAT

This extremely sweet dessert is best served with chilled semi-sweet white wine. It is not real nougat, but a variation on the theme. Making it takes skill and requires the use of a loaf tin or terrine, but the final result looks so spectacular that the effort is certainly worthwhile. It is important to use good-quality candied fruit. In Calabria, candied fruit nearly always includes thick pieces of the locally grown limes, oranges and tangerines, and is very special.

1 Line a 1.3kg/3lb loaf tin or pan or several smaller tins with clear film or plastic wrap, leaving plenty of overhang. Grease with almond oil.

2 Put the icing sugar in a large bowl. Stir in just enough lemon juice to make a mixture that resembles dough. It should be neither runny nor hard, but malleable enough to be kneaded.

3 Divide the mixture into three equal parts. Knead the lemon extract into the first part, the red food colouring into the second part and the cocoa into the third, making sure that the colourings and flavourings are evenly distributed in each case.

4 Mix the almonds and candied fruit in a bowl. Divide the mixture into three parts and add one part to each quantity of sugar paste.

5 Add one of the pieces of sugar paste to the tin and press it down to form an even layer. Mould the second piece of paste to the shape of the tin and press it evenly on top of the first layer. Top with the third layer of sugar paste.

6 Bring the surplus clear film lining over the paste to enclose it and then add a weight to compress the moulded mixture evenly. Chill in the refrigerator for 3 days.

7 Put the chocolate in a heatproof bowl over a small pan of boiling water. Immediately remove from the heat and leave for 5 minutes or until the chocolate has melted, stirring occasionally.

8 Remove the weight from the mould, unfold the covering, invert it on a board and unwrap it. Thickly spread the melted chocolate over the mould and chill until hard. Serve in thin slices.

SERVES 24

- almond oil, for greasing
- 1kg/2¼lb/9 cups icing/confectioners' sugar, sifted
- juice of 1 or 2 lemons (see Cook's Tip)
- 3 drops lemon extract
- 3 drops red food colouring
- 25g/1oz/4 tbsp unsweetened cocoa powder
- 50g/2oz/½ cup blanched almonds, roughly chopped
- 275g/10oz/2 cups assorted candied fruit, roughly chopped
- 225g/8oz dark/bittersweet chocolate, broken into pieces

COOK'S TIP

Lemons vary considerably in size and in the amount of juice they contain. Use just enough to make a malleable paste. To spread the paste in the pan or mould, use a metal spoon dipped in boiling water.

NUTRITIONAL INFORMATION

The nutritional analysis given for each recipe is calculated per portion (i.e. serving or item), unless otherwise stated. If the recipe gives a range, such as Serves 4–6, then the nutritional analysis will be for the smaller portion size, i.e. 6 servings. The analysis does not include optional ingredients, such as salt added to taste.

18 La Sfloglia Energy 439kcal/1858kJ; Protein 17.5g; Carbohydrate 77.7g, of which sugars 1.5g; Fat 8.6g, of which saturates 2.2g; Cholesterol 250mg; Calcium 177mg; Fibre 4.1g; Sodium 94mg.

18 Orecchiette Energy 1364kcal/5800kJ; Protein 37.6g; Carbohydrate 310.8g, of which sugars 6g; Fat 5.2g, of which saturates 0.8g; Cholesterol 0mg; Calcium 560mg; Fibre 16.5g; Sodium 12mg.

20 White Sauce Energy 1016kcal/4276kJ; Protein 25.4g; Carbohydrate 76g, of which sugars 30.3g; Fat 69.3g, of which saturates 44.2g; Cholesterol 203mg; Calcium 744mg; Fibre 2.5g; Sodium 302mg.

20 Basic Tomato Sauce Energy 199kcal/850kJ; Protein 7.7g; Carbohydrate 37.4g, of which sugars 35.7g; Fat 3.3g, of which saturates 1g; Cholesterol 0mg; Calcium 116mg; Fibre 16g; Sodium 131mg.

21 L'arrabiata Energy 543kcal/2260kJ; Protein 9.6g; Carbohydrate 27.3g, of which sugars 22.7g; Fat 44.9g, of which saturates 6.3g; Cholesterol 0mg; Calcium 100mg; Fibre 8.6g; Sodium 313mg.

21 Ragù Energy 459kcal/1908kJ; Protein 28.6g; Carbohydrate 9.7g, of which sugars 7.9g; Fat 30.6g, of which saturates 8.1g; Cholesterol 71mg; Calcium 54mg; Fibre 2.9g; Sodium 317mg.

25 Basic Polenta Energy 153kcal/642kJ; Protein 3.9g; Carbohydrate 30.5g, of which sugars 0g; Fat 1.4g, of which saturates 0g; Cholesterol 0mg; Calcium 1mg; Fibre 1.2g; Sodium 0mg.

60 Salsa Peverada Energy 206kcal/850kJ; Protein 7.7g; Carbohydrate 0g, of which sugars 0g; Fat 19.4g, of which saturates 3.4g; Cholesterol 117mg; Calcium 10mg; Fibre 0g; Sodium 303mg.

60 Pesto Energy 2080kcal/8573kJ; Protein 25.4g; Carbohydrate 8.1g, of which sugars 4.1g; Fat 216.5g, of which saturates 29.4g; Cholesterol 23mg; Calcium 455mg; Fibre 2.5g; Sodium 197mg.

61 Basic Pizza Dough Energy 243kcal/1034kJ; Protein 7.8g; Carbohydrate 52g, of which sugars 1g; Fat 1.9g, of which saturates 0.3g; Cholesterol 0mg; Calcium 97mg; Fibre 2.8g; Sodium 4mg.

61 Basic Bread Dough Energy 1652kcal/7011kJ; Protein 46.3g; Carbohydrate 350g, of which sugars 6.8g; Fat 17g, of which saturates 2.5g; Cholesterol 0mg; Calcium 639mg; Fibre 18.6g; Sodium 1984mg.

80 Bagna Càuda with Roasted Peppers Energy 559kcal/2312kJ; Protein 3g; Carbohydrate 15g, of which sugars 13g; Fat 55g, of which saturates 16g; Cholesterol 44mg; Calcium 26mg; Fibre 3.6g; Sodium 13mg.

82 Baked Chickpea Flour Pancakes Energy 202kcal/868kJ; Protein 7g; Carbohydrate 19g, of which sugars 1g; Fat 12g, of which saturates 2g; Cholesterol 0mg; Calcium 68mg; Fibre 4g; Sodium 15mg.

83 Cheese and Walnut Patties Energy 474kcal/1971kJ; Protein 26g; Carbohydrate 15g, of which sugars 3g; Fat 35g, of which saturates 16g; Cholesterol 73mg; Calcium 414mg; Fibre 1.5g; Sodium 659mg.

84 Piedmontese Fonduta Energy 768kcal/3181kJ; Protein 36g; Carbohydrate 6g, of which sugars 3g; Fat 67g, of which saturates 40g; Cholesterol 356mg; Calcium 1162mg; Fibre 0.2g; Sodium 958mg.

85 Parmesan and Truffle Canapés Energy 314kcal/1433kJ; Protein 12g; Carbohydrate 24g, of which sugars 2g; Fat 23g, of which saturates 14g; Cholesterol 62mg; Calcium 274mg; Fibre 2g; Sodium 404mg.

86 Cavour Artichokes Energy 264kcal/1106kJ; Protein 10g; Carbohydrate 2g, of which sugars 1g; Fat 25g, of which saturates 15g; Cholesterol 158mg; Calcium 162mg; Fibre 0.1g; Sodium 194mg.

87 Rabbit Antipasto Energy 468kcal/1937kJ; Protein 28g; Carbohydrate 4g, of which sugars 3g; Fat 38g, of which saturates 7g; Cholesterol 106mg; Calcium 67mg; Fibre 1.1g; Sodium 76mg.

88 Cheese and Mushroom Cannelloni Energy 787kcal/3279kJ; Protein 27g; Carbohydrate 42g, of which sugars 7g; Fat 58g, of which saturates 30g; Cholesterol 117mg; Calcium 526mg; Fibre 2.5g; Sodium 472mg.

90 Gnocchi with Gorgonzola Energy 646kcal/2705kJ; Protein 20g; Carbohydrate 71g, of which sugars 5g; Fat 33g, of which saturates 10g; Cholesterol 148mg; Calcium 350mg; Fibre 3.7g; Sodium 600mg.

92 Barolo Risotto Energy 772kcal/3237kJ; Protein 32g; Carbohydrate 87g, of which sugars 5g; Fat 23g, of which saturates 14g; Cholesterol 84mg; Calcium 244mg; Fibre 1.1g; Sodium 164mg.

94 Piedmontese Risotto Energy 430kcal/1979kJ; Protein 11g; Carbohydrate 63g, of which sugars 1g; Fat 14g, of which saturates 8g; Cholesterol 35mg; Calcium 127mg; Fibre 0.1g; Sodium 1013mg.

95 Chicken with Juniper Energy 365kcal/1525kJ; Protein 38g; Carbohydrate 7g, of which sugars 6g; Fat 16g, of which saturates 5g; Cholesterol 147mg; Calcium 53mg; Fibre 1.7g; Sodium 638mg.

96 Chicken Marengo Energy 974kcal/4056kJ; Protein 59g; Carbohydrate 33g, of which sugars 5g; Fat 65g, of which saturates 12g; Cholesterol 415mg; Calcium 158mg; Fibre 2.6g; Sodium 439mg.

98 Guinea Fowl with Barolo Energy 685kcal/2854kJ; Protein 40g; Carbohydrate 9g, of which sugars 4g; Fat 36g, of which saturates 16g; Cholesterol 119mg; Calcium 72mg; Fibre 0.9g; Sodium 210mg.

99 Veal with Marsala Energy 299kcal/1260kJ; Protein 35g; Carbohydrate 4g, of which sugars 2g; Fat 13g, of which saturates 8g; Cholesterol 107mg; Calcium 18mg; Fibre 0.2g; Sodium 93mg.

100 Braised Beef in Barolo Energy 906kcal/3777kJ; Protein 89g; Carbohydrate 7g, of which sugars 3g; Fat 48g, of which saturates 19g; Cholesterol 268mg; Calcium 47mg; Fibre 1g; Sodium 200mg.

102 Piedmontese Egg and Cheese Custard Energy 355kcal/1468kJ; Protein 8g; Carbohydrate 6g, of which sugars 6g; Fat 33g, of which saturates 19g; Cholesterol 229mg; Calcium 194mg; Fibre 0.4g; Sodium 90mg.

103 Salsa Verde Energy 125kcal/522kJ; Protein 3g; Carbohydrate 8g, of which sugars 1g; Fat 9g, of which saturates 1g; Cholesterol 49mg; Calcium 36mg; Fibre 0.6g; Sodium 138mg.

104 Baked Peaches Energy 217kcal/913kJ; Protein 4g; Carbohydrate 30g, of which sugars 28g; Fat 8g, of which saturates 3g; Cholesterol 6mg; Calcium 28mg; Fibre 2.9g; Sodium 7mg.

106 Pears Poached in Red Wine Energy 196kcal/826kJ; Protein 1g; Carbohydrate 29g, of which sugars 29g; Fat 0g, of which saturates 0g; Cholesterol 0mg; Calcium 27mg; Fibre 2.6g; Sodium 14mg.

107 Zabaglione Energy 134kcal/563kJ; Protein 3g; Carbohydrate 17g, of which sugars 17g; Fat 5g, of which saturates 2g; Cholesterol 202mg; Calcium 27mg; Fibre 0g; Sodium 12mg.

108 Piedmontese Chocolate Pudding Energy 409kcal/1712kJ; Protein 16g; Carbohydrate 55g, of which sugars 44g; Fat 15g, of which saturates 4g; Cholesterol 198mg; Calcium 184mg; Fibre 0.7g; Sodium 131mg.

110 Panna Cotta Energy 302kcal/1255kJ; Protein 4g; Carbohydrate 18g, of which sugars 18g; Fat 24g, of which saturates 15g; Cholesterol 69mg; Calcium 113mg; Fibre 0g; Sodium 39mg.

112 Chestnut, Cream, Meringue and Chocolate Mountain Energy 671kcal/2804kJ; Protein 4g; Carbohydrate 80g, of which sugars 55g; Fat 39g, of which saturates 23g; Cholesterol 86mg; Calcium 79mg; Fibre 3.8g; Sodium 40mg.

116 Recco's Olive Oil Focaccia Energy 511kcal/2163kJ; Protein 18g; Carbohydrate 94g, of which sugars 2g; Fat 9g, of which saturates 1g; Cholesterol 0mg; Calcium 184mg; Fibre 3.9g; Sodium 3448mg.

118 Tomato and Anchovy Pizza Energy 813kcal/3402kJ; Protein 19g; Carbohydrate 82g, of which sugars 8g; Fat 48g, of which saturates 7g; Cholesterol 12mg; Calcium 22mg; Fibre 5.3g; Sodium 908mg.

120 Ligurian Seafood Salad Energy 697kcal/2921kJ; Protein 96g; Carbohydrate 12g, of which sugars 0g; Fat 30g, of which saturates 5g; Cholesterol 578mg; Calcium 370mg; Fibre 0.1g; Sodium 3971mg.

122 Smooth Ligurian Fish Soup Energy 477kcal/2005kJ; Protein 33g; Carbohydrate 36g, of which sugars 3g; Fat 23g, of which saturates 3g; Cholesterol 23mg; Calcium 103mg; Fibre 2g; Sodium 485mg.

123 Genoese-style Trenette with Pesto Energy 1049kcal/ 4364kJ; Protein 19g; Carbohydrate 72g, of which sugars 5g; Fat 78g, of which saturates 10g; Cholesterol 6mg; Calcium 160mg; Fibre 5.3g; Sodium 62mg.

124 Genoese Tuna Energy 553kcal/2298kJ; Protein 37g; Carbohydrate 2g, of which sugars 1g; Fat 41g, of which saturates 7g; Cholesterol 42mg; Calcium 41mg; Fibre 1.2g; Sodium 77mg.

126 Whitebait with Lemon Energy 418kcal/1734kJ; Protein 23g; Carbohydrate 0g, of which sugars 0g; Fat 36g, of which saturates 6g; Cholesterol 116mg; Calcium 122mg; Fibre 0g; Sodium 250mg.

127 Stuffed Baby Squid Energy 521kcal/2191kJ; Protein 50g; Carbohydrate 26g, of which sugars 1g; Fat 25g, of which saturates 4g; Cholesterol 677mg; Calcium 89mg; Fibre 0.8g; Sodium 667mg.

128 Sea Bream with Pine Kernels and Olives Energy 373kcal/1550kJ; Protein 20g; Carbohydrate 12g, of which sugars 1g; Fat 24g, of which saturates 3g; Cholesterol 38mg; Calcium 66mg; Fibre 1.8g; Sodium 773mg.

129 Tomaselle Energy 502kcal/2096kJ; Protein 46g; Carbohydrate 10g, of which sugars 5g; Fat 28g, of which saturates 6g; Cholesterol 90mg; Calcium 277mg; Fibre 5.2g; Sodium 506mg.

130 Lasagna with Pesto and Potatoes Energy 600kcal/2526kJ; Protein 26g; Carbohydrate 61g, of which sugars 9g; Fat 30g, of which saturates 16g; Cholesterol 71mg; Calcium 591mg; Fibre 2.9g; Sodium 367mg.

134 Minestrone Soup Energy 386kcal/1625kJ; Protein 15g; Carbohydrate 54g, of which sugars 5g; Fat 13g, of which saturates 3g; Cholesterol 5mg; Calcium 171mg; Fibre 3.2g; Sodium 111mg.

136 Trout with a Gonzga-style Sauce Energy 330kcal/1382kJ; Protein 40.4g; Carbohydrate 7.5g, of which sugars 6.4g; Fat 13.6g, of which saturates 2.6g; Cholesterol 161mg; Calcium 90mg; Fibre 2.4g; Sodium 247mg.

137 Trout Dogana Style Energy 420kcal/1751kJ; Protein 30g; Carbohydrate 3g, of which sugars 3g; Fat 23g, of which saturates 4g; Cholesterol 101mg; Calcium 56mg; Fibre 0.7g; Sodium 103mg.

138 Bresaola with Parmesan and Rocket Energy 307kcal/1275kJ; Protein 35g; Carbohydrate 1g, of which sugars 1g; Fat 18g, of which saturates 5g; Cholesterol 17mg; Calcium 222mg; Fibre 0.2g; Sodium 142mg.

139 Steak Rolls with Fruit Mustard Energy 347kcal/825kJ; Protein 74g; Carbohydrate 4g, of which sugars 2g; Fat 49g, of which saturates 22g; Cholesterol 302mg; Calcium 158mg; Fibre 0.9g; Sodium 1018mg.

140 Stewed Ossobucco Energy 347kcal/1448kJ; Protein 28g; Carbohydrate 9g, of which sugars 7g; Fat 14g, of which saturates 3g; Cholesterol 105mg; Calcium 54mg;

Fibre 2g; Sodium 195mg.

141 Veal Chop Milanese Style Energy 527kcal/2221kJ; Protein 40g; Carbohydrate 22g, of which sugars 8g; Fat 32g, of which saturates 19g; Cholesterol 256mg; Calcium 232mg; Fibre 0.4g; Sodium 327mg.

142 Cold Veal with Tuna Mayonnaise Energy 669kcal/2779kJ; Protein 41g; Carbohydrate 6g, of which sugars 4g; Fat 45g, of which saturates 8g; Cholesterol 179mg; Calcium 47mg; Fibre 0.7g; Sodium 998mg.

144 Bollito Misto Energy 740kcal/3048kJ; Protein 76g; Carbohydrate 11g, of which sugars 6g; Fat 44g, of which saturates 12g; Cholesterol 332mg; Calcium 166mg; Fibre 1.4g; Sodium 1268mg.

146 Potato and Leek Frittata with Taleggio Energy 325kcal/1353kJ; Protein 22g; Carbohydrate 10g, of which sugars 4g; Fat 22g, of which saturates 9g; Cholesterol 263mg; Calcium 408mg; Fibre 2.5g; Sodium 341mg.

148 Classic Milanese Risotto Energy 484kcal/2023kJ; Protein 10g; Carbohydrate 64g, of which sugars 1g; Fat 20g, of which saturates 12g; Cholesterol 52mg; Calcium 105mg; Fibre 0.2g; Sodium 763mg.

150 Courgettes with Breadcrumbs Energy 191kcal/788kJ; Protein 4g; Carbohydrate 9g, of which sugars 7g; Fat 16g, of which saturates 2g; Cholesterol 0mg; Calcium 57mg; Fibre 2.4g; Sodium 4mg.

151 Daisy Cake Energy 386kcal/1620kJ; Protein 8g; Carbohydrate 32g, of which sugars 12g; Fat 26g, of which saturates 15g; Cholesterol 231mg; Calcium 65mg; Fibre 0.6g; Sodium 130mg.

152 Italian Apple Cake Energy 415kcal/1756kJ; Protein 8g; Carbohydrate 79g, of which sugars 56g; Fat 10g, of which saturates 5g; Cholesterol 114mg; Calcium 118mg; Fibre 3.6g; Sodium 235mg.

154 Italian Chocolate Cake Energy 757kcal/3181kJ; Protein 12g; Carbohydrate 90g, of which sugars 77g; Fat 42g, of which saturates 24g; Cholesterol 201mg; Calcium 87mg; Fibre 2.9g; Sodium 162mg.

158 Cured Ham and Melon Energy 392kcal/1661kJ; Protein 57g; Carbohydrate 19g, of which sugars 19g; Fat 10g, of which saturates 3g; Cholesterol 174mg; Calcium 74mg; Fibre 2.2g; Sodium 3647mg.

159 Mortadella, Mushrooms and Parmesan Energy 429kcal/1776kJ; Protein 19g; Carbohydrate 1g, of which sugars 1g; Fat 39g, of which saturates 14g; Cholesterol 64mg; Calcium 325mg; Fibre 0.6g; Sodium 655mg.

160 Ricotta Ravioli Energy 616kcal/2579kJ; Protein 28g; Carbohydrate 27g, of which sugars 2g; Fat 44g, of which saturates 26g; Cholesterol 350mg; Calcium 505mg; Fibre 0.7g; Sodium 379mg.

162 Anchovy and White Fish Ravioli Energy 425kcal/1791kJ; Protein 24g; Carbohydrate 55g, of which sugars 3g; Fat 14g, of which saturates 3g; Cholesterol 183mg; Calcium 104mg; Fibre 2.7g; Sodium 210mg.

164 Tortellini in Broth Energy 752kcal/3151kJ; Protein 48g; Carbohydrate 61g, of which sugars 6g; Fat 37g, of which saturates 14g; Cholesterol 353mg; Calcium 306mg; Fibre 3.5g; Sodium 619mg.

166 Classic Ragù Bolognese Energy 584kcal/2433kJ; Protein 28g; Carbohydrate 6g, of which sugars 5g; Fat 50g, of which saturates 28g; Cholesterol 249mg; Calcium 42mg; Fibre 1.3g; Sodium 821mg.

168 White Ragù with Garganelli Energy 869kcal/3654kJ; Protein 36g; Carbohydrate 80g, of which sugars 6g; Fat 43g, of which saturates 26g; Cholesterol 193mg; Calcium 76mg; Fibre 3.8g; Sodium 282mg.

170 Lasagna in the Ferrara Style Energy 953kcal/3996kJ; Protein 46g; Carbohydrate 62g, of which sugars 11g; Fat 57g, of which saturates 31g; Cholesterol 320mg; Calcium 521mg; Fibre 4.2g; Sodium 1051mg.

172 Romagnola-style Poached Sea Bass Energy 357kcal/1500kJ; Protein 58g; Carbohydrate 3g, of which sugars 3g; Fat 8g, of which saturates 1g; Cholesterol 240mg; Calcium 408mg; Fibre 0.6g; Sodium 216mg.

173 Monkfish Wrapped in Parma Ham Energy 390kcal/1630kJ; Protein 42g; Carbohydrate 0g, of which sugars 0g; Fat 25g, of which saturates 4g; Cholesterol 28mg; Calcium 16mg; Fibre 0g; Sodium 836mg.

174 Chicken Breast in the Modenese Style Energy 445kcal/1867kJ; Protein 43g; Carbohydrate 8g, of which sugars 1g; Fat 27g, of which saturates 16g; Cholesterol 173mg; Calcium 145mg; Fibre 0.3g; Sodium 276mg.

176 Bolognese Lamb Cutlets Energy 588kcal/2453kJ; Protein 43g; Carbohydrate 17g, of which sugars 0g; Fat 39g, of which saturates 14g; Cholesterol 192mg; Calcium 156mg; Fibre 0.6g; Sodium 690mg.

177 Fennel with Parmesan Energy 361kcal/1507kJ; Protein 12g; Carbohydrate 3g, of which sugars 2g; Fat 34g, of which saturates 22g; Cholesterol 96mg; Calcium 350mg; Fibre 3g; Sodium 250mg.

178 Courgette Tart Energy 790kcal/3308kJ; Protein 31g; Carbohydrate 42g, of which sugars 4g; Fat 57g, of which saturates 35g; Cholesterol 316mg; Calcium 573mg; Fibre 2.7g; Sodium 420mg.

194 Grilled Mixed Seafood Energy 367kcal/1530kJ; Protein 23.9g; Carbohydrate 16.8g, of which sugars 4.4g; Fat 23.1g, of which saturates 5.9g; Cholesterol 184mg; Calcium 299mg; Fibre 2.5g; Sodium 516mg.

196 Doge's Soup Energy 415kcal/1726kJ; Protein 10.7g; Carbohydrate 36.9g, of which sugars 4.1g; Fat 25.1g, of which saturates 5.8g; Cholesterol 48mg; Calcium 197mg; Fibre 1.6g; Sodium 200mg.

198 Bread Dumplings Energy 584kcal/2447kJ; Protein 18.5g; Carbohydrate 63.9g, of which sugars 5.8g; Fat 30.2g, of which saturates 16.7g; Cholesterol 255mg; Calcium 243mg; Fibre 4.6g; Sodium 763mg.

199 Venetian Bean and Pasta Soup Energy 456kcal/1920kJ; Protein 24.7g; Carbohydrate 59.9g, of which sugars 6.7g; Fat 14.8g, of which saturates 2.9g; Cholesterol 12mg; Calcium 122mg; Fibre 12.9g; Sodium 267mg.

200 Venetian Rice and Bean Soup Energy 703kcal/2922kJ; Protein 12.3g; Carbohydrate 74.2g, of which sugars 4.5g; Fat 39.4g, of which saturates 15.4g; Cholesterol 47mg; Calcium 49mg; Fibre 7.3g; Sodium 116mg.

202 Soft Ricotta Polenta Energy 653kcal/2732kJ; Protein 23.7g; Carbohydrate 38.9g, of which sugars 0.8g; Fat 45.6g, of which saturates 28.1g; Cholesterol 132mg; Calcium 299mg; Fibre 1.9g; Sodium 798mg.

204 Basic Polenta Energy 238kcal/992kJ; Protein 9.8g; Carbohydrate 24.4g, of which sugars 0g; Fat 11g, of which saturates 6.2g; Cholesterol 25mg; Calcium 168mg; Fibre 0.7g; Sodium 420mg.

205 Dressed Polenta Energy 770kcal/3200kJ; Protein 21.5g; Carbohydrate 68.8g, of which sugars 4.8g; Fat 44.2g, of which saturates 27g; Cholesterol 120mg; Calcium 306mg; Fibre 1.9g; Sodium 465mg.

206 Polenta Gnocchi Energy 557kcal/2320kJ; Protein 20.4g; Carbohydrate 62.3g, of which sugars 1.8g; Fat 24.6g, of which saturates 10.4g; Cholesterol 114mg; Calcium 174mg; Fibre 2.9g; Sodium 296mg.

208 Grilled Polenta with Mushrooms Energy 518kcal/2155kJ; Protein 18.9g; Carbohydrate 46.2g, of which sugars 0.3g; Fat 27.2g, of which saturates 16.1g; Cholesterol 69mg; Calcium 334mg; Fibre 2.5g; Sodium 397mg.

209 Savoury Polenta Cake Energy 599kcal/2494kJ; Protein 16.1g; Carbohydrate 61.4g, of which sugars 0.7g; Fat 32.1g, of which saturates 11.4g; Cholesterol 174mg; Calcium 54mg; Fibre 1.9g; Sodium 448mg.

210 Venetian Stewed Peas Energy 366kcal/1520kJ; Protein 24.8g; Carbohydrate 40.3g, of which sugars 9.5g; Fat 13g, of which saturates 6.6g; Cholesterol 22mg; Calcium 79mg; Fibre 21.5g; Sodium 133mg.

211 Venetian Rice and Peas Energy 680kcal/2832kJ; Protein 23.9g; Carbohydrate 73.4g, of which sugars 3.9g; Fat 32.2g, of which saturates 14g; Cholesterol 57mg; Calcium 299mg; Fibre 6.7g; Sodium 383mg.

212 Rice and Sausages Energy 995kcal/4133kJ; Protein 26.2g; Carbohydrate 85.9g, of which sugars 3.4g; Fat 57.5g, of which saturates 27.3g; Cholesterol 112mg; Calcium 312mg; Fibre 0.8g; Sodium 1360mg.

214 Risotto with Trout Energy 615kcal/2565kJ; Protein 29.9g; Carbohydrate 70.1g, of which sugars 0.3g; Fat 20.3g, of which saturates 11.2g; Cholesterol 139mg; Calcium 59mg; Fibre 0g; Sodium 229mg.

216 Risotto of the Serene Republic Guards Energy 580kcal/2421kJ; Protein 39g; Carbohydrate 61g, of which sugars 0.9g; Fat 19.5g, of which saturates 11.1g; Cholesterol 98mg; Calcium 213mg; Fibre 0.2g; Sodium 348mg.

217 Marinated Herring with Onions Energy 302kcal/1254kJ; Protein 19g; Carbohydrate 10.2g, of which sugars 7.3g; Fat 20.9g, of which saturates 3.9g; Cholesterol 36mg; Calcium 124mg; Fibre 2.4g; Sodium 146mg.

218 Sweet-and-sour Fried Sardines Energy 729kcal/3037kJ; Protein 41.5g; Carbohydrate 31.8g, of which sugars 27.9g; Fat 49.4g, of which saturates 7.5g; Cholesterol 0mg; Calcium 203mg; Fibre 3.4g; Sodium 213mg.

219 Whipped Salt Cod in the Venetian Style Energy 435kcal/1803kJ; Protein 30.7g; Carbohydrate 0.2g, of which sugars 0.2g; Fat 34.6g, of which saturates 4.8g; Cholesterol 77mg; Calcium 28mg; Fibre 0.3g; Sodium 102mg.

220 Salt Cod in the Vicenza Style Energy 560kcal/2334kJ; Protein 44.5g; Carbohydrate 22.7g, of which sugars 12.7g; Fat 32.9g, of which saturates 13.3g; Cholesterol 147mg; Calcium 267mg; Fibre 1.2g; Sodium 319mg.

221 Squid Cooked in its Own Ink Energy 254kcal/1065kJ; Protein 31.1g; Carbohydrate 2.7g, of which sugars 0.3g; Fat 11.8g, of which saturates 2g; Cholesterol 450mg; Calcium 43mg; Fibre 0.4g; Sodium 223mg.

222 Spiced Squid Casserole Energy 220kcal/924kJ; Protein 26.4g; Carbohydrate 5.9g, of which sugars 3.1g; Fat 10.3g, of which saturates 1.6g; Cholesterol 375mg; Calcium 33mg; Fibre 0.9g; Sodium 190mg.

223 Wrapped Scallops Energy 299kcal/1247kJ; Protein 30.7g; Carbohydrate 3.8g, of which sugars 0.4g; Fat 17.9g, of which saturates 5g; Cholesterol 77mg; Calcium 39mg; Fibre 0.2g; Sodium 764mg.

224 Scallops Cooked in the Venetian Style Energy 367kcal/1526kJ; Protein 24.7g; Carbohydrate 4.8g, of which sugars 1.2g; Fat 27g, of which saturates 3.9g; Cholesterol 47mg; Calcium 130mg; Fibre 2.5g; Sodium 197mg.

225 Fried Venetian Chicken Energy 821kcal/3405kJ; Protein 45.6g; Carbohydrate 14.5g, of which sugars 0.5g; Fat 64.9g, of which saturates 13.5g; Cholesterol 310mg; Calcium 52mg; Fibre 0.4g; Sodium 324mg.

226 Venetian Stuffed Chicken 601kcal/2489kJ; Protein 43.3g; Carbohydrate 0g, of which sugars 0g; Fat 47.4g, of which saturates 15.8g; Cholesterol 250mg; Calcium 16mg; Fibre 0g; Sodium 458mg.

227 Pork Cooked in Milk Energy 679kcal/2834kJ; Protein 77.1g; Carbohydrate 3.3g, of which sugars 3.3g; Fat 29.2g, of which saturates 14g; Cholesterol 231mg; Calcium 103mg; Fibre 0g; Sodium 280mg.

228 Venetian Stuffed Duck Energy 569kcal/2361kJ; Protein 35.3g; Carbohydrate 1.6g, of which sugars 1.5g; Fat 45g, of which saturates 13.7g; Cholesterol 280mg; Calcium 52mg; Fibre 0g; Sodium 426mg.

230 Guinea Fowl in Red Wine Energy 586kcal/2449kJ; Protein 59.1g; Carbohydrate 13.1g, of which sugars 6.1g; Fat 24.2g, of which saturates 10.5g; Cholesterol 37mg; Calcium 115mg; Fibre 1.6g; Sodium 417mg.

232 Lamb and Pork Pie Energy 358kcal/1500kJ; Protein 22.1g; Carbohydrate 31g, of which sugars 2.4g; Fat 17g, of which saturates 5.0g; Cholesterol 68mg; Calcium 72mg; Fibre 2.5g; Sodium 67mg.

234 Venetian Beef Stew Energy 467kcal/1946kJ; Protein 42.2g; Carbohydrate 8.6g, of which sugars 6.9g; Fat 20.3g, of which saturates 7.9g; Cholesterol 109mg; Calcium 44mg; Fibre 1.8g; Sodium 377mg

236 Paparele with Chicken Livers Energy 526kcal/2211kJ; Protein 25.7g; Carbohydrate 59.3g, of which sugars 1.0g; Fat 20.7g, of which saturates 11.6g; Cholesterol 351mg; Calcium 316mg; Fibre 3g; Sodium 330mg.

237 Liver Cooked in the Venetian Style Energy 465kcal/1932kJ; Protein 27.5g; Carbohydrate 17.1g, of which sugars 10.8g; Fat 24.2g, of which saturates 8.2g; Cholesterol 552mg; Calcium 61mg; Fibre 2.6g; Sodium 149mg.

238 Rice and Asparagus Frittata Energy 463kcal/1924kJ; Protein 24.2g; Carbohydrate 25.9g, of which sugars 2.6g; Fat 29.3g, of which saturates 15.4g; Cholesterol 358mg; Calcium 227mg; Fibre 1.5g; Sodium 728mg.

240 Radicchio Frittata Energy 539kcal/2236kJ; Protein 33.1g; Carbohydrate 0.9g, of which sugars 0.9g; Fat 45g, of which saturates 22g; Cholesterol 327mg; Calcium 807mg; Fibre 0g; Sodium 827mg.

241 Radicchio with Beans Energy 493kcal/2079kJ; Protein 34g; Carbohydrate 56.4g, of which sugars 4.4g; Fat 16.2g, of which saturates 5.4g; Cholesterol 27mg; Calcium 149mg; Fibre 20.3g; Sodium 52mg.

242 Venetian-Style Treviso Radicchio Energy 180kcal/743kJ; Protein 4.5g; Carbohydrate 4.1g, of which sugars 3.7g; Fat 16.3g, of which saturates 3.3g; Cholesterol 12mg; Calcium 52mg; Fibre 1.7g; Sodium 242mg.

243 Venetian-Style Stewed Button Onions Energy 402kcal/1676kJ; Protein 3.9g; Carbohydrate 52g, of which sugars 45.9g; Fat 20g, of which saturates 3.6g; Cholesterol 1mg; Calcium 84mg; Fibre 4.1g; Sodium 16mg.

244 Asparagus in the Venetian Style Energy 253kcal/1046kJ; Protein 14.5g; Carbohydrate 3.5g, of which sugars 3.3g; Fat 20.4g, of which saturates 4.1g; Cholesterol 285mg; Calcium 90mg; Fibre 3g; Sodium 107mg.

245 Venetian-style Braised Artichoke Hearts Energy 131kcal/542kJ; Protein 0.6g; Carbohydrate 0.8g, of which sugars 0.8g; Fat 14g, of which saturates 1.9g; Cholesterol 0mg; Calcium 46mg; Fibre 1.2g; Sodium 34mg.

246 Vicenza-style Stewed Cabbage Energy 333kcal/1378kJ; Protein 10g; Carbohydrate 20.5g, of which sugars 19.9g; Fat 23.7g, of which saturates 7.3g; Cholesterol 33mg; Calcium 189mg; Fibre 8.2g; Sodium 436mg.

247 Stewed Venetian Peppers Energy 248kcal/1025kJ; Protein 2.5g; Carbohydrate 12.4g, of which sugars 10.9g; Fat 20.2g, of which saturates 8.2g; Cholesterol 29mg; Calcium 33mg; Fibre 3.9g; Sodium 105mg.

248 Potato and Cheese Gratin Energy 424kcal/1771kJ; Protein 19.5g; Carbohydrate 26.9g, of which sugars 2.2g; Fat 26.2g, of which saturates 15.3g; Cholesterol 74mg; Calcium 382mg; Fibre 1.7g; Sodium 726mg.

250 Venetian Fritters Energy 150kcal/628kJ; Protein 2.1g; Carbohydrate 21.1g, of which sugars 7.5g; Fat 6.9g, of which saturates 0.8g; Cholesterol 0mg; Calcium 34mg; Fibre 0.8g; Sodium 8mg.

252 Venetian Spiced Biscuits Energy 109kcal/459kJ; Protein 2.6g; Carbohydrate 15.5g, of which sugars 9g; Fat 4.4g, of which saturates 1.1g; Cholesterol 10mg; Calcium 55mg; Fibre 0.9g; Sodium 37mg.

254 Venetian Biscuits Energy 78kcal/330kJ; Protein 1.6g; Carbohydrate 15.9g, of which sugars 3.2g; Fat 1.4g, of which saturates 0.8g; Cholesterol 3mg; Calcium 25mg; Fibre 0.5g; Sodium 11mg.

255 Polenta Cake Energy 560kcal/2345kJ; Protein 13g; Carbohydrate 69.7g, of which sugars 41.2g; Fat 26.4g, of which saturates 3.7g; Cholesterol 82mg; Calcium 130mg; Fibre 3.6g; Sodium 16mg.

256 Soft Pumpkin Cake Energy 280kcal/1164kJ; Protein 4.6g; Carbohydrate 17.4g, of which sugars 9.7g; Fat 20.6g, of which saturates 10.9g; Cholesterol 91mg; Calcium 72mg; Fibre 1.9g; Sodium 178mg.

258 Veronese Pasta Cake Energy 635kcal/2665kJ; Protein 13.1g; Carbohydrate 81.7g, of which sugars 46.4g; Fat 29g, of which saturates 9.4g; Cholesterol 88mg; Calcium 156mg; Fibre 3.2g; Sodium 84mg.

262 Trentino Barley Soup Energy 229kcal/969kJ; Protein 4.8g; Carbohydrate 45.1g, of which sugars 4.5g; Fat 4.6g, of which saturates 0.6g; Cholesterol 0mg; Calcium 33mg; Fibre 1.6g; Sodium 9mg.

263 Beetroot Dumplings Energy 423kcal/1771kJ; Protein 15.7g; Carbohydrate 37.7g, of which sugars 6.3g; Fat 24.5g, of which saturates 9.9g; Cholesterol 131mg; Calcium 200mg; Fibre 5.9g; Sodium 297mg.

264 Wholemeal and Oat Rolls Energy 378kcal/1602kJ; Protein 14.5g; Carbohydrate 69.9g, of which sugars 3.8g; Fat 6.5g, of which saturates 1.4g; Cholesterol 7mg; Calcium 104mg; Fibre 8.3g; Sodium 41mg.

265 Tyrolean Goulash with Polenta Energy 638kcal/2654kJ; Protein 63.1g; Carbohydrate 9.2g, of which sugars 5.6g; Fat 39g, of which saturates 13.1g; Cholesterol 164mg; Calcium 46mg; Fibre 1.4g; Sodium 527mg.

266 Stockfish in the Trentino Style Energy 300kcal/1256kJ; Protein 21.3g; Carbohydrate 27.7g, of which sugars 11.5g; Fat 12.3g, of which saturates 5.4g; Cholesterol 62mg; Calcium 159mg; Fibre 3.3g; Sodium 151mg.

268 Beef with a Shallot Vinaigrette Energy 279kcal/1159kJ; Protein 22.9g; Carbohydrate 1.2g, of which sugars 0.9g; Fat 20.3g, of which saturates 5.4g; Cholesterol 58mg; Calcium 9mg; Fibre 0.2g; Sodium 556mg.

269 Trentino Potato Fritters Energy 651kcal/2715kJ; Protein 12.3g; Carbohydrate 54.2g, of which sugars 5.1g; Fat 44.2g, of which saturates 9.2g; Cholesterol 18mg; Calcium 233mg; Fibre 3.2g; Sodium 209mg.

270 Pear and Amaretti Tarts Energy 521kcal/2192kJ; Protein 6.7g; Carbohydrate 83.5g, of which sugars 46.4g; Fat 19.8g, of which saturates 11.9g; Cholesterol 109mg; Calcium 112mg; Fibre 4g; Sodium 205mg.

274 The Jota of Trieste Energy 504kcal/2123kJ; Protein 29.8g; Carbohydrate 61.1g, of which sugars 4.4g; Fat 17.3g, of which saturates 3.4g; Cholesterol 12mg; Calcium 151mg; Fibre 19.8g; Sodium 663mg.

276 Giant Beetroot and Mascarpone Ravioli Energy 759kcal/3179kJ; Protein 23.5g; Carbohydrate 84.6g, of which sugars 7.9g; Fat 38.8g, of which saturates 22.4g; Cholesterol 280mg; Calcium 278mg; Fibre 4.5g; Sodium 422mg.

278 Mock Spider Crab in the Trieste Style Energy 207kcal/867kJ; Protein 13.1g; Carbohydrate 14.5g, of which sugars 0.5g; Fat 11.2g, of which saturates 2g; Cholesterol 110mg; Calcium 42mg; Fibre 0.4g; Sodium 261mg.

279 Parcels of Sole and Rocket Energy 174kcal/724kJ; Protein 18.9g; Carbohydrate 0.7g, of which sugars 0.6g; Fat 10.6g, of which saturates 1.5g; Cholesterol 52mg; Calcium 66mg; Fibre 0.5g; Sodium 410mg.

280 Polenta with Tomatoes Energy 336kcal/1401kJ; Protein 10.7g; Carbohydrate 40g, of which sugars 3.4g; Fat 14.5g, of which saturates 3.8g; Cholesterol 13mg; Calcium 184mg; Fibre 2.7g; Sodium 150mg.

282 Warm Cuttlefish Salad with Rocket Energy 243kcal/1011kJ; Protein 25.1g; Carbohydrate 0.7g, of which sugars 0.6g; Fat 12.4g, of which saturates 1.9g; Cholesterol 165mg; Calcium 137mg; Fibre 0.5g; Sodium 621mg.

284 Stuffed Savoy Cabbage Bundles Energy 756kcal/3143kJ; Protein 46.5g; Carbohydrate 30.9g, of which sugars 16.5g; Fat 50.3g, of which saturates 15.5g; Cholesterol 225mg; Calcium 290mg; Fibre 7g; Sodium 540mg.

286 Potato Fritters Energy 757kcal/3182kJ; Protein 12.3g; Carbohydrate 109.2g, of which sugars 34.1g; Fat 33.2g, of which saturates 6.8g; Cholesterol 107mg; Calcium 115mg; Fibre 4.1g; Sodium 103mg.

288 Candied Fruit and Nut Roll Energy 787kcal/3306kJ; Protein 19.2g; Carbohydrate 102.9g, of which sugars 35.3g; Fat 34.7g, of which saturates 12.8g; Cholesterol 210mg; Calcium 240mg; Fibre 4.8g; Sodium 274mg.

304 Tuscan Cold Summer Soup Energy 119kcal/494kJ; Protein 1.3g; Carbohydrate 7.2g, of which sugars 6.9g; Fat 9.7g, of which saturates 1.4g; Cholesterol 0mg; Calcium 33mg; Fibre 2.9g; Sodium 23mg.

305 Tomato and Bread Soup Energy 285kcal/1194kJ; Protein 5g; Carbohydrate 28g, of which sugars 7.2g; Fat 17.9g, of which saturates 2.5g; Cholesterol 0mg; Calcium 64mg; Fibre 2.6g; Sodium 243mg.

306 Tuscan Spelt Soup Energy 294kcal/1239kJ; Protein 7.1g; Carbohydrate 38.2g, of which sugars 10.1g; Fat 13.7g, of which saturates 2.6g; Cholesterol 8mg; Calcium 48mg; Fibre 3.6g; Sodium 189mg.

308 Tuscan Bean and Cabbage Soup Energy 354kcal/1482kJ; Protein 11.5g; Carbohydrate 43.8g, of which sugars 12g; Fat 15.9g, of which saturates 4.9g; Cholesterol 16mg; Calcium 151mg; Fibre 5.8g; Sodium 617mg.

310 Tuscan Liver Pâté Energy 472kcal/1979kJ; Protein 16.6g; Carbohydrate 48.7g, of which sugars 4.8g; Fat 23.8g, of which saturates 8.3g; Cholesterol 177mg; Calcium 124mg; Fibre 2.2g; Sodium 596mg.

311 Tuscan Bread and Tomato Salad Energy 238kcal/998kJ; Protein 5.3g; Carbohydrate 28g, of which sugars 5.9g; Fat 12.5g, of which saturates 1.9g; Cholesterol 0mg; Calcium 116mg; Fibre 3.2g; Sodium 259mg.

312 Tuscan Bread Fritters Energy 604kcal/2518kJ; Protein 9.3g; Carbohydrate 58.5g, of which sugars 1.1g; Fat 38.5g, of which saturates 5.4g; Cholesterol 0mg; Calcium 110mg; Fibre 2.3g; Sodium 6mg.

314 Wild Boar Maltagliati in the Arezzo Style Energy 539kcal/2268kJ; Protein 30.8g; Carbohydrate 62.2g, of which sugars 8.7g; Fat 16.6g, of which saturates 4.3g; Cholesterol 55mg; Calcium 49mg; Fibre 3.9g; Sodium 327mg.

316 Pasta and Chickpeas Energy 820kcal/3477kJ; Protein 45.4g; Carbohydrate 144.9g, of which sugars 12.2g; Fat 10.6g, of which saturates 1g; Cholesterol 0mg; Calcium 310mg; Fibre 21.6g; Sodium 83mg.

317 Polenta Gnocchi Energy 878kcal/3654kJ; Protein 33.4g; Carbohydrate 84g, of which sugars 1.3g; Fat 44.4g, of which saturates 21.5g; Cholesterol 128mg; Calcium 244mg; Fibre 2.9g; Sodium 478mg.

318 Spinach and Bread Gnocchi Energy 465kcal/1933kJ; Protein 22.5g; Carbohydrate 25.7g, of which sugars 4.3g; Fat 30.8g, of which saturates 17.5g; Cholesterol 202mg; Calcium 738mg; Fibre 5.3g; Sodium 879mg.

320 Risotto with Chianti Energy 507kcal/2110kJ; Protein 9.3g; Carbohydrate 41.7g, of which sugars 1.4g; Fat 19.7g, of which saturates 12.7g; Cholesterol 56mg; Calcium 181mg; Fibre 0.3g; Sodium 299mg.

321 Red Mullet in the Style of Livorno Energy 279kcal/1165kJ; Protein 24.9g; Carbohydrate 5.7g, of which sugars 2.9g; Fat 14.7g, of which saturates 1.4g; Cholesterol 0mg; Calcium 106mg; Fibre 0.9g; Sodium 133mg.

322 Stuffed Sardines Energy 621kcal/2594kJ; Protein 35.8g; Carbohydrate 37.2g, of which sugars 2.6g; Fat 37.7g, of which saturates 9.3g; Cholesterol 155mg; Calcium 343mg; Fibre 1.3g; Sodium 505mg.

323 Mackerel with Wild Fennel Energy 743kcal/3084kJ; Protein 57.7g; Carbohydrate 1.8g, of which sugars 1.4g; Fat 56g, of which saturates 11.1g; Cholesterol 159mg; Calcium 42mg; Fibre 0.4g; Sodium 189mg.

324 Tuscan Fish Stew Energy 585kcal/2458kJ; Protein 52.9g; Carbohydrate 46.8g, of which sugars 6.5g; Fat 19.8g, of which saturates 3.2g; Cholesterol 92mg; Calcium 168mg; Fibre 2.7g; Sodium 657mg.

326 Marinated Eels Energy 603kcal/2499kJ; Protein 37.4g; Carbohydrate 0g, of which sugars 0g; Fat 50.4g, of which saturates 10g; Cholesterol 338mg; Calcium 43mg; Fibre 0g; Sodium 200mg.

327 Jailed Octopus Energy 212kcal/888kJ; Protein 24.1g; Carbohydrate 0.2g, of which sugars 0.2g; Fat 12.8g, of which saturates 1.9g; Cholesterol 64mg; Calcium 61mg; Fibre 0.4g; Sodium 3mg.

328 Tuscan Pot Roast Energy 707kcal/2955kJ; Protein 81.7g; Carbohydrate 2.7g, of which sugars 2.3g; Fat 41.2g, of which saturates 20.6g; Cholesterol 254mg; Calcium 30mg; Fibre 0.7g; Sodium 537mg.

329 Florentine T-Bone Steak Energy 1008kcal/4182kJ; Protein 83.1g; Carbohydrate 0.7g, of which sugars 0.6g; Fat 74.5g, of which saturates 28.3g; Cholesterol 236mg; Calcium 74mg; Fibre 1.3g; Sodium 154mg.

330 Pork Sausages with Grapes Energy 638kcal/2648kJ; Protein 16.3g; Carbohydrate 29.7g, of which sugars 17.5g; Fat 51.3g, of which saturates 18.7g; Cholesterol 71mg; Calcium 75mg; Fibre 1.5g; Sodium 1142mg.

331 Florentine Roast Pork Loin Energy 369kcal/1541kJ; Protein 46.5g; Carbohydrate 0.5g, of which sugars 0.5g; Fat 14.2g, of which saturates 3.8g; Cholesterol 137mg; Calcium 23mg; Fibre 0g; Sodium 155mg.

332 Wild Boar Cacciatora Energy 430kcal/1791kJ; Protein 33.8g; Carbohydrate 7.5g, of which sugars 4.7g; Fat 23.5g, of which saturates 5.1g; Cholesterol 100mg; Calcium 39mg; Fibre 1.5g; Sodium 294mg.

334 Tuscan Rabbit Casserole Energy 265kcal/1106kJ; Protein 25.2g; Carbohydrate 0.4g, of which sugars 0.4g; Fat 12.5g, of which saturates 3.7g; Cholesterol 124mg; Calcium 17mg; Fibre 0g; Sodium 40mg.

335 Peas Cooked in Olive Oil Energy 280kcal/1157kJ; Protein 9g; Carbohydrate 21.3g, of which sugars 8.9g; Fat 18.4g, of which saturates 2.7g; Cholesterol 0mg; Calcium 49mg; Fibre 6.7g; Sodium 4mg.

336 Stewed Beans Energy 160kcal/669kJ; Protein 6.3g; Carbohydrate 14.6g, of which sugars 2.7g; Fat 8.9g, of which saturates 1.3g; Cholesterol 0mg; Calcium 19mg; Fibre 5.1g; Sodium 425mg.

337 Green Beans in the Florentine Style Energy 181kcal/747kJ; Protein 3.3g; Carbohydrate 10.2g, of which sugars 7.4g; Fat 14.5g, of which saturates 2.1g; Cholesterol 0mg; Calcium 62mg; Fibre 3.7g; Sodium 14mg.

338 Deep-fried Courgettes Energy 187kcal/774kJ; Protein 5.4g; Carbohydrate 11.5g, of which sugars 3.7g; Fat 13.5g, of which saturates 2.2g; Cholesterol 53mg; Calcium 90mg; Fibre 1.2g; Sodium 40mg.

339 Wild Mushroom Salad Energy 247kcal/1027kJ; Protein 22.3g; Carbohydrate 0.9g, of which sugars 0.5g; Fat 17.2g, of which saturates 10.4g; Cholesterol 50mg; Calcium 633mg; Fibre 2g; Sodium 556mg.

340 Tuscan Cream and Chocolate Pudding Energy 1087kcal/4507kJ; Protein 9.9g; Carbohydrate 56.5g, of which sugars 44.8g; Fat 96.3g, of which saturates 45.5g; Cholesterol 233mg; Calcium 147mg; Fibre 2.2g; Sodium 245mg.

342 Tuscan Honey Cookies Energy 461kcal/1950kJ; Protein 8.9g; Carbohydrate 91.3g, of which sugars 47.2g; Fat 9.2g, of which saturates 0.8g; Cholesterol 0mg; Calcium 150mg; Fibre 3.5g; Sodium 48mg.

344 Soft Almond Sweetmeats Energy 273kcal/1144kJ; Protein 5.5g; Carbohydrate 29g, of which sugars 28.5g; Fat 15.9g, of which saturates 1.2g; Cholesterol 0mg; Calcium 55mg; Fibre 1.4g; Sodium 14mg.

345 Tuscan Hard Dunking Cookies Energy 932kcal/3946kJ; Protein 19.7g; Carbohydrate 183.8g, of which sugars 107g; Fat 18.3g, of which saturates 2.5g; Cholesterol 152mg; Calcium 270mg; Fibre 4.8g; Sodium 68mg.

346 Soft Tuscan Rice Cake Energy 2838kcal/11969kJ; Protein 111.3g; Carbohydrate 438.1g, of which sugars 295.1g; Fat 71.6g, of which saturates 25.9g; Cholesterol 1783mg; Calcium 1850mg; Fibre 0.6g; Sodium 1307mg.

348 Tuscan Candied Fruit-and-nut Hard Cake Energy 9564kcal/40476kJ; Protein 91g; Carbohydrate 1911.9g, of which sugars 1748g; Fat 225.7g, of which saturates 17.4g; Cholesterol 0mg; Calcium 4054mg; Fibre 134.8g; Sodium 6443mg.

350 The Traditional Sweet Bread of Lucca Energy 291kcal/1233kJ; Protein 5.9g; Carbohydrate 57.4g, of which sugars 23.1g; Fat 5.8g, of which saturates 3.1g; Cholesterol 50mg; Calcium 88mg; Fibre 1.7g; Sodium 80mg.

352 Tuscan Grape-harvest Focaccia Energy 337kcal/1432kJ; Protein 7.4g; Carbohydrate 75.1g, of which sugars 17.9g; Fat 2.9g, of which saturates 0.3g; Cholesterol 0mg; Calcium 117mg; Fibre 2.9g; Sodium 4mg.

353 Rosemary and Sultana Rolls Energy 110kcal/463kJ; Protein 2.8g; Carbohydrate 17.3g, of which sugars 2.3g; Fat 3.8g, of which saturates 0.6g; Cholesterol 0mg; Calcium 37mg; Fibre 0.5g; Sodium 168mg.

356 Thick Onion Soup in a Cup Energy 368kcal/1526kJ; Protein 12.1g; Carbohydrate 23.8g, of which sugars 17.6g; Fat 25.7g, of which saturates 9.3g; Cholesterol 139mg; Calcium 218mg; Fibre 6.1g; Sodium 152mg.

358 Ancona Fish Soup Energy 389kcal/1627kJ; Protein 27.4g; Carbohydrate 29g, of which sugars 4.8g; Fat 18.9g, of which saturates 2.8g; Cholesterol 68mg; Calcium 46mg; Fibre 2.7g; Sodium 207mg.

359 Clear Chicken Soup with Passatelli Energy 188kcal/785kJ; Protein 16.5g; Carbohydrate 6.9g, of which sugars 0.9g; Fat 8.9g, of which saturates 5.3g, Cholesterol 38mg; Calcium 327mg; Fibre 1.2g; Sodium 290mg.

360 Chickpea and Pork Soup Energy 302kcal/1268kJ; Protein 17.6g; Carbohydrate 31.2g, of which sugars 7.7g; Fat 12.8g, of which saturates 2.8g; Cholesterol 22mg; Calcium 118mg; Fibre 6.8g; Sodium 149mg.

362 Stuffed Deep-fried Giant Olives Energy 602kcal/2488kJ; Protein 18.2g; Carbohydrate 6.2g, of which sugars 0.5g, Fat 55.6g, of which saturates 15.8g; Cholesterol 210mg; Calcium 151mg; Fibre 1.2g; Sodium 983mg.

364 Umbrian Easter Bread Energy 2030kcal/8543kJ; Protein 79.8g; Carbohydrate 261.7g, of which sugars 7.5g; Fat 81.3g, of which saturates 37.6g; Cholesterol 381mg; Calcium 1642mg; Fibre 9.7g; Sodium 1881mg.

366 Ravioli in the Pesaro Style Energy 513kcal/2155kJ; Protein 26.3g; Carbohydrate 61.2g, of which sugars 3.8g; Fat 19.8g, of which saturates 10g; Cholesterol 201mg; Calcium 489mg; Fibre 4g; Sodium 377mg.

368 Spaghetti with Wild Asparagus Energy 373kcal/1572kJ; Protein 13.9g; Carbohydrate 60.9g, of which sugars 7.7g; Fat 9.8g, of which saturates 1.4g; Cholesterol 0mg; Calcium 65mg; Fibre 5.5g; Sodium 11mg.

369 Tagliatelle with Cuttlefish and Shrimp Energy 630kcal/2654kJ; Protein 41.3g; Carbohydrate 67.4g, of which sugars 5.5g; Fat 20.5g, of which saturates 3g; Cholesterol 258mg; Calcium 152mg; Fibre 3.3g; Sodium 558mg.

370 Marche Baked Pasta Energy 474kcal/1984kJ; Protein 25.3g; Carbohydrate 33.2g, of which sugars 2.7g; Fat 24.9g, of which saturates 11.2g; Cholesterol 232mg; Calcium 297mg; Fibre 1.7g; Sodium 488mg.

372 Polenta and Beans Energy 458kcal/1926kJ; Protein 20.2g; Carbohydrate 70.4g, of which sugars 5.8g; Fat 11.1g, of which saturates 3.6g; Cholesterol 8mg; Calcium 82mg; Fibre 12.9g; Sodium 26mg.

374 Umbrian Stuffed Grilled Trout Energy 661kcal/2761kJ; Protein 40.9g; Carbohydrate 34.9g, of which sugars 1.2g; Fat 40.7g, of which saturates 6.2g, Cholesterol 147mg; Calcium 114mg; Fibre 1g; Sodium 475mg.

375 Salt Cod Fritters Energy 429kcal/1786kJ; Protein 39.9g; Carbohydrate 5.8g, of which sugars 0.1g; Fat 27.5g, of which saturates 3.1g; Cholesterol 128mg; Calcium 34mg; Fibre 0.2g; Sodium 137mg.

376 Guinea Fowl in a Pyramid Energy 476kcal/1999kJ; Protein 82.5g; Carbohydrate 0g, of which sugars 0g; Fat 16.1g, of which saturates 4.1g; Cholesterol 0mg; Calcium 105mg; Fibre 0g; Sodium 225mg.

377 Quail in the Todi Style Energy 631kcal/2628kJ; Protein 44.9g; Carbohydrate 1g, of which sugars 1g; Fat 31.4g, of which saturates 5.4g; Cholesterol 52mg; Calcium 54mg; Fibre 0.7g; Sodium 1671mg.

378 Chicken in the Style of Macerata Energy 765kcal/3174kJ; Protein 64.1g; Carbohydrate 0g, of which sugars 0g; Fat 56.3g, of which saturates 17.1g; Cholesterol 471mg; Calcium 40mg; Fibre 0g; Sodium 304mg.

379 Drunken Chicken Energy 862kcal/3621kJ; Protein 50.2g; Carbohydrate 74.8g, of which sugars 41.1g; Fat 24.9g, of which saturates 2.7g; Cholesterol 116mg; Calcium 151mg; Fibre 5.2g; Sodium 137mg.

380 Lamb with Black Truffle Energy 523kcal/2179kJ; Protein 47.2g; Carbohydrate 1.9g, of which sugars 0.2g; Fat 34g, of which saturates 10.7g; Cholesterol 213mg; Calcium 19mg; Fibre 0.9g; Sodium 171mg.

382 Frittata with Fresh Herbs Energy 235kcal/975kJ; Protein 13.7g; Carbohydrate 1.7g, of which sugars 0.4g; Fat 19.6g, of which saturates 4.3g; Cholesterol 381mg; Calcium 115mg; Fibre 0.2g; Sodium 145mg.

384 Black Truffle Frittata Energy 251kcal/1040kJ; Protein 14.6g; Carbohydrate 0.2g, of which sugars 0.1g; Fat 20.9g, of which saturates 4.7g; Cholesterol 428mg; Calcium 67mg; Fibre 0.3g; Sodium 160mg.

385 The Flag Energy 129kcal/538kJ; Protein 1.9g; Carbohydrate 10.7g, of which sugars 10.4g; Fat 9g, of which saturates 1.4g; Cholesterol 0mg; Calcium 17mg; Fibre 2.9g; Sodium 15mg.

386 Spelt with Vegetables Energy 305kcal/1288kJ; Protein 11.6g; Carbohydrate 50g, of which sugars 5.6g; Fat 7.9g, of which saturates 2.1g, Cholesterol 12mg; Calcium 68mg; Fibre 4.5g; Sodium 396mg.

387 Warm Spring Cabbage Salad Energy 404kcal/1991kJ; Protein 1.9g; Carbohydrate 6.2g, of which sugars 5.6g; Fat 50.2g, of which saturates 7g; Cholesterol 0mg; Calcium 56mg; Fibre 2.5g; Sodium 8mg.

388 Carnival Fritters Energy 359kcal/1506kJ; Protein 6.1g; Carbohydrate 45.7g, of which sugars 2.8g; Fat 18.2g, of which saturates 5.2g; Cholesterol 65mg; Calcium 87mg; Fibre 1.7g; Sodium 51mg.

389 Pasta with Sweet Walnut Sauce Energy 618kcal/2588kJ; Protein 15.1g; Carbohydrate 70.2g, of which sugars 16.5g; Fat 32.7g, of which saturates 6g; Cholesterol 14mg; Calcium 65mg; Fibre 3.8g; Sodium 76mg.

390 Snake-shaped Cake Energy 368kcal/1548kJ; Protein 5.8g; Carbohydrate 57.6g, of which sugars 36g; Fat 14.3g, of which saturates 1.5g; Cholesterol 0mg; Calcium 85mg; Fibre 2.6g; Sodium 8mg.

392 Spiced Umbrian Cake Energy 2407kcal/10011kJ; Protein 44.3g; Carbohydrate 161.5g, of which sugars 138.7g; Fat 177.6g, of which saturates 25.6g; Cholesterol 6mg; Calcium 400mg; Fibre 14.1g; Sodium 248mg.

408 Roman Egg and Cheese Soup Energy 245kcal/1030kJ; Protein 14.1g; Carbohydrate 27.5g, of which sugars 1.3g; Fat 9.4g, of which saturates 4.1g; Cholesterol 110mg; Calcium 246mg; Fibre 1.1g; Sodium 424mg.

409 Rice and Broad Bean Soup Energy 507kcal/2111kJ; Protein 14.4g; Carbohydrate 61.3g, of which sugars 3.1g; Fat 22.7g, of which saturates 5.8g; Cholesterol 13mg; Calcium 87mg; Fibre 8.5g; Sodium 50mg.

410 Vegetable Soup with Semolina Energy 204kcal/854kJ; Protein 8.6g; Carbohydrate 21.3g, of which sugars 6.6g; Fat 10g, of which saturates 6.1g; Cholesterol 27mg; Calcium 190mg; Fibre 2.6g; Sodium 202mg.

411 Baked Eggs with Tomatoes Energy 243kcal/1008kJ; Protein 13.4g; Carbohydrate 3.9g, of which sugars 3.9g; Fat 19.7g, of which saturates 4.4g; Cholesterol 381mg; Calcium 66mg; Fibre 1.3g; Sodium 151mg.

412 Deep-fried Mozzarella Sandwiches Energy 428kcal/1789kJ; Protein 18.9g; Carbohydrate 30.5g, of which sugars 2.7g; Fat 26.6g, of which saturates 10.4g; Cholesterol 129mg; Calcium 331mg; Fibre 1.9g; Sodium 539mg.

413 Roman Cheese and Ham Fritters Energy 436kcal/1800kJ; Protein 17g; Carbohydrate 0.2g, of which sugars 0.2g; Fat 40.2g, of which saturates 17.3g; Cholesterol 222mg; Calcium 310mg; Fibre 0g; Sodium 632mg.

414 Cheese Skewers with Anchovy Sauce Energy 712kcal/2971kJ; Protein 23.2g; Carbohydrate 49.7g, of which sugars 3g; Fat 48.2g, of which saturates 31g; Cholesterol 130mg; Calcium 401mg; Fibre 1.5g; Sodium 1161mg.

415 Scamorza Crostini Energy 340kcal/1415kJ; Protein 16.7g; Carbohydrate 14.7g, of which sugars 1.3g; Fat 24.2g, of which saturates 11.7g; Cholesterol 44mg; Calcium 317mg; Fibre 0.4g; Sodium 452mg.

416 Spaghetti with Oil and Garlic Energy 505kcal/2126kJ; Protein 12.8g; Carbohydrate 76.4g, of which sugars 3.3g; Fat 18.6g, of which saturates 2.6g; Cholesterol 0mg; Calcium 27mg; Fibre 3.3g; Sodium 3mg.

417 Puttanesca Pasta Energy 592kcal/2489kJ; Protein 14.5g; Carbohydrate 77g, of which sugars 6.1g; Fat 25.8g, of which saturates 3.5g; Cholesterol 0mg; Calcium 88mg; Fibre 5g; Sodium 726mg.

418 Rigatoni with Tomato and Ricotta Energy 443kcal/1867kJ; Protein 17.1g; Carbohydrate 61.7g, of which sugars 8.6g; Fat 15.9g, of which saturates 6.4g; Cholesterol 25mg; Calcium 136mg; Fibre 4.1g; Sodium 100mg.

419 Pasta Carbonara Energy 620kcal/2609kJ; Protein 32g; Carbohydrate 74.1g, of which sugars 3.3g; Fat 23.9g, of which saturates 9.3g; Cholesterol 194mg; Calcium 275mg; Fibre 2.9g; Sodium 890mg.

420 Bucatini with Amatriciana Sauce Energy 725kcal/3043kJ; Protein 31.9g; Carbohydrate 77.2g, of which sugars 6.4g; Fat 34.2g, of which saturates 11.5g; Cholesterol 68mg; Calcium 262mg; Fibre 3.9g; Sodium 1162mg.

421 Squid Risotto Energy 503kcal/2107kJ; Protein 26.8g; Carbohydrate 73.1g, of which sugars 1.7g; Fat 11.1g, of which saturates 1.7g; Cholesterol 281mg; Calcium 63mg; Fibre 0.9g; Sodium 198mg.

422 Roman Semolina Gnocchi Energy 441kcal/1848kJ; Protein 17.6g; Carbohydrate 40.6g, of which sugars 8.3g; Fat 24.5g, of which saturates 14.6g; Cholesterol 132mg; Calcium 418mg; Fibre 0.9g; Sodium 406mg.

424 Crazy Water Energy 314kcal/1317kJ; Protein 47.2g; Carbohydrate 5.4g, of which sugars 5.4g; Fat 11.5g, of which saturates 1.7g, Cholesterol 115mg; Calcium 54mg; Fibre 2.2g; Sodium 168mg.

425 Roman Roast Lamb Energy 493kcal/2057kJ; Protein 38.5g; Carbohydrate 0.7g, of which sugars 0.6g; Fat 31.4g, of which saturates 12.1g; Cholesterol 183mg; Calcium 34mg; Fibre 0.1g; Sodium 522mg.

426 Veal with Sage, Prosciutto and Mozzarella Energy 540kcal/2266kJ; Protein 73.4g; Carbohydrate 3.4g, of which sugars 0.5g; Fat 24g, of which saturates 14.4g; Cholesterol 198mg; Calcium 247mg; Fibre 0.1g; Sodium 752mg.

427 Roman Stewed Kidneys Energy 131kcal/551kJ; Protein 14.3g; Carbohydrate 6.6g, of which sugars 5.4g; Fat 5g, of which saturates 2g; Cholesterol 336mg; Calcium 27mg; Fibre 1.5g; Sodium 160mg.

428 Roman Braised Oxtail Energy 395kcal/1646kJ; Protein 32.4g; Carbohydrate 2.8g, of which sugars 2.7g; Fat 25.4g, of which saturates 10g; Cholesterol 124mg; Calcium 39mg, Fibre 0.9g; Sodium 213mg.

430 St Joseph's Day Choux Buns Energy 106kcal/441kJ; Protein 1.7g; Carbohydrate 4.9g, of which sugars 0.1g; Fat 9.1g, of which saturates 3.6g; Cholesterol 44mg; Calcium 14mg; Fibre 0.2g; Sodium 53mg.

431 Viterbo St Joseph's Day Rice Fritters Energy 730kcal/3059kJ; Protein 16.8g; Carbohydrate 104.2g, of which sugars 51.9g; Fat 27.2g, of which saturates 6.9g; Cholesterol 139mg; Calcium 267mg; Fibre 1.7g; Sodium 171mg.

434 Sardinian Focaccia Twist Energy 705kcal/2943kJ; Protein 22.1g; Carbohydrate 61g, of which sugars 2.9g; Fat 43g, of which saturates 7g; Cholesterol 64mg; Calcium 110mg; Fibre 2.4g; Sodium 927mg.

436 Sardinian Saffron Risotto Energy 540kcal/2250kJ; Protein 20.9g; Carbohydrate 70.8g, of which sugars 3.5g; Fat 17.7g, of which saturates 7.6g; Cholesterol 51mg; Calcium 133mg; Fibre 1g; Sodium 132mg.

438 Tuna in the Style of Alghero Energy 365kcal/1526kJ; Protein 40g; Carbohydrate 2.9g, of which sugars 2.1g; Fat 19.3g, of which saturates 3.6g; Cholesterol 47mg; Calcium 43mg; Fibre 0.7g; Sodium 196mg.

439 Sea Bass in the Oristano Style Energy 483kcal/ 2004kJ; Protein 30.4g; Carbohydrate 4.7g, of which sugars 3.5g; Fat 33.8g, of which saturates 4.9g; Cholesterol 120mg; Calcium 265mg; Fibre 2.6g; Sodium 1096mg.

440 Sea Bass in a Salt Crust Energy 215kcal/902kJ; Protein 40.8g; Carbohydrate 0.7g, of which sugars 0.6g; Fat 5.4g, of which saturates 0.8g; Cholesterol 160mg; Calcium 311mg; Fibre 1.7g; Sodium 177mg.

441 Sardinian Fish Stew Energy 610kcal/2557kJ; Protein 65.8g; Carbohydrate 34.8g, of which sugars 9.7g; Fat 23.9g, of which saturates 3.5g; Cholesterol 150mg; Calcium 137mg; Fibre 3.7g; Sodium 473mg.

442 Fregola with Mussels and Clams Energy 1194kcal/ 5061kJ; Protein 55.4g; Carbohydrate 197.4g, of which sugars 16.7g; Fat 21.4g, of which saturates 3.1g; Cholesterol 90mg; Calcium 201mg; Fibre 10.4g; Sodium 1177mg.

444 Spaghetti with Dried Fish Roe Energy 493kcal/ 2077kJ; Protein 17.2g; Carbohydrate 74.4g, of which sugars 3.5g; Fat 16.1g, of which saturates 2.2g; Cholesterol 74mg; Calcium 48mg; Fibre 3.4g; Sodium 31mg.

445 Chicken Steeped in Myrtle Energy 546kcal/2267kJ; Protein 51.7g; Carbohydrate 0g, of which sugars 0g; Fat 37.5g, of which saturates 10.4g; Cholesterol 275mg; Calcium 17mg; Fibre 0g; Sodium 188mg.

446 Mushroom and Meat Sardinian Impanadas Energy 672kcal/2795kJ; Protein 15.2g; Carbohydrate 49.2g, of which sugars 3.5g; Fat 47.4g, of which saturates 5.2g; Cholesterol 61mg; Calcium 101mg; Fibre 2.8g; Sodium 467mg.

448 Sardinian Honey Fritters Energy 1343kcal/5593kJ; Protein 16.5g; Carbohydrate 114.4g, of which sugars 13.3g; Fat 94.3g, of which saturates 44.6g; Cholesterol 129mg; Calcium 300mg; Fibre 4g; Sodium 382mg.

450 Sardinian Iced Cookies Energy 1321kcal/5514kJ; Protein 25.5g; Carbohydrate 122.1g, of which sugars 73.4g; Fat 84.6g, of which saturates 15.5g; Cholesterol 118mg; Calcium 268mg; Fibre 7.1g; Sodium 108mg.

454 Calzone with Tomato Sauce Energy 732kcal/3071kJ; Protein 20g; Carbohydrate 97.4g, of which sugars 9.7g; Fat 31.9g, of which saturates 8.7g; Cholesterol 22mg; Calcium 329mg; Fibre 7.8g; Sodium 1142mg.

456 Pizza Napoletana Energy 488kcal/2059kJ; Protein 12g; Carbohydrate 82.7g, of which sugars 10.4g; Fat 14.4g, of which saturates 1.2g; Cholesterol 0mg; Calcium 145mg; Fibre 5.1g; Sodium 382mg.

457 Molisan Bread and Tomato Salad Energy 395kcal/ 1636kJ; Protein 3.7g; Carbohydrate 19.1g, of which sugars 3.2g; Fat 34.3g, of which saturates 4.7g; Cholesterol 0mg; Calcium 58mg; Fibre 1.6g; Sodium 186mg.

458 Potato Croquettes Energy 502kcal/2095kJ; Protein 11.5g; Carbohydrate 46.2g, of which sugars 2.7g; Fat 31.4g, of which saturates 10.6g; Cholesterol 98mg; Calcium 175mg; Fibre 2.3g; Sodium 327mg.

459 Tomato, Mozzarella and Basil Salad Energy 326kcal/ 1350kJ; Protein 12.3g; Carbohydrate 3.1g, of which sugars 3.1g; Fat 29.5g, of which saturates 11g; Cholesterol 36mg; Calcium 233mg; Fibre 1g; Sodium 256mg.

460 Pasta with Tomatoes and Mozzarella Energy 657kcal/ 2766kJ; Protein 25.7g; Carbohydrate 85.7g, of which sugars 6g; Fat 25.9g, of which saturates 10.4g; Cholesterol 36mg; Calcium 260mg; Fibre 4g; Sodium 257mg.

461 Maccheroni with Seven Flavours Energy 456kcal/ 1928kJ; Protein 13.8g; Carbohydrate 81.1g, of which sugars 9.7g; Fat 10.7g, of which saturates 1.5g; Cholesterol 0mg; Calcium 70mg; Fibre 5.5g; Sodium 26mg.

462 Spaghetti with Clams Energy 629kcal/2651kJ; Protein 40.3g; Carbohydrate 77.7g, of which sugars 3.6g; Fat 19.5g, of which saturates 2.9g; Cholesterol 117mg; Calcium 177mg; Fibre 3.5g; Sodium 2107mg.

464 Sautéed Clams Energy 206kcal/870kJ; Protein 16.8g; Carbohydrate 20.4g, of which sugars 1g; Fat 5.2g, of which saturates 0.9g; Cholesterol 56mg; Calcium 124mg; Fibre 0.9g; Sodium 1194mg.

465 Peppered Mussels Energy 113kcal/469kJ; Protein 7.5g; Carbohydrate 1.5g, of which sugars 0g; Fat 8.5g, of which saturates 1.2g; Cholesterol 27mg; Calcium 23mg; Fibre 0g; Sodium 160mg.

466 Mixed Fry-up Energy 618kcal/2566kJ; Protein 29.1g; Carbohydrate 14g, of which sugars 9.2g; Fat 50.1g, of which saturates 11.7g; Cholesterol 182mg; Calcium 223mg; Fibre 1.5g; Sodium 232mg.

468 Rice Ring Mould with Prawns Energy 606kcal/ 2528kJ; Protein 27.8g; Carbohydrate 78.4g, of which sugars 2.6g; Fat 18.7g, of which saturates 10g; Cholesterol 110mg; Calcium 201mg; Fibre 1g; Sodium 1475mg.

470 Chicken Cacciatora Energy 405kcal/1686kJ; Protein 26g; Carbohydrate 4.3g, of which sugars 4g; Fat 29.7g, of which saturates 6.6g; Cholesterol 154mg; Calcium 26mg; Fibre 1.3g; Sodium 124mg.

471 Genovese Onion Sauce Energy 618kcal/2573kJ; Protein 56.8g; Carbohydrate 26.4g, of which sugars 18.7g; Fat 32.4g, of which saturates 5.8g; Cholesterol 210mg; Calcium 105mg; Fibre 4.7g; Sodium 288mg.

472 Stewed Beans with Bread Energy 444kcal/1858kJ; Protein 17.5g; Carbohydrate 37g, of which sugars 5.8g; Fat 26.2g, of which saturates 3.8g; Cholesterol 0mg; Calcium 87mg; Fibre 13.1g; Sodium 29mg.

473 Aubergines with Tomato and Mozzarella Energy 407kcal/1693kJ; Protein 26.8g; Carbohydrate 5.2g, of which sugars 5g; Fat 31.2g, of which saturates 15.6g; Cholesterol 67mg; Calcium 724mg; Fibre 3.6g; Sodium 667mg.

474 Courgettes with Tomato and Mozzarella Energy 649kcal/2682kJ; Protein 20.2g; Carbohydrate 15.4g, of which sugars 9.1g; Fat 56.6g, of which saturates 20.7g; Cholesterol 55mg; Calcium 357mg; Fibre 4g; Sodium 311mg.

475 Caprese Cake Energy 931kcal/3875kJ; Protein 17.3g; Carbohydrate 62.9g, of which sugars 59.5g; Fat 68.6g, of which saturates 26.7g; Cholesterol 218mg; Calcium 177mg; Fibre 3.7g; Sodium 301mg.

476 Neapolitan Easter Cake Energy 809kcal/3396kJ; Protein 14.7g; Carbohydrate 110g, of which sugars 62.6g; Fat 37.6g, of which saturates 16g; Cholesterol 190mg; Calcium 144mg; Fibre 2.2g; Sodium 435mg.

480 Pancakes in Chicken Broth Energy 270kcal/1123kJ; Protein 15.1g; Carbohydrate 9.3g, of which sugars 0.6g; Fat 19.6g, of which saturates 8.6g; Cholesterol 216mg; Calcium 280mg; Fibre 0.4g; Sodium 483mg.

481 Orange Antipasto Energy 147kcal/612kJ; Protein 3.2g; Carbohydrate 12.8g, of which sugars 12.8g; Fat 9.6g, of which saturates 1.2g; Cholesterol 0mg; Calcium 89mg; Fibre 2.6g; Sodium 243mg.

482 Ricotta Fritters Energy 737kcal/3071kJ; Protein 21.3g; Carbohydrate 53.8g, of which sugars 2.9g; Fat 50.1g, of which saturates 17.9g; Cholesterol 192mg; Calcium 198mg; Fibre 2.5g; Sodium 337mg.

484 Tagliolini with Ham, Onion and Chilli Energy 616kcal/ 2588kJ; Protein 16.7g; Carbohydrate 80.3g, of which sugars 7.8g; Fat 27.6g, of which saturates 3.9g; Cholesterol 11mg; Calcium 49mg; Fibre 4g; Sodium 231mg.

485 Drunken Prawns Energy 192kcal/798kJ; Protein 15g; Carbohydrate 2.9g, of which sugars 2.5g; Fat 8.7g, of which saturates 1.4g; Cholesterol 52mg; Calcium 113mg; Fibre 1g; Sodium 1021mg.

486 Stuffed Roast Turkey in the Molise Style Energy 839kcal/3513kJ; Protein 119.4g; Carbohydrate 14.7g, of which sugars 3.7g; Fat 33.2g, of which saturates 10.2g; Cholesterol 469mg; Calcium 157mg; Fibre 0.9g; Sodium 529mg.

488 Lamb with Cheese and Egg Energy 792kcal/3299kJ; Protein 63.3g; Carbohydrate 0.5g, of which sugars 0.4g; Fat 57g, of which saturates 20.9g; Cholesterol 333mg; Calcium 238mg; Fibre 0.4g; Sodium 702mg.

489 Potato, Onion and Tomato Bake Energy 473kcal/ 1978kJ; Protein 7.2g; Carbohydrate 55.6g, of which sugars 12.5g; Fat 26.2g, of which saturates 3.8g; Cholesterol 0mg; Calcium 65mg; Fibre 5g; Sodium 150mg.

490 Potatoes with Lentils Energy 405kcal/1705kJ; Protein 13.3g; Carbohydrate 57.3g, of which sugars 5.7g; Fat 15.2g, of which saturates 2.3g; Cholesterol 0mg; Calcium 52mg; Fibre 6.3g; Sodium 39mg.

491 Yellow Peppers with Capers Energy 168kcal/696kJ; Protein 2.9g; Carbohydrate 11.7g, of which sugars 11.2g; Fat 12.5g, of which saturates 1.7g; Cholesterol 0mg; Calcium 27mg; Fibre 2.9g; Sodium 164mg.

492 Christmas Chickpea Pastries Energy 131kcal/544kJ; Protein 3.4g; Carbohydrate 5.6g, of which sugars 1.2g; Fat 10.7g, of which saturates 5.5g; Cholesterol 48mg; Calcium 7mg; Fibre 0.4g; Sodium 261mg.

494 Chocolate-covered Almond Cake Energy 316kcal/ 1318kJ; Protein 7.4g; Carbohydrate 23.9g, of which sugars 12.1g; Fat 21.9g, of which saturates 9.7g; Cholesterol 142.1mg; Calcium 58.8mg; Fibre 0.9g; Sodium 121mg.

495 Abruzzese Ring Cookies Energy 275kcal/1155kJ; Protein 3.1g; Carbohydrate 39.3g, of which sugars 15.5g; Fat 11.9g, of which saturates 2.2g; Cholesterol 2mg; Calcium 52mg; Fibre 1g; Sodium 3mg.

510 Sicilian Onion and Tomato Pizza Energy 3119kcal/ 12997kJ; Protein 74.2g; Carbohydrate 236g, of which sugars 24.3g; Fat 215.3g, of which saturates 40.9g; Cholesterol 75mg; Calcium 1585mg; Fibre 16.8g; Sodium 2975mg.

512 Sicilian Fried Potato Rolls Energy 468kcal/1953kJ; Protein 15.4g; Carbohydrate 37.6g, of which sugars 2.4g; Fat 29.5g, of which saturates 9.2g; Cholesterol 126mg; Calcium 216mg; Fibre 2.1g; Sodium 461mg.

513 Baked Aubergines with Mozzarella Energy 458kcal/ 1897kJ; Protein 10.3g; Carbohydrate 10.9g, of which sugars 2g; Fat 41.9g, of which saturates 8.7g; Cholesterol 78mg; Calcium 141mg; Fibre 1.9g; Sodium 429mg.

514 Sicilian Rice Fritters Energy 260kcal/1084kJ; Protein 7g; Carbohydrate 29.5g, of which sugars 0.4g; Fat 12.7g, of which saturates 4.8g; Cholesterol 47mg; Calcium 89mg; Fibre 0.3g; Sodium 174mg.

516 Sicilian Mushroom Fritters Energy 66kcal/274kJ; Protein 1.9g; Carbohydrate 1.6g, of which sugars 0.1g; Fat 5.9g, of which saturates 1.1g; Cholesterol 18mg; Calcium 33mg; Fibre 0.4g; Sodium 42mg.

517 Anelli with Breadcrumbs Energy 650kcal/2748kJ; Protein 22g; Carbohydrate 107.7g, of which sugars 6.5g; Fat 17.6g, of which saturates 4.1g; Cholesterol 11mg; Calcium 230mg; Fibre 5.1g; Sodium 354mg.

518 Pasta with Fresh Sardines Energy 478kcal/2007kJ; Protein 20g; Carbohydrate 57.4g, of which sugars 9.1g; Fat 20.3g, of which saturates 3.1g; Cholesterol 0mg; Calcium 90mg; Fibre 3.4g; Sodium 226mg.

520 Vermicelli with Squid Ink Energy 383kcal/1603kJ; Protein 18.9g; Carbohydrate 53.5g, of which sugars 0.3g; Fat 9.1g, of which saturates 1.4g; Cholesterol 188mg; Calcium 40mg; Fibre 0.3g; Sodium 100mg.

522 Spaghetti with Capers and Yellow Pepper Energy 569kcal/2394kJ; Protein 14.4g; Carbohydrate 80.1g, of which sugars 9.1g; Fat 23.5g, of which saturates 3.2g; Cholesterol 0mg; Calcium 56mg; Fibre 5.6g; Sodium 384mg.

524 Baked Stuffed Sardines Energy 596kcal/2481kJ; Protein 36.1g; Carbohydrate 21.1g, of which sugars 9.8g; Fat 41.3g, of which saturates 6.8g; Cholesterol 0mg; Calcium 215mg; Fibre 1.3g; Sodium 467mg.

526 Trapani Fish Couscous Energy 315kcal/1315kJ; Protein 30.7g; Carbohydrate 26.7g, of which sugars 0.9g; Fat 10g, of which saturates 1.3g; Cholesterol 69mg; Calcium 43mg; Fibre 0.6g; Sodium 94mg.

528 Meatball and Ricotta Bake Energy 380kcal/1590kJ; Protein 29.5g; Carbohydrate 16.5g, of which sugars 2.1g; Fat 22.4g, of which saturates 11.3g; Cholesterol 223mg; Calcium 300mg; Fibre 0.8g; Sodium 457mg.

530 Beef Rolls with Artichokes Energy 420kcal/1744kJ; Protein 26.3g; Carbohydrate 10.1g, of which sugars 1.1g; Fat 30.7g, of which saturates 14.9g; Cholesterol 108mg; Calcium 28mg; Fibre 0.6g; Sodium 356mg.

532 Rice and Aubergine Bake Energy 371kcal/1544kJ; Protein 8.4g; Carbohydrate 38.6g, of which sugars 5.6g; Fat 20.2g, of which saturates 7.8g; Cholesterol 28mg; Calcium 152mg; Fibre 2.9g; Sodium 158mg.

534 Sicilian Fig Pastries Energy 423kcal/1783kJ; Protein 5.5g; Carbohydrate 70g, of which sugars 54g; Fat 13.9g, of which saturates 5.2g; Cholesterol 35mg; Calcium 117mg; Fibre 2.9g; Sodium 90mg.

536 Sicilian Orange Jelly Energy 151kcal/641kJ; Protein 9.5g; Carbohydrate 29.6g, of which sugars 29.6g; Fat 0.2g, of which saturates 0g; Cholesterol 0mg; Calcium 26mg; Fibre 0.2g; Sodium 20mg.

537 Sicilian Watermelon Ice Energy 294kcal/1243kJ; Protein 2.1g; Carbohydrate 58.6g, of which sugars 57.7g; Fat 7.3g, of which saturates 2.9g; Cholesterol 1mg; Calcium 52mg; Fibre 1.1g; Sodium 72mg.

538 Sicilian Cassata Energy 1078kcal/4564kJ; Protein 13.9g; Carbohydrate 211.6g, of which sugars 209.8g; Fat 22.8g, of which saturates 13.5g; Cholesterol 54mg; Calcium 134mg; Fibre 0g; Sodium 31mg.

542 Bread Soup with Potatoes and Rocket Energy 391kcal/1639kJ; Protein 9.8g; Carbohydrate 48.6g, of which sugars 4.7g; Fat 18.8g, of which saturates 2.8g; Cholesterol 0mg; Calcium 258mg; Fibre 4.4g; Sodium 452mg.

543 White Broad Bean Soup Energy 481kcal/2026kJ; Protein 27.6g; Carbohydrate 55.1g, of which sugars 3.1g; Fat 18.2g, of which saturates 2.6g; Cholesterol 0mg; Calcium 125mg; Fibre 19.6g; Sodium 23mg.

544 Broad Bean Purée Energy 314kcal/1317kJ; Protein 11.3g; Carbohydrate 32.7g, of which sugars 2.2g; Fat 16.3g, of which saturates 2.3g; Cholesterol 0mg; Calcium 50mg; Fibre 7.9g; Sodium 17mg.

545 Fried Onions with Capers and Chilli Energy 165kcal/681kJ; Protein 2.3g; Carbohydrate 14.3g, of which sugars 10.2g; Fat 11.4g, of which saturates 1.6g; Cholesterol 0mg; Calcium 49mg; Fibre 2.6g; Sodium 497mg.

546 Fried Priest Stranglers Energy 194kcal/811kJ; Protein 4.7g; Carbohydrate 23.3g, of which sugars 0.5g; Fat 9.8g, of which saturates 1.6g; Cholesterol 57mg; Calcium 51mg; Fibre 0.9g; Sodium 22mg.

548 Olive and Anchovy Bread Energy 482kcal/2013kJ; Protein 7.8g; Carbohydrate 51.8g, of which sugars 1g; Fat 28.4g, of which saturates 3.9g; Cholesterol 0mg; Calcium 117mg; Fibre 2.4g; Sodium 456mg.

550 Home-made Pasta with Chickpeas Energy 955kcal/4037kJ; Protein 38.6g; Carbohydrate 160.3g, of which sugars 6g; Fat 22.2g, of which saturates 2.8g; Cholesterol 0mg; Calcium 379mg; Fibre 17.5g; Sodium 53mg.

552 Orecchiette with Garlic and Chilli Energy 577kcal/2424kJ; Protein 12.7g; Carbohydrate 76g, of which sugars 5.2g; Fat 26.8g, of which saturates 3.7g; Cholesterol 0mg; Calcium 32mg; Fibre 3.3g; Sodium 39mg.

553 Orecchiette with Cauliflower Energy 636kcal/2680kJ; Protein 36.9g; Carbohydrate 81.6g, of which sugars 9.6g; Fat 20.2g, of which saturates 9g; Cholesterol 47mg; Calcium 424mg; Fibre 7.4g; Sodium 701mg.

554 Pasta with Potenza Ragù Energy 327kcal/1362kJ; Protein 28.3g; Carbohydrate 5.3g, of which sugars 4.5g; Fat 20.7g, of which saturates 7.1g; Cholesterol 84mg; Calcium 136mg; Fibre 2g; Sodium 334mg.

557 Pasta with Mussels Energy 452kcal/1910kJ; Protein 18.1g; Carbohydrate 68.3g, of which sugars 6.3g; Fat 13.8g, of which saturates 2g; Cholesterol 15mg; Calcium 128mg; Fibre 4.2g; Sodium 95mg.

558 Rice and Artichoke Timbale Energy 628kcal/2625kJ; Protein 25.9g; Carbohydrate 61.3g, of which sugars 7g; Fat 29.5g, of which saturates 13g; Cholesterol 146mg; Calcium 361mg; Fibre 0.4g; Sodium 632mg.

560 Red Mullet in a Parcel Energy 328kcal/1364kJ; Protein 24.5g; Carbohydrate 0.4g, of which sugars 0.3g; Fat 25.5g, of which saturates 2.9g; Cholesterol 0mg; Calcium 123mg; Fibre 1g; Sodium 411mg.

561 Pugliese Baked Bream Energy 456kcal/1894kJ; Protein 31.8g; Carbohydrate 0.4g, of which sugars 0.3g; Fat 36.5g, of which saturates 7.4g; Cholesterol 19mg; Calcium 340mg; Fibre 0.6g; Sodium 334mg.

562 Pugliese Fish Stew Energy 500kcal/2108kJ; Protein 40.7g; Carbohydrate 54.5g, of which sugars 5.6g; Fat 14.7g, of which saturates 2.1g; Cholesterol 75mg; Calcium 153mg; Fibre 3.4g; Sodium 644mg.

564 Stuffed Squid Energy 418kcal/1758kJ; Protein 37.7g; Carbohydrate 20.7g, of which sugars 7.4g; Fat 21.2g, of which saturates 5.9g; Cholesterol 456mg; Calcium 245mg; Fibre 2.6g; Sodium 508mg.

566 Salt Cod with Red Peppers Energy 207kcal/861kJ; Protein 25.1g; Carbohydrate 3.2g, of which sugars 3g; Fat 10.4g, of which saturates 1.5g; Cholesterol 61mg; Calcium 32mg; Fibre 1.2g; Sodium 85mg.

567 Chicken in a Lucanian Spicy Sauce Energy 483kcal/2004kJ; Protein 32.5g; Carbohydrate 8.4g, of which sugars 7g; Fat 31.2g, of which saturates 7.5g; Cholesterol 165mg; Calcium 38mg; Fibre 2.5g; Sodium 126mg.

568 Lucanian Chicken Pie Energy 670kcal/2808kJ; Protein 27g; Carbohydrate 66.3g, of which sugars 1.6g; Fat 33.9g, of which saturates 13g; Cholesterol 191mg; Calcium 196mg; Fibre 2.7g; Sodium 329mg.

570 Pugliese Beef Rolls Energy 324kcal/1346kJ; Protein 19.7g; Carbohydrate 5g, of which sugars 4.6g; Fat 25.2g, of which saturates 6.6g, Cholesterol 51mg; Calcium 184mg; Fibre 1.8g; Sodium 574mg.

572 Puglia Lamb Casserole Energy 397kcal/1657kJ; Protein 40.9g; Carbohydrate 1.9g, of which sugars 1.7g; Fat 25.2g, of which saturates 12.6g; Cholesterol 146mg; Calcium 271mg; Fibre 1g; Sodium 368mg.

573 Genzano Baked Lamb Energy 932kcal/3904kJ; Protein 57.1g; Carbohydrate 64.6g, of which sugars 4.2g; Fat 51.3g, of which saturates 16.3g; Cholesterol 190mg; Calcium 88mg; Fibre 3.5g; Sodium 482mg.

574 Chilli Frittata Energy 251kcal/1040kJ; Protein 15.2g; Carbohydrate 0g, of which sugars 0g; Fat 21.3g, of which saturates 6.9g; Cholesterol 257mg; Calcium 261mg; Fibre 0g; Sodium 292mg.

576 Stuffed Baked Peppers Pugliese-style Energy 716kcal/2982kJ; Protein 22.8g; Carbohydrate 52g, of which sugars 14.3g; Fat 47.7g, of which saturates 12g; Cholesterol 171mg; Calcium 432mg; Fibre 5.8g; Sodium 477mg.

578 Spinach Salad with Basil Energy 107kcal/443kJ; Protein 2.8g; Carbohydrate 6g, of which sugars 5g; Fat 8.1g, of which saturates 1.1g; Cholesterol 0mg; Calcium 139mg; Fibre 2.6g; Sodium 107mg.

579 Poor Woman's Courgettes Energy 244kcal/1004kJ; Protein 1.9g; Carbohydrate 1.9g, of which sugars 1.8g; Fat 25.4g, of which saturates 3.6g; Cholesterol 0mg; Calcium 33mg; Fibre 1.1g; Sodium 2mg.

580 Lucanian Vegetable Casserole Energy 961kcal/4012kJ; Protein 19.5g; Carbohydrate 98.1g, of which sugars 21.3g; Fat 57.2g, of which saturates 8.1g; Cholesterol 0mg; Calcium 261mg; Fibre 10.2g; Sodium 826mg.

582 Pugliese Almond Cookies Energy 148kcal/625kJ; Protein 3.5g; Carbohydrate 22g, of which sugars 11.1g; Fat 5.8g, of which saturates 0.5g; Cholesterol 0mg; Calcium 49mg; Fibre 1.2g; Sodium 2mg.

586 Green Cabbage Soup Energy 448kcal/1888kJ; Protein 24g; Carbohydrate 60.8g, of which sugars 11.7g; Fat 13.7g, of which saturates 6.5g; Cholesterol 29mg; Calcium 552mg; Fibre 6g; Sodium 864mg.

587 Aubergine Skin Salad Energy 172kcal/708kJ; Protein 2.5g; Carbohydrate 2g, of which sugars 1.2g; Fat 17.1g, of which saturates 2.4g; Cholesterol 0mg; Calcium 129mg; Fibre 1.8g; Sodium 105mg.

588 Anchovy Fritters Energy 416kcal/1753kJ; Protein 14.5g; Carbohydrate 64.9g, of which sugars 1.25g; Fat 12.7g, of which saturates 2.1g; Cholesterol 0mg; Calcium 141mg; Fibre 2.6g; Sodium 34.6mg.

589 Risotto with Stockfish Energy 565kcal/2361kJ; Protein 30.3g; Carbohydrate 76g, of which sugars 4.5g; Fat 12.1g, of which saturates 4.3g; Cholesterol 72mg; Calcium 52mg; Fibre 1.1g; Sodium 126mg.

590 Calabrian Baked Swordfish Energy 737kcal/3089kJ; Protein 57.4g; Carbohydrate 43.9g, of which sugars 1.8g; Fat 38g, of which saturates 11.9g; Cholesterol 118mg; Calcium 557mg; Fibre 1.9g; Sodium 1103mg.

591 Calabrian Tuna Steaks Energy 472kcal/1976kJ; Protein 51.7g; Carbohydrate 10.2g, of which sugars 4.2g; Fat 24.2g, of which saturates 5.1g; Cholesterol 64mg; Calcium 64mg; Fibre 1.5g; Sodium 380mg.

592 Stuffed Mussels with Tomato Sauce Energy 366kcal/1537kJ; Protein 21.2g; Carbohydrate 29g, of which sugars 6.5g; Fat 19.3g, of which saturates 3.1g; Cholesterol 125mg; Calcium 238mg; Fibre 3g; Sodium 441mg.

594 Calabrian Fish Patties Energy 346kcal/1450kJ; Protein 38.2g; Carbohydrate 17.3g, of which sugars 2.9g; Fat 14.2g, of which saturates 4g; Cholesterol 152mg; Calcium 87mg; Fibre 1.5g; Sodium 353mg.

595 Calabrian Turkey Steaks with Lime Energy 310kcal/1294kJ; Protein 32.9g; Carbohydrate 0.1g, of which sugars 0.1g; Fat 19.8g, of which saturates 3.4g; Cholesterol 92mg; Calcium 17mg; Fibre 0.1g; Sodium 82mg.

596 Calabrian Sweet-and-Sour Meatballs Energy 442kcal/1837kJ; Protein 23.1g; Carbohydrate 13.4g, of which sugars 3.8g; Fat 33.4g, of which saturates 8.2g; Cholesterol 116mg; Calcium 189mg; Fibre 2.4g; Sodium 275mg.

598 Calabrian Rabbit and Red Pepper Stew Energy 465kcal/1934kJ; Protein 31.8g; Carbohydrate 12.9g, of which sugars 12.1g; Fat 25.6g, of which saturates 5.9g; Cholesterol 147mg; Calcium 49mg; Fibre 3.4g; Sodium 68mg.

600 Yellow Pumpkin with Mint and Capers Energy 373kcal/1545kJ; Protein 3.5g; Carbohydrate 18.7g, of which sugars 3g; Fat 32.1g, of which saturates 4.2g; Cholesterol 0mg; Calcium 81mg; Fibre 2.2g; Sodium 155mg.

601 Celery in Tomato Sauce Energy 115kcal/480kJ; Protein 1.7g; Carbohydrate 7.6g, of which sugars 7.2g; Fat 8.9g, of which saturates 1.4g; Cholesterol 0mg; Calcium 26mg; Fibre 2.4g; Sodium 31mg.

602 Savoury Artichoke Cake Energy 441kcal/1847kJ; Protein 10.6g; Carbohydrate 49.1g, of which sugars 3.7g; Fat 23.8g, of which saturates 5.5g; Cholesterol 13mg; Calcium 185mg; Fibre 2.9g; Sodium 257mg.

604 Calabrian Pastries Energy 541kcal/2267kJ; Protein 10.7g; Carbohydrate 60.1g, of which sugars 40.4g; Fat 30g, of which saturates 3.8g; Cholesterol 24mg; Calcium 162mg; Fibre 4.5g; Sodium 22mg.

606 Honey-coated Fritters Energy 103kcal/431kJ; Protein 1.6g; Carbohydrate 13g, of which sugars 0.3g; Fat 5.3g, of which saturates 0.8g; Cholesterol 0mg; Calcium 23mg; Fibre 0.5g; Sodium 1mg.

608 Calabrian Lemon Tart Energy 605kcal/2539kJ; Protein 12.2g; Carbohydrate 80.5g, of which sugars 46.7g; Fat 28.3g, of which saturates 15.9g; Cholesterol 162mg; Calcium 149mg; Fibre 1.3g; Sodium 218mg.

610 Nun's Sighs Energy 571kcal/2414kJ; Protein 14.8g; Carbohydrate 100.7g, of which sugars 81.2g; Fat 14.9g, of which saturates 5.8g; Cholesterol 363mg; Calcium 228mg; Fibre 1g; Sodium 152mg.

612 Calabrian Frozen Nougat Energy 230kcal/974kJ; Protein 1.2g; Carbohydrate 51.4g, of which sugars 50.3g, Fat 3.5g, of which saturates 1.8g; Cholesterol 1mg; Calcium 30mg; Fibre 0.4g; Sodium 14mg.

INDEX

This edition is published by Lorenz Books
an imprint of Anness Publishing Ltd
info@anness.com
www.lorenzbooks.com
www.annesspublishing.com

Publisher: Joanna Lorenz
Editor and Designer: Lucy Doncaster
Photography: Martin Brigdale and Ian Garlick
Food Stylist: Valentina Harris
Index: Helen Snaith
Cover Design: Adelle Mahoney
Production Controller: Ben Worley

Parts of this book have been previously published in a separate series:
The Food and Cooking of Tuscany
The Food and Cooking of Sicily and Southern Italy
The Food and Cooking of Venice and the North-east of Italy
The Food and Cooking of Rome and Naples
The Food and Cooking of Milan and Bologna

PUBLISHER'S NOTE
Although the advice and information in this book are believed to be accurate and true at the time of going to press, neither the authors nor the publisher can accept any legal responsibility or liability for any errors or omissions that may have been made, nor for any inaccuracies, nor for any loss, harm or injury that comes about from following instructions or advice in this book.

PICTURE CREDITS
Shutterstock: 4–5, 6, 10–11, 10bl, 10br, 11tl, 11tr, 12–13, 14l, 20–1, 24, 25, 27, 28, 41, 45, 55t, 65tr, 65tl, 66–7, 76, 100bl, 148bl, 152br, 160bl, 188, 195br, 202br, 249b, 282br, 293br, 295t, 298t, 299br, 301tr, 333bl, 356br, 394–5, 400br, 403br, 403bl, 428br, 449bl, 501tr, 525bl, 526br, 583bl, 598br, 612br; iStock: 6, 16, 23, 31, 32, 35, 36, 39, 49, 52, 53tl, 57, 71tr, 72, 74tr, 74tl, 75, 77, 80bl, 88br, 91tl, 111bl, 120br, 130bl, 134br, 144bl, 175b, 185tr, 187tr, 191, 196br, 257br, 281bl, 296b, 306br, 346br, 365bl, 373bl, 396br, 401, 402tr, 404bl, 496–7, 500bl, 500br, 503tr, 503tl, 505bl, 505br, 506bl, 507tr, 521br, 522br, 530br, 547br, 548br, 557br, 570br, 592br, 608br; Alamy Stock Photos: 9, 40, 51, 77br, 300br, 405, 443br, 502.

PICTURE CAPTIONS
2–3 Italian food is notable for its use of simple, tasty and thrifty ingredients, which cooks combine to produce classic recipes that are so much more than the sum of their parts.
4–5 Grapes, along with olives, are perhaps Italy's most famous crop, and are put to splendid use both at the table and for making the country's many famous wines.
6 The stunning rolling countryside of Tuscany produces all manner of crops, from wheat to the region's famous grapes and olives.
12–13 Italian cooks know instinctively how to make the most of the simple, gutsy ingredients that grow so well and taste so good.
49 Wherever there is a spare patch of earth, Italians like to grow food – be it a vegetable patch in the countryside or a pot of basil on an urban balcony.
63 As in many parts of the world, bread is one of life's essentials in Italy, where cooks over many generations have transformed a mundane staple into a daily delicacy.
66 The rolling countryside of Piedmont is the perfect terroir for wine grapes, so it is little wonder that so many top-class wines are produced in the region.
182 Famous for its watery vistas and iconic gondolas, Venice – La Serenissima – is also home to an illustrious and incredibly diverse food culture.
290 Rich in architecture as well as agriculture, Tuscany is world-famous for its wine, olives and culture, and produces a wealth of robust traditional dishes.
394 The home of pizza, Naples is a chaotic, vibrant, intoxicating city that makes the very best of the simple yet tasty ingredients that abound in the region.
496 The sun-baked island of Sicily boasts numerous stunning seaside towns, such as Cefalù, shown here, where the daily catch from the sparkling Mediterranean is transformed into simple yet delectable dishes.

COOK'S NOTES
- For all recipes, quantities are given in both metric and imperial measures and, where appropriate, in standard cups and spoons. Follow one set of measures, but not a mixture, because they are not interchangeable.
- Standard spoon and cup measures are level. 1 tsp = 5ml, 1 tbsp = 15ml, 1 cup = 250ml/8fl oz.
- Australian standard tablespoons are 20ml. Australian readers should use 3 tsp in place of 1 tbsp for measuring small quantities of gelatine, flour, salt, etc.
- American pints are 16fl oz/2 cups. American readers should use 20fl oz/2.5 cups in place of 1 pint when measuring liquids.
- Electric oven temperatures in this book are for conventional ovens. When using a fan oven, the temperature will probably need to be reduced by about 10–20°C/20–40°F. Since ovens vary, you should check with your manufacturer's instruction book for guidance.
- Medium (US large) eggs are used unless otherwise stated.